R. Gupta's®

Principles & Practices of BANKING

For JAIIB and Diploma in Banking & Finance Examination

by

Abinash Kumar Mandilwar

M.Sc., MBA (Finance), M.Phil. (Management), CAIIB, Certified Credit Professional, CPD (IIBF), PGDFA, Diploma in Micro Finance, Diploma in Home Loan Advising, Certificate in AML & KYC, SME Finance, Trade Finance

Chief Manager, Bank of India, Kolkata

Updated Upto

FEBRUARY 2022

RAMESH PUBLISHING HOUSE, NEW DELHI

Published by
O.P. Gupta *for* Ramesh Publishing House

Admin. Office
12-H, New Daryaganj Road, Opp. Officers' Mess,
New Delhi-110002 ✆ 23261567, 23275224, 23275124

E-mail: info@rameshpublishinghouse.com
Website: www.rameshpublishinghouse.com

Showroom
• Balaji Market, Nai Sarak, Delhi-6 ✆ 23253720, 23282525
• 4457, Nai Sarak, Delhi-6, ✆ 23918938

First Edition : January, 2019
Second Edition : October, 2019
Third Edition (Revised) : February, 2022

Book Code: R-2007

ISBN: 978-93-89480-16-0

HSN Code: 49011010

Price: ₹ 545

Printed at: Deepak Offset, Delhi

समर्पण

ॐ भूर्भुवः स्व तत्सवितुर्वरेण्यं भर्गो
देवस्य धीमहि धियो यो नः प्रचोदयात।।

मेरी यह पुस्तक वेदमाता माँ गायत्री, हमारे परम पूज्य गुरुदेव पंडित श्रीराम शर्मा आचार्य, परम वन्दनीया माता भगवती देवी शर्मा, मेरे पूज्य पिताजी स्व॰ विश्वनाथ प्रसाद एवं मेरी परम आदरणीय माँ स्व॰ चन्द्रकान्ता देवी के चरणों में सादर समर्पित।

Preface

Banking Sector in India is changing rapidly. Core Banking Solution, Digital Banking and 24 × 7 Banking Services play the crucial role in modern banking development. Huge number of young staff are joining the banking industry. To meet the requirement of this generation of bankers a need was felt to equip them with the basics of banking. This book has been written specially for the young staff members. A keen attempt has been made to make the book useful. Besides, for the preparation of JAIIB Examination, this book is also very useful for Day to Day Banking and all Knowledge Based Examinations. It is with great hope and expectation that the book has been written which will help the young generation of proficient bankers.

A combination of subjective as well as objective material has been comprehensively dealt in this book. There is a need to publish a complete book covering all the aspects so that new recruits get updated without referring to many voluminous books. This book titled "JAIIB—Principles & Practices of Banking" has many unique features to its credit & consists of all topics/syllabi required for JAIIB/DB&F examination with clear concepts & simple language with latest changes (up to September 2019). It has been experienced that students need objective type questions beside subjective matter. This has been taken care of in this book. To prepare the students well, objective questions are also incorporated after every chapter. Two mock tests (100 questions each) for self-evaluation of preparation are given at the end of the book.

During preparation of this book, I have received tremendous support from my family members, friends & colleagues of BOI Staff Training College, especially my wife Mrs. Sumita Taterway (Ruby), my daughters Miss Tanya and Miss Pragya. Special thanks to Shri Anand Mohan Patel, Shri Ajay Kumar Sinha, and Shri N Srinivas (Faculty Members of Staff Training College, Bhopal) for their support, vetting & compilation of this book.

Any suggestions towards its further improvement will be thankfully acknowledged and incorporated in the next edition.

Date: 30-09-2019 — **Abinash Kr. Mandilwar**

About the Author

The author Abinash Kumar Mandilwar joined 'Bank of India' as Probationary Officer in 1995. He was born and completed his study as well as started his carrier in Patna, Bihar. A highly experienced banker, has been working in the bank for more than 24 years. He has held several important assignments which include 10 years as branch head before his current posting as Chief Manager and Faculty at Bank of India Staff Training College at Bhopal.

He is a Certified Associate of Indian Institute of Banking & Finance (CAIIB). His academics include Post Graduate in Chemistry, MBA (Finance), M. Phil. (Management), Honours Diploma in Computer Science., Post Graduate Diploma in Financial Advising, Certified Credit Professional, Diploma in Micro Finance, Diploma in Home Loan Advising, Diploma in Banking Oriented Paper in Hindi, Certificate in AML & KYC, Certificate in SME Finance, Certificate in Trade Finance, Certificate in Customer Service & Banking Codes and Standard. He was also awarded the Continuing Professional Development (CPD) Certification from IIBF in 2011.

As a faculty for more than 4 years at training college, is catering to training needs of managers in middle management/ Staff. He has vast experience of teaching on banking subject in Bank of India as well as associated Regional Rural Banks. He is also associated as a visiting faculty with other bank training institutes.

His articles have been published in different in house banking journals. His Power Point Presentations (PPTs) on various banking topics are appreciated by bankers on social media and Slideshare.net.

Sudeep Ratan Srivastava
Principal
Bank of India
Staff Training College, Bhopal

Foreword

The banking scenario has undergone tremendous changes during last few years. To cope up with such changes there is always a need to have standard and up to date medium of knowledge to be imparted to all those who are interested in banking subjects.

Further more for those joining the banks, need knowledge of various domains of banking to meet requirements of their day-do-day roles. To perform these roles effectively and efficiently, Indian Institute of Banking & Finance (IIBF) is conducting JAIIB course leading to Junior Associate of Indian Institute of Banking & Finance.

Keeping in view the above scenario, there was a long felt need to have a comprehensive, exhaustive and updated book for the new practitioners of banking as well as for those preparing themselves for the exams conducted by IIBF. The book covers the basic conceptual part of the subject 'Principles & Practices of Banking'. The language of the book is simple and lucid.

The book will be of great help to the new entrants in the banking industry especially for their orientation to the core operational areas of banking. The readers will also be introduced to the entire day-to-day banking updates.

I am confident that this book will be useful to all candidates who are appearing for the JAIIB/DB&F Examination and also to those general banking personnel who desire to update their knowledge on the subject. The book will help the new entrants who did not study such subjects in their academic life. The Test papers given at the end of each chapter will immensely be beneficial to the new entrants and will help them to prepare themselves for the JAIIB Exams. In short this is a concise text book which will help the readers prepare for their practical aspects of banking.

I wish the readers an interesting reading and a sound initiation into the world of banking.

Bhopal

Date: 07-09-2018

— **Sudeep Ratan Srivastava**

2007 (Cnt)–2

CONTENTS

MODULE B : FUNCTIONS OF BANKS

MODULE D : SUPPORT SERVICES—MARKETING OF BANKING SERVICES/PRODUCTS

MOCK TEST

RULES & SYLLABUS

JAIIB / DB&F

Paper-1 : Principles & Practices of Banking

OBJECTIVE

JAIIB aims at providing required level of basic knowledge in banking and financial services, banking technology, customer relations, basic accountancy and legal aspects necessary for carrying out day to day banking operations.

ELIGIBILITY

(i) The examination is open to the ordinary members of the Institute (Any person working in the banking and finance industry whose employer is an Institutional member of the Institute can apply for membership, for details visit IIBF website).

(ii) Candidates must have passed the 12th standard examination in any discipline or its equivalent. The Institute may, however at its discretion, allow any candidate from clerical or supervisory staff cadre of banks to appear at the examination on the recommendation of the Manager of the bank/officer-incharge of the bank's office where the candidate is working, even if he/she is not 12th standard pass or its equivalent.

(iii) Subordinate staff of recognized Banking / Financial Institutions in India, who are members of the Institute, are eligible to appear at the examination, provided they have passed the 12th standard examination or its equivalent.

SUBJECTS OF EXAMINATION

(1) Principles & Practices of Banking

(2) Accounting & Finance for Bankers

(3) Legal & Regulatory Aspects of Banking

There is no exemption in any of the subject/s for prior qualification/s.

PASSING CRITERIA

1. Minimum marks for pass in the subject is 50 out of 100.
2. Candidates securing at least 45 marks in each subject with an aggregate of 50% marks in all subjects of examination in a single attempt will also be declared as having completed the Examination.
3. Candidates will be allowed to retain credits for the subject they have passed in an attempt till the expiry of the time limit for passing the examination as mentioned below.

TIME LIMIT FOR PASSING THE EXAMINATION

1. Candidates will be required to pass the examination within a time limit of 2 years (*i.e.* 4 consecutive attempts).
2. Candidates not able to pass examination within stipulated time period of two years are required to re-enroll themselves afresh. Such candidates will not be granted credit/s for subjects passed, if any, earlier.

3. Time limit of 2 years will start from the date of application for First attempt.
   Attempts will be counted irrespective of whether a candidate appears at any examination or otherwise.

MEDIUM OF EXAMINATION

Candidates are allowed to attempt the examination either in Hindi or English, and should clearly fill in their choice of medium at the time of registration of application. In any case change of medium will not be allowed at a later stage.

PATTERN OF EXAMINATION

(i) Question Paper will contain approximately 120 objective type multiple choice questions for 100 marks including questions based on case studies/caselets. The Institute may however vary the number of questions to be asked for a subject.

(ii) The examination will be held in Online Mode only.

(iii) There will NOT be negative marking for wrong answers.

DURATION OF EXAMINATION:

The duration of the examination will be of 2 hours.

PERIODICITY AND EXAMINATION CENTRES

a) Examination will be conducted on pre-announced dates published on IIBF Web Site. Institute conducts examination on half yearly basis, however periodicity of the examination may be changed depending upon the requirement of banking industry.

b) List of Examination centers will be available on the website. (Institute will conduct examination in those centers where there are 20 or more candidates.)

SYLLABUS OF JAIIB / DB&F

Paper-1 : Principles & Practices of Banking

MODULE A – INDIAN FINANCIAL SYSTEM

✦ **Indian Financial System – An Overview**

Role of RBI, Commercial Banks, NBFCs, PDs, FIs, Cooperative Banks, CRR, SLR; Equity & Debt Market; IRDA

✦ **Banking Regulation**

Constitution, Objectives, Functions of RBI; Tools of Monetary Control; Regulatory Restrictions on Lending

✦ **Retail Banking, Wholesale and International Banking**

Retail Banking—Products, Opportunities; Wholesale Banking, Products; International Banking, Requirements of Importers & Exporters, Remittance Services; Universal Banking; ADRs; GDRs; Participatory Notes

✦ **Role of Money Markets, Debt Markets & Forex Market**

Types of Money & Debt Market Instruments incl. G-Secs; ADs, FEMA, LIBOR, MIBOR, etc.

✦ **Role and Functions of Capital Markets, SEBI**

Overview of Capital Market; Stock Exchange; Commonly used Terms; Types of Capital Issues; Financial Products/Instruments including ASBA, QIP; SEBI; Registration of Stock Brokers, Sub-brokers, Share Transfer Agents, etc QIBs

- **Mutual Funds & Insurance Companies, Bancassurance & IRDA**
  Types of Mutual Funds, its Management & its Role; Role & Functions of Insurance Companies; Bancassurance; IRDA
- **Factoring, Forfeiting Services and Off-Balance Sheet items**
  Types & advantages of Factoring & forfeiting services; Types of off balance sheet items
- **Risk Management, Basel Accords**
  Introduction to Risk Management; Basel I, II & III Accords
- **CIBIL, Fair Practices Code for Debt Collection, BCSBI**
  Role and Functions of CIBIL; Fair Practices Code for Debt Collection; Codes of BCSBI
- **Recent Developments in the Financial System**
  Structure, Reforms in the Indian Financial System; recent developments in Money, Debt, Forex Markets; Regulatory Framework; Payments and Settlement System

MODULE B – FUNCTIONS OF BANKS

- **Banker Customer Relationship**
  Types; Different Deposit Products & Services; Services to Customers & Investors
- **KYC / AML / CFT norms**
  PMLA Act; KYC Norms
- **Bankers' Special Relationship**
  Mandate; POA; Garnishee Orders; Banker's Lien; Right of Set off
- **Consumer Protection—COPRA, Banking Ombudsman Scheme**
  Operational Aspects of COPRA Act & Banking Ombudsman Scheme
- **Payment and Collection of Cheques and Other Negotiable Instruments**
  NI Act; Role & Duties of Paying & Collecting Banks; Endorsements; Forged Instruments; Bouncing of Cheques; Its Implications; Return of Cheques; Cheque Truncation System
- **Opening Accounts of various types of Customers**
  Operational Aspects of opening and Maintaining Accounts of Different Types of Customers including Aadhaar, SB Rate Deregulation
- **Ancillary Services**
  Remittances; Safe Deposit Lockers; Govt. Business; EBT
- **Cash Operations**
  Cash Management Services and its Importance
- **Principles of Lending, Working Capital Assessment and Credit Monitoring**
  Cardinal Principles; Non-fund Based Limits; WC; Term Loans; Credit Appraisal Techniques; Sources of WC Funds & its Estimation; Operating Cycle; Projected Net WC; Turnover Method; Cash Budget; Credit Monitoring & Its Management; Base Rate
- **Priority Sector Advances**
  Targets; Sub-Targets; Recent Developments
- **Agricultural Finance**
  Types of Agricultural Loans; Risk Mitigation in agriculture (NAIS, MSP etc.)

- **Micro, Small and Medium Enterprises**
  MSMED Act, 2006 Policy Package for MSMEs; Performance and Credit Rating Scheme; Latest Developments

- **Government Sponsored Schemes**
  SGSY; SJSRY; PMRY; SLRS

- **Self Help Groups**
  Need for & Functions of SHGs; Role of NGOs in Indirect Finance to SHGs; SHGs & SGSY Scheme; Capacity Building

- **Credit Cards, Home Loans, Personal Loans, Consumer Loans**
  Operational Aspects, Advantages, Disadvantages & Guidelines of Credit Cards; Procedure and Practices for Home Loans, Personal Loans and Consumer Loans

- **Documentation**
  Types of Documents; Procedure; Stamping; Securitisation

- **Different Modes of Charging Securities**
  Assignment; Lien; Set-off; Hypothecation; Pledge; Mortgage

- **Types of Collaterals and their Characteristics**
  Land & Buildings; Goods; Documents of Title to Goods; Advances against Insurance Policies, Shares, Book Debts, Term Deposits, Gold, etc; Supply Bills

- **Non-Performing Assets**
  Definition; Income Recognition; Asset Classification; Provisioning Norms; CDR
  Financial Inclusion
  BC; BF; Role of ICT in Financial Inclusion, Mobile based transactions, R SETI

- **Financial Literacy**
  Importance of financial literacy, customer awareness

MODULE C – BANKING TECHNOLOGY

- **Essentials of Bank Computerization**
  Computer Systems; LANs; WANs; UPS; Core Banking

- **Payment Systems and Electronic Banking**
  ATMs; HWAK; PIN; Electromagnetic Cards; Electronic Banking; Signature Storage & Retrieval System; CTS; Note & Coin Counting Machines; Microfiche;
  NPC; RUPAY

- **Data Communication Network and EFT systems**
  Components & Modes of Transmission; Major Networks in India; Emerging Trends in Communication Networks for Banking; Evolution of EFT System; SWIFT; Automated Clearing Systems; Funds Transfer Systems; Recent Developments in India

- **Role of Technology Upgradation and its impact on Banks**
  Trends in Technology Developments; Role & Uses of Technology Upgradation; Global Trends; Impact of IT on Banks

- **Security Considerations**
  Risk Concern Areas; Types of Threats; Control Mechanism; Computer Audit; IS Security; IS Audit; Evaluation Requirements

- **Overview of IT Act**
  Gopalakrishna Committee Recommendations

- **Preventive Vigilance in Electronic Banking**
  Phishing; Customer Education; Safety Checks; Precautions

MODULE D – SUPPORT SERVICES-MARKETING OF BANKING SERVICES/PRODUCTS

✦ **Marketing – An Introduction**
Concept; Management; Products & Services; Marketing Mix; Brand Image

✦ **Social Marketing / Networking**
Evolution, Importance & Relevance of Social Marketing / Networking

✦ **Consumer Behaviour and Product**
Consumer Behaviour; Product Planning, Development, Strategies, etc; CRM

✦ **Pricing**
Importance, Objectives, Factors, Methods, Strategies of Pricing; Bank Pricing

✦ **Distribution**
Distribution Channels; Channels for Banking Services; Net Banking; Mobile Banking

✦ **Channel Management**
Meaning, Levels, Dynamics, Advantages

✦ **Promotion**
Role of Promotion in Marketing; Promotion Mix

✦ **Role of Direct Selling Agent/Direct Marketing Agent in a Bank**
Definition; Relevance; Banker as DSA / DMA; Delivery Channels in Banks; Benefits

✦ **Marketing Information Systems–a Longitudinal Analysis**
Functions & Components of MKIS; MKIS Model; Use of Computers & Decision Models; Performance of MKIS; Advantages

MODULE E – ETHICS IN BANKS AND FINANCIAL INSTITUTIONS

✦ **Ethics, Business Ethics & Banking: An Integrated Perspective**
Business Ethics, Ethical Foundation and Banking Ethics in Global and Indian Contexts

✦ **Ethics at the Individual Level**
Values, Norms, Beliefs, Morality, Conflict, Integrity, Golden Rule, Dilemmas, Decision-Making.

✦ **Ethical Dimensions: Employees**
Obligation to Bank/ Third Parties, Abuse of Official Position, Sexual Harassment, Conflict of Interest, Fair Accounting Practices, HRM Ethics, Employees as Ethics Ambassadors & Managers as Ethical Leaders

✦ **Work Ethics and the Workplace**
Work Ethics, Benefits of Ethical Behaviour, Unethical Behaviour: Causes and Remedies, Code of Ethics Manual, Whistle-blowing in Banks, Whistle-blowing Laws in India

✦ **Banking Ethics: Changing Dynamics**
Ethics and Technology, Data Security and Privacy, Intellectual Property Rights, Patents and Proprietary Rights, Ethics of Information Security, Cyber Threats, Digital Rights Management

UPDATION

CHAPTER-12

Anti-money Laundering (AML) Standards & Know Your Customer (KYC) Norms 2021

Page-83 (1st column after para-2)

Reserve Bank of India (RBI) vide notification RBI/DBR/2015-16/18 dated February 25, 2016 (Updated as on May 10, 2021) has updated RBI updates Master Direction - Know Your Customer (KYC) Direction, 2016.

Page-85 (1st column after point-IV)

Beneficial Owner (BO)

(a) Where the **customer is a Company**, the beneficial owner is the natural person(s), who, whether acting alone or together, or through one or more juridical persons, has/have a controlling ownership interest or who exercise control through other means.

Explanation: For the purpose of this sub-clause-

1. "Controlling ownership interest" means ownership of/entitlement to more than 25 per cent of the shares or capital or profits of the company.
2. "Control" shall include the right to appoint majority of the directors or to control the management or policy decisions including by virtue of their shareholding or management rights or shareholders agreements or voting agreements.

(h) Where the **customer is a Partnership Firm**, the beneficial owner is the natural person(s), who, whether acting alone or together, or through one or more juridical person, has/have ownership of/entitlement to more than 15 per cent of capital or profits of the partnership.

(c) Where the **customer is an Unincorporated Association or Body of Individuals**, the beneficial owner is the natural person(s), who, whether acting alone or together, or through one or more juridical person, has/have ownership of/entitlement to more than 15 per cent of the property or capital or profits of the unincorporated association or body of individuals.

Explanation: Term 'Body of Individuals' includes societies. Where no natural person is identified under (a), (b) or (c) above, the beneficial owner is the relevant natural person who holds the position of senior managing official.

(d) Where the customer is a **Trust**, the identification of beneficial owner(s) shall include identification of the author of the trust, the trustee, the beneficiaries with 15% or more interest in the trust and any other natural person exercising ultimate effective control over the trust through a chain of control or ownership.

Page-85 (1st column)

Customer Acceptance Policy (CAP)

a. ....

h. REs shall apply the CDD procedure at the UCIC level. Thus, if an existing KYC compliant customer of a RE desires to open another account with the same RE, there shall be no need for a fresh CDD exercise.

i. CDD Procedure is followed for all the joint account holders, while opening a joint account.

j. Where Permanent Account Number (PAN) is obtained, the same shall be verified from the verification facility of the issuing authority.

k. Where an equivalent e-document is obtained from the customer, RE shall verify the digital signature as per the provisions of the Information Technology Act, 2000 (21 of 2000).

Page-85 (2nd column)

Risk Management (After 2nd para)

Provided that various other information collected from different categories of customers relating to the perceived risk, is non-intrusive and the same is specified in the KYC policy.

Page-86 (1st column)

Customer Identification Procedure (CPI) (After 2nd para)

Now, these six documents are considered as officially valid documents:

1. Passport (within validity)
2. Driving License (within validity)
3. Proof of possession of Aadhaar number
4. Voter's Identity Card
5. Job Card issued by NREGA
6. The letter issued by the National Population Register containing details of name, address or any other document as notified by the Central Government in consultation with the Regulator.

Where the OVD furnished by the customer does not have updated address, the following documents shall be deemed to be OVDs for the limited purpose of proof of address:

1. ....

Page-87 (1st column)

(After 1st para)

1. Individuals :

For undertaking CDD, REs shall obtain the following from an individual while establishing an account-based relationship or while dealing with the individual who is a beneficial owner, authorised signatory or the power of attorney holder related to any legal entity:

(a) the Aadhaar number where,

(i) he is desirous of receiving any benefit or subsidy under any scheme notified under section 7 of the Aadhaar (Targeted Delivery of Financial and Other subsidies, Benefits and Services) Act, 2016 (18 of 2016); or

(ii) he decides to submit his Aadhaar number voluntarily to a bank or any RE notified under first proviso to sub-section (1) of section 11A of the PML Act; or

the proof of possession of Aadhaar number where offline verification can be carried out; or

the proof of possession of Aadhaar number where offline verification cannot be carried out or any OVD or the equivalent e-document thereof containing the details of his identity and address; and

(b) the Permanent Account Number or Form No. 60 as defined in Income-tax Rules, 1962, and

(c) such other documents pertaining to the nature of business or financial status specified by the REs in their KYC policy.

2. CDD Measures for Sole Proprietary Firms: For opening an account in the name of a sole proprietary firm, CDD of the individual (proprietor) shall be carried out. In addition to the above, any two of the following documents as a proof of business/ activity in the name of the proprietary firm shall also be obtained:

(a) Registration certificate

(b) Certificate/licence issued by the municipal authorities under Shop and Establishment Act.

(c) Sales and income tax returns.

(d) CST/VAT/ GST certificate (provisional/final).

(e) Certificate/registration document issued by Sales Tax/Service Tax/Professional Tax authorities.

(f) IEC (Importer Exporter Code) issued to the proprietary concern by the office of DGFT or Licence/certificate of practice issued in the name of the proprietary concern by any professional body incorporated under a statute.

(g) Complete Income Tax Return (not just the acknowledgement) in the name of the sole proprietor where the firm's income is reflected, duly acknowledged by the Income Tax authorities.

(h) Utility bills such as electricity, water, landline telephone bills, etc.

In cases where the Regulated Entities (REs) are satisfied that it is not possible to furnish two such documents, Regulated Entities (REs) may, at their discretion, accept only one of those documents as proof of business/activity.

Provided Regulated Entities (REs) undertake contact point verification and collect such other information and clarification as would be required to establish the existence of such firm, and shall confirm and satisfy itself that the business activity has been verified from the address of the proprietary concern.

CDD Measures for Legal Entities

3. Company:

a) Certificate of incorporation

b) Memorandum and Articles of Association

c) Permanent Account Number of the company

d) A resolution from the Board of Directors and power of attorney granted to its managers, officers or employees to transact on its behalf

e) Documents, as specified in case of individualwho is a beneficial owner,, of the managers, officers or employees, as the case may be, holding an attorney to transact on the company's behalf.

4. Partnership Firm:

a) Registration certificate

b) Partnership deed

c) Permanent Account Number of the partnership firm

d) Documents, as specified in case of individualwho is a beneficial owner, of the person holding an attorney to transact on its behalf

5. Trust Documents:

a) Registration certificate

b) Trust deed

c) Permanent Account Number or Form No. 60 of the trust

d) Documents, as specified in case of individual who is a beneficial owner, of the person holding an attorney to transact on its behalf.

6. Association of Persons:

a) Resolution of the managing body of such association or body of individuals.

b) Permanent Account Number or Form No. 60 of the unincorporated association or a body of individuals.

c) Power of attorney granted to transact on its behalf.

d) Documents, as specified in case of individual who is a beneficial owner, of the person holding an attorney to transact on its behalf and

e) Such information as may be required by the RE to collectively establish the legal existence of such an association or body of individuals.

Explanation: Unregistered trusts/partnership firms shall be included under the term 'unincorporated association'.

7. Juridical Persons Not Specifically Covered in the earlier part, Such as Societies, Universities and Local Bodies Like Village Panchayats:

a) Document showing name of the person authorised to act on behalf of the entity;

b) Documents, as specified in case of individual who is a beneficial owner, of the person holding an attorney to transact on its behalf and

c) Such documents as may be required by the RE to establish the legal existence of such an entity/ juridical person.

CHAPTER-14 (NEW)

Consumer Protection Act, 2019, Banking Ombudsman Scheme (P.No.-95-102)

INTRODUCTION

The Consumer Protection Act has been enacted for the purpose of providing timely and effective administration and settlement of consumer disputes and related matters. The Government instead of bringing an amendment in the 1986 Act, enacted a new Act altogether so as to provide enhanced protection to the consumers taking into consideration the booming e-commerce industry and the modern methods of providing goods and services such as online sales, tele-shopping, direct selling and multi-level marketing in addition to the traditional methods.

The 2019 Consumer Protection Act brings about fundamental changes to the existing 1986 legislation. But it also envisages a Central Consumer Protection Authority and vests too much power and control in this authority without proposing adequate administrative safeguards.

CONSUMER PROTECTION ACT, 2019

The Consumer Protection Act was initially enacted in 1986 and implemented from April 15, 1987. A comprehensive amendment (The Consumer Protection (Amendment) Act 2002) has been passed on Dec. 17, 2002 (implemented effective from March 15, 2003, the 'World Consumer Rights Day').

Further, it was amended in 2019 as 'The Consumer Protection (Amendment) Bill, 2019'. The Consumer Protection Bill, 2019 was passed by the Indian Parliament on August 2019. The Act of Parliament received the assent of the President on the 9th August, 2019, and is hereby published for general information. This new act replaced the old Consumer Protection Act, 1986.

Consumer Protection Act, 2019 is a law to protect the interests of the consumers. This act was inevitable to resolve a large number of pending consumer complaints in consumer courts across the country. It has ways and means to solve the consumer grievances speedily.

AIM OF THE CONSUMER PROTECTION ACT, 2019

The basic aim of the Consumer Protection Act, 2019 to save the rights of the consumers by establishing authorities for timely and effective administration and settlement of consumers' disputes.

However, its practical implementation was far from fulfilling its desired objective of being a socio-economic legislation which sought "*to provide for better protection of the interests of consumers.*" While using the same phrase in its preamble, the 2019 Act, has substantially enhanced the scope of protection afforded to consumers, by bringing within its purview advertising claims, endorsements and product liability, all of which play a fundamental role in altering consumer behaviour and retail trends in the 21st century.

Definition of a Consumer

Consumer means any individual who:

1. Buys any goods for a consideration which has been paid or promised or partly paid and partly promised; or
2. Hires or avail of any services for a consideration which has been paid or promised or partly paid and partly promised, or under any system of deferred payment;
3. Includes any user of such goods other than the person who buys such goods or hires of any services for consideration paid; or
4. Promised or partly paid or partly promised, or under any system of deferred payment, when such use is made with the approval of such person.

Who is not a Consumer?

1. Person buying goods for resale;
2. Person buying goods for any commercial purpose;
3. Person receiving goods/services free or gifts;
4. Person enjoying personal service under a contract (service by employees/maid servants) etc.

Explanation: For the purposes regarding definition of consumer;

(a) The expression "commercial purpose" does not include use by a person of goods bought and used by him exclusively for the purpose of earning his livelihood, by means of self-employment;

(b) The expressions "buys any goods" and "hires or avails any services" includes offline or online transactions through electronic means or by teleshopping or direct selling or multi-level marketing;

Coverage: All goods and services including banking, insurance, transport, processing, electricity, professional such as physicians etc. in private, public and cooperative sectors are covered under this Act. All banking services are covered due to their being essential services.

"CONSUMER" DEFINITION CHANGES UNDER THE NEW ACT, 2019

Some major changes about the definition of "consumer" under the Consumer Protection Act, 2019 areas under:

- Those who make purchases online. Endorsement of goods and services, normally done by celebrities, are also covered within the ambit of the 2019 Act.
- In fact, an additional onus has been placed on endorsers, apart from manufacturers and service providers, to prevent false or misleading advertisements.
- In contrast to the 1986 Act, the definition of "goods" has been amended to include "food" as defined in the Food Safety and Standards Act, 2006. This would also bring the meteorically rising number of food delivery platforms within the fold of the 2019 Act.
- Interestingly, "telecom" has been added to the definition of "services" to bring telecom service providers within the purview of the 2019 Act. But surprisingly, such inclusion has not been worded as "telecommunication service" defined under the Telecom Regulatory Authority of India Act, which would have included internet, cellular and data services.
- A significant addition to the 2019 Act is the introduction of "product liability" whereby manufacturers and sellers of products or services have been made responsible to compensate for any harm caused to a consumer by defective products, manufactured or sold, or for deficiency in services.
- Another newly introduced concept is that of "unfair contracts" aimed to protect consumers from unilaterally skewed and unreasonable contracts which lean in favour of manufacturers or service providers.
- The definition of "unfair trade practices" has been enlarged to include electronic advertising which

is misleading, as well as refusing to take back or withdraw defective goods, or to withdraw or discontinue deficient services, and to refund the consideration within the period stipulated or in the absence of such stipulation, within a period of thirty days. It is now also an offence if any personal information, given in confidence and gathered in the course of a transaction, gets disclosed.

All these changes signify an attempt to create more transparency in the marketplace, through legislative protection, with a view to ensure that consumer interests are above all else.

RIGHTS OF CONSUMERS

The act provides following rights to the consumers:

- To have information about the quantity, quality, purity, potency, price, and standard of goods or services;
- To be protected from hazardous goods and services;
- To be protected from unfair or restrictive trade practices;
- To have a variety of goods or services at competitive prices;
- To have the right to consumer awareness.

Consumer Protection Council

To promote and protect the right of the consumers, councils are established. Their scope is not regarding directly dealing with the consumer complaints at initial or appellate scope but to promote and protect the rights of consumer.

1. **Central Consumer Protection Council:** The Central Government has established a council known as the Central Consumer Protection Council, called the Central Council. The Central Council consist of the following:
   (a) The Minister-In-charge of the Consumer Affairs in the Central Government shall be the Chairman of the council, and
   (b) Such member of other official or non-official members representing such interests as may be prescribed.

   The Central Council shall meet as and when necessary but at least once in a year.
2. **State Consumer Protection Council:** The State Government has established a council known as the State Consumer Protection Council, called the State Council. The State Council consist of the following:
   (a) The Minister-In-charge of the Consumer Affairs in the State Government shall be the Chairman of the council,
   (b) Such member of other official or non-official members representing such interests as may be prescribed by the State Government, and
   (c) Such member of other official or non-official members not exceeding ten as may be nominated by Central Government.

   The State Council shall meet as and when necessary but at least twice in a year.
3. **District Consumer Protection Council:** The State Government has established a council known as the District Consumer Protection Council in every district, called the District Council. The District Council consist of the following:
   (a) The Collector of the District shall be the Chairman of the council,
   (b) Such member of other official or non-official members representing such interests as may be prescribed by the State Government.

   The District Council shall meet as and when necessary but at least twice in a year.

CENTRAL CONSUMER PROTECTION AUTHORITY (CCPA)

One of the most significant additions to the 2019 Act is the proposal to establish Central Consumer Protection Authority (CCPA) with the following features:

- The Central Authority shall consist of a Chief Commissioner and such number of other Commissioners as may be prescribed, to be appointed by the Central Government to exercise the powers and discharge the functions under this Act.
- The Central Authority shall have an Investigation Wing headed by a Director General for the purpose of conducting inquiry or investigation under this Act as may be directed by the Central Authority.
- The CCPA has to regulate, protect and enforce the interest of the consumers and matters related to unfair trade practices.
- The CCPA has been provided with vast powers to inquire, investigate and take action against violations of the 2019 Act.

- Another significant power the CCPA has been showered with, is the power to take action and impose penalty against misleading and false advertisement as well as against any endorser of such advertisement, which means the CCPA can now initiate action against the celebrities who have endorsed such misleading and false advertisement provided such celebrities failed to carry out any due diligence before participating in such advertisements.
- The CCPA may impose a penalty of up to ₹ 10 lakhs for first violation and up to ₹ 50 lakhs on every subsequent violation on a manufacturer or an endorser, for a false or misleading advertisement.
- In addition to this, such manufacturer or endorser may be sentenced to imprisonment for upto two years.

PROHIBITION & PENALTY FOR A MISLEADING ADVERTISEMENT

The Central Consumer Protection Authority (CCPA) will have the power to impose fines on the endorser or manufacturer up to 2-year imprisonment for misleading or false advertisement (Like Laxmi DhanWarsha Yantra).

Worth to mention that repeated offense, may attract a fine of ₹ 50 lakh and imprisonment of up to 5 years.

CONSUMER DISPUTES REDRESSAL COMMISSION

The act has the provision of the establishment of the Consumer Disputes Redressal Commissions (CDRCs) at the national, state and district levels. The CDRCs will entertain complaints related to:

- Overcharging or deceptive charging,
- Unfair or restrictive trade practices,
- Sale of hazardous goods and services which may be hazardous to life,
- Sale of defective goods or services.

JURISDICTION UNDER THE CONSUMER PROTECTION ACT, 2019

The act has defined the criteria of Consumer Disputes Redressal Commission (CDRCs). As far as the Consumer Redressal Commissions are concerned, certain key changes have been brought by the 2019 Act such as:

- **Territorial Jurisdiction:** The 2019 Act now provides an added advantage to the consumers by providing for filing of complaints where the complainant resides or personally works for gain as against the 1986 Act which only provides for filing of complaint where the opposite party resides or carry on business. This would help in removing the difficulties faced by the consumers in seeking redressal of their grievances against businesses who may not have an office or branch in their state.
- **Pecuniary Jurisdiction:** The 2019 Act also changed the pecuniary jurisdiction for the District, State and National Commissions, respectively. The pecuniary limit for the District Commission has been increased to up to ₹ 1 Crore from up to ₹ 20 Lakhs; for State Commission it has been increased to up to ₹ 10 Crores from up to ₹ 1 Crore; and for National Commission the pecuniary jurisdiction has been increased to over and above ₹ 10 Crores as against ₹ 1 Crore in the 1986 Act. In addition to this, the 2019 Act has also changed the manner for determining the pecuniary jurisdiction for filing the Complaint. Now the pecuniary jurisdiction will be determined on the basis of the value of goods or services paid as consideration as against the 1986 Act wherein, the pecuniary jurisdiction was determined as per the value of goods and services as well as compensation claimed. This would help in doing away the practice of inflating the compensation claimed so as to bring the complaint within the jurisdiction of State or National Commission.
- **Alternate Dispute Resolution:** Another provision introduced by the 2019 Act to ensure speedy resolution of disputes is to provide for referring the disputes to mediation. As per the 2019 Act, the Consumer Commission shall refer the matter to mediation on written consent of both the parties. For this purpose, the 2019 Act also provides for establishment of a consumer mediation cell by the respective State Governments in each District Commission and State Commission as well as at the National Commission by the Central Government.
- **E-Complaints:** The 2019 Act also provides for filing of Complaints before the District Commissions electronically in accordance with the rules which are yet to be prescribed by the Government.

WHO CAN FILE A COMPLAINT?

A consumer (individually or jointly) himself or through any voluntary consumer Organisation, Central or State Governments can file a complaint. Limitation period is 2 years from the date of cause of action i.e. purchase of goods/hiring of services.

PROCEDURE FOR FILE A COMPLAINT

A simple written complaint in duplicate with full name and address of opposite party narrating facts of the complaint along with copies of the supporting documents and details of relief sought. No Court Fee is charged. Engaging of Lawyer is not necessary. Consumer or anyone can represent his case.

Consumer Can Fill His Complain in the Following Consumer Commission:

1. **District Commission:** A Consumer Disputes Redressal Commission to be known as the "District Commission" established by the State Government in each district of the State by notification. Each State Commission shall consist of a President and not less than two members. The District Commission shall have jurisdiction to entertain complaints where the value of the goods or services paid as consideration does not exceed ₹ 1 Crore.

   The Central Government may make rules to provide for the qualifications, method of recruitment, procedure for appointment, make rules to provide for salaries and allowances term of office, resignation and removal of the President and members of the District Commission.

2. **State Commission:** Each State Commission shall consist of a President and not less than four or not more than such number of members as may be prescribed in consultation with the Central Government, complaints where the value of the goods or services paid as consideration, exceeds rupees one crore, but does not exceed rupees ten crore:

   The Central Government may make rules to provide for the qualification for appointment, method of recruitment, procedure of appointment, term of office, resignation and removal of the President and members of the State Commission.

   The State Government may make rules to provide for salaries and allowances and other terms and conditions of service of the President and members of the State Commission.

3. **National Commission:** The National Commission shall consist of a President and not less than four or not more than such number of members as may be prescribed in consultation with the Central Government, complaints where the value of the goods or services paid as consideration, exceeds rupees one crore, but does not exceed rupees ten crore:

   The Central Government may, by notification, make rules to provide for qualifications, appointment, term of office, salaries and allowances, resignation, removal and other terms and conditions of service of the President and members of the National Commission.

   The President and members of the National Commission shall hold office not exceeding five years from the date on which he enters upon his office and up to age of seventy years in the case of the President and sixty-seven years in the case of any other member.

Commission	*Claim amount*	*Office Structure*
District Commission	Up to ₹ 1 Crore	Headed by President and 2 other members.
State Commission	More than ₹ 1 Crore up to ₹ 10 Crore	Headed by President and 4 other members.
National Commission	Above ₹ 10 Crore	Headed by President and 4 other members. Maximum age 70 years for President and 67 years for any other member.

ESTABLISHMENT OF CONSUMER MEDIATION CELL

Another provision introduced by the 2019 Act to ensure speedy resolution of disputes is to provide for referring the disputes to mediation. As per the 2019 Act, the Consumer Commission shall refer the matter to mediation on written consent of both the parties.

The State Government shall establish, by notification, a consumer mediation cell to be attached to each of the District Commissions and the State Commissions of that State. The Central Government shall establish, by notification, a consumer mediation cell to be attached to the National Commission and each of the regional Benches. Every consumer mediation cell shall maintain-

(a) a list of empanelled mediators;
(b) a list of cases handled by the cell;
(c) record of proceeding; and
(d) any other information as may be specified by regulations.

Pursuant to mediation, if an agreement is reached between the parties with respect to all of the issues involved in the consumer dispute or with respect to only some of the issues, the mediator shall prepare a settlement report of the settlement and forward the signed agreement along with such report to the concerned Commission. The District Commission or the State Commission or the National Commission, as the case may be, shall, within seven days of the receipt of the settlement report, pass suitable order recording such settlement of consumer dispute and dispose of the matter accordingly.

RELIEF BY DISTRICT COMMISSION

If, after the proceeding conducted the District Commission is satisfied about the complaint, it shall issue an order to the opposite party directing him:

- To remove the defect pointed out from the goods;
- To removal of deficiencies in services;
- To replacement by new goods free from defects;
- To refund of price/charges etc.;
- To pay such amount as may be awarded as compensation to the consumer for any loss or injury suffered by the consumer, due to the negligence of the opposite party.

OFFENCES AND PENALTIES

Some significant changes about the various types of penalties and punishments for different offences under the Consumer Protection Act, 2019 are as under;

1. **Penalty for Fails to Comply with any Order:** Whoever fails to comply with any order made by the District Commission or the State Commission or the National Commission, as the case may be, shall be punishable with imprisonment for a term which shall not be less than one month, but which may extend to three years, or with fine, which shall not be less than twenty-five thousand rupees, but which may extend to one lakh rupees, or with both.
2. **Penalty for Noncompliance of Direction of Central Authority:** Whoever, fails to comply with any direction of the Central Authority shall be punished with imprisonment for a term which may extend to six months or with fine which may extend to twenty lakh rupees, or with both.
3. **Punishment for False or Misleading Advertisement:** Any manufacturer or service provider who causes a false or misleading advertisement to be made which is prejudicial to the interest of consumers shall be punished with imprisonment for a term which may extend to two years and with fine which may extend to ten lakh rupees; and for every subsequent offence, be punished with imprisonment for a term which may extend to five years and with fine which may extend to fifty lakh rupees.
4. **Punishment for Manufacturing for Sale or Storing, Selling or Distributing or Importing Products Containing Adulterant or Importing Spurious Goods:** Whoever, by himself or by any other person on his behalf, manufactures for sale or stores or sells or distributes or imports any product containing an adulterant shall be punished, if such act:
   - does not result in any injury to the consumer, with imprisonment for a term which may extend to six months and with fine which may extend to one lakh rupees;
   - causing injury not amounting to grievous hurt to the consumer, with imprisonment for a term which may extend to one year and with fine which may extend to three lakh rupees;
   - causing injury resulting in grievous hurt to the consumer, with imprisonment for a term which may extend to seven years and with fine which may extend to five lakh rupees and non-bailable; and
   - results in the death of a consumer, with imprisonment for a term which shall not be less than seven years, but which may extend to imprisonment for life and with fine which shall not be less than ten lakh rupees and non-bailable.

The punishment in case of first conviction, suspend any licence issued to the person for a period up to two years, and in case of second or subsequent conviction, cancel the licence.

SUMMARY OF OFFENCE AND PUNISHMENT

Particulars	*Offence Type*	*Punishment Amount*	*Imprisonment Period*
Order made by the District/ State/National Commission	Found guilty	Min. ₹ 25000/- Max. ₹ 1 Lakh	Min. 1 month Max. 3 years
Direction of Central Authority	Fails to comply with any direction	Max. ₹ 20 Lakh	Max. 6 months
False or misleading advertisement	First time offence	Max. ₹ 10 Lakh	Max. 2 years
	every subsequent offence	Max. ₹ 50 Lakh	Max. 5 years

Manufacturing for sale or storing, selling or distributing or importing products containing adulterant or importing spurious goods. (1st conviction, suspend licence for a period up to two years, and in case of second or subsequent conviction, cancel the licence)	Does not result in any injury	Max. Rs. 1 Lakh	Max. 6 months
	Causing injury not amounting to grievous hurt	Max. Rs. 3 Lakh	Max. 1 year
	Causing injury resulting in grievous hurt	Max. Rs. 5 Lakh	Max. 7 years non-bailable
	Results in the death of a consumer	Min. Rs. 10 Lakh	Min. 7 years Max. Whole life non-bailable

APPEAL FILED BEFORE STATE COMMISSION OR NATIONAL COMMISSION

A person aggrieved by any order passed by the Central Authority may file an appeal to the National Commission within a period of thirty days from the date of receipt of such order.

Any person aggrieved by an order made by the District Commission may appeal against the order to the State Commission within 45 days from the date of order. Appeal to State Commission against the award of District Commission will be accepted after Deposit amount is 50% of that amount in the manner as may be prescribed.

Any person aggrieved by an order made by the State Commission may appeal against the order to the National Commission within 30 days from the date of order. Appeal to National Commission against the award of State Commission will be accepted after Deposit amount is 50% of that amount.

Any person aggrieved by an order made by the National Commission may appeal against the order to the Supreme Court within 30 days from the date of order. Appeal to Supreme Court against the award of National Commission will be accepted after Deposit amount is 50% of that amount.

An appeal filed before the State Commission or the National Commission, as the case may be, shall be heard as expeditiously as possible and every endeavour shall be made to dispose of the appeal within a period of ninety days from the date of its admission.

TIME LIMITS FOR DISPOSAL OF COMPLAIN

Endeavour is made to decide the complaint within the following time frame:

A : Admissibility of the complaint from date of receipt of the complaint: within 21 days;

B : Decision on complaint (Without analysis or testing of commodities): 3 months;

C : With analysis or testing of commodities: 5 months.

Action Taken on Complaint	*Time Limit*
Admission of complaint from the date of receipt of the complaint.	21 days
Disposal without analysis or testing of commodities	3 months
Disposal analysis or testing of commodities	5 months
Appeal against the order made by the District Commission to the State Commission.	45 days
Appeal against the order made by the State Commission to the National Commission.	30 days
Appeal against the order made by the National Commission to the Supreme Court.	30 days
Appeal against the order made by the Central Authority to the National Commission.	30 days
Decision should be taken on Appeals for admission or rejection.	90 days

Conclusively, the Consumer Protection Act, 2019 when compared with the 1986 Act shows that it provides for greater protection of consumer interests taking into consideration the current age of digitization. The 2019 Act also deals with the technological advancements in the industry, provides for easier filing of complaints and also imposes strict liability on businesses including, which, prima-facie, appears to be much more consumer-friendly than the 1986 endorsers for violating the interest of the consumers. However, the test of time will prove the fate of the 2019 Act as and when it is notified by the Central Government Act and also includes the current industry trends of e-commerce.

BANKING OMBUDSMAN SCHEME

Introduction: For the improvement of customer service in banking industry, RBI has provided a platform to customer for redressal of banking related dispute. RBI notified the Banking Ombudsman Scheme 2006 u/s 35A of Banking Regulation Act 1949. The scheme came into force effective from 01st Jan 2006. It covers all commercial banks, RRB's & scheduled primary Co-operative Banks. Presently the Banking Ombudsman Scheme 2006 (As amended up to July 1, 2017) is in operation.

Objective: The Scheme is introduced with the object of enabling resolution of complaints relating to certain services rendered by banks and to facilitate the satisfaction or settlement of such complaints. Resolution of complaints relating to banking services through conciliation & mediation between the bank and the aggrieved parties or by passing an award.

Eligibility of Ombudsman: The Reserve Bank may appoint one or more of its officers in the rank of Chief General Manager or General Manager for maximum period not exceeding 3 Years at a time.

Location of Office: The office of the Banking Ombudsman shall be located at such places as may be specified by the Reserve Bank. At present, twenty Banking Ombudsmen have been appointed with their offices located mostly in state capitals. All costs of the office are borne by RBI.

Jurisdiction: The Reserve Bank shall specify the territorial limits to which the authority of each Banking Ombudsman. A person makes a complaint to the Banking Ombudsman within whose jurisdiction the branch or office of the bank complained against is located. For Credit card, the jurisdiction is with reference to ombudsman having jurisdiction over the billing address of the card holder. For other accounts, it is as per location of the branch.

Grounds of Complaint

Any person may file a complaint with the Banking Ombudsman having jurisdiction on any one of the rounds alleging deficiency in banking services including internet banking or other services.

Procedure for Filing Complaint: Any person who has a grievance against a bank on any one or more of the grounds mentioned in the Scheme may, himself or through his authorised representative (other than an advocate), make a complaint on paper or through electronic media (e-mail), or forwarded by RBI or Central Govt. to the Banking Ombudsman.

The complaint in writing shall be duly signed by the complainant or his authorized representative and shall be, as far as possible, in the form specified in Annexure 'A' or as near as thereto as circumstances admit, stating clearly:

I. The name and the address of the complainant;
II. The name and address of the branch or office of the bank against which the complaint is made;
III. The facts giving rise to the complaint;
IV. The nature and extent of the loss caused to the complainant; and
V. The relief sought for.

Conditions for Complaint:

- Complain was made to the Bank and Bank had rejected or no reply was received within a month or complainant is not satisfied with the reply given by the bank;
- The complaint is made not later than one year after the complainant has received the reply of the bank to his representation or, where no reply is received, not later than one year and one month after the date of the representation to the bank; Complaint is not for issues already settled by ombudsman or for which proceeding before court or any other forum is pending or a decree or order has been passed;
- The complaint is not frivolous or vexatious in nature;
- The complaint is within limitation period under Indian limitation Act 1963.

Process of Redressal of Grievance: Banking Ombudsman sent a copy of the complaint to the bank and endeavour shall-be made for a settlement by agreement through conciliation or mediation. The proceedings shall be summary in nature.

Award by the Ombudsman: Where a complaint is not settled by agreement within a period of one month from the date of receipt of the complaint, Ombudsman may pass an Award or reject the complaint, on the basis of evidence, the principles of banking law and practice, directions and guidelines issued by RBI.

Amount of Award: Award shall specify the amount, to be paid by bank as compensation, not more than actual loss suffered as direct consequence of act of omission or commission of the bank or ₹ 20 lac (As amended up to July 1, 2017, earlier it was ₹ 10 lac), whichever is lower.

The Banking Ombudsman may award compensation not exceeding ₹ 1 lakh to the complainant for mental agony and harassment. The Banking Ombudsman will take into account the loss of the complainant's time, expenses incurred by the complainant, harassment and mental anguish suffered by the complainant while passing such award.

Effect of award: A copy of the Award shall be sent to the complainant and the bank. An award shall lapse and be of no effect unless the complainant furnishes to the bank concerned within a period of 30 days from the date of receipt of copy of the Award, a letter of acceptance of the Award in full and final settlement of his claim. The bank shall, unless it has preferred an appeal within one month from the date of receipt by it of the acceptance in writing of the Award by the complainant, comply with the Award and intimate compliance to the Banking Ombudsman.

Implementation: Customer has to send acceptance of the award within 30 days of date of receipt of the award. Bank is to implement the award within one month from the date of receipt of the acceptance from the complainant and intimate compliance to the Banking Ombudsman.

Rejection of the Complaint: If it frivolous, malafide or without sufficient cause or there is no loss or damage or inconvenience caused to the complainant or is beyond the pecuniary jurisdiction of ombudsman.

Appeal: Customer can appeal to appellate authority within 30 days of receipt of rejection to Dy. Governor RBI. Customer or bank can file the appeal to appellate authority (Dy. Governor RBI) against the award or decision of the Banking Ombudsman rejecting the complaint within 30 days of the date of receipt of the Award. Provided further that appeal may be filed by a bank only with the prior sanction of the Chairman or, in his absence, the Managing Director or the Executive Director or the Chief Executive Officer or any other officer of equal rank.

CHAPTER-20 (NEW)

Priority Sector Lending (P.No.-140-146)

PRIORITY SECTOR LENDING IN INDIA

The concept of 'Priority sector lending' focuses on the idea of directing the lending of the banks towards few specified sectors and activities in the economy. The term 'priority sector' indicates those activities which have national importance and have been assigned priority for development. These primarily include agriculture, small industries etc. The case has further been that these sectors and activities were neglected ones for the purpose of bank credit and therefore for the purposes of accessibility of credit, these neglected ones are considered to be at priority for providing credit.

Priority Sector Lending - Targets and Classification 2020

RBI has updated priority sector lending guidelines on 04.09.2020. These Directions shall be called the Reserve Bank of India (Priority Sector Lending - Targets and Classification) Directions, 2020. These Directions shall come into effect on the day they are placed on the official website of the Reserve Bank of India.

Applicability

The provisions of these Directions shall apply to every Commercial Bank [including Regional Rural Bank (RRB), Small Finance Bank (SFB), Local Area Bank] and Primary (Urban) Co-operative Bank (UCB) other than Salary Earners' Bank licensed to operate in India by the Reserve Bank of India.

Definitions/Clarifications

In these Directions, unless the context otherwise requires, the terms herein shall bear the meanings assigned to them below:

(i) 'Urban Co-operative Bank' or 'UCB' means a Primary Co-operative Bank as defined under Section 5(ccv) of the Banking Regulation Act, 1949 read with Section 56 of the Act.

(ii) "On-lending" means loans sanctioned by banks to eligible intermediaries for onward lending for creation of priority sector assets. The average maturity of priority sector assets thus created by the eligible intermediaries should be co-terminus with maturity of the bank loan.

(iii) Contingent liabilities/off-balance sheet items do not form part of priority sector achievement. However, foreign banks with less than 20 branches have an option to reckon the Credit Equivalent of Off-Balance Sheet Exposures (CEOBE) extended to borrowers for eligible priority sector activities for achievement of priority sector target, subject to the condition that the CEOBE (both priority sector and non-priority sector excluding interbank exposure) should be added to the Adjusted Net Bank Credit (ANBC) in the denominator for computation of PSL targets.

(iv) Off-balance sheet interbank exposures are excluded for computing CEOBE for the priority sector targets.

(v) The term "all-inclusive interest" includes interest (effective annual interest), processing fees and service charges.

TARGET/SUB-TARGET FOR PRIORITY SECTOR LENDING

The target set under priority sector lending are as under:

- Domestic commercial banks (excl. RRBs& SFBs) & foreign banks with 20 branches and above have to achieve the total Priority Sector

Target of 40 percent of Adjusted Net Bank Credit (ANBC) or Credit Equivalent Amount of Off-Balance Sheet Exposure (CEOBE), whichever is higher.

- Foreign banks with less than 20 branches have to achieve the total Priority Sector Target 40 per cent of ANBC or CEOBE whichever is higher; out of which up to 32% can be in the form of lending to Exports and not less than 8% can be to any other priority sector.
- Regional Rural Banks have to achieve the total Priority Sector Target 75 per cent of ANBC or CEOBE whichever is higher; However, lending to Medium Enterprises, Social Infrastructure and Renewable Energy shall be reckoned for priority sector achievement only up to 15 per cent of ANBC.
- Small Finance Banks have to achieve the total Priority Sector Target 75 per cent of ANBC as computed in para 6 below or CEOBE whichever is higher.

SUMMARY OF THE PRIORITY SECTOR LENDING TARGETS

Categories	Domestic commercial banks & foreign banks with 20 branches and above	Foreign banks with less than 20 branches	Regional Rural Banks	Small Finance Banks
Total Priority Sector	40 per cent of Adjusted Net Bank Credit (ANBC) or Credit Equivalent Amount of Off-Balance Sheet Exposure (CEOBE), whichever is higher.	40 per cent of ANBC or CEOBE whichever is higher; out of which up to 32% can be in the form of lending to Exports and not less than 8% can be to any other priority sector.	75 per cent of ANBC or CEOBE whichever is higher; However, lending to Medium Enterprises, Social Infrastructure and Renewable Energy shall be reckoned for priority sector achievement only up to 15 per cent of ANBC.	75 per cent of ANBC as computed in para 6 below or CEOBE whichever is higher.
Agriculture	18 per cent of ANBC or CEOBE, whichever is higher; out of which a target of 10 per cent# is prescribed for Small and Marginal Farmers (SMFs)	Not applicable	18 per cent ANBC or CEOBE, whichever is higher; out of which a target of 10 per cent# is prescribed for SMFs	18 per cent of ANBC or CEOBE, whichever is higher; out of which a target of 10 per cent# is prescribed for SMFs
Micro Enterprises	7.5 per cent of ANBC or CEOBE, whichever is higher	Not applicable	7.5 per cent of ANBC or CEOBE, whichever is higher	7.5 per cent of ANBC or CEOBE, whichever is higher
Advances to Weaker Sections	12 percent# of ANBC or CEOBE, whichever is higher	Not applicable	12 per cent# of ANBC or CEOBE, whichever is higher	12 per cent# of ANBC or CEOBE, whichever is higher

#Revised targets for Agriculture and SMFs will be implemented in a phased manner

The targets for lending to SMFs and for Weaker Sections shall be revised upwards from FY 2021-22 onwards as follows:

Categories	Primary Urban Co-operative Bank				
Total Priority Sector	40 per cent of ANBC or CEOBE, whichever is higher, which shall stand increased to 75 per cent of ANBC or CEOBE, whichever is higher, with effect from March 31, 2024. UCBs shall comply with the stipulated target as per the following milestones:				
	Existing target	**March 31, 2021**	**March 31, 2022**	**March 31, 2023**	**March 31, 2024**
	40%	45%	50%	60%	75%
Micro Enterprises	7.5 per cent of ANBC or Credit Equivalent Amount of Off-Balance Sheet Exposure, whichever is higher				
Advances to Weaker Sections	12 per cent# of ANBC or credit equivalent amount of Off-Balance Sheet Exposure, whichever is higher.				

#Revised targets for weaker sections will be implemented in a phased manner as indicated below

Financial Year	Small and Marginal Farmers target*	Weaker Sections target^
2020-21	8%	10%
2021-22	9%	11%
2022-23	9.5%	11.5%
2023-24	10%	12%

* *Not applicable to UCBs*
^ *Weaker Sections target for RRBs will continue to be 15% of ANBC or CEOBE, whichever is higher.*

Computation of ANBC are as under:

ADJUSTED NET BANK CREDIT (ANBC)	
Bank Credit in India (As prescribed in item No. VI of Form 'A' as on 31st March) under Sec 42 [2] of RBI Act, 1934.	I
Bills rediscounted with RBI and other approved Financial institutions	II
Net Bank Credit (NBC)	III (I-II)
Outstanding Deposits under RIDF and other eligible funds with NABARD, NHB, SIDBI and MUDRA Ltd in lieu of non-achievement of priority sector lending targets/sub-targets + outstanding PSLCs	IV
Eligible amount for exemptions on issuance of long term bands for infrastructure and affordable housing as per circular DBOD.BP.BC.No. 25/08.12.014/2014-15 dated July 15, 2014	V
Eligible advance extended in India against the incremental FCNR(B)/NRE deposits, qualifying for exemption from CRR/SLR requirements.	VI
Investments made by public sector banks in the Recapitalization Bonds floated by Government of India.	VII
Other investments eligible to be treated as priority sector (e.g. investments in securitised assets)	VIII
Face Value of securities acquired and kept under HTM category under the TLTRO 2.0 (Press Release 2019-2020/2237 dated April 17, 2020 read with Q.11 of FAQ and SLF-MF- Press Release 2019-2020/2276 dated April 27, 2020 and also Extended Regulatory Benefits under SLFMF Scheme vide Press Release 2019-2020/2294 dated April 30, 2020.	IX
Bonds/debentures in Non-SLR categories under HTM category	X
For UCBs: investments made after August 30, 2007 in permitted non SLR bonds held under 'Held to Maturity' (HTM) category	XI
ANBC (Other than UCBs)	III + IV- (V+VI+VII) +VIII - IX + X
ANBC for UCBs	III + IV - VI - IX + XI
*For the purpose of priority sector computation only. Banks should not deduct / net any amount like provisions, accrued interest, etc. from NBC.	

1. Sub-target Under Agriculture

The lending to agriculture sector will include Farm Credit (Agriculture and Allied Activities), lending for Agriculture Infrastructure and Ancillary Activities.

Domestic Commercial Banks, RRBs, Foreign Banks with 20 & Above Branches & Small Finance Banks: 18 per cent of ANBC or CEOBE, whichever is higher; out of which a target of 10 per cent is prescribed for Small and Marginal Farmers (SMFs), to be achieved by March 2024.

Computation of 10% loan to small and marginal farmers include the following:

- **Marginal Farmer:** Farmer Landholding up to 1 hectare.

- **Small Farmer:** Farmer Landholding up to 2 hectares.
- Landless agricultural labourers, tenant farmers, oral lessees and share-croppers.
- Loan to SHG or JLG engaged in agriculture and allied activities.
- Loans up to ₹ 2 lakh to individuals solely engaged in Allied activities without any accompanying land holding criteria.
- Loan to farmer producer companies of individual farmers and co-operative society having 75% Small and Marginal farmer engaged in agriculture activities.

The present distinction between direct and indirect agriculture is dispensed with. Instead, the lending to agriculture sector has been re-defined to include:

A. Farm Credit (which will include short-term crop loans and medium/long-term credit to farmers);

B. Farm Credit Loan to corporate farmer, farmer producer organization, Partnership forms, Cooperative societies;

C. Agriculture Infrastructure; and

D. Ancillary Activities.

A. Farm Credit Loans to Individual Farmers, SHG, JLG and Proprietorship Firms of Farmers Directly Engaged in Agriculture and Allied Activities. This will include:

- Short term loan for raising crops, i.e. Crop Loans;
- Medium & long-term loan to farmers for agriculture & allied activities;
- Loan to farmers for pre & post-harvest activities;
- Loans against pledge/hypothecation of agricultural produce (including warehouse receipts) for a period not exceeding 12 months subject to a limit up to ₹ 75 lakh against NWRs/eNWRs and up to ₹ 50 lakh against warehouse receipts other than NWRs/eNWRs.
- Loans to farmers under KCC Scheme;
- Loans to distress farmers indebted to non-institutional lenders;
- Loans to farmers for installation of stand-alone Solar Agriculture Pumps, solar power plants and for solarisation of grid connected Agriculture Pumps;
- Loan to small & marginal farmers to purchase of land for agriculture purpose.

B. Farm Credit Loan to Corporate Farmer, Farmer Producer Organization, Partnership Forms, Cooperative Societies Engaged in Agriculture and Allied Activities for Loans Limit up to 2 Crores Per Borrower. This will include:

- Crop Loans to farmer which will include traditional/Non-traditional plantations and horticulture, and loans to allied activities;
- Medium- & long-term loan to farmers for agriculture & allied activities;
- Loan to farmers for pre & post-harvest activities;
- Loans against pledge/hypothecation of agricultural produce (including warehouse receipts) for a period not exceeding 12 months subject to a limit up to ₹ 75 lakh against NWRs/eNWRs and up to ₹ 50 lakh against warehouse receipts other than NWRs/eNWRs.
- Loans up to ₹ 5 crore per borrowing entity to FPOs/FPCs undertaking farming with assured marketing of their produce at a pre-determined price;
- UCBs are not permitted to lend to co-operatives of farmers.

C. Agriculture Infrastructure: Loan for Aggregate Sanction Limit of ₹ 100 Crores Per Borrower from the Banking System.

- Loans for construction of storage facilities (Warehouse, Godowns, market yards) including cold storage units designed to store Agriculture produce, irrespective of their location;
- Soil conservation and watershed development;
- Plant tissue culture and agri-biotechnology, seed production, production of bio-pesticides, bio-fertilizer, and vermi composting;
- Loans for construction of oil extraction/processing units for production of bio-fuels, their storage and distribution infrastructure along with loans to entrepreneurs for setting up Compressed Bio Gas (CBG) plants.

D. Agriculture Ancillary Activities:

- Loans up to ₹ 5 crores to co-operative societies of farmers for disposing of the produce of farmers (Not applicable to UCBs);
- Loans for setting Agriclinics & Agribusiness Centre's;
- Loan sanction to MFIs for on lending Ag activities;

- Loans for Food & Agro-processing up to an aggregate sanction limit of ₹ 100 crores per borrower from the banking system;
- Loans up to ₹ 50 crore to Start-ups, as per definition of Ministry of Commerce and Industry, Govt. of India that are engaged in agriculture and allied services;
- Bank loans to Primary Agricultural Cooperative Society (PACS), Farmer's Service Societies (FSS) and Large sized Adivasi Multi-Purpose Scheme (LAMPS) for on lending to Agriculture;
- Outstanding deposits under RIDF and eligible funds with NABRD on account of priority sector shortfall.

2. Micro, Small and Medium Enterprises (MSMEs)

Bank loans to Micro, Small and Medium Enterprises, for both manufacturing and service sectors are eligible to be classified under the priority sector as per the following norms. Within the MSME target, Micro Enterprises will be 7.5% of ANBC or Off-Balance Sheet exposure, whichever is higher.

Revised MSME Classification applicable w.e.f 1st July 2020

Composite Criteria for Manufacturing Enterprises and Enterprises rendering Services: Investment and Annual Turnover

Classification	Micro	Small	Medium
Investment in Plant and Machinery or Equipment	Not more than ₹ 1 crore	Not more than ₹ 10 crore	Not more than ₹ 50 crore
Annual Turnover	Not more than ₹ 5 crore	Not more than ₹ 50 crore	Not more than ₹ 250 crore

A. Khadi and Village Industries Sector (KVI): All loan given to units of KVI sector will eligible for classification of 7.5% prescribed to Micro Enterprises.

B. Other Finance to MSMEs:

(a) Loans to person involve in assisting the Artisans, village and Cottage Industry.

(b) Loan to cooperative of producers in the Artisans, village and Cottage Industry (Not applicable for UCBs).

(c) Loan sanction to Banks, MFIs for on lending to MSE sectors.

(d) Credit outstanding under General Credit Cards (including Artisan Credit Card, Laghu Udyami Card, Swarojgar Credit Card, and Weaver's Card etc. in existence and catering to the non-farm entrepreneurial credit needs of individuals).

(e) Loans up to ₹ 50 crore to Start-ups, as per definition of Ministry of Commerce and Industry, Govt. of India that confirm to the definition of MSME;

(f) Overdraft to Pradhan Mantri Jan-Dhan Yojana (PMJDY) account holders as per limits and conditions prescribed by Department of Financial Services;

(g) Outstanding deposits with SIDBI and MUDRA Ltd. on account of priority sector shortfall.

3. Export Credit (not applicable to RRBs and LABs)

The Export Credit extended as per the details below would be classified as priority sector.

(a) **Domestic Commercial Banks/WoS of Foreign Banks/ SFBs/ UCBs:** Incremental export credit over corresponding date of the preceding year, up to 2 per cent of ANBC or CEOBE whichever is higher, subject to a sanctioned limit of up to ₹ 40 crore per borrower.

(b) **Foreign Banks with 20 and above Branches:** Incremental export credit over corresponding date of the preceding year, up to 2 per cent of ANBC or CEOBE whichever is higher.

(c) **Foreign Banks with Less Than 20 Branches:** Export Credit will be allowed up to 32% of ANBC or Off-Balance Sheet exposure, whichever is higher.

Export credit includes pre-shipment and post shipment export credit (excluding off-balance sheet items) as defined in Master Circular on Rupee / Foreign Currency Export Credit and Customer Service to Exporters issued by our Department of Banking Regulation.

4. Education

Loans to individuals for educational purposes, including vocational courses, not exceeding ₹ 20 lakh will be considered as eligible for priority sector classification. Loans currently classified as priority sector will continue till maturity.

5. Housing

The following housing loans are categorised as Priority Sector Advances:

(a) **Loan for Construction and Purchase:** Loans to individuals up to ₹ 35 lakh in metropolitan centres (with population of ten lakh and above) and loans up to ₹ 25 lakh in other centres for purchase/construction of a dwelling unit per family provided the overall cost of the dwelling unit in the metropolitan centre and at other centres should not exceed ₹ 45 lakh and ₹ 30 lakh respectively. Existing individual housing loans of UCBs presently classified under PSL will continue as PSL till maturity or repayment. The housing loans to banks' own employees will be excluded.

(b) **Loan for Repairs:** Loans for repairs to damaged dwelling units of families up to ₹ 10 lakh in metropolitan centres and up to ₹ 6 lakh in other centres.

(c) **Loan to Governmental Agency:** Bank loans to any governmental agency for construction of dwelling units or for slum clearance and rehabilitation of slum dwellers subject to dwelling units with carpet area of not more than 60 sq.m.

(d) **Loan for Housing Projects:** The loans sanctioned by banks for housing projects exclusively for the purpose of construction of houses for economically weaker sections and low-income groups, the total cost of which does not exceed ₹ 10 lakh per dwelling unit. For the purpose of identifying the economically weaker sections and low-income groups, the family income limit of ₹ 3 lakh for EWS and ₹ 6 lakh for LIG per annum, in alignment with the income criteria specified under the Pradhan Mantri Awas Yojana.

(e) **Loan to HFC:** Bank loans to Housing Finance Companies (HFCs), approved by NHB for their refinance, for on-lending for the purpose of purchase/construction/reconstruction of individual dwelling units or for slum clearance and rehabilitation of slum dwellers, subject to an aggregate loan limit of ₹ 20 lakh per borrower.

(f) Bank loans for affordable housing projects using at least 50% of FAR/FSI for dwelling units with carpet area of not more than 60 sq.m.

(g) Outstanding deposits with NHB on account of priority sector shortfall.

6. Social Infrastructure

Bank loans up to a limit of ₹ 5 crore per borrower for setting up schools, drinking water facilities and sanitation facilities including construction/refurbishment of household toilets and water improvements at household level, etc. and loans up to a limit of ₹ 10 crore per borrower for building health care facilities including under 'Ayushman Bharat' in Tier II to Tier VI centres.

In case of UCBs, the above limits are applicable only in centres having a population of less than one lakh.

Bank loans to MFIs extended for on-lending to individuals and also to members of SHGs/JLGs for water and sanitation facilities.

7. Renewable Energy

Bank loans up to a limit of ₹ 30 crore to borrowers for purposes like solar based power generators, biomass-based power generators, wind mills, micro-hydel plants and for non-conventional energy based public utilities, viz., street lighting systems and remote village electrification etc., will be eligible for Priority Sector classification.

For individual households, the loan limit will be ₹ 10 lakh per borrower.

8. Others

The following loans are also categorised as Priority Sector Advances:

(a) Loans not exceeding ₹ 1.00 lakh per borrower provided directly by banks to individuals and individual members of SHG/JLG, provided the individual borrower's household annual income in rural areas does not exceed ₹ 1.00 lakh and for non-rural areas it does not exceed ₹ 1.60 lakh, and loans not exceeding ₹ 2.00 lakh provided directly by banks to SHG/JLG for activities other than agriculture or MSME, viz., loans for meeting social needs, construction or repair of house, construction of toilets or any viable common activity started by the SHGs.

(b) Loans to distressed persons [other than distressed farmers indebted to non-institutional lenders] not exceeding ₹ 1.00 lakh per borrower to prepay their debt to non-institutional lenders.

(c) Loans sanctioned to State Sponsored Organisations for Scheduled Castes/ Scheduled Tribes for the specific purpose of purchase and supply of inputs and/or the marketing of the outputs of the beneficiaries of these organisations.

(d) Loans up to ₹ 50 crore to Start-ups, as per definition of Ministry of Commerce and Industry, Govt. of India that are engaged in activities other than Agriculture or MSME.

9. Weaker Sections

Priority sector loans to the following borrowers will be considered under Weaker Sections category. 12% of ANBC or Credit equivalent amount of Off- Balance Sheet exposure, whichever is higher have to achieve by 31 March 2024. (Not applicable to Foreign banks with less than 20 branches).

(a) Loan to Small and Marginal farmers;

(b) Beneficiaries under Government Sponsored Schemes such as National Rural Livelihood Mission (NRLM), National Urban Livelihood Mission (NULM), Differential Rate of Interest (DRI) scheme and Self Employment Scheme for Rehabilitation of Manual Scavengers (SRMS)

(c) Artisans, Village and cottage industries where individual credit limits do not exceed ₹ 1 lakh;

(d) Loan to individual SC & ST category;

(e) Loan to persons with disabilities;

(f) Loans to individual women beneficiaries up to ₹ 1 lakh per borrower. (For UCBs, existing loans to women will continue to be classified under weaker sections till their maturity/repayment.);

(g) Loans to distressed farmers indebted to non-institutional lenders;

(h) Loans to distressed persons other than farmers not exceeding ₹ 1 lakh per borrower to prepay their debt to non-institutional lenders;

(i) Overdraft limit to PMJDY account holder as per limits and conditions prescribed may be notified by Government of India from time to time;

(j) Minority communities as may be notified by Government of India from time to time.

Monitoring of Priority Sector Lending Targets

To ensure continuous flow of credit to priority sector, there will be more frequent monitoring of priority sector lending compliance of banks on 'quarterly' basis instead of annual basis as of now. The data on priority sector advances have to be furnished by banks at quarterly and annual intervals as per revised reporting formats, the guidelines for which will be issued separately.

Priority Sector Lending Certificates (PSLCs)

Priority Sector Lending Certificates (PSLCs) are a mechanism to enable banks to achieve the priority sector lending target and sub-targets by purchase of these instruments in the event of shortfall. This also incentivizes surplus banks as it allows them to sell their excess achievement over targets thereby enhancing lending to the categories under priority sector. Under the PSLC mechanism, the seller sells fulfilment of priority sector obligation and the buyer buys the obligation with no transfer of risk or loan assets.

Non-achievement of Priority Sector Targets

(i) Banks having any shortfall in lending to priority sector shall be allocated amounts for contribution to the Rural Infrastructure Development Fund (RIDF) established with NABARD and other funds with NABARD/NHB/SIDBI/ MUDRA Ltd., as decided by the Reserve Bank from time to time.

(ii) With effect from March 31, 2021, all UCBs (excluding those under all-inclusive directions) will be required to contribute to Rural Infrastructure Development Fund (RIDF) established with NABARD and other funds with NABARD / NHB / SIDBI / MUDRA Ltd., against their priority sector lending (PSL) shortfall vis-à-vis the prescribed target.

(iii) While computing priority sector target achievement, shortfall / excess lending for each quarter will be monitored separately. A simple average of all quarters will be arrived at and considered for computation of overall shortfall / excess at the end of the year. The same method will be followed for calculating the achievement of priority sector sub-targets.

(iv) The interest rates on banks' contribution to RIDF or any other funds, tenure of deposits, etc. shall be fixed by Reserve Bank of India from time to time.

(v) The mis-classifications reported by the Reserve Bank's Department of Supervision (DoS) (NABARD in respect of RRBs) would be adjusted/ reduced from the achievement of that year, to which the amount of misclassification pertains, for allocation to various funds in subsequent years.

(vi) Non-achievement of priority sector targets and sub-targets will be taken into account while granting regulatory clearances/approvals for various purposes.

CHAPTER-22 (NEW)

Micro, Small and Medium Enterprises (MSME) & CGTMSE (P.No.-156-163 Point 3&4)

Micro, Small & Medium Enterprises (MSME) is the pillar of economic growth of India. MSME's are the backbone of Indian industry. MSME has played a prominent role in the development of the country in terms of creating employment opportunities- MSMEs contribute 29 per cent to India's gross domestic product and comprise almost half of its exports. These units employ over 11 crore workers. Though India is still facing infrastructural problems, lack of proper market linkages, and challenges in terms of flow of institutional credit, it has seen a tremendous growth in this sector.

Micro, Small & Medium Enterprises Development (MSMED) Act, 2006

The Government of India has enacted the Micro, Small and Medium Enterprises Development (MSMED) Act, 2006 on June 16, 2006 which was notified on October 2, 2006. With the enactment of MSMED Act 2006, the paradigm shift that has taken place is the inclusion of the services sector in the definition of Micro, Small & Medium enterprises, apart from extending the scope to medium enterprises.

New Definition of Micro, Small and Medium Enterprises 2020

On 1st June, 2020 the Union Cabinet headed by Prime Minister Narendra Modi officially revised the MSME definition. The recent changes in the definition of micro, small, and medium-sized enterprises made as a part of the Atmanirbhar Bharat Abhiyaan relief package were approved.

Union Ministry of Micro, Small and Medium Enterprises has issued Gazette notification dated 01 June 2020 to pave way for implementation of the upward revision in the definition and criteria of MSMEs in the country. The new definition and criterion will come into effect from 1st July, 2020. Gazette Notification is as under:

"In exercise of the powers conferred by sub-section (1) read with sub-section (9) of section 7 of the 'Micro, Small and Medium Enterprises Development Act, 2006 (27 of 2006) and in supersession of the notification of the Government of India, Ministry of Small Scale Industries, dated the 29th September, 2006, published in the Gazette of India, Extraordinary, Part II, Section 3, Sub-section (ii), vide S.O. 1642(E), dated the 30th September 2006 except as respects things done or omitted to be done before such supersession, the Central Government, hereby notifies the following criteria for classification of micro, small and medium enterprises, namely:

(i) A micro enterprise, where the investment in Plant and Machinery or Equipment does not exceed one crore rupees and turnover does not exceed five crore rupees;

(ii) A small enterprise, where the investment in Plant and Machinery or Equipment does not exceed ten crore rupees and turnover does not exceed fifty crore rupees;

(iii) A medium enterprise, where the investment in Plant and Machinery or Equipment does not exceed fifty crore rupees and turnover does not exceed two hundred and fifty crore rupees."

EXCLUDED ITEMS FOR CALCULATING THE INVESTMENT IN PLANT AND MACHINERY

Exercise of the powers conferred by sub-section (1) of MSME Act 2006 herein referred to as the said Act, the Central Government specifies the following items, the cost of which shall be excluded while calculating the investment in plant and machinery in the case of the enterprises mentioned in Section 7(1)(a) of the said Act, namely:

(a) Equipment such as tools, jigs, dyes, moulds and spare parts for maintenance and the cost of consumables stores;

(b) Installation of plant and machinery;

(c) Research and development equipment and pollution controlled equipment

(d) Power generation set and extra transformer installed by the enterprise as per regulations of the State Electricity Board;

(e) Bank charges and service charges paid to the National Small Industries Corporation or the State Small Industries Corporation;

(f) Procurement or installation of cables, wiring, bus bars, electrical control panels (not mounded on individual machines), oil circuit breakers or miniature circuit breakers which are necessarily to be used for providing electrical power to the plant and machinery or for safety measures;

(g) Gas producer's plants;

(h) Transportation charges (excluding sales-tax or value added tax and excise duty) for indigenous machinery from the place of the manufacture to the site of the enterprise;

(i) Charges paid for technical know-how for erection of plant and machinery;

(j) Such storage tanks which store raw material and finished produces and are not linked with the manufacturing process; and

(k) Firefighting equipment.

While calculating the investment in plant and machinery refer to paragraph 1, the original price thereof, irrespective of whether the plant and machinery are new or second handed, shall be taken into account provided that in the case of imported machinery, the following shall be included in calculating the value, namely;

- Import duty (excluding miscellaneous expenses such as transportation from the port to the site of the factory, demurrage paid at the port);
- Shipping charges;
- Customs clearance charges; and
- Sales tax or value added tax.

OLD DEFINITION OF MSME TILL 30TH JUNE 2020

Sector	Enterprises for Manufacturing/ processing Units	Enterprises engaged in providing services
Micro Enterprise	Investment in plant & machinery not exceeding ₹ 25 lakh.	Investment in equipment not to exceed ₹ 10 lakh.
Small Enterprise	More than ₹ 25 lakh but not to exceed ₹ 5 crore.	More than ₹ 10 lakh but not to exceed ₹ 2 crore.
Medium Enterprise	More than ₹ 5 crore but not to exceed ₹ 10 crore.	More than ₹ 2 crore but not to exceed ₹ 5 crore.

REVISED MSME CLASSIFICATION APPLICABLE W.E.F 1ST JULY 2020

Composite Criteria for Manufacturing Enterprises and Enterprises Rendering Services: Investment and Annual Turnover			
Classification	**Micro**	**Small**	**Medium**
Investment in Plant and Machinery or Equipment	Not more than ₹ 1 crore	Not more than ₹ 10 crore	Not more than ₹ 50 crore
Annual Turnover	Not more than ₹ 5 crore	Not more than ₹ 50 crore	Not more than ₹ 250 crore

ISSUE OF ACKNOWLEDGEMENT OF LOAN APPLICATIONS TO MSME BORROWERS

Banks are advised to mandatorily acknowledge all loan applications, submitted manually or online, by their MSME borrowers and ensure that a running serial number is recorded on the application form as well as on the acknowledgement receipt. Banks are further advised to put in place a system of Central Registration of loan applications, online submission of loan applications and a system of e-tracking of MSME loan applications.

Collateral: Banks are mandated not to accept collateral security in the case of loans up to ₹ 10 lakh extended to units in the MSE sector. Banks are also advised to extend collateral-free loans up to ₹ 10 lakh to all units financed under the Prime Minister Employment Generation Programme (PMEGP) administered by KVIC.

Banks may, on the basis of good track record and financial position of the MSE units, increase the limit to dispense with the collateral requirement for loans up to ₹ 25 lakh (with the approval of the appropriate authority). Banks are advised to strongly encourage their branch level functionaries to avail of the Credit Guarantee Scheme cover, including making performance in this regard a criterion in the evaluation of their field staff.

Composite Loan: A composite loan limit of ₹ 1 crore can be sanctioned by banks to enable the MSE entrepreneurs to avail of their working capital and term loan requirement through Single Window.

Credit Guarantee Fund Trust Scheme for MSEs?

The Ministry of MSME, Government of India and SIDBI set up the Credit Guarantee Fund Trust for Micro and Small Enterprises (CGTMSE) with a view to facilitate flow of credit to the MSE sector without the need for collaterals/ third party guarantees. The Credit Guarantee scheme (CGS) seeks to reassure the lender that, in the event of a MSE unit, which availed collateral—free credit facilities, failing to discharge its liabilities to the lender, the Guarantee Trust would make good the loss incurred by the lender up to 85 per cent of the outstanding amount in default.

The CGTMSE would provide cover for credit facility up to ₹ 200 lakh which have been extended by lending institutions without any collateral security and/or third party guarantees. A guarantee and annual service fee is charged by the CGTMSE to avail of the guarantee cover.

TARGETS PRESCRIBED FOR LENDING BY BANKS TO MSMES

As per extant policy, certain targets have been prescribed for banks for lending to the Micro and Small enterprise (MSE) sector. Banks have been advised to achieve a 20 per cent year-on-year growth in credit to micro and small enterprises, a 10 per cent annual growth in the number of micro enterprise accounts and 60 per cent of total lending to MSE sector as on corresponding quarter of the previous year to Micro enterprises.

SPECIALISED MSME BRANCHES

Public sector banks have been advised to open at least one specialised branch in each district. Further, banks have been permitted to categorise their general banking branches having 60% or more of their advances to MSME sector as specialized MSME branches in order to encourage them to open more specialized MSME branches for providing better service to this sector as a whole.

CLUSTER FINANCING

Cluster based approach to lending is intended to provide a full-service approach to cater to the diverse needs of the MSE sector which may be achieved through extending banking services to recognized MSE clusters. A cluster based approach may be more beneficial:

(a) in dealing with well-defined and recognized groups;
(b) availability of appropriate information for risk assessment;
(c) monitoring by the lending institutions; and
(d) reduction in costs.

CREDIT RATING OF THE MSME BORROWERS

With a view to facilitating credit flow to the MSME sector and enhancing the comfort-level of the lending institutions, the credit rating of MSME units done by reputed credit rating agencies should be encouraged. Banks are advised to consider these ratings as per availability and wherever appropriate structure their rates of interest depending on the ratings assigned to the borrowing MSME units.

STREAMLINING FLOW OF CREDIT TO MICRO AND SMALL ENTERPRISES FOR FACILITATING TIMELY AND ADEQUATE CREDIT FLOW DURING THEIR 'LIFE CYCLE'

In order to provide timely financial support to Micro and Small enterprises facing financial difficulties during their 'Life Cycle', Banks are advised to review and tune their existing lending policies to the MSE sector by incorporating therein the following provisions so as to facilitate timely and adequate availability of credit to viable MSE borrowers especially during the need of funds in unforeseen circumstances:

(i) To extend standby credit facility in case of term loans;
(ii) Additional working capital to meet with emergent needs of MSE units;
(iii) Mid-term review of the regular working capital limits, where banks are convinced that changes in the demand pattern of MSE borrowers require increasing the existing credit limits of the MSMEs, every year based on the actual sales of the previous year;
(iv) Timelines for Credit Decisions.

DEBT RESTRUCTURING OF ADVANCES

A viable/potentially viable unit may apply for a debt restructuring if it shows early stage of sickness. In such cases the banks may consider to reschedule the debt for repayment, consider additional funds etc. A debt restructuring mechanism for units in MSME sector has been formulated and advised to all commercial banks.

FRAMEWORK FOR REVIVAL AND REHABILITATION OF MSME

The salient features of the Framework are as under:

(i) Before a loan account of an MSME turns into a Non-Performing Asset (NPA), banks or creditors should identify incipient stress in the account by creating three sub-categories under the Special Mention Account (SMA) category as given in the Framework.
(ii) Any MSME borrower may also voluntarily initiate proceedings under this Framework.
(iii) Committee approach to be adopted for deciding corrective action plan.
(iv) Time lines have been fixed for taking various decisions under the Framework.

BANKING CODES & STANDARD BOARD OF INDIA (BCSBI) FOR MSE

The Banking Codes and Standards Board of India (BCSBI) has formulated a Code of Bank's Commitment to Micro and Small Enterprises. The Code sets minimum standards of banking practices for banks to follow when they are dealing with Micro and Small Enterprises (MSEs) unit. It provides protection to MSEs and explains how banks are expected to deal with MSEs for their day-to-day operations and in times of financial difficulty.

THE CREDIT GUARANTEE SCHEME (CGS)

Businesses, especially MSMEs, require a steady source of finance if they are to meet the hiccups of kick-starting their business and growing it. Though business loans are available, they are difficult to obtain in when the MSME is in its nascent stage. The Credit Guarantee Scheme offers unsecured loan facilities to MSME businesses. MSME businesses can avail term loans or working capital loans under the scheme.

The Credit Guarantee Scheme (CGS) seeks to reassure the lender that, in the event of a MSE unit, which availed collateral-free credit facilities, fails to discharge its liabilities to the lender, the Guarantee Trust would make good the loss incurred by the lender up to 85 per cent of the outstanding amount in default.

CREDIT GUARANTEE FUND TRUST FOR MICRO & SMALL ENTERPRISES (CGTMSE)

Ministry of Micro, Small & Medium Enterprises (MSME), Government of India (GOI) and Small Industries Development Bank of India (SIDBI) set up Credit Guarantee Fund Trust for Small Industries (CGTSI) in August 2000. The GOI and SIDBI as settlors of the Trust have committed a corpus of ₹ 2,500 crore in the ratio of 4 : 1 to the CGTMSE, out of which ₹ 1,906 crore has been contributed till date. Credit Guarantee Fund Trust for Micro & Small Enterprises (CGTMSE) w.e.f. 2nd July 2007.

Policy Changes in CGTMSE in 2018: Following policy changes in Credit Guarantee Scheme were announced in an event "Rebooting CGTMSE" organized by Ministry of MSME and CGTMSE on February 20, 2018:

1. Charging Annual Guarantee Fees (AGF) on Outstanding Loan Amount rather than sanction amount.
2. Expanding the Coverage of the Credit Guarantee Scheme (CGS) to cover MSE Retail Traders segment.
3. Allowing loans with Partial Collateral Security under Credit Guarantee Scheme.
4. Increase in the extent of guarantee coverage to 75% from existing 50% for proposals above ₹ 50 lakh.
5. Enhancing IT infrastructure of the Trust to improve operational efficiencies and reduce the turnaround time for claim settlement.

The above-mentioned steps undertaken by the Trust are expected to greatly increase the attractiveness of the scheme and increase the operational efficiency of the Trust. This in turn is expected to increase the credit guarantees availed by MLIs and help in enhanced flow of credit to the MSE sector and betterment of the sector as a whole.

Eligible Lending Institutions Under the Scheme: All Scheduled Commercial Banks (either PSU, Private or Foreign Banks), selected Regional Rural Banks, selected state financial corporations or NBFC's or such of those institutions as may be directed by GOI can avail of guarantee cover in respect of their eligible credit facilities under the Scheme. Small Industries Development Bank of India (SIDBI), National Small Industries Corporation Ltd. (NSIC) and North Eastern Development Finance Corporation Ltd. (NEDFC) have been included as eligible institutions.

Eligibility of Borrowers for CGTMSE Coverage:

(a) All Credit Facilities sanctioned to Micro & Small units defined as per MSMED act 2006, on the basis of investment in Plant & Machineries/ Equipment.

(b) Units under both the sectors viz. Manufacturing and Services including Retail Trade, can be covered under CGTMSE.

(c) All the units should be engaged in the activity as approved by CGTMSE for coverage.

(d) All units should have a valid Udyog Adhaar No. (UAN).

(e) Maximum Quantum of loan to a single borrower eligible for coverage should not exceed ₹ 200 Lakhs.

(f) A borrower can be given benefit of coverage only once in his/her lifetime under CGTMSE cap of ₹ 200 lakh is removed by 06 December 2019 notification. Now the borrowers can avail incremental credit facilities (i.e. to the extent of reduction in the outstanding exposure limit) under Credit Guarantee Scheme of CGTMSE, subject to maximum cap of ₹ 200 lakh.

(g) For loans up to ₹ 10 Lakhs, no collateral security or third party guarantee should be obtained, to be eligible under the scheme.

(h) For loans above ₹ 10 Lakhs, Partial Collateral security may be obtained.

(i) Under the Credit Guarantee Scheme, the CGTMSE encourages composite credit being extended to a single borrower by a Bank. Joint financing by a financial institution (e.g. Small Industries Development Bank of India, National Small Industries Corporation, and North Eastern Development Finance Corporation Ltd. etc) and commercial bank can be covered under the scheme. For e.g. MSE unit is financed by term loan from State financial institution development financial institution and Working capital from a commercial bank. However, sharing of securities will not be permitted.

(j) Loan under Consortium are not eligible under the scheme.

(k) Loans to SHGs are not eligible under the scheme.

(l) Educational Institutions/Training Institutions are not covered under the Scheme

Credit Facilities & Parameters: Fund and non-fund based (Letters of Credit, Bank Guarantee etc.) credit facilities up to ₹ 200 lakh per eligible borrower are covered under the guarantee scheme provided they are extended purely on the project viability without collateral security or third party guarantee. A lender can extend either term loan or working capital facility alone and still be eligible for a guarantee cover if it meets the other eligibility parameters (wef 31.10.2018, CGTMSE has removed rate of interest limit cap of 14% for all eligible loan account).

CGTMSE Cover for Borrowers Engaged in Retail Trade: Credit Facility extended to borrowers engaged in Retail Trade activity will now be covered under CGTMSE scheme with effect from 28.02.2018 (credit facility eligible for coverage on or after 28.02.2018). The Details are hereunder:

(a) Exposure Limit for Credit facility of all Retail Trade segment will be up to ₹ 100 Lakh per MSE Borrowers (w.e.f 31.10.2018, CGTMSE has removed floor limit of ₹ 10 lakh in Retail Trade Segment).

(b) Extent of Guarantee coverage to such credit facility would be 50% of amount in default irrespective of the category of the borrower.

(c) Applicable Fee i.e. AGF will be charged at the rate of 2% of the guaranteed amount for the first year and on outstanding amount for the remaining tenure of the credit facility. Differential pricing structure depending upon NPA percentage and Claim payout ratio of the Member Lending Institution (MLI) will also be applicable on the AGF.

Security Accepted Under the Scheme: No Collateral Security for loans up to ₹ 10 Lakhs. Collateral Security would mean any asset other than business asset. Waiver of collateral security may be extended for loans over ₹ 10 Lakhs and upto ₹ 25 Lakhs subject to good track record and financial position of the borrower.

In view of several requests from various MLIs regarding coverage of Partial Collateral Security, it has been decided to make it effective from the date of issue of Circular. Therefore, the modification of allowing partial collateral security under the ambit of Credit Guarantee Scheme of CGTMSE is applicable to fresh credit facilities eligible for guarantee coverage by MLIs on or after February 28, 2018.

Modified AGF Structure-Standard Rate (SR): With a view to incentivize the borrowers with good repayment track record, AGF would be charged on the outstanding loan amount instead of guaranteed amount for credit facilities sanctioned / renewed to MSEs on or after April 01, 2018 as detailed below:

Credit Facility	Annual Guarantee Fee (AGF) [% p.a.]*	
	Women, Micro Enterprises and Units covered in North East Region	**Others**
Up to ₹ 5 Lakhs	1.00 + Risk Premium as per extant guidelines of the Trust	
Above ₹ 5 Lakhs and up to ₹ 50 Lakhs	1.35 + Risk Premium as per extant guidelines of the Trust	1.50 + Risk Premium as per extant guidelines of the Trust
Above ₹ 50 Lakhs and up to ₹ 200 Lakhs	1.80 + Risk Premium as per extant guidelines of the Trust	
**AGF will be charged on the guaranteed amount for the first year and on the outstanding amount for the remaining tenure of the credit facility.*		

MSE Retail Trade Activity: The AGF will be charged at 2% of the guaranteed amount for the first year and on the outstanding amount for the remaining tenure of the credit facility. Differential pricing structure depending upon NPA / Claim pay-out ratio of the MLI will also be applicable on the AGF as per CGTMSE Circular No.107/ 2015-16 dated January 28, 2016.

Additional risk premium of 15% will be charged on the applicable rate to MLIs who exceed the pay-out threshold limit of 2 times more than thrice in last 5 years. This premium will be applicable for all guarantee accounts irrespective of the sanction date.

Guarantee Cover: Guarantee cover for entire agreed tenure of the Term Credit/Composite Credit for the defaulted principal amount. Other Charges such as interest in term loan, Penal Interest, Commitment Charge, Service charge or any other expenses shall not qualify for guarantee cover. Lock in period is 18 months from date of last disbursement of loan or date of payment of guarantee fee whichever is later.

Extent of Guarantee Cover available w.e.f. 01/04/2018

Category	Up to ₹ 5.00 Lac	Above ₹ 5.00 Lac to ₹ 50.00 Lac	Above ₹ 50.00 Lac to Up to ₹ 200.00 Lac
Micro Enterprises	85% Maximum ₹ 4.25 lac	75% Maximum ₹ 37.50 lac	75% of amount default amount maximum ₹ 150.00 lac
Women/NE Region	85% Maximum ₹ 4.25 lac	80% Maximum ₹ 40 lac	75% of amount default amount maximum ₹ 150.00 lac
All others	85% Maximum ₹ 4.25 lac	75% Maximum ₹ 37.50 lac	75% of amount default amount maximum ₹ 150.00 lac

Salient Features and Limitation About Guarantee and Invoke of Guarantee are as under:

- Where working capital alone is financed, the tenure of guarantee cover is fixed for a block of 5 years. Thereafter the guarantee cover needs to be renewed for a further period of 5 years. A working capital account covered under CGTMSE can be renewed within 12 months from guarantee expiry date. Guarantee Fee has to be paid afresh for renewed guarantee cover thereafter for the next block of 5 years. Only Standard account at the end of the block of five years will be renewed and substandard accounts will be rejected.
- The Guarantee Cover shall run through the entire agreed tenure of the Term Credit in case Term Loan, sanctioned alone.
- In case of Composite Loan (wherein Cash Credit & Term loan are sanctioned together), the guarantee cover will run through the entire period of term loan or term loan termination date whichever is earlier. For example, if the term loan is repaid in 48/60/72 months from the guarantee start date the guarantee cover will expire for both Cash Credit and Term Loan in 48/60/72 months, as the case may be. The guarantee cover for Cash Credit a one will be renewed the reafter for a block of 5 years, subject to coverage for Cash Credit will be valid up to without cap of maximum tenure now from the original cover start date.

Invocation of Guarantee on Default of a Loan are as under:

- The lender shall prefer a claim on the defaulted account on recall of loan and initiation of recovery proceedings under due process of Law. The lender can, however, invoke the guarantee given by the Trust only after the lock-in period of 18 months either from the date of last disbursement of credit to the borrower or from the date of the guarantee cover coming into force in respect of the particular credit facility, whichever is later.
- After satisfying itself about the procedural aspects met by the lender, regarding lodgement/ preferment of claim for guarantee, the Trust will honour 75% of the guaranteed portion of the amount in default, subject to maximum of 75%/ 80%/85% of the amount in default. The balance 25% shall be paid on conclusion of the recovery proceedings.
- For the purpose of the scheme, issue of notice under Lok Adalat is sufficient to prove the legal proceedings have initiated.
- Mere issuance of recall notice under SARFAESI Act cannot be construed as initiation of legal proceedings for purpose of preferment of claim under CGS. Lending institution should take further action as contained in Section 13 (4) of the above Act.

NPA REPORTING AND CLAIM SETTLEMENT

NPA Reporting: If an account slipped to NPA, Branch has to report through Nodal official. Nodal official will generate the report and update on CGTMSE website. Branch has to report on or before last day of Next Quarter.

CGTMSE Guarantee Invocation Period: Guarantee of CGTMSE in respect of accounts covered under CGTMSE may be invoked if the following conditions are satisfied -

(a) Within a maximum period of one year from date of NPA, if NPA is after lock in period or within one year of expiry of lock-in period, if NPA is within lock-in period for accounts sanctioned before 01.01.2013.

(b) The Branch/Bank can invoke the guarantee in respect of credit facility within a maximum period of two years from date of NPA, if NPA is after lock-in period or within two years of expiry of lock-in period, if NPA is within lock-in period, for accounts sanctioned on or after 01.01.2013 but turned NPA before 15.03.2018.

(c) The Branch/Bank can invoke the guarantee in respect of credit facility within a maximum period of three years from the date of NPA, if NPA is after lock in period or within three years of expiry of lock in period, if NPA is within lock in period for accounts turned NPA on or after 15.03.2018, irrespective of sanction date.

Submission of Claim: Branch has to report the claim through Nodal official. Before claiming the credit facility has been recalled and the recovery proceeding has been initiated under due process of law. Mere issuance of recall notice under SARFAESI Act cannot be construed as initiation of legal proceedings for purpose of preferment of claim under CGS. Lending institution should take further action as contained in Section 13 (4) of the above Act.

Settlement of Claim: Settlement of claim is to be entered and verified by this menu. The CGTMSE shall pay 75% of guaranteed amount within 30 days.

The balance 25% will be paid on conclusion of recovery proceeding or after 3 years from decree of recovery, whichever is earlier. Any amount realized from sale of security should be remitted in full to the corporation after deducting our expenses etc.

Credit Guarantee Scheme for PM SVANidhi (CGS-PMS): Ministry of Housing and Urban Affairs (MoHUA), Government of India, had implemented a scheme titled "PM Street Vendor's Atma Nirbhar Nidhi (PM SVANidhi)", for providing credit to Street Vendors.

In this connection, a Credit Guarantee Scheme for PM SVANidhi (CGS-PMS) has been launched under which guarantee coverage would be provided to eligible Lending Institutions for facilitating credit support to eligible Street Vendors. The objective of the Credit Guarantee Scheme is to facilitate working capital loan upto ₹ 10,000. Further, as per PM SVANidhi Scheme, on timely or early repayment, the vendors will be eligible for the next loan with an enhanced limit of maximum of 200% of the earlier loan, subject to a ceiling of ₹ 20,000.

CGTMSE has its Registered Office at Mumbai and does not have any branches. Since the entire operations are online, CGTMSE is able to cater to the needs of its MLIs from Mumbai.

CHAPTER-23

Government Sponsored Schemes

Page-166 (2nd column)

Cash Credit Limit (CCL): In case of CCL, banks are advised to sanction minimum loan of ₹ 6 lakhs to each eligible SHGs for a period of 3 years with a yearly drawing power (DP). The drawing power may be enhanced annually based on the repayment performance of the SHG. The drawing power may be calculated as follows:

DP for First Year: 6 times of the existing corpus of minimum of ₹ 1 lakh whichever is higher.

DP for Second Year: 8 times of the corpus at the time review/enhancement or minimum of ₹ 2 lakh whichever is higher.

DP for Third Year: Minimum of ₹ 6 lakhs based on the Micro credit plan prepared by SHG and appraised by Federation/Support agency and the previous credit History.

DP for Fourth Year onwards: Minimum of ₹ 6 lakhs based on the Micro credit plan prepared by SHG and appraised by the Federations/ Support agency and the previous credit History.

Page-167 (1st column)

Repayment Schedule: Repayment of loan schedule will be as under;

1st **Dose**—repaid in 24-36 months in monthly / quarterly installments;

2nd **Dose**—repaid in 36-48 months in monthly / quarterly installments;

3rd **Dose**—repaid in 48-6. months in monthly / quarterly installments;

4th **Dose**—repaid between 60-84 months based on the cash flow in monthly / quarterly installments.

Page-167 (2nd column)

Eligibility for NULM Loan to SHG

The group enterprise should have minimum 2 members with a minimum of 70% members from urban poor families. The application / intent to set up a group enterprise by beneficiaries/group members should preferably be referred by the community structures viz. SHG/ALF formed under SJSRY/NULM.

Page-168 (1st column)

Project Cost: The maximum unit Project Cost for a group enterprise is ₹ 2 lakhs per member or ₹ 10 lakhs whichever is lower.

Margin Money: No margin money should be taken for a loan up to ₹ 50,000 and for higher amount loans, preferably 5% should be taken as margin money and it should in no case be more than 10% of the project cost.

MODULE–A

INDIAN FINANCIAL SYSTEM

MODERN FINANCIAL SYSTEM—AN OVERVIEW

INDIAN FINANCIAL SYSTEM

The financial system is the most important institutional and functional vehicle for economic transformation. Finance is a bridge between the present and the future. It is the mobilisation of savings and their efficient, effective and equitable allocation for investment. It is the success with which the financial system performs its functions that sets the pace for the achievement of broader national objectives.

The term financial system is a set of inter-related activities working together to achieve some predetermined purpose or goal. It includes different markets, the institutions, instruments, services and mechanisms which influence the generation of savings, investment, capital formation and growth.

History of Banking Sector in India

Banking in India, in the modern sense, originated in the last decades of the 18th century. Among the first banks were the Bank of Hindustan, which was established in 1770 and liquidated in 1829–32; and the General Bank of India, established in 1786 but failed in 1791.

The largest bank, and the oldest still in existence, is the State Bank of India. The three banks—Bank of Calcutta, Bank of Bombay and the Bank of Madras were merged in 1921 to form the Imperial Bank of India, which after India attained independence, became the State Bank of India in 1955. In 1960, the State Banks of India was given control of eight state-associated banks under the State Bank of India (Subsidiary Banks) Act, 1959. These were called associate banks of SBI. On 1st April, 2017, State Bank of India, which is India's largest Bank merged with five of its Associate Banks (State Bank of Bikaner & Jaipur, State Bank of Hyderabad, State Bank of Mysore, State Bank of Patiala and State Bank of Travancore) and Bharatiya Mahila Bank with itself. In 1969 the Indian government nationalised 14 major private banks, one of the big bank was Bank of India. In 1980, 6 more private banks were nationalised. These nationalised banks are the majority of lenders in the Indian economy.

The Indian banking sector is broadly classified into scheduled and non-scheduled banks. The scheduled banks are those which are included under the 2nd Schedule of the Reserve Bank of India Act, 1934. The scheduled banks are further classified into Nationalised banks; State Bank of India; Regional Rural Banks (RRBs); foreign banks; and other Indian private sector banks. The term commercial banks refer to both scheduled and non-scheduled commercial banks regulated under the Banking Regulation Act, 1949.

Definition of Banking

Section 5(B) of Banking Regulation Act, 1949 defines banking as "Accepting for the purpose of lending or investment of deposits of money from the public, repayable on demand and withdrawable by cheques, drafts, and orders or otherwise". Banking Company means any company which transacts the business of banking in India. Banks are governed by Reserve Bank of India Act (RBI Act) 1934 and Banking Regulation Act (BR Act) 1949. Nationalised banks are owned by Government of India and governed by directives issued by RBI.

Thus, the core business of the bank is to accept deposit from the public and lending to the public or investment of such deposit. The deposit may be repayable on demand or fixed for a time as agreed by the banker and the customer.

Role of Banking

Banks provide funds for business as well as personal needs of individuals. They play a significant role in the economy of a nation. Let us know about the role of banking.

- It encourages savings habit amongst people and thereby makes funds available for productive use.
- It acts as an intermediary between people having surplus money and those requiring money for various business activities.
- It facilitates business transactions through receipts and payments by cheques instead of currency.
- It provides loans and advances to businessmen for short term and long-term purposes.
- It also facilitates import-export transactions.
- It helps in national development by providing credit to farmers, small-scale industries and self-employed people as well as to large business houses which lead to balanced economic development in the country.
- It helps in raising the standard of living of people in general by providing loans for purchase of consumer durable goods, houses, automobiles, etc.

TYPES OF BANKS IN INDIA

There are various types of banks which operate in our country to meet the financial requirements of different categories of people engaged in agriculture, business, profession, etc. On the basis of functions, the banking institutions in India may be divided into the following types:

1. Central Bank (RBI, in India)
2. Commercial Banks (Public Sector Banks, Private Sector Banks, Foreign Banks)
3. Development Banks (IFCI, SFCs)
4. Co-operative Banks (Central Co-operative Banks, State Co-operative Banks)
5. Non-Banking Financial Companies (NBFC)

1. Central Bank (RBI, in India)

A bank which is entrusted with the functions of guiding and regulating the banking system of a country is known as its Central bank. Such a bank does not deal with the general public. It acts essentially as Government's banker, maintain deposit accounts of all other banks and advances money to other banks, when needed. The Central Bank provides guidance to other banks whenever they face any problem. It is therefore known as the banker's bank. The Reserve Bank of India is the central bank of our country. The Central Bank maintains record of Government revenue and expenditure under various heads. It also advises the Government on monetary and credit policies and decides on the interest rates for bank deposits and bank loans. In addition, foreign exchange rates are also determined by the central bank. Another important function of the Central Bank is the issuance of currency notes, regulating their circulation in the country by different methods. No other bank than the Central Bank can issue currency.

2. Commercial Banks

Commercial Banks are banking institutions that accept deposits and grant loans and advances to their customers. Commercial banks include Public sector banks, Private sector banks and Foreign banks.

(a) **Public Sector Banks:** These are banks where majority stake is held by the Government of India or Reserve Bank of India. Examples of public sector banks are: State Bank of India, Corporation Bank, Bank of Baroda and Dena Bank, etc.

(b) **Private Sectors Banks:** In case of private sector banks majority of share capital of the bank is held by private individuals. These banks are registered as companies with limited liability. For example: The ICICI Bank, Axis Bank, Federal Bank etc.

(c) **Foreign Banks:** These banks are registered and have their headquarters in a foreign country but operate their branches in our country. Some of the foreign banks operating in our country are Hong Kong and Shanghai Banking Corporation (HSBC), Citibank, American Express Bank, Standard & Chartered Bank, etc.

3. Development Banks

Business often requires medium and long-term capital for purchase of machinery and equipment, for using latest technology, or for expansion and modernization. Such financial assistance is provided by Development Banks. They also undertake other development measures like subscribing to the shares and debentures issued by companies, in case of under subscription of the issue by the public. Industrial Finance Corporation of India (IFCI) and State Financial Corporations (SFCs) are examples of development banks in India.

4. Co-operative Banks

People who come together to jointly serve their common interest often form a co-operative society under the Co-operative Societies Act. When a co-operative society engages itself in banking business it is called a Co-operative Bank. The society has to obtain a licence from the Reserve Bank of India before starting banking business. These are allowed to raise deposits from the public and give advances to the public. Any co-operative bank as a society has to function under the overall supervision of the Registrar, Co-operative Societies of the State. As regards banking business, the society must follow the guidelines set issued by the Reserve Bank of India.

5. Non-Banking Financial Companies (NBFC)

A Non-Banking Financial Company (NBFC) is a company registered under the Companies Act. 1956. Its principal business is receiving deposits from public and lending, investments in various types of securities, leasing, hire-purchase, bill discounting etc.

The Reserve Bank of India regulates and supervises Non-Banking Financial Companies which are into the business of (i) lending (ii) acquisition of shares, stocks, bonds, etc., or (iii) financial leasing or hire purchase. The Reserve Bank also regulates companies whose principal business is to accept deposits. (Section 45I (c) of the RBI Act, 1934)

INDIAN FINANCIAL SERVICES

Primary Dealers (PDs): Primary dealers deal in government securities and deal in both the primary and secondary markets. Their basic responsibility is to provide markets for government securities and strengthen the government securities market. Thus, PDs are acting as a market maker of government securities.

Payment and Settlement System: An efficient and effective Payment and Settlement System is a necessary condition for smooth functioning of financial system. The PSS Act, 2007 provides for the regulation and supervision of payment systems in India and designates the Reserve Bank of India as the authority for that purpose and all related matters. The Reserve Bank is authorized to exercise its powers and perform its functions and discharge its duties under this statute. The Act also provides the legal basis for "netting" and "settlement finality".

Management of Government Debt: Most of the Central Banks manage the issue and service of government debt. This involves price discovery, volumes to be raised, tenure of debt and matching it with overall cash management of the debt.

Cash Reserve Ratio: In terms of Section 42(1) of the RBI Act, 1934 the Reserve Bank, having regard to the needs of securing the monetary stability in the country, prescribes the CRR for SCBs without any floor or ceiling rate. CRR is the mandatory deposit (in Cash) held by the banks with RBI. It is a certain/Percentage of their demand and Time Liabilities (DTL). Non-maintenance of CRR will result in levy of penal interest by RBI. The decrease of CRR will result in pumping more liquidity in the banking system and increasing will squeeze the liquidity.

Statutory Liquidity Ratio (SLR): All commercial banks in the country have to maintain a stipulated proportion of their net demand and time liabilities in the form of liquid assets like cash, gold and unencumbered securities. Treasury bills, dated securities issued under market borrowing programme and market stabilisation schemes (MSS), etc also form part of the SLR. Banks have to report to the RBI every alternate Friday their SLR maintenance and pay penalties for failing to maintain SLR as mandated. The value of such assets of a SCB shall not be less than such percentage not exceeding 40 per cent of its total DTL in India as on the last Friday of the second preceding fortnight as the Reserve Bank may, by notification in the Official Gazette, specify from time to time.

EQUITY AND DEBT MARKET

The market in which shares are issued and traded, either through exchanges or over-the-counter markets. Also known as the stock market, it is one of the most vital areas of a market economy because it gives companies access to capital and investors a slice of ownership in a company with the potential to realize gains based on its future performance.

Stock Exchange: A stock exchange is a platform which provides services through stock brokers, to the investors/traders to buy/sell stocks, bonds and other securities. Trade on an exchange can be done only by its members, called stock brokers. The stock exchanges are regulated by the capital market regulator (SEBI).

Stock Brokers: These entities are members of stock exchange and are also required to be registered with the SEBI and be guided by the directives of SEBI. Stock brokers act as intermediaries between the buyer and the seller of stocks and other securities

Equity Shares: The equity holder, popularly known as shareholder is the part owner of the company. Depending upon the pattern of the share holding, the equity holder is entitled for dividends, and voting rights as members of the company. These shares can be obtained either through the Initial Public Offering (IPOs), Further/Follow-on Public Offering (FPOs) (primary markets) and can also be bought in the stock markets after the stocks are listed (Secondary markets).

Rights Issue (RIs): When a listed company wants to raise funds from the markets, one option available to the corporate is to arrange to issue additional/fresh stocks (shares/debentures) to the existing stock holders, known as Rights Issue. Rights Issues are offered to the existing shareholders whose names appear on a record date and in a particular ratio to the number of securities held by the shareholder.

Debentures: One of the options available for an investor is to invest in a company's debentures. A debenture holder enjoys a fixed rate of interest payable every half year/year, on a fixed date. The principal amount is repayable on the date of redemption. Debenture holders are creditors of the company.

Bonds: A bond is issued in the form of a negotiable certificate/ documents against indebtedness.

Commercial Paper (CP): Commercial papers are issued by companies with high credit ratings, in the form of promissory notes, at discount but repayable at par, to their holder at maturity. Commercial papers are money market instruments and issued as per the guidelines of the Reserve Bank of India.

Certificate of Deposit (CD): A certificate of deposit (which is also a money market instrument) is issued by a bank. It is issued at discount to be redeemable at par on the maturity date. The minimum investment is ₹ 100,000. It is issued for a minimum period of 7 days up to a maximum period of one year. It is issued in the form of usance promissory note. The CDs can be traded in the market from the date of issue. The CDs are issued as per the guidelines of the Reserve Bank of India.

MUTUAL FUNDS

Mutual Funds: Mutual Funds play a key role as a financial intermediary in the financial services sector. A mutual fund pools money from investors and invests in Stocks, Debt and other financial securities. SEBI Regulations 1993 defines a mutual fund as: "a fund established in the form of a trust by a sponsor to raise monies by the trustees through the sale of units to the public, under one of more schemes, for investing in securities in accordance with these regulations"

Net Asset Value (NAV): Mutual funds are required to declare the NAV for different schemes at regular intervals on their web sites. NAV is the net asset value of a particular fund, and the mutual funds calculate NAV on daily basis. The funds are bought and sold at the NAV, after the initial issue. NAV reflects the market conditions and may go up and down depending upon various factors. The redemption of units is based on the NAV of the particular scheme.

Foreign Institutional Investors (FII): As per SEBI (FII) Regulations 1995, Foreign Institutional investor means an institution established or incorporated outside India which proposes to make investments in India in securities. Foreign Institutional Investors need to be registered with SEBI to invest in the Indian equity and debt market.

CAPITAL MARKET— SOME INTERESTING FEATURES

De-mat Accounts: De-mat accounts are maintained in an electronic form. Dematerialization is the conversion of physical/ paper securities into the electronic form. The de-mat account is opened with a depository participant (e.g., a bank or a broker) who has an account with either Central Depository Services Limited (CDSL) or with National Securities Depository Limited (NSDL).

Registrars: Registrars maintain a register of share and debenture holders and process share and debenture allocation, when issues are subscribed. Registrar too need regulator's approval to do business.

MULTI COMMODITY EXCHANGE OF INDIA LTD (MCX)

MCX is an independent commodity exchange based in India. It was established in 2003 and is based in Mumbai. It is India's largest commodity derivatives exchange where the clearance and settlements of the exchange happens and the turnover of the exchange for quarter ended December 2017 was 12.82 trillion rupees. MCX offers options trading in gold and futures trading in non-ferrous metals, bullion, energy, and a number of agricultural commodities (mentha oil, cardamom, crude palm oil, cotton and others).

In 2016, MCX was seventh among the global commodity bourses in terms of the number of futures contracts traded, the latest yearly data from Futures Industry Association (FIA) showed. In 2017 MCX partnered with Thomson Reuters to develop India's first co-branded commodity index series, the iCOMDEX. iCOMDEX series consists of iCOMDEX Composite, iCOMDEX Base Metals, iCOMDEX Bullion, iCOMDEX Gold, iCOMDEX Copper and iCOMDEX Crude Oil. Recently, the exchange has set up a web-based application "ComRIS" (Commodity Receipts Information System) in order to maintain electronic record of commodities deposited at the Exchange accredited warehouses and ensure flow of real time information from the warehouses.

INSURANCE REGULATORY & DEVELOPMENT AUTHORITY OF INDIA (IRDAI)

It is an autonomous, statutory agency tasked with regulating and promoting the insurance and re-insurance industries in India. It is a regulator for insurance business, both general and life insurance. It was constituted by the Insurance Regulatory and Development Authority Act, 1999, an Act of Parliament passed by the Government of India. The agency's headquarters are in Hyderabad, Telangana, where it moved from Delhi in 2001. IRDAI is a 10-member body including the chairman, five full-time and four part-time members appointed by the government of India.

TEST YOURSELF

1. Which was the first Indian bank established in 1770?
   (a) General Bank of India
   (b) Bank of Hindustan
   (c) Bank of Calcutta
   (d) Bank of Bombay

2. The bank, which was not merged in 1921 to form the Imperial Bank of India?
   (a) Bank of Calcutta
   (b) Bank of Bombay
   (c) General Bank of India
   (d) Bank of Madras

3. In which year, the State Banks of India was given control of eight state-associated banks under the State Bank of India (Subsidiary Banks) Act?
   (a) 1959 (b) 1960
   (c) 1965 (d) 1969

4. The scheduled banks are those which are included under the ________ Schedule of the Reserve Bank of India Act, 1934.
   (a) 2nd (b) 3rd
   (c) 4th (d) 5th

5. Which is the role of RBI in India?
   (a) It acts essentially as Government's banker
   (b) RBI maintain deposit accounts of all other banks
   (c) RBI provides guidance to other banks whenever they face any problem
   (d) All of the above

6. RBI regulates and supervises Non-Banking Financial Companies which are into the business of ______.
   (a) acquisition of shares, stocks, bonds, etc.
   (b) lending
   (c) financial leasing or hire purchase
   (d) All of the above

7. Primary dealers deal in government securities and deal in ________.
   (a) primary markets
   (b) secondary markets
   (c) both the primary and secondary markets
   (d) None

8. The PSS Act, ________ provides for the regulation and supervision of payment systems in India.
   (a) 2005 (b) 2007
   (c) 2009 (d) 2010

9. Cash Reserve Ratio is defined In terms of ________.
   (a) Section 42(1) of the RBI Act, 1934
   (b) Section 42(1) of the BR Act, 1949
   (c) Section 24 of the RBI Act, 1934
   (d) Section 24(1) of the BR Act, 1949

10. The value of SLR of a SCB shall not be less than such percentage notified by RBI and not exceeding ________ per cent of its total DTL in India.
    (a) 25 (b) 30
    (c) 35 (d) 40

11. All commercial banks in the country have to maintain a stipulated proportion of their net demand and time liabilities as SLR in the form of liquid assets like ________.
    (a) Cash
    (b) Gold
    (c) Treasury bills
    (d) All of the above

12. The minimum investment in certificate of deposit is ________.
    (a) ₹ 25,000/- (b) ₹ 50,000/-
    (c) ₹ 100,000/- (d) ₹ 10,00,000/-

13. A certificate of deposit is issued for a minimum period of ______ up to a maximum period of ____.
    (a) 7 days, one year
    (b) 14 days, one year
    (c) 7 days, two years
    (d) 14 days, two years

14. MCX is an independent commodity exchange based in India. It was established in ______ and is based in Mumbai.
(a) 2002 (b) 2003
(c) 2004 (d) 2005

15. Which of the following can not be included in the money market?
(a) call or notice money
(b) corporate securities
(c) certificate of deposit
(d) treasury bills

16. Monetary control is exercised by RBI in India through:
(a) Payment system
(b) Issue of currency
(c) Cash reserves and liquid reserve ratios
(d) Repo rate and Reverse repo rate

17. The corporate securities are held in electronic form instead of physical form by:
(a) Registrars (b) Custodians
(c) Depositories (d) Mutual funds

18. Which of the following is the role of mutual funds?
(a) to promote unit based scheme to inculcate saving habit
(b) manage the funds of high net worth individuals
(c) pooling of investor money for investment in capital market and other securities
(d) All of the above

19. Urban cooperative banks are controlled by:
(a) NABARD
(b) Central Govt.
(c) State Govt. and RBI
(d) RBI

20. Supervision over the depositories and stock exchange is the role of:
(a) RBI (b) IRDAI
(c) AMFI (d) SEBI

ANSWER

1	2	3	4	5	6	7	8	9	10
(b)	(c)	(b)	(a)	(d)	(d)	(c)	(b)	(a)	(d)
11	**12**	**13**	**14**	**15**	**16**	**17**	**18**	**19**	**20**
(d)	(c)	(a)	(b)	(b)	(c)	(c)	(c)	(c)	(d)

BANKING REGULATIONS

INTRODUCTION

The Reserve Bank, as the central bank of the country, started their operations as a private shareholder's bank. RBI replaced the Imperial Bank of India and started issuing the currency notes and acting as the banker to the government. Imperial Bank of India was allowed to act as the agent of the RBI. RBI covered all over the undivided India. In order to have close integration between policies of the Reserve Bank and those of the Government, it was decided to nationalize the Reserve Bank immediately after the independence of the country. From 1st January 1949, the Reserve Bank began functioning as a State-owned and State-controlled Central Bank. To streamline the functioning of commercial banks, the Government of India enacted the Banking Companies Act,1949 which was later changed as the Banking Regulation Act 1949. RBI acts as a regulator of banks, banker to the Government and banker's bank. It controls financial system in the country through various measures.

RESERVE BANK OF INDIA

The Reserve Bank of India is a central bank and was established in 1st April 1935 in accordance with the provisions of Reserve Bank of India Act 1934. RBI works as a central bank where commercial banks are account holders. The central office of RBI is located at Mumbai since inception. It was inaugurated with share capital of ₹ 5 Crores divided into shares of ₹ 100 each fully paid up. RBI was Nationalised on 1st January 1949 on the basis of the Reserve Bank of India (Transfer to Public Ownership) Act, 1948. RBI is fully owned by the Government of India. The Reserve Bank of India has 20 regional offices, most of them in state capitals and 11 Sub-offices.

RBI is governed by a central board (headed by a governor) appointed by the central government of India. The general superintendence and direction of the bank is entrusted to central board, consists of:

(a) One Governor;

(b) Not more than four deputy Governors;

(c) Two Governmental official from the ministry of Finance;

(d) Ten nominated directors from various fields by the government to give representation to important elements in the economic life of the country, and

(e) The four-nominated director by the Central Government to represent the four local boards with the headquarters at Mumbai, Kolkata, Chennai and New Delhi.

Local Board consists of five members each central government appointed for a term of four years to represent territorial and economic interests and the interests of cooperative and indigenous banks.

Objectives of RBI

The main objectives of RBI may be stated as follows in specific terms:

- To maintain monetary stability such that the business and economic life of the country can deliver the welfare gains of a mixed economy;

- To maintain the financial stability and ensure sound financial institutions so that economic units can conduct their business with confidence;
- To maintain stable payment systems, so that financial transactions can be safely and efficiently executed;
- To ensure that credit allocation by the financial system broadly reflects the national economic priorities and social concerns;
- To regulate the overall volume of money and credit in the economy to ensure a reasonable degree of price stability;
- To promote the development of financial markets and systems to enable itself to operate/regulate efficiently.

ROLE OF RESERVE BANK OF INDIA

Chapter III of the RBI Act, 1934 describes role and functions of RBI. These functions are as under:

1. Monetary policy
2. Issuer of currency
3. Transact government business
4. Banker to banks
5. Regulator and supervisor of the financial system
6. Manager of Foreign Exchange
7. Supervisory Functions
8. Developmental role
9. Other Control and Supervisory Roles

1. Monetary Policy

Monitory policy refers to the use of instruments under the control of the Central Bank to regulate the availability, cost and use of money to maintain price stability, inflation and credit. The Central Government may, by notification in the Official Gazette, constitute a Committee to be called the Monetary Policy Committee of the Bank. The Monetary Policy Committee shall determine the Policy Rate required to achieve the inflation target. The Central Government shall, in consultation with the Bank, determine the inflation target in terms of the Consumer Price Index, once in every five years. The Central Government shall, upon such determination, notify the inflation target in the Official Gazette.

The primary objective of the monetary policy is to maintain price stability while keeping in mind the objective of growth; The decision of the Monetary Policy Committee shall be binding on the Bank. RBI use several direct and indirect instruments in the formulation and implementation of monetary policy.

Direct Instruments

(a) Cash Reserve Ratio (CRR): Cash Reserve Ratio is a certain percentage of bank deposits which banks are required to keep with RBI in the form of reserves or balances. Higher the CRR with the RBI lower will be the liquidity in the system and vice versa. RBI is empowered to vary CRR between 15 per cent and 3 per cent.

Maintenance of CRR on Daily Basis: With a view to providing flexibility to banks in choosing an optimum strategy of holding reserves depending upon their intra fortnight cash flows, all SCBs are required to maintain minimum CRR balances up to 95 per cent of the average daily required reserves for a reporting fortnight on all days of the fortnight with effect from the fortnight beginning September 21, 2013.

All SCBs are required to submit to Reserve Bank a provisional Return in Form 'A' within 7 days from the expiry of the relevant fortnight which is used for preparing press communique. The final Form 'A' Return is required to be submitted to RBI within 20 days from expiry of the relevant fortnight.

The Reserve Bank does not pay any interest on the CRR balances maintained by SCBs with effect from the fortnight beginning March 31, 2007.

Penalties: From the fortnight beginning June 24, 2006, penal interest is charged as under in cases of default in maintenance of CRR by SCBs:

(i) In case of default in maintenance of CRR requirement on a daily basis which is currently 95 per cent of the total CRR requirement, penal interest will be recovered for that day at the rate of three per cent per annum above the Bank Rate on the amount by which the amount actually maintained falls short of the prescribed minimum on that day and if the shortfall continues on the next succeeding day/s, penal interest will be recovered at the rate of five per cent per annum above the Bank Rate.

(ii) In cases of default in maintenance of CRR on average basis during a fortnight, penal interest will be recovered as envisaged in sub-section (3) of Section 42 of Reserve Bank of India Act, 1934.

SCBs are required to furnish the such as date, amount, percentage, reason for default in maintenance of requisite CRR and action taken to avoid recurrence of such default.

(b) Statutory Liquidity Ratio (SLR): All commercial banks in the country have to maintain a stipulated proportion of their net demand and time liabilities in the form of liquid assets like cash, gold and unencumbered securities. Treasury bills, dated securities issued under market borrowing programme and market stabilisation schemes (MSS), etc also form part of the SLR. Banks have to report to the RBI every alternate Friday their SLR maintenance, and pay penalties for failing to maintain SLR as mandated. The value of such assets of a SCB shall not be less than such percentage not exceeding 40 per cent of its total DTL in India as on the last Friday of the second preceding fortnight as the Reserve Bank may, by notification in the Official Gazette, specify from time to time.

Penalties: If a banking company fails to maintain the required amount of SLR, it shall be liable to pay to RBI in respect of that default, the penal interest for that day at the rate of three per cent per annum above the Bank Rate on the shortfall and if the default continues the next succeeding working day, the penal interest may be increased to a rate of five per cent per annum above the Bank Rate for the concerned days of default on the shortfall.

Indirect Instruments

(a) Liquidity Adjustment Facility: A liquidity adjustment facility (LAF) is a tool used in monetary policy that allows banks to borrow money through repurchase agreements. This arrangement allows banks to respond to liquidity pressures and is used by governments to assure basic stability in the financial markets. LAF is used to aid banks in adjusting the day to day mismatches in liquidity. LAF helps banks to quickly borrow money in case of any emergency or for adjusting in their SLR/CRR requirements. LAF consists of repo and reverse repo operations.

(b) Repo Rate and Reverse Repo Rate: Repo or repurchase option is a collaterised lending *i.e.,* banks borrow money from Reserve bank of India to meet short term needs by selling securities to RBI with an agreement to repurchase the same at pre-determined rate and date. The rate charged by RBI for this transaction is called the repo rate. Repo operations therefore inject liquidity into the system. Reverse repo operation is when RBI borrows money from banks by lending securities. The interest rate paid by RBI in this case is called the reverse repo rate.

(c) Open Market Operations (OMO): Open market operations refer to the buying and selling of government securities in the open market in order to expand or contract the amount of money in the banking system. Securities' purchases inject money into the banking system and stimulate growth, while sales of securities do the opposite and contract the economy.

(d) Marginal Standing Facility (MSF): RBI announced that MSF scheme has become effective from 9th May, 2011. Marginal Standing Facility is a liquidity support arrangement provided by RBI to commercial banks if the latter doesn't have the required eligible securities above the SLR limit. Under MSF, a bank can borrow one-day loans form the RBI, even if it doesn't have any eligible securities excess of its SLR requirement (maintains only the SLR). This means that the bank can't borrow under the repo facility. MSF, being a penal rate, is always fixed above the repo rate. The MSF would be the last resort for banks once they exhaust all borrowing options including the liquidity adjustment facility by pledging government securities, where the rates are lower in comparison with the MSF.

(e) Bank Rate: A bank rate is the interest rate at which a nation's central bank lends money to domestic banks, often in the form of very short-term loans. Managing the bank rate is method by which central banks affect economic activity.

2. Issuer of Currency

RBI shall have the sole right to issue bank notes in India. Bank notes shall be of the denominational values of 2, 5, 10, 20, 50, 100, 200, 500, 1000, 2000, 5000, and 10000 rupees or of such other denominational values, not exceeding ten thousand rupees, as the Central Government may, on the recommendation of the Central Board, specify in this behalf. Every bank note shall be legal tender at any place in India in payment or on account for the amount expressed therein, and shall be guaranteed by the Central Government.

3. Transact Government Business

The Reserve Bank shall undertake to accept monies for account of the Central Government and to make payments up to the amount standing to the credit of its account, and to carry out its exchange, remittance and other banking operations, including the management of the public debt of the Union.

4. Banker to Banks

An important role and function of RBI is to maintain the banking accounts of all scheduled banks and acts as the banker of last resort. RBI works as a central bank where commercial banks are account holders. It is the duty of the RBI to control the credit through the CRR, bank rate and open market operations.

5. Regulator and Supervisor of the Financial System

RBI prescribes broad parameters of banking operations within which the country's banking and financial system functions. Their main objective is to maintain public confidence in the system, protect depositor's interest and provide cost effective banking services to the public.

6. Manager of Foreign Exchange

The manager of exchange control department manages the foreign exchange, according to the foreign exchange management act, 1999. The manager's main objective is to facilitate external trade and payment and promote orderly development and maintenance of foreign exchange market in India. The RBI plays a crucial role in foreign exchange transactions. It does due diligence on every foreign transaction, including the inflow and outflow of foreign exchange. It takes steps to stop the fall in value of the Indian Rupee. The RBI also takes necessary steps to control the current account deficit. They also give support to promote export and the RBI provides a variety of options for NRIs.

7. Supervisory Functions

In addition to its traditional central banking functions, the Reserve Bank performs certain non-monetary functions of the nature of supervision of banks and promotion of sound banking in India. The Reserve Bank Act 1934 and the banking regulation act 1949 have given the RBI wide powers of supervision and control over commercial and co-operative banks, relating to licensing and establishments, branch expansion, liquidity of their assets, management and methods of working, amalgamation, reconstruction and liquidation. The RBI is authorized to carry out periodical inspections of the banks and to call for returns and necessary information from them. The nationalisation of 14 major Indian scheduled banks in July 1969 has imposed new responsibilities on the RBI for directing the growth of banking and credit policies towards more rapid development of the economy and realisation of certain desired social objectives.

8. Developmental Role

Being the banker of the Government of India, the RBI is responsible for implementation of the government's policies related to agriculture and rural development. The RBI also ensures the flow of credit to other priority sectors as well. Section 54 of the RBI gives stress on giving specialized support for rural development. Priority sector lending is also in key focus area of the RBI.

9. Other Control and Supervisory Roles

The other control and supervisory roles of the Reserve Bank of India is done through the following:

(a) **Issue of Licence:** Under the Banking Regulation Act 1949, the RBI has been given powers to grant licenses to commence new banking operations. The RBI also grants licenses to open new branches for existing banks. Under the licensing policy, the RBI provides banking services in areas that do not have this facility.

(b) **Directed credit for lending to Priority Sector and Weaker Sections:** RBI issues guidelines for lending to Priority Sector and Weaker Sections advances. Banks have to follow the guidelines and have to achieve Priority Sector and Weaker Sections advance targets.

(c) **Prudential Norms:** The RBI issues guidelines for credit control and management. The RBI is a member of the Banking Committee on Banking Supervision (BCBS). As such, they are responsible for implementation of international standards of capital adequacy norms and asset classification.

(d) **Corporate Governance:** The RBI has power to control the appointment of the chairman and directors of banks in India. The RBI has powers to appoint additional directors in banks as well.

(e) **KYC Norms:** To curb money laundering and prevent the use of the banking system for financial crimes, The RBI has "Know Your Customer" guidelines. Every bank has to ensure KYC norms are applied before allowing someone to open an account and monitoring transactions in the accounts.

(f) **Transparency Norms:** This means that every bank has to disclose their charges for providing services and customers have the right to know these charges.

(g) **Risk Management:** The RBI provides guidelines to banks for taking the steps that are necessary to mitigate risk. They do this through risk management in Basel Norms.

(h) **Audit and Inspection:** The procedure of audit and inspection is controlled by the RBI through off-site and on-site monitoring system. On-site inspection is done by the RBI on the basis of "CAMELS". Capital adequacy; Asset quality; Management; Earning; Liquidity; System and control.

(i) **Publish Periodicals**: Apart from the above, the RBI publishes periodical review and data related to banking. The RBI plays a very important role in every aspect related to banking and finance.

REGULATORY RESTRICTIONS ON LENDING

RBI provides a framework of the rules and regulations issued to Scheduled Commercial Banks on statutory and other restrictions on loans and advances. Banks should implement these instructions and adopt adequate safeguards in order to ensure that the banking activities undertaken by them are run on sound, prudent and profitable lines.

(a) A bank cannot grant any loans and advances on the security of its own shares.

(b) BR Act also lays down the restrictions on loans and advances to the directors and the firms in which they hold substantial interest.

(c) **Restrictions on Holding Shares in Companies:** While granting loans and advances against shares, statutory provisions contained in Sections 19(2) and 19(3) of the Banking Regulation Act, 1949 should be strictly observed.

(d) **Restrictions on Credit to Companies for Buy-back of their Securities**: In terms of provisions of the Companies Act, 2013, companies are permitted to purchase their own shares or other specified securities out of their free reserves, or securities premium account, or the proceeds of any shares or other specified securities, subject to compliance of various conditions specified therein. Therefore, banks should not provide loans to companies for buy-back of shares/securities.

(e) **Lending to directors and their relatives on reciprocal basis**: There have been instances where certain banks have developed an informal understanding or mutual/reciprocal arrangement among themselves for extending credit facilities to each other's directors, their relatives, etc.

(f) **Restrictions on Grant of Loans & Advances to Officers and Relatives of Senior Officers of Banks:** The statutory regulations and/or the rules and conditions of service applicable to officers or employees of public sector banks indicate, to a certain extent, the precautions to be observed while sanctioning credit facilities to such officers and employees and their relatives.

(g) The banks should desist from sanctioning advances against FDRs, or other term deposits of other banks.

(h) **Loans against Certificate of Deposits (CDs):** Banks may lend against CDs and buy back their own CDs, until further notice, only in respect of CDs held by mutual funds, subject to the provisions of paragraph 44(2) of the SEBI (Mutual Funds) Regulations, 1996.

(i) No bank should grant any loan / advance for subscription to Indian Depository Receipts (IDRs).

(j) No additional facilities should be granted by any bank/FI to the listed willful defaulters.

TEST YOURSELF

1. The Reserve Bank of India is a central bank and was established in ________.
(a) 1st April 1934 (b) 1st April 1935
(c) 1st Jan. 1934 (d) 1st Jan. 1935

2. Who issues a banking license to a multi-state cooperative society for undertaking banking business?
(a) State Govt. (b) Central Govt.
(c) RBI (d) NABARD

3. As per RBI Act 1934, originally which of the following is not the objective of creation of RBI:
(a) To regulate the issue of bank notes
(b) To regulate the banks in India in all their functions
(c) To keeping reserves for securing monetary stability in India
(d) To operate the currency and credit system of India to its advantage

4. RBI is under obligation to undertake banking business for the central govt. under the provisions of:
(a) Section 22 of RBI Act
(b) Section 21 of RBI Act
(c) Section 20 of RBI Act
(d) In public interest

5. In which of the following areas, RBI cannot issue directions to banks:
(a) Interest rates on deposits
(b) Interest rates on advances
(c) Margin on bank loans
(d) None of the above

6. On which of the following aspects, RBI does not have authority as far as banks are concerned:
(a) Collection and dissemination of credit information
(b) Moratorium, amalgamation and winding of the banks
(c) Imposition of penalties
(d) None of the above

7. RBI is empowered to vary CRR between _______ per cent and _______ per cent.
(a) 15, 3 (b) 15, 5
(c) 20, 3 (d) 20, 5

8. Each bank in its name must include, which of the following words under the provision of banking regulation Act.
(a) Bank (b) Banking company
(c) Banking (d) Any of the above

9. RBI was nationalised on _________ on the basis of the Reserve Bank of India (Transfer to Public Ownership) Act, 1948.
(a) 1st January 1948 (b) 1st April 1949
(c) 1st January 1949 (d) 1st April 1949

10. The Reserve Bank of India has __ regional offices, most of them in state capitals and __ Sub-offices.
(a) 18, 11 (b) 20, 11
(c) 22, 15 (d) 23, 15

11. All SCBs are required to submit to Reserve Bank a provisional Return of CRR in Form 'A' within ____from the expiry of the relevant fortnight.
(a) 5 days (b) 7 days
(c) 10 days (d) 14 days

12. In case of default in maintenance of CRR requirement on a daily basis which is currently 95 per cent of the total CRR requirement, penal interest will be recovered for that day at the rate of _____ per cent per annum above the Bank Rate on the amount by which the amount actually maintained falls short of the prescribed minimum on that day.
(a) two (b) three
(c) four (d) five

13. If a banking company fails to maintain the required amount of SLR, it shall be liable to pay to RBI in respect of that default, the penal interest for that day at the rate of _______ per cent per annum above the Bank Rate on the shortfall and if the default continues the next succeeding working day, the penal interest may be increased to a rate of _______ per cent per annum above the Bank Rate for the concerned days of default on the shortfall.
(a) two, three (b) three, four
(c) three, five (d) two, five

14. Monetary and credit policy is reviewed by RBI:
(a) on bi-monthly basis (b) once in a year
(c) thrice in a year (d) four times in a year

15. The foreign exchange reserves of India are managed by:
(a) RBI (b) Exim bank
(c) FEDAI (d) SEBI

16. The supervisory functions of RBI are looked after by:
(a) Inspection Department of RBI
(b) Board of Financial Supervision of RBI
(c) Supervision Authority of RBI
(d) Central Supervisor of Banking

17. RBI shall have the sole right to issue bank notes in India. Bank notes shall be of the maximum denominational values of _______.
(a) ₹ 2000 (b) ₹ 5000
(c) ₹ 10000 (d) ₹ 20000

18. Which is not the function of RBI?
(a) Transact government business
(b) Banker to banks
(c) Regulator and supervisor of the Stock exchange
(d) Manager of foreign exchange

19. For controlling inflationary or deflationary situations in India, RBI does not use tools of:
(a) Cash Reserve Ratio
(b) Statutory Reserve Ratio
(c) Liquidity Adjustment Facility
(d) Open Market Operation

20. The Central Board of RBI comprises, a Governor, _______ Deputy Governors and _______ Directors nominated directors from various fields by the government:
(a) 4, 10 (b) 4, 15
(c) 5, 10 (d) 5, 15

ANSWER

1	2	3	4	5	6	7	8	9	10
(b)	(c)	(b)	(c)	(d)	(d)	(a)	(d)	(c)	(b)
11	**12**	**13**	**14**	**15**	**16**	**17**	**18**	**19**	**20**
(b)	(b)	(c)	(a)	(a)	(b)	(c)	(c)	(c)	(a)

RETAIL BANKING, WHOLESALE AND INTERNATIONAL BANKING

RETAIL BANKING

Retail Banking as a business model is adopted by all the banks on account of multiple comfort factors for the banks viz. acquisition of a huge customer base, multiple product offerings, better pricing and profitability, scope for cross selling and up selling financial and beyond financial products for increased per customer revenue and of course better risk proposition. With the changing paradigm of technology as the driver for retail banking explosion, banks are embracing different strategies by redesigning their conventional business silos, re-engineering existing products and inventing products, services, channels, relationships to increase the share of the customers' wallet.

Retail banking can be defined as "Retail banking is typically mass-market banking where individual customers use local branches of larger commercial banks. Services offered include savings and checking accounts, mortgages, personal loans, agriculture and business loans, debit cards, credit cards and so on".

The concept of Retail Banking is not new to banks but is now viewed as an important and attractive market segment that offers opportunities for growth and profits. In retail banking all the needs of individual customers are taken care of in a well-integrated manner.

SCOPE FOR RETAIL BANKING IN INDIA

India is a densely populated developing country. Huge customer base and growing economic condition provide a large consumer market for banking services. Scope for retail banking in India is increasing day-by-day due to the following reasons:

1. All round increase in economic activity.
2. Increase in the purchasing power. The rural areas have the large purchasing power at their disposal and this is an opportunity to market Retail Banking.
3. India has 200 million households and 400 million middle class population more than 90% of the savings come from the house hold sector. Falling interest rates have resulted in a shift. "Now People Want to Save Less and Spend More."
4. Nuclear family concept is gaining much importance which may lead to large savings, large number of banking services to be provided are day-by-day increasing.
5. Tax benefits are available, for example, in case of housing loans the borrower can avail tax benefits for the loan repayment and the interest charged for the loan.

The Indian Banks are competing with one another to grab a pie of the retail banking sector, which has tremendous potential. Retail banking environment today is changing fast. The changing customer demographics demands to create a differentiated application based on scalable technology, improved service and banking convenience. Higher penetration of technology and increase in global literacy levels has set up the expectations of the customer higher than never before. Increasing use of modern technology has further enhanced reach and accessibility.

Retail banking in the country is characterized by multiple products, multiple channels and multiple customer groups. This multiplicity of the roles to be played by the retail bankers adds to the excitement as well as the challenges faced by the bankers. Today's retail banking sector is characterized by three basic features:

1. **Multiple Products:** Various types of Deposits, Credit Cards, Loans (Personal, Auto, Housing etc.) Insurance, mutual funds etc.
2. **Multiple Channels of Distribution:** Branch, Internet Banking, Mobile banking, Debit Cards, Call centers.
3. **Multiple Customer Groups:** Individual customers, Petty Businesses, Small and Medium Enterprises (SMEs).

Retail Products

The typical products offered in the Indian Retail Banking segment are:

Retail Deposit Products:

- Savings Bank Accounts;
- Current Deposit Accounts;
- Recurring Deposit Accounts;
- Fixed Deposit Accounts;
- Deposit Accounts for Salaried Class;
- Senior Citizen Deposit Accounts;
- Basic Savings Bank Accounts of PMJDY.

Retail Loan Products:

- Various type of Home Loans for purchase/ construction/repair of house or flat;
- Auto Loans for purchase of Vehicles;
- Consumer Loans for purchase of Consumer Durables;
- Personal Loans and Pensioner Loans for personal needs and consumption purposes;
- Education Loans for pursuing Higher Education;
- Trade related MSME Loans for setting up business, manufacturing unit, retail trade etc.;
- KCC and other agricultural and allied activity loans to farmers;
- Credit Cards etc.

Retail Services:

- Safe Deposit Lockers;
- Depository Services;
- Bancassurance Products etc.

Features of Retail Banking

One of the prominent features of Retail Banking products is that it is a volume driven business. Further, Retail Credit ensures that the business is widely dispersed among a large customer base unlike in the case of corporate lending, where the risk may be concentrated on a selected few plans. Ability of a bank to administer a large portfolio of retail credit products depends upon such factors:

1. **Strong Credit Assessment Capability:** Because of large volume good infrastructure is required. If the credit assessment itself is qualitative, then the need for follow up in the future reduces considerably.
2. **Sound Documentation:** A latest system for credit documentation is necessary pre-requisite for healthy growth of credit portfolio, as in the case of credit assessment. This will also minimize the need to follow up at future point of time.
3. **Strong Possessing Capability:** Since large volumes of transactions are involved, today transactions, maintenance of backups is required.
4. **Regular Constant Follow- up:** Ideally, follow up for loan repayments should be an ongoing process. It should start from customer enquiry and last till the loan is repaid fully.
5. **Skilled human Resource:** This is one of the most important pre-requisite for the efficient management of large and diverse retail credit portfolio. Only highly skilled and experienced man power can withstand the river of administrating a diverse and complex retail credit portfolio.
6. **Technological Support:** This is yet another vital requirement. Retail credit is highly technological and intensive in nature. Because of large volumes of business, the need to provide instantaneous service to the customer, faster processing, maintaining database, etc. is imperative.

Opportunities in Retail Banking

Retail banking has immense opportunities in a growing economy like India. As the growth story gets unfolded in India, retail banking is going to emerge a major driver. The rise of Indian middle class is an important contributory factor in this regard. The percentage of middle to high-income Indian households is expected to continue rising. The younger population not only wields increasing purchasing power, but as far as acquiring personal debt is concerned, they are perhaps more comfortable than previous generations. Improving consumer purchasing power, coupled with more liberal attitudes towards personal debt, is contributing to India's retail banking segment.

WHOLESALE BANKING AND INTERNATIONAL BANKING

Wholesale Banking

Wholesale banking refers to banking services between merchant banks and other financial institutions. This type of banking deals with larger clients, such as large corporations and other banks, whereas retail banking focuses more on the individual or small business. Wholesale banking services include currency conversion, working capital financing, large trade transactions and other types of services.

Wholesale banking involves providing banking services to other commercial banks, mortgage brokers, large corporate, mid-size companies, real estate developers, international trading businesses, institutional customers or other corporations. The services which come under the net of wholesale banking involves wholesaling, underwriting, market making, consultancy, mergers and acquisitions, joint ventures, fund management etc. The focus is on high-level clients and high-value transactions.

Products: The products offered can be classified into four groups, viz, Fund Based Services, Non- Fund Based Services, Value-Added Services and Internet Banking Services. Various types of these products offered by the most of the banks is mentioned below.

Fund Based Services:

(a) Long-Term Lending

(b) Short-Term Finance

(c) Working Capital Finance

(d) Bill Discounting

(e) Structured Finance

(f) Export Credit

Non-Fund Based Services:

(a) Bank Guarantee

(b) Letter of Credit

(c) Collection of Bills and Documents

Value-Added Services:

(a) Channel Financing

(b) Cash Management Service

(c) Syndication Service

(d) Forex Business

(e) Corporate Salary Account) Money Market Service

(g) Tax Collection

(h) Derivatives business

(i) Vendor Financing

Internet Banking Services:

(a) Payment Gateway Services

(b) Corporate Internet Banking

(c) Supply Chain Management

Wholesale Banking in India

India presents a strong case for the growth of wholesale banking due to continued globalisation of Indian companies. India being seen as a favourable investment destination, increase in infrastructure spending, stable government, robust markets, stable currency, low deficits, etc. Wholesale banking thus comprises a major share of the banking revenues due to the above factors and also due to an increased inclination of government towards mid-segment companies which have increasing banking requirements.

Wholesale clientele for banks are highly significant for banks to drive business. Banks provide various forms of banking solutions like project finance, leasing finance, working capital finance, merchant banking, syndication services etc. are also provided to clients. The major advantage in wholesale banking is that a client can have easy and one-place access to all its finances and their details. This makes internal stock transfers, fund transfers, allocations and distributions simpler. It however, it increases the risk it poses to the clients as all their funds are parked in one institution and the businesses depend on the financial health of the bank for smooth run. In cases of economic downturns, if the banks crash, all the dependent businesses come to a standstill instantly. Thus, businesses usually diversify into several financial institutions to remain afloat during any crisis.

International Banking

International markets, offer opportunities to the traders and corporate and multinational companies, to expand their business, across different parts of the globe. International investors explore more investment avenues for their investments. The international markets in the financial sector offers a wide range of opportunities for expansion of trade and financial activities across the borders of nations.

"International Banking" can be defined as a sub-set of commercial banking transactions and activity having a cross-border and/or cross currency element. Multinational banking refers to the location and ownership of banking facilities in a large number of countries and geographic regions. International banking comprises a range of transactions that can be distinguished from purely domestic operations by

(a) the currency of denomination of the transaction,
(b) the residence of the bank customer and
(c) the location of the booking office.

Banks are offering a lot of services to the International Business People. These services can be broadly classified as under.

Banking Services to Exporters

1. **Pre-shipment / Packing Credit:** Any loan or advance granted or any other credit provided by a bank to an exporter for financing the purchase, processing, manufacturing or packing of goods prior to shipment / working capital expenses towards rendering of services on the basis of letter of credit opened in his favour.
2. **Export Bill Negotiation:** Banks negotiate export bills drawn under LC, if the documents are found to be strictly in terms with the LC conditions and payment of the bills to the exporter is made even before the bills are realised from the importers.
3. **Export Bill Purchase and Discounting:** Even when the exports are not covered under letter of credit, Banks sanction credit limits and pay the value of invoice, immediately on shipment to the exporter at a discount. The export documents are presented and proceeds will be credited to the advance accounts on realisation.
4. **Bank Guarantee:** Banks issue guarantees in foreign currency on behalf of the exporter for approved purposes, subject to availability of credit limit or against 100% cash margin.
5. **Supplier Credit:** This facility provided to the Indian exporter to extend term credit to importers (Overseas) of eligible goods at the post shipment stage.
6. **LC Advising:** Bank takes responsibility to communicate the exporter under letter of credit and other required authorities. The advising bank is the party who sends documents under Letter of Credit to opening bank.
7. **LC Confirmation:** When exporter does not have confidence in the credit standing of a letter of credit opening bank, confirming bank confirms and guarantees to undertake the responsibility of payment or negotiation acceptance under the credit.

Banking Services to Importers

1. **Issue Letter of Credit:** Bank opens letter of credit on request of importers takes responsibility to pay amount on receipt of documents from supplier of goods (beneficiary under LC).
2. **Advance payments towards imports:** Whenever any advance payment to an overseas supplier is required to be made, bank provide advisory services and also assist in faster remittance to the suppliers.
3. **Collection of Bills:** Banks provides services of documentary collection and flexible method of payment for goods purchase from abroad.
4. **Bank Guarantee:** Banks issue guarantee in foreign currency on behalf of importers against 100% cash margin or under regular limit.
5. **Arranging for Buyer's and Supplier's Credit:** Banks offer a wide range of offshore financing options to importer and take care of their working capital requirements. Banks also arrange for financing import requirements of importers by way of supplier's credit and buyer's credit.

Remittances Services

1. **EEFC Account Services:** Banks provide facility to maintain an Exchange Earners Foreign Currency Accounts (EEFC Accounts) to his eligible customers in all permitted foreign currency.
2. **Receipt of Foreign Inward Remittances:** Banks receive remittances from abroad on behalf of his customers and credit to the beneficiaries' accounts.
3. **Outward Remittances:** As a Authorised Dealer (AD) in Foreign Exchange, banks provide remittance facility in foreign currency for any permitted purpose as per FEMA Guidelines up to the limit permitted by RBI.

UNIVERSAL BANKING

Universal banking is a banking system in which banks provide a wide variety of financial services, including commercial and investment services. Universal banking is common in some European countries, including Switzerland. In the United States, however, banks are required to separate their commercial and investment banking services. Proponents of universal banking argue that it helps banks better diversify risk. Detractors think dividing up banks' operations is a less risky strategy.

Universal banks may offer credit, loans, deposits, asset management, investment advisory, payment processing, securities transactions, underwriting and financial analysis. While a universal banking system allows banks to offer a multitude of services, it does not require them to do so. Banks in a universal system may still choose to specialize in a subset of banking services.

American Depositary Receipt (ADR)

American depositary receipts were introduced in 1927 as an easier way for U.S. investors to purchase stock in foreign companies. Non-U.S. companies also benefit from ADRs as it makes it easier to attract American investors. An American depositary receipt (ADR) is a negotiable certificate issued by a U.S. bank representing a specified number of shares (or one share) in a foreign stock traded on a U.S. exchange. ADRs are denominated in U.S. dollars, with the underlying security held by a U.S. financial institution overseas, and holders of ADRs realize any dividends and capital gains in U.S. dollars, but dividend payments in euros are converted to U.S. dollars, net of conversion expenses and foreign taxes. ADRs are listed on either the NYSE, AMEX or Nasdaq but they are also sold OTC.

Global Depository Receipt (GDR)

A global depository receipt (GDR) is a certificate issued by a depository bank, which purchases shares of foreign companies and deposits it on the account. They are the global equivalent of the original American depository receipts (ADR) on which they are based. GDRs represent ownership of an underlying number of shares of a foreign company and are commonly used to invest in companies from developing or emerging markets by investors in developed markets.

Participatory Notes

Participatory Notes, also referred to as "P-notes," are financial instruments used by investors or hedge funds that are not registered with the Securities and Exchange Board of India (SEBI) to invest in Indian securities. Any dividends or capital gains collected from the underlying securities go back to the investors. Indian regulators are against participatory notes because they fear that hedge funds acting through participatory notes will cause economic volatility in India's exchanges. Foreign institutional investors (FIIs) provide quick money entering the Indian capital market. Because of the short-term nature of investing, regulators have fewer guidelines for FIIs. To invest in Indian stock markets without the hassle of involvement with the regulatory approval process, FIIs trade P-notes.

P-notes are easily traded overseas through endorsement and delivery. They are popular because investors anonymously take positions in Indian markets, and hedge funds anonymously carry out their operations. Some entities route their investments through P-notes to take advantage of certain countries' tax laws.

TEST YOURSELF

1. Which is not a part of retail banking in India?
(a) Mortgages and personal loans
(b) Agriculture and business loans,
(c) Debit cards, credit cards
(d) Forex Business

2. Scope for retail banking in India is increasing day by day due to the following reasons. Find the incorrect statement.
(a) Increase in the purchasing power. The rural areas have the large purchasing power at their disposal and this is an opportunity to market Retail Banking.
(b) India has 200 million households and 400 million middle class population more than 90% of the savings come from the house hold sector.
(c) Joint family concept is gaining much importance which may lead to large savings, large number of banking services to be provided are day-by-day increasing.
(d) Tax benefits are available, for example, in case of housing loans the borrower can avail tax benefits for the loan repayment and the interest charged for the loan.

3. The loan limit under retail lending in India are generally varies from:
(a) ₹ 10000 to ₹ 1 Crore
(b) ₹ 1 Crore to ₹ 5 Crore
(c) ₹ 5 Crore to ₹ 10 Crore
(d) More than ₹ 10 Crore

4. Today's retail banking sector is characterized by three basic features. Which is the part of multiple channels of distribution:
(a) Branch (b) Internet banking
(c) Debit Cards (d) All of the above

5. Which is not a part of retail deposit schemes?
(a) Recurring Deposit (b) Salaried account
(c) NPS account (d) PMJDY

6. Which types of Retail Services are offered by the bank?
(a) Safe Deposit Lockers
(b) Depository Services
(c) Bancassurance Products
(d) All of the above

7. Participatory notes are like contract notes issued by:
(a) Foreign Institutional Investors (FIIs) to entities that want to invest in the Indian stock market
(b) Commercial banks to their investors
(c) Government for India to bank
(d) None

8. Which is a part Retail Loan Products by banks in India?
(a) Home loan (b) Agriculture loan
(c) MSME loan (d) All of the above

9. When banks have business relationship with the industrial and business entities, these type of banking is categorised as:
(a) Retail banking (b) Wholesale banking
(c) Universal banking (d) International banking

10. Which is not a part of Fund Based Services offered by bank:
(a) Long-Term Lending
(b) Collection of Bills and Documents
(c) Working Capital Finance
(d) Export Credit

11. Which is a part of Non-Fund Based Services offered by bank:
(a) Bank Guarantee
(b) Letter of Credit
(c) Collection of Bills and Documents
(d) All of the above

12. Which is not a part of Value-Added Services:
(a) Channel Financing
(b) Collection of Bills and Documents
(c) Syndication Service
(d) Cash Management Service

13. Which is a part of Value-Added Services:
(a) Forex Business
(b) Money Market Service
(c) Tax Collection
(d) All of the above

14. Internet Banking Services becomes the essential part of modern banking, it includes:
(a) Payment Gateway Services
(b) Corporate Internet Banking
(c) Supply Chain Management
(d) All of the above

15. A global depository receipt (GDR) is a certificate issued by a depository bank, which purchases shares of ______ and deposits it on the account.
(a) Foreign companies (b) Indian companies
(c) Local companies (d) Small companies

16. ADRs are denominated in ______, with the underlying security held by a U.S. financial institution overseas.
(a) Indian Rupee (b) Australian Dollar
(c) U.S. Dollars (d) Pound Sterling

17. Global depository receipts are normally traded on:
(a) US Stock Exchange
(b) European Stock Exchange
(c) Indian Stock Exchange
(d) International Stock Exchange

18. The term super financial hub in the context of banking, is called:
(a) Universal banking (b) Narrow banking
(c) Retail banking (d) Wholesale banking

19. Banking facilities provided to poor and deprived family of the country is called as:
(a) Narrow banking
(b) Financial inclusion
(c) Financial literacy
(d) Universal banking

20. Which of the following can issue participatory notes:
(a) SEBI (b) SGB Holders
(c) FII (d) FDI

ANSWER

1	2	3	4	5	6	7	8	9	10
(d)	(c)	(a)	(d)	(c)	(d)	(a)	(d)	(b)	(b)
11	**12**	**13**	**14**	**15**	**16**	**17**	**18**	**19**	**20**
(d)	(b)	(d)	(d)	(a)	(c)	(b)	(a)	(b)	(c)

ROLE OF MONEY MARKETS, DEBT MARKETS & FOREX MARKET

CALL MONEY MARKETS

Money market in India

Money markets is that segment of financial markets where borrowing and lending of the short-term funds takes place. The Money market in India correlation for short-term funds with maturity ranging from overnight to one year in India including financial instruments that are deemed to be close substitutes of money. Similar to developed economies the Indian money market is diversified and has evolved through many stages, from the conventional platform of treasury bills and call money to commercial paper, certificates of deposit, repos, forward rate agreements and most recently interest rate swaps. In our country, Money Markets are regulated by both RBI and SEBI.

Call Money/Notice Money/ Term Money Market

Call Money, Notice Money and Term Money markets are sub-markets of the Indian Money Market. These refer to the markets for very short-term funds. Call Money refers to the borrowing or lending of funds for 1 day. Notice Money refers to the borrowing and lending of funds for 2-14 days. Term money refers to borrowing and lending of funds for a period of more than 14 days.

India Debt Market

Debt market refers to the financial market where investors buy and sell debt securities, mostly in the form of bonds. These markets are important source of funds, especially in a developing economy like India. India debt market is one of the largest in Asia. Like all other countries, debt market in India is also considered a useful substitute to banking channels for finance. The most distinguishing feature of the debt instruments of Indian debt market is that the return is fixed. This means, returns are almost risk-free. This fixed return on the bond is often termed as the 'coupon rate' or the 'interest rate'. Therefore, the buyer (of bond) is giving the seller a loan at a fixed interest rate, which equals to the coupon rate.

Trading in Money Market

The Indian money market consists of diverse sub-markets, each dealing in a particular type of short-term credit. The trades are conducted both on telephone as well as on the NDS Call systems, which is an electronic screen based system set up by the RBI for negotiating money market deals between entities permitted to operate in the money market.

MONEY MARKET INSTRUMENTS IN INDIA

1. Treasury Bills (T-Bills)

Treasury bills are instrument of short-term borrowing by the Government of India, issued as promissory notes under discount. Treasury bills, also known as Zero Coupon Bonds are the instrument of short term borrowing with maturity period of less than one year. This instrument is issued by Reserve Bank of India on behalf of the Central

Government for fulfilling short term requirements of funds. They are issued at discount and are paid at par. The interest received on them is the discount, which is the difference between the price at which they are issued and their redemption value.

They have assured yield and negligible risk of default. The interest received on them is the discount, which is the difference between the price at which they are issued and their redemption value. They have assured yield and negligible risk of default. Under one classification, treasury bills are categorised as ad hoc, tap and auction bills. They are issued of ₹ 10,000 or in multiples thereof.

For example, suppose an investor purchases a 108 days Treasury bill for ₹ 138,000 having face value of ₹ 1,50,000. On maturity, he receives ₹ 1, 50,000. The difference of ₹ 12, 000 in the issue and redemption price is the interest received by him.

2. Certificate of Deposit

Certificate of Deposit (CD) is a negotiable money market instrument and issued in dematerialised form or as a Usance Promissory Note against funds deposited at a bank or other eligible financial institution for a specified time period. All scheduled commercial banks excluding Regional Rural Banks (RRBs) and Local Area Banks (LABs) and Select All India Financial Institutions permitted by RBI are eligible to issue certificates of deposits. The official document bears the maturity date the fixed rate of interest and the value.

Minimum Size of Issue and Denominations: Minimum amount of ₹ 100, 000 and multiples thereof.

Maturity: The maturity period of CDs issued by banks should not be less than 7 days and not more than one year, from the date of issue. The FIs can issue CDs for a period not less than 1 year and not exceeding 3 years from the date of issue.

Discount / Coupon Rate: CDs may be issued at a discount on face value. Banks / FIs are also allowed to issue CDs on floating rate basis provided the methodology of compiling the floating rate is objective, transparent and market-based. The issuing bank / FI is free to determine the discount / coupon rate.

Transferability: CDs in physical form are freely transferable by endorsement and delivery. CDs in demat form can be transferred as per the procedure applicable to other demat securities. There is no lock-in period for the CDs.

Loans / Buy-backs: Banks / FIs cannot grant loans against CDs. Furthermore, they cannot buy-back their own CDs before maturity. However, the RBI may relax these restrictions for temporary periods through a separate notification.

3. Commercial Paper

Commercial Paper is unsecured money market instrument issued in the form of promissory note. It was introduced in India in 1990 with a view to enabling highly rated corporate borrowers to diversify their sources of short-term borrowings and to provide an additional instrument to investors. Corporates, primary dealers (PDs) and the All-India Financial Institutions (FIs) are eligible to issue CP.

Subsequently, primary dealers and all-India financial institutions were also permitted to issue CP to enable them to meet their short-term funding requirements for their operations. The interest rate on commercial papers are usually linked to the yield on the one-year government bond. Not all the companies are eligible to issue CP.

Eligibility to issue CP: The tangible net worth of the company, as per the latest audited balance sheet, is not less than ₹ 4 crore. The company has been sanctioned working capital limit by bank/s or FIs and the borrower account of the company is classified as a Standard Asset by the financing bank/institution.

Characteristics of Commercial Paper: CP are negotiable instruments and hence they are flexible. All eligible participants should obtain credit rating for issuance of Commercial Paper either from Credit Rating Information Services of India Ltd. (CRISIL) or the Investment Information and Credit Rating Agency of India Ltd. (ICRA) or the Credit Analysis and Research Ltd. (CARE) or the FITCH Ratings India Pvt. Ltd. The minimum credit rating shall be A-2

Period of Maturity and Amount Prescribed for CP: CP can be issued for maturities between a minimum of 7 days and a maximum of up to one year from the date of issue. However, the maturity date of the CP should not go beyond the date up to which the credit rating of the issuer is valid. CP are issued in denominations of ₹ 5 lakh or multiples thereof.

Investor in CP: CP can be invested by individuals, banking companies, other corporate bodies (registered or incorporated in India) and unincorporated bodies, Non-Resident Indians (NRIs) and Foreign Institutional Investors (FIIs) etc. can invest in CPs.

However, investment by FIIs would be within the limits set for them by Securities and Exchange Board of India (SEBI) from time-to-time. However, these are risky instruments as they are not backed by assets. So, its investors who are less averse to risk should avoid this. Only blue chip companies, banks, corporation use this.

4. The Repo/Reverse Repo Market

Repo (repurchase agreement) was introduced in December 1992. Repo means selling a security under an agreement to repurchase it at a pre-determined date and rate. Repo transactions are affected between banks and financial institutions and among bank themselves, RBI also undertake Repo. in 1996, Reverse Repo was introduced. Reverse Repo means buying a security on a spot basis with a commitment to resell on a forward basis. Reverse Repo transactions are affected with scheduled commercial banks and primary dealers.

5. Collateralized Borrowing and Lending Obligation (CBLO)

A collateralized borrowing and lending obligation (CBLO) is a money market instrument that represents an obligation between a borrower and a lender as to the terms and conditions of a loan. Collateralized borrowing and lending obligations are used by those who have been phased out of or heavily restricted in the interbank call money market.

Collateralized borrowing and lending obligations (CBLOs) is operated by the Clearing Corporation of India Ltd. (CCIL) and Reserve Bank of India (RBI). The CBLO is a money market segment where short-term loans can be secured by financial institutions in order to cover their transactions. To gain access to these funds, the financial institution must provide eligible securities as collateral. Eligible securities for collateral include Central Government securities, such as Treasury Bills, with at least six months left to the maturity date.

FIXED INCOME MARKET IN INDIA

1. G-secs (Government Securities)

A Government Security (G-Sec) is a tradeable instrument issued by the Central Government or the State Governments. It acknowledges the Government's debt obligation. Such securities are short term (usually called treasury bills, with original maturities of less than one year) or long term (usually called Government bonds or dated securities with original maturity of one year or more). In India, the Central Government issues both, treasury bills and bonds or dated securities while the State Governments issue only bonds or dated securities, which are called the State Development Loans (SDLs). G-Secs carry practically no risk of default and, hence, are called risk-free gilt-edged instruments.

Treasury bills (T-bills) offer short-term investment opportunities, generally up to one year. They are thus useful in managing short-term liquidity. At present, the Government of India issues three types of treasury bills through auctions, namely, 91-day, 182-day and 364-day. Apart from purchasing government securities in the primary issuance, *i.e.*, through auctions/sales, all types of government paper can also be purchased from the secondary market. Primary Dealers also purchase and sell securities.

2. Corporate Bond Market

The corporate Debt Market in India is an efficient price discovery mechanism as well as market participation. Corporate bonds are debt securities issued by private and public corporations. Companies issue corporate bonds to raise money for a variety of purposes, such as building a new plant, purchasing equipment, or growing the business.

Indian firms are still seeking bank finance as the path to fulfil the funding requirements. An efficient bond market would help corporates reduce their financing cost and allow them to structure their asset-liability profiles better. A well developed corporate bond market is also necessary for long term financing of corporates.

When one buys a corporate bond, one lends money to the "issuer," the company that issued the bond. In exchange, the company promises to return the money, also known as "principal," on a specified maturity date. Until that date, the company usually pays you a stated rate of interest, generally semi-annually. While a corporate bond gives an IOU from the company, it does not have an ownership interest in the issuing company, unlike when one purchases the company's equity stock.

3. Interest Rate Derivatives

An interest-rate derivative is a financial instrument with a value that increases and decreases based on movements in interest rates. Interest-rate derivatives are often used as hedges by institutional investors, banks, companies and individuals to protect themselves against changes in market interest rates, but they can also be used to increase or refine the holder's risk profile.

An Interest Rate Futures contract is "an agreement to buy or sell a debt instrument at a specified future date at a price that is fixed today." The underlying security for Interest Rate Futures is either Government Bond or T-Bill. Exchange traded Interest Rate Futures on NSE are standardized contracts based on 6 year, 10 year and 13 year Government of India Security (NBF II) and 91-day Government of India Treasury Bill (91DTB). All futures contracts available for trading on NSE are cash settled.

Types of Interest Rate Derivatives

(A) Vanilla
(B) Quasi Vanilla
(C) Exotic derivatives

In context to the degree of complexity, there are three types of interest rate derivatives, each of which can be distinguished based on the extent of liquidity, tradability and complexity.

Where the vanilla type is the most basic and standard type of interest rate derivative with maximum liquidity, Quasi vanilla is the next level after vanilla type and is fairly liquid. The exotic derivatives are the most illiquid, more complex compared to the commonly traded vanilla derivatives.

Interest Rate Swap

A plain vanilla interest rate swap is the most basic and common type of interest-rate derivative. There are two parties to a swap: party one receives a stream of interest payments based on a floating interest rate and pays a stream of interest payments based on a fixed rate. Party two receives a stream of fixed interest rate payments and pays a stream of floating rate payments. Both payment streams are based on the same notional principal, and the interest payments are netted. Through this exchange of cash flows, the two parties aim to reduce uncertainty and the threat of loss from changes in market interest rates.

A swap can also be used to increase an individual or institution's risk profile, if they choose to receive the fixed rate and pay floating. This strategy is most common with companies that have a credit rating that allows them to issue bonds at a low fixed rate but prefer to swap to a floating rate to take advantage of market movements.

4. Inter Corporate Deposits

Section 186 of the Companies Act, 2013 has come up with the concept of loan and investment by the company. The new Act provides that inter-corporate investments not to be made through more than two layers of investment companies. Any amount received by a company from another company is not a deposit as per the provisions of Companies (Acceptance of Deposit) Rules, 2014. It may be a loan and generally termed as Inter-Corporate Deposits, yet they are not deposits under the Companies Act 2013.

The provision of Section 186 of the Companies Act, 2013 shall not have any effect in the below mentioned cases :

(i) A company from acquiring any other company incorporated in a country outside India if such other company has investment subsidiaries beyond two layers as per the laws of such country.

(ii) A subsidiary company from having any investment subsidiary for the purposes of meeting the requirements under any law or under any rule or regulation framed under any law for the time being in force.

FOREX (FOREIGN EXCHANGE) MARKET

General Features

Foreign exchange market is described as an OTC (Over the counter) market as there is no physical place where the participants meet to execute their deals. It is more an informal arrangement among the banks and brokers operating in a financing centre purchasing and selling currencies, connected to each other by telecommunications like telex, telephone and a satellite communication network, SWIFT.

The term foreign exchange market is used to refer to the wholesale a segment of the market, where the dealings take place among the banks. The retail segment refers to the dealings take place between banks and their customers. The retail segment refers to the dealings take place between banks and their customers. The retail segment is situated at a large number of places. They can be considered not as foreign exchange markets, but as the counters of such markets.

The leading foreign exchange market in India is Mumbai, Calcutta, Chennai and Delhi is other centers accounting for bulk of the exchange dealings in India. The policy of Reserve Bank has been to decentralize exchanges operations and develop broader based exchange markets. As a result of the efforts of Reserve Bank Cochin, Bangalore, Ahmedabad and Goa have emerged as new centre of foreign exchange market.

Hours Market

The markets are situated throughout the different time zones of the globe in such a way that when one market is closing the other is beginning its operations. Thus, at any point of time one market or the other is open. Therefore, it is stated that foreign exchange market is functioning throughout 24 hours of the day. However, a specific market will function only during the business hours. Some of the banks having international network and having centralized control of funds management may keep their foreign exchange department in the key centre open throughout to keep up with developments at other centers during their normal working hours. In India, the market is open for the time the banks are open for their regular banking business. No transactions take place on Saturdays.

LIBOR

LIBOR, the acronym for London Interbank Offer Rate, is the global reference rate for unsecured short-term borrowing in the interbank market. It acts as a benchmark for short-term interest rates. It is used for pricing of interest rate swaps, currency rate swaps as well as mortgages. It is an indicator of the health of the financial system and provides an idea of the trajectory of impending policy rates of central banks.

LIBOR is administered by the ICE Benchmark Administration (IBA) and is based on five currencies: the U.S. dollar (USD), euro (EUR), pound sterling (GBP), Japanese yen (JPY), and Swiss franc (CHF). The LIBOR serves seven different maturities: overnight, one week, and 1, 2, 3, 6 and 12 months. There are a total of 35 different LIBOR rates each business day. The most commonly quoted rate is the three-month U.S. dollar rate (usually referred to as the "current LIBOR rate").

MIBOR

MIBOR is the acronym for Mumbai Interbank Offer Rate, the yardstick of the Indian call money market. It is the rate at which banks borrow unsecured funds from one another in the interbank market. At present, it is used as a reference rate for floating rate notes, corporate debentures, term deposits, interest rate swaps and forward rate agreements. The pricing of overnight indexed swaps, a type of overnight interest rate swap used for hedging interest rate risk is based on overnight MIBOR.

The MIBOR was launched on June 15, 1998 by the Committee for the Development of the Debt Market, as an overnight rate. The NSEIL launched the 14-day MIBOR on November 10, 1998, and the one month and three-month MIBORs on December 1, 1998. Since the launch, MIBOR rates have been used as benchmark rates for the majority of money market deals made in India.

THE FOREIGN EXCHANGE MANAGEMENT ACT, 1999

Introduction

The Foreign Exchange Management Act, 1999 (FEMA) is an Act of the Parliament of India "to consolidate and amend the law relating to foreign exchange with the objective of facilitating external trade and payments and for promoting the orderly development and maintenance of foreign exchange market in India". It was passed in the winter session of Parliament in 1999, replacing the Foreign Exchange Regulation Act (FERA). This act makes offences related to foreign exchange civil offenses. It extends to the whole of India. It enabled a new foreign exchange management regime consistent with the emerging framework of the World Trade Organisation (WTO). It also paved the way for the introduction of the Prevention of Money Laundering Act, 2002.

Dealing in foreign exchange: A person has to obtain the general or special permission of the Reserve Bank for carry out the following activities:

(*a*) Deal in or transfer any foreign exchange or foreign security to any person other than an authorised person;

(*b*) Make any payment to any person resident outside India;

(*c*) Receive otherwise through an authorised person, any payment on behalf of any person resident outside India;

(*d*) Enter into any financial transaction in India as consideration of a right to acquire, any asset outside India by any person.

Holding of foreign exchange: No person resident in India shall be acquire, hold, own, possess or transfer any foreign exchange, foreign security or any immovable property situated outside India, unless permitted by RBI.

Current account transactions: Any person may sell or draw foreign exchange to or from an authorised person if such sale or draw is a current account transaction, Provided that the Central Government may, in public interest and in consultation with the Reserve Bank, impose such reasonable restrictions for current account transactions as may be prescribed.

Capital account transactions: A transaction which alters the assets or liabilities, including contingent liabilities, outside India of a person resident in India or assets or liabilities in India of person resident outside India, is called capital account transaction. As per Section 6, any person may sell or draw foreign exchange to or from an authorised person for a capital account transaction. Reserve Bank may in consultation with the Central Government, specify:

(a) Any class or classes of capital account transactions which are permissible;

(b) The limit up to which foreign exchange shall be admissible for such transactions:

(c) Any class or classes of capital account transactions which are permissible;

(d) The limit up to which foreign exchange shall be admissible for such transactions:

"Provided, Reserve Bank or the Central Government shall not impose any restriction on the draw of foreign exchange for payments due on account of amortization of loans or for depreciation of direct investments in the ordinary course of business transaction."

Restriction on Capital Account Transactions: Reserve Bank may, by regulations, prohibit, restrict or regulate the following-

(a) Transfer or issue of any foreign security by a person resident in India;

(b) Transfer or issue of any security by a person resident outside India;

(c) Transfer or issue of any security or foreign security by any branch, office or agency in India of a person resident outside India;

(d) Any borrowing or lending in foreign exchange in whatever form or by whatever name called;

(e) Any borrowing or lending in rupees in whatever form or by whatever name called between a person resident in India and a person resident outside India;

(f) Deposits between persons resident in India and persons resident outside India;

(g) Export, import or holding of currency or currency notes;

(h) Transfer of immovable property outside India, other than a lease not exceeding five years, by a person resident in India;

(i) Acquisition or transfer of immovable property in India, other than a lease not exceeding five years, by a person resident outside India;

(j) Giving of a guarantee or surety in respect of any debt, obligation or other liability incurred;

(i) By a person resident in India and owed to a person resident outside India; or

(ii) By a person resident outside India.

Reserve Bank's powers to issue directions to authorised person (Section 11): Reserve Bank, may give to the authorised persons, any direction in regard to making of payment or the doing or desist from doing any act relating to foreign exchange or foreign security, direct any authorised person to furnish such information, in such manner, as it deems fit.

Penalty on authorized person: Whereany authorised person contravenes any direction given by the Reserve Bank under this Act or fails to file any return as directed by the Reserve Bank, the Reserve Bank may, after giving reasonable opportunity of being heard, impose on the authorised person a penalty which may extend to ₹ 10000 and in the case of continuing contravention with for every day during which such contravention continues.

Power of Reserve Bank to inspect authorised person (Sec 12): Reserve Bank may undertake an inspection of the business of any authorised person for the purpose of verifying the correctness of any statement, information or particulars furnished to the Reserve Bank, obtaining any information or particulars which such authorised person has failed to furnish on being called upon to do so.

Contravention and Penalties: If any person contravenes any provisions of this Act, or contravenes any rule, regulation, notification, direction or order issued in exercise of the powers under this Act, or contravenes any condition subject to which an authorisation is issued by the Reserve Bank, he shall, upon adjudication, be liable to a penalty up to *thrice the sum involved* in such contravention where such amount is quantifiable, or up to ₹ 2 lac where the amount is not quantifiable.

Such contravention is a continuing one, further penalty which may extend to ₹ 5000 for every day after the first day during which the contravention continues.

If any person fails to make full payment of the penalty imposed on him under section 13 within a period of 90 days from the date on which the notice for payment of such penalty is served on him, he shall be liable to civil imprisonment u/s 14.

Power to compound contravention: U/s 15, any contravention under section 13 may, on an application made by the person committing such contravention, be compounded within 180 days from the date of receipt of application by the Director of Enforcement or such other officers of the Directorate of Enforcement and officers of the Reserve Bank as may be authorised in this behalf by the Central Government.

Adjudication and Appeal: U/s 16, Central Government may appoint officers of the Central Government, as the Adjudicating Authorities for holding an inquiry. Adjudicating Authority may direct the said person to furnish a bond or guarantee,

- No Adjudicating Authority shall hold an enquiry except upon a complaint in writing made by any officer authorised by a general or special order by the Central Government. Adjudicating Authority shall have the powers of a civil court.
- All proceedings before it shall be deemed to be judicial proceedings within the meaning of sections 193 and 228 of the Indian Penal Code.
- Adjudicating Authority shall deal with the complaint to dispose of the complaint finally within one year from the date of receipt of the complaint.

Appellate Tribunal (Sec 18): The Central Government shall, establish an Appellate Tribunal to be known as the Appellate Tribunal for Foreign Exchange to hear appeals against the orders of the Adjudicating Authorities and the Special Director (Appeals). Appellate Tribunal shall consist of a Chairperson and such number of Members as the Central Government may deem fit.

Directorate of Enforcement: U/s 36, Central Government shall establish a Directorate of Enforcement with a Director and other officers. U/s 37, the Director of Enforcement and other officers of Enforcement, not below the rank of an Assistant Director, shall take up for investigation, the contravention referred to in section 13.

TEST YOURSELF

1. Call Money, Notice Money and Term Money markets are sub-markets of the Indian Money Market. These refer to the markets for ________ funds.
(a) Long Term (b) Medium term
(c) Very short-term (d) All of these

2. ________ is a fund between banks, which is lending and borrowing for one day (overnight).
(a) Call money (b) Notice money
(c) Term money (d) Debt money

3. Term money refers to borrowing and lending of funds for a period of more than ________.
(a) 7 days (b) 14 days
(c) 30 days (d) 90 days

4. The most distinguishing feature of the debt instruments of Indian debt market is that the return is fixed. This means, returns are almost ________. This fixed return on the bond is often termed as the 'coupon rate' or the 'interest rate'.
(a) high risk (b) medium risk
(c) low risk (d) risk-free

5. Treasury bills are issued of ________ or in multiples thereof.
(a) ₹ 10,000 (b) ₹ 50,000
(c) ₹ 100,000 (d) ₹ 1000,000

6. The maturity period of CDs issued by banks should not be less than 7 days and not more than______, from the date of issue.
(a) 3 months (b) 6 months
(c) one-year (d) two years

7. Eligibility to issue Commercial Paper (CP) is the tangible net worth of the company, as per the latest audited balance sheet, is not less than ________.
(a) ₹ 1 crore (b) ₹ 2 crore
(c) ₹ 4 crore (d) ₹ 5 crore

8. Commercial Paper can be issued for maturities between a minimum of ________ and a maximum of up to one year from the date of issue.
(a) 7 days (b) 14 days
(c) 30 days (d) 90 days

9. Which is not a correct statement about the Repo and Reverse Repo Market?
(a) Repo (repurchase agreement) was introduced in December 1995.
(b) Repo means selling a security under an agreement to repurchase it at a pre-determined date and rate.
(c) Repo transactions are affected between banks and financial institutions and among bank themselves, RBI also undertake Repo.
(d) Reverse Repo means buying a security on a spot basis with a commitment to resell on a forward basis.

11. Which is not a correct statement about CBLO?
(a) CBLO stands for 'Collateralized Borrowing and Lending Obligations'.
(b) CBLO is operated by the Clearing Corporation of India Ltd. (CCIL) and Reserve Bank of India (RBI).
(c) The CBLO is a money market segment where long-term loans can be secured by financial institutions in order to cover their transactions.
(d) To gain access to these funds, the financial institution must provide eligible securities as collateral.

11. A Government Security (G-Se(c) is a tradeable instrument issued by ________. It acknowledges the Government's debt obligation.
(a) the Central Government only
(b) the State Governments only
(c) the Central Government or the State Governments
(d) None of the above

12. When one buys a corporate bond, one lends money to the "issuer," the company that issued the bond. In exchange, the company promises to return the money, also known as ________ on a specified maturity date.
(a) principal
(b) profit
(c) bond price
(d) maturity value

13. An interest-rate derivative is a financial instrument with a value that increases and decreases based on movements in _________.

(a) the period (b) interest rates
(c) price (d) security

14. Which is not a types of Interest rate derivatives?

(a) Vanilla
(b) Semi Vanilla
(c) Quasi Vanilla
(d) Exotic derivatives

15. LIBOR is not based on which currencies?

(a) U.S. dollar (USD) (b) Euro (EUR)
(c) Pound sterling (GBP) (d) Yuan

16. Under FEMA 1999, which of the following is included in the definition of authorised person?

(a) A bank only
(b) A bank or financial institution only
(c) A bank, a financial institution, a money changer or dealer authorised by Govt.
(d) A bank, a financial institution, a money changer or dealer authorised by RBI

17. The term repatriation to India, as per FEMA 1999 means:

(a) Bringing foreign exchange into India
(b) Remitting foreign exchange outside India
(c) Starting business in India by using foreign exchange funds
(d) Any of the above

18. A foreign exchange transaction other than by which there may be a change in asset or liabilities outside India of a person resident in India as per FEMA 1999, is called:

(a) Capital account transaction
(b) Foreign direct investment
(c) Foreign currency transaction
(d) Current account transaction

19. As per FEMA 1999, no person resident in India shall be acquire, hold, own, possess or transfer any foreign exchange, foreign security or any immovable property situated outside India, unless permitted by _________.

(a) Central Government
(b) RBI
(c) President of India
(d) Minister of external affairs

20. For contravention of provision of FEMA, penalty can be levied _________ where amount is quantifiable:

(a) Equal to the amount
(b) Double the amount
(c) Thrice the amount
(d) Four times of amount

ANSWER

1	2	3	4	5	6	7	8	9	10
(c)	(a)	(b)	(d)	(a)	(c)	(c)	(a)	(a)	(c)
11	**12**	**13**	**14**	**15**	**16**	**17**	**18**	**19**	**20**
(c)	(a)	(b)	(b)	(d)	(d)	(a)	(d)	(b)	(c)

CAPITAL MARKETS, SEBI

CAPITAL MARKET

Introduction

Economic environment of a nation is largely characterized by the efficient mobilization and usage of financial resources. A favorable economic environment attracts investments, which in turn influences the development of the economy. The quantity and quality of assets in a nation at a specific time is one of the essential criteria for the assessment of economic development. Assets in an economy is broadly divided according to their characteristics into Physical, Financial and intangible assets. Financial assets help the physical assets to generate activity.

Capital Market in India

The capital market is a vital of the financial system. Capital market provides the support of capitalism to the country. The wave of economic reforms initiated by the government has influenced the functioning and governance of the capital market. The Indian capital market is also undergoing structural transformation since liberalisation. The chief aim of the reforms exercise is to improve market efficiency, make stock market transactions more transparent, curb unfair trade practices and to bring our financial markets up to international standards.

Financial market can be classified as under:

1. Money Market
2. Debt Market
3. Capital Market
4. Forex Market

The promoters of a business can raise the funds for investing in business, through many ways like borrowing from banks and financial institutions, invest their own money and also raise funds by inviting public to invest in the form of shares, debentures etc.

Capital Market is a market where investors/ buyers, and issuers of securities/ sellers engage in issue/ subscription/ trade of financial securities like shares, bonds etc. This market helps in channelizing surplus funds from investors to the institutions in an organized manner, which then invests them into productive use. This market mostly deals in long term securities

It consists of two types viz., Primary market and Secondary market.

Primary Market

In this market, securities (shares, debentures, bonds etc) are offered to the public for subscription with a view to raise capital fund. The public issues are to be handled as per the guidelines of the regulator of Capital market, *i.e.*, the Securities Exchange Board of India (SEBI) and applicable legal framework like the Companies Act. There are number of facilitators (intermediaries) in the primary market like merchant bankers, issue manager, lead arranger and others, who through their services facilitate the public issue at different stages, to enable the investors to decide and invest in a company. Banks participate in the capital market as banker to the issue, arrangers, underwriters etc.

In the primary market, issues are classified into public, rights or preferential issues (also known as private placements). The public and rights issues involve a detailed procedure, whereas in case of private placements or preferential issues, the procedures are relatively simpler.

Public issues can be classified into Initial Public Offerings (IPOs) and Further/Follow-on Public Offerings (FPOs). When an unlisted company makes either a fresh issue of shares or an offer for sale of its existing shares or both for the first time to the public, it is called IPO. On the other hand, a company which is already a listed company, either makes a fresh issue of securities to the public or an offer for sale to the public through an offer document, it is known as FPO.

Secondary Market

Secondary market refers to a market where securities are traded after being initially offered to the public in the primary market and/or listed on the Stock Exchange. Majority of the trading is done in the secondary market. It essentially comprises of the stock exchanges which provide platform for trading of securities and a host of intermediaries who assist in trading of securities and clearing and settlement of trades. The securities are traded, cleared and settled as per prescribed regulatory framework under the supervision of the Exchanges and SEBI.

STOCK EXCHANGE

A stock exchange is a platform which provides services through stock brokers, to the investors/traders to buy/ sell stocks, bonds and other securities. Trade on an exchange can be done only by its members, called stock brokers. The stock exchanges are regulated by the capital market regulator (SEBI). The stock exchanges also provide clearing facilities for settlement of payments and delivery of securities.

The BSE and NSE

Most of the trading in the Indian stock market takes place on its two stock exchanges: the Bombay Stock Exchange (BSE) and the National Stock Exchange (NSE). The BSE has been in existence since 1875 and Ahmedabad Stock Exchange in 1894 were the oldest stock exchanges in India. After liberalization and setting up of National Stock Exchange (NSE) which was founded in 1992 and started trading in 1994, finally, 22 other Exchanges in various cities sprang up. However, NSE and BSE are the major stock exchanges accounted for 99.98% of the total turnover in India. Both exchanges follow the same trading mechanism, trading hours, settlement process, etc.

Depository: Depository is an institution or a kind of organization which holds securities with it in which trading is done like shares, debentures, derivatives, commodities etc. There are two depositories in India:

(a) National Securities Depository Limited (NSDL)

(b) Central Depository Services Limited (CDSL)

Depository Participant (DP): A DP is an agent of the depository (NSDL/CDSL). It is an intermediary between the depository and the investor. A DP can offer depository related services only after obtaining a certificate of registration from SEBI.

De-mat Accounts: De-mat accounts are maintained in an electronic form. Dematerialization is the conversion of physical/ paper securities into the electronic form. The de-mat account is opened with a depository participant (e.g., a bank or a broker) who has an account with either Central Depository Services Limited (CDSL) or with National Securities Depository Limited (NSDL).

Instruments of Capital Market

The various capital market instruments used by corporate entities for raising resources are as follows:

1. Equity: Equity is the ownership interest in a company of holders of its common and preferred stocks, The various types of equity shares are as follows:

(i) Equity Shares: The equity holder, popularly known as shareholder is the part owner of the company. Depending upon the pattern of the shareholding, the equity holder is entitled for dividends, and voting rights as members of the company. These shares can be obtained either through the Initial Public Offering (IPOs), Further/ Follow-on Public Offering (FPOs) (primary markets) and can also be bought in the stock markets after the stocks are listed (Secondary markets).

(ii) Rights Issue (RIs): When a listed company wants to raise funds from the markets, one option available to the corporate is to arrange to issue additional/fresh stocks (shares/debentures) to the existing stock holders, known as Rights Issue. Rights Issues are offered to the existing shareholders whose names appear on a record date and in a particular ratio to the number of securities held by the shareholder.

(iii) Bonus Shares: Shares issued by the companies to their shareholders free of cost by capitalization of accumulated reserves from the profits earned in the earlier years.

(iv) Preferred Stock/Preference Shares: The preference shareholders do not have the right to vote. The investors who hold the preference shares enjoy the following:

(a) entitled for fixed dividend over other equity shareholders.

(b) In case of surplus, preference is given in distribution of income, over equity share holders

(c) In case of liquidation, their claims would rank above the equity shareholders but only after the company's creditors, bond and debenture holders.

(v) Cumulative Preference Shares. A type of preference shares on which dividend accumulates if remains unpaid. All arrears of preference dividend have to be paid out before paying dividend on equity shares.

(vi) Cumulative Convertible Preference Shares: A type of preference shares where the dividend payable on the same accumulates, if not paid. After a specified date, these shares will be converted into equity capital of the company.

(vii) Participating Preference Shares: The right of certain preference shareholders to participate in profits after a specified fixed dividend contracted for is paid. Participation right is linked with the quantum of dividend paid on the equity shares over and above a particular specified level.

2. Security Receipts: Security receipt means a receipt or other security, issued by a securitisation company or reconstruction company to any qualified institutional buyer pursuant to a scheme, evidencing the purchase or acquisition by the holder thereof, of an undivided right, title or interest in the financial asset involved in securitisation.

3. Government Securities (G-Secs): These are sovereign (credit risk- free) coupon bearing instruments which are issued by the Reserve Bank of India on behalf of Government of India, in lieu of the Central Government's market borrowing programme. These securities have a fixed coupon that is paid on specific dates on half-yearly basis.

4. Debentures: Bonds issued by a company bearing a fixed rate of interest usually payable half yearly on specific dates and principal amount repayable on particular date on redemption of the debentures. Debentures are normally secured/ charged against the asset of the company in favour of debenture holders.

5. Bonds: A bond is issued in the form of a negotiable certificate/ documents against indebtedness. Bonds can be classified differently as per their characteristics, viz as coupon, zero coupon, convertible and non-convertible etc.

(i) Coupon Bonds: When an investor invests in a bond, he gets his return on investment, based on the coupon rate (interest at a pre-fixed rate).

(ii) Zero Coupon Bonds: A bond which is issued at a discount and repaid at a face value is called a Zero-Coupon Bond. No periodic interest is payable. The investor on the date of redemption gets the face value of the bond and the difference between the face value and the issue price, is the return on investment for the investor.

(iii) Convertible Bonds: The investor gets an option to convert the bond into equity at a fixed conversion price.

(iv) Non-convertible Bonds: The investor does not have the option to convert the bond into equity.

6. Commercial Paper (CP): Commercial papers are issued by companies with high credit ratings, in the form of promissory notes, at discount but repayable at par, to their holder at maturity. Commercial papers are money market instruments and issued as per the guidelines of the Reserve Bank of India.

7. Treasury Bills: These are short-term bearer discount security, issued by the Government (through RBI) as a means of meeting its cash requirements.

Commonly Used Terms in the Capital Market

Security Transaction Tax (STT): STT is a kind of turnover tax where the investor has to pay a small tax on the total consideration paid or received in a share transaction.

STT was introduced in the Budget of 2004 and implemented in October 2004. The objective behind the levy is to mitigate tax evasion as the same is taxed at source. Stocks, futures, option, mutual funds and exchange traded funds come under the ambit of STT. The STT applicable in the case of intra-day transaction will be different from the one applicable in the case of delivery transaction. Likewise, the STT applicable in the case of buying a security will be different from the one applicable in the case of selling the security.

Rolling Settlement: In a rolling settlement, each trading day is considered as a trading period and trades executed during the day are settled based on net obligations for the day. In India, trades in rolling settlement are settled on a T+2 basis *i.e.*, on the 2nd working day after a trade.

Pay-In Day and Pay-Out Day: Pay-in day is the day when the securities sold are delivered to the exchange by the sellers and funds for the securities purchased are made available to the exchange by the buyers. Pay-out day is the day the securities purchased are delivered to the buyers and the funds for the securities sold are given to the sellers by the exchange. At present, the pay-in and pay-out happens on the 2nd working day after the trade is executed on the exchange, that is, settlement cycle is on T+2 rolling settlement.

Auction: On account of non-delivery of securities by the trading member on the pay-in day, securities are put up for auction by the exchange. This ensures that buying trading member receives the securities. The Exchange purchases the requisite quantity in auction market and gives them to the buying trading member.

Securities Lending Scheme: Securities lending is the act of loaning a stock, derivative or other security to an investor or firm. Securities lending requires the borrower to put up collateral, whether cash, security or a letter of credit. When a security is loaned, the title and the ownership are also transferred to the borrower.

Eligibility norms for making capital issues as per SEBI

SEBI has stipulated the eligibility norms for companies planning an IPO. There is no entry norm for a listed company making a rights issue. The norms for an IPO are as follows:

Entry Norm I (Profitability Route): Norms are as under:

(a) Net tangible assets of at least ₹ 3 crore in each of the preceding three full years of which not more than 50% are held in monetary assets. However, the limit of 50% on monetary assets shall not be applicable in case the public offer is made entirely through offer for sale.

(b) Minimum of ₹ 15 crore as average pre-tax operating profit in at least three years of the immediately preceding five years.

(c) Net worth of at least ₹ 1 crore in each of the preceding three full years.

(d) If there has been a change in the company's name, at least 50% of the revenue for preceding one year should be from the new activity denoted by the new name.

(e) The issue size should not exceed 5 times the pre-issue net worth.

Alternative routes: To provide sufficient flexibility and also to ensure that genuine companies are not limited from fund raising on account of strict parameters, SEBI has provided the alternative route to the companies not satisfying any of the above conditions, for accessing the primary market, as under:

Entry Norm II (QIB Route): Issue shall be through book building route, with at least 75% of net offer to the public to be mandatory allotted to the Qualified Institutional Buyers (QIBs). The company shall refund the subscription money if the minimum subscription of QIBs is not attained.

For FPO's: A listed issuer making a public issue (Further Public Offer *i.e.*, FPO) is required to satisfy the following requirements:

(a) If the company has changed its name within the last one year, at least 50% revenue for the preceding 1 year should be from the activity suggested by the new name.

(b) The aggregate of the proposed issue and all previous issues made in the same financial year in terms of issue size does not exceed five times its pre-issue net worth as per the audited balance sheet of the preceding financial year.

Any listed company not fulfilling these conditions shall be eligible to make a public issue (*i.e.*, FPO) by complying with QIB Route as specified for IPOs *i.e.*, issue shall be through book building route, with at least 75% to be mandatory allotted to the Qualified Institutional Buyers (QIBs).

Application Supported by Blocked Amount (ASBA)

ASBA means "Application Supported by Blocked Amount". ASBA is an application containing an authorization to block the application money in the bank account, for subscribing to an issue. If an investor is applying through ASBA, his application money shall be debited from the bank account only if his/her application is selected for allotment after the basis of allotment is finalized, or the issue is withdrawn/failed.

Under ASBA facility, investors can apply in any public/ rights issues by using their bank account. Investor submits the ASBA form (available at the designated branches of the banks acting as SCSB) after filling the details like name of the applicant, PAN number, demat account number, bid quantity, bid price and other relevant details, to their banking branch by giving an instruction to block the amount in their account. In turn, the bank will upload the details of the application in the bidding platform. Investors shall ensure that the details that are filled in the ASBA form are correct otherwise the form is liable to be rejected.

SEBI has been specifying the investors who can apply through ASBA. In public issues w.e.f. May 1, 2010 all the investors can apply through ASBA. It is mandatory for all public issues opening on or after January 01, 2016. In rights issues, all shareholders of the company as on record date are permitted to use ASBA for making applications provided he/she/it:

- ❍ is holding shares in dematerialized form and has applied for entitlements or additional shares in the issue in dematerialized form;
- ❍ has not renounced its entitlements in full or in part;
- ❍ is not a renounce;
- ❍ who is applying through blocking of funds in a bank account with the SCSB.

Advantage an investor has in applying through ASBA: Applying through ASBA facility has the following advantages:

(i) The investor continues to earn interest on the application money as the same remains in the bank account.

(ii) The investor does not have to bother about refunds, as in ASBA only that much money to the extent required for allotment of securities, is taken from the bank account only when his application is selected for allotment after the basis of allotment is finalized.

(iii) The application form is simpler.

Qualified Institutional Placement (QIP)

A QIP is a capital raising tool wherein a listed company can issue equity shares, fully and partly convertible debentures, or any security (other than warrants) that is convertible to equity shares. Apart from preferential allotment, this is the only other speedy method of private placement whereby a listed company can issue shares or convertible securities to a select group of investors. But unlike in an IPO or an FPO (further public offer), only institutions or qualified institutional buyers (QIBs) can participate in a QIP issuance. QIBs include mutual funds, domestic financial institutions such as banks and insurance companies, venture capital funds, foreign institutional investors, and others.

Securities and Exchange Board of India (SEBI)

The Securities and Exchange Board of India (SEBI) is the designated regulatory body for the finance and investment markets in India. The board plays a vital role in maintaining stable and efficient financial and investment markets by creating and enforcing effective regulation in India's financial marketplace.

The SEBI was established in 1988 but was only given regulatory powers on April 12, 1992, through the Securities and Exchange Board of India Act, 1992. It plays a key role in ensuring the stability of the financial markets in India, by attracting foreign investors and protecting Indian investors. SEBI was built by the Government of India. Its headquarters is located at the Bandra Kurla Complex Business District found in Mumbai. It also has northern, eastern, southern and western regional offices.

SEBI's management is composed of its own members. Its management team consists of a chairman nominated by the Union Government of India, two members who are officers from the Union Finance Ministry, one member from the Reserve Bank of India and five other members who are also nominated by the Union Government of India.

Functions and Responsibilities: SEBI's Preamble describes in detail the functions and powers of the board. Its Preamble states that SEBI must "protect the interests of investors in securities and to promote the development of, and to regulate the securities market and for matters connected there with or incidental there to." In this light, as a board, SEBI must be responsive and proactive to the needs and interest of the groups that constitute India's financial and investment markets: the investors, the market intermediaries and the issuers of securities.

SEBI is allowed to approve by-laws of stock exchanges. It is its job to require the stock exchange to follow its by-laws. SEBI also inspects the books of accounts of financial intermediaries and asks for regular returns from recognized stock exchanges. SEBI's role covers compelling particular companies to list their shares in stock exchanges. Aside from these, SEBI is tasked to manage the registration of brokers.

Ultimately, the board has three powers: quasi-judicial, quasi-legislative and quasi-executive. SEBI has the right to draft regulations under its legislative capacity, conduct investigations and impose action under its executive function, and pass new rules and orders under its judicial capacity. Despite these powers, the results of SEBI's functions still have to go through the Securities Appellate Tribunal and the Supreme Court of India.

Stock Broker: A stockbroker, also called a Registered Representative, investment advisor or simply, broker, is a professional individual who executes buy and sell orders for stocks and other securities through a stock market, or over the counter, for a fee or commission. Stockbrokers are usually associated with a brokerage firm and handle transactions for retail and institutional customers. Brokerage firms and broker-dealers are also often referred to as stockbrokers.

Sub-Broker: A "Sub-broker" means any person not being a member of a Stock Exchange who acts on behalf of a member as an agent or otherwise for assisting the investors in buying, selling or dealing in securities through such Member. All the sub-brokers are required to obtain a Certificate of Registration from SEBI without which they are not permitted to deal in securities. SEBI has directed that no broker shall deal with a person who is acting as a sub-broker unless he is registered with SEBI and it shall be the responsibility of the member-broker to ensure that his clients are not acting in the capacity of a sub-broker unless they are registered with SEBI as a sub-broker. It is mandatory for Members to execute an agreement with all the sub-brokers. The agreement specifies the rights and responsibilities of members as well as sub-brokers.

Share Transfer Agent: A transfer agent is a trust company, bank or similar financial institution assigned by a corporation to maintain records of investors and account balances. The transfer agent records transactions, cancels and issues certificates, processes investor mailings and deals with other investor problems (e.g., lost or stolen certificates). A transfer agent works closely with a registrar to ensure that investors receive interest payments and dividends when they are due and to send monthly investment statements to mutual fund shareholders.

Qualified Institutional Buyer (QIBs)

Qualified Institutional Buyers are those institutional investors who are generally perceived to possess expertise and the financial muscle to evaluate and invest in the capital markets. In terms of DIP Guidelines, a 'Qualified Institutional Buyer' shall mean:

(a) Public financial institution as defined in section 4A of the Companies Act, 1956;

(b) Scheduled commercial banks;

(c) Mutual funds;

(d) Foreign institutional investor registered with SEBI;

(e) Multilateral and bilateral development financial institutions;

(f) Venture capital funds registered with SEBI;

(g) Foreign Venture capital investors registered with SEBI;

(h) State Industrial Development Corporations;

(i) Insurance Companies registered with the Insurance Regulatory and Development Authority of India (IRDAI);

(j) Provident Funds with minimum corpus of ₹ 25 crores;

(k) Pension Funds with minimum corpus of ₹ 25 crores.

These entities are not required to be registered with SEBI as QIBs. Any entities falling under the categories specified above are considered as QIBs for the purpose of participating in primary issuance process.

TEST YOURSELF

1. Initial Public offering (IPO) means that an unlisted company makes for the first time to the public ________.
(a) a fresh issue of shares
(b) an offer for sale of its existing shares
(c) both of the above
(d) None of the above

2. Which is a part of financial market of India?
(a) Money Market (b) Debt Market
(c) Capital Market (d) All of these

3. De-mat accounts are maintained in an ________ form.
(a) electronic (b) paper
(c) physical (d) any of these

4. Which is the oldest Stock Exchange in India?
(a) Bombay Stock Exchange (BSE)
(b) National Stock Exchange (NSE)
(c) Ahmedabad Stock Exchange
(d) Kolkata Stock Exchange

5. The issue of new securities to existing shareholder at a ratio to those already held is known as ________.
(a) Bonus issue
(b) Right issue
(c) Preference issue
(d) None of these

6. Shares issued by the companies to their shareholders free of cost by capitalization of accumulated reserves from the profits earned in the earlier years is called:
(a) Bonus issue (b) Right issue
(c) Preference issue (d) Debentures

7. A type of preference shares where the dividend payable on the same accumulates, if not paid. After a specified date, these shares will be converted into equity capital of the company is called:
(a) Cumulative Preference Shares
(b) Cumulative Convertible Preference Shares
(c) Participating Preference Shares
(d) Debentures

8. Government securities (G-Secs) are sovereign (credit risk-free) coupon bearing instruments which are issued by the _______ on behalf of Government of India.
(a) SBI (b) SEBI
(c) RBI (d) Stock exchange

9. A ________ is issued in the form of a negotiable certificate/ documents against indebtedness.
(a) Bond (b) Debentures
(c) G-Secs (d) Bonus issue

10. A bond which is issued at a discount and repaid at a face value is called a _______.
(a) Convertible Bonds
(b) Non-Convertible Bonds
(c) Coupon Bond
(d) Zero-Coupon Bond

11. ________ are issued by companies with high credit ratings, in the form of promissory notes, at discount but repayable at par, to their holder at maturity.
(a) Bond (b) Debentures
(c) G-Secs (d) Commercial papers

12. In India, trades in rolling settlement are settled on a T+2 basis *i.e.*, on the _______ after a trade.
(a) 2nd day (b) 3rd day
(c) 2nd working day (d) next working day

13. On account of non-delivery of securities by the trading member on the pay-in day, securities are put up for _______ by the exchange.
(a) settlement (b) auction
(c) pay out (d) security

14. SEBI has stipulated the eligibility norms for companies planning an IPO. Which is not a correct statement regarding Entry Norm I (Profitability Route)?
(a) Net tangible assets of at least ₹ 5 crore in each of the preceding three full years of which not more than 50% are held in monetary assets.
(b) Minimum of ₹ 15 crore as average pre-tax operating profit in at least three years of the immediately preceding five years.
(c) Net worth of at least ₹ 1 crore in each of the preceding three full years.
(d) The issue size should not exceed 5 times the pre-issue net worth.

15. SEBI has been specifying the investors who can apply through ASBA. In public issues w.e.f. May 1, 2010 all the investors can apply through ASBA. It is mandatory for all public issues opening on or after _______.
(a) January 01, 2015 (b) April 01, 2015
(c) January 01, 2016 (d) April 01, 2016

16. Headquarters of SEBI is located at _______.
(a) Mumbai (b) New Delhi
(c) Kolkata (d) Ahmedabad

17. SEBI board has which types of powers?
(a) quasi-judicial (b) quasi-legislative
(c) quasi-executive (d) All of these

18. All the sub-brokers are required to obtain a _______ from SEBI without which they are not permitted to deal in securities.
(a) Certificate of Incorporation
(b) Certificate of Registration
(c) Certificate of Permission
(d) All the above

19. The holder of the _______ bond gets the equity shares on redemption of the bond.
(a) Convertible Bonds
(b) Non-Convertible Bonds
(c) Coupon Bond
(d) Zero-Coupon Bond

20. Which of the following has the authority to suspend trading of the securities of the particular company at a stock exchange?
(a) SEBI (b) Central Govt.
(c) RBI (d) All the above

ANSWER

1	2	3	4	5	6	7	8	9	10
(c)	(d)	(a)	(a)	(b)	(a)	(b)	(c)	(a)	(d)
11	**12**	**13**	**14**	**15**	**16**	**17**	**18**	**19**	**20**
(d)	(c)	(b)	(a)	(c)	(a)	(d)	(b)	(a)	(a)

MUTUAL FUNDS & INSURANCE COMPANIES, BANCASSURANCE & IRDA

MUTUAL FUND

Introduction: Mutual Funds play a key role as a financial intermediary in the financial services sector. A mutual fund pools money from investors and invests in Stocks, Debt and other financial securities. SEBI Regulations 1993 defines a mutual fund as: "a fund established in the form of a trust by a sponsor to raise monies by the trustees through the sale of units to the public, under one of more schemes, for investing in securities in accordance with these regulations".

A mutual fund is an investment vehicle made up of a pool of moneys collected from many investors for the purpose of investing in securities such as stocks, bonds, money market instruments and other assets. Mutual funds are operated by professional money managers, who allocate the fund's investments and attempt to produce capital gains and/or income for the fund's investors. A mutual fund's portfolio is structured and maintained to match the investment objectives stated in its prospectus.

Management of Mutual Funds: Mutual funds give small or individual investors access to professionally managed portfolios of equities, bonds and other securities. Each shareholder, therefore, participates proportionally in the gains or losses of the fund. Mutual funds invest in a wide amount of securities, and performance is usually tracked as the change in the total market cap of the fund, derived by aggregating performance of the underlying investments.

Mutual fund units, or shares, can typically be purchased or redeemed as needed at the fund's current net asset value (NAV) per share, which is sometimes expressed as NAVPS. A fund's NAV is derived by dividing the total value of the securities in the portfolio by the total amount of shares outstanding.

Types of Mutual Funds in India

There are many different types of mutual funds categorised based on structure, asset class and investment objectives. Choosing the right type of fund for your investment needs will depend on your investment goal.

1. Types of Mutual Funds based on Structure

a) **Open-Ended Funds:** These are funds in which units are open for purchase or redemption through the year. All purchases/redemption of these fund units are done at prevailing NAVs. Basically these funds will allow investors to keep invest as long as they want. There are no limits on how much can be invested in the fund. They are an ideal investment for those who want investment along with liquidity because they are not bound to any specific maturity periods. Which means that investors can withdraw their funds at any time they want thus giving them the liquidity they need.

b) **Close-Ended Funds:** These are funds in which units can be purchased only during the initial offer period. Units can be redeemed at a specified maturity date. To provide for liquidity, these schemes are often listed for trade on a stock exchange. Unlike open ended mutual funds, once the units or stocks are bought, they cannot be sold back to the mutual fund, instead they need to be sold through the stock market at the prevailing price of the shares.

c) **Interval Funds:** These are funds that have the features of open-ended and close-ended funds in that they are opened for repurchase of shares at different intervals during the fund tenure. The fund management company offers to repurchase units from existing unit holders during these intervals. If unit holders wish to they can off load shares in favour of the fund.

2. Types of Mutual Funds based on Asset Class

a) **Equity Funds:** These are funds that invest in equity stocks/shares of companies. These are considered high-risk funds but also tend to provide high returns.

b) **Debt Funds:** These are funds that invest in debt instruments e.g. company debentures, government bonds and other fixed income assets. They are considered safe investments and provide fixed returns.

c) **Money Market Funds:** These are funds that invest in liquid instruments e.g. T-Bills, CPs etc. They are considered safe investments for those looking to park surplus funds for immediate but moderate returns. They are a perfect option for investors who want to invest their abundant funds.

d) **Balanced or Hybrid Funds:** These are funds that invest in a mix of asset classes. In some cases, the proportion of equity is higher than debt while in others it is the other way round. Risk and returns are balanced out this way. This is so because the debt markets offer a lower risk than the equity market.

3. Types of Mutual Funds based on investment objective

a) **Growth Funds:** Under these schemes, money is invested primarily in equity stocks with the purpose of providing capital appreciation. They are considered to be risky funds ideal for investors with a long-term investment timeline. Since they are risky funds they are also ideal for those who are looking for higher returns on their investments.

b) **Income Funds:** Under these schemes, money is invested primarily in fixed-income instruments e.g. bonds, debentures etc. with the purpose of providing capital protection and regular income to investors.

c) **Liquid Funds:** Under these schemes, money is invested primarily in short-term or very short-term instruments e.g. T-Bills, CPs etc. with the purpose of providing liquidity. They are considered to be low on risk with moderate returns and are ideal for investors with short-term investment timelines.

d) **Tax-Saving Funds (ELSS):** These are funds that invest primarily in equity shares. Investments made in these funds qualify for deductions under the Income Tax Act. They are considered high on risk but also offer high returns if the fund performs well.

e) **Capital Protection Funds:** These are funds where funds are split between investment in fixed income instruments and equity markets. This is done to ensure protection of the principal that has been invested.

f) **Fixed Maturity Funds:** Fixed maturity funds are those in which the assets are invested in debt and money market instruments where the maturity date is either the same as that of the fund or earlier than it.

g) **Pension Funds:** Pension funds are mutual funds that are invested in with a really long term goal in mind. They are primarily meant to provide regular returns around the time that the investor is ready to retire. The investments in such a fund may be split between equities and debt markets where equities act as the risky part of the investment providing higher return and debt markets balance the risk and provide lower but steady returns. The returns from these funds can be taken in lump sums, as a pension or a combination of the two.

4. Types of Mutual Funds based on specialty

a) **Sector Funds:** These are funds that invest in a particular sector of the market e.g. Infrastructure funds invest only in those instruments or companies that relate to the infrastructure sector. Returns are tied to the performance of the chosen sector. The risk involved in these schemes depends on the nature of the sector.

b) **Index Funds:** These are funds that invest in instruments that represent a particular index on an exchange so as to mirror the movement and returns of the index e.g. buying shares representative of the BSE Sensex.

c) **Fund of funds:** These are funds that invest in other mutual funds and returns depend on the performance of the target fund. These funds can also be referred to as multi manager funds. These investments can be considered relatively safe because the funds that investors invest in actually hold other funds under them thereby adjusting for risk from any one fund.

d) **Commodity focused Stock Funds:** These funds don't invest directly in the commodities. They invest in companies that are working in the commodities market, such as mining companies or producers of commodities. These funds can, at times, perform the same way the commodity is as a result of their association with their production.

e) **Market Neutral Funds:** The reason that these funds are called market neutral is that they don't invest in the markets directly. They invest in treasury bills, ETFs and securities and try to target a fixed and steady growth.

f) **Gift Funds:** Gift funds are mutual funds where the funds are invested in government securities for a long term. Since they are invested in government securities, they are virtually risk free and can be the ideal investment to those who don't want to take risks.

New Fund Offer (NFO): A new fund offer (NFO) is the first subscription offering for any new fund offered by an investment company. A new fund offer occurs when a fund is launched, allowing the firm to raise capital for purchasing securities. Mutual funds are one of the most common new fund offerings marketed by an investment company. The initial purchasing offer for a new fund varies by the fund's structuring.

Net Asset Value (NAV): Mutual funds invest the money collected from the investors in securities markets. In simple words, Net Asset Value is the market value of the securities held by the scheme. Since market value of securities changes every day, NAV of a scheme also varies on day-to-day basis. The NAV per unit is the market value of securities of a scheme divided by the total number of units of the scheme on any particular date. The NAV of the schemes need to be published on a daily basis by the mutual funds at least in two daily newspapers.

Role of Mutual Fund in the Indian Capital Market

The Capital Market of any country is one of the principal drivers of economic growth and development. The Indian Capital Market has witnessed a remarkable transformation both in qualitative and quantitative terms. The Indian Capital Market has grown tremendously in every sphere- be it the amount of capital raised through Initial Public Offers (IPOs), exchange trading turnovers, the market indices, market capitalizations, access to foreign market to mobilize resources, listing of securities at overseas bourses or foreign institutional investment and resource mobilization through Mutual Funds. It has seen a phenomenal development.

SEBI has made it mandatory for any entity/person engaged in marketing and selling of mutual fund products to pass the Association of Mutual Fund in India (AMFI) certification test (Advisors Module) and obtain a registration number from AMFI.

INSURANCE COMPANIES

History of Insurance in India: In India, insurance has a deep-rooted history. It finds mention in the writings of Manu (Manusmrithi), Yagnavalkya (Dharmasastra) and Kautilya (Arthasastra). Ancient Indian history has preserved the earliest traces of insurance in the form of marine trade loans and carriers' contracts. Insurance in India has evolved over time heavily drawing from other countries, England in particular. 1818 saw the advent of life insurance business in India with the establishment of the Oriental Life Insurance Company in Calcutta. This Company however failed in 1834. In 1829, the Madras Equitable had begun transacting life insurance business in the Madras Presidency.

In 1914, the Government of India started publishing returns of Insurance Companies in India. The Indian Life Assurance Companies Act, 1912 was the first statutory measure to regulate life business. In 1928, the Indian Insurance Companies Act was enacted to enable the Government to collect statistical information about both life and non-life business transacted in India by Indian and foreign insurers including provident insurance societies. In 1938, with a view to protecting the interest of the Insurance public, the earlier legislation was consolidated and amended by the Insurance Act, 1938 with comprehensive provisions for effective control over the activities of insurers.

An Ordinance was issued on 19th January, 1956 nationalising the Life Insurance sector and Life Insurance Corporation came into existence in the same year. The LIC absorbed 154 Indian, 16 non-Indian insurers as also 75 provident societies—245 Indian and foreign insurers in all. The LIC had monopoly till the late 90s when the Insurance sector was reopened to the private sector.

Opening Up of the Insurance Sector: The IRDA opened up the market in August 2000 with the invitation for application for registrations. The Authority has the power to frame regulations under Section 114 A of the Insurance Act, 1938 and has from 2000 onwards framed various regulations ranging from registration of companies for carrying on insurance business to protection of policyholders' interests.

In December, 2000, the subsidiaries of the General Insurance Corporation of India were restructured as independent companies and at the same time GIC was converted into a national re-insurer. Parliament passed a bill de-linking the four subsidiaries from GIC in July, 2002.

The proposal to raise FDI cap has been passed in 2014 when the UPA Government came up with Insurance Laws (Amendment) Bill to hike foreign holding in insurance joint ventures to 49 per cent from the existing 26 per cent.

Today as on 30th September 2017 there are 33 general insurance companies including the ECGC and Agriculture Insurance Corporation of India and 24 life insurance companies operating in the country.

The insurance sector is an enormous one and is growing at a speedy rate of 15-20%. Together with banking services, insurance services add about 7% to the country's GDP. A well-developed and evolved insurance sector is a boon for economic development as it provides long-term funds for infrastructure development at the same time strengthening the risk-taking ability of the country.

Definition of Insurance: Insurance is a promise of compensation for specific potential future losses in exchange for a periodic payment. Insurance is designed to protect the financial well-being of an individual, company or other entity in the case of unexpected loss. Some forms of insurance are required by law, while others are optional. Agreeing to the terms of an insurance policy creates a contract between the insured and the insurer. In exchange for payments from the insured (called premiums), the insurer agrees to pay the policy holder a sum of money upon the occurrence of a specific event.

Seven Fundamental Principles Governing Insurance Contract

The main objective of every insurance contract is to give financial security and protection to the insured from any future uncertainties. Insured must never ever try to misuse this safe financial cover. Seeking profit opportunities by reporting false occurrences violates the terms and conditions of an insurance contract. This breaks trust, results in breaching of a contract and invites legal penalties.

An insurer must always investigate any doubtable insurance claims. It is also a duty of the insurer to accept and approve all genuine insurance claims made, as early as possible without any further delays and annoying hindrances.

The seven principles of insurance are :

1. Principle of Utmost Good Faith,
2. Principle of Insurable Interest,
3. Principle of Indemnity,
4. Principle of Contribution,
5. Principle of Subrogation,
6. Principle of Loss Minimization, and
7. Principle of Causa Proxima (Nearest Cause).

1) **Principal of Utmost Good Faith:** Both parties, insurer and insured should enter into contract in good faith. Insured should provide all the information that impacts the subject matter. Insurer should provide all the details regarding insurance contract.

   For example: Niraj took a health insurance policy. At the time of taking policy, he was a smoker and he didn't disclose this fact. He got cancer. Insurance company won't pay anything as John didn't reveal the important facts.

2) **Principle of Insurable Interest:** Insured must have the insurable interest on the subject matter. In case of life insurance spouse and dependents have insurable interest in the life of a person. Corporations also have insurable interests in the life of its employees. In case of life or marine insurance, insured must be the owner both at the time of entering of entering into the insurance contract and at the time of accident.

3) **Principle of Indemnity:** Insured can't make any profit from the insurance contract. Insurance contract is meant for coverage of losses only. Indemnity means a guarantee to put the insured in the position as he was before accident. This principle doesn't apply to life insurance contracts.

4) **Principle of Contribution:** In case the insured took more than one insurance policy for same subject matter, he/she can't make profit by making claim for same loss more than once.

   For example: Raj has a property worth ₹ 5,00,000. He took insurance from Company A worth ₹ 3,00,000 and from Company B- ₹ 1,00,000. In case of accident, he incurred a loss of ₹ 3,00,000 to the property. Raj can claim ₹ 3,00,000 from A but after that he can't make profit by making a claim from Company B. Now Company A can make a claim from Company B to for proportional loss claim value.

5) **Principle of Subrogation:** After the insured gets the claim money, the insurer steps into the shoes of insured. After making the payment insurance claim, the insurer becomes the owner of subject matter.

   For example: Ram took a insurance policy for his Car. In an accident his car totally damaged. Insurer paid the full policy value to insured. Now Ram can't sell the scrap remained after the scrap.

6) **Principle of Loss Minimisation:** This principle states that the insured must take all the necessary steps to minimize the losses to insured assets.

For example: Ram took insurance policy for his house. In a cylinder blast, his house burnt. He should have called nearest fire station so that the loss could be minimised.

7) **Principle of Causa Proxima:** Word "Cause Proxima" means "Nearest Cause". An accident may be caused by more than one cause. In case property insured for only one cause. In such case nearest cause of the accident is found out. Insurer pays the claim money only if the nearest cause is insured.

TYPES AND CLASSIFICATION OF INSURANCE

Insurance is classified into life insurance and non-life insurance. Life insurance aims at providing financial security to the individuals and their dependents. Life insurance deals with the insurance of individuals, group and pension plan. Non-life insurance refers to the property, liability and miscellaneous insurance.

Types of Insurance Business

1. **Life Insurance**
2. **Health Insurance**
3. **Travel Insurance**
4. **Vehicle Insurance**
5. **Property Insurance**

1. Life Insurance Products: Life insurance benefit patterns have fit into one or combination of three classes:

a) Term Life Insurance policies
b) Money-back Policies
c) Whole Life Insurance policies
d) Unit-linked Investment Policies (ULIP)
e) Pension policies
f) Endowment Life Insurance policies

a) **Term Insurance Policies:** The basic principle of a term insurance policy is to secure the immediate needs of nominees or beneficiaries in the event of sudden or unfortunate demise of the policy holder. The policy holder does not get any monetary benefit at the end of the policy term except for the tax benefits he or she can choose to avail of throughout the tenure of the policy. In the event of death of the policy holder, the sum assured is paid to his or her beneficiaries. Term insurance policies are also relatively cheaper to acquire as compared to other insurance products.

b) **Money-back Policies:** Money back policies are basically an extension of endowment plans wherein the policy holder receives a fixed amount at specific intervals throughout the duration of the policy. In the event of the unfortunate death of the policy holder, the full sum assured is paid to the beneficiaries. The terms again might slightly vary from one insurance company to another.

c) **Whole Life Policies:** A whole life insurance plan covers the insured over his life. The primary feature of this product is that the validity of the policy is not defined so the policyholder enjoys the life cover throughout his life.

d) **Unit-linked Investment Policies (ULIP):** Unit linked insurance policies again belong to the insurance-cum-investment category where one gets to enjoy the benefits of both insurance and investment. While a part of the monthly premium pay-out goes towards the insurance cover, the remaining money is invested in various types of funds that invest in debt and equity instruments. ULIP plans are more or less similar in comparison to mutual funds except for the difference that ULIPs offer the additional benefit of insurance.

e) **Pension Policies:** Pension policies let individuals determine a fixed stream of income post retirement. This basically is a retirement planning investment scheme where the sum assured or the monthly pay-out after retirement entirely depends on the capital invested, the investment timeframe, and the age at which one wishes to retire. There are again several types of pension plans that cater to different investment needs. Now it is recognized as insurance product and being regulated by IRDAI.

f) **Endowment Policies:** An endowment policy is an investment product that you buy from a life assurance company. They are set up as regular savings plans and at the end of a set period pay out a lump sum. The policy includes life assurance, so it will also pay out if you die during the term.

2. Health Insurance: Health insurance, also called, medical insurance or simply mediclaim, covers the cost of an individual's medical and surgical expenses. The individual pays a fixed sum (premium), every year for the health cover. Health insurance is a type of insurance coverage that pays for medical and surgical expenses incurred by the insured. Health insurance can reimburse the insured for expenses incurred from illness or injury, or pay the care provider directly. It is often included in employer benefit packages as a means of enticing quality employees. The cost of health insurance pre-miums is deductible to the payer, and benefits received are tax-free.

National Health Protection Scheme: The Modi government's ambitious National Health Protection Scheme (NHPS) to cover 10 crore poor families with ₹ 5 lakh health insurance may be lurching for funds as allocations hardly cover the programmes potential expenditure costs.

The government announced an allocation of ₹ 2000 crore for the scheme in 2018-19 but said more funds would be made available as the programme is rolled out over the year. The government has kept some cushion to fund the scheme as it replaced the current 3 per cent education cess with 4 per cent health and education cess with an aim to garner additional ₹ 11,000 crore. The government indicated that it will bank on economies of scale to bring down the premium costs along with possibly asking states to share a portion of the premium.

3. Travel Insurance: Travel Insurance is an indispensable companion if you are travelling overseas. Comprehensive plans are offered by the leading Insurance companies in India giving you emergency, accidental as well as health coverage. Medical expenses abroad can burn a hole in not just your travel budget but it can put you in a long term financial debt. Insurance coverage insure you for Medical expenses, Dental expenses, Loss of passport, Loss of checked baggage, Medical evacuation, Compassionate visit, Accidental death or disability, Trip cancellation, Trip curtailment, Personal theft, etc during your journey outside India.

4. Vehicle Insurance: Vehicle insurance (also known as car insurance, motor insurance or auto insurance) is insurance for cars, trucks, motorcycles, and other road vehicles. Its primary use is to provide financial protection against physical damage or bodily injury resulting from traffic collisions and against liability that could also arise from incidents in a vehicle. Vehicle insurance may additionally offer financial protection against theft of the vehicle, and against damage to the vehicle sustained from events other than traffic collisions, such as keying, weather or natural disasters, and damage sustained by colliding with stationary objects. The specific terms of vehicle insurance vary with legal regulations in each region.

5. Property Insurance: Property insurance provides protection against most risks to property, such as fire, theft and some weather damage. This includes specialized forms of insurance such as fire insurance, flood insurance, earthquake insurance, home insurance, or boiler insurance. Property is insured in two main ways—open perils and named perils.

Open perils cover all the causes of loss not specifically excluded in the policy. Common exclusions on open peril policies include damage resulting from earthquakes, floods, nuclear incidents, acts of terrorism, and war. Named perils require the actual cause of loss to be listed in the policy for insurance to be provided. The more common named perils include such damage-causing events as fire, lightning, explosion, and theft.

Group Insurance: Group Insurance covers a defined group of people, for example members of a professional association, or a society or employees of an organization. Group Insurance may offer life cover, health cover, and/or other types of personal insurance. Most insurance companies in India have introduced group insurance policies to meet insurance needs of specific groups including professionals, employers-employees, co-operative societies, among others. Group insurance has several advantages chief among which a life cover is made available to members irrespective of age, gender, socio economic background or profession, so long as they belong to the group that is applying for insurance.

Micro Insurance: Insurance Regulatory and Development Authority of India (IRDAI) has created a special category of insurance policies called micro-insurance policies to promote insurance coverage among economically vulnerable sections of society. The IRDA Micro-insurance Regulations, 2005 defines and enables micro-insurance.

For the insurance linked social security schemes that the government had announced in the 2015 Budget the Pradhan Mantri Suraksha Bima Yojana (PMSBY) and Pradhan Mantri Jeevan Jyoti Bima Yojana (PMJJBY). Prime Minister Narendra Modi has launched three new social security schemes (PM Bima Yojana) in Kolkata. **The new government schemes** are aimed at the unorganized sector and economically weaker sections of the society. However, benefits of the scheme can be availed by any strata of the society.

Pradhan Mantri Jeevan Jyoti Bima Yojana (PMJJBY): PMJJBY is a lucrative life insurance plan, wherein the insured receives ₹ 2 Lakh cover against an annual premium of ₹ 330 each year. The life risk cover will get terminated after 55 years. The scheme is applicable to all bank account holders in the age 18-50 years.

Pradhan Mantri Suraksha Bima Yojana (PMSBY): PMSBY offers 1 year accidental death and disability cover worth ₹ 2 Lakh for an annual premium of ₹ 12. Under the disability cover, insured will receive ₹ 1 Lakh. This is a yearly renewable scheme and can continue to give benefits as long as the insurer desires. People with multiple bank accounts can enroll in these schemes via any one of the savings accounts.

Bancassurance

Bancassurance is a French term referring to the selling of insurance through a bank's established distribution channels. In other words, we can say Bancassurance is the provision of insurance (assurance) products by a bank. The usage of the word picked up as banks and insurance companies merged and banks sought to provide insurance, especially in markets that have been liberalised recently.

Bancassurance is the selling of insurance and banking products through the same channel, most commonly through bank branches. Selling insurance, means distribution of insurance and other financial products through Banks. Bancassurance concept originated in France and soon became a success story even in other countries of Europe. In India a number of insurers have already tied up with banks and some banks have already flagged off bancassurance through select products.

Bancassurance has become significant. Banks are now a major distribution channel for insurers, and insurance sales a significant source of profits for banks. The latter partly being because banks can often sell insurance at better prices (*i.e.*, higher premiums) than many other channels, and they have low costs as they use the infrastructure (branches and systems) that they use for banking.

Bancassurance primarily rests on the relationship the customer has developed over a period of time with the bank. And pushing risk products through banks is a much more cost-effective affair for an insurance company compared to the agent route, while, for banks, considering the falling interest rates, fee based income coming in at a minimum cost is more than welcome.

Insurance Regulatory and Development Authority of India (IRDAI)

On the recommendations of the Malhotra Committee report, in 1999, the Insurance Regulatory and Development Authority(IRDA) was constituted as an autonomous body to regulate and develop the insurance industry. The IRDAI was incorporated as a statutory body in April, 2000. The key objectives of the IRDAI include promotion of competition so as to enhance customer satisfaction through increased consumer choice and lower premiums, while ensuring the financial security of the insurance market.

Duties, Powers and Functions of IRDAI: Section 14 of the IRDA Act, 1999 lays down the duties, powers and functions of IRDAI.

a) Registering and regulating insurance companies;
b) Protecting policy holders' interests;
c) Licensing and establishing norms for insurance intermediaries;
d) Promoting professional organisations in insurance;
e) Regulating and overseeing premium rates and terms of non-life insurance covers;
f) Specifying financial reporting norms of insurance companies;
g) Regulating investment of policy holders' funds by insurance companies;
h) Ensuring the maintenance of solvency margin by insurance companies;
i) Ensuring insurance coverage in rural areas and of vulnerable sections of society.

TEST YOURSELF

1. A mutual fund is set up in the form of _____.
(a) a society (b) a company
(c) a trust (d) a firm

2. A mutual fund in which units can be purchased only during the initial offer period is called:
(a) Open-Ended Funds (b) Close-Ended Funds
(c) Interval Funds (d) All of the above

3. Investments made in mutual funds qualify for deductions under the Income Tax Act is called:
(a) Income Funds (b) Liquid Funds
(c) Index Funds (d) ELSS

4. Which type of fund invests in debt securities with very short maturities?
(a) Growth fund
(b) Bond fund
(c) Money market mutual fund
(d) Income fund

5. Which type of fund is most likely to have the lowest management fee?
(a) Index fund (b) Equity income fund
(c) Equity growth fund (d) Bond fund

6. Shares of closed-end funds often sell:
(a) at the net asset value, plus a load fee
(b) at a discount to the net asset value
(c) at a premium to the net asset value
(d) exactly at the net asset value

7. Closed-end funds have lower cash requirements than open-end funds because:
(a) open-end funds pay more taxes than closed-end funds
(b) closed-end funds have limited lifetimes
(c) open-end funds tend to invest in less liquid assets
(d) open-end funds allow investors to redeem their shares at any time

8. As per SEBI guideline, a person engaged in the marketing and selling of mutual fund products is required to pass a certification test and obtain a registration number from:
(a) AMFI (b) SEBI
(c) NSE (d) IIBF

9. The aim of balanced funds is to provide ________.
(a) growth
(b) regular income
(c) both growth and regular income
(d) none

10. The first insurance company 'Oriental Life Insurance Company' was started in India in 1818 at:
(a) Kolkata (b) Chennai
(c) Mumbai (d) Ahmedabad

11. An Ordinance was issued on 19th January, ________ nationalising the Life Insurance sector and Life Insurance Corporation came into existence in the same year.
(a) 1950 (b) 1956
(c) 1961 (d) 1969

12. Which is not the principles of insurance contract?
(a) Principle of Utmost Good Faith
(b) Principle of Insurable Interest
(c) Principle of Honesty
(d) Principle of Subrogation

13. As on 30 September 2017, the total number of insurance companies in the life insurance business including LIC is operating in India is ________.
(a) 24 (b) 25
(c) 27 (d) 28

14. The proposal to raise FDI cap has been passed in 2014 when the UPA Government came up with Insurance Laws (Amendment) Bill to hike foreign holding in insurance joint ventures to ________ per cent from the existing 26 per cent.
(a) 40 (b) 49
(c) 51 (d) 75

15. Which is the primary legislation that deals with insurance business in India is ________.
(a) Insurance Act, 1938
(b) IRDA Act, 1999
(c) LIC of India Act
(d) Both Insurance Act, 1938 & IRDA Act, 1999

16. Which is not a correct statement about Term Insurance Policies?
(a) The basic principle of a term insurance policy is to secure the immediate needs of nominees or beneficiaries in the event of sudden or unfortunate demise of the policy holder.
(b) The policy holder does not get any monetary benefit at the end of the policy term.
(c) In Term insurance policies are also relatively cheaper to acquire as compared to other insurance products.
(d) None of these

17. The Government's ambitious National Health Protection Scheme (NHPS) to cover 10 crore poor families with ________ health insurance may be lurching for funds as allocations hardly cover the programmes potential expenditure costs.
(a) ₹ 1 lakh (b) ₹ 2 lakh
(c) ₹ 5 lakh (d) ₹ 10 lakh

18. PMJJBY is a lucrative life insurance plan, wherein the insured receives ₹ 2 Lakh cover against an annual premium of ₹ 330 each year. The life risk cover will get terminated after ________.
(a) 50 years (b) 55 years
(c) 58 years (d) 60 years

19. PMSBY offers 1 year accidental death and disability cover worth ₹ 2 Lakh for an annual premium of ₹ 12. Under the disability cover, insured will receive Rs ________.
(a) 30,000 (b) 50,000
(c) 1 Lakh (d) 2 Lakh

20. Which is not a correct statements about function and duty of IRDAI?
(a) Registering and regulating insurance companies
(b) Protecting insurance company's' interests
(c) Licensing and establishing norms for insurance intermediaries
(d) Promoting professional organisations in insurance

ANSWER

1	2	3	4	5	6	7	8	9	10
(c)	(b)	(d)	(c)	(a)	(b)	(d)	(a)	(c)	(a)
11	**12**	**13**	**14**	**15**	**16**	**17**	**18**	**19**	**20**
(b)	(c)	(a)	(b)	(d)	(d)	(c)	(b)	(c)	(b)

FACTORING, FORFEITING SERVICES AND OFF-BALANCE SHEET ITEMS

FACTORING

Factoring Finance in India: Factoring is one of the upcoming sources of finance for SMEs in India. It is particularly, relevant if a company is growing on a daily basis and when new customers are added regularly; there are chances of ending up with huge invoices. This problem often directs many businesses to look for alternative source of finance like factoring.

What is Factoring? Factoring is a financial option for the management of receivables. In simple definition it is the conversion of credit sales into cash. In factoring, a financial institution (factor) buys the accounts receivable of a company (Client) and pays up to 80% (rarely up to 90%) of the amount immediately on agreement. Factoring company pays the remaining amount (Balance 20% minus finance cost minus operating cost) to the client when the customer pays the debt. Collection of debt from the customer is done either by the factor or the client depending upon the type of factoring.

The account receivable in factoring can either be for a product or service. Examples are factoring against goods purchased, factoring in construction services (in government contracts it is assured that the government body can pay back the debt in the stipulated period of factoring and hence contractors can submit the invoices to get cash instantly), factoring against medical insurance etc. Let us see how factoring is done against an invoice of goods purchased.

The different types of Factoring

a) **Recourse and Non-recourse Factoring**: In this type of arrangement, the financial institution, can resort to the firm, when the debts are not recoverable. So, the credit risk associated with the trade debts are not assumed by the factor.

On the other hand, in non-recourse factoring, the factor cannot recourse to the firm, in case the debt turn out to be irrecoverable.

b) **Disclosed and Undisclosed Factoring**: The factoring in which the factor's name is indicated in the invoice by the supplier of the goods or services asking the purchaser to pay the factor, is called disclosed factoring.

Conversely, the form of factoring in which the name of the factor is not mentioned in the invoice issued by the manufacturer. In such a case, the factor maintains sales ledger of the client and the debt is realized in the name of the firm. However, the control is in the hands of the factor.

c) **Domestic and Export Factoring**: When the three parties to factoring, *i.e.*, customer, client, and factor, reside in the same country, then this is called as domestic factoring.

Export factoring, or otherwise known as cross-border factoring is one in which there are four parties involved, *i.e.*, exporter (client), the importer (customer), export factor and import factor. This is also termed as the two-factor system.

d) **Advance and Maturity Factoring**: In advance factoring, the factor gives an advance to the client, against the uncollected receivables.

In maturity factoring, the factoring agency does not provide any advance to the firm. Instead, the bank collects the sum from the customer and pays to the firm, either on the date on which the amount is collected from the customers or on a guaranteed payment date.

Advantage of Factoring: Advantage of the factoring options are as follows:

1. It is help to improve the current ratio. Improvement in the current ratio is an indication of improved liquidity. Enables better working capital management. This will enable the unit to offer better credit terms to its customers and increase orders.
2. It is increase in the turnover of stocks. The turnover of stock into cash is speeded up and this results in larger turnover on the same investment.
3. It ensures prompt payment and reduction in debt.
4. It helps to reduce the risk. Present risk in bills financing like finance against accommodation bills can be reduced to minimum.
5. It is help to avoid collection department. The client need not undertake any responsibility of collecting the dues from the buyers of the goods.

Limitations of Factoring: Factoring option has some limitation, which are as follows:

1. Factoring is a high risk area, and it may result in over dependence on factoring, mismanagement, over trading of even dishonesty on behalf of the clients.
2. It is uneconomical for small companies with less turnover.
3. The factoring is not suitable to the company's manufacturing and selling highly specialized items because the factor may not have sufficient expertise to assess the credit risk.
4. The developing countries such as India are not able to be well verse in factoring. The reason is lack of professionalism, non-acceptance of change and developed expertise.

FORFEITING SERVICES

FORFEITING: Forfeiting in French means to give up one's right. Thus, in forfeiting the exporter hands over the entire export bill with the forfeiter and obtains payments. The exporter has given up his right on the importer which is now taken by the forfeiter. By doing so, the exporter is benefited as he gets immediate finance for his exports. The risk of his exports is now borne by the forfeiter. In case if the importer fails to pay, recourse cannot be made on the exporter. Commercial banks act as forfeiters by purchasing account receivables from the exporter. There is not much risk involved for the forfeiter as the export is done against the L/C (Letter of credit), issued by importer's bank.

Forfeiting Process: The following are the forfeiting process or parties involved in forfeiting.

1. Before resorting to forfeiting, the exporter approaches the forfeiting company with the details of his export and the details of the importer and the importing country.
2. On approval by the forfeiter, along with the terms and conditions, a sale contract is entered into between the exporter and importer.
3. On execution of the export, the exporter submits the bill to the forfeiter and obtains payment. In this way, the three parties involved in the forfeiting process are the exporter, the importer and the forfeiter.
4. If the exports are done against Document Acceptance Bill, it has to be signed by the importer and since the importer's bank has guaranteed through the LC, it will be easy for the forfeiter to collect payment.
5. All the trade documents, connected with exports, are handed over by the exporter to his bank which in turn hands over the documents to the importer's bank.
6. The proof of all these documents will be submitted by the exporter to the forfeiter who will make payment for the export.
7. The cost of forfeiting is included in the bill. The exporter may not lose much as the interest will be included in the invoice and recovered from the importer. However, the forfeiter is exposed to the risk of fluctuations in the exchange rate, interest rate and commercial risk, and to cover these risks, he charges suitably.

Advantages of Forfeiting: The following are some of the advantages of forfeiting.

1. It provides immediate funds to the exporter who is saved from the risk of the defaulting importer.
2. It is an earning to commercial banks who by taking the bills of highly valued currencies can gain on the appreciation of currencies.
3. The forfeiter can also discount these bills in the foreign market to meet more demands of the exporters.

4. There is very little risk for the forfeiter as both importer's bank and exporter's banks are involved.
5. Letter of Credit plays a major role for the forfeiter. Moreover, he enters into an agreement with the exporter on his terms and conditions and covers his risks by separate charges.
6. As forfeiting provides 100% finance to exporter against his exports, he can concentrate on his other exports.

Disadvantages or Drawbacks of Forfeiting: The following are some of the disadvantages of forfeiting.

1. Forfeiting is not available for deferred payments especially while exporting capital goods for which payment will be made on a deferred basis by the importer.
2. There is discrimination between Western countries and the countries in the Southern Hemisphere which are mostly underdeveloped (countries in South Asia, Africa and Latin America).
3. There is no International Credit Agency which can guarantee for forfeiting companies which affects long-term forfeiting.
4. Only selected currencies are taken for forfeiting as they alone enjoy international liquidity.

Forfeiting in India: For a long time, Forfeiting was unknown to India. Export Credit Guarantee Corporation was guaranteeing commercial banks against their export finance. However, with the setting up of export-import banks, since 1994 forfeiting is available on liberalized basis.

The exim bank undertakes forfeiting for a minimum value of ₹ 5 lakhs. For this purpose, the exporter has to execute a special Promote in favour of the exim bank. The exporter will first enter into an agreement with the importer as per the quotation given to him by the exim bank. The exim bank on its part, gets quotation from the forfeiting agency abroad. Thus, the entire forfeiting process is completed by exporter agreeing to the terms of the exim bank and signing the Promote.

Forfeiting business in India will pick up only when there is trading of foreign bills in international currencies in India for which the value of domestic currency has to be strengthened. This would be possible only with increasing exports. At present, India's share stands at 1.7 per cent in the world exports. Perhaps, this will bring a push to the forfeiting market.

OFF-BALANCE SHEET ITEMS

Off balance sheet (OBS) items refer to assets or liabilities that do not appear on a company's balance sheet but that are nonetheless effectively assets or liabilities of the company. These items are not assets or liabilities to be reported in the balance sheet as on the date of balance sheet, but may get converted into an asset or liability at a later date, depending on the happening of a certain event. These items are contingent upon certain breach of commitments and are also called 'Contingent Liabilities'. These contingent liabilities have to be disclosed as 'Notes to the Balance Sheet'. But once these commitments crystalize, these also become part of the assets or liabilities of the bank and have to be shown in the balance sheet.

Banks classify their off-balance sheet exposure into three broad categories:

1. Full risk (credit substitute): Standby letter of credit, money guarantees etc.
2. Medium risk (not direct credit substitute): Bid bonds, letter of credit, indemnities and warrantees etc.
3. Low risk: Reverse repos, currency swaps, options, futures etc.

GUARANTEES

Bank Guarantee: Bank guarantee is one of the facilities that banks extend to their customer. A contract of guarantee is a contract to perform the promise, or discharge the liability, of a third person in case of his default.

A bank guarantee is a promise from a bank that the liabilities of a debtor will be met in the event that debtor fails to fulfil your contractual obligations. It is a promise from a bank or other lending institution that if a particular borrower defaults on a loan, the bank will cover the loss.

Guarantee Parties Involved: The parties to the contract of guarantee are:

a) **Applicant:** The principal debtor: The person at whose request the guarantee is executed.
b) **Beneficiary:** The person to whom the guarantee is given and who can enforce it in case of default.
c) **Guarantor:** The person who undertakes to discharge the obligations of the applicant in case of his default.

Thus, a contract of guarantee is a collateral contract, consequential to a main contract between the applicant and the beneficiary. Guarantee issued must be unconditional and for:

- Definite period
- Definite amount
- Definite purpose

Types Of Bank Guarantees: Guarantee may be based on location of beneficiary, Purpose and Currency:

Inland: Issued within India in favour of beneficiary located in India for any contract or purpose originating within India.

Foreign: Issued in India in favour of beneficiary located in any other country in Foreign Currency.

As per nature of contract, Bank Guarantees are classified in three types;

1) **Financial Guarantee:** Financial Guarantees are issued by bank on behalf of customer's requirement to deposit a cash security or earnest money. Most Government department insist that before contract is awarded to contractor, insist on an Earnest Money Deposit. Issued in respect of Excise / Custom Duties and Octroi under dispute etc. Issued in respect liabilities towards tax, excise duties, custom duties etc. to Govt. authorities in relation of specific transaction; Issued for covering payments for supplies/ services favouring Oil Companies, SAIL, Railways etc.
2) **Performance Guarantee:** Performance Guarantees are issued by the bank on behalf of its customer whereby the bank assures a third party, which the customer will perform the contract as per condition stipulated in the contract. These are issued on behalf of customer, who enters into contracts to do certain things on or before a given date. It involves a contractual obligation.
3) **Deferred Payment Guarantee:** It is issued in favour of suppliers to guarantee payment of installments for capital goods purchased on deferred payment basis. Under this type of guarantee, the banker guarantees payment of instalment spread over a period. It required when goods or machinery are purchased on long term credit and payment is made through cheque or bills of different dates. In this case, generally the payment terms are as under:
   - Advance payment of ten to fifteen per cent of the value of goods is made by the borrower.
   - Another ten to fifteen per cent of the value of goods is paid on receipt of documents under letter of credit.
   - The balance amount is paid in installments spread over a period of one to five years, which is secured by 'Deferred Payment Guarantee'.

LETTER OF CREDIT

Letter of Credit is a guarantee letter issued by a bank in international trade in favour of the exporter that a buyer's payment will be paid on time. In the event that the buyer is unable to make payment on the purchase, the bank will be required to cover the full or remaining amount of the purchase. Now in simple words, If LC opened on seller name as beneficiary, seller will receive amount though the buyer's bank (opening bank) on the agreed time.

Advantage of Letter of Credit: Letters of credit are often used in international transactions to ensure that payment will be received. Due to the nature of international dealings including factors such as distance, differing laws in each country and difficulty in knowing each party personally, the use of letters of credit has become a very important aspect of international trade. The bank also acts on behalf of the buyer (holder of letter of credit) by ensuring that the supplier will not be paid until the bank receives a confirmation that the goods have been shipped.

Parties of Letter of Credit

Applicant: Applicant is the party who opens Letter of Credit. He is the buyer / importer of the goods (generally borrower of the issuing bank). The applicant arranges to open letter of credit with his bank as per the terms and conditions of Purchase order and business contract between buyer and seller. The applicant has to make payment if documents as per LC are delivered, whether the goods are as per contract between the buyer and beneficiary or not.

Beneficiary Party: The seller or exporter is the beneficiary in whose favour the letter of credit is issued. It gets payment against documents as per LC from the nominated bank within validity period for negotiation,

Issuing Bank: Issuing Bank is the bank that opens letter of credit. Letter of credit is created by issuing bank who takes responsibility to pay amount on receipt of documents from supplier of goods (beneficiary under LC).

Advising Bank: Advising bank, as a part of letter of credit takes responsibility to communicate with necessary parties under letter of credit and other required authorities. The advising bank is the party who sends documents under Letter of Credit to opening bank.

Confirming Bank: Confirming bank as a party of letter of credit confirms and guarantees to undertake the responsibility of payment or negotiation acceptance under the credit.

Negotiating Bank: Negotiating Bank, who negotiates documents delivered to bank by beneficiary of LC.

Negotiating bank is the bank that verifies documents and confirms the terms and conditions under LC on behalf of beneficiary to avoid discrepancies.

Reimbursing Bank: Reimbursing bank is the party who authorized to honour the reimbursement claim of negotiation/ payment/ acceptance.

Types of Letter of Credit

Different types of LC are as under:

Revocable & Irrevocable LCs: In revocable LC, the buyer and the bank that established the LC are able to manipulate the LC or make corrections without informing or getting permissions from the seller. According to the UCPDC 600, all LCs are irrevocable, hence this type of LC is obsolete. Irrevocable LC is a letter of credit that does not allow the issuing bank to make any changes without the approval of the beneficiary, applicant bank and confirming bank, if any.

Deferred or Usance LC: A letter of credit, which ensures payment after a certain period of time. The date of payment is accepted by both buyer and seller. The bank may review the documents early but the payment to the beneficiary is made after the agreed to time passes. It is also known as Usance LC.

Sight LC: A letter of credit that demand payment on the submission of the required documents. The bank reviews the documents and pays the beneficiary if the documents meet the conditions of the letter.

With & Without Recourse LCs: Where the beneficiary holds himself liable to the holder of the bill if dishonoured, it is considered with-recourse LC. Where he does not hold himself liable, the credit is said to be without-recourse LC. As per RBI directive (Jan 23, 2003), banks should not open such LCs. Under LC, the Banks can negotiate bills bearing the 'without recourse' clause.

A Restricted LC: It is one wherein a specified bank is designated to pay, accept or negotiate payment will be made. The confirming bank's liability is similar to the issuing bank. The confirming bank has to negotiate documents if tendered by the beneficiary.

Transferable LCs: It is an LC, where the beneficiary is entitled to transfer the LC, in whole or in part, to the 2nd beneficiary/s (supplier of beneficiary). The 2nd beneficiary, however, cannot transfer it further, but it can transfer the unused portion, back to the original beneficiary. It is transferable only once.

A Back to Back Credit: A pair of LCs in which one is to the benefit of a seller who is not able to provide the corresponding goods for unspecified reasons. In that event, a second credit is opened for another seller to provide the desired goods. Back-to-back is issued to facilitate intermediary trade. Intermediate companies such as trading houses are sometimes required to open LCs for a supplier and receive Export LCs from buyer.

A Red Clause LC: It referred to a packing or anticipatory credit, has a clause permitting the correspondent bank in the exporter's country to grant advance to beneficiary at issuing bank's responsibility. These advances are adjusted from proceeds of the bills negotiated.

A Green Clause LC: It permits the advances for storage of goods in a warehouse in addition to pre-shipment advance. It is an extension of the red clause LC.

Standby Credits: It is similar to performance bond or guarantee, but issued in the form of LC. The beneficiary can submit his claim by means of a draft accompanied by the requisite documentary evidence of performance, as stipulated in the credit.

Documentary Credits: When LC specifies that the bills drawn under LC must-accompany documents of title to goods such as RRs or MIRs or Bills of lading etc. It is termed as Documentary Credit. If any such documents are not called, the credit is said to be Clean Credit.

Revolving Credits: These LCs provide that the amount of drawings made there under would be reinstated and made available to the beneficiary again and again for further drawings during the currency of credit provided the applicant makes the payment of documents earlier negotiated. At times, an overall turnover cap is also stipulated.

Procedure for Opening Letter of Credit: Buyer entered in to a contract with overseas supplier to import machinery at his factory. As per their contract, buyer needs to open a Letter of credit (LC) in favour of exporter/seller. Banker has to verify the following documents of the buyer/importer:

- IEC No. of the buyer,
- Whether Goods/Services under LC is permitted under Foreign Trade Policy or not,
- Import License of the buyer if applicable,
- FEMA Guidelines about the items imported.

The customer's financial standing, line of business, frequency of imports, sales, account turnover, satisfactory track record of importer for import of goods, etc. are also scrutinised.

Forward Exchange Contract

A forward exchange contract is a special type of foreign currency transaction. Forward exchange contracts are agreements between two parties to exchange two designated currencies at a specific time in the future. These contracts always take place on a date after the date that the spot contract settles and are used to protect the buyer from fluctuations in currency prices.

Forward Rate Agreements and Interest Rate Swaps

A Forward Rate Agreement or an Interest Rate Swap provides means for hedging the interest rate risk arising on account of lendings or borrowings made at fixed/ variable interest rates.

A Forward Rate Agreement (FRA) is a financial contract between two parties to exchange interest payments for a 'notional principal' amount on settlement date, for a specified period from start date to maturity date. Accordingly, on the settlement date, cash payments based on contract (fixed) and the settlement rate, are made by the parties to one another. The settlement rate is the agreed bench-mark/ reference rate prevailing on the settlement date.

An Interest Rate Swap (IRS) is a financial contract between two parties exchanging or swapping a stream of interest payments for a 'notional principal' amount on multiple occasions during a specified period. Such contracts generally involve exchange of a 'fixed to floating' or 'floating to floating' rates of interest. Accordingly, on each payment date - that occurs during the swap period - cash payments based on fixed/ floating and floating rates, are made by the parties to one another.

TEST YOURSELF

1. Which is not a part of Factoring service?
(a) Management of receivables
(b) Hands over the entire export bill
(c) Discounting of bills
(d) Collection of bills

2. The without recourse factoring means:
(a) Where the factor is not responsible for the loss of the seller on account of his actions
(b) Where the factor assumes the risk of default in payment by the buyer
(c) Where the risk of default in payment by the buyer is that of the seller
(d) Where all the risk associated with the factoring is that of the buyer

3. To be eligible for factoring facility, the seller's eligibility criteria normally relate to:
(a) Minimum track record of certain years of existence in business
(b) Consistence profitability
(c) Positive minimum net worth
(d) All of the above

4. Which are the most commonly forfeited debt instrument under the forfeiting?
(a) Bills receivables
(b) Promissory notes and debentures
(c) Bills of exchange and promissory notes
(d) All of the above

5. Under forfeiting, the exporter is able to transfer which of the following risk?
(a) Interest rate risk
(b) Currency risk
(c) Credit risk and political risk
(d) All of the above

6. Which of the following is an off-balance sheet exposure?
(a) Clean overdraft
(b) Credit balance in overdraft account
(c) Bid bond
(d) Overdraft on current deposit account

7. Normally a bank guarantee cannot be issued for more than
(a) 3 years (b) 5 years
(c) 10 years (d) 15 years

8. If a customer requires to deposit earnest money with government department, which type of guarantee will be issued by bank?
(a) Financial guarantee
(b) Performance guarantee
(c) Deferred payment guarantee
(d) None of the above

9. How many parties are there in the bank guarantee?
(a) 2 (b) 3
(c) 4 (d) 5

10. When goods or machinery are purchased by customer on long term credit and payment is to be made in installments which type of guarantee is to be issued by the bank?
(a) Financial guarantee
(b) Performance guarantee
(c) Deferred Payment guarantee
(d) None of the above

11. Under deferred payment guarantee, the liability of the bank is ________.
(a) Primary (b) Secondary
(c) As per contract term (d) All of the above

12. In case of invocation of guarantee by the beneficiary, bank should make the payment ______.
(a) Immediately without delay and demur
(b) After informing the matter to controlling office
(c) After consulting the applicant
(d) After due verification of terms of contract

13. How the amount of guarantee to be issued by the bank is determined?
(a) It is determined on the basis of security available
(b) It is determined by the beneficiary
(c) It is as per contract between the beneficiary and the applicant
(d) Based on the cash margin available

14. Who request his banker to open a Letter of Credit?
(a) Buyer (b) Seller
(c) Exporter (d) Any one

15. Which of the followings are advantage of the buyer or importer?
(a) No cash advance payment has to be made to the seller
(b) Possibility to stipulate favourable terms and condition to protect his interest
(c) Shipment schedule ensured
(d) All of the above

16. The LC issuing bank is also called ______.
(a) Importer's bank or the opening bank
(b) Negotiating bank
(c) Advising Bank
(d) Confirming bank

17. Who is entitled to receive the payment on delivering of documents stipulated in a LC?
(a) Beneficiary
(b) Negotiating Bank
(c) Advising Bank
(d) Confirming Bank

18. Which is the role of Negotiating Bank?
(a) The bank that hands over the LC to the beneficiary
(b) Negotiates documents delivered to bank by beneficiary of LC.
(c) The bank that opens the LC
(d) None of the above

19. The letter of credit where packing or anticipatory credit is available against the LC is called ______.
(a) Transferable LC (b) Red clause LC
(c) Back to back LC (d) Revolving LC

20. Back to back letter of credit means
(a) A revolving credit
(b) Another credit behind the credit issued
(c) Issuance of another credit on the security of the original letter of credit
(d) LC which is backed by a tangible security

21. A letter of credit is a ______.
(a) Negotiable Instrument
(b) Not negotiable Instrument
(c) Quasi negotiable Instrument
(d) None of the above

22. Transferable letter of credit can be transferred:
(a) Any number of times
(b) Only once
(c) 2 times
(d) As per instruction of issuer

23. Who is entitled to receive the payment on delivering of documents stipulated in a LC?
(a) Beneficiary (b) Negotiating bank
(c) Advising Bank (d) Confirming bank

24. A ______ is a financial contract between two parties to exchange interest payments for a 'notional principal' amount on settlement date, for a specified period from start date to maturity date.
(a) Forward Rate Agreement (FRA)
(b) Interest Rate Swap (IRS)
(c) Factoring
(d) Forfeiting

ANSWER

1	2	3	4	5	6	7	8	9	10
(b)	(b)	(d)	(c)	(d)	(c)	(c)	(a)	(b)	(c)
11	12	13	14	15	16	17	18	19	20
(a)	(a)	(c)	(a)	(d)	(a)	(a)	(b)	(b)	(c)
21	22	23	24						
(b)	(b)	(a)	(a)						

RISK MANAGEMENT, BASEL ACCORDS

RISK MANAGEMENT

Introduction: Banking sectors plays a pivotal role in the management of the economy of a country. It is the key driver of economic growth of the country and has a dynamic role to play in converting the idle capital resources for their optimum utilization so as to attain maximum productivity. In fact, the foundation of a sound economy depends on how sound the Banking sector is and vice versa.

Risk Management in Banks: Today, The Indian Economy is in the process of becoming a world class economy. The Indian banking industry is making great advancement in terms of quality, quantity, expansion and diversification and is keeping up with the updated technology, ability, stability and thrust of a financial system, where the commercial banks play a very important role, emphasize the very special need of a strong and effective control system with extra concern for the risk involved in the business. Globalization, Liberalization and Privatization have opened up a new methods of financial transaction where risk level is very high. In banks and financial institutions risk is considered to be the most important factor of earnings. Therefore they have to balance the relationship between risk and return. In reality we can say that management of financial institution is nothing but a management of risk.

What is Risk? Risk refers to 'a condition where there is a possibility of undesirable occurrence of a particular result which is known or best quantifiable and therefore insurable'. A risk can be defined as an unplanned event with financial consequences resulting in loss or reduced earnings. An activity which may give profits or result in loss may be called a risky proposition due to uncertainty or unpredictability of the activity of trade in future.

In other words, it can be defined as the uncertainty of the outcome. As risk is directly proportionate to return, the more risk a bank takes, it can expect to make more money.

Type of Risks in Bank: The major risks in banking business as commonly referred can be broadly classified into:

1. **Liquidity Risk**
2. **Interest Rate Risk**
3. **Market Risk**
4. **Credit or Default Risk**
5. **Operational Risk**

1. Liquidity Risk: The liquidity risk of banks arises from funding of long-term assets by short-term liabilities, thereby making the liabilities subject to roll-over or re-financing risk.

The liquidity risk in banks manifest in different dimensions :

(a) **Funding Risk:** Funding Liquidity Risk is defined as the inability to obtain funds to meet cash flow obligations. For banks, funding liquidity risk is crucial. This arises from the need to replace net outflows due to unanticipated withdrawal/ non-renewal of deposits (wholesale and retail).

(b) **Time Risk:** Time risk arises from the need to compensate for non-receipt of expected inflows of funds *i.e.*, performing assets turning into non-performing assets.

(c) **Call Risk:** Call risk arises due to crystallisation of contingent liabilities. It may also arise when a bank may not be able to undertake profitable business opportunities when it arises.

2. Interest Rate Risk: Interest Rate Risk arises when the Net Interest Margin or the Market Value of Equity (MVE) of an institution is affected due to changes in the interest rates. IRR can be viewed in two ways–its impact is on the earnings of the bank or its impact on the economic value of the bank's assets, liabilities and Off-Balance Sheet (OBS) positions. Interest rate Risk can take different forms.

3. Market Risk: The risk of adverse deviations of the mark-to-market value of the trading portfolio, due to market movements, during the period required to liquidate the transactions is termed as Market Risk. This risk results from adverse movements in the level or volatility of the market prices of interest rate instruments, equities, commodities, and currencies. It is also referred to as Price Risk.

The term Market risk applies to

(i) That part of IRR which affects the price of interest rate instruments,
(ii) Pricing risk for all other assets/ portfolio that are held in the trading book of the bank,
(iii) Foreign Currency Risk.

(a) **Forex Risk:** Forex risk is the risk that a bank may suffer losses as a result of adverse exchange rate movements during a period in which it has an open position either spot or forward, or a combination of the two, in an individual foreign currency.

(b) **Market Liquidity Risk:** Market liquidity risk arises when a bank is unable to conclude a large transaction in a particular instrument near the current market price.

4. Credit or Default Risk: Credit risk is more simply defined as the potential of a bank borrower or counter-party to fail to meet its obligations in accordance with the agreed terms. For most banks, loans are the largest and most obvious source of credit risk. It is the most significant risk, more so in the Indian scenario where the NPA level of the banking system is significantly high.

Now, let's discuss the two variants of credit risk:

(a) Counterparty Risk: This is a variant of Credit risk and is related to non-performance of the trading partners due to counterparty's refusal and or inability to perform. The counter party risk is generally viewed as a transient financial risk associated with trading rather than standard credit risk.

(b) Country Risk: This is also a type of credit risk where non-performance of a borrower or counter-party arises due to constraints or restrictions imposed by a country. Here, the reason of non-performance is external factors on which the borrower or the counter-party has no control.

Credit Risk depends on both external and internal factors. The internal factors include Deficiency in credit policy and administration of loan portfolio, Deficiency in appraising borrower's financial position prior to lending, Excessive dependence on collaterals and Bank's failure in post-sanction follow-up, etc.

The major external factors are the state of Economy, Swings in commodity price, foreign exchange rates and interest rates, etc.

Credit Risk can't be avoided but can be mitigated by applying various risk-mitigating processes :

- Banks should assess the credit-worthiness of the borrower before sanctioning loan *i.e.*, Credit rating of the borrower should be done before hand. Credit rating is the main tool of measuring credit risk and it also facilitates pricing the loan.
- By applying a regular evaluation and rating system of all investment opportunities, banks can reduce its credit risk as it can get vital information of the inherent weaknesses of the account.
- Banks should fix prudential limits on various aspects of credit – benchmarking Current Ratio, Debt-Equity Ratio, Debt Service Coverage Ratio, Profitability Ratio etc.
- There should be maximum limit exposure for single/ group borrower.
- There should be provision for flexibility to allow variations for very special circumstances.
- Alertness on the part of operating staff at all stages of credit dispensation – appraisal, disbursement, review/ renewal, post-sanction follow-up can also be useful for avoiding credit risk.

5. Operational Risk: Basel Committee for Banking Supervision has defined operational risk as 'the risk of loss resulting from inadequate or failed internal processes, people and systems or from external events'. Managing operational risk has become important for banks due to the following reasons:

- Higher level of automation in rendering banking and financial services,
- Increase in global financial inter-linkages,

- Scope of operational risk is very wide because of the above-mentioned reasons.

Two of the most common operational risks are discussed below :

(a) Transaction Risk: Transaction risk is the risk arising from fraud, both internal and external, failed business processes and the inability to maintain business continuity and manage information.

(b) Compliance Risk: Compliance risk is the risk of legal or regulatory sanction, financial loss or reputation loss that a bank may suffer as a result of its failure to comply with any or all of the applicable laws, regulations, codes of conduct and standards of good practice. It is also called integrity risk since a bank's reputation is closely linked to its adherence to principles of integrity and fair dealing.

6. Other Risks: Apart from the above-mentioned risks, following are the other risks confronted by Banks in course of their business operations :

(a) Strategic Risk: Strategic Risk is the risk arising from adverse business decisions, improper implementation of decisions or lack of responsiveness to industry changes.

(b) Reputation Risk: Reputation Risk is the risk arising from negative public opinion. This risk may expose the institution to litigation, financial loss or decline in customer base.

Risk Management in India: Risk Management is actually a combination of management of uncertainty, risk, equivocality and error. Uncertainty–where the outcomes cannot be estimated even randomly, arises due to lack of information and this uncertainty gets transformed into risk (where the estimation of outcome is possible) as information gathering progresses.

Initially, the Indian banks have used risk control systems that kept pace with legal environment and Indian accounting standards, But with the growing pace of deregulation and associated changes in the customer's behaviour, banks are exposed to mark-to-market accounting.

Therefore, the challenge of Indian banks is to establish a coherent framework for measuring and managing risk consistent with corporate goals and responsive to the developments in the market. As the market is dynamic, banks should maintain vigil on the convergence of regulatory frameworks in the country, changes in the international accounting standards and finally and most importantly changes in the clients' business practices.

THE BASEL COMMITTEE ON BANKING SUPERVISION

The Basel Committee on Banking Supervision (BCBS) is the primary global standard setter for the prudential regulation of banks and provides a forum for cooperation on banking supervisory matters. Its mandate is to strengthen the regulation, supervision and practices of banks worldwide with the purpose of enhancing financial stability. Its 45 members comprise central banks and bank supervisors from 28 jurisdictions. Basel is a city found in Basel-City, Switzerland. The Basel Committee on Banking Supervision (BCBS) was founded in 1974. In 2014 it celebrated its 40th year anniversary.

The Basel Committee 1974 – 2014 work on developing banking regulation can be broken into the five following regulatory waves. Name for regulatory waves are proposed to reflect the dominating core document that occupied the mind of central and/or commercial bankers at the time.

1. 1974 – 1986 – Concordat;
2. 1987 – 1998 – Basel-I;
3. 1999 – 2008 – Basel-II;
4. 2009 – 2011 – Basel-III;
5. 2012 – 2014 – Post-Basel-III.

BASEL-I ACCORD

Basel-I is a set of international banking regulations put forth by the Basel Committee on Bank Supervision (BCBS) that sets out the minimum capital requirements of financial institutions with the goal of minimizing credit risk. Banks that operate internationally are required to maintain a minimum amount (8%) of capital based on a per cent of risk-weighted assets. Basel-I is the first of three sets of regulations known individually as Basel-I, II and III and together as the Basel Accords.

The BCBS aims to enhance "financial stability by improving supervisory know-how and the quality of banking supervision worldwide." This is done through regulations known as accords. Basel-I was the first accord. It was issued in 1988 and focused mainly on credit risk by creating a bank asset classification system.

Bank Asset Classification System: The Basel-I classification system groups a bank's assets into five risk categories, classified as percentages: 0%, 10%, 20%, 50% and 100%. A bank's assets are placed into a category based on the nature of the debtor.

The 0% risk category is comprised of cash, central bank and government debt, and any Organization for Economic Cooperation and Development (OECD) government debt. Public sector debt can be placed in the 0%, 10%, 20% or 50% category, depending on the debtor. Development bank debt, OECD bank debt, OECD securities firm debt, non-OECD bank debt (under one year of maturity), non-OECD public sector debt and cash in collection comprises the 20% category. The 50% category is residential mortgages, and the 100% category is represented by private sector debt, non-OECD bank debt (maturity over a year), real estate, plant and equipment, and capital instruments issued at other banks.

The bank must maintain capital (Tier 1 and Tier 2) equal to at least 8% of its risk-weighted assets. For example, if a bank has risk-weighted assets of $100 million, it is required to maintain capital of at least $8 million.

Implementation of Basel-I: The BCBS regulations do not have legal force. Members are responsible for their implementation in their home countries. Basel-I originally called for the minimum capital ratio of capital to risk-weighted assets of 8% to be implemented by the end of 1992. In September 1993, the BCBS issued a statement confirming that G10 countries' banks with material international banking business were meeting the minimum requirements set out in Basel-I.

BASEL-II ACCORD

Basel-II is a set of international banking regulations put forth by the Basel Committee on Bank Supervision, which leveled the international regulation field with uniform rules and guidelines. Basel-II expanded rules for minimum capital requirements established under Basel-I, the first international regulatory accord, and provided framework for regulatory review, as well as set disclosure requirements for assessment of capital adequacy of banks. The main difference between Basel-II and Basel-I is that Basel-II incorporates credit risk of assets held by financial institutions to determine regulatory capital ratios.

Basel-II is a second international banking regulatory accord that is based on three main pillars: minimal capital requirements, regulatory supervision and market discipline. Minimal capital requirements play the most important role in Basel-II and obligate banks to maintain minimum capital ratios of regulatory capital over risk-weighted assets. Because banking regulations significantly varied among countries before the introduction of Basel accords, a unified framework of Basel-I and, subsequently, Basel-II helped countries alleviate anxiety over regulatory competitiveness and drastically different national capital requirements for banks.

Basel-II uses a "Three Pillars" Concept

(1) Minimum capital requirements (addressing risk),

(2) Supervisory review and

(3) Market discipline.

The Basel-I accord dealt with only parts of each of these pillars. For example: with respect to the first Basel-II pillar, only one risk, credit risk, was dealt with in a simple manner while market risk was an afterthought; operational risk was not dealt with at all.

The First Pillar-Minimum Capital Requirements: Basel-II provides guidelines for calculation of minimum regulatory capital ratios and confirms the definition of regulatory capital and 8% minimum coefficient for regulatory capital over risk-weighted assets. Basel-II divides the eligible regulatory capital of a bank into three tiers. The higher the tier, the less subordinated securities a bank is allowed to include in it. Each tier must be of certain minimum percentage of the total regulatory capital and is used as a numerator in the calculation of regulatory capital ratios.

Tier-1 capital is the more strict definition of regulatory capital that is subordinate to all other capital instruments, and includes shareholders' equity, disclosed reserves, retained earnings and certain innovative capital instruments. Tier-2 is Tier-1 instruments plus various other bank reserves, hybrid instruments, and medium and long-term subordinated loans. Tier-3 consists of Tier-2 plus short-term subordinated loans.

The capital base of the bank consists following three types of capital elements. Tier-1, Tier-2, and Tier-3 capital. The sum of Tier-1, Tier-2, and Tier-3 elements will be eligible for inclusion in the capital base, subject to the following limits :

a) The total of Tier-2 (supplementary) elements will be limited to a maximum of 100 per cent of the total of Tier-1 element.

b) Subordinate term debt will be limited to a maximum of 50 per cent of Tier-1 elements.

c) Tier-3 capital will be limited to 250 per cent of a bank's Tier-1 capital that is required to support market risk.

d) Where general provisions/general loan-loss reserves include amounts reflecting lower valuations of asset or latent but unidentified losses present in the balance sheet, the amount of such provision or reserves will be limited to a maximum of 1.25 percentage points.

e) Asset revaluation reserves, which take the form of latent gains on unrealized securities, will be subject to a discount of 55 per cent.

Elements of Tier-1 Capital: The elements of Tier-1 capital include:

(i) Paid-up capital (ordinary shares), statutory reserves, and other disclosed free reserves, if any;

(ii) Perpetual Non-cumulative Preference Shares (PNCPS) eligible for inclusion as Tier-I capital -subject to laws in force from time to time;

(iii) Innovative Perpetual Debt Instruments (IPDI) eligible for inclusion as Tier-I capital; and

(iv) Capital Reserves representing surplus arising out of sale proceeds of assets.

Elements of Tier-2 Capital: The elements of Tier-2 capital include undisclosed reserves, revaluation reserves, general provisions and loss reserves, hybrid capital instruments, subordinated debt and investment reserve account.

(a) Undisclosed Reserves: They can be included in capital, if they represent accumulations of post-tax profits and are not encumbered by any known liability and should not be routinely used for absorbing normal loss or operating losses.

(b) Revaluation Reserves: It would be prudent to consider revaluation reserves at a discount of 55 per cent while determining their value for inclusion in Tier-II capital. Such reserves will have to be reflected on the face of the Balance Sheet as revaluation reserves.

(c) General Provisions and Loss Reserves: Such reserves can be included in Tier-II capital if they are not attributable to the actual diminution in value or identifiable potential loss in any specific asset and are available to meet unexpected losses. Adequate care must be taken to see that sufficient provisions have been made to meet all known losses and foreseeable potential losses before considering general provisions and loss reserves to be part of Tier-II capital. General provisions/loss reserves will be admitted up to a maximum of 1.25 per cent of total risk weighted assets.

'Floating Provisions' held by the banks, which is general in nature and not made against any identified assets, may be treated as a part of Tier-II capital within the overall ceiling of 1.25 per cent of total risk weighted assets.

Excess provisions which arise on sale of NPAs would be eligible Tier-II capital subject to the overall ceiling of 1.25% of total Risk Weighted Assets.

(d) Hybrid Debt Capital Instruments: Those instruments which have close similarities to equity, in particular when they are able to support losses on an ongoing basis without triggering liquidation, may be included in Tier-II capital. At present the following instruments have been recognized and placed under this category:

(i) Debt capital instruments eligible for inclusion as Upper Tier-II capital; and

(ii) Perpetual Cumulative Preference Shares (PCPS)/Redeemable Non-Cumulative Preference Shares (RNCPS) / Redeemable Cumulative Preference Shares (RCPS) as part of Upper Tier-II Capital.

(e) Subordinated Debt: Refers to the status of the debt. In the event of the bankruptcy or liquidation of the debtor, subordinated debt only has a secondary claim on repayments, after other debt has been repaid.

Elements of Tier-3 Capital: Tertiary capital held by banks to meet part of their market risks, that includes a greater variety of debt than Tier-1 and Tier-2 capitals. Tier 3 capital debts may include a greater number of subordinated issues, undisclosed reserves and general loss reserves compared to Tier-2 capital.

Tier-3 capital is used to support market risk, commodities risk and foreign currency risk. To qualify as Tier-3 capital, assets must be limited to 250% of a bank's Tier-1 capital, be unsecured, subordinated and have a minimum maturity of two years.

The Second Pillar–Supervisory Review Process: This is a regulatory response to the first pillar, giving regulators better 'tools' over those previously available. This section discusses the key principles of supervisory review, risk management guidance and supervisory transparency and accountability produced by the Committee with respect to banking risks, including guidance relating to, among other things, the treatment of interest rate risk in the banking book, credit risk (stress testing, definition of default, residual risk, and credit concentration risk), operational risk, enhanced cross-border communication and cooperation, and securitisation.

I. Importance of Supervisory Review: The supervisory review process of the Framework is intended not only to ensure that banks have adequate capital to support all the risks in their business, but also to encourage banks to develop and use better risk management techniques in monitoring and managing their risks.

The supervisory review process recognises the responsibility of bank management in developing an internal capital assessment process and setting capital targets that are commensurate with the bank's risk profile and control environment. In the framework, bank management continues to bear responsibility for ensuring that the bank has adequate capital to support its risks beyond the core minimum requirements.

Supervisors are expected to evaluate how well banks are assessing their capital needs relative to their risks and to intervene, where appropriate. This interaction is intended to foster an active dialogue between banks and supervisors such that when deficiencies are identified, prompt and decisive action can be taken to reduce risk or restore capital. Accordingly, supervisors may wish to adopt an approach to focus more intensely on those banks with risk profiles or operational experience that warrants such attention.

The committee recognises the relationship that exists between the amount of capital held by the bank against its risks and the strength and effectiveness of the bank's risk management and internal control processes. However, increased capital should not be viewed as the only option for addressing increased risks confronting the bank. Other means for addressing risk, such as strengthening risk management, applying internal limits, strengthening the level of provisions and reserves, and improving internal controls, must also be considered. Furthermore, capital should not be regarded as a substitute for addressing fundamentally inadequate control or risk management processes.

There are three main areas that might be particularly suited to treatment under Pillar-2: risks considered under Pillar-1 that are not fully captured by the Pillar-1 process (e.g. credit concentration risk); those factors not taken into account by the Pillar-1 process (e.g. interest rate risk in the banking book, business and strategic risk); and factors external to the bank (e.g. business cycle effects). A further important aspect of Pillar-2 is the assessment of compliance with the minimum standards and disclosure requirements of the more advanced methods in Pillar-1, in particular the IRB framework for credit risk and the Advanced Measurement Approaches for operational risk. Supervisors must ensure that these requirements are being met, both as qualifying criteria and on a continuing basis.

Four key principles of supervisory review: The Committee has identified four key principles of supervisory review, which complement those outlined in the extensive supervisory guidance that has been developed by the Committee, the keystone of which is the Core Principles for Effective Banking Supervision and the Core Principles Methodology. 172 A list of the specific guidance relating to the management of banking risks is provided at the end of this Part of the Framework.

Principle-1: Banks should have a process for assessing their overall capital adequacy in relation to their risk profile and a strategy for maintaining their capital levels.

Principle-2: Supervisors should review and evaluate banks' internal capital adequacy assessments and strategies, as well as their ability to monitor and ensure their compliance with regulatory capital ratios. Supervisors should take appropriate supervisory action if they are not satisfied with the result of this process.

Principle-3: Supervisors should expect banks to operate above the minimum regulatory capital ratios and should have the ability to require banks to hold capital in excess of the minimum.

Principle-4: Supervisors should seek to intervene at an early stage to prevent capital from falling below the minimum levels required to support the risk characteristics of a particular bank and should require rapid remedial action if capital is not maintained or restored.

The Third Pillar-Market Discipline: This pillar aims to complement the minimum capital requirements and supervisory review process by developing a set of disclosure requirements which will allow the market participants to gauge the capital adequacy of an institution.

Market discipline supplements regulation as sharing of information facilitates assessment of the bank by others, including investors, analysts, customers, other banks, and rating agencies, which leads to good corporate governance. The aim of Pillar-3 is to allow market discipline to operate by requiring institutions to disclose details on the scope of application, capital, risk exposures, risk assessment processes, and the capital adequacy of the institution. It must be consistent with how the senior management, including the board, assess and manage the risks of the institution.

When market participants have a sufficient understanding of a bank's activities and the controls it has in place to manage its exposures, they are better able to distinguish between banking organizations so that they can reward those that manage their risks prudently and penalize those that do not.

These disclosures are required to be made at least twice a year, except qualitative disclosures providing a summary of the general risk management objectives and policies which can be made annually. Institutions are also required to create a formal policy on what will be disclosed and controls around them along with the validation and frequency of these disclosures. In general, the disclosures under Pillar-3 apply to the top consolidated level of the banking group to which the Basel-II framework applies.

BASEL-III ACCORD

Basel-III released in December, 2010 is the third in the series of Basel Accords. These accords deal with risk management aspects for the banking sector. In a nut shell we can say that Basel-III is the global regulatory standard (agreed upon by the members of the Basel Committee on Banking Supervision) on bank capital adequacy, stress testing and market liquidity risk. (Basel-I and Basel-II are the earlier versions of the same, and were less stringent)

According to Basel Committee on Banking Supervision "Basel-III is a comprehensive set of reform measures, developed by the Basel Committee on Banking Supervision, to strengthen the regulation, supervision and risk management of the banking sector".

Thus, we can say that Basel-III is only a continuation of effort initiated by the Basel Committee on Banking Supervision to enhance the banking regulatory framework under Basel-I and Basel-II. This latest Accord now seeks to improve the banking sector's ability to deal with financial and economic stress, improve risk management and strengthen the banks' transparency.

Objectives / aims of the Basel-III measures: Basel-III measures aim to:

a) Improve the banking sector's ability to absorb shocks arising from financial and economic stress, whatever the source
b) Improve risk management and governance
c) Strengthen banks' transparency and disclosures.

Thus we can say that Basel-III guidelines are aimed at to improve the ability of banks to withstand periods of economic and financial stress as the new guidelines are more stringent than the earlier requirements for capital and liquidity in the banking sector.

The basic structure of Basel-III remains unchanged with three mutually reinforcing pillars.

Pillar-1 : Minimum Regulatory Capital Requirements based on Risk Weighted Assets (RWAs): Maintaining capital calculated through credit, market and operational risk areas.

Pillar-2 : Supervisory Review Process: Regulating tools and frameworks for dealing with peripheral risks that banks face.

Pillar-3 : Market Discipline : Increasing the disclosures that banks must provide to increase the transparency of banks.

Major Changes Proposed in Basel-III over earlier Accords *i.e.*, Basel-I and Basel-II

(a) **Better Capital Quality:** One of the key elements of Basel-III is the introduction of much stricter definition of capital. Better quality capital means the higher loss-absorbing capacity. This in turn will mean that banks will be stronger, allowing them to better withstand periods of stress.

(b) **Capital Conservation Buffer:** Another key feature of Basel-III is that now banks will be required to hold a capital conservation buffer of 2.5%. The aim of asking to build conservation buffer is to ensure that banks maintain a cushion of capital that can be used to absorb losses during periods of financial and economic stress.

(c) **Countercyclical Buffer:** This is also one of the key elements of Basel-III. The countercyclical buffer has been introduced with the objective to increase capital requirements in good times and decrease the same in bad times. The buffer will slow banking activity when it overheats and will encourage lending when times are tough *i.e.* in bad times. The buffer will range from 0% to 2.5%, consisting of common equity or other fully loss-absorbing capital.

(d) **Minimum Common Equity and Tier-1 Capital Requirements:** The minimum requirement for common equity, the highest form of loss-absorbing capital, has been raised under Basel-III from 2% to 4.5% of total risk-weighted assets. The overall Tier-1 capital requirement, consisting of not only common equity but also other qualifying financial instruments, will also increase from the current minimum of 4% to 6%. Although the minimum total capital requirement will remain at the current 8% level, yet the required total capital will increase to 10.5% when combined with the conservation buffer.

(e) **Leverage Ratio:** A review of the financial crisis of 2008 has indicted that the value of many assets fell quicker than assumed from historical experience. Thus, now Basel-III rules include a leverage ratio to serve as a safety net. A leverage ratio is the relative amount of capital to total assets (not risk-weighted). This aims to put a cap on swelling of leverage in the banking sector on a global basis. 3% leverage ratio of Tier-1 will be tested before a mandatory leverage ratio is introduced in January 2018.

(f) **Liquidity Ratios:** Under Basel-III, a framework for liquidity risk management will be created. A new Liquidity Coverage Ratio (LCR) and Net Stable Funding Ratio (NSFR) are to be introduced in 2015 and 2018, respectively.

(g) **Systemically Important Financial Institutions (SIFI):** As part of the macro-prudential framework, systemically important banks will be expected to have loss-absorbing capability beyond the Basel-III requirements. Options for implementation include capital surcharges, contingent capital and bail-in-debt.

Over View for the RBI Guidelines for Implementation of Basel-III guidelines: The final guidelines have been issued by Reserve Bank of India for implementation of Basel-III guidelines on 2nd May, 2012. Major features of these guidelines are:

(a) These guidelines would become effective from January 1, 2013 in a phased manner. This means that as at the close of business on January 1, 2013, banks must be able to declare or disclose capital ratios computed under the amended guidelines. The Basel-III capital ratios will be fully implemented as on March 31, 2018.

(b) The capital requirements for the implementation of Basel-III guidelines may be lower during the initial periods and higher during the later years. Banks needs to keep this in view while Capital Planning;

(c) Guidelines on operational aspects of implementation of the Countercyclical Capital Buffer. Guidance to banks on this will be issued in due course as RBI is still working on these. Moreover, some other proposals viz. 'Definition of Capital Disclosure Requirements', 'Capitalization of Bank Exposures to Central Counterparties' etc., are also engaging the attention of the Basel Committee at present. Therefore, the final proposals of the Basel Committee on these aspects will be considered for implementation, to the extent applicable, in future.

(d) For the financial year ending March 31, 2013, banks will have to disclose the capital ratios computed under the existing guidelines (Basel-II) on capital adequacy as well as those computed under the Basel-III capital adequacy framework.

(e) The guidelines require banks to maintain a Minimum Total Capital (MTC) of 9% against 8% (international) prescribed by the Basel Committee of Total Risk Weighted Assets. This has been decided by Indian regulator as a matter of prudence. Thus, its requirement in this regard remained at the same level. However, banks will need to raise more money than under Basel-II as several items are excluded under the new definition.

(f) Of the above, Common Equity Tier-1 (CET-1) capital must be at least 5.5% of RWAs;

(g) In addition to the Minimum Common Equity Tier-1 capital of 5.5% of RWAs, (international standards require these to be only at 4.5%) banks are also required to maintain a Capital Conservation Buffer (CCB) of 2.5% of RWAs in the form of Common Equity Tier-1 capital. CCB is designed to ensure that banks build up capital buffers during normal times (*i.e.*, outside periods of stress) which can be drawn down as losses are incurred during a stressed period. In case such buffers have been drawn down, the banks have to rebuild them through reduced discretionary distribution of earnings. This could include reducing dividend payments, share buybacks and staff bonus.

(h) Indian banks under Basel-II are required to maintain Tier-1 capital of 6%, which has been raised to 7% under Basel-III. Moreover, certain instruments, including some with the characteristics of debts, will not be now included for arriving at Tier-1 capital;

(i) The new norms do not allow banks to use the consolidated capital of any insurance or non-financial subsidiaries for calculating capital adequacy.

(j) **Leverage Ratio:** Under the new set of guidelines, RBI has set the leverage ratio at 4.5% (3% under Basel-III). Leverage ratio has been introduced in Basel-III to regulate banks which have huge trading book and off balance sheet derivative positions. However, In India, most of banks do not have large derivative activities so as to arrange enhanced cover for counterparty credit risk. Hence, the pressure on banks should be minimal on this count.

(k) **Liquidity norms:** The Liquidity Coverage Ratio (LCR) under Basel-III requires banks to hold enough unencumbered liquid assets to cover expected net outflows during a 30-day stress period. In India, the burden from LCR stipulation will depend on how much of CRR and SLR can be offset against LCR. Under present guidelines, Indian banks already follow the norms set by RBI for the statutory liquidity ratio (SLR) – and cash reserve ratio (CRR), which are liquidity buffers. The SLR is mainly government securities while the CRR is mainly cash. Thus, for this aspect also Indian banks are better placed over many of their overseas counterparts.

(l) **Countercyclical Buffer:** Economic activity moves in cycles and banking system is inherently pro-cyclic. During upswings, carried away by the boom, banks end up in excessive lending and unchecked risk build-up, which carry the seeds of a disastrous downturn. The regulation to create additional capital buffers to lend further would act as a break on unbridled bank-lending. The detailed guidelines for these are likely to be issued by RBI only at a later stage.

Countercyclical Capital Buffer: In addition to the capital conservation buffer, Basel-III introduces another capital buffer, a countercyclical capital buffer within a range of 0-2.5% of RWAs inform of Common Equity or other fully loss absorbing capital will be implemented according to national circumstances. The purpose of countercyclical capital buffer is to achieve the broader macro-prudential goal of protecting the banking sector from periods of excess aggregate credit growth. For any given country, this buffer will only be in effect when there is excess credit growth that results in a system-wide build-up of risk. The countercyclical capital buffer, when in effect, would be introduced as an extension of the capital conservation buffer range.

Credit value Adjustment Risk Capital: At present, the counterparty credit risk in the trading book covers only the risk of default of the counterparty. The reform package includes an additional capital charge for Credit Value Adjustment (CVA) risk which captures risk of mark-to-market losses due to deterioration in the credit worthiness of a counterparty. The risk of interconnectedness among larger financial firms (defined as having total assets greater than or equal to $100 billion) will be better captured through a prescription of 25% adjustment to the asset value correlation (AVC) under IRB approaches to credit risk. In addition, the guidelines on counterparty credit risk management with regard to collateral, margin period of risk and central counterparties and counterparty credit risk management requirements have been strengthened.

Revised Basel-III Transitional Arrangements: In terms of Basel-III Capital Regulation issued by RBI, the Capital Conservation Buffer (CCB) is scheduled to be implemented from March 31, 2015 in phases and would be fully implemented as on March 31, 2019. However RBI vide circular dated 27.03.2014 has advised that the implementation of CCB will be begin as on March 31, 2016. Consequently, Basel III Capital Regulation will be fully implemented as on March 31, 2019.

TEST YOURSELF

1. Which is not a correct statement about the Risk?
(a) Risk refers to a condition where there is a possibility of undesirable occurrence of a particular result
(b) A risk can be defined as a planned event with financial consequences resulting in loss or reduced earnings.
(c) Risk can be defined as the uncertainty of the outcome.
(d) As risk is directly proportionate to return, the more risk a bank takes, it can expect to make more money.

2. The ________ of banks arises from funding of long-term assets by short-term liabilities, thereby making the liabilities subject to rollover or refinancing risk.
(a) liquidity risk (b) credit risk
(c) market risk (d) operational Risk

3. Which is not a type of liquidity risk?
(a) Funding Liquidity Risk
(b) Time risk
(c) Call risk
(d) Interest Rate Risk

4. ________ is the risk that a bank may suffer losses as a result of adverse exchange rate movements during a period.
(a) Liquidity risk (b) Credit risk
(c) Forex risk (d) Operational risk

5. ________ is defined as the potential of a bank borrower or counterparty to fail to meet its obligations in accordance with the agreed terms.
(a) Liquidity risk (b) Credit risk
(c) Market risk (d) Operational risk

6. Operational risk is the risk of loss arising from various types of ________.
(a) human error
(b) failed system and procedure in the bank
(c) breakdown in internal control
(d) All of the above

7. ________ is the risk arising from fraud, both internal and external, failed business processes and the inability to maintain business continuity and manage information.
(a) Transaction risk (b) Credit risk
(c) Market risk (d) Operational risk

8. ________ arises when a bank is unable to conclude a large transaction in a particular instrument near the current market price.
(a) Transaction risk b) Credit risk
(c) Market liquidity risk d) Operational risk

9. At organizational level in each bank, the overall responsibility of risk management is assigned to:
(a) Board of Director
(b) Risk Management Organization
(c) Risk Management Committee
(d) Risk Management Sub-committee of Board of Director

10. Basel is a city found in Basel-City, ________.
(a) Brazil (b) Switzerland
(c) France (d) USA

11. The Basel Committee 1974–2014 work on developing banking regulation can be broken into the five following regulatory waves. Find the incorrect match:
(a) 1974 – 1998 – Basel-I
(b) 1999 – 2008 – Basel-II
(c) 2009 – 2011 – Basel-III
(d) 2012 – 2014 – Post-Basel-III.

12. The Basel-I classification system groups a bank's assets into five risk categories, classified as percentages ________. A bank's assets are placed into a category based on the nature of the debtor.
(a) 0%, 10%, 25%, 50% and 100%
(b) 0%, 10%, 20%, 50% and 100%
(c) 0%, 20%, 40%, 60% and 100%
(d) 0%, 10%, 50%, 100% and 200%

13. Basel-I originally called for the minimum capital ratio of capital to risk-weighted assets of ________ to be implemented by the end of 1992.
(a) 7% (b) 8%
(c) 9% (d) 10%

14. Which is not the part of Basel II "three pillars" concept?
(a) Minimum capital requirements (addressing risk)
(b) Supervisory review
(c) Disclosure norms
(d) Market discipline

15. Basel-II provides guidelines for calculation of minimum regulatory capital ratios. The sum of Tier-1, Tier-2, and Tier-3 elements will be eligible for inclusion in the capital base, Find the wrong limits:
(a) The total of Tier-2 (supplementary) elements will be limited to a maximum of 100 per cent of the total of Tier-1 element.
(b) Subordinate term debt will be limited to a maximum of 50 per cent of Tier-1 elements.
(c) Tier-3 capital will be limited to 200 per cent of a bank's Tier-1 capital that is required to support market risk.
(d) Asset revaluation reserves, which take the form of latent gains on unrealized securities, will be subject to a discount of 55 per cent.

16. Which of the elements of Tier-2 capital other than undisclosed reserves?
(a) Revaluation Reserves
(b) Hybrid Debt Capital Instruments
(c) Subordinated Debt
(d) All of the above

17. Basel-III released in ________ is the third in the series of Basel Accords.
(a) December, 2008 (b) December, 2010
(c) November, 2012 (d) November, 2014

18. The first pillar under Basel-II taken about ______.
(a) Minimum capital requirements (addressing risk)
(b) Supervisory review
(c) Disclosure norms
(d) Market discipline

19. The risks considered for capital requirements under Basel-II are ______.
(a) credit risk, market risk, operational risk
(b) transaction risk, credit risk, liquidity risk,
(c) market risk, operational risk, forex risk
(d) liquidity risk, market risk, operational risk

20. The minimum total capital under Basel-III is ____ % of total risk weighted assets.
(a) 7% (b) 8%
(c) 9% (d) 10%

ANSWER

1	2	3	4	5	6	7	8	9	10
(b)	(a)	(d)	(a)	(b)	(d)	(a)	(c)	(c)	(b)
11	**12**	**13**	**14**	**15**	**16**	**17**	**18**	**19**	**20**
(a)	(b)	(b)	(c)	(c)	(d)	(b)	(a)	(a)	(c)

CIBIL, FAIR PRACTICES CODE FOR DEBT COLLECTION, BCSBI

CREDIT INFORMATION COMPANIES IN INDIA

Introduction: With many applicants looking for a loan, banks were increasingly finding it difficult to carry out intensive background checks regarding the credit-worthiness of the applicant. A Credit Information Company (CIC) is an independent organization licensed by the Reserve Bank of India (RBI) that signs up banks, NBFCs and financial institutions as its members and aggregates data and identity information for individual consumers and businesses from its members. Credit reporting is very important in today's financial system and is considered a primary factor while evaluating the credit worthiness of customers and monitoring the credit circumstances of consumers and businesses. This information enables lenders to function more efficiently and at a lower cost than is otherwise possible.

Credit Information Companies (CIC's): CIC or Credit Information Companies are an independent third-party institution that collects financial data regarding loans, credit cards and more about individuals and shares it with its members. Banks, Non-Banking Financial institutions are usually the customers of Credit Information Companies. The Credit Card Company collects financial information about all these individuals and forms a credit report based on their financial history. This credit report plays a very important role as it helps banks and other financial institutions determine the credit worthiness of an individual applying for a loan or credit card with them.

Credit Information Companies Regulation Act (CIC Act): Credit Information Companies in India are licensed by the Reserve Bank of India and governed by the Credit Information Companies Regulation Act, 2005 and various other rules and regulations issued by the Reserve Bank of India. The CIC Act, 2005 is a legislation that is enacted by the Government of India, in order to regulate the actions of the Credit Card Companies in India. Following the CIC Act, 2005, the RBI and the Government of India enacted the CIC Act, 2006.

How do Credit Information Companies work? Credit Information Companies comply public data, credit transactions and payment histories of individuals and companies. The data is collected from various authentic sources and the companies form a credit report based on the collected data. The credit companies also create a score based on the credit report of an individual or an organisation. Usually credit score ranges between 350 to 850, anything above 750 is considered as a good score. The credit report and credit score plays a very important rule in an individual's financial journey as banks refer to this report and score to decide the creditworthiness of an individual before granting a loan or credit card.

Who are credit information company's customers? Credit information companies service individuals (wanting to access their own credit reports), lenders who access credit reports of their existing customers and prospective customers who are applying for new loans or credit cards and businesses who are borrowing from banks and financial institutions to keep a check on their reported credit history.

What information does a credit information company provide? A credit information company provides:

To the Lender:

- A consolidated view of a consumer to a lender across all reported loans held
- The repayment history as reported by the subscribing lenders
- The identification information, address and other demographic information as reported by member institutions
- Top line indicators (derived attributes) based on the information provided by the data contributing members

To the individual/business/consumer:

- An ability for the consumer to access his credit record as seen by the lender to ensure that the information reported is accurate.
- Keeping a tab on one's credit-worthiness and repayment track record.

Who should buy a credit report? Every individual who is looking to borrow should ideally go in for a credit report. One should scrutinize the same for errors and keep checking his report from time to time. Ideally, one should pull out a credit report every quarter. The cost of each report will be ₹ 138 (including taxes/handling charges). This is a small price to pay for the assurance that your credit record is reflected correctly. To get yours today, click on Forms Credit Report Request.

How do I correct my credit report? In case an individual finds that his credit report is not updated, he can approach the respective financial institution or credit bureau to update the credit reports. The financial institution or credit bureau should take appropriate steps to update the credit information within 30 days after being requested to do so. The credit bureau can make changes in the individual's credit information only after such changes have been authorized by the concerned financial institution.

Credit Information Companies in the country

This credit rating would enable the bank or the institution to take a decision on whether they should lend money to the said individual or not. Herewith are a list of 4 credit information companies. These are approved by the Reserve Bank of India.

1. CIBIL : CIBIL which stands for Credit Information Bureau (India) Limited, is an ISO 27001 : 2005 company. A first of its kind, it is India's premier Credit Information Company (CIC). Founded in the year 2000, it has established itself as a key participant of the Indian financial system. The company records credit related information of individuals as submitted by registered member institutions. CIBIL works in association with Trans Union International Inc. and Dun and Bradstreet.

CIBIL has two major segments viz. the Consumer Bureau and the Commercial Bureau. The Consumer Bureau maintains credit records of individuals while the Commercial Bureau maintains credit records of institutions/companies.

CIBIL Shareholding Pattern: As India's leading CIC (Credit Information Company), CIBIL enjoys considerable clout in the Indian credit system. CIBIL has a diverse ownership structure consisting of well-known banking and non-banking companies. Its major stakeholder is Trans Union International Inc. with about 66% of the total share. The remaining 34% is held by 8 other parties with stakes ranging between 1% to 6% each.

CIBIL TransUnion Score: An individual's or company's credit history is evaluated to generate a Credit Information Report (CIR) from which is derived a credit score known as the CIBIL TransUnion Score. This report and score form an integral part of a lender's credit approval process. Credit scores range between 300 and 900. The higher the score, the more credit worthy the borrower is, which translates to quick approvals and better interest rates.

CIBIL provides credit reports and scores to those who inquire for them. This includes individuals, institutions and lenders. When an application for a loan or credit card is submitted, lenders check the applicant's credit scores to ascertain whether it satisfies eligibility criteria. In general, a score of 750 or higher is considered good.

Analysis of CIBIL Score:

Score	Analysis
–1	Borrower has no history of borrowings with any member of CIBIL.
300 – 600	In general, credit cards and loans are not provided to people in this slab.
601 – 750	This is intermediate range of scores and will allow to borrow from various lenders, however banks may refer to overall financial position.
750 +	Scores above 750 considered to be good and will help getting loan or a credit card with ease.

Reasons for Low CIBIL Score: These are the important reason for low CIBIL Score:

- Cheque Bounce/ dishonors;
- Irregular Loan Payments;
- Defaulting on Credit Card bills / making late payments or consistent part payments;
- Defaulting as a Guarantor.

Advantages of Higher CIBIL Score: Followings are the main Advantages of Higher CIBIL Score to individual/business/consumer:

- Quick processing of loan and credit card applications;
- More negotiating power;
- Easy availability of credit such as Loans;
- Assurance of Safety.

2. Equifax Credit Information Services (ECIS) : Equifax Credit Information Services Private Limited (ECIS), a credit bureau/consumer credit company (CIC) licensed by the Reserve Bank of India (Certificate of Registration, under the Credit Information Companies Regulation Act 2005, was obtained in March 2010) is the Indian arm of Equifax Incorporated, a consumer credit reporting agency, founded in 1899 in the US with its operations currently spread across 15 countries. ECIS is a joint venture between Equifax Inc and seven Indian financial institutions namely, Bank of Baroda, State Bank of India, Kotak Mahindra Prime Ltd, Bank of India, Sundaram Finance Limited, Union Bank of India and Religare Finvest Limited. With around 1300 registered members, Equifax is currently headquartered in Mumbai with branch offices located in Delhi and Bengaluru.

3. Experian : Experian is one of the world's foremost credit information services companies offering a wide range of business tools to their clients based all across the globe. Widely known to be among the planet's most innovative companies according to Forbes magazine, the company is licensed by the Reserve Bank of India and assists clients by providing a wealth of analytical as well as data tools, which help them manage their businesses in a more efficient and effective manner. Experian is also the first credit information company to be licensed by Credit Information Companies (Regulation) Act 2005 (CICRA 2005) and currently operate two firms within India, namely:

- Experian Credit Information Company of India Private Ltd
- Experian Services India Private Ltd

Experian has tied up with more than 2,900 financial institutions, counting public sector banks, telecom companies, micro finance institutions as well as non-banking financial companies. The company, which is ISO 27000:2013 certified, provides its customers with credit information as per guidelines issued by the Credit Information Companies (Regulation) Act of 2005.

4. CRIF High Mark : CRIF High Mark Credit Information Services Along with providing Credit score and report to consumers, the company caters to all borrower segments such as MSME and Commercial borrowers, Retail consumers, Microfinance borrower. The most popular of these is CIBIL, which also provides you information on your credit rating for a charge. Most banks and lenders prefer to go to credit rating companies, to ensure that there are no defaults in the future and the customer is credit worthy. This is particularly true for largest ticket size loans like home loans, credit cards and personal loans. There could be in the future other credit card companies that spring-up from time to time.

FAIR PRACTICES CODE FOR DEBT COLLECTION (JANUARY 2018)

Introduction: The Bank is committed to following fair practices especially with regard to collection and recovery of its dues from its borrowers (herein after referred to as "customer"). At the same time the Bank is also committed to follow fair practices in this regard to foster customer confidence and to retain the image of the Bank as an institution, which is fair in its dealings even with defaulters.

Preamble: This Code for Collection of Dues and Repossession of Security (CDRS) is a non-statutory code issued on voluntary basis. Bank adopts this Code for Collection of Dues and Repossession of Security. It lays down guidelines to have fairness and transparency in the collection, recovery and repossession of security.

Applicability: It applies to the Bank and the agents engaged by it for the purpose of collection, recovery and repossession of securities.

Dues Collection Policy Statement: Although the Bank is committed to collection /recovery of its dues and repossession of securities, the dignity of and respect for the customer is central to the Debt Collection Policy. Bank's dues collection policy is built on courtesy, fair treatment and persuasion. The bank shall not follow policies, which are unduly coercive in collection of dues.

Security Repossession Policy Statement: The Bank's Security Repossession Policy aims at recovery of dues in the event of default and is not aimed at whimsical deprivation of the property. The Bank shall resort to repossession of the securities only when the collection/ recovery of dues is not forthcoming in spite of request made and the policy for repossession shall be in accordance with the terms and conditions of the loan documents and within the legal framework. The policy recognises fairness and transparency in repossession, valuation and realisation of securities.

General Guidelines: We will follow collection of dues and security repossession policy in consonance with the law. The policy will be displayed on our website and a copy of the same will be made available at our branch for perusal. All the members of the staff or any person authorised to represent the Bank in collection/ recovery of dues and/or Repossession of Securities shall follow the guidelines as set out below:

a) Whenever we give loans, we will explain to you the repayment schedule viz. amount, tenure and periodicity of repayment. However, if you do not adhere to the repayment schedule, a defined process in accordance with the laws of the land will be followed for recovery of dues.

b) We will have a Board approved policy for Collection of Dues and Security Repossession as also appointment of Recovery Agents.

c) All relevant laws, regulations, guidelines and conditions of approval, licensing or registration will be taken into account while appointing Recovery Agents.

d) We will ensure that our Recovery Agents are properly trained to handle their responsibilities with care and sensitivity. We will also ensure that they do not exceed their brief.

e) Our collection policy is built on courtesy, fair treatment and persuasion. We believe in fostering customer confidence and long-term relationship.

f) We will provide you with all the information regarding your dues and will endeavour to give sufficient notice for payment of dues.

g) We will have a system of checks before passing on a default case to recovery agencies so that you are not inconvenienced on account of lapses on our part.

h) We will write to you when we initiate recovery proceedings against you and will inform you of the name of the recovery agency / agent, to whom your case has been assigned as also their address and telephone numbers.

i) We will provide details of the recovery agency firms/companies engaged by us on our website.

j) We will also make available, on request, details of the recovery agency firms/companies relevant to you at our branch.

k) Our staff or any person authorized to represent us in collection of dues and/or security repossession will identify himself/herself and produce the authority letter issued by us and upon request show you his/her identity card issued by the bank or under authority of the bank.

l) All the members of our staff or any person authorised to represent us in collection and / or security repossession would follow the guidelines set out below:

   i. You would be contacted ordinarily at the place of your choice and in the absence of any specified place at the place of your residence and if unavailable at your residence, at the place of business/occupation.

   ii. Their identity and authority to represent us would be made known to you.

   iii. Your privacy would be respected.

   iv. Interaction with you would be in a civil manner.

   v. Normally our representatives will contact you between 07.00 hrs and 19.00 hrs, unless the special circumstances of your Code of Bank's Commitment to Customers – January 2018 business or occupation require otherwise.

   vi. Your requests to avoid calls at a particular time or at a particular place would be honoured as far as possible.

   vii. Time and number of calls and contents of conversation would be documented.

   viii. All assistance would be given to resolve disputes or differences regarding dues in a mutually acceptable and in an orderly manner.

   ix. During visits to your place for dues collection, decency and decorum would be maintained. Our officials / agents will not resort to intimidation or harassment of any kind, either verbal or physical against any person, including acts intended to humiliate publicly or intrude the privacy of your family members, referees and friends, making threatening and anonymous calls or making false and misleading representations. However, it is your responsibility to keep updating your contact details. In case the bank is unable to contact you at the details provided, the bank will access information available from public sources and approach your friends / relatives to trace you.

   x. Inappropriate occasions such as bereavement in the family or other important family functions like marriages would be avoided for making calls / visits to collect dues.

   xi. We will investigate any complaint from you about unfair practices of our recovery agents.

BANKING CODES AND STANDARDS BOARD OF INDIA (JAN. 2018)

Introduction: RBI constituted committee on Procedures and Performance Audit of Public Services in November 2003, under the chairmanship of Shri S. S. Tarapore (former Dy. Governor) to address the issues relating to availability of adequate banking services to the common man. Therefore, RBI, in its Monetary Policy Statement in April, 2005 announced setting up of the Banking Codes and Standards Board of India (BCSBI) in order to ensure that comprehensive code of conduct for fair treatment of customer was evolved and adhered to. The BCSBI has been registered as a separate society under the Society Registration Act, 1860. Commercial banks, RRBs and Urban Banks are its members.

The BCSBI functions as an autonomous body to monitor and assess the compliance with codes. This is a Code of Customer Rights, which sets minimum standards of banking practices we will follow as a member of BCSBI while dealing with individual customers. It provides protection to customers and explains how a member bank is required to deal with customers in its day-to-day operations.

The Code does not replace or supersede regulatory or supervisory instructions of the Reserve Bank of India (RBI) and we will comply with such instructions/directions issued by RBI from time to time. The Code may have set higher standards than those prescribed in the regulatory instructions and such higher standards will prevail as the Code represents the best practices voluntarily agreed to by us as our commitment to you.

Objectives of the Code: The Code has been developed to:

a) Promote good and fair banking practices by setting minimum standards in our dealings with you;
b) Increase transparency so that you can have a better understanding of what you can reasonably expect from us;
c) Encourage market forces, through competition, to achieve higher operating standards;
d) Promote a fair and cordial relationship between you and your bank;
e) Foster confidence in the banking system;
f) Promote safe and fair customer dealing in case of banking in a digitized environment;
g) Increase awareness of customers and to enhance customer protection.

Application of the Code: This Code applies to all the products and services listed below, whether they are provided by our branch or agents acting on our behalf, whether across the counter, over the phone, by post, through interactive electronic devices, on the internet or by any other method. However, all products discussed here may or may not be offered by us.

a) Current accounts, savings accounts, term deposits, recurring deposits, PPF accounts and all other deposit accounts;
b) Payment services such as pension, payment orders, remittances by way of demand drafts, wire transfers and all electronic transactions e.g. RTGS, NEFT, IMPS, UPI;
c) Banking services related to Government transactions;
d) Demat accounts, Equity, Government bonds;
e) Indian currency notes/coins exchange facility;
f) Collection of cheques, safe custody services, safe deposit locker facility;
g) Loans, overdrafts and guarantees;
h) Foreign exchange services including money changing;
i) Third party insurance and investment products marketed through our branch and/or our authorised representatives or agents;
j) Card products including credit cards, debits cards, ATM cards, smart cards and POS services (including credit cards offered by our subsidiaries/companies promoted by us);
k) Digital Products such as e-wallet, Mobile Banking, internet banking, UPI, BHIM, Aadhaar Pay.

Right to Fair Treatment: Act fairly and reasonably in all our dealings with you by:

a) Providing minimum banking facilities of receipt and payment of cash / cheques, remittances, exchange of soiled notes, etc. at the bank's counter and also providing cashless transactions through alternate delivery channels.
b) Meeting the commitments and standards set in this Code, for the products and services we offer, and in the procedures and practices we follow.
c) Making sure our products and services meet relevant laws and regulations in letter and spirit and are appropriate to your needs and in line with the banking scenario, including digital banking.
d) Ensuring that our dealings with you rest on ethical principles of integrity and transparency.
e) Offering digital banking and payment systems in a secure, convenient and robust technological environment.
f) Not discriminating against you on the basis of age, race, gender, marital status, religion, disability or financial status when offering and delivering our products and services.
g) Promoting good and fair banking practices by setting minimum standards in all dealings with you.
h) Promoting a fair and equitable relationship with you.
i) Training our staff attending to you adequately and appropriately and ensuring that our staff attends to you promptly and courteously and to deal quickly and sympathetically with things that may go wrong by correcting mistakes and handling your complaints expeditiously.

Right to Transparency, Fair and Honest Dealing: We will help you to understand how our financial products and services work by:

a) Giving you timely and adequate information about them and the necessary safeguards in any one or more of the following languages—Hindi, English or the appropriate local language.

b) Ensuring that our advertising and promotional literature is clear and not misleading. We will make every effort to ensure that the contracts or agreements we frame are transparent, easily understood by and well communicated to you. The product's price, the associated risks, the terms and conditions that govern use over the product's life cycle Code of Bank's Commitment to Customers – January 2018 and mutual responsibilities will be clearly disclosed. We will ensure that you are not subjected to unfair business or marketing practices, coercive contractual terms, negative confirmations or misleading representations. For achieving this, we will be following the practices and procedures given in Chapter 3 on Information Transparency and Chapter 4 on Advertising, Marketing and Sales.

c) Ensuring that you are given complete information about our products and services, minimum balance requirements, the interest rates and service charges, besides the terms and conditions applicable to them in a transparent manner through the following methods as per your preference.
   i. By sending SMS or e-mails
   ii. Through electronic or print media
   iii. Display on our website
   iv. Display on branch notice board

   [Display on website and branch notice board will be in addition to the other modes of information dissemination mentioned above.]

d) Giving you information on the facilities provided to you and how you can avail of these and whom and how you may contact for addressing your queries.

e) Displaying in our branch, for your information
   i. Services we provide.
   ii. Minimum balance requirement, if any, for Savings Bank Accounts and Current Accounts and the charges for non-maintenance thereof.
   iii. Information available in booklet form.

f) Displaying on our website our policies on
   i. Deposits
   ii. Cheque collection
   iii. Grievance Redressal
   iv. Compensation
   v. Collection of Dues and Security Repossession
   vi. Charter of Customer Rights
   vii. Customer Protection Policy (including protection from cyber fraud)
   viii. Limited Liability in respect of unauthorized electronic banking transactions
   ix. Facilities for senior citizens and differently abled persons.

g) To increase awareness of the Code among customers we will
   i. provide you with a copy of the Code when you open an account with us and otherwise on request.
   ii. make available this Code at our every branch and on our website.
   iii. ensure that our staff are trained to provide relevant information about the Code and to effectively put the Code in to practice.
   iv. hold customer meetings on provisions of the Code periodically.

Code of Bank's Commitment to Micro and Small Enterprises: This is a Code, reflecting the bank's positive commitment to its Micro and Small Enterprise (MSE) customers to provide easy, speedy and transparent access to banking services in their day-do-day operations and in times of financial difficulty. This Code is not only a Charter of Rights of the MSE but also enshrines his obligations vis-a-vis his bank.

Code of Bank's Commitment to Customers: This is a Code of Customer Rights, which sets minimum standards of banking practices member banks have to follow while they deal with individual customer. It provides protection to customers and explains how banks are expected to deal with customers in their day-to-day operations.

TEST YOURSELF

1. Credit Information Companies in India are licensed by the Reserve Bank of India and governed by the Credit Information Companies Regulation Act, ______.
(a) 2003 (b) 2005
(c) 2006 (d) 2008

2. How many Credit Information Companies work in India?
(a) 2 (b) 3
(c) 4 (d) 5

3. CIBIL founded in the year ______.
(a) 2000 (b) 2002
(c) 2006 (d) 2008

4. CIBIL is a bureau refers to ______.
(a) Consumer Bureau
(b) Commercial Bureau
(c) Both Consumer Bureau and the Commercial Bureau
(d) None of these

5. CIBIL has a diverse ownership structure consisting of well-known banking and non-banking companies. Its major stakeholder is Trans Union International Inc. with about ______ of the total share.
(a) 23% (b) 34%
(c) 51% (d) 66%

6. CIBIL Trans Union Credit scores range between ____.
(a) 200 and 800 (b) 200 and 900
(c) 300 and 800 (d) 300 and 900

7. In general, a CIBIL TransUnion Credit score of _____ or higher is considered good.
(a) 600 (b) 650
(c) 750 (d) 800

8. Which of not the reasons for Low CIBIL Score?
(a) Cheque Bounce/ dishonors
(b) Irregular Loan Payments
(c) Defaulting as a Guarantor
(d) None of these

9. What is the meaning of –1 CIBIL Score?
(a) Borrower has good credit history, he is eligible for loan
(b) Borrower has bad credit history, he is not eligible for loan
(c) Borrower has no history of borrowings with any member of CIBIL
(d) None of these

10. Along with the CIBIL, which Credit Information Services is not work in India?
(a) Equifax (b) Moody
(c) CRIF High Mark (d) Experian

11. Equifax is currently headquartered in ______.
(a) Mumbai (b) Delhi
(c) Bangalore (d) Kolkata

12. Code for Collection of Dues and Repossession of Security (CDRS) is a ______ code issued on ______ basis.
(a) non-statutory, voluntary
(b) statutory, voluntary
(c) non-statutory, compulsory
(d) statutory, compulsory

13. Normally our representatives will contact you between ______, unless the special circumstances of your Code of Bank's Commitment to Customers.
(a) 06 am and 07 pm (b) 07 am and 07 pm
(c) 06 am and 08 pm (d) 07 am and 08 pm

14. The BCSBI has been established on the recommendation of ______.
(a) R.V. Gupta Committee
(b) S.S. Tarapore Committee
(c) Narshimham Committee
(d) V.K. Nair Committee

15. RBI, in its Monetary Policy Statement in April ______ announced setting up of the Banking Codes and Standards Board of India (BCSBI).
(a) 2005 (b) 2006
(c) 2007 (d) 2008

16. Banking Codes and Standards Board of India (BCSBI) is registered as ______.
(a) Firm (b) Company
(c) Govt. undertaking (d) Society

17. Which is not the objectives of the BCSBI Code?
(a) Promote good and fair banking practices by setting minimum standards in our dealings with you
(b) Promote a fair and cordial relationship between you and your bank
(c) Increase awareness of customers and to enhance customer protection
(d) None of the above

18. BCSBI Code is not applies to the products ______.
(a) Current accounts, savings accounts, term deposits
(b) Banking services related to Government transactions
(c) Demat accounts, Equity, Government bonds
(d) None of the above

19. As per BCSBI the interest rates and service charges, besides the terms and conditions applicable to them in a transparent manner through the following methods as per your preference.
(a) By sending SMS or e-mails
(b) Display on our website
(c) Display on branch notice board
(d) All the above

20. Bank's Code for Customer Service which is a voluntary code is issued by______.
(a) RBI (b) IBA
(c) BCSBI (d) Central Govt.

ANSWER

1	2	3	4	5	6	7	8	9	10
(b)	(c)	(a)	(c)	(d)	(d)	(c)	(d)	(c)	(b)
11	**12**	**13**	**14**	**15**	**16**	**17**	**18**	**19**	**20**
(a)	(a)	(b)	(b)	(a)	(d)	(d)	(d)	(d)	(c)

RECENT DEVELOPMENTS IN THE FINANCIAL SYSTEM

INSOLVENCY AND BANKRUPTCY CODE 2016

The Insolvency and Bankruptcy Code, 2016 (IBC) is the bankruptcy law of India which seeks to consolidate the existing framework by creating a single law for insolvency and bankruptcy. The Insolvency and Bankruptcy Code, 2016 was introduced in Lok Sabha in December 2015. It was passed by Lok Sabha on 5 May 2016. The Code received the assent of the President of India on 28 May 2016. Certain provisions of the Act have come into force from 5 August and 19 August 2016. The Insolvency and Bankruptcy Code (Amendment) Act, 2017 of Parliament received the assent of the President on the 18th January, 2018.

The bankruptcy code is a one stop solution for resolving insolvencies which at present is a long process and does not offer an economically viable arrangement. A strong insolvency framework where the cost and the time incurred is minimized in attaining liquidation has been long overdue in India. The code will be able to protect the interests of small investors and make the process of doing business a less cumbersome process. One of the essential business supporting element is a mechanism to settle failed or bankrupt entities without causing damage to any players in the economy. Continuation of financially non-viable businesses leads to locking of funds and physical assets. Similarly, it may lead to stress for the lender who have provided loan to the distressed business entity. For this, a bankruptcy code in the form of set of laws for the resolution of failed entities/individuals is needed.

What is Bankruptcy? Bankruptcy is a financial condition where a firm/individual is unable to repay debts to creditors. Under India's Insolvency and Bankruptcy Code 2016, a bankrupt entity is a debtor who has been adjudged as bankrupt by an adjudicating authority through passing a bankruptcy order.

Need for Bankruptcy Code: In every economy, there should be a legal procedure accompanied by institutions that collectively can resolve or settle the problems of failed institutions. An early resolution with sound principles will help the related parties like banks not to suffer from the failure of the business entity to whom they have provided a loan. Similarly, the Insolvency and Bankruptcy Procedures will help to ensure confidence of banks, foreign investors, and associated companies in crisis mitigation mechanism related to business entities in the country.

A situation where investable money locked for a long time in litigations is the least preferred situation for business partners and lenders. Use of the bankruptcy procedure also may help the failing entity to resolve its problems early without going to a worst case scenario.

Insolvency and Bankruptcy Code 2016: For establishing an insolvency regulation related to entities and individuals, the Parliament has enacted Insolvency and Bankruptcy Code 2016. The Code offers a uniform, comprehensive insolvency legislation encompassing all companies, partnerships and individuals (other than financial firms). For financial firms like banks, insolvency is a much delicate issue and for this a separate resolution regime will be enacted later.

The Code provides clear, coherent and speedy process for early identification of financial distress and resolution of entities if the underlying business is found to be viable. It suggests two options – a restructuring if the firm is viable and liquidation if it is not financially viable. Resolution should be done quickly and judiciously to ensure that business is not stuck.

The new code will replace existing bankruptcy laws and cover companies, limited liability partnerships, partnership firms, other corporate persons, and individuals, and any other body specified by the Government. There are Sick Industrial Companies Act, the Recovery of Debt Due to Banks and Financial Institutions Act, and Securitization and Reconstruction of Financial Assets and Enforcement of Security Interest Act, 2002 (SARFAESI). Besides, DRTs, Lok Adalats are also dealing with bankruptcy procedures. All these will be substituted/guided by the Insolvency and Bankruptcy Code on bankruptcy matters as it consolidates/improves the existing laws.

Features of Insolvency and Bankruptcy Code 2016: The Code specifies a timeframe 180 days after the process is initiated, plus a 90 days extension for resolving insolvency.

A major feature of the Code is that it creates a four pillars of institutional infrastructure for administering the bankruptcy procedure. These entities/agencies are:

1) **Insolvency and Bankruptcy Board of India:** is the regulator that will oversee the new entities.
2) **Insolvency Professionals:** will conduct the insolvency resolution process, take over the management of a company, assist creditors in the collection of relevant information, and manage the liquidation process,
3) **Insolvency Professional Agencies:** will examine and certify the insolvency professionals, and
4) **Information Utilities:** collect, collate and disseminate financial information related to debtors.

An important pre-requisite for the success of the code is the presence of sophisticated institutions and professionals who should facilitate the resolution procedure. Highly skilled insolvency professionals and matured institutions critical for making the entire process workable.

How insolvency procedures are conducted under the new law?

- As per the new law, when a loan default occurs, either the borrower or the lender approaches the NCLT or DRT (Debt Recovery Tribunal) for initiating the resolution process. The Code provides two options if a firm files insolvency: first is an Insolvency Resolution Process, during which creditors assess whether the debtor's financial position is viable for him to continue and if so, they have to search options for the rescue of the firm. The second option is liquidation.
- The adjudicating authority for insolvency issues of a Company/LLP is prescribed to be the NCLT and National Company Law Appellate Tribunal (NCLAT), and for individuals and partnership firms, it is the extant DRT and Debt Recovery Appellate Tribunal (DRAT).
- Next step is that creditors appoint an interim Insolvency Professional (IP) to take control of the debtor's assets and company's operations, collect financial information of the debtor from information utilities, and constitute the creditors' committee.
- Third step is that the committee has to then take decisions regarding insolvency resolution by a 66% majority. While the new IBC ordinance benefits home buyers, promoters will not really lose out. So long as the promoter is not a willful defaulter, he will still be given a fair chance of resolution rather than liquidation under CIRP. To provide a shot in the arm to promoters grappling with insolvency, the government has reduced the threshold of voting for all major decision of the committee of creditors to 66% from the earlier 75%. This too will encourage speedy resolution of insolvencies, in genuine cases.
- During the insolvency resolution period, the management of the debtor is placed in the hands of a resolution professional.
- Fourth step is that once the resolution is passed; the committee has to decide on the restructuring process through either a revised repayment plan or liquidation of the assets of the company. If no decision is made, the debtor's assets will be liquidated to repay the debt.
- The final step is that the resolution plan will be sent to the tribunal for final approval, and implemented once approved.
- The bankruptcy code has provisions to address cross-border insolvency through bilateral agreements with other countries.
- The Code proposes shorter time duration for the completion of insolvency process. Filing for bankruptcy has to be done in three months and other procedures like filing claims and appeals are also to be done quickly. The entire process will be completed within 180 days.

- Workers' interests are highly protected under the law. Here, the money due to workers and employees from the provident fund, the pension fund and gratuity fund shouldn't be included in the estate of the bankrupt company or individual. Similarly, in case of liquidation, workers' salaries for up to 24 months will get first priority, ahead of secured creditors.
- Anyone who was declared is not allowed to hold public office, and politicians and government officials cannot hold any public office if they are declared bankrupt.
- The Insolvency and Bankruptcy Code is thus a comprehensive and systemic reform that ensures speedy solution to insolvency and bankruptcy. Such a swift procedure will help creditors considerable as well as avoid distressed firms negatively affecting the economic and financial activities. The Code is big stride for ease of doing business in India.

Priority of Claims: The Code significantly changes the priority waterfall for distribution of liquidation proceeds. After the costs of insolvency resolution (including any interim finance), secured debt together with workmen dues for the preceding 24 months rank highest in priority. Central and state Government dues stand below the claims of secured creditors, workmen dues, employee dues and other unsecured financial creditors. Under the earlier regime, Government dues were immediately below the claims of secured creditors and workmen in order of priority.

CHEQUE TRUNCATION SYSTEM

Truncation is the process of stopping the flow of the physical cheque issued by a drawer at some point by the presenting bank en-route to the paying bank branch. In its place an electronic image of the cheque is transmitted to the paying branch through the clearing house, along with relevant information like data on the MICR band, date of presentation, presenting bank, etc. Cheque truncation thus obviates the need to move the physical instruments across bank branches, other than in exceptional circumstances for clearing purposes. This effectively eliminates the associated cost of movement of the physical cheques, reduces the time required for their collection and brings elegance to the entire activity of cheque processing.

Cheque Truncation in India: Cheque Truncation speeds up the process of collection of cheques resulting in better service to customers, reduces the scope of loss of instruments in transit, lowers the cost of collection of cheques, and removes reconciliation-related and logistics-related problems, thus benefitting the system as a whole.

With the other major products being offered in the form of RTGS and NEFT, the Reserve Bank has created the capability to enable inter-bank and customer payments online and in near-real time. However, cheques continue to be the prominent mode of payments in the country. Reserve Bank of India has therefore decided to focus on improving the efficiency of the cheque clearing cycle. Offering Cheque Truncation System (CTS) is a step in this direction.

In addition to operational efficiency, CTS offers several benefits to banks and customers, including human resource rationalization, cost effectiveness, business process re-engineering, better service, adoption of latest technology, etc. CTS, thus, has emerged as an important efficiency enhancement initiative undertaken by Reserve Bank in the Payments Systems arena.

Status of CTS Implementation in the Country: CTS has been implemented in New Delhi, Chennai and Mumbai with effect from February 1, 2008, September 24, 2011 and April 27, 2013 respectively. After migration of the entire cheque volume from MICR system to CTS, the traditional MICR-based cheque processing has been discontinued across the country.

Benefits of CTS to Customers of Banks: The benefits are many. With the introduction of imaging and truncation, the physical movement of instruments is stopped. The electronic movement of images can facilitate reduction in the clearing cycles as well. Moreover, there is no fear of loss of instruments in transit. Further, limitations of the existing clearing system in terms of geography or jurisdiction can be removed, thus enabling consolidation and integration of multiple clearing locations managed by different banks with varying service levels into a nation-wide standard clearing system with uniform processes and practices.

Under grid-based Cheque Truncation System clearing, all cheques drawn on bank branches falling within in the grid jurisdiction are treated and cleared as local cheques. No outstation cheque collection charges/Speed Clearing charges to be levied if the collecting bank and the paying bank are located within the jurisdiction of the same CTS grid even though they are located in different cities.

CTS also benefits issuers of cheques. The Corporates if needed can be provided with images of cheques by their bankers for internal requirements, if any.

CTS thus brings elegance to the entire activity of cheque processing and clearing. The benefits from CTS could be summarized as follows :

- Shorter clearing cycle;
- Superior verification and reconciliation process;
- No geographical restrictions as to jurisdiction;
- Operational efficiency for banks and customers alike;
- Reduction in operational risk and risks associated with paper clearing;
- No collection charges for collection of cheque drawn on a bank located within the grid.

CURRENCY-COUNTING MACHINE

A currency-counting machine is a machine that counts money—either stacks of banknotes or loose collections of coins. Counters may be purely mechanical or use electronic components. The machines typically provide a total count of all money, or count off specific batch sizes for wrapping and storage.

Currency counters are commonly used in vending machines to determine what amount of money has been deposited by customers.

In some modern automated teller machines, currency counters allow for cash deposits without envelopes, since they can identify which bills have been inserted instead of just how many. The user is given the chance to review the automatic counter's idea of the quantity and kinds of the inserted banknotes before the deposit is complete.

RuPay

The Indian market offers huge potential for cards penetration despite the challenges. RuPay Cards will address the needs of Indian consumers, merchants and banks. The benefits of RuPay debit card are the flexibility of the product platform, high levels of acceptance and the strength of the RuPay brand-all of which will contribute to an increased product experience.

Lower Cost and Affordability: Since the transaction processing will happen domestically, it would lead to lower cost of clearing and settlement for each transaction. This will make the transaction cost affordable and will drive usage of cards in the industry.

Customized Product Offering: RuPay, being a domestic scheme is committed towards development of customized product and service offerings for Indian consumers.

Protection of Information related to Indian Consumers: Transaction and customer data related to RuPay card transactions will reside in India.

Provide Electronic product options to untapped/ unexplored consumer segment: There are under-penetrated/untapped consumers segments in rural areas that do not have access to banking and financial services. Right pricing of RuPay products would make the RuPay cards more economically feasible for banks to offer to their customers. In addition, relevant product variants would ensure that banks can target the hitherto untapped consumer segments.

Inter-operability between payment channels and products: RuPay card is uniquely positioned to offer complete inter-operability between various payments channels and products. NPCI currently offers varied solutions across platforms including ATMs, mobile technology, cheques etc and is extremely well placed in nurturing RuPay cards across these platforms.

BHIM (BHARAT INTERFACE FOR MONEY)

BHIM is a mobile app developed by NPCI, based on the Unified Payment Interface (UPI) and was launched on 30 December 2016. It is intended to facilitate e-payments directly through banks and as part of the drive towards cashless transactions. BHIM allow users to send or receive money to other UPI payment addresses or scanning QR code or account number with IFSC code or MMID (Mobile Money Identifier) Code to users who do not have a UPI-based bank account. BHIM allows users to check current balance in their bank accounts and to choose which bank account to use for conducting transactions, although only one can be active at any time. Users can create their own QR code for a fixed amount of money, which is helpful in merchant transactions.

INNOVATIONS IN BRANCH BANKING THROUGH AI (ARTIFICIAL INTELLIGENCE) AND INTELLIGENT ROBOTIC ASSISTANT

As per latest RBI reports, AI (Artificial Intelligence) and robotics have the potential to transform data analytics and customer experience in banking. Until recently, application of robotics was unheard of in banking and was considered for application primarily in the manufacturing & medical sectors. With use of Intelligent Robotic Assistant (IRA), robotics are being brought into the mainstream of customer service and support. IRA is designed to assist branch staff in large branches, which have high footfalls, by guiding customers to carry out their banking transactions. AI is becoming an integral part of the banking system, functions, processes and customer interactions. Both Robotics and AI will help banks manage both internal and external customers much more effectively and help reduce operational costs exponentially in the future. The potential of AI and Robotics based solutions is enormous and will revolutionize the way people do banking.

TEST YOURSELF

1. The Insolvency and Bankruptcy Code, 2016 was introduced in Lok Sabha in December ______.
(a) 2014 (b) 2015
(c) 2016 (d) 2017

2. Bankruptcy is a financial condition where a ______ is unable to repay debts to creditors.
(a) firm (b) individual
(c) company (d) Any of the above

3. The adjudicating authority for insolvency issues of a ______ is prescribed to be the NCLT and National Company Law Appellate Tribunal (NCLAT).
(a) Company (b) LLP
(c) Partnership firms (d) Both 'a' and 'b'

4. The adjudicating authority for insolvency issues for individuals and partnership firms, it is the extant DRT and Debt Recovery Appellate Tribunal (DRAT).
(a) Individuals (b) LLP
(c) Partnership firms (d) Both 'a' and 'c'

5. Which is the regulator that will oversee the new entities?
(a) Insolvency and Bankruptcy Board of India
(b) Insolvency Professionals
(c) Insolvency Professional Agencies
(d) Information Utilities

6. Which agencies will examine and certify the insolvency professionals?
(a) Insolvency and Bankruptcy Board of India
(b) Insolvency Professionals
(c) Insolvency Professional Agencies
(d) Information Utilities

7. As per The Insolvency and Bankruptcy Code, 2016 the committee has to then take decisions regarding insolvency resolution by a ______ majority.
(a) 66% (b) 70%
(c) 75% (d) 80%

8. The Code proposes shorter time duration for the completion of insolvency process. Filing for bankruptcy has to be done in ______ and other procedures like filing claims and appeals are also to be done quickly.
(a) two months (b) three months
(c) nine months (d) twelve months

9. The entire process of The Insolvency and Bankruptcy Code, 2016 will be completed within ______
(a) 90 days (b) 120 days
(c) 180 days (d) 270 days

10. After the costs of insolvency resolution (including any interim finance), secured debt together with workmen dues for the preceding ______ rank highest in priority.
(a) 6 months (b) 12 months
(c) 24 months (d) 36 months

11. BHIM is a mobile app developed by NPCI, based on the ______ and was launched on 30 December 2016.
(a) UPI (b) Paytm
(c) Paypal (d) None of the above

12. The benefits of RuPay debit card are the flexibility of the product platform, high levels of acceptance. Find the benefits of RuPay:
(a) Lower cost and affordability
(b) Customized product offering
(c) Protection of information related to Indian consumers
(d) All of the above

13. Which is not used as a magnetic stripe card?
(a) Credit Card (b) Charge Card
(c) Electronic Purse (d) All of the above

14. The principle here is that a prepaid area is set aside to store electronic units of time or electronic tickets, etc., for a specific service or item is called:
(a) Electronic Cheque (b) Electronic Cash
(c) Electronic Token (d) Electronic Card

15. At present, by utilising remote banking facility, corporate customers will be able to get which of the following services:
(a) Getting their current balance or statement of accounts
(b) Opening letter of credits
(c) Ordering intra-bank and inter-bank fund transfers
(d) All of the above

16. Which are the benefits from CTS (Cheque Truncation Systems)?
(a) Shorter clearing cycle
(b) Superior verification and reconciliation process
(c) No geographical restrictions
(d) All of the above

ANSWER

1	2	3	4	5	6	7	8	9	10
(b)	(d)	(d)	(d)	(a)	(c)	(a)	(b)	(c)	(c)
11	**12**	**13**	**14**	**15**	**16**				
(a)	(d)	(d)	(c)	(d)	(d)				

MODULE–B

FUNCTIONS OF BANKS

BANKER-CUSTOMER RELATIONSHIP

INTRODUCTION

Relationship between a banker and customer comes into existence when the banker agrees to open an account in the name of customer. The relationship between a banker and a customer depends on the activities, products or services provided by bank to its customers or availed by the customer. Thus the relationship between a banker and customer is the transactional relationship. Bank's business depends much on the strong bondage with the customer. Trust plays an important role in building healthy relationship between a banker and customer.

Banking: The Banking Regulations Act 1949, Sec.5 (b) defines the term banking as "Banking means accepting, for the purpose of lending or investment, of deposits of money from the public repayable on demand or otherwise and withdrawable by cheque, draft, and order or otherwise."

Sec.5 (c) of BR Act defines "banking company" as a company that transacts the business of banking in India. Since a banker or a banking company undertakes banking related activities we can derive the meaning of banker or a banking company from Sec 5(b) as a body corporate that:

(a) Accepts deposits from public.
(b) Lends to the borrower or
(c) Invests the money so collected by way of deposits.
(d) Allows withdrawals of deposits on demand or by any other means.

Accepting deposits from the 'public' means that a bank accepts deposits from anyone who offers money for the purpose. Unless a person has an account with the bank, it does not accept deposit. For depositing or borrowing money there has to be an account relationship with the bank. A bank can refuse to open an account for undesirable persons. It is banks right to open an account. Reserve Bank of India has stipulated certain norms.

"Know Your Customer" (KYC) guidelines for opening account and banks have to strictly follow them. In addition to the activities mentioned in Sec. 5 (b) of B R Act, banks can also carry out activities mentioned in Sec. 6 of the Act.

DEFINITION OF CUSTOMER

The term Customer has not been defined by any act. In simple words a customer is such a person to whom you extend your services in return of consideration. A customer is a person who maintains an account with the bank without taking into consideration the duration and frequency of operation of his account. To be a customer for any bank the individual should have an account with the bank. The individual should deal with the bank in its nature of regular banking business.

Those who do not maintain any account relationship with the bank but frequently visit branch of a bank for availing banking facilities such as for purchasing a draft, encashing a cheque, etc. Technically they are not customers, as they do not maintain any account with the bank branch. The term 'customer' is used only with respect to the branch, where the account is maintained. He cannot be treated as a 'customer' for other branches of the same bank. However with the implementation of 'Core Banking Solution' the customer is the customer of the bank and not of a particular branch as he can operate his account from any branch of the bank and from anywhere. In the event of arising any cause of action, the customer is required to approach the branch with which it had opened account and not with any other branch.

As per 'Know Your Customer' guidelines issued by Reserve Bank of India, customer has been defined as:

a) A person or entity that maintains an account and/or has a business relationship with the bank;

b) One on whose behalf the account is maintained (*i.e.* the beneficial owner);

c) Beneficiaries of transactions conducted by professional intermediaries, such as Stock Brokers, Chartered Accountants, Solicitors etc. as permitted under the law, and

d) Any person or entity connected with a financial transaction, which can pose significant reputational or other risks to the bank, say, a wire transfer or issue of a high value demand draft as a single transaction.

BANKER-CUSTOMER RELATIONSHIP

It obviously means that to become a customer account relationship is must. Account relationship is a contractual relationship. Banking is a trust-based relationship. There are numerous kinds of relationship between the bank and the customer. The relationship between a banker and a customer depends on the type of transaction. Thus the relationship is based on contract, and on certain terms and conditions.

These relationships confer certain rights and obligations both on the part of the banker and on the customer. However, the personal relationship between the bank and its customers is the long lasting relationship. Some banks even say that they have generation-to-generation banking relationship with their customers.

Classification of Relationship: The relationship between banker and customer is of utmost importance. The relationship between a bank and its customers can be broadly categorized in to General Relationship and Special Relationship.

General Relationship

If we look at Sec 5(b) of Banking Regulation Act, we would notice that bank's business is accepting of deposits for the purposes of lending. Thus, the relationship arising out of these two main activities are known as General Relationship.

1. **Debtor and Creditor:** When a 'customer' opens an account with a bank, he fills in and signs the account opening form. By signing the form he enters into an agreement/contract with the bank. When customer deposits money in his account the bank becomes a debtor of the customer and customer a creditor. The money so deposited by customer becomes bank's property and bank has a right to use the money as it likes. The bank is not bound to inform the depositor the manner of utilization of funds deposited by him. Bank does not give any security to the depositor *i.e.,* debtor. The bank has borrowed money and it is only when the depositor demands, banker pays. Bank's position is quite different from normal debtors.

   While issuing Demand Draft, Mail / Telegraphic Transfer, bank becomes a debtor as it owns money to the payee/ beneficiary.

2. **Creditor and Debtor:** Lending money is the most important activities of a bank. The resources mobilized by banks are utilized for lending operations. Customer who borrows money from bank owns money to the bank. In the case of any loan/advances account, the banker is the creditor and the customer is the debtor. The relationship in the first case when a person deposits money with the bank reverses when he borrows money from the bank. Borrower executes documents and offer security to the bank before utilizing the credit facility.

Special Relationship

In addition to these two activities banks also undertake other activities mentioned in Sec.6 of Banking Regulation Act. In addition to opening of a deposit/loan account banks provide variety of services, which makes the relationship more wide and complex. Depending upon the type of services rendered and the nature of transaction, the banker acts as a bailee, trustee, principal, agent, lessor, custodian etc.

1. **Trustee and Beneficiary (Bank as a Trustee and Customer as a Beneficiary):** As per Sec. 3 of Indian Trust Act 1882, a "trust" is an obligation annexed to the ownership of property, and arising out of a confidence reposed in and accepted by the owner, or declared and accepted by him, for the benefit of another, or of another and the owner. Thus, trustee is the holder of property on behalf of a beneficiary.

   In case of trust, banker customer relationship is a special contract. When a person entrusts valuable items with another person with an intention that such items would be returned on demand to the keeper the relationship becomes of a trustee and trustier. Customers keep certain valuables or securities with the bank for safekeeping or deposits certain money for a specific purpose (Escrow accounts) the banker in such cases acts as a trustee. Banks charge fee for safekeeping valuables

2. **Bailee and Bailor (Bank-Bailee and Customer-Bailor):** Sec.148 of Indian Contract Act, 1872, defines "Bailment" "Bailor" and "Bailee". A "Bailment" is the delivery of goods by one person to another for some purpose, upon a contract that they shall, when the purpose is accomplished, be returned or otherwise disposed of according to the directions of the person delivering them. The person delivering the goods is called the "Bailor". The person to whom they are delivered is called, the "Bailee".

   Banks secure their advances by obtaining tangible securities. In some cases physical possession of securities goods (Pledge), valuables, bonds etc., are taken. While taking physical possession of securities the bank becomes bailee and the customer bailor. Banks also keeps articles, valuables, securities etc., of its customers in Safe Custody and acts as a Bailee. As a bailee the bank is required to take care of the goods bailed.

3. **Lessor and Lessee (Bank-Lessor and Customer-Lessee):** Sec.105 of 'Transfer of property Act 1882' defines lease, Lessor, lessee, premium and rent. As per the section "A lease of immovable property is a transfer of a right to enjoy such property, made for a certain time, express or implied, or in perpetuity, in consideration of a price paid or promised, or of money, a share of crops, service or any other thing of value, to be rendered periodically or on specified occasions to the transferor by the transferee, who accepts the transfer on such terms."

Definition of Lessor, lessee, premium and rent:

(1) The transferor is called the lessor,

(2) The transferee is called the lessee,

(3) The price is called the premium, and

(4) The money, share, service or other thing to be so rendered is called the rent.

Providing safe deposit lockers is as an ancillary service provided by banks to customers. While providing Safe Deposit Vault/locker facility to their customers' bank enters into an agreement with the customer. The agreement is known as "Memorandum of letting" and attracts stamp duty.

The relationship between the bank and the customer is that of lessor and lessee. Banks lease (hire lockers to their customers) their immovable property to the customer and give them the right to enjoy such property during the specified period *i.e.*, during the office/ banking hours and charge rentals. Bank has the right to break-open the locker in case the locker holder defaults in payment of rent. Banks do not assume any liability or responsibility in case of any damage to the contents kept in the locker. Banks do not insure the contents kept in the lockers by customers.

4. **Agent and Principal (Bank-Agent and Customer-Principal):** Sec. 182 of 'The Indian Contract Act, 1872' defines "an agent" as a person employed to do any act for another or to represent another in dealings with third persons. The person for whom such act is done or who is so represented is called "the Principal".

   Thus an agent is a person, who acts for and on behalf of the principal and under the latter's express or implied authority and the acts done within such authority are binding on his principal and, the principal is liable to the party for the acts of the agent.

   Banks collect cheques, bills, and makes payment to various authorities' viz., rent, telephone bills, insurance premium etc., on behalf of customers. Banks also abides by the standing instructions given by its customers. In all such cases bank acts as an agent of its customer, and charges for these services. As per Indian contract Act agent is entitled to charges. No charges are levied in collection of local cheques through clearing house. Charges are levied in only when the cheque is returned in the clearinghouse.

5. **Indemnity holder and Indemnifier (Bank-Indemnity holder and Customer-Indemnifier):** The dictionary meaning of the word Indemnity means 'security or protection against a loss or other financial burden'. As per Section 124 of the Indian Contract Act 1872 the definition of the Indemnity is as follows. *'A contract by which one party promises to save the other from loss caused to him by the contract of the promisor himself, or by the conduct of any other person, is called a "contract of indemnity".* Right of indemnity-holder is defined in Section 124 of the Indian Contract Act 1872. An indemnity is an obligation by a person to provide compensation for a particular loss suffered by another person. In case of banking, the relationship happens in

transactions of issue duplicate demand draft, TDR, deceased account payment etc. In that case indemnifier will compensate any loss arising from the wrong or excess payment. In these case bank is Indemnity Holder (Promisee) and customer is Indemnifier (Promisor).

6. **Hypothecator and Hypothecatee (Bank-Hypothecatee and Customer- Hypothecator)**: The relationship between customer and banker can be that of Hypothecator and Hypothecatee. This happens when the customer hypothecates certain movable or non-movable property or assets with the banker in order to get a loan. In this case, the customer became the Hypothecator, and the Banker became the Hypothecatee.

7. **Pledger and Pledgee (Bank-Pledgee or Pawnee and Customer-Pledger or Pawnor):** The relationship between customer and banker can be that of Pledger and Pledgee. This happens when customer pledges (promises) certain assets or security with the bank in order to get a loan. In this case, the customer becomes the Pledger or Pawnor, and the bank becomes the Pledgee or Pawnee. Under this agreement, the assets or security will remain with the bank until a customer repays the loan.

8. **Mortgagor and Mortgagee (Bank- Mortgagee and Customer- Mortgagor)**: As per section 58 of Transfer of Property Act 1882, mortgage is transfer of interest in specific immovable property for the purpose of securing the payment of money advanced or to be advanced by way of loan, an existing or future debt or the performance of an engagement which may give rise to pecuniary liability. The mortgagor only pats with the interest in the property and not the ownership. The transferor of interest in property, is called a mortgagor and the transferee is called a mortgagee. In this case, the customer became the Mortgagor, and the Banker became the Mortgagee.

9. **As a Custodian:** A custodian is a person who acts as a caretaker of something. Banks take legal responsibility for a customer's securities. While opening a D-Mat account bank becomes a custodian.

10. **As a Guarantor:** Banks give guarantee on behalf of their customers and enter in to their shoes. Guarantee is a contingent contract. As per Sec 31, of Indian contract Act guarantee is a "contingent contract". Contingent contract is a contract to do or not to do something, if some event, collateral to such contract, does or does not happen.

11. **Advisor and Client (Bank-Advisor and Customer-client):** When a customer invests in securities, the banker acts as an advisor. The advice can be given officially or unofficially. While giving advice the banker has to take maximum care and caution. Here, the banker is an Advisor, and the customer is a Client.

VARIOUS TYPES OF RELATIONSHIPS

Type of Transaction	*Bank*	*Customer*
Deposit in bank	Debtor	Creditor
Loan from bank	Creditor	Debtor
Safe Deposit vault (SDV Locker)	Lessor	Lessee
Safe Custody	Bailee	Bailor
Issue of Draft	Debtor	Creditor
Payee of a Draft	Trustee	Beneficiary
Collection of Cheque	Agent	Principal
Pledge	Pledgee (Pawnee)	Pledger (pawnor)
Mortgage	Mortgagee	Mortgagor
Hypothecation	Hypothecatee	Hypothecator
Sale/purchase of security on behalf of customer	Agent	Principal
Money deposited, but no instructions for its disposal	Trustee	Beneficiary
Article/Goods left by mistake by customer	Trustee	Beneficiary

Termination of relationship between a Banker and a Customer

It would thus be observed that banker customer relationship is transactional relationship. The relationship between a bank and a customer ceases on:

(a) The death, insolvency, lunacy of the customer;

(b) The customer closing the account *i.e.*, Voluntary termination;

(c) Liquidation of the company;

(d) The closing of the account by the bank after giving due notice;

(e) The completion of the contract or the specific transaction.

Various Deposit Products and Services

The main function of the banks are to mobilise deposit from public and lend that deposit to individual, firms and corporate institutions. Banks offers various types of deposit products which can be broadly classified as Demand Deposits and Term/Time Deposits. Difference between Demand Deposits and Term/Time Deposits are as follows.

Demand Deposits	***Term or Time Deposits***
Payable on demand	Fixed for a definite term or time.
Low interest or no interest paid. It also called CASA or Low cost deposit.	High rate of interest, Vary as per deposit tenure.
It includes SB deposit, Current Deposit, Unclaimed Deposit, Overdue TDR, Credit balance in CC and OD accounts.	It includes all term deposits includes RD, FDR for the period of Minimum 7 days to maximum 10 years.
Interest on savings account is calculated on a daily basis. Banks are free to pay interest half yearly or quarterly basis.	Generally, interest is compounding and payable quarterly.

Current Account

A current account is always a Demand Deposit and the bank is obliged to pay the money on demand. These deposits are the most liquid deposits and there are no limits for number of transactions or the amount of transactions in a day. Current Accounts are basically meant for businessmen and are never used for the purpose of investment or savings. Most of the current account are opened in the names of firm / company accounts. Cheque book facility is provided and the account holder can deposit all types of the cheques and drafts in their name or endorsed in their favour by third parties. No interest is paid by banks on these accounts. On the other hand, banks charges certain service charges, on such accounts.

Saving Accounts

These deposits accounts are one of the most popular deposits for individual accounts. These accounts not only provide cheque facility but also have a lot of flexibility for deposits and withdrawal of funds from the account. Savings deposits are subject to restrictions on the number of withdrawals as well as on the amounts of withdrawals during any specified period. From 25th October, 2011, RBI has deregulated Saving Fund account interest rates and now banks are free to decide the same within certain conditions imposed by RBI. Minimum balances may be prescribed in order to offset the cost of maintaining and servicing such deposits. Savings deposits are deposits that accrue interest at a fixed rate set by the commercial banks. The interest amount earned in savings account must be filed for Income Tax Returns as Income from other sources. But, TDS is not applicable for a savings account as per Section 194 A of IT Act. Savings Bank Account Interest amount exceeding ₹ 10,000 will be taxed at marginal tax rate of the concerned account holder. Under directions of RBI, now banks are also required to open Small accounts.

SMALL ACCOUNTS

A 'Small Account' means a savings account in which:

- The account should be considered as a normal banking service available to all;
- No requirement of minimum balance;
- The aggregate of all credits in a financial year does not exceed rupees one lakh;
- The aggregate of all withdrawals and transfers in a month does not exceed rupees ten thou-sand; and
- The balance at any point of time does not exceed rupees fifty thousand.
- Foreign remittances are not credited to a small account.

TERM DEPOSITS

Term deposits are fixed for a definite term. Minimum period as per RBI is 7 days. Maximum period as per

IBA is 10 years. Features of Term Deposits are as under:

- Accounts may be opened by individuals, firms or corporates.
- Term deposits receipts are not transferable.
- Amount is payable on maturity. The interest is cumulative on quarterly rests.
- Interest rate on term deposits is decided by Asset Liability Management Committee of the bank.
- If due date of term deposit is on a holiday, banks will make payment on next working day or thereafter and will pay the interest for the holiday to depositor at contracted rate irrespective of when the payment is taken.
- Depositor can request for addition or deletion of names in the deposit but at least one of the original depositors must remain. If loan has been raised against term deposit, name of a minor can be added only when loan has been adjusted.
- If interests paid on term deposit is more than ₹ 10000 or above in a financial year, TDS is deducted @10% if PAN is submitted and @20% if PAN is not submitted. If 15G/H along with PAN is submitted by individual, TDS will not be deducted by bank.
- As per Section 269 T of Income Tax Act, if the principal plus interest of term deposit is ₹ 20,000 or above, the payment should be made through credit to account or issuing account payee cheque or DD. It should not be paid in cash.
- In case of premature payment of FDR, penalty may be decided by the bank. Many banks has removed penal charge on premature closure of TDR. However, penalty cannot be charged in case of premature payment in case of death of depositor.
- In case of death of depositor, interest for overdue period will be paid at saving rate if depositor died after maturity date. If depositor dies before maturity of FDR, interest for overdue period will be paid at FD rate as on date of maturity for the period overdue amount remained with the bank.
- FDR can be renewed on due date even in the absence of FDR. It will be renewed for the period indicated by customer. If no period is indicated, it will be renewed for a term equal to the original term.
- Term deposits are classified into various schemes such as:
    a) Fixed Deposit (Interest payable every 6 months),
    b) Monthly Interest Deposit (Interest payable monthly),
    c) Quarterly Interest Deposit (Interest payable quarterly),
    d) Short-Term Deposits (Period of deposit minimum 7 days to less than one year)
    e) Recurring Deposit (Equal monthly installment deposited for minimum 6 months to maximum 120 months)
    f) Flexi Recurring Deposit (In addition to monthly installment (Core Deposit) an option to deposit excess amount as per bank's scheme during the stipulated tenure.

NON-RESIDENT EXTERNAL DEPOSIT ACCOUNTS

NRO, NR(E)RA and FCNR(B) Accounts: There are several kinds of accounts available for non-resident Indians, Persons of Indian Origin and Overseas Citizens of India. They are as follows:

Non-Resident Ordinary Accounts (NRO): NRIs can open Non-Resident Ordinary (NRO) deposit accounts for collecting their funds from local bonafide transactions. NRO accounts being Rupee accounts, the exchange rate risk on such deposits is borne by the depositors themselves. When a resident becomes an NRI, his existing Rupee accounts are designated as NRO. Such accounts also serve the requirements of foreign nationals resident in India. AD Category-I banks may permit foreign nationals who have come to India on employment and are eligible to open/hold a resident savings bank account to re-designate their resident account maintained in India as NRO account on leaving the country after their employment to enable them to receive their legitimate dues subject to certain conditions. NRO accounts can be maintained as current, saving, recurring or term deposits.

Non-Resident (External) Rupee Account- NRE Account: The Non-Resident (External) Rupee Account NR(E)RA scheme, also known as the NRE scheme, was introduced in 1970. Any NRI can open an NRE account with funds remitted to India through a bank abroad. This is a repatriable account and transfer from another NRE account or FCNR(B) account is also permitted. An NRE rupee account may be opened as current, savings or term deposit. Local payments can be freely made from NRE accounts. Since this account is maintained in Rupees, the depositor is exposed to exchange risk. NRIs/PIOs have the option to credit the current income to their Non-Resident (External) Rupee accounts, provided the authorised dealer is satisfied that the credit represents current income of the non-resident account holders and income-tax thereon has been deducted/provided for.

Foreign Currency Non-Resident Account- FCNR(B) Account: Foreign Currency Non-Resident Account Bank or FCNR (B) was first introduced in 1993. It replaced the existing FCNR (A) scheme. FCNR (B) accounts are maintained only in the form of term deposits of one to five years. Recurring Deposits are not being accepted under the Scheme. Repatriation of funds in foreign currencies is permitted. Transfer of funds from existing NRE accounts to FCNR (B) accounts and vice versa of the same account holder is permissible without prior approval of RBI. Earlier this account is opened by the NRIs in 6 designated currencies only, but Based on the recommendations of the Committee to Review the Facilities for Individuals under FEMA, 1999, Foreign Exchange Department (FED) has permitted banks to accept FCNR (B) deposits in any permitted currency with effect from October 19, 2011.

SERVICES TO CUSTOMERS AND INVESTORS

Some Banks also provides a comprehensive range of services to the corporate sector, besides augmenting revenue earning for the banks.

1. Merchant Banking: A merchant bank is a company that deals mostly in international finance, business loans for companies and underwriting. These banks are experts in international trade, which makes them specialists in dealing with multinational corporations.

Merchant Banking is a combination of Banking and consultancy services. It provides consultancy to its clients for financial, marketing, managerial and legal matters. Consultancy means to provide advice, guidance and service for a fee. It helps a businessman to start a business. It helps to raise (collect) finance. It helps to expand and modernize the business. It helps in restructuring of a business. It helps to revive sick business units. It also helps companies to register, buy and sell shares at the Stock exchange.

To illustrate the role of a merchant bank, suppose a multinational corporation XYZ is considering the purchase of a smaller company in another country. Company XYZ will likely solicit the services of a merchant bank for advice on how to best approach the acquisition process. In addition, the merchant bank may also assist in the financing of the acquisition, providing underwriting or loan services.

2. Lease Financing: Leasing has emerged as an important source of long term financing of the corporate enterprises during the recent few years. Lease financing is one of the important sources of medium- and long-term financing where the owner of an asset gives another person, the right to use that asset against periodical payments. The owner of the asset is known as lessor and the user is called lessee.

In other words, in a lease agreement the lessor, *i.e.*, the owner of the asset permits the lessee to use the asset for a specified payment but retains the title over the property. A lease thus is an agreement between the lessor and the lessee.

The lease agreement also sets forth the period covered by the lease, cancellation provisions, rental payments, additional rents or purchase options, allocations of maintenance and other expenses and other features of the agreement. Since leasing represents an alternative to ownership, leasing can be viewed as a Specialised means for generating funds. In exchange for the use of the asset the company can issue a claim against its future cash flows, long term debt equity or lease obligations. Viewed in this way leasing is strictly a financing decision. But it should also be remembered that it is not a way of avoiding financing.

It is financing because if the company chooses leasing instead of owning the asset by means of borrowing it incurs a contractual obligation to make payments of fixed amounts at specified times. The lease, therefore, is analogous to any other financial claim issued by the company. The important question is the cost of the lease in relation to other financing alternatives to register, buy and sell shares at the stock exchange.

TEST YOURSELF

1. The Banking Regulations Act 1949, Sec. 5 (b) defines the banking function are:
(a) Accepts deposits from public
(b) Lends to borrower
(c) Invests the money so collected by way of deposits
(d) All of the above

2. In deposit accounts, the relationship between bank and customer is:
(a) Debtor and Creditor
(b) Creditor and Debtor
(c) Trustee and Beneficiary
(d) Bailee and Bailor

3. When a bank lends money to the borrower, the relationship between bank and customer is:
(a) Debtor and Creditor
(b) Creditor and Debtor
(c) Trustee and Beneficiary
(d) Bailee and Bailor

4. Banker customer relationship comes to an end under which of the following circumstances?
(a) Death of the customer
(b) Insolvency of the customer

(c) Insanity of the customer
(d) All of the above

5. While taking physical possession of securities the bank becomes _______ and the customer _______.
(a) Bailee, Bailor (b) Bailor, Bailee
(c) Trustee, Beneficiary (d) Beneficiary, Trustee

6. If a TDR of a bank is lost by the customer, Which document required to be executed?
(a) Guarantee letter (b) Promissory note
(c) Indemnity letter (d) Agreement letter

7. Source of credit information are:
(a) Inspection to residence and business premises of applicant
(b) On interview with applicant and verification of documents submitted
(c) CIBIL report
(d) All of the above

8. Merchant bankers are _______.
(a) Financial brokers
(b) Financial intermediaries
(c) Credit appraisers
(d) Underwriters

9. The transferor of _______ in property, is called a mortgagor and the transferee is called a mortgagee.
(a) ownership (b) possession
(c) interest (d) All of the above

10. When a bank collects the cheque on behalf of a customer the relation between bank and customer is:
(a) Agent, Principal (b) Creditor and Debtor
(c) Trustee and Beneficiary (d) Bailee and Bailor

11. Term deposits are fixed for a definite term. Minimum period as per RBI is _______. Maximum period as per IBA is _______.
(a) 7 days, 20 years
(b) 14 days, 10 years
(c) 7 days, 10 years
(d) 14 days, No limit prescribed

12. Which is a type of term deposit?
(a) Monthly Interest Deposit
(b) Short-Term Deposits
(c) Flexi Recurring Deposit
(d) All of the above

13. Which is not a part of demand deposit?
(a) Savings account (b) Current Account
(c) Recurring Deposit (d) All of the above

14. A non-resident Indians can open which type of deposit account in foreign currency?
(a) NRO account (b) NR(E)RA account
(c) FCNR((B) Accounts (d) All of the above

15. Hybrid deposit means _______.
(a) Combination of SB and CD accounts
(b) Combination of Demand and Term deposit
(c) Combination of Monthly Income Scheme and Quarterly Income Scheme
(d) None of the above

16. Pragya deposits ₹ 10000 with the bank for remittance by way of tele graphic transfer for credit in Tanya's account at other city. The relationship between bank and customer is:
(a) Agent, Principal
(b) Debtor and Creditor
(c) Trustee and Beneficiary
(d) Bailee and Bailor

17. For a loan to be raised in case of need, a person assigns his insurance policy in favour of a bank, the relationship between bank and customer is:
(a) Agent, Principal
(b) Debtor and Creditor
(c) Trustee and Beneficiary
(d) Assignor and Assignee

18. When customer pledges (promises) certain assets or security with the bank in order to get a loan. In this case, the customer becomes the _______, and the bank becomes the _______.
(a) Pawnor, Pawnee
(b) Debtor and Creditor
(c) Trustee and Beneficiary
(d) Assignor and Assignee

19. Disadvantage to Leasing _______.
(a) Deprivation of asset ownership
(b) Deprivation of asset in case of default
(c) Attachment on owner going insolvent
(d) All of the above

20. A NRE account can be opened by _______.
(a) Foreign national only
(b) Foreign Institutional investors only
(c) NRI and Foreign national
(d) NRI and PIO

ANSWER

1	2	3	4	5	6	7	8	9	10
(d)	(a)	(b)	(d)	(a)	(c)	(d)	(b)	(c)	(a)
11	**12**	**13**	**14**	**15**	**16**	**17**	**18**	**19**	**20**
(c)	(d)	(c)	(c)	(b)	(b)	(d)	(a)	(d)	(d)

ANTI-MONEY LAUNDERING (AML) STANDARDS & KNOW YOUR CUSTOMER (KYC) NORMS

THE PREVENTION OF MONEY LAUNDERING ACT (PMLA), 2002

Introduction: Banks were advised to follow certain customer identification procedure for opening of accounts and monitoring transactions of a suspicious nature for the purpose of reporting it to appropriate authority. The Prevention of Money Laundering Act (PMLA), 2002 is an Act of the Parliament of India enacted in January, 2003. The Act along with the Rules framed has come into force with effect from 1st July, 2005. These 'Know Your Customer' guidelines have been revisited in the context of the Recommendations made by the Financial Action Task Force (FATF) on Anti Money Laundering (AML) standards and on Combating of Financing of Terrorism (CFT). PMLA (Amendment) Act, 2012 as passed by Lok Sabha on 29/11/2012 has come into force from 15th February 2013.

The Prevention of Money Laundering (Maintenance of Records) Rules 2005 have been amended vide Gazette Notification dated 1st June 2017 by Ministry of Finance.

Objective: The objectives of the Act are as under:

a) To prevent banks from being used, intentionally or unintentionally, by criminals for Money Laundering or terrorist financing activities;

b) To enable banks to know/ understand their customer and their financial dealings better;

c) To put in place a proper control mechanism for detecting and reporting suspicious transaction in accordance with the statutory and regulatory provision;

d) To enhance method for fraud Prevention;

e) To ensure compliance with guidelines issued by the regulators including FIU-IND & RBI.

Obligation under PML Act 2002: PMLA Act 2002 places certain obligation on every banking company, financial institution and intermediary, which include:

I. Appointment of Principal Officers. The Principal Officer shall be responsible for ensuring compliance, monitoring transactions, and sharing and reporting information as required under the law/regulations. The name, designation and address of the Principal Officer shall be communicated to the FIU-IND;

II. A "Designated Director" shall be nominated by the Board. The name, designation and address of the Designated Director shall be communicated to the FIU-IND;

III. Maintaining record of prescribed transactions;

IV. Furnishing information of transaction to the specified authority;

V. Verifying & maintaining record of the identity of its clients;

VI. Preserving records for 5 years from the date of each transaction between bank & clients or for 5 years after business relationship ended.

MONEY LAUNDERING

Definition of Money Laundering: Sec. 3 of PML Act defines 'money laundering' as: "whosoever directly or indirectly attempts to indulge or knowingly assists or knowingly is a party or is actually involved in any process or activity connected with the proceeds of crime and projecting it as untainted property shall be guilty of the offence of money-laundering". In India AML activities are monitored by FIU-IND as per PML Act. Any act or attempted act to conceal or disguise the identity of illegally obtained proceeds so that they appear to have originated from legitimate sources.

In other words, it is the process used by criminals through which they make "dirty" money appear "clean".

Punishment for Money-Laundering: Punishment for non-adherence of the Act would be rigorous imprisonment for not less than 3 years but up to 7 years. If in case of offences done under Narcotic Drugs and Psychotropic Substance Act 1985 the maximum punishment may extend to 10 years.

Combating the Financing of Terrorism (CFT) measures: Money to fund terrorist activities moves through the global financial system via wire transfers and in and out of personal and business accounts. It can sit in the accounts of illegitimate charities and be laundered through buying and selling securities and other commodities, or purchasing and cashing out insurance policies.

Before opening of the new account branches should ensure the name is not listed in the following list available on RBI website:-

I. The ISIL (Da'esh) & Al-Qaida Sanctions List
II. The 1988 Sanction List

Ways of Money Laundering

Stages of Money Laundering: The money laundering cycle can be broken down into three distinct stages; however, it is important to remember that money laundering is a single process. The stages of money laundering include the:

- **Placement**: Entry of funds in to the system at this stage, the launderer inserts the dirty money into a legitimate financial institution.
- **Layering**: Making a series of transactions to distance fund from the point of entry. Layering involves sending the money through various financial transactions to change its form and make it difficult to know.
- **Integration**: At the integration stage, the money re-enters the mainstream economy in legitimate-looking form. It appears to come from a legal transaction.

Other ways of money laundering: various ways of money laundering are as under:

- **Smurfing:** In banks, large cash transaction requires reporting. To avoid such reporting, large deposit are divided into multiple smaller transactions. After deposit, the smurfer purchases draft at other places which is deposited into other accounts.
- **Front Companies:** Front companies are used to place and layer illicit proceeds. A front company can be used to protect a parent company, thus concealing illegal activities.
- **Shell and Nominee Company:** Shell nominee companies are anonymous corporate structures that provide for anonymous ownership. These companies have various combination of nominee directors and ownership of stock by bearer shares. They do not have commercial manufacturing business.
- **Black salaries:** A company may have unregistered employees without a written contract and pay them cash salaries. Dirty money might be used to pay them.

Risk Perception in Money Laundering

Bank is exposed to the following risks:

- **Reputational Risk:** Risk of loss due to severe impact on bank's reputation which is most valuable asset of the organization.
- **Compliance Risk:** Risk of loss due to failure to comply with key regulations governing the bank's operations.
- **Operational Risk:** The risk of direct or indirect loss resulting from inadequate or failed internal processes, people and systems or from external events.
- **Legal Risk:** Risk of loss due to any legal action the bank or its staff may face due to failure to comply with the law resulting in adverse judgments, unenforceable contracts, fines and penalties, generating losses, increased expenses for an institutions or even closure of such institutions.

KNOW YOUR CUSTOMER

For the purpose of this policy, according to RBI guidelines, a 'Customer is defined as under:

I. A person or entity that maintains an account and/or has a business relationship with the bank;

II. One, on whose behalf the account is maintain (*i.e.,* the beneficial owner);

III. Beneficiaries of the transactions conducted by professional intermediaries, such as Stock Brokers, Chartered Accountants, Solicitors etc, as permitted by law; and

IV. Any person or firm or entity connected with a financial transaction.

Key Elements of KYC Policy

The key elements of policy are:

- **Customer Acceptance Policy (CAP)**
- **Risk Management (RM)**
- **Customer Identification Procedure (CIP)**
- **Monitoring of Transactions (TM)**

Customer Acceptance Policy (CAP)

Banks should develop clear customer acceptance policies and procedures for making relationship with customers, As per RBI guideline:

a. No account is opened in anonymous or fictitious/ benami name;

b. No account is opened where the bank is unable to apply appropriate CDD measures, either due to non-cooperation of the customer or non-reliability of the documents/information furnished by the customer;

c. No transaction or account based relationship is undertaken without following the CDD procedure;

d. The mandatory information to be sought for KYC purpose while opening an account and during the periodic updation, is specified;

e. 'Optional'/additional information, is obtained with the explicit consent of the customer after the account is opened;

f. Circumstances in which, a customer is permitted to act on behalf of another person/entity, is clearly spelt out;

g. Suitable system is put in place to ensure that the identity of the customer does not match with any person or entity, whose name appears in the sanctions lists circulated by Reserve Bank of India;

Customer Acceptance Policy shall not result in denial of banking/financial facility to members of the general public, especially those, who are financially or socially disadvantaged.

Risk Management

Customers shall be categorised as low, medium and high risk category, based on the assessment and risk perception of the banks.

Risk categorisation shall be undertaken based on parameters such as customer's identity, social/financial status, nature of business activity, and information about the clients' business and their location etc. While considering customer's identity, the ability to confirm identity documents through online or other services offered by issuing authorities may also be factored in.

Low Risk Category Customers:

- Individuals (other than High Net Worth/ NRI customer) have known source of fund;
- Salaried employee, whose salary structure is well defined;
- Pensioners, benefit recipients;
- People belonging to lower economic strata of society showing small balances;
- Govt. department and govt. owned companies, Regulators, Statutory Bodies etc;
- Customer with a long term and active business relationship;
- Customer other than High & Medium risk.

Medium Risk Customer:

- NBFC;
- Builders;
- Stock Brokers.

High Risk Customer:

- Nonresident customer;
- HNI, Non-face to face customer;
- Trust, Charities, NGOs;
- Sleeping Partner firms, Investment Company;
- Donation receiving organization, Religious institution;
- Shopping malls, Jewelers;
- Petrol pump, Liquor stores;
- Antique dealers, Arms dealer, Agent, Brokers, Bullion dealers;
- Politically Exposed Persons of foreign origin;
- Customer with dubious reputation etc.;
- Companies having close family share holding etc.;
- Person living in High Risk Countries.

Periodic updation shall be carried out at least once in every two years for high risk customers, once in every eight years for medium risk customers and once in every ten years for low risk customers.

Customer Identification Procedure (CIP)

Customer identification means undertaking client due diligence measures while commencing an account-based relationship including identifying and verifying the customer and the beneficial owner on the basis of one of the OVDs. Banks/FIs need to obtain sufficient information to establish, to their satisfaction, the identity of each new customer, whether regular or occasional, and the purpose of the intended nature of the banking relationship.

"Officially Valid Document" (OVD): The officially valid documents will serve the purpose for both identification of customer and also the address proof of customer.

'Officially Valid Document' (OVD) definition amended vide Gazette Notification dated 1st June 2017 by Ministry of Finance – the Permanent Account Number (PAN) Card; and the letter issued by the Unique Identification Authority of India have been removed from this definition. Now, these five documents are considered as officially valid documents:

1. Passport (within validity)
2. Driving License (within validity)
3. Voter's Identity Card
4. Job Card issued by NREGA
5. The letter issued by the National Population Register containing details of name, address or any other document as notified by the Central Government in consultation with the Regulator

The Government has since amended the Prevention of Money Laundering (Maintenance of Records) Rules, 2005 providing additional relaxations for the purpose of proof of address in addition to the relaxations in proof of identity under 'simplified measures' as contained in paragraph 2(d) of PML Rules. Thus, for the limited purpose of proof of address the following additional documents are deemed to be OVDs under 'simplified measures' for 'Low Risk Customer'.

1. Utility bill which is not more than two months old of any service provider (electricity, telephone, post-paid mobile phone, piped gas, water bill);
2. Property or Municipal Tax receipt;
3. Bank account or Post Office savings bank account statement;
4. Pension or family pension payment orders (PPOs) issued to retired employees by Government Departments or Public Sector Undertakings, if they contain the address;
5. Letter of allotment of accommodation from employer issued by State or Central Government departments, statutory or regulatory bodies, public sector undertakings, scheduled commercial banks, financial institutions and listed companies. Similarly, leave and license agreements with such employers allotting official accommodation; and
6. Documents issued by Government departments of foreign jurisdictions and letter issued by Foreign Embassy or Mission in India.

E-KYC: In order to reduce the risk of identity fraud, document forgery & paperless KYC verification, Unique Identification Authority of India (UIDAI) has launched its E-KYC service. The E-KYC service is accepted as a valid process for KYC verification under PMLA. While using E-KYC service of UIDAI, the individual user has to authorize the UIDAI, by explicit consent, to release his/her identity/ address through biometric authentication to the bank branch. The UIDAI then release the data name, age, gender, and photograph of the individual to bank. E-Aadhaar downloaded from UIDAI website may be accepted as an officially valid documents.

Walk-in Customers: In case of transactions carried out by a non-account based customer, that is a walk-in customer, where the amount of transaction is equal to or exceeds ₹ 50,000/- whether conducted as a single transaction or several transactions that appear to be connected, the customer's identity and address should be verified. However, if a bank has reason to believe that a customer is intentionally structuring a transaction into a series of transactions below the threshold of ₹ 50000 the bank should verify the identity and address of the customer and also consider filing a suspicious transaction report to FIU-IND.

Banks should ensure that any remittance of funds by way of demand draft, mail/telegraphic transfer or any other mode and issue of travelers' cheques for value of ₹ 50,000/- and above is effected by debit to the customer's account or against cheques and not against cash payment

Customer Due Diligence (CDD) means identifying and verifying the customer and the beneficial owner using 'Officially Valid Documents' as a 'proof of identity' and a 'proof of address'.

Documents needed for verification of various types of clients:

1. Individuals :

Where the client is an individual, who is eligible to be enrolled for an Aadhaar number, he shall for the purpose of sub-rule (1) submit to the reporting entity,—

(a) The Aadhaar number issued by the Unique Identification Authority of India; and

(b) The Permanent Account Number or Form No. 60 as defined in Income-tax Rules, 1962,

And such other documents including in respect of the nature of business and financial status of the client as may be required by the reporting entity:

Provided that where an Aadhaar number has not been assigned to a client, the client shall furnish proof of application of enrolment for Aadhaar and in case the Permanent Account Number is not submitted, one certified copy of an 'officially valid document' shall be submitted.

a) One certified copy of an 'officially valid document' containing of his identity &address

b) One recent photograph

Notwithstanding anything contained in sub-rules, an individual who desires to open a small account in a banking company may be allowed to open such an account on production of a self-attested photograph and affixation of signature or thumb print, as the case may be, on the form for opening the account:

Provided that the designated officer of the banking company, while opening the small account, certifies under his signature that the person opening the account has affixed his signature or thump print, as the case may be, in his presence;

2. Company:

a) Certificate of incorporation;

b) Memorandum and Articles of Association;

c) A resolution from the Board of Directors

d) Aadhaar numbers; and

e) Permanent Account Numbers or Form 60 as defined in the Income-tax Rules, 1962,

3. Partnership Firm:

a) Registration certificate;

b) Partnership deed; and

c) Aadhaar numbers; and

d) Permanent Account Numbers or Form 60 as defined in the Income-tax Rules, 1962,

4. Trust Documents:

a) Registration certificate;

b) Trust deed;

c) Aadhaar numbers; and

d) Permanent Account Numbers or Form 60 as defined in the Income-tax Rules, 1962,

5. Association of Persons:

a) Resolution of the managing body of such association or body of individuals;

b) Power of attorney granted to him to transact on its behalf;

c) Aadhaar numbers; and

d) Permanent Account Numbers or Form 60 as defined in the Income-tax Rules, 1962,

e) Information as may be required by the banking company or the financial institution or the intermediary to collectively establish the legal existence of such an association or body of individuals.

Partial freezing/closure of Non-KYC compliance account: In the case of non-compliance of KYC and/or undertaking Re-KYC exercise guideline account, RBI advised the bank to take the following steps:

1. Initially, a notice of 3 moths should be given for KYC compliance,
2. It should be followed reminder for further 3 months,
3. Thereafter, Partial freeze the debit and allowing credit only,
4. If partial freeze continue for 6 months and accounts are still non- KYC complaint, both credit and debit freeze and may be close the account.
5. Closer of account shall be approved by Branch Manager.
6. Reason for partial freeze and closure should be communicated to account holder.

Change of Address, Transfer of Account & Close Relative Address Proof: RBI has relaxed norms of furnishing address proof. Only one documentary proof of address (either current or permanent) may be submitted. In case of address proof mentioned as per 'Proof of Address' undergoes a change, fresh address proof may be submitted within a period of six months.

At the time of close relatives e.g. Wife, children & parents bank can obtain KYC documents of relative with whom the prospective customer living along with a declaration from the relative that the said person is staying with him/her.

Monitoring of Transactions

Bank has to monitor the transaction of its accounts and concerned report has to submit to FIU-IND periodically.

1) **Cash Transaction Report:** Cash transactions of above ₹ 10 lakhs or its equivalent in foreign currency. Series of cash transactions connected to each other, of below ₹ 10 lakhs or its equivalent in foreign currency within a month and the aggregate value of such doubtful transactions in cash or otherwise.

2) **Non-Profit Organisation:** The report of all transactions involving receipts by non-profit organizations of value more than rupees ten lakh or its equivalent in foreign currency should be submitted every month to the Director, FIU-IND by 15th of the succeeding month in the prescribed format.

3) **Suspicious Transactions Report (STR):** The Suspicious Transaction Report (STR) should be furnished within 7 days of arriving at a conclusion that any transaction, whether cash or non-cash, or a series of transactions integrally connected are of suspicious nature.

4) **Cross Boarder Wire Transfer (CBWT):** Bank has to submit to FIU-IND all Cross Boarder Wire Transfer (CBWT) for the value of more than five lakhs rupees or its equivalent in foreign currency either the origin or destination of funds in India.

5) **Counterfeit Currency Report (CCR):** Counterfeit Currency Report (CCR) to be submitted within 7 working days from the date of occurrence of transaction (Process same as STR). Branch to ZO 2 days. Up to 4 pieces FIR need not be filed. Instead a consolidated monthly statement is send to police with counterfeit current notes. For 5 pieces and above FIR has to be filed.

Transaction coverage	***Name of Report***	***Period***
Large Cash transaction of above ₹ 10 lakhs/month	CTR	Within 15 days of close of each month
Suspicious Transactions	STR	Within 7 days of confirmation of suspicion
Counterfeit Currency Notes	CCR	Within 7 days of detection
Cross Boarder Wire Transfer	CBWT	Within 15 days of close of each month
Non-Profit Organization report Receipt more than ₹ 10 lakhs	NPOTR	Within 15 days of close of each month

FINANCIAL INTELLIGENCE UNIT- INDIA

FIU-IND is a central agency. It is an independent body and report directly to the Economic Intelligence Council headed by Finance Minister. FIU-IND receives CTR, STR, CCR, NPOTR, CBWT reports. It analyzes information received by banks and suggests AML related crime. It monitors and identifies strategic key areas on AML trends, typologies & developments. The Director of FIU-IND is vested with the power of a civil court under the code of civil procedure. He has the power to seize, direct, penalize reporting entities and its employee for breach or violation of PML Act.

Money Mule: In a money mule transaction, an individual with a bank account is recruited to receive cheque deposits or wire transfers and then transfer these funds to accounts held on behalf of another person or to other individuals, minus a certain commission payment. When caught, they face legal action for being part of such fraud. Many a times the address and contact details of such mules are found to be fake or not up to date. Which makes it difficult to locate the Account Holder. RBI has desire that banks should strictly adhere to the guidelines on KYC/AML/CFT to avoid money mules.

CKYCR: Central KYC Registry is a centralized repository of KYC records of customers in the financial sector with uniform KYC norms and inter-usability of the KYC records across the sector with an objective to reduce the burden of producing KYC documents and getting those verified every time when the customer creates a new relationship with a financial entity.

CDD Procedure and sharing KYC information with Central KYC Records Registry (CKYCR): Banks shall capture the KYC information for sharing with the CKYCR in the manner mentioned in the Rules, as required by the revised KYC templates prepared for 'individuals' and 'Legal Entities' as the case may be. Government of India has authorised the Central Registry of Securitisation Asset Reconstruction and Security Interest of India (CERSAI), to act as, and to perform the functions of the CKYCR vide Gazette Notification No. S.O. 3183(E) dated November 26, 2015.

TEST YOURSELF

1. The Prevention of Money Laundering Act 2002 along with the Rules framed has come into force with effect from ________.
   (a) 1st July, 2002
   (b) 1st June, 2003
   (c) 1st July, 2005
   (d) 1st April, 2006

2. The objective of the PMLA 2002 is:
   (a) To prevent banks from being used, intentionally or unintentionally, by criminals for Money Laundering or terrorist financing activities.
   (b) To enable banks to know/ understand their customer and their financial dealings better.
   (c) To enhance method for fraud Prevention and to ensure compliance with guidelines issued by the regulators including FIU-IND & RBI.
   (d) All of the above

3. PMLA Act 2002 places certain obligation on every banking company, financial institution and intermediary, which include:
   (a) Appointment of Principal Officers. The Principal Officer shall be responsible for ensuring compliance, monitoring transactions, and sharing and reporting information as required under the law/regulations. The name, designation and address of the Principal Officer shall be communicated to the FIU-IND.
   (b) A "Designated Director" shall be nominated by the Board. The name, designation and address of the Designated Director shall be communicated to the FIU-IND. Maintaining record of prescribed transactions,
   (c) Verifying & maintaining record of the identity of its clients,
   (d) All of the above

4. As per PMLA Act 2002, preserving records for ________ from the date of each transaction between bank & clients or for 5 years after business relationship ended.
   (a) 3 years (b) 5 years
   (c) 8 years (d) 10 years

5. Which of the following is not correct statement as per PMLA 2002?
   (a) Sec.3 of PML Act defines 'money laundering'
   (b) In India AML activities are monitored by FIU-IND
   (c) Money Laundering is the process used by criminals through which they make "clean" money appear "dirty"
   (d) Money Laundering is defined as 'Any act or attempted act to conceal or disguise the identity of illegally obtained proceeds so that they appear to have originated from legitimate sources'

6. Punishment for non-adherence of the Act would be rigorous imprisonment for not less than ________ years but up to ________ years.
   (a) 3, 5 (b) 3, 7
   (c) 5, 7 (d) 5, 10

7. The money laundering cycle can be broken down into three distinct stages; the correct stages of money laundering are the:
   (a) Placement: Integration: Layering:
   (b) Layering: Placement Integration:
   (c) Placement: Layering: Integration
   (d) Integration: Layering: Placement

8. At the ________ stage, the money re-enters the mainstream economy in legitimate-looking form. It appears to come from a legal transaction.
   (a) Placement (b) Integration
   (c) Layering (d) Smurfing

9. In banks, large cash transaction requires reporting. To avoid such reporting, large deposit are divided into multiple smaller transactions. This process of money laundering is called:
   (a) Placement (b) Integration
   (c) Layering (d) Smurfing

10. All cash transaction of the value of more than ______ or its equivalent in foreign currency are covered by the act.
    (a) 5 lac (b) 10 lac
    (c) 20 lac (d) 50 lac

11. 'Officially Valid Document' (OVD) definition amended vide Gazette Notification dated 1st June 2017 by Ministry of Finance–the ________; and the letter issued by the ________ have been removed from this definition.
    (a) PAN Card, Aadhar
    (b) Driving license, Passport
    (c) Voter ID card, Ration card
    (d) PAN card, Passport

12. Which of the documents required compulsorily for opening of a Partnership Firm account
    (a) Registration certificate
    b) Partnership deed
    (c) Aadhaar numbers; and Permanent Account Numbers or Form 60
    (d) All of the above

13. Banks/FIs should introduce a system of maintaining proper record of transactions prescribed under Rule 3 of PML Rules, 2005. Those records are:
(a) All cash transactions of the value of more than Rupees Ten Lakhs or its equivalent in foreign currency within a month
(b) All transactions involving receipts by non-profit organisations of value more than rupees ten lakhs or its equivalent in foreign currency
(c) All cash transactions, where forged or counterfeit currency notes or bank notes have been used as genuine
(d) All of the above

14. Which types of risk is not involved with money laundering?
(a) Reputational Risk (b) Compliance Risk
(c) Credit Risk (d) Operational Risk

15. Which are the key elements of KYC policy?
(a) Customer Acceptance Policy (CAP)
(b) Risk management (RM)
(c) Customer Identification Procedure (CIP)
(d) All of the above

16. As per KYC policy, Bank has not to open account to following name:
(a) Anonymous name
(b) Fictitious name
(c) Political party
(d) Criminal background

17. Which is not categorised as Medium Risk Customer?
(a) NBFC (b) Bullion dealers
(c) Builders (d) Stock Brokers

18. Which is categorised as Low Risk Customer?
(a) Statutory Bodies
(b) Trust
(c) Charities
(d) Nonresident customer

19. The Director of FIU-IND is vested with the power of a ________ under the code of civil procedure.
(a) Civil Court (b) High Court
(c) Supreme Court (d) CBI Court

20. The Suspicious Transaction Report (STR) should be furnished within ________ of arriving at a conclusion that any transaction, whether cash or non-cash, or a series of transactions integrally connected are of suspicious nature.
(a) 3 days (b) 7 days
(c) 15 days (d) 30 days

ANSWER

1	2	3	4	5	6	7	8	9	10
(c)	(d)	(d)	(b)	(c)	(b)	(c)	(b)	(d)	(b)
11	**12**	**13**	**14**	**15**	**16**	**17**	**18**	**19**	**20**
(a)	(d)	(d)	(c)	(d)	(c)	(b)	(a)	(a)	(b)

BANKER'S SPECIAL RELATIONSHIP

INTRODUCTION

Normally, customer operates himself his bank account. There are many situations in one's life where an individual possessing properties, bank accounts, etc. may not be in a position to perform his duties due to reasons like being abroad, ill, old etc. In such situations if the transaction requires the presence of the individual who is not able to be present personally, then the only way out is to give the powers to act on behalf of the individual to another person. This is when a Power of Attorney deed is to be created. It is very common these days to give the powers to a trustworthy person to conduct the registrations, or sale or rent out etc. if you are busy with your other schedules.

For banking operation, the customer may authorise, for his convenience, an agent or nominee to operate on his account. Such an authority is given either by way of Mandate Letter or Power of Attorney. By mandate letter the particular banker is informed that certain powers have been delegated whereas a power of attorney acts as a general notice and authority.

MANDATE LETTERS

A letter of mandate is addressed by a customer to the bank informing that powers to operate the account (ordinary deposit account) have been delegated by the customer (the mandator) to a particular person (the mandatory). Such letters of mandate do not attract stamp duty.

As far as possible, branches should require customers to execute powers of attorney when they desire to authorise their agent or nominee to operate on their account on a more or less permanent basis. The procedure of obtaining mandate letters instead of powers of attorney should, as far as possible, be limited to operations on ordinary credit accounts.

POWER OF ATTORNEY

A Power of Attorney is a legal document by which one person gives the right to perform or powers of transacting in matters relating to property, banking, legal and judicial proceedings, tax payments, etc. to another person due to certain reasons like being out of country, or getting old, or not able to look after one's duties in those matters etc. A power of Attorney is an authority given by a written formal instrument whereby one person termed the donor or principal authorises another person termed the done, attorney or agent to act on his behalf.

Powers of Attorney on Bank Accounts: A power of attorney may be special or general. A special power of attorney authorises a person to act in a single transaction whereas authority to act in more than one transaction such as a bank account or generally, is a general power of attorney. The power of attorney is a stamped document. A power to operate an account will not include, by itself, a power to overdraw or borrow money. Authority or power to borrow by the attorney should definitely/explicitly be stated/embodied in the instrument. Drawing on an overdraft account is borrowing.

Types of Power of Attorney

Power of Attorney can be of mainly two type;

1. **General Power of Attorney:** A person can give to another person a complete general right or power to act lawfully with respect to his property or bank accounts or tax payments, or registration work or to sue a third party etc. It is commonly termed as General Power of Attorney.

Either you can give a General Power of Attorney for all your properties, banking transactions, tax matters, registration, legal disputes and court matters etc. or you can give a general power to any one category like only for all property matters or only for all Banking processes etc. This type of power is very wide and has lot of risk if the attorney is not a trustworthy person.

2. **Special Power of Attorney:** The other type of power granted is the special power which means it is granted for only a specific task or work. A special power of attorney is to be made by a person when any particular or specific task or act is to be done. Once the particular act is completed the special power of attorney comes to an end.

   This is generally used when you want to rent out your property or appear for the registration of any property or appear in a court on behalf of the Principal or to appear before the Tax authorities etc.

GARNISHEE ORDER

A Garnishee Order is an order issued by court under provisions of Order 21, Rule 46 of the Code of Civil Procedure, 1908. The bank upon whom the order is served is called Garnishee. The depositor who owes money to another person is called judgement debtor. Features of the Garnishee Order are as under;

- Garnishee Order applies to existing debts as also debts accruing due *i.e.*, SB/CD, RD/FD.
- Garnishee Order applies only to those accounts of Judgement Debtor which have credit balance.
- The relationship between bank and judgement debtor is of debtor and creditor. Bank is the debtor of Judgement Debtor who is a creditor of the bank.
- Garnishee Order does not apply to money deposited subsequent to receipt of Garnishee Order. It also does not apply to cheques sent for collection but yet to be realized. But if credit was allowed in the account before realization with power to withdraw to customer, Garnishee order will be applicable on this amount.
- Garnishee Order does not apply to unutilized portion of overdraft or cash credit account of the borrower as no debt is due to judgement debtor. For example, if limit is ₹ 4 crore and outstanding is debit ₹ 3 crore, Garnishee order is not applicable on the balance ₹ 1 crore.
- Bank can exercise right of set off before applying Garnishee Order.
- Garnishee Order is applicable only if both debts are in same right and same capacity.
- Garnishee Order issued in a single name does not apply to accounts in the joint names of judgement debtor with other person(s). But if Garnishee Order is issued in joint names, it will apply to individual accounts also of the same debtors. When Garnishee Order is in the name of a partner it will not apply to partnership account but when Garnishee Order is in the name of firm, accounts of individual partners are covered.
- If amount is not specified in the order, then it will be applicable on the entire balance in the account. However, if it is for specific amount, the cheques can be paid from the balance available after setting aside the amount as mentioned in the Garnishee Order.
- Not applicable on fixed deposits taken as security for some loan.
- If loan given against fixed deposits, applicable on the amount after adjusting the loan.

INCOME TAX ATTACHMENT ORDERS

Income Tax Authorities issue Attachment Orders in terms of Section 226(3) of Income Tax Act, 1961. On receipt of this order, banker is required to remit the desired amount to income tax authorities. Feature of the Attachment Orders are as under;

- An order without mentioning the amount is not a valid order.
- Attachment Order is different from Garnishee order in following respects (*a*) Attachment order applies to money deposited in the account after receipt of order also till it is fully satisfied whereas Garnishee order does not apply to subsequent deposits. (*b*) Attachment Order in single name applies to joint accounts also proportionately unless the contrary is proved whereas Garnishee order in single name does not apply to joint accounts. However, right of set off is available to bank before applying the order.
- In case banker fails to comply with Attachment Order, it will be liable for the amount of order and deemed as an assessee in default.
- When both Garnishee Order and Attachment Order are received simultaneously, priority should be given to Attachment Order.

BANKER'S RIGHT OF SET OFF

The right of set off is also called the right to combine Accounts. The banker can set off the balance or money in a Deposit Account against the debt due to him in an Advance Account of the customer, subject to the following:

(a) The debt due to the banker must be a sum certain due and recoverable at the date of set off. This means, a notice of demand calling upon the customer to repay the advance should be given before the right is exercised. The notice should state that on the failure of the borrower to repay the debt within the time stipulated, the Bank will take all or any of such steps for the recovery of the advance as the Bank is entitled under the security documents and law, including the exercise of its right of set off.

(b) If the customer has one account of his own money and another as Trustee, the banker cannot set off a credit balance in the Trust Account against the debit balance in his personal account.

(c) There should not be any agreement, express or implied, inconsistent with the right of set off.

(d) The creditor and the debtor should be one and the same person or one and the same set of persons. If the deposit account is in the names of A and B of whom only A is indebted to the Bank, no right of set off can be exercised.

LIEN

Lien is the right of one person to retain goods and securities in his possession belonging to another until certain legal debts due to the person retaining the goods are satisfied. In other words, it is the right of the creditor to retain the goods and securities in his possession, belonging to a debtor, until the debt due is paid.

Banker's lien: As a general rule, the right of lien does not give the person exercising the right, any power or right to sell or dispose of the securities retained. But in case of a bank, it is otherwise. A banker's lien is more than a general lien.

It is an implied pledge and the banker has a right to sell the property after reasonable notice, provide the property comes into his hands in the ordinary course of his business.

Section 171 of the contract act lays down that a banker's lien can be applied if:

- The property is in the hands of the banker in the capacity of his customer's bankers;
- The instruments of the money or goods with the banker are not for a specific purpose inconsistent with lien;
- The possession of the instruments has been obtained lawfully as a banker;
- There exists no implied or expressed agreement contrary to the lien.

RIGHT OF APPROPRIATION

Section 59, 60, 61 of Indian Contract Act, deal with appropriation of payments. If a customer maintains more than one account with a bank and he deposits some amount then he has the first right to indicate to which account the amount should be credited. If he does not exercise this right, then bank can credit the amount to any of his accounts including an account which is time barred by limitation.

Clayton's rule is related to appropriation of payments and is applicable in case of running borrowal accounts like cash credit or overdraft. This rule is applicable in case of death, insolvency, insanity of a joint borrower or partner or guarantor or retirement of a partner or revocation of guarantee by guarantor. As per Clayton's rule, credit entry will set off debits in the chronological order of time. This means that first item on the debit side will be discharged first by a credit and so on. For example in a firm's cash credit account, there was a debit balance of ₹ 5 lac when one of the partners died. The bank continued operations in the account. ₹ 4 lac were deposited and ₹ 3 lac were withdrawn. The estate of deceased partner is liable only for one lac *i.e.,* ₹ 5 lac minus ₹ 4 lac.

TEST YOURSELF

1. Charge created on paper securities such as Shares, debenture, bonds Mutual fund is:

(a) Hypothecation (b) Assignment
(c) Lien (d) Pledge

2. Lien is the ________ of one person to retain goods and securities in his possession belonging to another until certain legal debts due to the person retaining the goods are satisfied.

(a) right (b) interest
(c) obligation (d) instrument

3. A special power of attorney authorises a person to act in a ________ transaction.

(a) general (b) special
(c) single (d) multiple

4. Which is not a correct statements about Garnishee Order?

(a) Garnishee Order applies to existing debts as also debts accruing due i.e. SB/CD, RD/FD.
(b) Garnishee Order applies only to those accounts of Judgement Debtor which have credit balance.
(c) The relationship between bank and judgement debtor is of debtor and creditor. Bank is the debtor of Judgement Debtor who is a creditor of the bank.
(d) Bank cannot exercise right of set off before applying Garnishee Order.

5. Which is correct statements about Attachment Order?
(a) An order without mentioning the amount is not a valid order.
(b) In case banker fails to comply with Attachment Order, it will be liable for the amount of order and deemed as an assessee in default.
(c) When both Garnishee order and Attachment Order are received simultaneously, priority should be given to attachment order.
(d) All of the above

6. Particular lien gives the creditor right to retain ______ increase the expenses incurred is not valid.
(a) All goods (b) Specific goods
(c) Some goods (d) Ordered goods

7. The right of ______ is also called the right to combine Accounts.
(a) Set off (b) Lien
(c) Garnishee (d) Attachment

8. A Garnishee Order is an order issued by ______.
(a) Police officer (b) Court
(c) Revenue officer (d) CBI

9. Mandate is a ______ agreement.
(a) memorandum (b) stamped
(c) unstamped (d) letter

10. A power of attorney may be ______.
(a) Specific (b) General
(c) both (d) none

11. Attachment order is issued by ______.
(a) Court (b) Income Tax officer
(c) GST officer (d) Both (b) and (c)

12. A Garnishee Order is an order issued by court. The depositor who owes money to another person is called ______.
(a) Judgement debtor (b) Judgement creditor
(c) Garnishee (d) Garnisher

13. A mandate in a partnership account can be cancelled by:
(a) All the partners
(b) Any one of the partners
(c) Majority of the partners
(d) Court

14. A power of attorney can be registered with:
(a) Registrar of companies
(b) Registrar of firms
(c) Registrar of assurance (sub-Registrar)
(d) All of the above

15. A mandate is ______.
(a) A promise to pay a loan
(b) An authority of principal to his agent for operating the account
(c) An order of the banker to customer
(d) None

16. Before exercising its right of set-off, a banker is to see that:
(a) The amount of loan must be certain and due for payment
(b) Both the accounts must be in the same capacity
(c) There should be a contract to the contrary
(d) All of the above

17. Clayton's rule applies to the following type of loan accounts:
(a) Demand loans (b) Term loans
(c) Cash credit (d) All of the above

18. A sum of Rs. 50000 is lying in the account of a deceased customer and attachment order has been received:
(a) Attachment order will not be applicable
(b) Attachment order will apply after legal heir's consent
(c) Attachment order will be applicable
(d) Attachment order will be returned

19. Section 171 of the contract act lays down that a banker's lien can be applied if:
(a) The property is in the hands of the banker in the capacity of his customer's bankers
(b) The instruments of the money or goods with the banker are not for a specific purpose inconsistent with lien;
(c) The possession of the instruments has been obtained lawfully as a banker;
(d) All of the above

20. If a customer maintains more than one account with a bank and he deposits some amount then he has the first right to indicate to which account the amount should be credited. This right is called:
(a) Power of Attorney (b) Right of Set-off
(c) Lien (d) Right of Appropriation

ANSWER

1	2	3	4	5	6	7	8	9	10
(c)	(a)	(c)	(d)	(d)	(b)	(a)	(b)	(c)	(c)
11	**12**	**13**	**14**	**15**	**16**	**17**	**18**	**19**	**20**
(d)	(a)	(b)	(c)	(b)	(d)	(c)	(c)	(d)	(d)

CONSUMER PROTECTION ACT (COPRA), BANKING OMBUDSMAN SCHEME

INTRODUCTION

An Act to provide for better protection of the interests of consumers and for that purpose to make provision for the establishment of consumer councils and other authorities for the settlement of consumers' disputes and for matters connected therewith.

CONSUMER PROTECTION ACT (COPRA)

The Consumer Protection Act (COPRA) was initially enacted in 1986 and implemented from April 15, 1987. A comprehensive amendment (The Consumer Protection (Amendment) Act 2002) has been passed on Dec 17, 2002 (implemented effective from March 15, 2003, the 'World Consumer Rights Day'). Further, it was amended in 2011 as 'The Consumer Protection (Amendment) Bill, 2011'. It extends to the whole of India except the State of Jammu and Kashmir.

Consumer Protection Council

To promote and protect the right of the consumers, councils are established. Their scope is not regarding directly dealing with the consumer complaints at initial or appellate scope but to promote and protect the rights of consumer.

1. Central Consumer Protection Council: The Central Government has established a council known as the Central Consumer Protection Council, called the Central Council. The Central Council consist of the following:

a) The Minister-In-charge of the Consumer Affairs in the Central Government shall be the Chairman of the council, and

b) Such member of other official or non-official members representing such interests as may be prescribed.

The Central Council shall meet as and when necessary but at least once in a year.

2. State Consumer Protection Council: The State Government has established a council known as the State Consumer Protection Council, called the State Council. The State Council consist of the following:

a) The Minister-In-charge of the Consumer Affairs in the State Government shall be the Chairman of the council,

b) Such member of other official or non-official members representing such interests as may be prescribed by the State Government, and

c) Such member of other official or non-official members not exceeding ten as may be nominated by Central Government.

The State Council shall meet as and when necessary but at least twice in a year.

3. District Consumer Protection Council: The State Government has established a council known as the District Consumer Protection Council in every district, called the District Council. The District Council consist of the following:

a) The Collector of the District shall be the Chairman of the council,

b) Such member of other official or non-official members representing such interests as may be prescribed by the State Government, and

The State Council shall meet as and when necessary but at least twice in a year.

Definition of a Consumer

Consumer means any individual who:

1. Buys any goods for a consideration which has been paid or promised or partly paid and partly promised; or
2. Hires or avail of any services for a consideration which has been paid or promised or partly paid and partly promised, or under any system of deferred payment;
3. Includes any user of such goods other than the person who buys such goods or hires of any services for consideration paid; or
4. Promised or partly paid or partly promised, or under any system of deferred payment, when such use is made with the approval of such person.

Who is not a Consumer?

1. Person buying goods for resale;
2. Person buying goods for any commercial purpose;
3. Person receiving goods/services free or gifts;
4. Person enjoying personal service under a contract (service by employees/maid servants) etc.

Coverage: All goods and services including banking, insurance, transport, processing, electricity, professional such as physicians etc. in private, public and cooperative sectors are covered under this Act. All banking services are covered due to their being essential services.

Who can file a Complaint? A consumer (individually or jointly) himself or through any voluntary consumer Organisation, Central or State Governments can file a complaint. Limitation period is 2 years from the date of cause of action *i.e.* purchase of goods/hiring of services.

Procedure for file a Complaint: A simple written complaint in duplicate with full name and address of opposite party narrating facts of the complaint along with copies of the supporting documents and details of relief sought. No Court Fee is charged. Engaging of Lawyer is not necessary. Consumer or anyone can represent his case.

Consumer can fill his Complain in the following Consumer Forum:

1) **District Forum:** A Consumer Disputes Redressal Forum to be known as the "District Forum" established by the State Government in each district of the State by notification. Subject to the other provisions of this Act. The District Forum shall have jurisdiction to entertain complaints where the value of the goods or services and the compensation, if any, claimed does not exceed ₹ 20 lakh.

   Each District Forum shall consist of a person who is, or has been, or is qualified to be a District Judge, who shall be its President and two other members, one of whom shall be a woman. Every member of the District Forum shall hold office for a term of 5 years or up to the age of 65 years, whichever is earlier.

2) **State Commission:** Each State Commission shall consist of a person who is or has been a Judge of a High Court, appointed by the State Government, who shall be its President and not less than two, and not more than such number of members, as may be prescribed, and one of whom shall be a woman. They will be not less than thirty-five years of age. Every member of the State Commission shall hold office for a term of 5 years or up to the age of 67 years, whichever is earlier.

3) **National Commission:** The National Commission shall consist of a person who is or has been a Judge of the Supreme Court, to be appointed by the Central Government, who shall be its President and not less than four, and not more than such number of members, as may be prescribed, and one of whom shall be a woman. They will be not less than thirty-five years of age.

Forum	*Claim amount*	*Office Structure*
District Forum	Up to ₹ 20 lakh	Headed by President (qualified to be a District Judge) & 2 other members (1 Woman).
State Commission	More than ₹ 20 lakh up to ₹ 100 lakh	Headed by President (has/had been High Court Judge) & 2 other members (1 Woman). They will be not less than thirty-five years of age.
National Commission	Above ₹ 100 lakh	Headed by President (has/had been Judge of Supreme Court) & 4 members (1 Woman). They will be not less than thirty-five years of age.

Relief by COPRA: If, after the proceeding conducted the Forumis satisfied about the complaint, it shall issue an order to the opposite party directing him:

- To remove the defect pointed out from the goods;
- To removal of deficiencies in services;
- To replacement by new goods free from defects;
- To refund of price/ charges etc.;
- To pay such amount as may be awarded by it as compensation to the consumer for any loss or injury suffered by the consumer, due to the negligence of the opposite party;

Penalty: Penalty for non-compliance of order is imprisonment for not less than one month and up to 3 years/fine not less than ₹ 2,000/- and up to ₹ 10,000/- or both.

If the complaint is found to be of frivolous nature, fine up to ₹ 10,000/- or imprisonment for not less than one month but up to 3 years.

Appeal: Any person aggrieved by an order made by the District Forum may appeal against the order to the State Commission within 30 days from the date of order in all cases. Appeal to State Commission against the award of District Forum will be accepted after Deposit amount is 50% of the Claim amount or ₹ 25,000/- whichever is less.

Any person aggrieved by an order made by the State Commission may appeal against the order to the National Commission within 30 days from the date of order in all cases. Appeal to National Commission against the award of State Commission will be accepted after Deposit amount is 50% of the Claim amount or ₹ 35,000/- whichever is less.

Any person aggrieved by an order made by the National Commission may appeal against the order to the Supreme Court within 30 days from the date of order in all cases. Appeal to Supreme Court against the award of National Commission will be accepted after Deposit amount is 50% of the Claim amount or Rs. 50,000/- whichever is less.

Time limits for disposal - Endeavour is made to decide the complaint within the following time frame:

A : Admissibility of the complaint from date of receipt of the complaint: within 21 days.

B : Decision on complaint: Without analysis or testing of commodities: 3 months

C : With analysis or testing of commodities: 5 months

Action	*Time*
Admission of complaint from the date of receipt of the complaint.	21 days
Disposal without analysis or testing of commodities	3 months
Disposal analysis or testing of commodities	5 months
Disposal should be done at State/National Commission	3 months
Decision should be taken on Appeals for admission/rejection	90 days

BANKING OMBUDSMAN SCHEME

Introduction: For the improvement of customer service in banking industry, RBI has provided a platform to customer for redressal of banking related dispute. RBI notified the Banking Ombudsman Scheme 2006 u/s 35A of Banking Regulation Act 1949. The scheme came into force effective from 01st Jan 2006. It covers all commercial banks, RRB's & scheduled primary Co-operative Banks. Presently the Banking Ombudsman Scheme 2006 (As amended up to July 1, 2017) is in operation.

Objective: The Scheme is introduced with the object of enabling resolution of complaints relating to certain services rendered by banks and to facilitate the satisfaction or settlement of such complaints. Resolution of complaints relating to banking services through conciliation & mediation between the bank and the aggrieved parties or by passing an award.

Eligibility of Ombudsman: The Reserve Bank may appoint one or more of its officers in the rank of Chief General Manager or General Manager for maximum period not exceeding 3 Years at a time.

Location of Office: The office of the Banking Ombudsman shall be located at such places as may be specified by the Reserve Bank. At present, twenty Banking Ombudsmen have been appointed with their offices located mostly in state capitals. All costs of the office are borne by RBI.

Jurisdiction: The Reserve Bank shall specify the territorial limits to which the authority of each Banking Ombudsman. A person makes a complaint to the Banking Ombudsman within whose jurisdiction the branch or office of the bank complained against is located. For Credit card, the jurisdiction is with reference to ombudsman having jurisdiction over the billing address of the card holder. For other accounts, it is as per location of the branch.

Grounds of Complaint

Any person may file a complaint with the Banking Ombudsman having jurisdiction on any one of the rounds alleging deficiency in banking services including internet banking or other services.

Procedure for Filing Complaint: Any person who has a grievance against a bank on any one or more of the grounds mentioned in the Scheme may, himself or through his authorised representative (other than an advocate), make a complaint on paper or through electronic media (e-mail), or forwarded by RBI or Central Govt. to the Banking Ombudsman.

The complaint in writing shall be duly signed by the complainant or his authorized representative and shall be, as far as possible, in the form specified in Annexure 'A' or as near as thereto as circumstances admit, stating clearly:

I. The name and the address of the complainant;

II. The name and address of the branch or office of the bank against which the complaint is made;

III. The facts giving rise to the complaint;

IV. The nature and extent of the loss caused to the complainant; and

V. The relief sought for.

Conditions for Complaint:

- Complain was made to the Bank and Bank had rejected or no reply was received within a month or complainant is not satisfied with the reply given by the bank;
- The complaint is made not later than one year after the complainant has received the reply of the bank to his representation or, where no reply is received, not later than one year and one month after the date of the representation to the bank; Complaint is not for issues already settled by ombudsman or for which proceeding before court or any other forum is pending or a decree or order has been passed;
- The complaint is not frivolous or vexatious in nature;
- The complaint is within limitation period under Indian limitation Act 1963.

Process of Redressal of Grievance: Banking Ombudsman sent a copy of the complaint to the bank and endeavour shall-be made for a settlement by agreement through conciliation or mediation. The proceedings shall be summary in nature.

Award by the Ombudsman: Where a complaint is not settled by agreement within a period of one month from the date of receipt of the complaint, Ombudsman may pass an Award or reject the complaint, on the basis of evidence, the principles of banking law and practice, directions and guidelines issued by RBI.

Amount of Award: Award shall specify the amount, to be paid by bank as compensation, not more than actual loss suffered as direct consequence of act of omission or commission of the bank or ₹ 20 lac (As amended up to July 1, 2017, earlier it was ₹ 10 lac), whichever is lower.

The Banking Ombudsman may award compensation not exceeding ₹ 1 lakh to the complainant for mental agony and harassment. The Banking Ombudsman will take into account the loss of the complainant's time, expenses incurred by the complainant, harassment and mental anguish suffered by the complainant while passing such award.

Effect of award: A copy of the Award shall be sent to the complainant and the bank. An award shall lapse and be of no effect unless the complainant furnishes to the bank concerned within a period of 30 days from the date of receipt of copy of the Award, a letter of acceptance of the Award in full and final settlement of his claim. The bank shall, unless it has preferred an appeal within one month from the date of receipt by it of the acceptance in writing of the Award by the complainant, comply with the Award and intimate compliance to the Banking Ombudsman.

Implementation: Customer has to send acceptance of the award within 30 days of date of receipt of the award. Bank is to implement the award within one month from the date of receipt of the acceptance from the complainant and intimate compliance to the Banking Ombudsman.

Rejection of the Complaint: If it frivolous, malafide or without sufficient cause or there is no loss or damage or inconvenience caused to the complainant or is beyond the pecuniary jurisdiction of ombudsman.

Appeal: Customer can appeal to appellate authority within 30 days of receipt of rejection to Dy. Governor RBI. Customer or bank can file the appeal to appellate authority (Dy. Governor RBI) against the award or decision of the Banking Ombudsman rejecting the complaint within 30 days of the date of receipt of the Award. Provided further that appeal may be filed by a bank only with the prior sanction of the Chairman or, in his absence, the Managing Director or the Executive Director or the Chief Executive Officer or any other officer of equal rank.

TEST YOURSELF

Consumer Protection Act (COPRA)

1. A comprehensive amendment (The Consumer Protection (Amendment) Act 2002) has been passed on Dec 17, 2002 implemented effective from March 15, 2003. The day March 15 is celebrated as:
(a) World Consumer Day
(b) World Consumer Rights Day
(c) India Consumer Rights Day
(d) COPRA establishment day

2. The objectives of the Consumer Protection Act (COPRA) is to promote and protect the rights of the consumers such as:
(a) The right to be protected against the marketing of goods and services which are hazardous to life and property
(b) The right to be informed about the quality, quantity, potency, purity, standard and price of goods or services, as the case may be so as to protect the consumer against unfair trade practices
(c) The right to consumer education
(d) All of the above

3. As per Consumer Protection Act (COPRA), Consumer means any individual who?
(a) Buys any goods for a consideration which has been paid or promised or partly paid and partly promised, or
(b) Hires or avail of any services for a consideration which has been paid or promised or partly paid and partly promised, or under any system of deferred payment and,
(c) Promised or partly paid or partly promised, or under any system of deferred payment. when such use is made with the approval of such person,
(d) All of the above

4. As per Consumer Protection Act (COPRA), who is not a consumer?
(a) Person buying goods for resale, or Person buying goods for any commercial purpose.
(b) Person receiving goods/services free or gifts.
(c) Person enjoying personal service under a contract (service by employees/maid servants)
(d) All of the above

5. As per Consumer Protection Act (COPRA), which are covered under this Act:
(a) All goods and services including banking & insurance,
(b) Professional such as physicians etc.
(c) All of the above
(d) None of the above

6. Consumer Protection Act has been enacted in bank with which of the following main objectives:
(a) Protection of interest of banks
(b) Protection of interest of consumers that include bank customers also
(c) Create tribunals to deal with bank recovery purpose
(d) All of the above

7. As per Consumer Protection Act (COPRA), who can file a complaint?
(a) A consumer (individually or jointly) himself
(b) Through any voluntary consumer Organisation,
(c) Through Central or State Governments can file a complaint.
(d) All of the above

8. For filling a complaint under COPRA, Limitation period is ________ from the date of cause of action i.e. purchase of goods/hiring of services.
(a) 2 years (b) 1 years
(c) 6 months (d) No time limitation

9. Which is the correct statement about COPRA?
(a) A simple written complaint in duplicate with full name and address of opposite party narrating facts of the complaint along with copies of the supporting documents required.
(b) Prescribed Court Fee is charged.
(c) Engaging of Lawyer is necessary.
(d) All of the above

10. The terms 'goods' as per COPRA means which of the following ________.
(a) Movable and immovable property
(b) Actionable claim
(c) Goods as stated in Indian Contract Act
(d) Goods as stated in Sale of Goods Act

11. Consumer can fill his complain in which the following consumer forum?
(a) District Forum
(b) State Commission
(c) National Commission
(d) All of the above

12. Which is the correct statement about consumer forums?
(a) Complain can be filled at District Forum, if claimed does not exceed ₹ 20 lakh.
(b) Complain can be filled at State Commission, if claimed does not exceed ₹ 20 lakh but up to ₹ 50 lac
(c) Complain can be filled at National Commission, if claimed exceed ₹ 50 lakh
(d) All of the above

13. Under Consumer Protection Act, the Central Government has established a council known as:
(a) National Commission
(b) State Commission
(c) Central Consumer Protection Council
(d) All of the above

14. Who acts as the chairman of State Consumer Protection Council?
(a) The Minister-In-charge of the Consumer Affairs in the Central Government
(b) The Minister-In-charge of the Consumer Affairs in the State Government
(c) Secretary of the Consumer Affairs in the State Government
(d) Chief Justice of High Court

15. Who makes the appointment the member of District Forum?
(a) Supreme Court (b) High court
(c) State Govt. (d) Central Govt.

16. Which of the following is correct with regard to term of office of the member of district forum?
(a) 3 years or up to age of 60 years
(b) 3 years or up to age of 65 years
(c) 5 years or up to age of 60 years
(d) 5 years or up to age of 65 years

17. On receipt of complaint by district forum and after a direction to the opposite party, it is to submit its version within _____.
(a) 15 days (b) 30 days
(c) 45 days (d) 60 days

18. If, after the proceeding conducted the Forum is satisfied about the complaint, it shall issue an order to the opposite party directing him:
(a) To remove the defect pointed out from the goods, or to removal of deficiencies in services,
(b) To replacement by new goods free from defects, or to refund of price/ charges etc.
(c) To pay such amount as may be awarded by it as compensation to the consumer for any loss or injury suffered by the consumer, due to the negligence of the opposite party;
(d) All of the above

19. Penalty for non-compliance of order of the forum is _____.
(a) Imprisonment for not less than one month and up to 3 years/fine not less than ₹ 2,000/- and up to ₹ 10,000/- or both.
(b) Imprisonment for not less than one month and up to 2 years/fine not less than ₹ 2,000/- and up to ₹ 10,000/- or both.
(c) Imprisonment for not less than one month and up to 3 years/fine not less than ₹ 5,000/- and up to ₹ 10,000/- or both.
(d) Imprisonment for not less than one month and up to 3 years/fine not less than ₹ 2,000/- and up to ₹ 100,000/- or both.

20. Any person aggrieved by an order made by the State Commission may appeal against the order to the National Commission within 30 days from the date of order in all cases. Appeal to National Commission against the award of State Commission will be accepted after Deposit amount is _____.
(a) 50% of the Claim amount or ₹ 25,000/- whichever is less.
(b) 50% of the Claim amount or ₹ 35,000/- whichever is less.
(c) 50% of the Claim amount or ₹ 50,000/- whichever is less.
(d) 25% of the Claim amount or ₹ 35,000/- whichever is less.

ANSWER

1	2	3	4	5	6	7	8	9	10
(b)	(d)	(d)	(d)	(c)	(b)	(d)	(a)	(a)	(d)
11	**12**	**13**	**14**	**15**	**16**	**17**	**18**	**19**	**20**
(d)	(a)	(a)	(b)	(c)	(d)	(b)	(d)	(a)	(b)

Banking Ombudsman Scheme

1. RBI notified the Banking Ombudsman Scheme 2006 u/s __________.
(a) 34A of Banking Regulation Act 1949
(b) 35A of Banking Regulation Act 1949
(c) 34A of RBI Act 1934
(d) 35A of RBI Act 1934

2. The scheme came into force effective from ______.
(a) 01st Jan 2006 (b) 01st April 2006
(c) 01st Jan 2007 (d) 01st April 2007

3. Banking Ombudsman Scheme 2006 covers:
(a) Commercial banks
(b) RRB's
(c) Scheduled primary Co-operative Banks
(d) All of the above

4. The Reserve Bank may appoint one or more of its officers in the rank of __________
(a) Chief General Manager
(b) General Manager
(c) Dy. Governor
(d) Either 'a' or 'b'

5. The Reserve Bank may appoint one or more of its officers for maximum period not exceeding ______ at a time.
(a) 3 Years (b) 4 Years
(c) 5 Years (d) 6 Years

6. All costs of the Banking Ombudsman office are borne by ________.
(a) State Bank of India
(b) All Commercial banks of the area
(c) RBI
(d) All Commercial Banks & RRB of the area

7. Which is correct statement about Jurisdiction of Banking Ombudsman? A person makes a complaint to the Banking Ombudsman within whose jurisdiction?
(a) For Credit card, the jurisdiction is with reference to ombudsman having jurisdiction over the billing address of the card holder.
(b) For other accounts, it is as per location of the branch.
(c) For other accounts, it is as per location of the administrative office of the bank
(d) Both 'a' and 'b'

8. Which is correct about grounds of Complaint for Banking Ombudsman?
(a) Non-payment or inordinate delay in the payment or collection of cheques, drafts, bills etc.;
(b) Failure to provide or delay in providing a banking facility (other than loans and advances) promised in writing by a bank or its direct selling agents;
(c) Delays, non-credit of proceeds to parties' accounts, non-payment of deposit or non-observance of the Reserve Bank directives
(d) All of the above

9. Any person who has a grievance against a bank on any one or more of the grounds mentioned in the Scheme may, make a complain __________.
(a) Himself
(b) Through his authorised representative
(c) Through an advocate
(d) Either 'a' or 'b'

10. Which is correct statement about complaint at Banking Ombudsman?
(a) Any person who has a grievance makes a complaint by on paper to the Banking Ombudsman.
(b) Any person who has a grievance makes a complaint through electronic media (e-mail) to the Banking Ombudsman.
(c) Any person who has a grievance makes a complaint forwarded by RBI or Central Govt. to the Banking Ombudsman.
(d) All of the above

11. Who is the appellate authority for Banking Ombudsman under the scheme?
(a) Dy. Governor of RBI (b) Governor of RBI
(c) High court (d) Supreme court

12. Conditions for complaint at Banking Ombudsman under the scheme is:
(a) Complain was made to the Bank and Bank had rejected or no reply was received within a month or complainant is not satisfied with the reply given by the bank.
(b) The complaint is made not later than one year after the complainant has received the reply of the bank.
(c) Complaint is not for issues already settled by ombudsman or for which proceeding before court or any other forum is pending or a decree or order has been passed.
(d) All of the above

13. The maximum amount of the banking ombudsman award as compensation is:
(a) ₹ 5 lac (b) ₹ 10 lac
(c) ₹ 20 lac (d) No limit

14. Which is the major amendment in 2017 in Banking Ombudsman Scheme 2006?

(a) The maximum amount of the award as compensation increased from ₹ 5 lac to ₹ 10 lac
(b) The maximum amount of the award as compensation increased from ₹ 10 lac to ₹ 20 lac
(c) The maximum amount of the award as compensation increased from ₹ 5 lac to ₹ 20 lac
(d) None of the above

15. The Banking Ombudsman may reject a complaint at any stage if it appears to him that the complaint made is:

(a) That it is not pursued by the complainant with reasonable diligence
(b) Requiring consideration of elaborate documentary and oral evidence and the proceedings before the Banking Ombudsman are not appropriate for adjudication of such complaint
(c) In the opinion of the Banking Ombudsman there is no loss or damage or inconvenience caused to the complainant.
(d) Any of the above

16. What is the limitation period for filling an appeal against the order of Banking Ombudsman?

(a) 30 days (b) 45 days
(c) 60 days (d) 90 days

17. The Banking Ombudsman may award compensation not exceeding ________ to the complainant for mental agony and harassment.

(a) ₹ 1 lac (b) ₹ 5 lac
(c) ₹ 10 lac (d) ₹ 20 lac

18. Appeal against the order of banking ombudsman may be filed by a bank only with the prior sanction of the ________ or any other officer of equal rank.

(a) Chairman (b) MD or CEO
(c) ED (d) Any of the above

19. Customer and bank have to send acceptance of the award within ________ of date of receipt of the award.

(a) 15 days (b) 30 days
(c) 60 days (d) 90 days

20. Bank is to implement the award within ________ from the date of receipt of the acceptance from the complainant and intimate compliance to the Banking Ombudsman.

(a) One-month
(b) Three-month
(c) Six-month
(d) Decided by Banking Ombudsman

ANSWER

1	2	3	4	5	6	7	8	9	10
(b)	(a)	(d)	(d)	(a)	(c)	(d)	(d)	(d)	(d)
11	**12**	**13**	**14**	**15**	**16**	**17**	**18**	**19**	**20**
(a)	(d)	(c)	(b)	(d)	(a)	(a)	(d)	(b)	(a)

PAYMENT & COLLECTION OF CHEQUES AND OTHER NEGOTIABLE INSTRUMENTS

NEGOTIABLE INSTRUMENTS

Introduction: In India, the Negotiable Instruments Act was passed during 1881 which came into force from March 01, 1882. It extends to the whole of India. According to Section 13 (a) of the Act, Negotiable Instruments means Promissory Note (PN), Bill of Exchange (BOE) and Cheque. Cheque is the primary instrument for banking transaction. Banker has a statutory obligation to make payment of a cheque drawn on an account, if cheque is otherwise in order and there is sufficient balance in the account.

Different types of Negotiable Instruments: Following negotiable instruments are defined under NI Act.

1. Promissory Notes: Section 4 of the Act defines, "A promissory note is an instrument in writing (note being a bank-note or a currency note) containing an unconditional undertaking, signed by the maker, to pay a certain sum of money to or to the order of a certain person, or to the bearer of the instruments." Example- If A writes "I promise to pay B or order ₹ 5000".

An instrument to be a promissory note must possess the following elements:

a) It must be in writing;
b) It must certainly an express promise or clear understanding to pay a certain sum of money;
c) The promise should be to pay money and money only;
d) Promise to pay must be unconditional;
e) It should be signed by the maker;
f) The maker & Payee must be certain.

2. Bill of Exchange: Section 5 of the Act defines, "A bill of exchange is an instrument in writing containing an unconditional order, signed by the maker, directing a certain person to pay a certain sum of money only to, or to the order of a certain person or to the bearer of the instrument".

A bill of exchange, therefore, is a written acknowledgment of the debt, written by the creditor and accepted by the debtor. There are usually three parties to a bill of exchange drawer, acceptor or drawee and payee. Drawer himself may be the payee.

For example, Mahesh directed to Ramesh for payment of ₹ 1000 to Suresh "I shall be highly obliged if you make it convenient to pay ₹ 1000 to Suresh".

Essential conditions of a bill of exchange;

a) It must be in writing;
b) It must be signed by the drawer;
c) The drawer, drawee and payee must be certain;
d) The sum payable must also be certain;
e) It should be properly stamped;
f) It must contain an express order to pay money and money alone.

3. Cheques: Section 6 of the Act defines "A cheque is a bill of exchange drawn on a specified banker, and not expressed to be payable otherwise than on demand".

A cheque is bill of exchange with two more qualifications, namely,

a) It is always drawn on a specified banker, and

b) It is always payable on demand.

Consequently, all cheque are bill of exchange, but all bills are not cheque. A cheque must satisfy all the requirements of a bill of exchange; that is, it must be signed by the drawer, and must contain an unconditional order on a specified banker to pay a certain sum of money to or to the order of a certain person or to the bearer of the cheque. It does not require acceptance.

Parties to Bill of Exchange or a Cheque:

- **Drawer:** The maker of a bill of exchange or a cheque is called the 'drawer'.
- **Drawee:** The person directed to pay the money by the drawer is called the 'drawee',
- **Payee:** The person named in the instrument, to whom or to whose order the money is directed to be paid by the instrument is called the 'payee'. He is the real beneficiary under the instrument.
- **Endorser:** When the holder transfers or endorses the instrument to anyone else, the holder becomes the 'endorser'.
- **Endorsee:** The person to whom the bill is endorsed is called an 'endorsee'.
- **Holder:** A person who is legally entitled to the possession of the negotiable instrument in his own name and to receive the amount thereof, is called a 'holder'. He is either the original payee, or the endorsee. In case the bill is payable to the bearer, the person in possession of the negotiable instrument is called the 'holder'.
- **Holder in Due Course:** Defined in Section 9 of the NI Act. Holder in due course is a person who became possessor of a NI for valuable consideration, in good faith, before becoming due, and without having any reason to believe that the person transferring the instrument was not entitled thereto. If before the amount mentioned in it became payable, and without having sufficient cause to believe that any defect existed in the title of the person from whom he derived his title.

Presentation for Acceptance: As per Section 61, a usance bill payable after sight and bills payable on a fixed date (and not demand bills) require to be presented to drawee for acceptance to make him liable and also for calculation of due date.

Negotiation: When a promissory note, bill of exchange or cheque is transferred to any person so as to constitute that person the holder thereof, the instrument is said to be negotiated.

Negotiation of a Bearer Instruments: A bearer instrument is negotiated by mere delivery and no endorsement is required.

Negotiation of an Order Instrument: An order instrument can be negotiated by endorsement followed by delivery. It may be noted that legal heirs cannot complete the negotiation of a negotiable instrument with endorsement by the deceased merely by delivery.

ENDORSEMENT OF CHEQUES

Signing of an instrument on the back or on a slip of paper annexed thereto for the purpose of negotiation is called endorsement (Section 15). The person who transfers the instrument is called endorser and the person to whom it is transferred is called endorsee. Various types of endorsements are as under:

a) **Blank Endorsement**: In a blank endorsement the endorser just signs his name without indicating endorsee. It can be converted into full by writing name of a person above signatures. The effect of an endorsement in blank is that it makes an instrument drawn originally payable to order to bearer instrument for the purpose of negotiation which can be further negotiated by mere delivery.

b) **Endorsement in Full:** When, the endorser indicates the name of the endorsee it is called full endorsement.

c) **Sans Recourse Endorsement:** An endorsement in which endorser excludes his liability is termed 'sans recourse' or 'without recourse' endorsement. In case of dishonour of instrument, the amount cannot be recovered from such endorser.

d) **Facultative:** An endorsement in which endorser waives the notice of dishonour is called Facultative endorsement, but this is not applicable to other parties to the instrument.

e) **Restrictive Endorsement**: An endorsement which restricts further right of negotiation is called as restrictive endorsement. For example if it is written in the endorsement as "Pay to Hari for my use" it is restrictive endorsement.

f) **Conditional Endorsement:** When along with endorsement, condition is imposed by endorser. For example, pay to C on completion of studies. Paying bank not to ensure compliance of condition. Condition binds endorser and endorsee only.

g) **Back to Back Endorsement**: An endorsement in which the endorser himself becomes endorsee is called as back to back endorsement and in such a case, the endorsee can recover the amount only from parties prior to his own endorsement.

h) **Negotiation Back:** When the drawer of a cheque himself becomes endorsee, it is called "Negotiation Back" and this cheque is treated as satisfied.

i) **Partial Endorsement**: The endorsement can be made only for full amount but in case part payment has been received and a note to that effect is made on the instrument, then the same can be endorsed for the balance amount.

j) **Forged Endorsement:** When endorsement is made by a person other than Holder by forging signatures of Holder Title does not pass to any person on the basis of such endorsement. A person getting instrument after such endorsement does not become holder.

k) **Regularity of Endorsement:** Paying bank gets protection u/s 85(1) only when endorsement is regular (may not be genuine).

CROSSING OF THE CHEQUES

General Crossing

Where a cheque bears across its face an addition of the words "& company" or any abbreviation thereof, between two parallel transverse lines, or of two parallel transverse lines simply, either with or without the words "not negotiable," that addition shall be deemed a crossing, and the cheque shall be deemed to be crossed generally.

The effect of general crossing of the cheque is that the same should not paid over the counter and only paid through a bank account only.

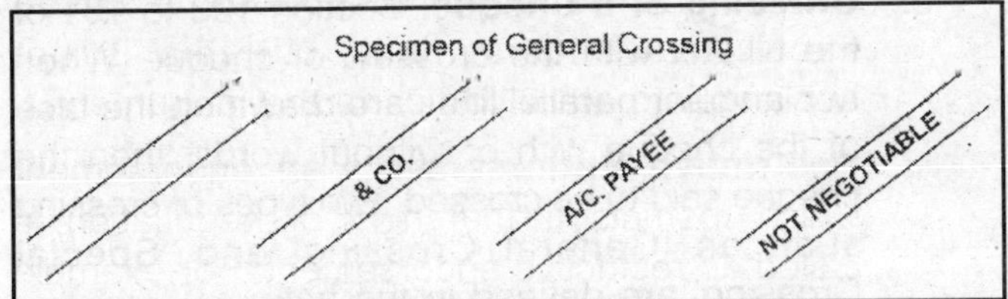

Special Crossing

If the cheque bears across its face, in addition of the crossing, the name of the banker, the cheque is deemed to have been crossed specially to that banker.

The effect of this crossing is that, the proceeds of the cheque should be paid only to that banker. Because of this reason, the banks put the crossing stamp on the cheques received by them for collection.

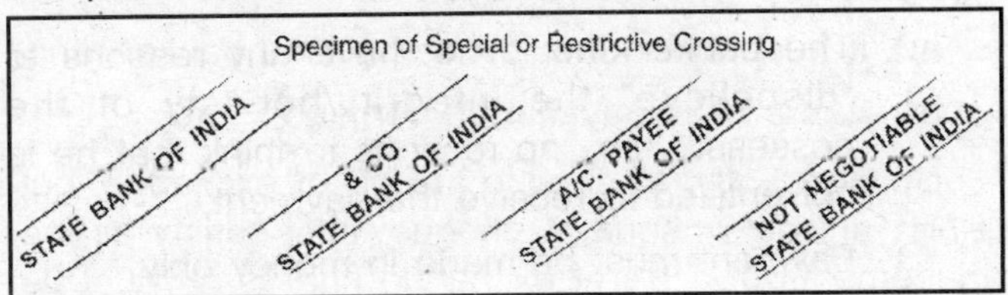

Not Negotiable Crossing: The type of crossing would remove the negotiable characteristic of the instrument and the transferee cannot have a better title than what the transferor had. Section 130 of the NI Act define that "A person taking a cheque crossed generally or specially, bearing in either case the words "not negotiable," shall not have, and shall not be capable of giving, a better title to the cheque than that which the person from whom he took it had."

Account Payee Crossing: In order to add more protection, to the cheque sometimes the word like "A/c Payee" or "Payee's A/c only" are added to the crossing. This type of crossing has not been provided for the Negotiable Instrument Act but it is a practice widely followed. These words constitute a direction to the collecting bank to collect proceeds in the payee's account only and such instruction do not take away characteristic of negotiability.

Crossing after Issue of the Cheque:

- If the cheque is not crossed, the holder of the cheque may cross it either generally or specially;
- If the cheque is crossed generally, the holder may cross it specially;
- The holder may add the words "Not Negotiable" to the crossing.

Protection only for Crossed Cheque: Protection is not available for an un-crossed cheque. Hence it is always advisable for banker to cross all cheques paid in for collection.

Payment in due Course: As per Section 10 of N.I. Act 'payment in due course means payment according to the apparent tenor of the instrument in good faith and without negligence to any person in possession thereof under circumstances which do not afford a reasonable ground for believing that he is not entitled to receive payment of the amount therein mentioned'.

Section 85 of NI Act conditions to be satisfied for being a payment in due course.

- Payment is in accordance with the apparent tenor of the instrument;
- Payment must be in good faith and Without negligence;

- Payment must be made to the person in possession of the instrument;
- The banker should not have any reasons to "disbelieve" the integrity/honesty of the possessor, *i.e.,* no reasons to think that he is not entitled to receive the payment;
- Payment must be made in money only.

PAYING BANKER

Duty of the Paying Banker: The implied duty of a paying banker, however, is dependent on certain other important condition. Conditions for honouring customer cheques are as under:

1. **The Cheque must be in the Proper Form:** It must be satisfying the condition specify in the Negotiable Instrument Act. As per Section 6, a cheque is a bill of exchange drawn on a specified banker and not expressed to be payable otherwise than on demand. It includes electronic image of truncated cheque and also an electronic cheque. RBI decided to prescribe certain benchmark towards achieving standardization of cheques known as 'CTS-2010 standard' specification. No changes/correction should be carried out on the CTS cheques (other than for date validation purpose, if required) for the any change in payee's name; amount etc, fresh cheque forms should be used by customers.
2. **Drawer's Signature must tally with the Specimen Signature:** In the case of drawer's signature do not tally with the ones on bank record, the banker should obtain fresh set of signatures and should not pay the cheques on which the signatures are different from the bank's record.
3. **The Cheque must not be either Stale or Postdated:** The cheque must be present within the validity period. After the validity period cheque becomes stale cheque, it cannot be paid. As per RBI direction u/s 35A, Banking Regulation Act, validity of the cheque, demand draft and banker's cheque will be valid for 3 months with effect from April 01, 2012. After a cheque becomes stale, it can be revalidated any number of times. A postdated cheque is one which bears date later than which the cheque actually drawn. If cheque is undated, holder can fill the date. A cheque bearing the date prior to actual date of signing or opening of account is called antedated cheque, which is valid and can be paid till it becomes stale.
4. **Sufficient Fund available in Account:** The banker is bound to pay the cheque drawn by his customer. There should be sufficient credit balance available or up to drawing limit which is given by the banker in the customer's account. The fund available in the customer's account should also be properly available for the payment of the cheque. The funds may not be available to pay the cheque if:-
   a) The banker has exercised his right of set off for amounts due from the customer or
   b) There is an attachment order from court, Income Tax officer or any other lawful authority restraining the bank from paying the money.
5. **The amount expressed in word and figure should be matched:** The amount expressed in cheque differ in word and figure, it should not be paid and return with mark 'word and figure differ'. However, Section 18 of NI Act provides that where there is a difference between the amount in words and the amount in figures, the amount in words is the amount payable.
6. **If mutilated cheque is presented for payment:** A cheque is mutilated when it has been cut or torn or a part of it is missing. Mutilation may be accidental or intentional. When it is accidental, the banker should get the drawer's confirmation before honouring it. If it is intentional, banker should refuse payment with mark 'mutilated cheque' or 'mutilation required confirmation'.
7. **The Cheque must be properly Endorsed:** In the case of bearer cheque, endorsement is not applicable. In the case of an order cheque, endorsement may be done. An order cheque may be made payable to the bearer by an endorsement in blank. Only a regular endorsed order cheque should be honoured by banker.
8. **Crossing of a Cheque**: Section 123 to 131 of the NI Act with the crossing of cheque. When two angular parallel lines are drawn on the face of the cheque with or without words, then the cheque said to be crossed. Two types of crossing such as 'General Crossing' and 'Special Crossing' are defined in the act.
9. **Inchoate Instruments**: As per Section 20 of the NI Act, an instrument on which date, payee or amount is not mentioned is called as inchoate or incomplete instrument. Incomplete cheque can be completed by the Holder and the completion so made will not be treated as material alteration. An instrument without signatures is not treated as an instrument at all.

10. **Ambiguous Instruments:** Where the instrument is drawn in such a manner that it can be construed both as PN or BE.

 In the following cases, the instrument is taken as ambiguous;

 a) Where drawer and drawee are the same person.

 b) Where drawee is a fictitious person. Eg. Lord Krishna etc

 c) Where drawee is a person incapable of entering into a contract.

Liability of the Paying Banker: A banker justify to refuge payment of a cheque drawn on him in certain circumstances. A banker's obligation to honour the customer's cheques is terminated on the happening of any of the following events:

1. If banker received a notice from the customer to stop payment of a cheque in writing;
2. Notice of the customer's death;
3. Notice of the customer's insanity;
4. Notice of the customer's bankruptcy;
5. Knowledge of any defect in the title of the person presenting the cheque;
6. Notice of a Garnishee Order/Attachment Order.

Banker's liability in case of wrongful Dishonour: Before dishonouring a cheque on the ground of customer's credit not being sufficient, or with the remark that the customer has "insufficient fund", the banker should be careful. In this case banker would be liable, if step taken by him proves to be erroneous.

Payment of a forged Cheque: A cheque with the forged signature of a drawer must not be paid by a banker. The payment of such cheque is deemed as payment without the authority of the customer. The paying banker is not given any protection under law on the payment of a forged cheque. The banker's liability remains even if the signature is cleverly forged and it is difficult to detect it with reasonable care. In case of forged cheque, the banker cannot escape from liability, even if, the customer was negligent in keeping the cheque book under lock and key as required by the rule of the bank.

COLLECTING BANKER

Responsibility of Collecting Banker: A banker (agent) who collects the cheque and credits to his customer's account (Principal) while collecting crossed cheque is given protection under Section 131 of the Negotiable Instrument Act. According to the section *'A banker who has in good faith and without negligence received payment for a customer of a cheque crossed generally or specially to himself shall not, in case the title to the cheque proves defective, incur any liability to, the true owner of the Cheque by reason only of having received such payment'.*

Conversion: Conversion means illegal interference in the property of another person. If a bank collects the cheque for his customer belonging to some other person and the customer has no title to that cheque, bank shall be liable for conversion. Bank will, however be having statutory protection under Section 131 of the Negotiable Instrument Act if certain conditions are satisfy.

The above section protects a collecting banker when it collects a crossed cheques bearing a forged endorsement, or in respect of which a customer has no title or a defective title. It may be noted here that to claim protection, the collecting banker must comply strictly with the provisions of the section. These are as under:

a) **The collecting banker should have acted in Good Faith and without Negligence:** The most important point for banker is to remember when he is collecting cheque is that he must act in good faith without negligence. It is deemed to be done in good faith where it is done bonafide and honestly. But section 131 requires him to act without negligence also. Without negligence means with reasonable care (without doubt about the genuineness of the title of the customer to the instrument). The account should be opened with proper KYC. Collection of large amount cheques in new accounts without proper scrutiny means negligence.

b) **Banker should receive payment for a Customer:** Customer means having an account in the bank. Section 131 applies only to the crossed cheque collected for a customer. Therefore, if the banker collects cheques for any person other than a customer, he cannot claim protection and he will be held liable to the true owner in case the title of the person for he collects the cheque prove defective.

c) **Examination of Endorsement:** The collecting banker must satisfy himself that all the endorsements on the cheque are regular.

d) **Protection only for Crossed Cheque:** Protection is not available for an un-crossed cheque. Hence it is always advisable for banker to cross all cheques paid in for collection.

e) **Collation of Cheques crossed 'Not Negotiable':** In certain cheques we can see the wording 'Not Negotiable', especially some cheques drawn by LIC. Not Negotiable crossing is only an indication to the collecting banker and it has nothing to do with the paying banker. Not Negotiable crossing does not restrict the transferability of cheques, but the only thing is that the transferee will not get a better title than what the transferor had. In other words, if it is a stolen or forged cheque, the transferee or the "holder in due course" will also get a defective title.

f) **Collation of Cheques Crossed 'Not Transferable':** A collecting banker is guilty of negligence when he collects a 'Not Transferable' cheque to any person other than the payee.

g) **General Crossing and Special Crossing:** Before accepting a cheque for collection, the bank should ensure that the cheque is either crossed generally or specially crossed to the collecting bank itself. If the cheque is specially crossed by another bank, then such cheque should not be accepted for collection.

h) **Cheque payable to a Partnership Firm or a Company collected in the personal account of the Partner or the Director:** The protection is not available when the collecting bank collecting cheques made payable to the partnership firm or the company's cheque for the personal accounts of the partner of the firm or private accounts of the director of the company.

i) **Collection of Cheque payable to a Customer in his official capacity for his Personal Account:** The banker should not collect the cheque payable to a customer in his official capacity for his private account. For instance, a cheque payable to 'Mr. XYZ, Income Tax Commissioner' should not be collected for the personal account of Mr. XYZ.

Duties of the Collecting Banker: A banker is bound to show a reasonable care in collection of his customer's cheques and bills. Otherwise, he may be held liable for any loss suffered by the customer. In the case of a cheque entrusted with the banker for collection, he is expected to present it to the drawee banker within a reasonable time. Under Section 84 of the NI Act duties of the collecting banker are as under:

a) They must present the cheque within reasonable time. In determining what a reasonable time is, regard shall be had to the nature of the instrument, the usage of trade and of bankers, and the facts of the particular case.

b) To hand over the proceeds after realisation without delay.

c) Duty to open the account with reference and sufficient documentary proof. RBI has insisted that the bank should open an account of a new customer only after the new account holder has been properly verified. Besides introduction, photograph, sufficient documentary proof for constitution and address to be obtained under the applicable KYC norms.

d) Extra precaution must be taken by a banker while collecting the high value cheque in new open account. In the case of especially new open accounts, the banker should make discreet enquiries as to the source of income, and the banker should desist from handling such cheques.

e) Status of the customer's account should be verified. The collecting banker is required to take into account the status of the customer and the various transactions taking place in his account to observe the standard of living conditions of the customer. If a man of small means and small income tenders cheques for huge amounts, naturally the banker should make discreet enquiries as to the source of income, and the banker should desist from handling such cheques. It may lead to negligence or conversion.

f) Duty of the prudent banker to verify the instrument or any apparent defects in the instrument.

g) The banker has to ensure crossing and special crossing of the cheque prior to send for collection.

CHEQUE TRUNCATION

Truncation is the process of stopping the flow of the physical cheque issued by a drawer at some point by the presenting bank en-route to the paying bank branch. In its place an electronic image of the cheque is transmitted to the paying branch through the clearing house, along with relevant information like data on the MICR band, date of presentation, presenting bank, etc. Cheque truncation thus obviates the need to move the physical instruments across bank branches, other than in exceptional circumstances for clearing purposes. This effectively eliminates the associated cost of movement of the physical cheques, reduces the time required for their collection and brings elegance to the entire activity of cheque processing.

Importance of Cheque Truncation in India: Cheque Truncation speeds up the process of collection of cheques resulting in better service to customers, reduces the scope of loss of instruments in transit, lowers the cost of collection of cheques, and removes reconciliation-related and logistics-related problems, thus benefitting the system as a whole.

With the other major products being offered in the form of RTGS and NEFT, the Reserve Bank has created the capability to enable inter-bank and customer payments online and in near-real time. However, cheques continue to be the prominent mode of payments in the country. Reserve Bank of India has therefore decided to focus on improving the efficiency of the cheque clearing cycle. Offering Cheque Truncation System (CTS) is a step in this direction.

In addition to operational efficiency, CTS offers several benefits to banks and customers, including human resource rationalisation, cost effectiveness, business process re-engineering, better service, adoption of latest technology, etc. CTS, thus, has emerged as an important efficiency enhancement initiative undertaken by Reserve Bank in the Payments Systems arena.

Status of CTS Implementation in the Country: CTS has been implemented in New Delhi, Chennai and Mumbai with effect from February 1, 2008, September 24, 2011 and April 27, 2013 respectively. After migration of the entire cheque volume from MICR system to CTS, the traditional MICR-based cheque processing has been discontinued across the country.

Benefits of CTS to Customers of Banks: The benefits are many. With the introduction of imaging and truncation, the physical movement of instruments is stopped. The electronic movement of images can facilitate reduction in the clearing cycles as well. Moreover, there is no fear of loss of instruments in transit. Further, limitations of the existing clearing system in terms of geography or jurisdiction can be removed, thus enabling consolidation and integration of multiple clearing locations managed by different banks with varying service levels into a nation-wide standard clearing system with uniform processes and practices.

Under grid-based Cheque Truncation System clearing, all cheques drawn on bank branches falling within in the grid jurisdiction are treated and cleared as local cheques. No outstation cheque collection charges/Speed Clearing charges to be levied if the collecting bank and the paying bank are located within the jurisdiction of the same CTS grid even though they are located in different cities.

CTS also benefits issuers of cheques. The Corporates if needed can be provided with images of cheques by their bankers for internal requirements, if any.

CTS thus brings elegance to the entire activity of cheque processing and clearing. The benefits from CTS could be summarized as follows :

a) Shorter clearing cycle;
b) Superior verification and reconciliation process;
c) No geographical restrictions as to jurisdiction;
d) Operational efficiency for banks and customers alike;
e) Reduction in operational risk and risks associated with paper clearing;
f) No collection charges for collection of cheque drawn on a bank located within the grid.

Precautions Required to be Taken by the Banks: Banks should exercise care while affixing stamps on the cheque forms, so that it does not interfere with the material portions such as date, payee's name, amount and signature. The use of rubber stamps, etc, should not overshadow the clear appearance of these basic features in image. It is necessary to ensure that all essential elements of a cheque are captured in an image during the scanning process and banks / customers have to exercise appropriate care in this regard.

TEST YOURSELF

1. In India, the Negotiable Instruments Act was passed during 1881 which came into force from ________.
(a) March 01, 1881 (b) March 01, 1882
(c) January 01, 1881 (d) January 01, 1882

2. Originally, it had 137 Section. Five Section were added in 1988, and again five Section were added during December 2002. At present it has ________.
(a) 147 sections and 17 Chapters
(b) 149 sections and 17 Chapters
(c) 149 sections and 18 Chapters
(d) 147 sections and 18 Chapters

3. The Negotiable Instruments Act extends to the ________.
(a) Whole of India, except the state of J & K
(b) Whole of India, except NE state
(c) Whole of India,
(d) Whole of India, except the state of Tamil Nadu

4. According to Section 13 (a) of the Act, Negotiable Instruments means:
(a) Promissory Note (PN)
(b) Bill of Exchange (BOE)
(c) Cheque
(d) All of the above

5. Bill of exchange is defined under which section of the NI Act ________.
(a) Section 4 (b) Section 5
(c) Section 6 (d) Section 7

6. Which of the following elements must possess in a Promissory Note?
(a) It must be in writing,
(b) It must certainly an express promise or clear understanding to pay a certain sum of money,
(c) Promise to pay must be unconditional,
(d) All of the above

7. Maker of the bill of exchange is also referred to as:
(a) Payee (b) Drawee
(c) Drawer (d) None

8. An Inchoate instrument is the one which ______.
(a) Amount is left blank
(b) Name of the payee is left blank
(c) Date is not filled
(d) Any or all of the above

9. Negotiation in an order Cheque is Completed by ______.
(a) Only delivery
(b) Endorsement only
(c) Endorsement & Delivery
(d) Order Cheque is not Negotiable

10. Which of the following is a characteristic of payment in due course under negotiable instrument act, 1881?
(a) Payment in good faith
(b) Payment without negligence
(c) Payment as per apparent tenor of the instrument
(d) All of the above

11. A negotiable instrument can be endorsed by ______.
(a) Singing on the back of the instrument
(b) Signing on a separate piece of paper called as 'allonge' if space is insufficient at the back of the instrument
(c) Both 'a' & 'b'
(d) Neither 'a' nor 'b'

12. If a cheque is payable to Anil or order and Anil only signs on a back of the instrument, such a chain is ______.
(a) Partial endorsement
(b) Blank endorsement
(c) Full endorsement
(d) Conditional endorsement

13. Who can cross a cheque?
(a) Drawer of the cheque
(b) Holder of the cheque
(c) A banker who receive the cheque for collection
(d) All of the above

14. What constitutes special crossing?
(a) Drawing two parallel transverse lines on the face of the cheque
(b) Writing a/c payee only on the face of the cheque
(c) Drawing two parallel transverse lines on the face of the cheque and writing the name of the bank in between
(d) Writing the words not negotiable on the face of the cheque

15. Which of the following does not constitute a material alteration?
(a) Change in date
(b) Conversion of order cheque to bearer cheque
(c) Conversion of a bearer cheque to a crossed cheque
(d) All of the above

16. Number of parties in a bill of exchange is ______.
(a) 2 (b) 3
(c) 4 (d) None

17. Which of the following bills is/are allowed grace period under section 22 of NI Act?
(a) Usance bill (b) Demand bill
(c) Both (d) None of the above

18. Present validity period of cheque, as per RBI and w.e.f. 01.04.2012 is ______.
(a) 2 months (b) 3 months
(c) 4 months (d) 6 months

19. 'Pay to Alok only'. Such Endorsement is ______.
(a) Partial endorsement
(b) Restrictive endorsement
(c) Full endorsement
(d) Conditional endorsement

20. If the cheque is dishonoured wrongly, the drawer banker is liable for damages to whom?
(a) Payee (b) Drawer
(c) Holder (d) None of the above

21. As per RBI direction u/s 35A, Banking Regulation Act, validity of the cheque, demand draft and banker's cheque will be valid for ______ months with effect from April 01, 2012.
(a) 1 (b) 3
(c) 6 (d) 12

22. A cheque is presented for payment where amount is written in figure is Hindi and other particulars in English. What the banker should do?
(a) Bank can pay the cheque as it can be drawn in any language
(b) All particulars should be in same language
(c) Request the drawer to reissue the cheque
(d) None of the above

23. If alteration in the amount of the cheque is authenticated by the drawer:
(a) It can be paid normally
(b) It can't be paid, As per RBI direction alteration is only allowed in date for revalidation

(c) It can be paid normally, if alteration is authenticated by drawer properly
(d) It can't be paid, As per RBI direction alteration is only allowed in payee name

24. Your branch has received a cheque of ₹ 50,000/- drawn in favour of Lord Krishna or order for payment, across the counter. What would you do with the cheque?
(a) It will be paid after obtaining the identification of the person obtaining the payment
(b) It will be paid to a person in whose favour endorsement done by Lord Krishna appears
(c) It will be paid to a person whose name is stated by the drawer for obtaining payment on behalf of the payee
(d) It will be returned, as it is drawn in favour of a fictitious name

25. A cheque for ₹ 10000/- dated 15/02/2017, presented for the payment on 25/02/2017. It is observed that the cheque book from which the cheque was issued, issued to customer on 20/02/2017. What the bank should do?
(a) Such cheque cannot be paid
(b) Upon drawer's confirmation, it can be paid
(c) Cheque would be paid if otherwise in order
(d) It should be returned unpaid

26. The duties of paying banker for payment of cheque and protection has been laid down in ________.
(a) NI Act
(b) Indian Contract Act
(c) RBI Act
(d) Banking Regulation Act

27. Maximum time frame for collection of cheques drawn on state capitals/major cities/other locations are ____/____/____ days respectively.
(a) 7/10/14 (b) 4/7/10
(c) 10/14/21 (d) 7/14/21

28. On which of the following a collecting bank will get protection against conversion u/s 131 of NI Act?
(a) Crossed Draft
(b) Crossed DP Note
(c) Crossed Bill of Exchange
(d) Crossed Cheque

29. When a bank is collecting a cheque of a newly opened SB account as first entry in the account, find the correct statement:
(a) Banker would not get protection because it has not collected the cheque for a customer
(b) Banker will get protection if the account is opened after complying with KYC requirement
(c) Banker will not get protection because the first entry in the account is not in cash
(d) Both 'a' & 'c'

30. In case of collection of cheque and bills, the relationship of the banker with the customer is that of ________.
(a) Banker as agent and customer trustee
(b) Banker as trustee and customer debtor
(c) Banker as debtor and customer creditor
(d) Banker as agent and customer principal

31. A customer of your branch Mahesh, deposited a cheque, which he steals from another person named Mahesh. Your branch collects this cheque without being aware about the defect. Find the correct statement:
(a) Collecting bank is negligent
(b) Collecting bank will get protection if it has collected the cheque in good faith and without negligence
(c) Collecting bank is responsible for conversion
(d) Collecting bank is negligent but will get protection

32. A cheque is in favour of a Trust. The trustee wants to deposit this cheque in his personal account. The collecting bank ________.
(a) Must be collected in Trust account only
(b) Need not enquire before its collection
(c) May be collected in personal account if Trustee request
(d) Should know the customer is enough

ANSWER

1	2	3	4	5	6	7	8	9	10
(b)	(a)	(c)	(d)	(b)	(d)	(c)	(d)	(c)	(d)
11	**12**	**13**	**14**	**15**	**16**	**17**	**18**	**19**	**20**
(c)	(b)	(d)	(c)	(c)	(b)	(a)	(b)	(b)	(b)
21	**22**	**23**	**24**	**25**	**26**	**27**	**28**	**29**	**30**
(b)	(a)	(b)	(d)	(c)	(a)	(a)	(d)	(b)	(a)
31	**32**								
(b)	(a)								

OPENING ACCOUNTS OF VARIOUS TYPES OF CUSTOMERS

TYPES OF BANK CUSTOMERS

Introduction: Bank is an important service sector organisation. Customers play the most significant part in bank. In fact, the customer is the actual boss in a deal and is responsible for the actually profit for the organization. Customer is the one who uses the banking products and services and judges the quality of those products and services. Hence, it's important for an organization to retain customers or make new customers and flourish business. To manage customers, organizations should follow some sort of approaches like segmentation or division of customers into groups because each customer has to be considered valuable and profitable.

For a bank it is advantageous to have different types of clients because, as will receive deposits and provide loans for both business and individuals. Banking relationship is a contract between the Bank & the Customer. Therefore, for establishing relationship with the customer, Bank has to ensure that the customer is legally capable of entering into a valid contract & he has applied to the Bank in the proper form (Indian Contract Act, 1872).

During the opening of accounts, the banker deals with different types of customers. The banker should acquaint himself with various laws governing different types of customers. The customers can be classified as follows:

1. Personal Accounts:

Banker should take care and verify the certain fact while opening of accounts of individual. As per Indian Contract Act 1872, a person is competent to enter into a valid contract and open a bank account provided:

- Individual should be major, *i.e.* of 18 years of age.
- He should be sound mind,
- He is otherwise not disqualified by any law,
- He should not be an insolvent,
- Drunken person is not legally competent to enter into a contract,
- He should be in good sense while lending a loan and entering into a contract,

(a) Accounts of Single Individual: This is purely a personal account in the name of an individual and is normally operated upon by the account holder himself. The account holder may authorise another person to operate on his account. For this purpose, he gives a Mandate or executes a Power of Attorney in favour of such a person.

In order to avoid legal complications that may arise after the death of the account holder, it is desirable to suggest opening of a joint account in the names of two individuals (unless it is essential in certain circumstances to open an account in the single name only), and/or to obtain proper nomination.

(b) Joint Accounts of Individuals: A joint account is opened in the names of more than one individual for convenience of operations and/ or to avoid legal complications upon death of one of the joint account holders. A joint account is neither a partnership nor a trust account. It is important to obtain clear and unambiguous instructions regarding the mode of operation and repayment of balance of a joint account in the event of death of one or more joint account holder(s). Different types of operational instructions are as under:

(i) Jointly or Survivor (ii) Either or Survivor
(iii) Former or Survivor (iv) Any one or Survivor

One or more of the joint account holders can authorise operation on the account on his/their behalf by giving a Mandate or executing a Power of Attorney, but, such Mandate or Power of Attorney must be given by all the parties to the accounts. Addition/deletion of any name, material alteration, closure of account & operational instructions in the joint account can be changed by all the account holders jointly. However, in joint accounts with operational instructions "Former or Survivor", instructions can be changed/revoked only by Former.

(c) Illiterate Person: Illiterate person is a person who cannot read or write. Such persons are competent to enter in to a valid contract. The account (other than Current Account) of such a person may be opened provided he calls on the Bank with a latest passport size photograph. Photograph is essential for identification. Thereupon, his thumb impression or mark should be obtained on the account opening form/card in the presence of the Bank's official. Such thumb impressions or marks affixed by illiterate persons on instruments are equivalent to their signatures. Any withdrawal/repayment of deposit amount and/or interest by way of withdrawal form or otherwise should similarly be affixed with the thumb impression or mark of the depositor.

(d) Blind Persons: Blind Persons can operate the account in bank. Signature of Thumb impression of blind person in the A/c opening form to be witnessed by a person. who should certify that contents of the A/c opening form were explained to the blind person in his presence. The sign may be authorised by bank officer and a witness known to both the bank and the blind person. He should always visit the branch for cash withdrawal. As per all banking facilities including net banking, ATM, Cheque Book, Locker facility, loans to be offered to visually challenged customers without discrimination.

(e) Minors' Accounts: A minor is a person below the age of 18 years. A minor is under legal incapacity to contract by himself and, therefore, a guardian recognised by law along can deal with the person and property of the minor. The term "guardian" includes a natural guardian or guardian appointed by the Court of Law. Ordinarily, an account of a minor is opened and operated upon by the natural guardian of the minor or by the guardian appointed by the Court.

According to RBI guidelines (RBI/2013-14/581DBOD. No.Leg.BC.108/09.07.005/2013-14) with a view to promote the objective of financial inclusion and also to bring uniformity among banks in opening and operating minors' accounts, banks are advised as under:

(a) A savings/fixed/recurring bank deposit account can be opened by a minor of any age through his/her natural or legally appointed guardian.

(b) Minors above the age of 10 years may be allowed to open and operate savings bank accounts independently, if they so desire. Banks may, however, keeping in view their risk management systems, fix limits in terms of age and amount up to which minors may be allowed to operate the deposit accounts independently. They can also decide, in their own discretion, as to what minimum documents are required for opening of accounts by minors.

(c) On attaining majority, the erstwhile minor should confirm the balance in his/her account and if the account is operated by the natural guardian / legal guardian, fresh operating instructions and specimen signature of erstwhile minor should be obtained and kept on record for all operational purposes.

Banks are free to offer additional banking facilities like internet banking, ATM/ debit card, cheque book facility etc., subject to the safeguards that minor accounts are not allowed to be overdrawn and that these always remain in credit.

It is permissible to open any type of deposit account in the name of and/or to be operated upon by a minor within the framework of rules of business of the Bank as outlined hereunder, but no Current Account should be opened.

According to Section 26 of NI Act, a minor can draw, endorse or negotiate a cheque or a bill but he cannot be held liable on such cheques or bill. Minor can be admitted to the benefits of partnership with the consent of other partners but cannot be made liable for the losses. A minor may be appointed as an agent on behalf of his principal but legally he cannot be held responsible to his principal.

When the minor becomes major he has the sole right to operate the account and guardian's power ceases. The payment should be made to the erstwhile minor upon provided his identity. When the account is operated upon by the guardian on behalf of the minor a Balance Confirmation Letter duly signed by the erstwhile minor and verified by the guardian. If account is operated by the minor himself, the erstwhile minor should be asked to sign a Balance Confirmation Letter.

2. Hindu Undivided Family (HUF)

'Hindu Undivided Family' otherwise known as 'Joint Hindu Family' property, business or ancestral estates and its common possession, enjoyment ownership is the basis of formation of HUF. As per Hindu law, the Hindus, Sikhs & Jains can form HUF.

HUF is governed basically by two schools of thought. In Bengal, it is governed by Dayabhag Law. In other parts of India, it is governed by Mitakshara Law. The law governing Hindu Undivided Family is codified under Hindu Code and now, succession among Hindu is governed by Hindu Succession Act, 1956. Parts of this Act was amended in 2005 by the Hindu Succession (Amendment) Act, 2005. Creation of Hindu Law under which all major members of the family get right by birth in the ancestral property of the family.

HUF property is managed by senior most major male member called 'Manager' or 'Karta'. Upon death of Karta, next senior male coparcener becomes Karta. Joint owner of HUF are known as coparceners. It consists of one common living ancestor and his all male & female (female from Sept. 2005) descendent up to three generations next to him. HUF cannot enter into a partnership as per Supreme Court judgement of 1998.

HUF account is operated by Karta. Karta has authority to borrow money for the family necessities & for ancestral family business. Documents are to be executed by Karta. All major coparceners are to be made guarantors. The liability of the 'Karta' is unlimited, whereas the liability of the coparceners is limited to their shares in the joint family estate.

3. Proprietorship Firm

Business is wholly owned by an individual. In law, there is no difference between proprietor & the firm. In all respects, it is an account in the name of an individual only except that it is operated upon by the proprietor on behalf of firm. The firm should have PAN or GST Number. Proprietorship letter in bank's Performa is to be obtained. Proof of proprietorship may be obtained. Creditors have recourse not only against assets of the firm but also against private assets of the proprietor. Proprietor can authorize another person to operate the account through Mandate or Power of Attorney.

4. Partnership Firm

Partnership is the relation between persons who have agreed to share profits of business carried on by all or any one them acting for all (Indian Partnership Act 1932). As per RBI instruction now Registration Certificate and Partnership deed to be obtained. As per Indian Companies Act 2013, Maximum number of partner can be up to 100 in a firm (Earlier number of partner was restricted to 20 for other businesses & 10 for banking business). Partnership is not a distinct legal person from the partners who have made partnership firm. HUF cannot enter into a partnership as per Supreme Court judgement of 1998. The firm should have PAN or GST Number. A partner cannot delegate his authority to operate the account.

A minor cannot be a partner, but he can be admitted for his benefit in an existing partnership firm. The particulars of minor partner, particularly the DOB should be properly recorded.

In case of death/retirement/insolvency of a partner account should be stopped, if the balance is in debit and a fresh account should opened after fresh sanction of limit. In case of dispute when one partner revokes the authority against the other partner, operation in the account should be stopped.

Dissolution of the Partnership firm can takes place by following ways:

a) By mutual consent;
b) Death/insolvency/retirement of a partner;
c) Operation of Law (insolvency of all partners, business becoming unlawful, dissolution by a competent court; and
d) In case of automatic dissolution.

5. Limited Liability Partnership (LLP)

A limited liability partnership (LLP) is a partnership in which some or all partners (depending on the jurisdiction) have limited liabilities. LLP is governed by limited liability partnership Act 2008. Liability is limited to the extent of his contribution in the LLP. Minimum 2 designated partner and no limit on maximum number of Partners. A partner is not liable for another partner's misconduct or negligence, except in certain cases. LLP is a legal entity separate from its partner. It has own assets in his name, sure and be sued. Since LLP contains element of both 'a corporate structure' as well as 'a partnership firm structure' LLP is called a hybrid between a company and a partnership. It has perpetual succession (death of a partner does not affect the existence of LLP). Partners have a right to manage the business directly. Firms and companies can get themselves converted into LLP. LLP cannot raise fund from public.

6. Companies

Companies are defined in Indian Company Act 1956. As per the provision of Company Act 2013 (implemented with effect from 1st April 2014), recognizes a joint Stock Company is a legal person with perpetual entity & is distinct from its members. A company or association of persons can be created at law as legal person so that the company in itself can accept limited liability for civil responsibility. Because companies are legal persons, they also may associate and register themselves as companies otherwise it will be treated as illegal. Address of the registered office is compulsory. It is the address at which all the documents & notices may be served upon the company. Cheques favouring company are not to be credited to the personal accounts of the Directors or other officers of the company.

Following documents are required for account opening of a company:

a) **Certificate of Incorporation:** Issued by Registrar of Companies. It is conclusive proof for incorporation of the company & compliance of all formalities by promoters.

b) **Certificate of commencement of business:** A company having share capital cannot commence business until it has obtained the certificate to commence business (COB) from the concerned Registrar of Companies. Certificate of commencement of business is not required by Private Ltd. Co. as its shares are closely held & it can commence business on its incorporation.

c) **Memorandum of Association:** Company's fundamental & unalterable law. Embodies Company's name, Authorized capital, Objectives of the company, Liability of shareholders.

d) **Article of Association**: Regulations controlling internal management of the company. Rights & powers of the Directors, rules about conduct of company meetings & business, Procedure for borrowing & limit on borrowing etc.

e) **Copy of Board Resolution**: Certified copy of Board Resolution authorizing to borrow from the Bank with details of limit, security etc., Persons who are authorized to sign the security documents & operate the Bank Account, persons in whose presence Seal of the company will be affixed to the security documents.

f) **Company Common Seal**: Common Seal if any, of the company available should be embossed on bank's documents. As per Companies (Amendment) Act, 2015 and RBI instruction Company Common Seal is not necessary, if other documents available during current account opening.

Different types of Companies in India

(*i*) **Private Company**: Private Company has share holders with limited liability and its shares may not be offered to the general public. Private Limited Company having a no minimum paid-up share capital limitation now. (As per Companies (Amendment) Act, 2015, paid-up share capital of one lakh rupee or such higher paid-up share capital as may be prescribed is omitted now). It has minimum two members and maximum member restricted to two hundred and Minimum two directors and no maximum number of directors is restricted.

(ii) **Public Company:** Public company means a company which is not a private company and has no minimum paid-up share capital limitation now (As per Companies (Amendment) Act, 2015, paid-up share capital of five lakh rupee or such higher paid-up share capital as may be prescribed is omitted now). Shares are offered to the public & are listed on stock exchange. Minimum seven members, no limit of maximum number. Minimum 3 directors, maximum 15 director limits. Provided that a company may appoint more than fifteen directors after passing a special resolution (As per Companies Act 2013, no Central Govt. permission required now). At least one-woman director shall be on Board. Certificate of commencement of business is must to do any type of business.

(iii) **Government Company:** "Government Company" means any company in which not less than fifty one per cent of paid-up share capital is held by the Central Government, or by any State Government, or partly by the Central Government and partly by one or more State Governments and includes a company which is a subsidiary company of such a Government company.

(iv) **One Person Company:** The Companies Act 2013 Act introduces a new type of entity to the existing list *i.e.,* apart from forming a public or private limited company, the 2013 act enables the formation of a new entity a 'one-person company' (OPC). An OPC means a company with only one person having a sole member [section 3(1) of 2013 Act]. An OPC can be formed only by an Indian Resident and citizen.

(v) **Other Companies:** As per Companies act 1956, companies can be classified on the basis of time, place of incorporation and nature of working share capital as follows:

a) **Foreign Company:** It means a company incorporated outside India and having a place of business in India whether by itself or through an agent, physically or through electronic mode and conduct any business activity in India in any other manner.

b) **Existing Company:** A company which is established before the Company Act 1956 is called Existing Company.

c) **Holding Company:** A company is known as the holding company of another company if it has control over another company.

d) **Subsidiary Company:** A company is known as subsidiary of another company when control is exercised by the latter over the former called a subsidiary company. A company is to be deemed to be subsidiary company of another.

7. **Trust:** Trusts are governed by the Indian Trust Act, 1882. A trust is created when ownership of a property is transferred to someone for holding or managing it for benefit of another person(s). Trust may be public charitable trust or private trust (for benefit of private individuals). Trusts managed by trustees. Loan can be granted if it is for the purpose of the trust. Trustee is authorised to borrow as per the trust deed. Original Trust Deed to be examined before financing. Certificate of Registration under Public Trust Act to be examined & copy to be kept on record.

8. **Clubs & Societies:** Clubs& Societies are non-profit making organisation and represent a group of persons. These are normally incorporated under Cooperative Society Act. Clubs can be registered under Society Act 1860, or Company Act 1956. These get the status of a legal entity only after their incorporation in their own name. These are governed by rules & regulations (bye laws). Certified true copy of resolution. Cheques favouring society, club, association not to be collected in individual accounts of office bearers or employees.

Deregulation of Savings Bank Deposit Interest Rate

As per RBI guidelines, it has been decided to deregulate the savings bank deposit interest rate with immediate effect. Accordingly, the following Guidelines will be effective from October 25, 2011:

Banks are free to determine their savings bank deposit interest rate, subject to the following two conditions:

(a) First, each bank will have to offer a uniform interest rate on savings bank deposits up to ₹ 1 lakh, irrespective of the amount in the account within this limit.

(b) Second, for savings bank deposits over ₹ 1 lakh, a bank may provide differential rates of interest, if it so chooses, subject to the condition that banks will not discriminate in the matter of interest paid on such deposits, between one deposit and another of similar amount, accepted on the same date, at any of its offices.

The above revised Guidelines would be applicable to savings bank deposits of resident Indians only. Interest rate on Non-Resident (External) Accounts Scheme and Ordinary Non-Resident Deposit under savings account, which has been prescribed at 4 per cent per annum at present, will continue to be regulated until further review.

TEST YOURSELF

1. As per Indian Contract Act 1872, who is not competent to contract?
   (a) Minor (b) Insolvent
   (c) Insane (d) All of the above

2. For opening of bank account, registration of a partnership firm is:
   (a) Optional
   (b) Compulsory
   (c) Not required
   (d) As per partnership deed

3. As per Indian Companies Act 2013, Maximum number of partners in a firm can be:
   (a) 10 (b) 20
   (c) 100 (d) 200

4. If partnership deed is silent about operation of the account, then the account will be operated by:
   (a) Any of the partner
   (b) All partners jointly
   (c) First partner as per deed
   (d) As per instruction of the partners

5. If bank finance to the partnership firm, the liability of a partner for the loan is:
   (a) Unlimited
   (b) Limited to their share in the business
   (c) Limited
   (d) No liability of partners

6. In a Government company, number of shares held by the Government at least:
   (a) 50% (b) 51%
   (c) 75% (d) 100%

7. HUF property is managed by 'Manager' or 'Karta'. Who becomes the 'Manager' or 'Karta'?
   (a) Senior most major male member
   (b) Senior most major female member

(c) Appointed by all major coparceners
(d) Any of the major coparceners

8. If bank finance to the limited liability partnership firm, the liability of a partner for the loan is:
(a) Unlimited
(b) Limited to their share in the business
(c) Limited
(d) No liability of partners

9. Embodies Company's name, Authorized capital, Objectives of the company, Liability of share holders are written in:
(a) Certificate of Incorporation
(b) Memorandum of Association
(c) Article of Association
(d) None of the above

10. A company which is established before the Company Act 1956 is called ________.
(a) Holding Company (b) Subsidiary Company
(c) Existing Company (d) Foreign Company

11. Which is the correct statement about 'Public Company?
(a) Its share is listed in stock exchange
(b) Minimum seven members, no limit of maximum number
(c) Minimum three directors, maximum no limit
(d) All of the above

12. As per Indian Contract Act 1872, a person who is competent to enter into a valid contract:
(a) He is otherwise disqualified by any law
(b) He should not be a solvent
(c) Drunken person is legally competent to enter into a contract
(d) He should be in good sense while lending a loan and entering into a contract

13. Which is not correct about Illiterate person?
(a) Illiterate persons are competent to enter in to a valid contract
(b) Photograph is essential for identification
(c) Normally, Left Hand Thumb impression (LHT) of male & Right Hand Thumb impression (RHT) of female is to be obtained
(d) None of the above

14. Which is not correct about Proprietor firm?
(a) In law, there is no difference between proprietor & the firm.
(b) Creditors have recourse not only against assets of the firm but also against private assets of the proprietor.
(c) Bank insists that proprietor should execute the security documents in the capacity as Proprietor on behalf of the firm as well as in his individual capacity.
(d) Proprietor cannot authorize another person to operate the account through Mandate or Power of Attorney.

15. Which is not correct about limited liability partnership (LLP)?
(a) LLP is governed by limited liability partnership Act 2008.
(b) Minimum 3 designated partner and no limit on maximum number of Partners.
(c) LLP is a legal entity separate from its partner.
(d) LLP cannot raise fund from public.

16. Which is not necessary for financing a Private Company?
(a) Memorandum of Association
(b) Article of Association
(c) Certificate of commencement of business
(d) Board resolution

17. A company is known as the ________ of another company if it has control over another company.
(a) holding company (b) Existing company
(c) Other company (d) Foreign company

18. Which is not a statutory company in India?
(a) Reserve Bank of India
(b) Tata Iron & Steel Company
(c) The Life Insurance Corporation of India
(d) The Food Corporation of India

19. Which is not correct about Trust?
(a) Trusts are governed by the Indian Trust Act, 1982.
(b) Trust may be public charitable trust or private trust (for benefit of private individuals).
(c) Loan can be granted if it is for the purpose of the trust. Trustee is authorised to borrow as per the trust deed.
(d) Certificate of Registration under Public Trust Act to be examined & copy to be kept on record.

20. While giving a loan to a club or society or school the bank should study:
(a) Bye-laws (b) Copy of resolution
(c) Rules & Regulation (d) All of the above

ANSWER

1	2	3	4	5	6	7	8	9	10
(d)	(b)	(c)	(b)	(a)	(b)	(a)	(b)	(b)	(c)
11	**12**	**13**	**14**	**15**	**16**	**17**	**18**	**19**	**20**
(d)	(d)	(d)	(d)	(b)	(c)	(a)	(b)	(a)	(d)

ANCILARY SERVICES

INTRODUCTION

The basic function of a bank is acceptance of deposits of money from the public for the purpose of lending and investment. Besides these functions, banks also provide some ancillary services. Remittances, Safe Deposit Lockers, Portfolio Management, and Merchant Banking are the example of ancillary services provided by the bank in India.

REMITTANCES

Remittance means transfer of fund from one branch of a bank to another branch of the same bank or different bank. Customers prefer cheques and banker's cheque for remittance fund within the city. Customers use various modes of remittance facility such as Demand Draft, RTGS, NEFT, and MT etc. for remitting their fund from one city to another. Now a days, internet banking and mobile banking options are available 24 hours from home.

DEMAND DRAFT (DD) AND BANKER'S CHEQUE

Demand Draft is a most common Negotiable Instrument used for remittance of fund. When it is used in the same city it is called banker's cheque. Demand draft is an order drawn by one branch of the bank upon another instructing the other branch to pay a certain sum of money only or to the order of a certain person. A bank cannot make its demand draft payable to bearer as it may be used as a currency note. This will be a violation of Sec.31 the RBI Act 1934. Other features of demand draft are as under;

- DD/TT/MT etc. are modes of remittances. DD is valid for a period of 3 months and it requires revalidation thereafter;
- Demand draft or Pay order of ₹ 50,000 & above in a day should be issued to the debit of an account or cheque and not against cash;
- Duplicate DD have to be issued to the purchaser within 14 days (fortnight) of the request subject to completion of formalities;
- Duplicate DD up to ₹ 5000 should be issued without awaiting non-payment advice from the drawee branch;
- In case duplicate DDs are not issued within the stipulated period, banks are required to pay interest for the period of delay at rates applicable to term deposits of corresponding maturities;
- When a duplicate DD has been issued at the request of purchaser/beneficiary, the original should not be paid but returned with the remarks. "Duplicate since issued";
- In case both original as well as duplicate DDs are presented to the drawee branch for payment it should pay duplicate DD and return original with the reason 'DD reported lost and duplicate since issued and paid';
- The payment of a demand draft cannot be stopped.

NATIONAL ELECTRONIC FUNDS TRANSFER (NEFT) SYSTEM

NEFT system is a nationwide funds transfer system to facilitate transfer of funds from any bank branch to any other bank branch. Salient features of the system are given below:

Introduction: National Electronic Funds Transfer (NEFT) is a nation-wide payment system facilitating one-to-one funds transfer. Under this scheme, individuals, firms and corporates can electronically transfer funds from any bank branch to any individual, firm or corporate having an account with any other bank branch in the country. Even such individuals who do not have a bank account (walk-in customers) can also deposit cash at the NEFT-enabled branches with instructions to transfer funds using NEFT. However, such cash remittances will be restricted to a maximum of ₹ 50,000/- per transaction. However, it is necessary for the beneficiary to have an account with the NEFT enabled destination bank branch in the country.

Amount: There is no value limit for individual transactions. Thus there is no minimum or maximum amount to be remitted.

Restriction on centres: There is no restriction of centres or of any geographical area within the country. The settlement of funds between originating and receiving banks takes places centrally at Mumbai, whereas the branches participating in NEFT can be located anywhere across the length and breadth of the country.

Settlement Timings: NEFT operates in half hourly batches. There are twenty three settlements on weekdays other than second & fourth Saturday.

Period of Credit: The beneficiary should get credit within 2 hours from the time of completion of batch *i.e.*, on B+2 basis on the same day.

Non-credit to beneficiary: If it is not possible to afford credit to the account of the beneficiary for whatever reason, destination banks are required to return the transaction (to the originating branch) within two hours of completion of the batch in which the transaction was processed.

Transfer funds from / to NRE and NRO accounts: NEFT can be used to transfer funds from or to NRE and NRO accounts in the country.

Remittance Abroad: NEFT system can be used only for remitting Indian Rupee among the participating banks within the country. Foreign remittances can neither be received nor sent abroad using the NEFT. However, remittances can be sent to Nepal under the Indo-Nepal Remittance Facility Scheme (maximum amount ₹ 50,000/-).

The remitting customer can track the remitting transaction through the remitting branch only, as the remitting branch is informed about the status of the remitted transactions.

REAL TIME GROSS SETTLEMENT (RTGS)

The acronym 'RTGS' stands for Real Time Gross Settlement, which can be defined as the continuous (real-time) settlement of funds transfers individually on an order by order basis (without netting). 'Real Time' means the processing of instructions at the time they are received rather than at some later time; 'Gross Settlement' means the settlement of funds transfer instructions occurs individually (on an instruction by instruction basis). Considering that the funds settlement takes place in the books of the Reserve Bank of India, the payments are final and irrevocable.

Salient features of RTGS are as under;

1. "RIGS" stands for Real Time Gross Settlement. RTGS system is a funds transfer mechanism where transfer of money takes place from one bank to another on a "real time" and on "gross" basis.
2. This is the fastest possible money transfer system through the banking channel.
3. Settlement in "real time" means payment transaction is not subjected to any waiting period. The transactions are settled as soon as they are processed.
4. "Gross settlement" means the transaction is settled on one to one basis without bunching with any other transaction. Considering that money transfer takes place in the books of the Reserve Bank of India, the payment is taken as final and irrevocable.
5. RTGS helps in preventing Systemic and Settlement Risks. There are 22 digits in UTR (Unique Transaction Reference Number).
6. The RTGS system is primarily meant for large value transactions. The minimum amount to be remitted through RTGS is ₹ 2 lakh. There is no upper ceiling for RTGS transactions.
7. The originating member should ensure two factor authentications by adopting maker-checker principle while originating a payment transaction.
8. The originating member should release the payment message from their system to the RTGS central system within 30 minutes of debiting a customer's account.
9. Credit received by the RTGS member should be credited to the account of the beneficiary based on the account number in the payment message within 30 minutes of the receipt of the message at the Member Interface.
10. The RTGS service window for customer's transactions is available to banks from 9.00 hours to 16.30 hours on week days for settlement at the RBI end.

Difference between IFS Code and MICR: Indian Financial System Code (IFSC) is an alpha numeric code designed to uniquely identify the bank-branches in India. This is a 11 digit code with first 4 characters representing the banks code, the next character reserved as control character (Presently 0 appears in the fifth position) and remaining 6 characters to identify the branch. This is used by RTGS and NEFT. The MICR code has 9 digits to identify the bank-branch. Each three digits in code signifies the information about City, Bank Name, and Branch Code. IFSC code is printed on cheques leaves issued to their customers.

ELECTRONIC BENEFIT TRANSFER (EBT) SCHEME

The key driver of our country's vision of inclusive growth is Financial Inclusion. The Central and State Governments have institutionalized several welfare schemes like social security pensions, Mahatma Gandhi National Rural Employment Guarantee Scheme (MNREGS), National Old Age Pension (NOAPS) insurance scheme etc. for the benefit of the poor. The Reserve Bank, therefore, as part of its Financial Inclusion initiative encouraged governments to disburse social security payments through the banking channel leveraging Electronic Benefit Transfers for financial intermediation. EBT is one of the products offered under Financial Inclusion, which facilitates payments to reach the intended beneficiaries through bank accounts. This relieves State Government functionaries of cost and time involved in administering the high volume small value payments. Provision of door step banking services in remote areas entails a cost on the banks. The payment of commission by the State Governments for EBT transactions makes the model economically viable and also helps banks to extend their penetration to remote villages. It also provides banks with a business opportunity of linking credit products to the payments. The Committee (Chairman Dr. R.B. Burman) had recommended the "One District-One Bank model" to be used for implementation of the EBT Scheme. Based on the recommendations, a few State Governments in Haryana, Karnataka, AP, Odisha, Chhattisgarh, Himachal Pradesh, Uttarakhand, Bihar, Punjab, etc. implemented the "One District-One Bank EBT model' in select districts on a pilot basis.

Electronic Benefit Transfer (EBT) Scheme using the "One District–One Bank Model" In this model, a designated bank has the mandate to disburse government payments at the door step of the beneficiary, electronically, through hand held devices using biometric smart cards at the locations of BCs of the bank. However, difficulties as explained below have been expressed by various stakeholders in scaling up one district one bank model of EBT.

a) No designated bank by itself may have the adequate branch/BC network to reach the entire district.
b) Even if the designated bank is somehow able to undertake EBT in the district, it may not be able to provide all other financial services like deposits, OD, remittance and GCCs/KCCs to the customers. It may also not be able to provide banking services to non-government beneficiaries.
c) The designated bank may deploy BCs in the villages only on 2-3 pre-notified days in a month for disbursing the amount of social security payments in cash to the EBT beneficiaries.
d) The designated banks may also not be able to provide banking services to non-government beneficiaries. This inhibition could be due to the fact that under roadmap to reach about 72,800 villages of above 2000 population by March 2012, the SLBCs have generally adopted Service Area Approach (SAA) for allotment of unbanked villages to banks. This has caused overlap of villages between the EBT mandated bank and FIP mandated bank. While there is no bar at this stage of Financial Inclusion, going forward this may lead to viability issues, which requires to be addressed.
e) EBT beneficiaries will be required to open accounts with other banks for their regular banking transactions. Beneficiaries will end up managing more than one account/smart card while accessing services from different banks.
f) The one bank - one district model will thus take away freedom from public to bank with the Bank of their choice keeping in view better service, etc.
g) In the absence of whole range of banking services mentioned above the BC/branch at these locations would not be viable.

Keeping in view the need to spread the banking habits to all villages, it is advised that one district–many banks – one leader bank model may be adopted henceforth for EBT implementation. In this model, all the banks present in the district participate in EBT, though for administrative convenience the State Government deals only with one leader bank. State Government shall designate the leader bank, in consultation with the Regional Office of RBI and the SLBC, who will obtain the funds from the State Government and in turn will arrange to transfer funds through interbank transfer to other banks for credit to the accounts of ultimate beneficiaries' account on a commission basis. The commission paid by the State Government may be from the amount which will accrue to them due to non-incurring of expenses involved in manually administering high volumes of small value payments. The revenue sharing model is to be decided mutually amongst participating banks. Today, with the availability of various modes of EFT like RTGS, NEFT and NECS, the leader bank is in a position to transfer funds to other participating banks speedily and cost effectively.

MOBILE BANKING TRANSACTIONS IN INDIA

RBI issued a set of operating guidelines (Oct 08, 2008) for banks, u/s 18 of the Payment and Settlement Systems Act, 2007 (Act 51 of 2007). Mobile banking transactions means undertaking banking transactions using mobile phones by bank customers that involve credit/debit to their accounts. Regulatory & Supervisory Issues for Mobile banking transactions are as under;

1. Banks licensed and supervised in India and have a physical presence in India only, can offer mobile banking services.
2. The services are restricted to customers of banks and/or holders of debit/credit cards issued as per the extant RBI guidelines.
3. Only Rupee based domestic services can be provided (cross border inward and outward transfers strictly prohibited).
4. Banks may use services of Business Correspondent for extending this facility.
5. Banks shall file Suspicious Transaction Report to Financial Intelligence Unit-India as in the case of normal banking transactions.

Inter-Operability: Banks offering mobile banking service must ensure that customers having mobile phones of any network operator are in a position to avail of the service. Restriction to the customers of a particular mobile operator(s) is permissible during the initial stages of offering the service, up to a maximum period of 6 months.

Transaction Limit in Mobile Banking: As per discretion of the bank (earlier it was a daily cap of ₹ 50,000). Banks may also fix per transaction limit depending on the bank's own risk perception of the customer.

Technology/Security Standard: Transactions up to ₹ 5000 can be without end-to-end encryption. Banks can provide fund transfer services which facilitate transfer of funds from their accounts for delivery in cash to the recipients (at ATMs or through any agent(s) appointed by the bank as business correspondents):

(i) Max value shall be ₹ 10000/- per transaction.
(ii) Banks may cap the velocity of transactions, subject to a max value of ₹ 25,000 per month, per customer.

INTERNET BANKING

Internet banking one of the popular e-banking modes has changed the banking operations and offer virtual banking services to the clients on 24 x 7 basis. It is also called as convenient banking, since the customer (account holder) can have access to his bank account from anywhere at any time, through the bank's web site. The customer is allowed online access to account details and payment and funds transfer facilities. Net banking services of a bank can be accessed through a Personal Identification Number (PIN) and access password as in the case of ATMs. In net banking the advantage for the bank customer is that funds can be transferred from the client's bank account to another account with the same bank or another bank through NEFT/RTGS. Another method of funds transfer facility is online payment of taxes. Bank customer can pay various taxes like income tax, GST, etc.; Net banking can be used as a channel by the customer to pay the utility bills (electricity bills, telephone bills, etc.) on line. Customers can make use of net banking to pay the insurance premiums and similar other payments.

Mail Transfer (MT) and Telegraphic Transfer (TT): Mail Transfer and Telegraphic Transfer is another method of sending money from one place to another place by using the letter (mail). The mail transfer (MT) is possible only when the sender (remitter) and the receiver (remittee) both are having bank accounts in the same bank, but at different branches. In this, the remitter has to inform his bank to transfer a certain amount from his account to another person's account in other branch of the same bank. The details of the remittee (receiver) such as his name, account number, the branch where he has account, etc. must be provided to the bank. This is, however, a dying product and many banks like State Bank of India have since withdrawn this.

SAFE DEPOSIT LOCKER

The Bank provides as one of the customer services, the facility of Safe Deposit Vault at its several Branches. The main advantage of having a Safe Deposit Locker is that a customer is able to keep together in one place all his valuables and confidential documents safe from fire, theft and away from prying eyes. The relationship between bank and customer in case of Safe Deposit Vault is Lessor and Lessee. The relationship between bank and customer in case of safe custody of articles, is Bailee and Bailor. Safe Deposit Vault is governed by provisions of Transfer of Property Act.

The locker should be made available only to a renter who maintains a current account or an introduced savings account with the branch. This will help the branch in establishing the identity of the renter and the cost of servicing the locker can be minimized by taking standing instructions (which should be obtained) for recovery of rent. Needless to add, the accounts must be KYC compliant. If all the lockers are rented, banks to maintain wait list for locker allotment. Bank should not insist for any deposit at the time of hiring the locker. Bank may obtain a Fixed Deposit which would cover 3 years rent and the charges for breaking open the locker in case of an eventuality.

There are two types of keys of lockers. Master Key (or Custodian Key) is held by the Custodian. Without first operating this key in the lock, the renter cannot operate his key and open the locker. Renter's Key of the locker to be allotted to the renter. Identification Code of the bank / branch should be embossed on all the locker keys with a view to facilitate Authorities in identifying the ownership of the locker keys. Pass Word is a confidential word known only to the Bank and the renter which helps the Bank to identify the renter and serves as an additional precaution in case of doubt. The pass word is recorded on the specimen signature card.

If a locker is in joint names with operating instructions as either or survivor, and one of them reports loss of key, the operation of the locker should be allowed to both on joint basis. All other particulars such as appropriate special instructions regarding operation of the locker by renters must be recorded in clear and unambiguous manner under initials of all the renters.

When an article is found in the vault, every attempt should be made to trace the owner. When the owner claims the article, it may be given to him after proper enquiry and verification and upon obtaining an appropriate letter from him.

Where the lockers have remained unoperated for more than three years for medium risk category or one year for a higher risk category, banks should immediately contact the locker-hirer and advise him to either operate the locker or surrender it. In case the locker-hirer does not respond nor operate the locker, banks should consider opening the lockers after due notice to him even if the rent is paid regularly. Banks should not open sealed/closed packets left with them for safe custody or found in locker while releasing them to the nominee(s) and surviving locker hirers / depositor of safe custody article.

Locks of the lockers must be changed under the following circumstances, as a precautionary measure, to protect the renter as well as the Bank :

(a) When a locker is surrendered;

(b) When a locker is exchanged;

(c) When an overdue locker is drilled open;

(d) When a locker is drilled open due to loss of key;

(e) Cancellation of the name of a joint renter or a representative;

(f) Transfer of locker from one Branch to another.

PENSION PAYMENTS & GOVERNMENT BUSINESS

The Reserve Bank of India carries out the general banking business of the Central and State Governments through its own offices and through the offices of the agency banks appointed under Section 45 of the RBI Act, 1934, by mutual agreement. RBI pays agency commission (also called turnover commission) to the agency banks for the government business handled by them.

Government Transactions Eligible for Agency Commission: Transactions relating to the following government business undertaken by agency banks are eligible for agency commission:

a) Revenue receipts and payments on behalf of the Central/State Government;

b) Pension payments in respect of Central / State Governments;

c) Special Deposit Scheme (SDS) 1975;

d) Public Provident Fund (PPF) Scheme, 1968;

e) Senior Citizen Savings Scheme (SCSS), 2004;

f) Kisan Vikas Patra, 2014 and Sukanya Samriddhi Account;

g) Any other item of work specifically advised by Reserve Bank as eligible for agency commi-ssion (viz. Relief Bonds/ Savings Bonds etc. transactions).

Whenever agency banks collect stamp duty through physical mode or e-mode (challan based), they are eligible for payment of agency commission, provided the agency banks do not collect any charges from the members of public or receive remuneration from the State Government for doing this work.

If the agency bank is engaged by the State Government as Franking Vendor and it collects stamp duty from the public for franking the documents, it will not be eligible for agency commission since the State Government is paying commission to it as Franking Vendor. However, the agency bank which-collects the stamp duty paid by the Franking Vendor for credit to the Treasury through challan in physical or e-mode for purchase of the franking bar, would be eligible for agency commission since it is a regular payment of Stamp Duty as stated above.

Pension Payment Order is the basic document sanctioning pension to a retired employee. Life certificate is obtained in November every year. Pension for the month of March is credited in the month of April. Thus, in the month of April, pension is credited twice in the account of the pensioner. Pension account is opened in the name of pensioner. It can be opened jointly with the spouse either as 'either or survivor or "former or survivor provided the pensioner gives an undertaking that the pension disbursing authority will be discharged by credit pension to the joint account.

Agency banks would be eligible to claim agency commission for pension transactions at the rate of ₹ 65/- per transaction only when the entire work relating to disbursement of pension including pension calculation is attended to by them. If the work relating to pension calculations, etc., is attended to by the concerned Government Department/Treasury and the bank branches are required only to credit the amount of pension to the pensioners' accounts maintained with them by a single debit to Government Account, such transaction is to be categorised under 'other than pension payment' and would be eligible for payment of agency commission @ 5.5 paise per ₹ 100/- turnover w.e.f. July 1, 2012.

Turnover commission is payable to an agency bank at the full rate provided the transactions are handled by the bank at all stages. Where, however, the work is shared between two banks, the turnover commission is shared between the banks in the proportion of 75:25. Thus, broadly, the turnover commission is payable to the agency banks as detailed below:

a) At the full rate, in cases where the transactions are handled by the bank at all stages, *i.e.*, up to the stage of dispatch of scrolls and challans / cheques to the Pay and Accounts Offices, and treasuries/sub-treasuries.
b) At 75% of the applicable rate, where the dealing branch is required to account for the transaction by passing on the scrolls and documents to the local/nearest branch of Reserve Bank of India or any agency bank conducting government business.
c) At 25% of the applicable rate, in the case of agency branch which received the scrolls and documents from dealing branches of other banks and is responsible for the account of these transactions and dispatching of the scrolls and documents to the Pay and Accounts Offices, Treasuries, etc.

The number of transactions eligible for payment of agency commission should not exceed 14 per pensioner per year. This includes one monthly credit for payment of net pension and a maximum of two per year for payment of arrears on account of increase in dearness relief, if applicable. Cases involving payment of arrears on account of late start/restart of pension qualifies as a single transaction for claiming of agency commission. In other words, any payment of arrears on account of late start/restart of pension should be treated as a single credit transaction and not as separate monthly credits.

PORTFOLIO MANAGEMENT

The Bank provides as one of the customer services, the facility of Portfolio Management. Portfolio management is the art and science of making decisions about investment mix and policy, matching investments to objectives, asset allocation for individuals and institutions, and balancing risk against performance. Portfolio management is all about determining strengths, weaknesses, opportunities and threats in the choice of debt vs. equity, domestic vs. international, growth vs. safety, and many other trade-offs encountered in the attempt to maximize return at a given appetite for risk.

The key to effective portfolio management is the long-term mix of assets. Asset allocation is based on the understanding that different types of assets do not move in concert, and some are more volatile than others. Asset allocation seeks to optimize the risk/return profile of an investor by investing in a mix of assets that have low correlation to each other. Investors with a more aggressive profile can weight their portfolio toward more volatile investments. Investors with a more conservative profile can weight their portfolio toward more stable investments.

MERCHANT BANKING

A merchant bank is a company that deals mostly in international finance, business loans for companies and underwriting. These banks are experts in international trade, which makes them specialists in dealing with multinational corporations.

Merchant Banking is a combination of Banking and consultancy services. It provides consultancy to its clients for financial, marketing, managerial and legal matters. Consultancy means to provide advice, guidance and service for a fee. It helps a businessman to start a business. It helps to raise (collect) finance. It helps to expand and modernize the business. It helps in restructuring of a business. It helps to revive sick business units. It also helps companies to register, buy and sell shares at the Stock exchange.

To illustrate the role of a merchant bank, suppose a multinational corporation XYZ is considering the purchase of a smaller company in another country. Company XYZ will likely solicit the services of a merchant bank for advice on how to best approach the acquisition process. In addition, the merchant bank may also assist in the financing of the acquisition, providing underwriting or loan services.

TEST YOURSELF

1. Which is not a Negotiable Instrument for remittances?
   (a) Demand Draft (b) Banker's Cheque
   (c) Cheque (d) None
2. DD is valid for a period of ________ and it requires revalidation thereafter.
   (a) 1 months (b) 3 months
   (c) 6 months (d) 12 months
3. Demand draft or Pay order of ________ & above in a day should be issued to the debit of an account or cheque and not against cash.
   (a) ₹ 10,000 (b) ₹ 20,000
   (c) ₹ 50,000 (d) ₹ 100,000
4. Duplicate DD have to be issued to the purchaser within ________ of the request subject to completion of formalities.
   (a) 14 days (b) 21 days
   (c) 30 days (d) 45 days
5. In case both original as well as duplicate DDs are presented to the drawee branch for payment. What steps bank has to take?
   (a) Bank should pay original DD and return duplicate with the reason 'DD reported lost and duplicate since issued and paid'.
   (b) In case both original as well as duplicate DDs are presented to the drawee branch for payment it should pay duplicate DD and return original with the reason 'DD reported lost and duplicate since issued and paid'.
   (c) Banker should return the both DDs.
   (d) Banker should contact purchaser of DD for further action.
6. Walk-in customers can also deposit cash at the NEFT-enabled branches with instructions to transfer funds using NEFT. However, such cash remittances will be restricted to a maximum of ________ per transaction.
   (a) ₹ 10,000 (b) ₹ 20,000
   (c) ₹ 50,000 (d) ₹ 100,000
7. Settlement Timings of the NEFT operates in ________ batches.
   (a) half hourly (b) hourly
   (c) two hourly (d) three hourly
8. Period of Credit in case of NEFT, the beneficiary should get credit within ________ from the time of completion of batch *i.e.*, on B+2 basis on the same day.
   (a) 1 hour (b) 2 hours
   (c) 4 hours (d) 6 hours
9. Which is not a correct statement about NEFT?
   (a) There is no value limit for individual transactions. Thus there is no minimum or maximum amount to be remitted.
   (b) There are twenty four settlements on weekdays other than second & fourth Saturday.
   (c) NEFT can be used to transfer funds from or to NRE and NRO accounts in the country.
   (d) NEFT system can be used only for remitting Indian Rupee among the participating banks within the country.
10. The originating member should release the payment message from their system to the RTGS central system within ________ of debiting a customer's account.
    (a) 30 minutes (b) 60 minutes
    (c) 120 minutes (d) 180 minutes
11. The RTGS system is primarily meant for large value transactions. The minimum amount to be remitted through RTGS is ________.
    (a) ₹ 50000 (b) ₹ 1 lakh
    (c) ₹ 2 lakh (d) ₹ 5 lakh
12. Which is not a correct statement about RTGS?
    (a) This is the fastest possible money transfer system through the banking channel.
    (b) Settlement in "real time" means payment transaction is not subjected to any waiting period.
    (c) There is no upper ceiling for RTGS transactions.
    (d) The RTGS service window for customer's transactions is available to banks from 10.00 hours to 16.30 hours on week days for settlement at the RBI end
13. RTGS helps in preventing Systemic and Settlement Risks. There are ________ in UTR (Unique Transaction Reference Number).
    (a) 15 digits (b) 20 digits
    (c) 22 digits (d) 24 digits
14. IFSC is a ________ digit code with first ________ characters representing the banks code, the next character reserved as control character (Presently 0 appears in the fifth position) and remaining ________ characters to identify the branch.
    (a) 12, 4, 7 (b) 11, 4, 6
    (c) 10, 4, 6 (d) 11, 5, 6
15. IFSC is used by
    (a) RTGS
    (b) NEFT
    (c) Both RTGS and NEFT
    (d) Draft

16. The MICR code has 9 digits to identify the bank-branch. Each three digits in code signifies the information about City, Bank Name, and Branch Code.
(a) State, city, and Branch Code
(b) State, Bank Name, and Branch Code
(c) Bank Name, City, and Branch Code
(d) City, Bank Name, and Branch Code

17. Which is not a correct statement about Mobile Banking?
(a) Banks licensed and supervised in India and have a physical presence in India only, can offer mobile banking services.
(b) The services are not restricted to customers of banks and/or holders of debit/credit cards issued as per the extant RBI guidelines.
(c) Only Rupee based domestic services can be provided cross border inward and outward transfers strictly prohibited.
(d) Banks may use services of Business Correspondent for extending this facility.

18. Safe Deposit Vault is governed by provisions of ________.
(a) Transfer of Property Act
(b) Indian Contract Act
(c) NI Act
(d) Banking Regulation Act

19. The relationship between bank and customer in case of Safe Deposit Vault is:
(a) Principal and Agent (b) Lessor and Lessee
(c) Bailee and Bailor (d) Debtor and Creditor

20. Locks of the lockers must be changed under which of the following circumstances:
(a) When a locker is surrendered
(b) When an overdue locker is drilled open
(c) When a locker is drilled open due to loss of key
(d) All of the above

ANSWER

1	2	3	4	5	6	7	8	9	10
(d)	(b)	(c)	(a)	(b)	(c)	(a)	(b)	(b)	(a)
11	**12**	**13**	**14**	**15**	**16**	**17**	**18**	**19**	**20**
(c)	(d)	(c)	(b)	(c)	(d)	(b)	(a)	(b)	(d)

CASH OPERATIONS

CASH MANAGEMENT SERVICES

Introduction: The fundamental objective of cash management is 'optimisation of liquidity through an improved flow of funds'. In today's highly competitive environment, where time is considered as money, deployment of staff to render basic routine tasks does not make economic sense. Cash management today is not what it used to be. Electronic banking, which began as a passive desktop access to bank balances, is emerging into complex processes of liquidity management through numerous techniques.

Importance of Cash Management for a Corporate Entity: Good cash management is a conscious process of knowing when, where, and how a company's cash needs will occur; knowing what the best sources for meeting additional cash needs; and being prepared to meet these needs when they occur by keeping good relationships with bankers and other creditors.

Scientific cash management results in

a) significant savings in time,
b) decrease in interest costs,
c) less paper work and
d) greater accounting accuracy.

Proper cash management creates more control over time and funds; provides timely access to information; enables easy employee related payments; supports electronic payments; produces faster electronic reconciliation; allows for detection of bookkeeping errors; reduces the number of cheques issued and earns interest income or reduces interest expense. Corporations with subsidiaries worldwide, can pool everything internationally so that the company can off-set the debts with the surplus moneys from various subsidiaries. The end result will transform treasury function as a profit-centre by optimising cash and put it to good use. Creative and pro-active cash management solutions can contribute dramatically to a company's profitability and to its competitive edge. The ultimate purpose of proper management of liquidity, needless to emphasise, is to improve the overall productivity of funds.

Importance of Fee-based Services Segment to Banks: Deregulation and new technology have eroded banks' comparative advantages and made it easier for non-bank competitors to enter into hitherto exclusive banks' domains. In response, banks have shifted their sales mix toward non-interest income by selling 'non-bank' fee-based financial services by charging explicit fees for services. According to another study titled 'Fee-Based Financial Services Markets: New Opportunities and Threats In the Internet Age' by Killen Associates again, the market for retail and commercial fee-based financial services will exceed that for interest-based services globally.

Banks want such services to be their primary profit source for certain reasons. This revenue is more stable over time, assures a steady income and more importantly, leads to a strong relationship with the corporate client.

Types of Cash Management Services

A number of banks in India are offering wide-ranging cash management services to their corporate clients. All the three categories of banks *viz.,* nationalised banks, private banks, and foreign banks operating in India are active in the cash management segment. Indian banks are offering services like;

- Electronic funds transfer services;
- Provision of cash related MIS reports;
- Cash pooling services;
- Cash collection services;
- Debit transfer services;
- Guaranteed credit arrangements;
- Sweep products;
- Tax payment services;
- Receivables and payables management.

Foreign banks operating in India are offering regional and global treasury management services, liquidity management services, card services, electronic banking services, e-commerce solutions, account management services, collection management services, cash delivery management services and investment solutions.

The Reserve Bank of India has been taking a number of initiatives, which will facilitate the active involvement of commercial banks in the sophisticated cash management segment. One of the pre-requisites to ensure faster and reliable mobility of funds in a country is to have an efficient payment system. With the help of the systems already put in place in India and which are coming into being, both banks and corporates can exercise effective control over the cash management.

A FRAMEWORK TO PROVIDE EFFECTIVE CASH MANAGEMENT SERVICES

Companies seek to achieve synergies by implementing a simplified account structure and through rationalising the number of banks used. In advising companies on the optimal account structure, it is important to bear in mind the nature of company's funds flows. The aim is to maximise control, efficiency and return. Banks need to work with its clients to ensure that arrangements are in place to assist them in maximising returns from an otherwise idle funds.

Provision of CMS by Banks-Challenges and Issues: The conventional formal line between treasury and control and between cash and accounting strategies is fading. Now, bankers and controllers are working together closely in seeking solutions in the complex cash management function. In today's world, the key differentiator between a successful bank and other bank is the stress each lays on technology. As such, let me turn your attention to the numerous challenges bankers need to address squarely, while gearing up to provide cash management services in a technology dominated environment.

Need to Comprehend the Client's Line of Activity: Bankers need to really understand the accounting and control side of its client business. The bankers should see themselves as strategic partners in company's growth and need to spend a lot of time learning about the concerned industry.

Provision of Other Advisory Services to Clients: Companies would like to see banks solve certain other related problems. Changing systems is a major initiative with far-reaching implications to the companies so banker cannot afford to make a mistake. As the technology changes almost monthly, companies do expect bankers to tell them what to do and where to spend their money. Bankers cannot build a standard solution always, because the customers do not pose standard problems. Bankers have to customise the solution that will resemble what the customer is wishing for.

Decisions Regarding Sourcing of Software: The three sources of software applications for on-line banking and on-line cash management in particular, are

1) built in-house,
2) bought from independent software vendors and
3) outsourced to a trusted third party.

Large banks prefer to build applications in-house owing to their belief that it provides them with competitive advantage.

Special Consideration to Small and Medium Companies: When the corporate scene in India is dominated by a multitude of small and medium companies, a legitimate question that arises is, are the high-tech banking cash management services just for the large companies or do they have any immediate practical value for smaller companies also? Although technology and size may not go together banks have to cost-justify the cash management services companies use. No doubt, banks did invest a lot in the technology-based services. But with the advent of the Internet and other tools, banks should strive to make accessible cash management services to middle and small companies without totally phasing out their existing hardware.

Need to Work as a Team: When banks develop cash management solutions, they have to necessarily work directly with corporate financial controllers and their staff. When outsourcing is involved, with something as complex as payables or receivables the corporate teams get bigger and more varied. Besides financial controllers, banks have to work with systems people and sometimes marketing people.

Concerns About Security and Risk Management: Corporate treasury information is quite sensitive. Corporations lose large amounts due to internal and external fraud. Security and trust are critical issues when it comes to electronic transmission and retrieval of important and sensitive information such as corporate treasury data. Commercial cash management is one of the most risky forms of Internet banking, therefore, it requires strong security and trust elements.

Need to Work with Technology Vendors: A growing number of non-bank vendors also offer payment-related services to corporate clients in Western countries. Banks bring the strong relationships with customers that they have built over time. No single player can do it alone in the future because there are so many dimensions to technology and different industries need different solutions. Alliances will have to be forged, so that vendors with different technological pieces will work together to provide integrated solutions. There is no question that banks and other third-party processors are going to compete, but there may be even greater opportunities for them to work together.

TEST YOURSELF

1. Good cash management is a conscious process of:
   (a) knowing when, where, and how a company's cash needs will occur
   (b) knowing what the best sources for meeting additional cash needs
   (c) being prepared to meet these needs when they occur by keeping good relationships with bankers and other creditors
   (d) All of the above
2. Which is not a Scientific cash management results in:
   (a) significant savings in time
   (b) decrease in interest costs,
   (c) more paper work
   (d) greater accounting accuracy
3. Indian banks are offering cash management services like;
   (a) Electronic funds transfer services
   (b) Provision of cash related MIS reports
   (c) Cash pooling services
   (d) All of the above
4. Indian banks are not offering which type of cash management services?
   (a) Cash collection services
   (b) Guaranteed credit arrangements
   (c) Tax payment services
   (d) None of the above
5. The three sources of software applications for on-line banking and on-line cash management in particular, are:
   (a) built in-house
   (b) bought from independent software vendors and
   (c) outsourced to a trusted third party
   (d) all of the above
6. Which of the following can be considered as part of cash management services?
   (a) maintaining minimum cash balance at bank branch
   (b) providing all denomination of currency notes in an ATM
   (c) providing solutions of a large company to optimize the liquidity
   (d) all of the above

ANSWER

1	2	3	4	5	6
(d)	(c)	(d)	(d)	(d)	(c)

PRINCIPLES OF LENDING, WORKING CAPITAL ASSESSMENT AND CREDIT MONITORING

PRINCIPLES OF LENDING

Introduction: The basic function of a bank is acceptance of deposits of money from the public for the purpose of lending and investment. Banks should deploy such funds very carefully. While deploying funds as loans and advances, banks should ensure that certain lending principles are followed by them. Banks should give importance to the principles of lending based on the following concepts: Safety, Liquidity, Purpose, Diversity, Security and Profitability. Banks should also ensure that a good credit monitoring system is in place both at pre-sanction and post-sanction levels.

Principles of Lending

The lending business of the banks carry certain inherent risks and bank must aware about the risk whenever it wants to lend. Hence, lending activity has to necessarily adhere to certain principles. Lending principles can be classified as:

1. Project Report: While financing a loan, bank should assess the project report on the basis of following aspects:

(a) Safety of Funds (b) Profitability
(c) Liquidity (d) Purpose of the loan
(e) Risk Spread (f) Security

2. Borrowers Profile: While financing a loan, bank should assess the Borrowers Profile and credit worthiness of a person on the basis of following aspects:

(a) Character (b) Capacity
(c) Capital,

IMPORTANT ASPECTS FOR PROJECT REPORT ASSESSMENT

a) **Safety:** When banker lends certain money, the first and foremost principle of lending is to ensure the safety of the funds. By safety is meant that the borrower is in a position to repay the loan, alongwith interest, according to the terms of the loan contract. The repayment of the loan depends upon the borrower's (i) capacity to pay, and (ii) willingness to pay. The former depends upon his tangible assets and the success of his business, if he is successful in his efforts, he earns profits and can repay the loan promptly. Otherwise, the loan is recovered out of the sale proceeds of his tangible assets. The willingness to pay depends upon the honesty and character of the borrower. He should be a person of integrity, good character and reputation.

b) **Liquidity:** Banks are essentially to think that money lent is not going to be locked for a long time. Therefore, they lend most of the funds for short periods and mainly for working capital purposes. The banker must ensure that the borrower is able to repay the loan on demand or within a short period. This depends upon the nature of assets owned by the borrower and pledged to the banker.

c) **Profitability:** Commercial banks are profit-earning institutions and the nationalized banks are no exception to this. They must deploy their funds profitably so as to earn sufficient income out of which to pay interest to the depositors, salaries to the staff and to meet various other establishment expenses and distribute dividends to the shareholders. The rates of interest charged by banks were in the past primarily dependent on the directives issued by the Reserve Bank. Now banks are free to determine their own rates of interest on advances. The variations in the rates of interest charged from different customers depend upon the degree of risk involved in lending to them. A customer with high reputation is charged the lower rate of interest as compared to an ordinary customer. The sound principle of lending is not to sacrifice safety or liquidity for the sake of higher profitability.

d) **Purpose of the Loan:** While lending his funds, the banker enquires from the borrower the purpose for which he seeks the loan. Loans are not advanced for speculative and unproductive purposes. After the nationalization of major banks loans for initial expenditure to start small trades, businesses, industries, education, housing, medical expenses or any bonafide purposes etc., are also given by the banks.

e) **Principle of Diversification of Risks:** An industry or trade may face recessionary conditions and the price of the goods and commodities may sharply fall. Natural calamities like floods and earthquakes, and political disturbances in certain parts of the country may ruin even a prosperous business. To safeguard his interest against such unforeseen contingencies, the banker follows the principle of diversification of risks based on the famous maxim "do not keep all the eggs in one basket." It means that the banker should not grant advances to a few big firms only or to concentrate them in a few industries or in a few cities or regions of the country only. The advances, on the other hand, should be over a reasonably wide area, distributed amongst a good number of customers belonging to different trades and industries. The banker, thus, diversifies the risk involved in lending. If a big customer meets misfortune, or certain trades or industries are affected adversely, the overall position of the bank will not be in jeopardy.

f) **Security:** This is also a cardinal principle of sound lending. A prudent banker always tries to select the borrower very carefully and takes tangible assets as securities to safeguard his interests. Tangible assets are no doubt valuable and the banker feels safe while granting advances on the security of such assets, yet some risk is always involved therein.

IMPORTANT ASPECTS FOR BORROWERS PROFILE

The credit-worthiness of a person means that he deserves a certain amount of credit, which may safely be granted to him. Such credit-worthiness is judged by the banker on the basis of his (*a*) character, (*b*) capacity, and (*c*) capital.

(a) **Character:** In assessing the credit-worthiness of a person, the first consideration is that of the character of the person concerned. The word character implies and includes a number of personal characteristics of a person, *e.g.*, his honesty, integrity, regularity and promptness in fulfilling his promises and repaying his dues, sense of responsibility, good habits and the reputation and goodwill which he enjoys in the eyes of others. If a person possesses all these qualities, without any doubt or suspicion in the minds of others, he possesses an excellent character and will be considered creditworthy by the banker.

(b) **Capacity:** The success of an enterprise largely depends upon the ability, competence and experience of the entrepreneur. If the borrower possesses necessary technical skill, managerial ability and experience to run a particular industry or trade, success of such unit may be taken for granted (barring some unforeseen circumstances) and the banker will consider him a deserving case for granting an advance. The significance of this factor is now growing as the banks are willing to grant unsecured loans to technicians and competent persons on the basis of soundness of their business projects, irrespective of their own capital.

(c) **Capital:** The importance attached by the banker to the adequacy of capital of the borrower is not without significance. Banks are the repositories of the public money and lend the borrowed money. The banker, therefore, does not lend money to an entrepreneur who does not have adequate funds of his own. In case of failure of the business enterprise, the banker will be able to realize his money if the borrower's own capital is sufficient.

Though all the above-mentioned factors are important and taken into account by the banker at the time of assessing the credit-worthiness of the borrower, their relative importance differs from banker to banker and from borrower to borrower.

NON-FUND BASED LIMITS

Involve Immediate outflow of funds. The banker undertakes a risk to pay the amounts on happening of a contingency. Non-based facilities can be of following types among other:

(a) Bank Guarantees

(b) Letter of Credit

(a) Bank Guarantees

As part of Non-fund-based facilities, banks issue guarantees on behalf of their clients. A Bank Guarantee is a commitment given by a banker to a third party, assuring her/ him to honour the claim against the guarantee in the event of the non- performance by the bank's customer. A Bank Guarantee is a legal contract which can be imposed by law. The banker as guarantor assures the third party (beneficiary) to pay him a certain sum of money on behalf of his customer, in case the customer fails to fulfil his commitment to the beneficiary.

General Guidelines: As regards the purpose of the guarantee, as a general rule, the banks should confine themselves to the provision of financial guarantees and exercise due caution with regard to performance guarantee business.

As regards maturity, as a rule, banks should guarantee shorter maturities and leave longer maturities to be guaranteed by other institutions. No bank guarantee should normally have a maturity of more than 10 years. However, in view of the changed scenario of the banking industry where banks extend long term loans for periods longer than 10 years for various projects, it has been decided to allow banks to also issue guarantees for periods beyond 10 years. While issuing such guarantees, banks are advised to take into account the impact of very long duration guarantees on their Asset Liability Management. Further, banks may evolve a policy on issuance of guarantees beyond 10 years as considered appropriate with the approval of their Board of Directors.

Norms for Unsecured Advances & Guarantees: RBI guidelines dated July 1, 2015 are as under:

(i) Until June 17, 2004, banks were required to limit their commitments by way of unsecured guarantees in such a manner that 20 per cent of a bank's outstanding unsecured guarantees plus the total of its outstanding unsecured advances should not exceed 15 per cent of its total outstanding advances. In order to provide further flexibility to banks on their loan policies, the above limit on unsecured exposure of banks was withdrawn and banks' Boards have been given the freedom to fix their own policies on their unsecured exposures. "Unsecured exposure" is defined as an exposure where the realisable value of the security, as assessed by the bank/ approved valuers / Reserve Bank's inspecting officers, is not more than 10 per cent, ab-initio, of the outstanding exposure. Exposure shall include all funded and non-funded exposures (including underwriting and similar commitments). 'Security' will mean tangible security properly charged to the bank and will not include intangible securities like guarantees, letter of comfort, etc.

(ii) For determining the amount of unsecured advances for reflecting in schedule 9 of the published balance sheet, the rights, licenses, authorisations, etc., charged to the banks as collateral in respect of projects (including infrastructure projects) financed by them, should not be reckoned as tangible security. Banks, may however, treat annuities under build-operate –transfer (BOT) model in respect of road/ highway projects and toll collection rights where there are provisions to compensate the project sponsor if a certain level of traffic is not achieved, as tangible securities, subject to the condition that banks' right to receive annuities and toll collection rights is legally enforceable and irrevocable.

(iii) All exemptions allowed for computation of unsecured advances stand withdrawn.

Precautions for Issuing Guarantees: Banks should adopt the following precautions while issuing guarantees on behalf of their customers.

(i) As a rule, banks should avoid giving unsecured guarantees in large amounts and for medium and long-term periods. They should avoid undue concentration of such unsecured guarantee commitments to particular groups of customers and/or trades.

(ii) Unsecured guarantees on account of any individual constituent should be limited to a reasonable proportion of the bank's total unsecured guarantees. Guarantees on behalf of an individual should also bear a reasonable proportion to the constituent's equity.

(iii) In exceptional cases, banks may give deferred payment guarantees on an unsecured basis for modest amounts to first class customers who have entered into deferred payment arrangements in consonance with Government policy.

(iv) Guarantees executed on behalf of any individual constituent, or a group of constituents, should be subject to the prescribed exposure norms.

(v) It is essential to realise that guarantees contain inherent risks and that it would not be in the bank's interest or in the public interest, generally, to encourage parties to over-extend their commitments and embark upon enterprises solely relying on the easy availability of guarantee facilities.

(b) Letters of Credit (LCs)

A Letter of Credit is issued by a bank at the request of its customer (importer) in favour of the beneficiary (exporter). It is an undertaking/ commitment by the bank, advising/informing the beneficiary that the documents under a LC would be honoured, if the beneficiary (exporter) submits all the required documents as per the terms and conditions of the LC.

Guidelines for Grant of LCs Facility

Primary (urban) co-operative banks should not normally grant LC facilities in respect of parties who maintain only nominal current accounts. In case of borrowers maintaining only current accounts, who approach for opening of LCs, banks should invariably ascertain from the existing bankers of the borrowers the reasons as to why they are not extending LC facilities to the concerned borrowers. Banks should open LCs in respect of such parties only after making proper enquiries in regard to the antecedents of the borrowers from the bankers with whom the parties are enjoying main limits, their financial position and their ability to retire the bills. They should also prescribe a suitable margin and obtain other security, as necessary.

How LC Limit is Assessed?

Suppose a constituent makes a total purchase of ₹ 120 crores out of which he imports 50 % (₹ 60 crores). Now, he approaches us to open an LC for his requirement.

How to calculate the LC Limit?

1.	Average monthly import purchase (60 /12)	=	₹ 5 crores
2.	Import duty element say	=	₹ 1 crore
3.	Actual monthly import (5 -1)	=	₹ 4 crore
4.	Purchase of documents on D/A basis say	=	₹ 2.50 crore
5.	Purchase of documents on D/P basis say	=	₹ 1.50 crore
6.	Transit period for imports say	=	2 months
7.	Usance period for imports	=	2 months
8.	Total Lead time (6 + 7)	=	4 months
9.	LC requirement on DA basis = ₹ 2.50 crore x 4 months	=	₹ 10 crore
10.	+ LC requirement on DP basis = ₹ 1.50 crores x 2 months	=	₹ 3 crore
TOTAL L/C REQUIREMENT	= (₹ 10 crore + ₹ 3 crore)	=	Rs. 13 crore.

LCs for Commodities covered under Selective Credit Controls: There is no restriction for the banks in opening LCs for import of essential items. However, banks are not permitted to open inland LCs, providing a clause therein which would enable other banks to discount usance bills under the LCs.

Safeguards in Opening of LCs: Before opening LCs, banks should ensure that:

(i) LCs are issued in security forms only;

(ii) Large LCs are issued under two authorised signatures where one of the signatures for LCs should be from the Head Office/Controlling Office. As the need for large LCs may not arise overnight, with the availability of courier service, speed post service etc., this procedure may not result in delay. In the LCs itself a column may be provided to indicate the authority who had sanctioned it together with the particulars thereof;

(iii) LCs are not issued for amounts out of proportion to the borrowers' genuine requirements and these are opened only after ensuring that the borrowers have made adequate arrangements for retiring the bills received under LCs out of their own resources or from the existing borrowing arrangements;

(iv) Where LCs are for purchase of raw materials, borrowers do not maintain unduly high inventory of raw materials in relation to the norms / past trends. Where such LCs are to be opened on D/A basis, credit on the relative purchase is duly taken into account for the purpose of working out drawing power in cash credit accounts;

(v) In the case of borrowers having banking arrangements on a consortium basis, the LCs are opened within the sanctioned limit on the basis of the agreed share of each of the banks. Member-banks should not, however, open LCs outside the sanctioned limits without the knowledge of the lead bank/other banks;

(vi) If there is no formal consortium arrangement for financing the borrower, LCs should not be opened by the existing bank or a new bank, without the knowledge of the other banks;

(viii) LCs for acquisition of capital goods should be opened only after banks have satisfied themselves about tying up of funds for meeting the relative liability by way of providing for long term funds or term loans from financial institutions / banks;

(viii) In no case, working capital limits should be allowed to be utilised for retiring bills pertaining to acquisition of capital assets.

(ix) Banks should not extend any non-fund based facilities or additional / ad-hoc credit facilities to parties who are not their (the bank's) regular constituents for their production finance requirements; nor should they discount bills drawn under LCs or otherwise for beneficiaries who are not their regular clients. In case it becomes unavoidably necessary to provide such a facility to a party not being a regular client, banks should invariably seek the prior concurrence of the existing banker of the borrowers and also make proper enquiries in regard to the antecedents of the borrowers, their financial position and ability to retire the bills etc. in time.

(x) With effect from March 30, 2012 in case of bills drawn under LCs restricted to a particular UCB, and the beneficiary of the LC is not a borrower who has been granted regular credit facility by that UCB, the UCB concerned may, as per their discretion and based on their perception about the credit worthiness of the LC issuing bank, negotiate such LCs, subject to the condition that the proceeds will be remitted to the regular banker of the beneficiary of the LC. However, the prohibition regarding negotiation of unrestricted LCs for borrowers who have not been sanctioned regular credit facilities will continue to be in force.

(xi) UCBs negotiating bills as above, under restricted LCs, would have to adhere to the instructions of the Reserve Bank / RCS or CRCS regarding share linking to borrowing and provisions of Co-operative Societies Act on membership.

WORKING CAPITAL-APPRAISAL & ASSESSMENT

Working Capital: Working capital is required for day-to-day operations of an enterprise. Working capital is also called gross current assets.

An enterprise starts from cash and goes through a cycle of raw material, work in process, finished goods, receivables and then again cash. This cash to cash cycle is known as Operating Cycle. It is during this operating cycle that an enterprise needs working capital to support its operations smoothly. So operating cycle is the time lag between the cash investment in purchase of raw material and realizing cash through sale of finished goods.

Before we venture into the appraisal and assessment part, let us familiarize ourselves with a few terminologies and ratios pertaining to the topic which will pave the way for our comprehending the concept in a better way.

1. **Gross Working Capital:** It is nothing but the total current assets invested in the enterprise.
2. **Working Capital Gap:** Current Assets-Current Liabilities (excluding bank finance)
3. **Net Working Capital or Margin:** Current Assets-Current Liabilities (including bank finance). It is the promoter's contribution.
4. **Raw Material Holding:**

$$\frac{\text{Raw Material Stock}}{\text{Annual Consumption of RM}} \times 365 \text{ days}$$

5. **Debtor's Velocity Ratio:**

$$\frac{\text{Receivables}}{\text{Credit sales}} \times 365 \text{ days}$$

6. **Creditor's Velocity Ratio:**

$$\frac{\text{Payables or Creditors}}{\text{Credit Purchases}} \times 365 \text{ days}$$

5 and 6 are also called debtor's collection period and creditor's payment period.

Current Assets are those assets which can be converted into cash within one accounting year. These include cash, raw materials, finished goods, receivables, advance for raw material, prepaid expenses etc.

Current Liabilities are those items which are required to be repaid within one accounting year. These include creditors, bills payables, outstanding expenses, advances received etc.

Assessment of Working Capital: Banks in India have evolved their own method of lending as they have been given free hand by the RBI to decide their own lending method. Normally banks used Turnover Method based on Nayak Committee Recommendations and Tandon Committee Recommendations for calculation of MPBF limit. In case of seasonal activities, especially in the agro-based sector, the bank finance for working capital is assessed on the basis of monthly cash budget method. There are two prevalent methods being adopted by almost all the banks at present.

1. Turnover Method based on Nayak Committee Recommendations: Under this method WC proposals up to ₹ 5 crores are assessed. We finance 20% of projected annual sales turnover. Margin will be 5% of the gross projected turnover. Assumption is that operating cycle will be of 3 months requiring 25% of annual sales turnover. Under this method, the margin is 20% and Current Ratio is 1.25. If NWC or promoter's contribution is more than 5%, the same will be reckoned as margin resulting in lowering of assessed limit.

Recently, Department of Financial Services (DFS), Government of India issued an advisory to banks to increase working capital limits for small industry (MSE). IBA hence advised that bank may revisit their policy and revise guidelines implemented recently specially for MSEs under turnover assessment working capital limits enhanced from minimum 20% to 25% of the projected turnover in individual cases up to ₹ 5 crores with proportionate increase in margin. Besides to encourage digital transaction, it is also advised banks to increase working capital assessment from 20% to 30% of the digital portion projected turnover for credit limit in individual cases upto ₹ 5 crores with proportionate increase in margin.

2. Tandon Committee Recommendations: As per the recommendations of Tandon Committee, the corporates should be discouraged from accumulating too much of stocks of current assets and should move towards very lean inventories and receivable levels. The committee even suggested the maximum levels of Raw Material, Stock-in-process and Finished Goods which a corporate operating in an industry should be allowed to accumulate these levels were termed as inventory and receivable norms. Depending on the size of credit required, the funding of these current assets (working capital needs) of the corporates could be met by one of the following methods:

MPBF or First Method of Lending: Banks can work out the working capital gap, *i.e.*, total current assets less current liabilities other than bank borrowings (called Maximum Permissible Bank Finance or MPBF) and finance a maximum of 75 per cent of the gap; the balance to come out of long-term funds, *i.e.*, owned funds and term borrowings. This approach was considered suitable only for very small borrowers *i.e.*, where the requirements of credit were less than ₹ 10 lakh.

Suppose Current Assets is ₹ 100 lakh and Current Liability is ₹ 40 lakh

Current Asset	₹ 100 lakh
Current Liability	₹ 40 lakh
Working Capital Gap	₹ 100 lakh – ₹ 40 lakh = ₹ 60 lakh
Margin 25% of Working Capital Gap	25% of ₹ 60 lakh = ₹ 15 lakh
MPBF as per First Method of Lending	₹ 60 lakh – ₹ 15 lakh = ₹ 45 lakh

MPBF or Second Method of Lending: Under this method, it was thought that the borrower should provide for a minimum of 25% of total current assets out of long-term funds *i.e.*, owned funds plus term borrowings. A certain level of credit for purchases and other current liabilities will be available to fund the buildup of current assets and the bank will provide the balance (MPBF). Consequently, total current liabilities inclusive of bank borrowings could not exceed 75% of current assets. RBI stipulated that the working capital needs of all borrowers enjoying fund based credit facilities of more than ₹ 10 lakh should be appraised (calculated) under this method.

Suppose Current Assets is ₹ 100 lakh and Current Liability is ₹ 40 lakh

Current Asset	₹ 100 lakh
Current Liability	₹ 40 lakh
Working Capital Gap	₹ 100 lakh – ₹ 40 lakh = ₹ 60 lakh
Margin 25% of Current Asset	25% of ₹ 100 lakh = ₹ 25 lakh
MPBF as per Second Method of Lending	₹ 60 lakh – ₹ 25 lakh = ₹ 35 lakh

Third Method of Lending: Under this method, the borrower's contribution from long term funds will be to the extent of the entire CORE CURRENT ASSETS, which has been defined by the Study Group as representing the absolute minimum level of raw materials, process stock, finished goods and stores which are in the pipeline to ensure continuity of production and a minimum of 25% of the balance current assets should be financed out of the long term funds plus term borrowings. (This method was not accepted for implementation and hence is of only academic interest).

3. Cash Budget Method: Calculated on the basis of peak level cash deficit. Peak level cash deficit will be ascertained from projected Cash Budget Statement submitted by the borrower.

In case of seasonal activities, especially in the agro-based sector, the bank finance for working capital is assessed on the basis of monthly cash budget and the relative cash deficiency on a monthly basis. Under this method, all estimated/projected cash receipts (inflow) on a monthly basis is arranged in a tabular form and the monthly cash outflows are also similarly shown against each month. The deficit or surplus of each month is worked out and the peak deficit amount is considered to be the working capital limit to be provided by the bank.

	May	*Jun*	*Jul*	*Aug*	*Sep*	*Oct*
A. Cash Rec. FromCash Sales	41	52	44	28	08	12
B. Cash paid to Creditor, Exp.	31	56	62	65	29	22
C. Net Cash Flow	10	–4	–18	–37	–21	–10
D. Cash at start of Month	6	18	28	24	6	5
E. Cumulative Cash (C+D)	16	14	10	–13	–15	–05
F. Min. Bal. Required	05	05	05	05	05	05
G. Surplus / Deficit	11	09	05	–18	–20	–10
Limit Required.	–	–	–	**18**	**20**	**10**

MARGINAL COST OF FUNDS BASED LENDING RATE (MCLR)

The MCLR methodology for fixing interest rates for advances was introduced by the Reserve Bank of India with effect from April 1, 2016. MCLR refers to the minimum interest rate of a bank below which it cannot lend, except in some cases allowed by the RBI. It is an internal benchmark or reference rate for the bank. MCLR describes the method by which the minimum interest rate for loans is determined by a bank - based on marginal cost or the additional or incremental cost of arranging one more rupee to the prospective borrower. MCLR is based on cost of funds for banks and is derived as the sum of marginal cost of funds, negative carry because of CRR, operating costs of banks and tenor premium. Banks publish MCLR for at least five durations which are overnight MCLR, 1 month MCLR, 3 month MCLR, 6 month MCLR and 1 year MCLR. However, banks may publish MCLR base rates for more than five periods. The banks may revise the MCLR rate every month. Interest rate on each floating rate loan would be reset on based on the duration of the MCLR to which it is linked.

Reasons for Introducing MCLR: RBI decided to shift from base rate to MCLR because the rates based on marginal cost of funds are more sensitive to changes in the policy rates. This is very essential for the effective implementation of monetary policy. Prior to MCLR system, different banks were following different methodology for calculation of base rate /minimum rate – that is either based on average cost of funds or marginal cost of funds or blended cost of funds. Thus, MCLR aims

- To improve the transmission of policy rates into the lending rates of banks;
- To bring transparency in the methodology followed by banks for determining interest rates on advances;
- To ensure availability of bank credit at interest rates which are fair to borrowers as well as banks;
- To enable banks to become more competitive and enhance their long run value and contribution to economic growth.

CREDIT MONITORING

Credit Monitoring can be defined as a supervision of a loan account on an ongoing basis keeping a continuous watch / vigil over the functioning of a borrower's unit to confirm that the account conform to the various ass-umptions made at the time of sanction. In other words credit monitoring is to maintain asset quality of the Bank.

Asset Quality of a Bank: A good sanction can become a bad loan, if not properly disbursed. But a bad decision cannot take care of credit monitoring.

Need for Credit Monitoring: Credit monitoring has become most important in view of system driven NPAs & growing NPAs. To guard against the human tendency to deviate from the stipulated terms in case of necessity, which, is particular, exists in case of advances. Need for Credit Monitoring are as under:

- Prevention is better than cure;
- To avoid slippage of accounts into NPA;
- To ensure end use of funds;
- To ensure compliance of terms of sanction;
- Banking is depending on projections, assumptions, estimates, hence monitoring of advance is essential;
- A good sanction can become bad if not properly disbursed & supervised.

When does the Credit Monitoring Start? Credit Monitoring starts from the moment the possibility of a new advance is visualized. The principles of good lending, identifying genuine borrower, and availability of adequate security, collectively known as due diligence are of paramount importance for credit monitoring.

TYPES OF CREDIT MONITORING

Credit Monitoring can be classified as two types:

(a) **Portfolio Monitoring.**

(b) **Account Specific Monitoring.**

FOUR STAGES OF MONITORING: Credit Monitoring has to be done on the following stages:

1. **Pre-Sanction-Application received**
2. **Post Sanction-Pre disbursement**
3. **Post Sanction-During Disbursement**
4. **Post Sanction-Post Disbursement**

1. **Pre Sanction Stage-Application received:** In this stage following matters should be monitored and verified:
   - Complete and Proper Application Form;
   - Assets and liabilities statements along with supporting documents;
   - Interview with the Borrower/Guarantor;
   - Inspection of borrower's residence, work place, guarantor's place;
   - Inspection of the immovable property, (if proposed). Mortgaged Property to be inspected by two officers, Keeping in mind the advocate's / valuer's findings;
   - Due Diligence: PAN / ITR / CIBIL / CERSAI / ROC / RBI / ECGC Defaulters list;
   - Due diligence exercise from outside agencies;
   - Balance Sheet (If applicable-Audited);
   - Full KYC documents;
   - Collection and scrutiny of required data.
   - Existing Bank Statement/Status of account etc;

During the Processing of application and preparation of proposal, the following matters should also be keeping in mind in Pre-Sanction Stage:

- Study of Pre-sanction inspection & Mortgaged property inspection report;
- Study and approval of Search/Valuation Report;
- Credit Rating Exercise (In applicable Models);
- Scheme related guidelines;
- Government Policy;
- MOF Directives;
- Business related Risk;
- Balance Sheet Analysis;
- Credit Rating Norms;
- Industry wise Policy;
- RBI Guidelines;
- Prudential Norms etc. Balance sheet to be cross checked with ROC. (Read Auditor's Note Carefully-Verification of CA Authenticity).

2. **Monitoring at Post Sanction-Pre Disbursement Stage:** In this stage following matters should be monitored and verified:

- Preparation of proposal in prescribed format and sanction thereof at appropriate level;
- Read the Process Note Minutely;
- What are the terms and conditions are stipulated?
- Issuance of sanction letter conveying all terms and conditions as per sanction and acceptance of terms & conditions of sanction by the borrower;
- Recovery of Charges;
- Obtaining/ Scrutiny of Legal Opinion Report and Valuation report.

- ❍ Proper documentation (including check list);
- ❍ Creation of Mortgage Charge and its registration with the Sub-Registrar;
- ❍ Charges to be registered with ROC in respect of company account;
- ❍ Execution of proper security documents including creation of mortgage as per sanction terms;
- ❍ Vetting of security documents by panel advocate. (If applicable);
- ❍ Online Registration of Equitable Mortgage with CERSAI (Central Registry of Securitizations Asset Reconstruction & Security Interest of India) under SARFAESI within 30 days;
- ❍ Correct data entry-account opening; (Recording of documents);
- ❍ Safe keeping of documents.

3. **Post Sanction-During Disbursement Stage:** In this stage following matters should be monitored and verified:
   - ❍ The disbursements should be commensurate with the progress of the project / business activity, also taking into account the extent of margin brought in by the promoters up to a given point of time;
   - ❍ Status Reports on the suppliers;
   - ❍ Direct disbursement to suppliers/service providers. Avoid Cash disbursement;
   - ❍ Verification of end use of funds through inspection, records, books of accounts;
   - ❍ Implementation Certificate from approved Architect/Valuer & Certificate from company's Statutory Auditors about cost incurred on project;
   - ❍ Compliance with terms of sanction;
   - ❍ Completion of project & readiness to commence commercial activity;
   - ❍ Stock/Book debts inspection;
   - ❍ Rate of Interest and further changes;
   - ❍ Security offered;
   - ❍ Insurance of the property financed and security offered;
   - ❍ Terms of repayment;
   - ❍ Other terms and conditions.

4. **Post Disbursement Monitoring-Post Disbursement Monitoring:** In this stage it should be monitored and verified in two following way:

   a) **Immediate after Post Disbursement Monitoring:**
   - Compliance of various Post-disbursement conditions. Charge with ROC / RTA / CERSAI. ROC, CERSAI, MOD within 30 days.
   - Fresh search report to be obtained from ROC.
   - Verification of end use of funds immediately after disbursement. By carrying out Post Sanction Inspection.
   - Insurance of charged assets.
   - If account is covered under CGTMSE or any other guarantee schemes, the relevant formalities to be completed.

   b) **Regular-Credit Monitoring:** This type of monitoring required on regular basis after disbursement of loan account:
   - Periodical Inspections (verification of relevant records) and follow up for recovery of overdue, if any;
   - Obtaining Stock and Book Debts Statement and their verification particularly of Book Debts which is a major area of concern;
   - Follow up of Review of all accounts;
   - Submission of Staff Accountability Report;
   - Stock Audit by Chartered Accountants for credit limit;
   - If PDCs are given ensure these are encased in time;
   - Even when one instalment is delayed customer to be reminded politely;
   - Obtaining periodical renewal documents as per limitation act;
   - Check TOD/TOL/Insurance due etc.
   - Insurance for full value & with Bank's Hypothecation Clause.
   - Bank's name to be displayed at prominent place of the business.
   - Verification of Transactions and Turnover in the account.

Monitoring Action Plan: Major slippage are due to wilful default and diversion/siphoning of funds by the

Borrowers. It could have been avoided if there is adequate monitoring of the accounts through regular inspections and proper scrutiny of operations in the accounts. Business related genuine transaction should be allowed. Non business related cheque shall be returned (by keeping the borrower informed). Borrower be advised to close the account as per RBI guidelines. A discussion with the borrower could lead to a definite correction path and accounts are restored to quality credit assets only by alert attention. Constant dialogue with the borrower and/or guarantor to find out ways and means to rectify the causes that hinder smooth functioning of unit.

TEST YOURSELF

1. Under Turnover method, working capital assessment\ can be calculated up to:
(a) ₹ 50.00 lakh (b) ₹ 1.00 crore
(c) ₹ 5.00 crore (d) All limits.

2. No bank Guarantee should normally have a maturity of more than:
(a) 5 Years (b) 10 Years
(c) 20 Years (d) No such bar

3. Cash Budget Method for assessment of Working Capital is done for:
(a) Peak Level Cash Deficit
(b) Purchase of Current Assets
(c) It is for all Working capital limit
(d) As required by Tondon Committee

4. Credit Monitoring starts from the moment:
(a) The loan sanctioned
(b) The account converts as SMA 1
(c) The loan disbursed
(d) The possibility of a new advance is visualized.

5. Vetting of the document is being carried out by:
(a) A senior officer
(b) Empaneled Lawyer
(c) Any Lawyer
(d) Chartered Accountant

6. Submission of Audited Financial Statement is required for limit of:
(a) ₹ 5.00 lakh and more
(b) ₹ 7.50 lakh and more
(c) ₹ 10.00 lakh and more
(d) ₹ 25.00 lakh and more

7. Current Assets means any asset which can be converted in to cash within 12 months from the date of:
(a) Date of last day of financial year
(b) Date of first day of financial year
(c) 1st April of each year
(d) Balance Sheet

8. Net Working capital means:
(a) Current Assets – Current Liabilities
(b) Total Current Liabilities
(c) Total Current Assets
(d) Goodwill

9. Bank Guarantee is not written in Balance Sheet as:
(a) It is a contingent liability
(b) It is not a liability
(c) It is an asset
(d) It is backed by security

10. What is Gross Working Capital represents?
(a) Current Assets – Current Liabilities
(b) Current Liabilities
(c) Current Assets
(d) Current Assets + Goodwill

11. What is Net Working Capital represents?
(a) Margin of working capital
(b) Current assets-current liabilities (excluding bank finance
(c) Current assets-current liabilities (including bank finance).
(d) Both (a) & (c)

12. Formula for calculating drawing power in cash credit account is:
(a) Value of secured stock less margin
(b) Value of secured stock available
(c) Value of secured stock plus margin
(d) Balance in the account less margin

13. Collateral security means:
(a) Goods pledged in bank in cash credit account
(b) Gold available on Gold Loan account
(c) All security other than collateral security
(d) NSC available in loan against NSC account

14. When more than one banks are allowing credit facilities to one party in coordination with each other under a formal arrangement, this type of finance is called:
(a) Consortium
(b) Multiple
(c) Syndication
(d) Participation

15. Which of the committee did not recommend the concept of working capital term loan?
(a) Chore Committee
(b) Tondon Committee
(c) Kapoor Committee
(d) Nayak Committee

16. Current assets of a company is ₹ 1000 lakh, current liabilities is ₹ 100 lakh. What will be the MPBF as per 1st method of Tondan Committee?
(a) ₹ 675 lakh (b) ₹ 650 lakh
(c) ₹ 625 lakh (d) ₹ 750 lakh

17. Minimum number of banks, which can participate in consortium advance is?
(a) 2 (b) 3
(c) 4 (d) 5

18. Cash Budget Method is calculated on the basis of
(a) Maximum cash deficit
(b) Peak level cash surplus
(c) Minimum cash deficit
(d) Peak level cash deficit

19. Pre-sanction inspection of loan proposal refers to:
(a) Verification of all securities proposed to be offered
(b) Obtention of market report of the borrower and guarantor
(c) Verification of project and concerned documents
(d) All of the above

20. What is the net working capital (margin) requirement under second method of lending:
(a) 25% of total assets
(b) 25% of total current assets
(c) 25% of working capital gap
(d) 25% of current liabilities

ANSWER

1	2	3	4	5	6	7	8	9	10
(c)	(b)	(a)	(d)	(b)	(c)	(d)	(a)	(a)	(c)
11	**12**	**13**	**14**	**15**	**16**	**17**	**18**	**19**	**20**
(d)	(a)	(c)	(a)	(b)	(a)	(a)	(d)	(d)	(a)

PRIORITY SECTOR ADVANCES

PRIORITY SECTOR LENDING IN INDIA

Introduction: The concept of 'Priority sector lending' focuses on the idea of directing the lending of the banks towards few specified sectors and activities in the economy. The term 'priority sector' indicates those activities which have national importance and have been assigned priority for development. These primarily include agriculture, small industries etc. The case has further been that these sectors and activities were neglected ones for the purpose of bank credit and therefore for the purposes of accessibility of credit, these neglected ones are considered to be at priority for providing credit.

History and Journey of Priority Sector Lending in India

Post-independence era, the most primary sector of economy at that point in time *i.e.*, agriculture was in need of funds but it was not the desired avenue for the commercial banks to extend credit due to multiplicity of factors prevalent at those times. The government initiatives such as green revolution etc. also led to significant increase in the demand for credit by the farmers and the cooperative societies and the State Bank of India could not manage to meet the requirements of credit due to its increased demand.

National Credit Council was set up in 1968 to estimate the demand for bank credit from the different sectors of the economy. The Banking Laws (Amendment) Act was passed in this regard in 1968 which came into force on 1-2-1969. 14 banks were nationalised in 1969. In 1972, the description of the priority sector was formalised on the basis of the report submitted by the Informal Study Group on Statistics relating to advances to the priority sector constituted by the RBI in May 1971. Initially, there was no specific target set for lending to the priority sectors but in November 1974, the banks were advised to raise the share of these sectors in their aggregate advances to the level of 33.3 per cent by March 1979. In 1974 only, the private banks were also advised by the RBI to reach a level of not less than one third of their total outstanding by March 1980 at par with the public sector banks.

In 1980, on the basis of the recommendations of the Working Group on the Modalities of priority sector lending by banks chaired by Dr. K.S. Krishnaswamy, all commercial banks were advised to achieve the target of PSL at 40 per cent of the bank advances by 1985. Not only that but also the sub-targets were also specified for lending to agriculture and the weaker sections within the category of priority sector.

Since then, there have been several changes in the practice of priority sector lending which include changes in the scope of priority sector lending by inclusion of various other sectors from time to time and also the scope of targets and sub-targets under applicable to the various bank groups have also been modified from time to time as per the instructions of the RBI. Major changes were done on recommendation of the M V Nair Committee revised guideline issued with effect from July 20, 2012. In which Foreign Banks with 20 branches and above had to achieve the total Priority Sector Target of 40 per cent of ANBC or Credit Equivalent Amount of Off-Balance Sheet Exposure, whichever is higher within a maximum period of five years starting from April 1, 2013 and ending on March 31, 2018 as per the action plans submitted by them and approved by RBI. After March 31, 2018, RBI will review the position.

TARGET/SUB-TARGET FOR PRIORITY SECTOR LENDING

An Internal Working Group (IWG) was set up by RBI in July 2014 to revisit the existing priority sector lending guidelines. On the basis of recommendation of IWG, RBI issued details guidelines on Priority Sector Lending on 7th July 2016. RBI has issued latest priority sector lending guidelines on 01.03.2018. The target set under priority sector lending are as under:

- Domestic scheduled commercial banks have to achieve the total Priority Sector Target of 40 per cent of Adjusted Net Bank Credit [ANBC or Credit Equivalent Amount of Off-Balance Sheet Exposure, whichever is higher.
- Foreign banks with 20 branches and above have to achieve the total Priority Sector Target of 40 per cent of Adjusted Net Bank Credit [ANBC or Credit Equivalent Amount of Off-Balance Sheet Exposure, whichever is higher within a maximum period of five years starting from April 1, 2013 and ending on March 31, 2018 as per the action plans submitted by them and approved by RBI.
- Foreign banks with less than 20 branches have to achieve the total Priority Sector Target 40 per cent of Adjusted Net Bank Credit [ANBC] or Credit Equivalent Amount of Off-Balance Sheet Exposure, whichever is higher; to be achieved in a phased manner by 2020.
- Regional Rural Banks have to achieve the total Priority Sector Target 75 per cent of their advances with effect from 1st January 2016.
- The priority sector non-achievement will be assessed on quarterly average basis at the end of the respective year from 2016-17 onwards, instead of annual basis as at present.

SUMMARY OF THE PRIORITY SECTOR LENDING TARGETS

Banks	***Targets***
Domestic scheduled commercial banks	40% of ANBC or Credit equivalent amount of Off-Balance Sheet exposure, whichever is higher. Besides these targets, Banks have to also achieve sub-target of given in guidelines.
Foreign banks with 20 branches and above	40 per cent of Adjusted Net Bank Credit [ANBC or Credit Equivalent Amount of Off-Balance Sheet Exposure, whichever is higher up to 2018. The sub-targets would be made applicable post 2018 after a review in 2017.
Foreign banks with less than 20 branches	40 per cent of Adjusted Net Bank Credit [ANBC] or Credit Equivalent Amount of Off-Balance Sheet Exposure, whichever is higher; to be achieved in a phased manner by 2020. Sub-target is Not Applicable.
Regional Rural Banks	75 per cent of their advances with effect from 1st January 2016.

Computation of ANBC and Off–Balance Sheet Exposures are as under:

ADJUSTED NET BANK CREDIT (ANBC)

Bank Credit in India (As prescribed in item No. VI of Form 'A' as on 31st March) under Sec 42 [2] of RBI Act, 1934.	I
Bills rediscounted with RBI and other approved Financial institutions	II
Net Bank Credit (NBC)	III (I-II)
Investment in non-SLR bonds in HTM category + Other investments eligible to be treated as PSAs + O/s Deposits under RIDF, other eligible funds with NABARD, NHB and SIDBI on a/c of PSA shortfall + o/s PSLCs	IV
Eligible amount for exemptions on issuance of long term bands for infrastructure and affordable housing as per circular DBOD.BP.BC.No. 25/08.12.014/2014-15 dated July 15, 2014	V
Eligible advance extended in India against the incremental FCNR(B)/NRE deposits, qualifying for exemption from CRR/SLR requirements.	VI
Adjusted Net Bank Credit (ANBC)	III+IV-V-VI
Off–Balance Sheet Exposures: - An asset or Debt that does not appear on a bank's balance sheet. Which is written in foot note in Balance Sheet. Such as: LC, BG, Forward contract etc.	

The Total Priority Sector target of 40 per cent of ANBC or Credit Equivalent Amount of Off-Balance Sheet Exposure, whichever is higher for foreign banks with less than 20 branches has to be achieved in a phased manner as under:

Financial year	*Targets*
2015-16	32
2016-17	34
2017-18	36
2018-19	38
2019-20	40

1. SUB-TARGET UNDER AGRICULTURE

Domestic commercial Banks/Foreign Banks with 20 & above branches: 18% of ANBC or Off-Balance Sheet exposure, whichever is higher. Within the 18% target of agriculture, target of 8% is prescribed for Small & Marginal Farmer, to be achieved 8% by March 2017.

Computation of 8% loan to small and marginal farmers include the following :

- **Marginal Farmer:** Farmer Landholding up to 1 hectare;
- **Small Farmer:** Farmer Landholding up to 2 hectares;
- Landless agricultural labourers, tenant farmers, oral lessees and share-croppers;
- Loan to SHG or JLG engaged in agriculture and allied activities.
- Loan to farmer producer companies of individual farmers and co-operative society having 75% Small and Marginal farmer engaged in agriculture activities.

The present distinction between direct and indirect agriculture is dispensed with. Instead, the lending to agriculture sector has been re-defined to include:

A. Farm Credit (which will include short-term crop loans and medium/long-term credit to farmers);
B. Farm Credit Loan to corporate farmer, farmer producer organization, Partnership forms, Cooperative societies;
C. Agriculture Infrastructure; and
D. Ancillary Activities.

A. Farm Credit Loans to individual farmers, SHG, JLG, directly engaged in Agriculture and Allied Activities. This will include:

- Short term loan for raising crops, *i.e.*, Crop Loans;
- Medium & long-term loan to farmers for agriculture & allied activities;
- Loan to farmers for pre & post-harvest activities;
- Loan to farmers up to ₹ 50 lakhs against agriculture produce (including warehouse receipt) for 12 months;
- Loans to farmers under KCC Scheme;
- Loans to distress farmers indebted to non-institutional lenders;
- Loan to small & marginal farmers to purchase of land for agriculture purpose.

B. Farm Credit Loan to corporate farmer, farmer producer organization, Partnership forms, Co-operative societies engaged in Agriculture and Allied activities for Loans limit up to ₹ 2 crores per borrower. This will include:

- Crop Loans to farmer which will include traditional/Non-traditional plantations and horticulture, and loans to allied activities;
- Medium & long term loan to farmers for agriculture & allied activities;
- Loan to farmers for pre & post-harvest activities;
- Loan to farmers up to ₹ 50 lakhs against agriculture produce (including warehouse receipt) for 12 months.

C. Agriculture Infrastructure: Loan for aggregate sanction limit of ₹ 100 crores per borrower from the banking system.

- Loans for construction of storage facilities (Warehouse, Godowns, market yards) including cold storage units designed to store Agriculture produce, irrespective of their location;
- Soil conservation and watershed development;
- Plant tissue culture and agri-biotechnology, seed production, production of bio-pesticides, bio-fertilizer, and vermi composting.

D. Agriculture Ancillary Activities:

- Loans up to ₹ 5 crores to co-operative societies of farmers for disposing of the produce of farmers;
- Loans for setting Agriclinics & Agribusiness Centre's;
- Loan sanction to MFIs for on lending Ag activities;
- Loans for Food & Agro-processing up to an aggregate sanction limit of ₹ 100 crores per borrower from the banking system;
- Bank loans to Primary Agricultural Cooperative Society (PACS), Farmer's Service Societies (FSS) and Large sized Adivasi Multi-Purpose Scheme (LAMPS) for on lending to Agriculture;
- Outstanding deposits under RIDF and eligible funds with NABRD on account of priority sector shortfall.

2. MICRO, SMALL AND MEDIUM ENTERPRISES (MSMES)

Bank loans to Micro, Small and Medium Enterprises, for both manufacturing and service sectors are eligible to be classified under the priority sector as per the following norms. Within the MSME target, Micro Enterprises will be 7.5% of ANBC or Off- Balance Sheet exposure, whichever is higher to be achieved 7.5% by March 2017.

CLASSIFICATION OF MSME

Sector	*Enterprises for Manufacturing/ Processing Units*	*Enterprises Engaged in Providing Services*
Micro Enterprise	Investment in plant & machinery not exceeding ₹ 25 lakh.	Investment in equipment not to exceed ₹ 10 lakh.
Small Enterprise	More than ₹ 25 lakh but not to exceed ₹ 5 crores.	More than ₹ 10 lakh but not to exceed ₹ 2 crores.
Medium Enterprise	More than ₹ 5 crores but not to exceed ₹ 10 crores.	More than ₹ 2 crores but not to exceed ₹ 5 crores.

A. Manufacturing Enterprises: The Micro, Small and Medium Enterprises engaged in the manufacture or production of goods to any industry as per MSMED Act 2006.

B. Service Enterprises: All bank loans without any cap finance to Micro and Small Enterprises and Medium Enterprises engaged in providing or rendering of services and defined in terms of investment in equipment under MSMED Act, 2006. As per RBI circular dated 01.03.2018, cap for financing under MSME sector has been removed.

C. Khadi and Village Industries Sector (KVI): All loan given to units of KVI sector will eligible for classification of 7.5% prescribed to Micro Enterprises.

D. Other Finance to MSMEs:

a) Loans to person involve in assisting the Artisans, village and Cottage Industry.

b) Loan to cooperative of producers in the Artisans, village and Cottage Industry.

c) Loan sanction to Banks, MFIs for on lending to MSE sectors.

d) Credit outstanding under General Credit Cards (including Artisan Credit Card, Laghu Udyami Card, Swarojgar Credit Card, and Weaver's Card etc. in existence and catering to the non-farm entrepreneurial credit needs of individuals).

e) Outstanding deposits with SIDBI on account of priority sector shortfall.

3. EXPORT CREDIT

The Export Credit extended as per the details below would be classified as priority sector.

a) **Domestic Commercial Banks:** Incremental export credit over corresponding date of preceding year, up to 2% of ANBC or Off-Balance Sheet exposure, whichever is higher, effective from April 1, 2015 subject to sanction limit of ₹ 25 crores per borrower to unit having turnover of up to ₹ 100 crores.

b) **Foreign Banks with 20 & above Branches:** Incremental export credit over corresponding date of preceding year, up to 2% of ANBC or Off-Balance Sheet exposure, whichever is higher, effective from April 1, 2017.

c) **Foreign Banks with less than 20 Branches:** Export Credit will be allowed up to 32% of ANBC or Off-Balance Sheet exposure, whichever is higher.

Export credit includes pre-shipment and post shipment export credit (excluding off-balance sheet items) as defined in Master Circular on Rupee / Foreign Currency Export Credit and Customer Service to Exporters issued by our Department of Banking Regulation.

4. EDUCATION

Loans to individuals for educational purposes including vocational courses upto ₹ 10 lakh irrespective of the sanctioned amount will be considered as eligible for priority sector.

5. HOUSING

The following housing loans are categorised as Priority Sector Advances;

a) **Loan for Construction and Purchase:** Loans to individuals up to ₹ 35 lakh in metropolitan centres (with population of ten lakh and above) and loans up to ₹ 25 lakh in other centres for purchase/construction of a dwelling unit per family provided the overall cost of the dwelling unit in the metropolitan centre and at other centres should not exceed ₹ 45 lakh and ₹ 30 lakh respectively. The housing loans to banks' own employees will be excluded.

b) **Loan for Repairs:** Loans for repairs to damaged dwelling units of families up to ₹ 5 lakh in metropolitan centres and up to ₹ 2 lakh in other centres.

c) **Loan to Governmental Agency:** Bank loans to any governmental agency for construction of dwelling units or for slum clearance and rehabilitation of slum dwellers subject to a ceiling of ₹ 10 lakh per dwelling unit.

d) **Loan for Housing Projects:** The loans sanctioned by banks for housing projects exclusively for the purpose of construction of houses for economically weaker sections and low income groups, the total cost of which does not exceed ₹ 10 lakh per dwelling unit. For the purpose of identifying the economically weaker sections and low income groups, the family income limit of ₹ 3 lakh for EWS and ₹ 6 lakh for LIG per annum, irrespective of the location, is prescribed.

e) **Loan to HFC:** Bank loans to Housing Finance Companies (HFCs), approved by NHB for their refinance, for on-lending for the purpose of purchase/construction/reconstruction of individual dwelling units or for slum clearance and rehabilitation of slum dwellers, subject to an aggregate loan limit of ₹ 10 lakh per borrower.

f) The eligibility under priority sector loans to HFCs is restricted to five per cent of the individual bank's total priority sector lending, on an ongoing basis.

g) Outstanding deposits with NHB on account of priority sector shortfall.

6. SOCIAL INFRASTRUCTURE

Bank loans up to a limit of ₹ 5 crores per borrower for building social infrastructure for activities namely schools, health care facilities, drinking water facilities and sanitation facilities in Tier II to Tier VI centres.

7. RENEWABLE ENERGY

Bank loans up to a limit of ₹ 15 crores to borrowers for purposes like solar based power generators, biomass-based power generators, wind mills, micro-hydel plants and for non-conventional energy based public utilities *viz.* street lighting systems, and remote village electrification. For individual households, the loan limit will be ₹ 10 lakh per borrower.

8. OTHERS

The following loans are also categorised as Priority Sector Advances

a) Loans not exceeding ₹ 50,000/- per borrower provided directly by banks to individuals and their SHG/JLG, provided the individual borrower's household annual income in rural areas does not exceed ₹ 100,000/- and for non-rural areas it does not exceed ₹ 1,60,000/-.

b) Loans to distressed persons other than farmers not exceeding ₹ 100,000/- per borrower to prepay their debt to non-institutional lenders.

c) Overdrafts extended by banks upto ₹ 5,000/- under Pradhan Mantri Jan-DhanYojana (PMJDY) accounts provided the borrowers household annual income does not exceed ₹ 100,000/- for rural areas and ₹ 1,60,000/- for non-rural areas.

d) Loans sanctioned to State Sponsored Organisations for Scheduled Castes/Scheduled Tribes for the specific purpose of purchase and supply of inputs and/or the marketing of the outputs of the beneficiaries of these organisations.

9. WEAKER SECTIONS

Priority sector loans to the following borrowers will be considered under Weaker Sections category. 10% of ANBC or Credit equivalent amount of Off- Balance Sheet exposure, whichever is higher. Foreign branch having 20 branch and above have to achieve by 31 March 2018.

a) Loan to Small and Marginal farmers;

b) Beneficiaries of NRLM, NULM, SRMS, SHG & DRI Scheme;

c) Artisans, Village and cottage industries where individual credit limits do not exceed ₹ 1 lakh;

d) Loan to individual SC & ST category;

e) Loan to persons with disabilities;

f) Loans to individual women beneficiaries up to ₹ 1 lakh per borrower etc.;

g) Loans to distressed farmers indebted to non-institutional lenders;

h) Loans to distressed persons other than farmers not exceeding ₹ 1 lakh per borrower to prepay their debt to non-institutional lenders;

i) OD up to ₹ 5000 under PMJDY having annual income ₹ 1 lakh in rural and ₹ 1.60 lakh non-rural areas;

j) Minority communities as may be notified by Government of India from time to time.

Monitoring of Priority Sector Lending targets

To ensure continuous flow of credit to priority sector, there will be more frequent monitoring of priority sector lending compliance of banks on 'quarterly' basis instead of annual basis as of now. The data on priority sector advances have to be furnished by banks at quarterly and annual intervals as per revised reporting formats, the guidelines for which will be issued separately.

Non-achievement of Priority Sector targets

Scheduled Commercial Banks having any shortfall in lending to priority sector shall be allocated amounts for contribution to the Rural Infrastructure Development Fund (RIDF) established with NABARD and other Funds with NABARD/NHB/SIDBI, as decided by the Reserve Bank from time to time. For the year 2015-16, the shortfall in achieving priority sector target/sub-targets will be assessed based on the position as on March 31, 2016. From financial year 2016-17 onwards, the achievement will be arrived at the end of financial year based on the average of priority sector target /sub-target achievement as at the end of each quarter. The interest rates on banks' contribution to RIDF or any other Funds, tenure of deposits, etc. shall be fixed by Reserve Bank of India from time to time.

The misclassifications reported by the Reserve Bank's Department of Banking Supervision would be adjusted/ reduced from the achievement of that year, to which the amount of declassification/ misclassification pertains, for allocation to various funds in subsequent years.

Non-achievement of priority sector targets and sub-targets will be taken into account while granting regulatory clearances/approvals for various purposes.

TEST YOURSELF

1. In November 1974, the banks were advised to raise the share of priority sectors in their aggregate advances to the level of ________ by March 1979.

(a) 30 per cent (b) 33.3 per cent
(c) 40 per cent (d) 50 per cent

2. Foreign banks with less than 20 branches have to achieve the total Priority Sector Target 40 per cent of ANBC to be achieved in a phased manner by ________.

(a) 2018 (b) 2019
(c) 2020 (d) 2021

3. Regional Rural Banks have to achieve the total Priority Sector Target ________ of their advances with effect from 1st January 2016.

(a) 40 per cent (b) 50 per cent
(c) 60 per cent (d) 75 per cent

4. What is the meaning of ANBC?

(a) All New Banking Credit
(b) Adjusted Net Bank Credit
(c) Agriculture Net Banking Credit
(d) Advanced Non Bank Credit

5. Within the 18% target of agriculture, target of 8% is prescribed for Small & Marginal Farmer, to be achieved ________ by March 2017.

(a) 7% (b) 8%
(c) 10% (d) 12%

6. The lending to agriculture sector under Priority Sector has been re-defined to include:

(a) Farm Credit to individual and corporate
(b) Agriculture Infrastructure
(c) Ancillary Activities in Agriculture
(d) All of the above

7. Loan to farmers up to ₹ ________ against agriculture produce (including warehouse receipt) for 12 months is classified under Priority Sector.

(a) 5 lakhs (b) 10 lakhs
(c) 50 lakhs (d) 100 lakhs

8. Agriculture infrastructure: Loan for aggregate sanction limit of ₹ 100 crore per borrower from the banking system. Find the correct purposes:

(a) Loans for construction of storage facilities (Warehouse, Godowns, market yards) including cold storage units designed to store Agriculture produce, irrespective of their location.
(b) Soil conservation and watershed development
(c) Plant tissue culture and agri-biotechnology, seed production, production of bio-pesticides, bio-fertilizer, and vermi composting
(d) All of the above

9. Which is not correct for Priority Sector Target in Agriculture Ancillary activities:

(a) Loans up to ₹ 50 crore to co-operative societies of farmers for disposing of the produce of farmers
(b) Loans for setting Agriclinics & Agribusiness Centre's
(c) Loan sanction to MFIs for on lending Ag activities
(d) Loans for Food & Agro-processing up to an aggregate sanction limit of ₹ 100 crore per borrower from the banking system

10. Within the MSME target, Micro Enterprises will be ________ of ANBC or Off-Balance Sheet exposure, whichever is higher to be achieved.
(a) 7% (b) 7.5%
(c) 8% (d) 10%

11. Investment in plant & machinery more than ₹ 25 lakh but not to exceed ₹ 5 crore is classified as:
(a) Manufacturing Micro Enterprise
(b) Services Small Enterprise
(c) Manufacturing Small Enterprise
(d) Manufacturing Medium Enterprise

12. Export Credit target for Domestic commercial Banks: Incremental export credit over corresponding date of preceding year, up to 2% of ANBC subject to sanction limit of ₹ ________ per borrower to unit having turnover of up to ₹ ________.
(a) 25 crore, 100 crore (b) 20 crore, 100 crore
(c) 10 crore, 50 crore (d) 12 crore, 50 crore

13. Education Loans to individuals for educational purposes including vocational courses up to ______ irrespective of the sanctioned amount will be considered as eligible for priority sector.
(a) ₹ 10 lakh in India (b) ₹ 20 lakh in abroad
(c) ₹ 10 lakh (d) ₹ 20 lakh

14. Housing Loan for Repairs for priority sector, loans for repairs to damaged dwelling units up to ______ in metropolitan centres and up to ______ in other centres.
(a) ₹ 4 lakh, ₹ 2 lakh
(b) ₹ 5 lakh, ₹ 2 lakh
(c) ₹ 5 lakh, ₹ 3 lakh
(d) ₹ 10 lakh, ₹ 5 lakh

15. Bank loans to any governmental agency for construction of dwelling units or for slum clearance and rehabilitation of slum dwellers subject to a ceiling of ________ per dwelling unit.
(a) ₹ 10 lakh (b) ₹ 15 lakh
(c) ₹ 20 lakh (d) ₹ 25 lakh

16. Bank loans up to a limit of ₹ 5 crore per borrower for building social infrastructure for activities namely schools, health care facilities, drinking water facilities and sanitation facilities in ________.
(a) Tier I to Tier V centers
(b) Tier II to Tier V centers
(c) Tier II to Tier VI centers
(d) Tier III to Tier VI centers

17. Priority Sector limit for Renewable Energy up to a limit of ________ to borrowers for purposes like solar based power generators, biomass based power generators, wind mills, micro-hydel plants and for non-conventional energy based public utilities.
(a) ₹ 1 crore (b) ₹ 5 crore
(c) ₹ 10 crore (d) ₹ 15 crore

18. Priority sector loans to the following borrowers will not be considered under Weaker Sections category.
(a) Loan to individual SC & ST category
(b) Loan to persons with disabilities
(c) Loans to individual women beneficiaries up to ₹ 2 lac per borrower
(d) Loans to distressed farmers indebted to non-institutional lenders

19. Scheduled Commercial Banks having any shortfall in lending to priority sector shall be allocated amounts for contribution to the ________.
(a) RIDF (b) SIDBI
(c) NHB (d) Any of the above

20. Rural Infrastructure Development Fund (RIDF) was established with:
(a) NABARD
(b) NHB
(c) SIDBI
(d) All of the above

ANSWER

1	2	3	4	5	6	7	8	9	10
(b)	(c)	(d)	(b)	(c)	(d)	(c)	(d)	(a)	(b)
11	**12**	**13**	**14**	**15**	**16**	**17**	**18**	**19**	**20**
(c)	(a)	(c)	(b)	(a)	(c)	(d)	(c)	(d)	(a)

AGRICULTURAL FINANCE

AGRICULTURAL LOANS

Introduction: India is an agriculture base country. More than 60% population of India depends on agriculture directly and indirectly. Nearly 83% of Indian farmers are small and marginal farmer. But, the contribution of agriculture sector is less than 15% in GDP. Government of India targeted to doubling the income of Indian farmers up to 2022. An agriculturist has to have necessary capital to purchase/employ these inputs and services. However, our unpredictable monsoons, limited area under assured irrigation and uneconomic land holdings do not leave sufficient marketable surplus with the agriculturists, especially the small and marginal ones with the result that most of them are not in a position to earn enough to take up the developmental activities on their own. Meeting the credit requirements of such needy agriculturists has, therefore, become one of the important national priorities.

Agricultural Credit can also be classified according to the length of repayment period.

Short Term Advances: Finance for working capital, e.g., purchase of crop production inputs and services, feed/fodder for farm animals, purchase / storage of farm inputs for supply to agriculturists, etc. is termed as Short-Term Finance. Repayment of short term finance of a direct nature is generally linked with marketing of crop/ animal produce and can stretch upto 18 months depending upon the gestation period. These advances are given either as Demand Loan or Cash Credit. Indirect short term finance is generally in the form of revolving limit.

Medium Term Advances: Advances of an investment nature granted for development of farm/allied activities, where accrual of income sufficient to repay the advance takes place between 3 to 7 years, are called Medium Term Advances. If the repayment is contemplated within a period of 3 years, such advances are generally granted as Demand Loans. In case the repayment period exceeds 3 years, credit in the form of Term Loans is considered.

Long Term Advances: Where there is a need to spread the repayment over 8 to 15 years because of a longer gestation period and/or insufficient income generation during the initial stages, advances are considered of Long Term nature.

PRADHAN MANTRI KISAN SAMPADA YOJANA

Government of India (GOI) has approved a new Central Sector Scheme–Pradhan Mantri Kisan SAMPADA Yojana (Scheme for Agro-Marine Processing and Development of Agro-Processing Clusters) with an allocation of ₹ 6,000 crore for the period 2016-20 coterminous with the 14th Finance Commission cycle. The scheme will be implemented by Ministry of Food Processing Industries (MoFPI). Pradhan Mantri Kisan SAMPADA Yojana.

PM Kisan SAMPADA Yojana is a comprehensive package which will result in creation of modern infrastructure with efficient supply chain management from farm gate to retail outlet. It will not only provide a big boost to the growth of food processing sector in the country but also help in providing better process to farmers and is a big step towards doubling of farmers income, creating huge employment opportunities especially in the rural areas, reducing wastage of agricultural produce, increasing the processing level and enhancing the export of the processed foods.

The following schemes will be implemented under PM Kisan SAMPADA Yojana:

1) Mega Food Parks;
2) Integrated Cold Chain and Value Addition Infrastructure;
3) Creation/Expansion of Food Processing & Preservation Capacities;
4) Infrastructure for Agro-processing Clusters;
5) Creation of Backward and Forward Linkages;
6) Food Safety and Quality Assurance Infrastructure;
7) Human Resources and Institutions.

PM Kisan SAMPADA Yojana is expected to leverage investment of ₹ 31,400 crore for handling of 334 lakh MT agro-produce valued at INR 1,04,125 crore, benefiting 20 lakh farmers and generating 5,30,500 direct/indirect employment in the country by the year 2019-20.

KISAN CREDIT CARD (KCC)

KCC was first introduced in 1994. The Kisan Credit Card has emerged as an innovative credit delivery mechanism to meet the production credit requirements of the farmers in a timely and hassle-free manner. The GOI, Ministry of Finance constituted a Working Group under the chairmanship of Shri T M Bhasin, Chairman & Managing, Indian Bank to review the KCC Scheme. Based on the recommendations of the Working Group which were accepted by the GOI, the revised KCC Scheme is effective from 12 May 2012.

Applicability of the Scheme: The Revised KCC Scheme detailed in the ensuing paragraphs is to be implemented by Commercial Banks, RRBs, and Cooperatives. The scheme provides broad guidelines to the banks for operationalising the KCC scheme.

Objectives/Purpose: Kisan Credit Card Scheme aims at providing adequate and timely credit support from the banking system under a single window to the farmers for their cultivation & other needs as indicated below:

a) To meet the short-term credit requirements for cultivation of crops;
b) Post-harvest expenses;
c) Produce Marketing loan;
d) Consumption requirements of farmer household;
e) Working capital for maintenance of farm assets and activities allied to agriculture, like dairy animals, inland fishery etc.;
f) Investment credit requirement for agriculture and allied activities like pump sets, sprayers, dairy animals etc.

Note: The aggregate of components 'a' to 'e' above will form the short term credit limit portion and the aggregate of components under 'f' will form the long term credit limit portion..

Eligibility: Following farmers are eligible under the scheme:

(i) All Farmers–Individuals / Joint borrowers who are owner cultivators;
(ii) Tenant Farmers, Oral Lessees & Share Croppers;
(iii) SHGs or Joint Liability Groups of Farmers including tenant farmers, share croppers etc.

Fixation of Credit limit/Loan amount: The credit limit under the Kisan Credit Card may be fixed as under:

For Marginal Farmers: A flexible limit of ₹ 10,000 to ₹ 50,000 be provided (as Flexi KCC) based on the land holding and crops grown including post-harvest warehouse storage related credit needs and other farm expenses, consumption needs, etc., plus small term loan investments like purchase of farm equipment, establishing mini dairy/backyard poultry as per assessment of Branch Manager without relating it to the value of land. The composite KCC limit is to be fixed for a period of five years on this basis. Wherever higher limit is required due to change in cropping pattern and/or scale of finance, the limit may be arrived at as per the estimation.

All Farmers other than Marginal Farmers: Limit is arrived as per scale of finance.

The Short-term Limit to be arrived for the First Year: Scale of finance for the crop (as decided by District Level Technical Committee) x Extent of area cultivated + 10% of limit towards post-harvest/household /consumption requirements + 20% of limit towards repairs and maintenance expenses of farm assets + crop insurance, PAIS & asset insurance.

Limit for Second & Subsequent Year: First year limit for crop cultivation purpose arrived at as above plus 10% of the limit towards cost escalation / increase in scale of finance for every successive year (2nd, 3rd, 4th and 5th year) and estimated Term loan component for the tenure of Kisan Credit Card, *i.e.*, five years.

Term Loans: Term loan for investments towards land development, minor irrigation, purchase of farm equipment and allied agricultural activities. The banks may fix the quantum of credit for term and working capital limit for agricultural and allied activities, etc. The long-term loan limit is based on the proposed investments during the five-year period and the bank's perception on the repaying capacity of the farmer.

Maximum Permissible Limit: The short-term loan limit arrived for the 5th year plus the estimated long-term loan requirement will be the Maximum Permissible Limit (MPL) and treated as the Kisan Credit Card Limit.

Disbursement: ATM card must be issued in all KCC accounts. The short-term component of the KCC limit is in the nature of revolving cash credit facility. There should be no restriction in number of debits and credits. However, each instalment of the drawable limit drawn in a particular year will have to be repaid within 12 months. The drawing limit for the current season/ year could be allowed to be drawn using any of the following delivery channels.

- **a.** Operations through branch;
- **b.** Operations using Cheque facility;
- **c.** Withdrawal through ATM / Debit cards;
- **d.** Operations through Business Correspondents and ultra-small branches;
- **e.** Operation through PoS available in Sugar Mills/ Contract farming companies, etc., especially for tie-up advances;
- **f.** Operations through PoS available with input dealers;
- **g.** Mobile based transfer transactions at agricultural input dealers and mandies.

Note: (e), (f) & (g) to be introduced as early as possible so as to reduce transaction costs of both the bank as well as the farmer.

Rate of Interest (ROI): Rate of Interest will be linked to MCLR and is left to the discretion of the banks.

Interest Subvention: Interest Subvention of 2% p.a. will be available to banks on the KCC Scheme. As per RBI communication Ref No. RPCD:FSD:BC:71/ 05.04.02/2013-14 dated 04/12/2013 for computation of Interest subvention on KCC limit, only following activities are considered.

- a) Short term credit requirements for cultivation of crops
- b) Post-harvest expenses

Additional Interest subvention @3% will be available to the prompt paying farmers from the date of disbursement of crop loan to the actual date of repayment by farmers or up to date fixed by bank for repayment of crop loan whichever is earlier.

Repayment Period: Each withdrawal under the short term sub-limit as estimated under (a) to (e) of Para 3 above, be allowed to be liquidated in 12 months without the need to bring the debit balance in the account to zero at any point of time. No withdrawal in the account should remain outstanding for more than 12 months.

The term loan component will be normally repayable within a period of 5 to 9 years depending on the type of activity/investment as per the existing guidelines applicable for investment credit.

Margin for Crop Loan: No separate margin insisted as the margin is inbuilt while fixing of Scale of Finance by District Level Technical Committee (DLTC).

Margin for Term Loan: Up to ₹ 1.60 lac: NIL, For limit more than ₹ 1.60 lac: 15-25%.

Security: Security requirement may be as under:

- **i)** Hypothecation of crops up to card limit of ₹ 1.60 lac as per the extant RBI guidelines.
- **ii)** **With tie-up for Recovery:** Banks may consider sanctioning loans on hypothecation of crops upto card limit of ₹ 3.00 lakh without insisting on collateral security.
- **iii)** Collateral security may be obtained at the discretion of Bank for loan limits above ₹ 1.00 lakh in case of non tie-up and above ₹ 3.00 lakh in case of tie-up advances.
- **iv)** In States where banks have the facility of on-line creation of charge on the land records, the same shall be ensured.

Other Features: Other Features in the KCC uniformity to be adopted in respect of following:

- **i)** Interest Subvention/Incentive for prompt repayment as advised by Government of India and / or State Governments. The bankers will make the farmers aware of this facility;
- **ii)** The KCC holder should have the option to take benefit of Crop Insurance, Assets Insurance, Personal Accident Insurance Scheme (PAIS), and Health Insurance (wherever product is available and have premium paid through his KCC account);
- **iii)** One-time documentation at the time of first availment and thereafter simple declaration (about crops raised / proposed) by farmer from the second year onwards;
- **iv)** No bank's charges as PPC/DOC etc. up to ₹ 3.00 lacs card limit;
- **v)** KCC short term limit fetch interest for credit balance at SB interest rate.

Selected Activities under Agricultural Finance

Besides the KCC Scheme, banks financed to all the purpose of direct and indirect agriculture and allied activities. RBI and NABARD design most of the agriculture loan schemes and monitoring the implementation. Some of the loan schemes are as under;

1. **FARM MECHANISATION SCHEME:** With the advent of modern farm practices, the use of improved inputs and services has come to acquire a prominent place in Indian agriculture. Bank financing for purchase of all the mechanical instruments used in by farmer such as machinery/ implements like Tractors, Power Tillers, seed drill, seed-cum-fertilizer drill, planters, power sprayers, seed cleaners, weed removers, power threshers, chaff cutters, cane crushers, harvester combines etc. under Farm Mechanisation Scheme.

   Eligibility: Farmer & group of farmers having own land.

   Quantum of Finance: As per cost of the vehicle and machinery.

2. **DAIRY DEVELOPMENT SCHEME :** Dairying is an important source of subsidiary income to small/marginal farmers and agricultural labourers. In addition to milk, the manure from animals provides a good source of organic matter for improving soil fertility and crop yields. The gobar gas from the dung is used as fuel for domestic purposes as also for running engines for drawing water from well. The surplus fodder and agricultural by-products are gainfully utilised for feeding the animals. India is endowed with the largest livestock population in the world. In milk production India stood first in the world. It accounts for about 57.3 per cent of the world's buffalo population (Top position in the world) and 14.7 per cent of the cattle population.

   Purpose: To establish a dairy unit and for dairy schemes with large outlays, detailed project reports will have to be prepared. Bank loan is available for following purpose.

   a) To establish small dairy unit with 2 to 4 milch cattle.
   b) To establish new medium / large unit.
   c) Collection, processing, distribution of milk & manufacturing of milk products.
   d) Purchase of improved/crossbred milch cattle.
   e) Construction of cattle shed.
   f) Milk processing facilities, etc

   Eligibility: Farmers, Agriculture labourers, Co-operative Society Limited Co. etc.

   Margin: Up to ₹ 1.60 lac: Nil, For limit more than ₹ 1.60 lac: 15-25%.

   Repayment: 5 to 6 years with 2 to 3 months moratorium period.

   Insurance: The animals and capital assets may be insured annually or long-term master policy, where ever it is applicable.

3. **MINOR IRRIGATION SCHEME:** The objective of the Minor Irrigation schemes should be to meet genuine credit needs of the farmers for development of farm irrigation facilities to improve cropping intensity, better yields and incremental income from the farm.

   Purpose: Loan can be financed for the purpose of Lift irrigation, well irrigation, electric motor & pump set, diesel engine, construction of pump house, construction of water delivering channel, payment of deposits to state electricity board, sprinkler irrigation, drip irrigation etc.

   Eligibility: Individual farmers, Group of farmers, co-operative societies of farmers.

   Quantum: As per unit cost approved by NABARD for that area.

   Technical Feasibility: Availability and suitability of water in adequate quantity during cropping seasons for irrigation purpose. Minimum land area of the farmer-borrower for effective use of the irrigation scheme. Availability of BIS certification on equipment to ensure quality.

   Financial Viability: The financial viability of the irrigation schemes should be assessed keeping in view of the capital cost vis-à-vis expected incremental income from the farm. The assessment should clearly indicate that the net incremental income on account of improved agronomic practices would be adequate to service the loan with interest within a reasonable period apart from the farmer getting a fair return on the investment.

4. **POULTRY BROILER FARMING SCHEME:** Poultry meat is an important source of high quality proteins, minerals and vitamins to balance the human diet. Specially developed varieties of chicken (broilers) are now available with the traits of quick growth and high feed conversion efficiency. Depending on the farm size, broiler farming can be a main source of family income or can provide subsidiary income and gainful employment to farmers throughout the year. Poultry manure is of high fertilizer value which can be used for increasing yield of all crops.

The advantages of broiler farming are :

a) Initial investment is lower than layer farming

b) Rearing period is 5-6 weeks only;

c) More number of flocks can be taken in the same shed;

d) Broilers have high feed conversion efficiency *i.e.*, the amount of feed required for unit body weight gain is lower in comparison to other livestock;

e) Faster return from the investment;

f) Demand for poultry meat is more compared to sheep/goat meat.

Scope for Broiler Farming and its National Importance: India has made tremendous progress in broiler production during the last three decades and the broiler population in the country stood at 4600 million. Today India is the fifth largest producer of broiler meat in the world with an annual production of 4.8 million MT. Broiler farming has been given considerable importance in the national policy and has a good scope for further development in the years to come.

5. AGRI-CLINIC & AGRI-BUSINESS CENTRE (ACABC) SCHEME

The scheme aims to promote the establishment of Agri-Clinics and Agri-Business Centres (ACABC) all over the country.

Agri-Clinics: Agri-Clinics are envisaged to provide expert advice and services to farmers on various aspects to enhance productivity of crops/animals and increase the incomes of farmers. Agri-clinics provide support in the following areas:

- Soil health;
- Cropping practices;
- Plant protection;
- Crop insurance;
- Post-harvest technology;
- Clinical services for animals, feed and fodder management;
- Prices of various crops in the market, etc.

Agri-Business Centres: Agri-Business Centres are commercial units of agri-ventures established by trained agriculture professionals. Such ventures may include maintenance and custom hiring of farm equipment, sale of inputs and other services in agriculture and allied areas, including post-harvest management and market linkages for income generation and entrepreneurship development.

The scheme covers full financial support for training and handholding, provision of loan and credit-linked back ended composite subsidy.

Objectives of the Scheme:

- To supplement efforts of public extension by necessarily providing extension and other services to the farmers on payment basis or free of cost as per business model of agripreneur, local needs and affordability of target group of farmers.
- To support agricultural development.
- To create gainful self-employment opportunities for unemployed agricultural graduates, agricultural diploma holders, intermediate in agriculture and biological science graduates with Post Graduation in agri-related courses.

Eligibility Criteria for Candidate: Candidates should hold one of the following degrees.

- Graduate in Agriculture and allied subject;
- Diploma (with at least 50% marks) / Post Graduate Diploma in Agriculture and allied subject;
- Having more than 60% content in agriculture and allied subject;
- Agriculture related courses at intermediate (*i.e.*, plus two) level, with at least 55% marks;
- Biological science graduate with Post Graduate in agriculture and allied subject.

Training: National Institute of Agricultural Extension Management (MANAGE) will be responsible for providing training to eligible candidates, through Nodal Training Institute (NTIs) and motivating them for setting up of Agri-Clinic and Agri-Business Centre.

Quantum of loan: Individual: ₹ 20 lakhs, (₹ 25 lakhs for deserving case). Group of five: ₹ 100 lakhs (one of them must be from management)

Margin: Up to 5 lakh – Nil, (beyond 15% to 25%) 50% margin money provided by NABARD for SC/ST/Women/NE States/Hill areas.

6. RURAL GODOWNS:

It is a well-known fact that small farmers of the country do not have the economic strength to retain their farm produce with them till the market prices become favourable. There has been a felt need in the country to provide the farming community with facilities for scientific storage so that wastage and produce deterioration are avoided and enable farmers to meet their credit requirement without being compelled to sell their produce at unfavourable prices. A network of rural godowns will enable small farmers to enhance their holding capacity in order to sell their produce at fair prices and avoid distress sales.

Objectives of the Scheme: Grameen Bhandaran Yojana, for Construction/Renovation of Rural Godowns was introduced in 2001-2002.

1. Creation of scientific storage capacity with allied facilities in rural areas to meet the requirements of farmers for storing farm produce, processed farm produce and agricultural inputs.
2. Promotion of grading, standardisation and quality control of agricultural produce to improve marketability.
3. Prevention of distress sale immediately after harvest by providing the facility of pledge financing and marketing credit.
4. Strengthening of agricultural marketing infrastructure in the country with the introduction of a national system of warehouse receipts, in respect of agricultural commodities stored in such godowns.
5. Reverse the declining trend of investment in agriculture sector by encouraging private and cooperative sectors to invest in storage infrastructure in the country.

MINIMUM SUPPORT PRICE (MSP)

MSP is a form of market intervention by the Government of India to insure agricultural producers against any sharp fall in farm prices. The minimum support prices are announced by the Government of India at the beginning of the sowing season for certain crops on the basis of the recommendations of the Commission for Agricultural Costs and Prices (CACP). MSP is price fixed by Government of India to protect the producer-farmers- against excessive fall in price during bumper production years. The minimum support prices are a guarantee price for their produce from the Government. The major objectives are to support the farmers from distress sales and to procure food grains for public distribution. In case the market price for the commodity falls below the announced minimum price due to bumper production and glut in the market, government agencies purchase the entire quantity offered by the farmers at the announced minimum price.

PRADHAN MANTRI FASAL BIMA YOJANA (PMFBY)

Agriculture in India is wholly dependent on nature. Crop insurance scheme has been implemented to protect the farmers from perils of nature. The Central Govt. has announced a new format of Crop Insurance in name of "Pradhan Mantri Fasal Bima Yojana (PMFBY)", to be implemented from 1st April' 2016. PMFBY will provide a comprehensive insurance cover against failure of the crop thus helping in stabilising the income of the farmers and encourage them for adoption of innovative practices.

Objective of the Scheme: Pradhan Mantri Fasal Bima Yojana (PMFBY) aims at supporting sustainable production in agriculture sector by way of :

a) Providing financial support to farmers suffering crop loss/damage arising out of unforeseen events;
b) Stabilising the income of farmers to ensure their continuance in farming;
c) Encouraging farmers to adopt innovative and modern agricultural practices;
d) Ensuring flow of credit to the agriculture sector, which will contribute to food security, crop diversification and enhancing growth and competitiveness of agriculture sector besides protecting farmers from production risks.

Crops Insured: The scheme can cover all the crops, Food & Oilseeds crops and Annual Commercial/ Horticultural Crops for which past yield data is available and grown during the Notified Season, in a Notified Area and for which yield estimation at the Notified Area level will be available based on requisite number of Crop Cutting Experiments (CCEs) being a part of the General Crop Estimation Survey (GCES).

FARMERS TO BE COVERED: All farmers including sharecroppers, tenant farmers growing the notified crops in the notified areas

a. **On a Compulsory Basis:** All farmers growing notified crops and availing Seasonal Agricultural Operations (SAO) loans from Financial Institutions *i.e.*, Loanee Farmers. Such other farmers whom the government may decide to include from time to time.
b. **On a Voluntary Basis:** All other farmers growing notified crops (*i.e.*, Non- Loanee Farmers) who opt for the scheme. Special efforts shall be made to ensure maximum coverage of SC/ ST/Women farmers under the scheme.

Implementing Agency: The scheme will be implemented by AIC and other empanelled private general insurance companies. Selection of Implementing Agency

(IA) will be done by the concerned State Government through bidding. The existing State Level Co-ordination Committee on Crop Insurance (SLCCCI), Sub-Committee to SLCCCI, District Level Monitoring Committee (DLMC) shall be responsible for proper management of the Scheme.

RISKS COVERED

Following stages of the crop and risks leading to crop loss are covered under the scheme.

a) **Prevented Sowing/Planting Risk:** Insured area is prevented from sowing/planting due to deficit rainfall or adverse seasonal conditions.

b) **Standing Crops:** On notified area basis losses due to non-preventable risks, such as:
   (i) Natural Fire and Lightning
   (ii) Storm, Hailstorm, Cyclone, Typhoon, Tempest, Hurricane, Tornado etc.
   (iii) Flood, Inundation and Landslide
   (iv) Drought, Dry spells
   (v) Pests/ Diseases etc.

c) **Post-Harvest Losses:** Coverage is available only up to a maximum period of two weeks from harvesting for those crops which are allowed to dry in cut and spread condition in the field after harvesting against specific perils of cyclone and cyclonic rains and unseasonal rains.

d) **Localized Calamities:** Loss/ damage resulting from occurrence of identified localized risks of hailstorm, landslide, and Inundation affecting isolated farms in the notified area.

General Exclusions: Losses arising out of war and nuclear risks, malicious damage and other preventable risks shall be excluded.

Insurance Amount: In case of loanee farmers under compulsory component, the sum insured would be equal to scale of finance for that crop as fixed by DLTC which may extend up to the value of the threshold yield of the insured crop at the option of insured farmer. For farmers covered on voluntary basis the sum-insured is up. to the value of threshold yield *i.e.*, threshold yield × (MSP or gate price) of the insured crop.

Premium Rate: Premium Rates are as follows.

Season	*Crops*	*Premium rate*
1. Kharif	Food & Oilseeds crops (all cereals, millets, pulses) & oilseeds.	2.0% of SI or Actuarial rate, whichever is less.
2. Rabi	Food & Oilseeds crops (all cereals, millets, pulses) & oilseeds.	1.5% of SI or Actuarial rate, whichever is less.
3. Kharif & Rabi	Annual Commercial or Horticultural crops.	5.0% of SI or Actuarial rate, whichever is less.

Insurance Premium: The premium rate would be a flat rate or actuarial rate whichever is lower. The flat rates of insurance premium for different crops are as under:

- The difference between premium rate and the rate of insurance charges payable by farmers shall be treated as rate of normal premium subsidy, which shall be shared equally by the centre and state.
- Now, no subsidy in premium is allowed in respect of Small & Marginal farmers.

Coverage of Non-Loanee Farmers:

a) A non-loanee farmer seeking coverage has to submit a declaration within the cut-off date to any bank branch along with premium.

b) He should open a SB account with this branch.

c) The non-loanee farmer should submit Xerox copies of his land record for verification.

d) The nodal branch should remit the premium for non-loanee farmers by means of a separate draft.

e) The non-loanee farmers can also send the premium directly to Insurance Agency.

Indemnity Level (IL) and Threshold Yield (TY): Three levels of Indemnity, viz., 70%, 80% and 90% corresponding to crop Risk in the areas shall be available for all crops. The Threshold Yield (TY) shall be the bench-mark yield level at which insurance protection shall be given to all the insured farmers in an Insurance Unit. The Threshold Yield for a crop in an Insurance Unit shall be based on average yield of last seven years excluding two years of declared calamity if any, multiplied by the level of indemnity of the area.

$$\text{Threshold Yield} = \frac{\text{Sum [Last 7 years of Yield (Minus two notified calamity years if any)]}}{\text{5 or 7 (as the case may be)}} \times \text{Level of Indemnity}$$

Assessment & Claim Procedure: Yield losses at Notified Area level: Once the yield data is received from the State/UT Govt. as per the prescribed cut-off dates, claims will be processed, approved and settled by IA.

If the 'Actual Yield' (AY) per hectare of the insured crop for the defined area [on the basis of requisite number of Crop Cutting Experiments (CCEs)] in the insured season, falls short of the specified threshold yield (TY) Yield' (RY), all the insured farmers growing that crop in the defined area are deemed to have suffered shortfall in their yield.

The scheme seeks to provide protection against such contingency to all insured farmers of an Insurance Unit.

Claim Pay-outs based on Yield losses shall be calculated as per the following formula :

$$\text{Claims Pay-out} = \frac{\text{Shortfall in yield}}{\text{Threshold yield}} \times \text{Sum insured}$$

Where, Shortfall in yield = (Threshold yield – Actual yield)

PROCEDURE FOR ASSESSMENT, PROCESSING & APPROVAL OF CLAIMS

Assessment of Prevented Sowing: In case of majority of insured crops of a notified area are prevented from sowing/planting the insured crops due to adverse weather conditions that will be eligible for indemnity claims up to maximum of 25% of the sum-insured.

Localized Calamity Loss Assessment: Loss assessment and modified indemnity procedures in case of occurrence of localized perils, such as hailstorm, landslide, flood, and inundation shall be for a cluster of affected farms or affected village and the settlement of claims, if any, will be each insured farmer covered under assessment.

Post-Harvest Loss Assessment: Loss assessment and indemnity procedures in case of occurrence of Post-Harvest Loss shall be for a cluster of affected farms or affected village and the settlement of claims, if any, will be each insured farmer covered under assessment.

N.B.: The District Administration will assist IA in assessing the extent of loss.

Sharing of Risk: The difference between premium rate and the rate of Insurance charges payable by farmers shall be treated as Rate of Normal Premium Subsidy, which shall be shared equally by the Centre and State.

The liability of the Insurance companies in case of catastrophic losses computed at the national level for an agricultural crop season, shall be up to 350% of total premium collected (farmer share plus Govt. subsidy) or 35% of total Sum Insured (SI), of all the insurance companies combined, whichever is higher. The losses at the national level in a crop season beyond this ceiling shall be met by equal contribution (*i.e.*, on 50:50 basis) from the Central Government and the concerned State Governments.

Weather Based Crop Insurance Scheme (WBCIS)

The structure of farmer's premium under WBCIS will be at par with the proposed PMFBY. The criteria of selection of implementing agency and area allocation will be same as PMFBY. The other broad features will remain same.

TEST YOURSELF

1. Which of the following schemes will be implemented under PM Kisan SAMPADA Yojana?
(a) Mega Food Parks
(b) Integrated Cold Chain and Value Addition Infrastructure
(c) Creation/Expansion of Food Processing & Preservation Capacities
(d) All of the above

2. The revised KCC Scheme is effective from ____.
(a) 12 May 2012 (b) 12 May 2013
(c) 12 May 2014 (d) 12 May 2015

3. Kisan Credit Card Scheme aims at providing adequate and timely credit support to the farmers for their cultivation & other needs. Find the correct purposes:
(a) Post-harvest expenses
(b) Produce Marketing loan
(c) Consumption requirements of farmer household
(d) All of the above

4. Which of the following are not eligible under the KCC scheme?
(a) All Farmers–Individuals/Joint borrowers who are owner cultivators;
(b) Tenant Farmers, Oral Lessees & Share Croppers;
(c) Farmers club
(d) SHGs or JLG of Farmers including tenant farmers, share croppers etc.

5. Which is not a correct statements regarding the KCC scheme?
(a) For Marginal Farmers, a flexible limit of ₹ 10,000 to ₹ 50,000 be provided based on the land holding.
(b) All farmers other than marginal farmers, limit is arrived as per scale of finance.
(c) KCC Drawing Limit will be fixed for 5 years
(d) None of the above

6. Which of the following mode available for disbursement in all KCC accounts?
(a) Operations using Cheque facility
(b) Withdrawal through ATM / Debit cards

(c) Operations through PoS available with input dealers
(d) All of the above

7. Banks may consider sanctioning KCC loans on hypothecation of crops up to card limit of ______ without insisting on collateral security in case of tie-up advances.
(a) ₹ 1.00 lakh (b) ₹ 2.00 lakh
(c) ₹ 3.00 lakh (d) ₹ 5.00 lakh

8. As per RBI guideline, no bank's charges as PPC/ DOC etc. up to ______ KCC limit.
(a) ₹ 1.00 lakh (b) ₹ 3.00 lakh
(c) ₹ 4.00 lakh (d) ₹ 5.00 lakh

9. Collateral security and margin for loan to agriculture are exempted for loan:
(a) up to ₹ 10000 (b) up to ₹ 25000
(c) up to ₹ 160000 (d) up to ₹ 200000

10. Additional Interest subvention @ ______ will be available to the prompt paying farmers from the date of disbursement of crop loan to the actual date of repayment by farmers or up to date fixed by bank for repayment of crop loan whichever is earlier.
(a) 2% (b) 3%
(c) 4% (d) 7%

11. Under Dairy Development Scheme, minimum number of milch cattle is financed for small dairy unit:
(a) 1 (b) 2
(c) 4 (d) 10

12. Under Dairy Development Scheme, the loan cannot financed to:
(a) Agriculture labourers (b) Co-operative Society
(c) Limited Company (d) Charitable Trust

13. Under Minor Irrigation schemes, Loan cannot be financed for the purpose of
(a) Power threshers
(b) Construction of pump house,
(c) Electric motor & pump set
(d) Lift irrigation

14. Agri-clinics provide support in which of the following areas?
(a) Soil health (b) Cropping practices
(c) Plant protection (d) All of the above

15. Objectives of the Agri-Clinics and Agri-Business Centres (ACABC) scheme are:
(a) To supplement efforts of public extension by necessarily providing extension and other services to the farmers on payment basis or free of cost as per business model of agripreneur, local needs and affordability of target group of farmers
(b) To support agricultural development
(c) To create gainful self-employment opportunities for unemployed agricultural graduates, agricultural diploma holders, intermediate in agriculture and biological science graduates with Post Graduation in agri-related courses.
(d) All of the above

16. Quantum of loan for Agri-Clinics and Agri-Business Centres to Individual will be:
(a) ₹ 10 lakhs (b) ₹ 15 lakhs
(c) ₹ 20 lakhs (d) ₹ 50 lakhs

17. Pradhan Mantri Fasal Bima Yojana (PMFBY), to be implemented from ______.
(a) 1st Jan. 2016 (b) 1st April 2016
(c) 1st Jan. 2017 (d) 1st April' 2017

18. Pradhan Mantri Fasal Bima Yojana (PMFBY) aims at supporting sustainable production in agriculture sector by way of:
(a) Providing financial support to farmers suffering crop loss/damage arising out of unforeseen events
(b) Stabilising the income of farmers to ensure their continuance in farming
(c) Encouraging farmers to adopt innovative and modern agricultural practices
(d) All of the above

19. Which of the following stages of the crop and risks leading to crop loss are not covered under the PMFBY scheme.
(a) Prevented Sowing/ Planting Risk
(b) Malicious Damage
(c) Post-Harvest Losses
(d) Localized Calamities

20. Premium Rates under the PMFBY scheme for Kharif Season are ______ of SI or Actuarial rate, whichever is less.
(a) 1.5% (b) 2.0%
(c) 2.5% (d) 5%

ANSWER

1	2	3	4	5	6	7	8	9	10
(d)	(a)	(d)	(c)	(c)	(d)	(c)	(b)	(c)	(b)
11	**12**	**13**	**14**	**15**	**16**	**17**	**18**	**19**	**20**
(b)	(d)	(a)	(d)	(d)	(c)	(b)	(d)	(b)	(b)

MICRO, SMALL AND MEDIUM ENTERPRISES

MICRO, SMALL & MEDIUM ENTERPRISES (MSMED)

Introduction: MSME is the pillar of economic growth in many developed and developing countries in the world. Often rightly termed as "the engine of growth" for India, MSME has played a prominent role in the development of the country in terms of creating employment opportunities—MSME has employed more than 80 million people, the estimated contribution of MSME sector (including service segment) to GDP is about 40 per cent and the share of MSMEs in India's total export for the year 2014-15 was 44.70 per cent. Though India is still facing infrastructural problems, lack of proper market linkages, and challenges in terms of flow of institutional credit, it has seen a tremendous growth in this sector.

The advantage of this sector is it requires less investment, thus creating employment on a large scale, and reducing the employment and underemployment problems. Moreover, this sector has survived almost all threats emerging out of still completion from both domestic and international market.

Micro, Small & Medium Enterprises Development (MSMED) Act, 2006

The Government of India has enacted the Micro, Small and Medium Enterprises Development (MSMED) Act, 2006 on June 16, 2006 which was notified on October 2, 2006. With the enactment of MSMED Act 2006, the paradigm shift that has taken place is the inclusion of the services sector in the definition of Micro, Small & Medium enterprises, apart from extending the scope to medium enterprises. The MSMED Act, 2006 has modified the definition of micro, small and medium enterprises engaged in manufacturing or production and providing or rendering of services. The Reserve Bank has notified the changes to all scheduled commercial banks.

Definition of Micro, Small and Medium Enterprises: As per MSMED Act, 2006, MSME Sectors are classified as Manufacturing Enterprises and Service Enterprises.

(a) Manufacturing Enterprises: Enterprises engaged in the manufacture or production, processing or preservation of goods as specified below:

i) A micro enterprise is an enterprise where investment in plant and machinery does not exceed ₹ 25 lakh;

ii) A small enterprise is an enterprise where the investment in plant and machinery is more than ₹ 25 lakh but does not exceed ₹ 5 crore; and

iii) A medium enterprise is an enterprise where the investment in plant and machinery is more than ₹ 5 crore but does not exceed ₹ 10 crore.

Exercise of the powers conferred by sub-section (1) of 2006) herein referred to as the said Act, the Central Government specifies the following items, the cost of which shall be excluded while calculating the investment in plant and machinery in the case of the enterprises mentioned in Section 7(1)(a) of the said Act, namely:

a) Equipment such as tools, jigs, dyes, moulds and spare parts for maintenance and the cost of consumables stores;

b) Installation of plant and machinery;

c) Research and development equipment and pollution controlled equipment

d) Power generation set and extra transformer installed by the enterprise as per regulations of the State Electricity Board;

e) Bank charges and service charges paid to the National Small Industries Corporation or the State Small Industries Corporation;

f) Procurement or installation of cables, wiring, bus bars, electrical control panels (not mounded on individual machines), oil circuit breakers or miniature circuit breakers which are necessarily to be used for providing electrical power to the plant and machinery or for safety measures;

g) Gas producer's plants;

h) Transportation charges (excluding sales-tax or value added tax and excise duty) for indigenous machinery from the place of the manufacture to the site of the enterprise;

i) Charges paid for technical know-how for erection of plant and machinery;

j) Such storage tanks which store raw material and finished produces and are not linked with the manufacturing process; and

k) Firefighting equipment.

While calculating the investment in plant and machinery refer to paragraph 1, the original price thereof, irrespective of whether the plant and machinery are new or second handed, shall be taken into account provided that in the case of imported machinery, the following shall be included in calculating the value, namely;

i) Import duty (excluding miscellaneous expenses such as transportation from the port to the site of the factory, demurrage paid at the port);

ii) Shipping charges;

iii) Customs clearance charges; and

iv) Sales tax or value added tax.

(b) Service Enterprises: Enterprises engaged in providing or rendering of services and whose investment in equipment (original cost excluding land and building and furniture, fittings and other items not directly related to the service rendered or as may be notified under the MSMED Act, 2006) as specified below:

i) A micro enterprise is an enterprise where the investment in equipment does not exceed ₹ 10 lakhs;

ii) A small enterprise is an enterprise where the investment in equipment is more than ₹ 10 lakh but does not exceed ₹ 2 crores; and

iii) A medium enterprise is an enterprise where the investment in equipment is more than ₹ 2 crores but does not exceed ₹ 5 crores.

Sector	***Enterprises for Manufacturing/ Processing Units***	***Enterprises Engaged in Providing Services***
Micro Enterprise	Investment in plant & machinery not exceeding ₹ 25 lakh.	Investment in equipment not to exceed ₹ 10 lakh.
Small Enterprise	More than ₹ 25 lakh but not to exceed ₹ 5 crore.	More than ₹ 10 lakh but not to exceed ₹ 2 crore.
Medium Enterprise	More than ₹ 5 crore but not to exceed ₹ 10 crore.	More than ₹ 2 crore but not to exceed ₹ 5 crore.

PRIORITY SECTOR TARGETS FOR MSME SECTOR

Advances to Micro, Small and Medium Enterprises (MSME) sector shall be reckoned in computing achievement under the overall Priority Sector target of 40 per cent of Adjusted Net Bank Credit (ANBC) or credit equivalent amount of Off-Balance Sheet Exposure, whichever is higher, as per the extant guidelines on priority sector lending.

Domestic Commercial Banks are required to achieve a sub-target of 7.5 per cent of ANBC or Credit Equivalent Amount of Off-Balance Sheet Exposure, whichever is higher, for lending to Micro Enterprises from March 2017. The sub-target for Micro Enterprises for foreign banks with 20 branches and above operating in India would be made applicable post 2018 after a review in 2017. However, this sub-target for lending to Micro Enterprises is not applicable to foreign banks with less than 20 branches operating in India.

In terms of the recommendations of the Prime Minister's Task Force on MSMEs, banks are advised to achieve:

(i) 20 per cent year-on-year growth in credit to micro and small enterprises,

(ii) 10 per cent annual growth in the number of micro enterprise accounts and

(iii) 60% of total lending to MSE sector as on preceding March 31st to Micro enterprises

Issue of Acknowledgement of Loan Applications to MSME Borrowers: Banks are advised to mandatorily acknowledge all loan applications, submitted manually or online, by their MSME borrowers and ensure that a running serial number is recorded on the application form as well as on the acknowledgement receipt. Banks are further advised to put in place a system of Central Registration of loan applications, online submission of loan applications and a system of e-tracking of MSE loan applications.

Collateral: Banks are mandated not to accept collateral security in the case of loans up to ₹ 10 lakh extended to units in the MSE sector. Banks are also advised to extend collateral-free loans up to ₹ 10 lakh to all units financed under the Prime Minister Employment Generation Programme (PMEGP) administered by KVIC.

Banks may, on the basis of good track record and financial position of the MSE units, increase the limit to dispense with the collateral requirement for loans up to ₹ 25 lakh (with the approval of the appropriate authority). Banks are advised to strongly encourage their branch level functionaries to avail of the Credit Guarantee Scheme cover, including making performance in this regard a criterion in the evaluation of their field staff.

Composite Loan: A composite loan limit of ₹ 1 crore can be sanctioned by banks to enable the MSE entrepreneurs to avail of their working capital and term loan requirement through Single Window.

REVISED GENERAL CREDIT CARD (GCC) SCHEME

In order to enhance the coverage of GCC Scheme to ensure greater credit linkage for all productive activities within the overall Priority Sector guidelines and to capture all credit extended by banks to individuals for non-farm entrepreneurial activity, the GCC guidelines were revised on December 2, 2013.

CREDIT LINKED CAPITAL SUBSIDY SCHEME (CLSS)

Government of India, Ministry of Micro, Small and Medium Enterprises had launched Credit Linked Capital Subsidy Scheme (CLSS) for Technology Upgradation of Micro and Small Enterprises subject to the following terms and conditions:

i) Ceiling on the loan under the scheme is ₹ 1 crore.
ii) The rate of subsidy is 15% for all units of micro and small enterprises up to loan ceiling at Sr. No. (i) above.
iii) Calculation of admissible subsidy will be done with reference to the purchase price of plant and machinery instead of term loan disbursed to the beneficiary unit.
iv) SIDBI and NABARD will continue to be implementing agencies of the scheme.

Streamlining flow of credit to Micro and Small Enterprises (MSEs) for facilitating timely and adequate credit flow during their 'Life Cycle': In order to provide timely financial support to Micro and Small enterprises facing financial difficulties during their 'Life Cycle', Banks are advised to review and tune their existing lending policies to the MSE sector by incorporating therein the following provisions so as to facilitate timely and adequate availability of credit to viable MSE borrowers especially during the need of funds in unforeseen circumstances:

i) To extend standby credit facility in case of term loans
ii) Additional working capital to meet with emergent needs of MSE units
iii) Mid-term review of the regular working capital limits, where banks are convinced that changes in the demand pattern of MSE borrowers require increasing the existing credit limits of the MSMEs, every year based on the actual sales of the previous year.
iv) Timelines for Credit Decisions

Delayed Payment: In the Micro, Small and Medium Enterprises Development (MSMED), Act 2006, the provisions of the Interest on Delayed Payment Act, 1998 to Small Scale and Ancillary Industrial Undertakings, have been strengthened as under:

i) The buyer has to make payment to the supplier on or before the date agreed upon between him and the supplier in writing or, in case of no agreement, before the appointed day. The period agreed upon between the supplier and the buyer shall not exceed forty five days from the date of acceptance or the day of deemed acceptance.
ii) In case the buyer fails to make payment of the amount to the supplier, he shall be liable to pay compound interest with monthly rests to the supplier on the amount from the appointed day or, on the date agreed on, at three times of the Bank Rate notified by Reserve Bank.
iii) For any goods supplied or services rendered by the supplier, the buyer shall be liable to pay the interest as advised at (ii) above.

iv) In case of dispute with regard to any amount due, a reference shall be made to the Micro and Small Enterprises Facilitation Council, constituted by the respective State Government.

Further, banks are advised to fix sub-limits within the overall working capital limits to the large borrowers specifically for meeting the payment obligation in respect of purchases from MSMEs.

CREDIT RATING OF THE MICRO SMALL BORROWERS

With a view to facilitating credit flow to the MSME sector and enhancing the comfort-level of the lending institutions, the credit rating of MSME units done by reputed credit rating agencies should be encouraged. Banks are advised to consider these ratings as per availability and wherever appropriate. Credit rating is not mandatory but it is in the interest of the MSE borrowers to get their credit rating done as it would help in credit pricing of the loans taken by them from banks.

CREDIT GUARANTEE FUND TRUST FOR MICRO & SMALL ENTERPRISES (CGTMSE)

Ministry of Micro, Small & Medium Enterprises (MSME), Government of India (GOI) and Small Industries Development Bank of India (SIDBI) set up Credit Guarantee Fund Trust for Small Industries (CGTSI) in August 2000. The GOI and SIDBI as settlors of the Trust have committed a corpus of ₹ 2,500 crore in the ratio of 4:1 to the CGTMSE, out of which ₹ 1,906 crore has been contributed till date. Credit Guarantee Fund Trust for Micro & Small Enterprises (CGTMSE) w.e.f. 2nd July 2007.

The Ministry of MSME, Government of India and SIDBI set up the Credit Guarantee Fund Trust for Micro and Small Enterprises (CGTMSE) with a view to facilitate flow of credit to the MSE sector without the need for collaterals/ third party guarantees. The main objective of the scheme is that the lender should give importance to project viability and secure the credit facility purely on the primary security of the assets financed. The Credit Guarantee scheme (CGS) seeks to reassure the lender that, in the event of a MSE unit, which availed collateral-free credit facilities, fails to discharge its liabilities to the lender, the Guarantee Trust would make good the loss incurred by the lender up to 85 per cent of the outstanding amount in default.

Objective: Credit Guarantee Schemes are globally treated as instruments of credit enhancement for targeted sections. The Scheme is intended to encourage Member Lending Institutions to rely in their appraisal essentially on the viability of the project and the security of primary collateral of assets financed. The other objective is to encourage lenders availing of guarantee facility to extend composite credit facilities to borrowers comprising both working capital and term loans. The CGS seeks to reassure lenders that, in the event of a default by MSE unit covered by the guarantee, the Guarantee Trust would meet the loss incurred by the lender up to 85 per cent of the outstanding amount in default. All commercial banks included in the Second Schedule to the RBI Act, 1934, and such other institution(s) as may be notified by the Government of India from time to time are eligible to become MLIs.

Eligible Lending Institutions under the Scheme: All Scheduled Commercial Banks (either PSU, Private or Foreign Banks), selected Regional Rural Banks, selected state financial corporations or NBFC's or such of those institutions as may be directed by GOI can avail of guarantee cover in respect of their eligible credit facilities under the Scheme. Small Industries Development Bank of India (SIDBI), National Small Industries Corporation Ltd. (NSIC) and North Eastern Development Finance Corporation Ltd. (NEDFC) have been included as eligible institutions.

Policy Changes in CGTMSE in 2018: Following policy changes in Credit Guarantee Scheme were announced in an event "Rebooting CGTMSE" organized by Ministry of MSME and CGTMSE on February 20, 2018 :

1. Charging Annual Guarantee Fees (AGF) on Outstanding Loan Amount rather than sanction amount.
2. Expanding the Coverage of the Credit Guarantee Scheme (CGS) to cover MSE Retail Traders segment.
3. Allowing loans with Partial Collateral Security under Credit Guarantee Scheme.
4. Increase in the extent of guarantee coverage to 75% from existing 50% for proposals above ₹ 50 lakh.
5. Enhancing IT infrastructure of the Trust to improve operational efficiencies and reduce the turn around time for claim settlement.

The above mentioned steps undertaken by the Trust are expected to greatly increase the attractiveness of the scheme and increase the operational efficiency of the Trust. This in turn is expected to increase the credit guarantees availed by MLIs and help in enhanced flow of credit to the MSE sector and betterment of the sector as a whole.

Eligibility of Borrowers for CGTMSE Coverage:

a) All Credit Facilities sanctioned to Micro & Small units defined as per MSMED act 2006, on the basis of investment in Plant & Machineries/Equipment.

b) Units under both the sectors viz. Manufacturing and Services including Retail Trade, can be covered under CGTMSE.

c) All the units should be engaged in the activity as approved by CGTMSE for coverage.

d) All units should have a valid Udyog Adhaar No. (UAN).

e) Maximum Quantum of loan to a single borrower eligible for coverage should not exceed ₹ 200 Lakhs.

f) A Borrower can be given benefit of coverage only once in his/her lifetime under CGTMSE aggregating from all lenders up to maximum amount of ₹ 200 Lakhs, including previous sanctioned limits (even if closed) and present sanctioned limit.

g) For loans up to ₹ 10 Lakhs, no collateral security or third party guarantee should be obtained, to be eligible under the scheme.

h) For loans above ₹ 10 Lakhs, Partial Collateral security may be obtained. The details of the same has been explained in para 10, under Hybrid model of the scheme.

i) Under the Credit Guarantee Scheme, the CGTMSE encourages composite credit being extended to a single borrower by a Bank. Joint financing by a financial institution (*e.g.* Small Industries Development Bank of India, National Small Industries Corporation, and North Eastern Development Finance Corporation Ltd. etc.) and commercial bank can be covered under the scheme. For e.g. MSE unit is financed by term loan from State financial institution/development financial institution and Working capital from a commercial bank. However, sharing of securities will not be permitted.

j) Loan under Consortium are not eligible under the scheme.

k) Loans to SHGs are not eligible under the scheme.

l) Educational Institutions/Training Institutions are not covered under the Scheme.

Credit Facilities & Parameters: Fund and non-fund based (Letters of Credit, Bank Guarantee etc.) credit facilities up to ₹ 200 lakh per eligible borrower are covered under the guarantee scheme provided they are extended purely on the project viability without collateral security or third party guarantee. A lender can extend either term loan or working capital facility alone and still be eligible for a guarantee cover if it meets the other eligibility parameters (w.e.f. 31.10.2018, CGTMSE has removed rate of interest limit cap of 14% for all eligible loan account).

CGTMSE Cover for Borrowers Engaged in Retail Trade: Credit Facility extended to borrowers engaged in Retail Trade activity will now be covered under CGTMSE scheme with effect from 28.02.2018 (credit facility eligible for coverage on or after 28.02.2018). The Details are hereunder:

(a) Exposure Limit for Credit facility of Retail trade segment will be upto ₹ 100 Lac per MSE Borrowers.

(b) Extent of Guarantee coverage to such credit facility would be 50% of amount in default irrespective of the category of the borrower.

(c) Applicable Fee *i.e.*, AGF will be charged at the rate of 2% of the guaranteed amount for the first year and on outstanding amount for the remaining tenure of the credit facility. Differential pricing structure depending upon NPA percentage and Claim payout ratio of the Member Lending Institution (MLI) will also be applicable on the AGF.

Security Accepted Under the Scheme: No collateral Security for loans upto ₹ 10 Lakhs. Collateral Security would mean any asset other than business asset. Waiver of collateral security may be extended for loans over ₹ 10 Lakhs and upto ₹ 25 Lakhs subject to good track record and financial position of the borrower.

In view of several requests from various MLIs regarding coverage of Partial Collateral Security, it has been decided to make it effective from the date of issue of Circular. Therefore, the modification of allowing partial collateral security under the ambit of Credit Guarantee Scheme of CGTMSE is applicable to fresh credit facilities eligible for guarantee coverage by MLIs on or after February 28, 2018.

Modified AGF Structure-Standard Rate (SR): With a view to incentivize the borrowers with good repayment track record, AGF would be charged on the outstanding loan amount instead of guaranteed amount for credit facilities sanctioned / renewed to MSEs on or after April 01, 2018 as detailed below:

Annual Guarantee Fee (AGF) [% p.a.]*

Credit Facility	*Women, Micro Enterprises and Units covered in North East Region*	*Others*
Up to ₹ 5 Lakhs	1.00 + Risk Premium as per extant guidelines of the Trust	
Above ₹ 5 Lakhs and up to ₹ 50 Lakhs	1.35 + Risk Premium as per extant guidelines of the Trust	1.50 + Risk Premium as per extant guidelines of the Trust
Above ₹ 50 Lakhs and up to ₹ 200 Lakhs	1.80 + Risk Premium as per extant guidelines of the Trust	
*AGF will be charged on the guaranteed amount for the first year and on the outstanding amount for the remaining tenure of the credit facility.		

MSE Retail Trade Activity: The AGF will be charged at 2% of the guaranteed amount for the first year and on the outstanding amount for the remaining tenure of the credit facility. Differential pricing structure depending upon NPA / Claim pay-out ratio of the MLI will also be applicable on the AGF as per CGTMSE Circular No.107/ 2015-16 dated January 28, 2016.

Additional risk premium of 15% will be charged on the applicable rate to MLIs who exceed the pay-out threshold limit of 2 times more than thrice in last 5 years. This premium will be applicable for all guarantee accounts irrespective of the sanction date.

Guarantee Cover: Guarantee cover for entire agreed tenure of the Term Credit/ Composite Credit for the defaulted principal amount. Other Charges such as interest in term loan, Penal Interest, Commitment Charge, Service charge or any other expenses shall not qualify for guarantee cover. Lock in period is 18 months from date of last disbursement of loan or date of payment of guarantee fee whichever is later.

Extent of Guarantee Cover available w.e.f. 01/04/2018

CATEGORY	UP TO ₹ 5.00 LAC	Above ₹ 5.00 LAC TO ₹ 50.00 LAC	Above ₹ 50.00 LAC TO UP TO ₹ 200.00 LAC
Micro Enterprises	85% Maximum ₹ 4.25 lac	75% Maximum ₹ 37.50 lac	75% of amount default amount maximum ₹ 150.00 lac
Women/NE Region	85% Maximum ₹ 4.25 lac	80% Maximum ₹ 40 lac	75% of amount default amount maximum ₹ 150.00 lac
All Others	85% Maximum ₹ 4.25 lac	75% Maximum ₹ 37.50 lac	75% of amount default amount maximum ₹ 150.00 lac

Salient features and limitation about guarantee and invoke of guarantee are as under:

- Where working capital alone is financed, the tenure of guarantee cover is fixed for a block of 5 years. Thereafter the guarantee cover needs to be renewed for a further period of 5 Years. However the maximum tenure for which the guarantee cover will run in case of working capital loan is 10 Years, including intervening renewals/enhancement. A working capital account covered under CGTMSE can be renewed within 12 months from guarantee expiry date. Guarantee Fee has to be paid afresh for renewed guarantee cover thereafter for the next block of 5 years. Only Standard account at the end of the block of five years will be renewed and substandard accounts will be rejected.
- The Guarantee Cover shall run through the entire agreed tenure of the Term Credit in case Term Loan, sanctioned alone.
- In case of Composite Loan (where in Cash Credit & Term loan are sanctioned together), the guarantee cover will run through the entire period of term loan or term loan termination date which ever is earlier. For example, if the term loan is repaid in 48/60/72 months from the guarantee

start date the guarantee cover will expire for both Cash Credit and Term Loan in 48/60/72 months, as the case may be. The guarantee cover for Cash Credit alone will be renewed thereafter for a block of 5 years, subject to coverage for Cash Credit will be valid upto maximum tenure of 10 Years from the original cover start date.

- However, in case of composite loan, if the term loan period exceeds ten years, cover for term loan will continue for the whole ten or of term loan but for Working Capital, the tenure of cover will be restricted to maximum period of ten years.

Claim Settlements on default of a Loan are as under:

- The lender shall prefer a claim on the defaulted account on recall of loan and initiation of recovery proceedings under due process of Law. The lender can, however, invoke the guarantee given by the Trust only after the lock-in period of 18 months either from the date of last disbursement of credit to the borrower or from the date of the guarantee cover coming into force in respect of the particular credit facility, whichever is later.
- After satisfying itself about the procedural aspects met by the lender, regarding lodgement/ preferment of claim for guarantee, the Trust will honour 75% of the guaranteed portion of the amount in default, subject to maximum of 75%/ 80%/85% of the amount in default. The balance 25% shall be paid on conclusion of the recovery proceedings.
- For the purpose of the scheme, issue of notice under Lok Adalat is sufficient to prove the legal proceedings have initiated.
- Mere issuance of recall notice under SARFAESI Act cannot be construed as initiation of legal proceedings for purpose of preferment of claim under CGS. Lending institution should take further action as contained in Section 13 (4) of the above Act.

CGTMSE has its Registered Office at Mumbai and does not have any branches. Since the entire operations are online, CGTMSE is able to cater to the needs of its MLIs from Mumbai.

SPECIALISED MSME BRANCHES

Public sector banks have been advised to open at least one Specialised branch in each district. Further, banks have been permitted to categories their general banking branches having 60% or more of their advances to MSME sector as specialized MSME branches in order to encourage them to open more Specialised MSME branches for providing better service to this sector as a whole. As per the policy package announced by the Government of India for stepping up credit to MSME sector, the public sector banks will ensure specialized MSME branches in identified clusters/centres with preponderance of small enterprises to enable the entrepreneurs to have easy access to the bank credit and to equip bank personnel to develop requisite expertise. The existing Specialised SSI branches, if any, may also be pre-designated as MSME branches. Though their core competence will be utilized for extending finance and other services to MSME sector, they will have operational flexibility to extend finance/render other services to other sectors/borrowers.

CLUSTER APPROACH

All SLBC Convenor banks are advised to incorporate in their Annual Credit Plans, the credit requirement in the clusters identified by the Ministry of Micro, Small and Medium Enterprises, Government of India. They are also encouraged to extend banking services in such clusters/ agglomerations which have come up and identified subsequently by SLBC/DCC members.

1. As per Ganguly Committee recommendations (September 4, 2004), banks are advised that a full-service approach to cater to the diverse needs of the SSI sector (now MSE sector) may be achieved through extending banking services to recognized MSE clusters by adopting a 4-C approach namely, Customer focus, Cost control, Cross sell and Contain risk. A cluster-based approach to lending may be more beneficial:
   a) in dealing with well-defined and recognized groups;
   b) availability of appropriate information for risk assessment and
   c) monitoring by the lending institutions.

   Clusters may be identified based on factors such as trade record, competitiveness and growth prospects and/or other cluster specific data.
2. All SLBC Convenor banks were advised vide letter RPCD.PLNFS.No.10416/06.02.31/ 2006-07 dated May 8, 2007 to review their institutional arrangements for delivering credit to the MSME sector, especially in 388 clusters identified by United Nations Industrial Development Organisation (UNIDO) spread over 21 states in various parts of the country. A list of SME clusters as identified by UNIDO has been furnished in Annex II.

3. The Ministry of Micro, Small and Medium Enterprises has approved a list of clusters under the Scheme of Fund for Regeneration of Traditional Industries (SFURTI) and Micro and Small Enterprises Cluster Development Programme (MSE-CDP) located in 121 Minority Concentration Districts. Accordingly, appropriate measures have been taken to improve the credit flow to the identified clusters of micro and small entrepreneurs from the Minority Communities residing in the minority concentrated districts of the country.

4. In terms of recommendations of the Prime Minister's Task Force on MSMEs banks should open more MSE focused branch offices at different MSE clusters which can also act as Counselling Centres for MSEs. Each lead bank of a district may adopt at least one MSE cluster.

TEST YOURSELF

1. MSMED Act, 2006 was notified in India on ______.
   (a) April 1, 2006 (b) October 2, 2006
   (c) April 1, 2007 (d) October 2, 2007

2. What is the definition of Micro Enterprises in manufacturing sector?
   (a) Investment in plant and machinery does not exceed ₹ 25 lakh
   (b) Investment in plant and machinery is more than ₹ 25 lakh but does not exceed ₹ 5 crore
   (c) Investment in equipment does not exceed ₹ 10 lakhs
   (d) Investment in equipment is more than ₹ 10 lakh but does not exceed ₹ 2 crores

3. What is the definition of Small Enterprises in service sector?
   (a) Investment in plant and machinery does not exceed ₹ 25 lakh
   (b) Investment in plant and machinery is more than ₹ 25 lakh but does not exceed ₹ 5 crore
   (c) Investment in equipment does not exceed ₹ 10 lakhs
   (d) Investment in equipment is more than ₹ 10 lakh but does not exceed ₹ 2 crores

4. Within the MSME target, Micro Enterprises will be ______ of ANBC or Off-Balance Sheet exposure, whichever is higher to be achieved.
   (a) 7% (b) 7.5%
   (c) 8% (d) 10%

5. Investment in plant & machinery more than ₹ 5 crores but not to exceed ₹ 10 crore is classified as:
   (a) Manufacturing Micro Enterprise
   (b) Services Small Enterprise
   (c) Manufacturing Small Enterprise
   (d) Manufacturing Medium Enterprise

6. As per RBI norms, banks are mandated not to accept collateral security in the case of loans up to extended to units in the MSE sector.
   (a) ₹ 1 lakh (b) ₹ 5 lakh
   (c) ₹ 10 lakh (d) ₹ 20 lakh

7. As per RBI norms, a composite loan limit of ______ can be sanctioned by banks to enable the MSE entrepreneurs to avail of their working capital and term loan requirement through Single Window.
   (a) ₹ 20 lakh (b) ₹ 50 lakh
   (c) ₹ 1 crore (d) ₹ 5 crore

8. GOI had launched Credit Linked Capital Subsidy Scheme (CLSS) for Technology Upgradation of Micro and Small Enterprises subject to the following terms and conditions:
   (a) Ceiling on the loan under the scheme is ₹ 1 crore.
   (b) The rate of subsidy is 15% for all units of micro and small enterprises up to loan ceiling.
   (c) SIDBI and NABARD will continue to be implementing agencies of the scheme.
   (d) All of the above

9. What is the meaning of CGTMSE?
   (a) Credit Guarantee Trust for Micro & Small Enterprises
   (b) Credit Guarantee Trust for Medium & Small Enterprises
   (c) Credit Guarantee Fund Trust for Micro & Small Enterprises
   (d) Credit Guarantee Fund Trust for Medium & Small Enterprises

10. Who has set up Credit Guarantee Fund Trust for Small Industries (CGTSI) in August 2000?
    (a) Government of India (GOI)
    (b) Small Industries Development Bank of India (SIDBI)
    (c) Government of India (GOI) and Industries Development Bank of India (IDBI)
    (d) Government of India (GOI) and Small Industries Development Bank of India (SIDBI)

11. The GOI and SIDBI as settlors of the Trust have committed a corpus of ₹ 2,500 crore in the ratio of to the CGTMSE.

(a) 4 : 1 (b) 1 : 4
(c) 1 : 2 (d) 2 : 1

12. Credit Guarantee Fund Trust for Micro & Small Enterprises (CGTMSE) for MSE loans is effected from which date?

(a) 2nd July 2006 (b) 2nd July 2007
(c) 2nd July 2008 (d) 2nd July 2010

13. What is benefit for banks, if banks financed under CGTMSE Scheme?

(a) 'Zero' risk weight for guarantee cover available
(b) For CGTMSE covered NPA Accounts, no provisioning required for cover portion
(c) In NPA account claim settlement to the extent of 75% of eligible amount is Immediate within 30 days.
(d) All of the above

14. CGTMSE is applicable to those loan account if:

(a) No primary Security obtained
(b) No third party guarantee taken
(c) Sanctioned Limit up to ₹ 200 lac
(d) Any credit facility having ROI more than 14%

15. CGTMSE is not correct to loan account:

(a) Both Term Loan and Working Capital covered.
(b) Both Fund Based & Non Fund Based covered.
(c) Loan under Consortium are also eligible under the scheme.
(d) All of the above

16. Which is not excluded schemes under CGTMSE?

(a) Consortium Finance
(b) SRTO
(c) Educational Institutions
(d) Self Help Group

17. Presently, the maximum coverage available under CGTMSE Scheme:

(a) ₹ 50 lakh (b) ₹ 62.50 lakh
(c) ₹ 100 lakh (d) ₹ 150 lakh

18. Which is not correct statements about CGTMSE guarantee fee?

(a) Annual Service Fee Payable on the ledger outstanding
(b) Annual Service Fee Payable as on 31st March every year.
(c) Guarantee fee up to ₹ 5 lakh for Women & N E Region is 1.35% + RP
(d) Guarantee fee above ₹ 50 lakh for others is 1.80% + Risk Premium

19. Lock in period in CGTMSE claim lodgment is ______ from date of last disbursement of loan or date of payment of guarantee fee whichever is later.

(a) 12 months (b) 18 months
(c) 24 months (d) 36 months

20. Which is correct statements about CGTMSE guarantee cover?

(a) Guarantee cover for entire agreed tenure of the Term Credit/ Composite Credit for the defaulted principal amount.
(b) The guarantee cover for Cash Credit alone will be renewed thereafter for a block of 5 years, subject to coverage for Cash Credit will be valid up to maximum tenure of 10 Years from the original cover start date.
(c) Other Charges such as interest in term loan, Penal Interest, Commitment Charge, Service charge or any other expenses shall not qualify for guarantee cover.
(d) All of the above

ANSWER

1	2	3	4	5	6	7	8	9	10
(b)	(a)	(d)	(b)	(d)	(c)	(c)	(d)	(c)	(d)
11	**12**	**13**	**14**	**15**	**16**	**17**	**18**	**19**	**20**
(a)	(b)	(d)	(a)	(c)	(b)	(d)	(c)	(b)	(d)

GOVERNMENT SPONSORED SCHEMES

GOVERNMENT SPONSORED SCHEMES

The Central Government and the respective State Government is implementing various schemes through banks for the upliftment of the downtrodden by providing financial assistance in the form of subsidized loans. The individuals/Groups of individuals will be selected by the various channelizing agencies and banks will provide loans to candidates sponsored by these agencies.

DEENDAYAL ANTYODAYA YOJANA-NATIONAL RURAL LIVELIHOODS MISSION (DAY-NRLM)

Introduction: Government of India launched Swarnjayanti Gram Swarozgar Yojana (SGSY) scheme after restructuring the Integrated Rural Development Programme (IRDP) from April 1, 1999 in the rural area of the country. SGSY was effective up to 31st March 2013. The Ministry of Rural Development, Government of India launched a new programme known as National Rural Livelihoods Mission (NRLM) by restructuring and replacing the Swarnjayanti Gram Swarozgar Yojana (SGSY) scheme with effect from April 01, 2013.

NRLM was renamed as DAY-NRLM (Deendayal Antyodaya Yojana-National Rural Livelihoods Mission) w.e.f. March 29, 2016 and is the flagship program of Govt. of India for promoting poverty reduction through building strong institutions of the poor, particularly women, and enabling these institutions to access a range of financial services and livelihoods services.

Objective: DAY-NRLM is designed to be a highly intensive program and focuses on intensive application of human and material resources in order to mobilize the poor into functionally effective community owned institutions, promote their financial inclusion and strengthen their livelihoods.

Poverty reduction by building strong institutions of the poor (particularly women) and enabling these institutions to repeatedly access, a range of financial services (particularly bank loans) till they attain sustainable livelihood.

The blocks and districts in which all the components of DAY-NRLM will be implemented, either through the SRLMs (State Rural Livelihood Mission) or partner institutions or NGOs, will be the intensive blocks and districts, whereas remaining will be non-intensive blocks and districts.

Women SHGs and their Federations: Feature of women SHG Group are as under;

a) Women SHGs under DAY-NRLM consist of 10-20 persons. In case of special SHGs *i.e.*, groups in the difficult areas, groups with disabled persons, and groups formed in remote tribal areas, this number may be a minimum of 5 persons.

b) DAY-NRLM promotes affinity based women Self -help groups.

c) Only for groups to be formed with Persons with disabilities, and other special categories like elders, transgenders, DAY-NRLM will have both men and women in the self-help groups.

d) SHG is an informal group and registration under any Societies Act, State cooperative Act or a partnership firm is not mandatory. However, Federations of Self Help Groups formed at village, Gram Panchayat, Cluster or higher level may be registered under appropriate acts prevailing in their States.

FINANCIAL ASSISTANCE

These financial assistances will be provided to the SHGs.

Revolving Fund (RF): DAY-NRLM would provide Revolving Fund (RF) support to SHGs in existence for a minimum period of 3 to 6 months and follow the norms of good SHGs, If they follow 'Panchasutra'– 1. Regular meetings, 2. Regular savings, 3. Regular-internal lending, 4. Regular recoveries and 5. Maintenance of proper books of accounts.

Only such SHGs that have not received any RF earlier will be provided with RF, as corpus, with a minimum of ₹ 10,000 and up to a maximum of ₹ 15,000 per SHG. The purpose of RF is to strengthen their institutional and financial management capacity and build a good credit history within the group.

Capital Subsidy has been discontinued under DAY-NRLM: No Capital Subsidy will be sanctioned to any SHG from the date of implementation of DAY-NRLM.

Community Investment support Fund (CIF): CIF will be provided to the SHGs in the intensive blocks, routed through the Village level / Cluster level Federations, to be maintained in perpetuity by the Federations. The CIF will be used, by the Federations, to advance loans to the SHGs and/or to undertake the common/collective socio-economic activities.

Introduction of Interest subvention: DAY-NRLM has a provision for interest subvention, to cover the difference between the Lending Rate of the banks and 7%, on all credit from the banks/financial institutions availed by women SHGs, for a maximum of ₹ 3,00,000 per SHG. This will be available across the country in two ways:

(i) In 250 identified districts, banks will lend to the women SHGs @7% up to an aggregated loan amount of ₹ 3,00,000/-. The SHGs will also get additional interest subvention of 3% on prompt payment, reducing the effective rate of interest to 4%.

(ii) In the remaining districts also, all women SHGs under DAY-NRLM are eligible for interest subvention to the extent of difference between the lending rates and 7% for the loan up to ₹ 3,00,000, subjected to the norms prescribed by the respective SRLMs. This part of the scheme will be operationalized by SRLMs.

Role of Banks: Banks have to open Savings Bank accounts for all women SHGs, SHGs with members of Disability and the Federations of the SHGs. SHGs and their federations may be encouraged to transact through their respective saving account on regular basis. The KYC norms specified by RBI are applicable for identification of the customers. Eligibility Criteria:

i) SHG should be in active existence for minimum 6 months;

ii) Practicing 'Panchasutras';

iii) Existing defunct SHGs are eligible if they are revived and continue to be active for a minimum period of 3 months.

Lending Norms: Emphasis is laid on the multiple doses of assistance under DAY-NRLM. This would mean assisting an SHG over a period of time, through repeat doses of credit, to enable them to access higher amounts of credit for taking up sustainable livelihoods and improve on the quality of life. SHGs can avail either Term Loan (TL) or a Cash Credit Limit (CCL) loan or both based on the need. In case of need, additional loan can be sanctioned even though the previous loan is outstanding. In case of CCL, banks are advised to sanction minimum loan of ₹ 5 lakhs to each eligible SHGs for a period of 5 years with a yearly drawing power (DP). The drawing power may be enhanced annually based on the repayment performance of the SHG.

Cash Credit Limit (CCL): In case of CCL, banks are advised to sanction minimum loan of ₹ 5 lakhs to each eligible SHGs for a period of 5 years with a yearly drawing power (DP). The drawing power may be enhanced annually based on the repayment performance of the SHG. The drawing power may be calculated as follows:

DP for First Year: 6 times of the existing corpus of minimum of ₹ 1 lakh whichever is higher.

DP for Second Year: 8 times of the corpus at the time review/enhancement or minimum of ₹. 2 lakh whichever is higher.

DP for Third Year: Minimum of ₹ 3 lakhs based on the Micro credit plan prepared by SHG and appraised by Federation/Support agency and the previous credit History.

DP for Fourth Year onwards: Minimum of ₹ 5 lakhs based on the Micro credit plan prepared by SHG and appraised by the Federations/Support agency and the previous credit History.

Term Loan: In case of Term Loan, banks are advised to sanction loan amount in doses as mentioned below:

First Dose: 6 times of the existing corpus of minimum of ₹ 1 lakh whichever is higher.

Second Dose: 8 times of the existing corpus or minimum of ₹ 2 lakh whichever is higher.

Third Dose: Minimum of ₹ 3 lakhs based on the Micro credit plan prepared by the SHGs and appraised by the Federations/Support agency and the previous credit History.

Fourth Dose: Minimum of ₹ 5 lakhs based on the Micro credit plan prepared by the SHGs and appraised by the Federations/Support agency and the previous credit History.

Banks should take necessary measures to ensure that eligible SHG are provided with repeat loans. Banks are advised to work with DAY-NRLM to institutionalize as mechanism for online submission of loan application of SHGs for tracking and timely disposal of application.

Purpose of loan and repayment: The loan amount will be distributed among members based on the Micro Credit Plan prepared by the SHGs. The loans may be used by members for meeting social needs, high cost debt swapping, construction or repair of house, construction of toilets and taking up sustainable livelihoods by the individual members within the SHGs or to finance any viable common activity started by the SHGs.

Repayment Schedule: Repayment of loan schedule will be as under;

1st **Dose**—repaid in 6-12 months in monthly / quarterly installments;

2nd **Dose**—repaid in 12-24 months in monthly / quarterly installments;

3rd **Dose**—repaid in 24-36 months in monthly / quarterly installments;

4th **Dose**—repaid between 3-6 years based on the cash flow in monthly / quarterly installments.

Security and Margin: No collateral and no margin will be charged up to ₹ 10.00 lakhs limit to the SHGs. No lien should be marked against savings bank account of SHGs and no deposits should be insisted upon while sanctioning loans.

Dealing with Defaulters: Non-willful defaulters should not be debarred from receiving the loan. Willful defaulters should not be financed (Willful defaulters' members of a group can be allowed to benefit from the thrift and credit activities of the group including the corpus built up with the assistance of Revolving Fund).

DEENDAYAL ANTYODAYA YOJANA—NATIONAL URBAN LIVELIHOODS MISSION (DAY-NULM)

Launching & Implementing Agency: Government of India, Ministry of Housing and Urban Poverty Alleviation has restructured the existing Swarna Jayanti Shahari Rozgar Yojana (SJSRY) and launched the NULM w.e.f. 24.09.2013. Scheme is operative in all districts headquarters irrespective is population and all cities with population of 1 lakh or more and that SJSRY was to remain operational till March 31, 2014. The Self Employment Programme (SEP) component of NULM will focus on providing financial assistance through a provision of interest subsidy on loans to support establishment of individuals and Group Enterprises and SHGs of urban poor.

Target and Features of NULM are as under:

- Minimum percentage of women beneficiaries under Self Employment Programme (SEP) shall not be less than 30%,
- SC/ST must be benefited at least to the extent of the proportion of their strength in the city/ town population of poor,
- 3 per cent of the physical and financial targets for PWD,
- 15 per cent of the physical and financial targets for minority community.
- No minimum educational qualifications and training requirement.
- If project require skills for running the proposed micro-enterprise, training under EST& individual and group entrepreneurs.
- In addition to skill training of the beneficiaries, the ULB will also arrange to conduct EDP Programme for 3-7 days.

Interest Subvention: The difference between 7% p.a. and the prevailing It is to be provided to banks under NULM. After disbursement of loan to the beneficiaries, the concerned branch of the bank will send details of disbursed loan cases to ULB along with details of interest subsidy amount. Claim of interest subvention-quarterly basis.

Eligibility for NULM Loan to Individual: An urban poor individual for setting up a micro-enterprise for self-employment. Beneficiary should have attained 18 years age.

Project Cost: The maximum unit project cost for individual micro-enterprises cases is ₹ 2.00 lakhs.

Collateral on Bank Loan: No collateral required. Banks are mandated not to accept collateral security in the cases of loans up to ₹ 5 lakhs extended to units in the MSE Sector. Therefore, only the assets created would be hypothecated/mortgaged/pledged to banks for advancing loans.

Repayment: 5 to 7 years after initial moratorium of 6-18 months as per norms of the banks.

Eligibility for NULM Loan to SHG

The group enterprise should have minimum 5 members with a minimum of 70% members from urban poor families. The application / intent to set up a group enterprise by beneficiaries/group members should preferably be referred by the community structures viz. SHG/ALF formed under SJSRY/NULM.

Age: All members of the group enterprise should have attained an age of 18 years at the time of applying for bank loan.

Project Cost: The maximum unit Project Cost for a group enterprise is ₹ 10 lakhs.

Loan: Project cost less the beneficiary contribution (as specified by bank) would be made available as loan amount to the group enterprise by the bank.

Collateral on Bank Loan: No collateral guarantee required. Only assets created would be hypothecated/ mortgaged/ pledged to banks for advancing loans. The banks may approach CGTMSE guarantee.

Repayment: 5 to 7 years after initial moratorium of 6-18 months as decided by banks.

The indicative composition of the Task Force is as follows:

Sr. No.	TASK Force at ULB level	Role
1.	Chief Executive Officer (CEO) ULB / Municipal Commissioner of ULB / or any representative authorized by CEO ULB	Chairman
2.	Lead District Manager (LDM)	Member
3.	City Project Officer (CPO), ULB / or any authorized representative of ULB	Member Convener
4.	Representative from District Industries Centre (DIC)	Member
5.	Senior Branch Managers (Max-2) of banks	Member
6.	Representatives (2) of Area Level Federation/City Level Federation	Member

SELF EMPLOYMENT SCHEME FOR REHABILITATION OF MANUAL SCAVENGERS (SRMS)

Definition of Manual Scavenger: "Manual scavenger" means a person engaged or employed, at the commencement of this Act or at any time thereafter, by an individual or a local authority or an agency or a contractor, for manually cleaning, carrying, disposing of, or otherwise handling in any manner, human excreta in an insanitary latrine or in an open drain or pit into which human excreta from the insanitary latrines is disposed of, or on a railway track or in such other spaces or premises, as the Central Government or a state Government may notify, before the excreta fully decomposes in such manner as may be prescribed, and the expression "manual scavenging".

Cash Assistance: The identified manual scavengers, one from each family, would be eligible receiving Cash Assistance of ₹ 40,000 immediately after identification. The beneficiary would be allowed to withdraw the amount in monthly installments of maximum of ₹ 7000.

Maximum Project Cost: ₹ 10 lakh for any activities under ISB and ₹ 15 Lakh, in case of sanitation related projects *i.e.*, vacuum loader, suction machine with vehicle/ Garbage disposal vehicle, Pay & Use toilets etc.

Provision of Capital subsidy based on project cost-Back-end Capital Subsidy as given below:

Range of Project Cost (₹)	Rate of Subsidy
Upto ₹ 2,00,000/-	50% of project cost
₹ 2,00,001 to ₹ 5,00,000/-	₹ 1 lakh + 33.3% of project cost
₹ 5,00,001 to ₹ 10,00,000/-	₹ 2 lakh + 25% of project cost
₹ 10,00,001 to ₹ 15,00,000/-	₹ 3, 25,000/-

Rate of Interest to be Charged from Beneficiaries : 5% for PC up to ₹ 25,000/- (4% for women), and 6% for PC above ₹ 25,000/-

Provision of Interest Subsidy, Depending on the Amount of Loan : No change – Gap between the actual rate of interest charged by bank and the rate of interest at which the loan is to be provided under the Scheme.

Maximum Period of Training : 2 years.

Stipend During Training : ₹3,000/- p.m.

Repayment Period Including the Moratorium period which is Up to Two Years :

For projects costing up to ₹ 5 lakhs - 5 years.

For projects costing more than ₹ 5 lakhs - 7 years.

Penal Provisions for Misuse of Funds : Penal provisions for misuse of funds by beneficiaries, provided under the Scheme. Entire amount of subsidy with a penal interest of 6% will be recovered.

DIFFERENTIAL RATE OF INTEREST (DRI)

Differential Rate of Interest (DRI) Scheme: The scheme is in operation since 1972 but has been amended on 12.06.2007. Objective of the scheme is to assist poorest of the poor and bring them above the poverty line.

Purpose of Loan: For productive activities, pursuing higher education by indigent students, purchase of limbs, hearing aids, wheel chair for PWD.

Quantum of Loan: Maximum ₹ 15,000/- (additional ₹ 5000/- to PWD for artificial limbs/Braille typewriter etc.);

Target: Minimum 40% to SC/ST beneficiaries and 2/3rd of the sanction should be routed through rural and semi-urban branches.

Eligibility Norms for DRI Scheme are as under:

- Individuals whose family income does not exceed ₹ 18000/- p.a. in rural areas;
- Individuals whose family income does not exceed ₹ 24000/- p.a. in semi-urban and urban areas.
- Individual whose land holding does not exceed 1 acre of irrigated and 2.5 acres of un-irrigated land.
- No ceiling for :
  - SC/ST engaged in agriculture and allied activities.
  - People engaged in Cottage and Rural industries;
  - Persons with Disability pursuing gainful employment;
  - Orphanages and women's home;
  - State owned corporations/cooperative societies including State corporations for Supreme Court/ST's/Cooperative Societies, Large sized Adivasi Multipurpose Cooperative Societies for Tribal areas.

Security: Hypothecation of assets created out of bank loan. No collateral.

Subsidy: No subsidy, No margin.

Rate of Interest: 4% p.a. simple.

Repayment: Depending upon income generated. Maximum 5 years including moratorium period up to 2 years depending upon the type of activity and income generation. For the beneficiaries under IAY, it may be extended up to 7 years.

Classification: Weaker Section Advance.

PRIME MINISTER'S EMPLOYMENT GENERATION PROGRAMME (PMEGP)

Introduction: PMEGP is a new MSME Scheme of Govt. of India by merging REGP and PMRY scheme launched on 04-04-2008. State Khadi & V.I. Board and District Industries Centre of State Government have also been associated in implementation of the programme. Special Package of subsidy to promote rural industrialization. Empowering entrepreneurs through Skill Development and entrepreneurial development programme (EDP).

Objective of the Scheme: To provide continuous and sustainable employment to a large segment of traditional and prospective artisans, of rural and urban unemployed youth in the country for their better livelihood.

To increase the wage-earning capacity of artisans and contribute to increase in the growth rate of rural and urban employment. To facilitate participation of financial institutions for higher credit flow to only new micro enterprises.

Eligible Borrowers: Individuals, SHGs (of BPL), Charitable Trust, Institutions under Society Registration Act., Production based Co-operative Societies. Beneficiary should have attained 18 years age.

Education Qualification: VIII Std. Passed only for project costing above ₹ 10.00 lakhs in manufacturing and above ₹ 5.00 lakhs for Service Sector. Otherwise no minimum education qualification required.

Definition of Family: Beneficiary & spouse. Only one person from family eligible.

Repayment: 3 to 7 years with moratorium prescribed.

Project: No income ceiling for setting up of projects. Assistance under the Scheme is available only to new units to be established. Existing units or units already availed any Govt. Subsidy either under State / Central Govt. Schemes are not eligible.

Documents Required: Following certificate should be submitted along with application;

1) Age proof certificate;
2) Caste certificate if beneficiaries are from special categories (SC/ST/Minority/Ex-Servicemen etc.);
3) Educational qualification certificate if beneficiaries opting project cost above ₹ 10.00 lakhs in case manufacturing and above ₹ 5.00 lakhs for service sector;
4) 2-3 weeks EDP training certificate if already undergone such training.

Implementing Agencies and Facilitators: For easy approach and accessibility, first three agencies and following facilitators will work in each district.

a) Khadi & Village Industries Commission;
b) Khadi & Village Industries Boards;
c) District Industrial Centres of State Govts;
d) Rajiv Gandhi Udyami Mitra Yojana;
e) Ministry of Women & Child Development;
f) Panchayati Raj Institutions;
g) KVI Federations;
h) Nehru Yuva Kendra Sangathan;
i) Army Wives Welfare Association.

Financing Agencies: Scheme is financed by any of the following;

- All Public-Sector Banks;
- All Regional Rural Banks;
- Small Industries Development Bank of India (SIDBI);

- Co-operative Banks approved by a committee headed by the Secretary, Industries of the State;
- Private Sector Commercial Banks approved by a committee headed by the Secretary, Industries of the State.

Eligible Industry: Any industry including Coir Based projects excluding those mentioned in the negative list. Maximum project cost for ₹ 25.00 lakhs in case of manufacturing and ₹ 10.00 lakhs for Service Sector.

Negative List of the Activities: Following activities are not eligible under the scheme;

a) Any Industry/business connected with Meat (slaughter) *i.e.,* processing, canning and/or serving items like Beedi / Pan / Cigar / Cigarette etc. any Hotel or Dhaba or sales outlet serving liquor, preparation / producing tobacco as raw materials, tapping of toddy for sale.

b) Any industry / business connected with cultivating of crops / plantation like Tea, Coffee, Rubber etc. sericulture (cotton rearing), Horticulture, Floriculture, Animal Husbandry like Pisciculture, Piggery, Poultry, Harvester machines etc.

c) Manufacture of Polythene carry bags of less than 20 microns thickness and manufacture of carry bags or containers made up of recycled plastic for storing, carrying, dispensing or packaging of food stuff and any other item which causes environmental problems.

d) Industries such as processing of Pashmina Wool and such other products like hand spinning and hand weaving, taking advantage of Khadi Programme under the purview of Certification Rules and availing sales rebate.

e) Rural Transport (except Auto rickshaw in Andaman & Nicobar Islands, House boat, Shikara & Tourist Boats in Jammu & Kashmir and Cycle Rickshaw).

Implementing Agency: Rural area as declared under KVIC Act 2006–Scheme to be implemented by KVIC, KVIB and DIC. Urban area-Only DIC.

Margin & Financial Assistance

Categories of Beneficiaries under PMEGP	*Beneficiary's Contribution of Project Cost*	*Rate of Subsidy of Project Cost*	
Area (location of project/unit)		***Urban***	***Rural***
General Category	10%	15%	25%
Special (including SC/ST/OBC/Minorities/Women, Ex-Servicemen, Physically handicapped, NER, Hill and Border areas etc.)	05%	25%	35%

Bank Finance: The Bank will sanction 90% of the project cost in case of General category beneficiary and 95% in case special category of beneficiary / institutions. The Bank will disburse full amount suitably for setting up of the project.

Selection of Beneficiaries: Project proposals will be invited from potential beneficiaries at District level through Print and Electronic Media by KVIC/KVIBs and DIC at periodic intervals.

Facilitating agencies may also collect applications and submit the same to the KVIC, KVIB and DICs for placing the same before District Task Force Committee. To ensure the transparency in identification of the beneficiaries, Panchayati Raj Institutions to be involved in the process of selection.

Process to Apply for Loan: Prescribed application may be downloaded from KVIC website or from any field offices of KVIC or KVIB or DICs. The application along with required certificate may be submitted to any one of the Offices of KVIC or KVIB or DICs. The application will be placed before District Task Force Committee headed by District Magistrate/Deputy Commissioner/ Collector of respective Offices. Personal Interview will be conducted by District Task Force Committee.

Application Selection: Selection will be made on the basis of background and personal interview. The District task force will forward its recommendation to KVIC /KVIB /DICs within a period of one month of the meeting. The same will be forwarded by the implementing agencies to Financing Branch of the Bank within 15 days of receipt of the same.

Operational Procedure: The Bank will take their own credit decision on selection of projects. In case of any rejection, the same will be intimated to the District Task Force with reasons. After sanctioning of project, the beneficiary has to deposit 5% or 10% of the project cost as the case may be, in the bank. First instalment of loan will be released to Beneficiaries only after completion of EDP training. Project cost will include capital expenditure and one cycle of working capital.

Entrepreneurs Development Programme (EDP) training for 2-3 weeks is compulsory before disbursement of loan. EDP training will be provided by the following Training Institutions :

a) Departmental and Non-Departmental Training Centers of KVIC /KVIB,
b) Accredited training Centers,
c) EDP Institute of National repute like NIESBUD, NIMSME, IIE, EDI etc.

Skill Development: District Task Force will recommend needy entrepreneurs for skill development programme. Skill Development/Skill Up gradation will be provided as per requirement to the entrepreneurs by Training Centre accredited with Ministry of MSME and reputed institutions of KVIC/KVIB/State Govts., DIC.

Subsidy Release & Adjustment: The subsidy claim will be submitted online through Financing Bank after release of first instalment of loan. The Financing Branch will forward the same to the respective Nodal branch. The Nodal Branch after being satisfied that the unit fulfills the criteria under PMEGP will release the subsidy to the Financing Branch.

The original claim format to be forwarded to respective office *i.e.*, KVIC/KVIB/DIC by the Nodal Branch of the Bank keeping a copy with them. Acknowledgement letter in the prescribed format will be issued by the KVIC/KVIB/DIC to the Nodal Branch on receipt of original claim format.

The lock in period of subsidy is of 3 years in the TDR in the name of beneficiary. No interest will be paid on the TDR and no interest will be charged on loan to the corresponding amount of TDR. Subsidy will be adjusted only after physical verification.

TEST YOURSELF

1. NRLM was renamed as DAY-NRLM (Deendayal-Antyodaya Yojana-National Rural Livelihoods Mission) w.e.f. ________

(a) March 29, 2014 (b) March 29, 2015
(c) March 29, 2016 (d) March 29, 2017

2. Feature of women SHG Group are as under:

(a) Women SHGs under DAY-NRLM consist of 10-20 persons.
(b) In case of special SHGs *i.e.*, groups in the difficult areas, groups with disabled persons, and groups formed in remote tribal areas, this number may be a minimum of 5 persons.
(c) Only for groups to be formed with Persons with disabilities, and other special categories like elders, transgender, DAY-NRLM will have both men and women in the self-help groups.
(d) All of the above

3. DAY-NRLM would provide Revolving Fund (RF) support to SHGs in existence for a minimum period of ________ and follow the norms of good SHGs.

(a) 1 to 2 months (b) 1 to 3 months
(c) 3 to 6 months (d) 6 to 9 months

4. Which is the part of 'Panchasutra' for SHG?

(a) Regular meetings
(b) Regular savings
(c) Regular internal lending
(d) All of the above

5. Only such SHGs that have not received any RF earlier will be provided with RF, as corpus, with a minimum of ________ and up to a maximum of ________ per SHG.

(a) ₹ 10,000, ₹ 15,000
(b) ₹ 10,000, ₹ 25,000
(c) ₹ 20,000, ₹ 50,000
(d) ₹ 25,000, ₹ 50,000

6. Which type of Subsidy will be given to any SHG from the date of implementation of DAY-NRLM.

(a) Only Capital Subsidy
(b) Only Interest Subsidy
(c) Both Capital and Interest Subsidy
(d) No any Subsidy available

7. Banks have to open Savings Bank accounts for all SHGs, If:

(a) SHG should be in active existence for minimum 6 months;
(b) Practicing 'Panchasutras'
(c) Existing defunct SHGs are eligible if they are revived and continue to be active for a minimum period of 3 months.
(d) All of the above

8. Under DAY-NRLM scheme 2nd dose of CIF will be ________ of existing corpus and proposed saving during the next 12 months or ₹ 2 lakh, whichever is higher.

(a) 3 times (b) 8 times
(c) 10 times (d) 12 times

9. The maximum unit project cost under DAY-NULM scheme for individual micro-enterprises cases is ______.

(a) ₹ 2.00 lakhs (b) ₹ 5.00 lakhs
(c) ₹ 10.00 lakhs (d) ₹ 20.00 lakhs

10. The identified manual scavengers, one from each family, would be eligible receiving Cash Assistance of ______ immediately after identification under SRMS.

(a) ₹ 20,000/- (b) ₹ 25,000/-
(c) ₹ 40,000/- (d) ₹ 50,000/-

11. Rate of Interest to be charged from beneficiaries under SRMS @ ______ for PC above ₹ 25,000/-

(a) 4% (b) 6%
(c) 7% (d) 8%

12. Eligibility Norms for DRI Scheme are:

(a) Individuals whose family income does not exceed ₹ 18000/- p.a. in rural areas;
(b) Individuals whose family income does not exceed ₹ 24000/- p.a. in semi-urban and urban areas.
(c) Individual whose land holding does not exceed 1 acre of irrigated and 2.5 acres of un-irrigated land.
(d) All of the above

13. Rate of Interest under DRI scheme is:

(a) 4% p.a. (b) 4% p.a. simple
(c) 5% p.a. simple (d) 6% p.a. simple

14. PMEGP is a new MSME Scheme of Govt. of India by merging REGP and PMRY scheme launched on ______.

(a) 04-04-2006 (b) 04-04-2008
(c) 04-04-2010 (d) 04-04-2012

15. Education Qualification required under PMEGP is:

(a) VIII Std. Passed in all cases
(b) X Std. Passed in all cases
(c) VIII Std. Passed only for project costing above ₹ 10.00 lakhs in manufacturing and above ₹ 5.00 lakhs for Service Sector.
(d) X Std. Passed only for project costing above ₹ 10.00 lakhs in manufacturing and above ₹ 5.00 lakhs for Service Sector.

16. Definition of Family is applicable for PMEGP Scheme is:

(a) Beneficiary & spouse
(b) Beneficiary, spouse & children
(c) Beneficiary, spouse & parents
(d) Beneficiary, spouse dependent children

17. Rural area, PMEGP Scheme to be implemented by:

(a) KVIC (b) KVIB
(c) DIC (d) All of the above

18. Subsidy available under PMEGP scheme for General Category in Rural area is ______ Project Cost.

(a) 15% (b) 25%
(c) 30% (d) 35%

19. Minimum margin under PMEGP scheme for SC/ST Category is ______ Project Cost.

(a) 5% (b) 10%
(c) 15% (d) 20%

20. Which of the following activities are eligible under the PMEGP scheme;

(a) Any Industry/business connected with Meat (slaughter)
(b) Any industry/business connected with cultivating of crops/plantation like Tea, Coffee, and Rubber etc
(c) Manufacture of Polythene carry bags of less than 20 microns thickness
(d) Shikara & Tourist Boats in Jammu & Kashmir

ANSWER

1	2	3	4	5	6	7	8	9	10
(c)	(d)	(c)	(d)	(a)	(b)	(d)	(b)	(a)	(c)
11	**12**	**13**	**14**	**15**	**16**	**17**	**18**	**19**	**20**
(b)	(d)	(b)	(b)	(c)	(a)	(d)	(b)	(a)	(d)

SELF HELP GROUPS

IMPORTANCE OF SHG IN INDIA

Despite the vast expansion of the formal credit system in the country, the dependence of the rural poor on moneylenders somehow continued in many areas, especially for marginal farmers, landless labourers, petty traders and rural artisans belonging to socially and economically backward classes. NABARD launched a pilot project to cover Self-Help Groups (SHGs) promoted by Non-Governmental Organizations, banks and other agencies under the pilot project and supported it by way of refinance. In India about 85% of the groups linked with the banks were formed exclusively by women. The quick studies conducted by NABARD in a few states to assess the impact of the linkage project brought out encouraging and positive features like increase in loan volume of the SHGs, nearly 100% recovery performanceand gradual increase in the income level of the SHG members.

SELF HELP GROUP

A self-help group (SHG) is a village-based financial intermediary usually composed of 10-20 local women. It is affinity based homogeneous group of women or men.

In case of special SHGs *i.e.,* groups in the difficult areas, groups with disabled persons, and groups formed in remote tribal areas, this number may be a minimum of 5 persons. Members make small regular savings contributions over a few months until there is enough capital in the group to begin lending. Funds may then be lent back to the members or to others in the village for any purpose.

Objectives of SHG: Objective of the formation of SHG are as under;

- To create an appropriate & sensitive forum for addressing the need of people;
- To inculcate saving habits in the community;
- To generate the sense of collective action;
- To improve socio-economic status;
- To access the outside resources.

Activities of SHGs

The members of the SHG have to adopt some rules and regulations. SHG has to follow 'Panchasutra' : 1. Regular meetings, 2. Regular savings, 3. Regular internal lending, 4. Regular recoveries and 5. Maintenance of proper books of accounts. These important activities are as under;

1. **Meeting:** The group should meet regularly at least once in monthly. Full attendance in all the group meetings will make it easy for the SHG to stabilise and start working to the satisfaction of all. The group should have fixed date and fix a common place to conduct the meeting. Membership register, minutes register etc. are to be kept up to date by the group, by making the entry regularly.
2. **Savings:** Savings should be deposited by all members in the meeting itself. No interest will be paid to the members for their money with the group. Simple and clear books for all transactions to be maintained.
3. **Resolution from the SHG:** The SHG has to pass a resolution in the group meeting, signed by all members should be mention in the register.

4. **Saving Accounts:** For opening of the saving account with the bank, a resolution should be passed and the resolution is filled with the bank. The SHG should authorise at least three members, any two of whom, to jointly operate upon their account.
5. **Conduct of Internal Lending by SHG:** After saving for the minimum period of two to three months, the common savings fund should be used by the SHG for lending their own members. Interest should be charged on intra lending fund. Timely recovery of lending amount is necessary. Intra lending and recovery register should be maintain. The purpose, terms and condition for lending to its member, rate of interest etc. are decided by the group members during its meetings.

SHG-BANK LINKAGE PROGRAMME

The Reserve Bank of India has, from time to time, issued a number of guidelines/instructions to banks on SHG-Bank Linkage Programme.

Separate Segment under Priority Sector: It was decided that the banks should report their lending to SHGs for on-lending to members of SHGs under the respective categories, viz. 'Advances to SHGs' irrespective of the purposes for which the members of SHGs have been disbursed loans. All loan to SHG is categorised as weaker sections.

Opening of Savings Bank, A/c: The SHGs registered or unregistered which are engaged in promoting savings habits among their members would be eligible to open savings bank accounts with banks. These SHGs need not necessarily have already availed of credit facilities from banks before opening savings bank accounts. KYC verification of all the members of SHG need not be done while opening the savings bank account of the SHG as KYC verification of all the office bearers would suffice. Further, it is clarified that no separate KYC verification of the members or office bearers is necessary at the time of credit linking of SHGs.

Margin and Security Norms: As per operational guidelines of NABARD, SHGs may be sanctioned savings linked loans by banks (varying from a saving to loan ratio of 1:1 to 1:4). However, in case of matured SHGs, loans may be given beyond the limit of four times the savings as per the discretion of the bank. The flexibility allowed to the banks in respect of margin, security norms, etc. under the pilot project continues to be operational under the linkage programme even beyond the pilot phase.

Documentation: A simple system requiring minimum procedures and documentation is a precondition for augmenting flow of credit to SHGs. Keeping in view the nature of lending and status of borrowers, banks should strive to remove all operational irritants and make arrangements to expeditiously sanction and disburse credit by delegating adequate sanctioning powers to branch managers. The loan application forms, procedures and documents should be made simple. It would help in providing prompt and hassle-free credit.

Presence of Defaulters in SHGs: The defaults by a few members of SHGs and/or their family members to the financing bank should not ordinarily come in the way of financing SHGs per se by banks provided the SHG is not in default to it. However, the bank loan may not be utilized by the SHG for financing a defaulter member to the bank.

Capacity Building and Training: An important step in the Linkage Programme would be the training of the field level officials and sensitization of the controlling and other senior officials of the bank. Considering the need and magnitude of training requirements of bank officers/staff both at field level and controlling office level, the banks may initiate suitable steps to internalize the SHGs linkage project and organize exclusive short duration programmes for the field level functionaries. In addition, suitable awareness/sensitization programmes may be conducted for their middle level controlling officers as well as senior officers.

Monitoring and Review of SHG Lending: Having regard to the potential of the SHGs, banks may have to closely monitor the progress regularly at various levels. In order to give a boost to the ongoing SHG bank linkage programme for credit flow to the unorganized sector, banks were advised in January 2004 that monitoring of SHG bank linkage programme may be made a regular item on the agenda for discussion at the SLBC and DCC meetings. It should be reviewed at the highest corporate level on a quarterly basis. Further the progress of the programme may be reviewed by the banks at regular intervals.

Encourage SHG Linkage: Banks should provide adequate incentives to their branches in financing the Self-Help Groups (SHGs) and establish linkages with them, making the procedures absolutely simple and easy while providing for total flexibility in such procedures to suit local conditions. The group dynamics of working of the SHGs may be left to themselves and need neither be regulated nor formal structures imposed or insisted upon. The approach to financing of SHGs should be totally hassle-free and may include consumption expenditures.

Interest Rates: The interest rate applicable to loans given by banks to Self Help Groups/member beneficiaries would be left to their discretion.

Service/Processing Charges: No loan related service charges/inspection charges should be levied on priority sector loans up to ₹ 25,000. In the case of eligible priority sector loans to SHGs/ JLGs, this limit will be applicable per member and not to the group as a whole.

Total Financial Inclusion and Credit Requirement of SHGs

Banks have been advised to meet the entire credit requirements of SHG members, as envisaged in the Paragraph 93 of the Union Budget announcement made by the Honourable Finance Minister for the year 2008-09 where in it was stated as under: "Banks will be encouraged to embrace the concept of Total Financial Inclusion. Government will request all scheduled commercial banks to follow the example set by some public-sector banks and meet the entire credit requirements of SHG members, namely, (a) income generation activities, (b) social needs like housing, education, marriage, etc. and (c) debt swapping".

TEST YOURSELF

1. _______ launched a pilot project to cover Self-Help Groups (SHGs) promoted by Non-Governmental Organizations, banks and other agencies under the pilot project and supported it by way of refinance.
(a) NABARD (b) Govt. of India
(c) RBI (d) SIDBI

2. A self-help group (SHG) is a village-based financial intermediary usually composed of _______ local women.
(a) 5–10 (b) 5–20
(c) 10–20 (d) 10–15

3. In case of special SHGs *i.e.*, groups in the difficult areas, groups with disabled persons, and groups formed in remote tribal areas, this number may be a minimum of _______.
(a) 4 persons (b) 5 persons
(c) 6 persons (d) 7 persons

4. Objective of the formation of SHG are as under:
(a) To create an appropriate & sensitive forum for addressing the need of people
(b) To inculcate saving habits in the community
(c) To generate the sense of collective action
(d) All of the above

5. The members of the SHG have to adopt some rules and regulations. SHG has to follow 'Panchasutra'. Which are the part of Panchasutra
(a) Regular meetings
(b) Regular savings
(c) Regular internal lending
(d) All of the above

6. Banks have to open Savings Bank accounts for all SHGs, If:
(a) SHG should be in active existence for minimum 6 months;
(b) Practicing 'Panchasutras'
(c) Existing defunct SHGs are eligible if they are revived and continue to be active for a minimum period of 3 months.
(d) All of the above

7. The group members of SHG should meet regularly at least _______.
(a) once in a month (b) twice in a month
(c) once in a quarter (d) twice in a quarter

8. For opening of the saving account with the bank, a resolution should be passed and the resolution is filled with the bank. The SHG should authorise at least _______ members, any two of whom, to jointly operate upon their account.
(a) two (b) three
(c) four (d) five

9. All loan to SHG is categorised as _______.
(a) Agriculture loan (b) MSME loan
(c) Weaker sections loan (d) KCC loan

10. Government will request all scheduled commercial banks to follow the example set by some public-sector banks and meet the entire credit requirements of SHG members, namely,
(a) Income generation activities
(b) Debt swapping
(c) Social needs like housing, education, marriage, etc.
(d) All of the above

11. No loan related service charges/inspection charges should be levied on priority sector loans up to _______.
(a) ₹ 10,000 (b) ₹ 25,000
(c) ₹ 50,000 (d) ₹ 100,000

12. As per operational guidelines of NABARD, SHGs may be sanctioned savings linked loans by banks varying from a saving to loan ratio of 1:1 to _______.
(a) 1 : 2 (b) 1 : 3
(c) 1 : 4 d) 1 : 5

ANSWER

1	2	3	4	5	6	7	8	9	10	11	12
(a)	(c)	(b)	(d)	(d)	(d)	(a)	(b)	(c)	(d)	(b)	(c)

CREDIT CARDS, HOME LOANS, PERSONAL LOANS, CONSUMER LOANS

CREDIT CARD OPERATIONS

Purpose: To provide a framework of rules/regulations/standards/practices to the Home Loans, Personal Loans, Consumer Loans and credit card issuing banks and to the credit card issuing NBFCs to ensure that the same are in alignment with the best customer practices. Banks should adopt adequate safeguards and implement the following guidelines in order to ensure that their card operations are run on sound, prudent and customer friendly manner.

Credit Card Operations of Banks

Credit card is the one of the delivery channels of the banking services. Due to the advancement of technology and easy accessibility to credit, the credit cards are gaining popularity now a day. Experience has shown that the quality of banks' credit card portfolios mirrors the economic environment in which they operate, and there is a strong correlation between an economic downturn and deterioration in the quality of such portfolios. The deterioration may become even more serious if banks have relaxed their credit underwriting criteria and risk management standards as a result of intense competition in the market. It is therefore important for banks to maintain prudent policies and practices for managing the risks of their credit card business which are relevant to the market environment that they operate in.

Issue of Cards: Banks in India can undertake credit card business either departmentally or through a subsidiary company set up for the purpose. They can also undertake domestic credit card business by entering into tie-up arrangement with one of the banks already having arrangements for issue of credit cards.

Prior approval of the Reserve Bank is not necessary for banks desirous of undertaking credit card business either independently or in tie-up arrangement with other card issuing banks. Banks can do so with the approval of their Boards. However, only banks with net worth of ₹ 100 crore and above should undertake credit card business. Banks desirous of setting up separate subsidiaries for undertaking credit card business would, however, require prior approval of the Reserve Bank.

Each bank must have a well-documented policy and a Fair Practices Code for credit card operations. The Fair Practices Code should incorporate the various guidelines on the subject issued by RBI from time to time, as well as the relevant Guidelines contained in this Master Circular. Banks which have adopted the "Code of Bank's Commitment to Customers" (Code) of The Banking Codes and Standards Board of India (BCSBI) may also incorporate the principles enunciated therein, as amended from time to time, in their Fair Practices Code. The Fair Practices Code should be available on the website of the Bank/NBFC.

Banks/NBFCs should ensure prudence while issuing credit cards and independently assess the credit risk while issuing cards to persons, especially to students and others with no independent financial means.

As holding several credit cards enhances the total credit available to any consumer, banks/NBFCs should assess the credit limit for a credit card customer having regard to the limits enjoyed by the cardholder from other banks on the basis of self- declaration/ credit information obtained from a CIC. While issuing cards, the terms and conditions for issue and usage of a credit card should be mentioned in clear and simple language (preferably in English, Hindi and the local language) comprehensible to a card user.

Types of Credit Cards

Banks may issue credit cards including co-branded credit cards, corporate credit cards to the employees of their corporate customers, as well as add-on credit cards. However, while issuing co-branded credit cards, banks must undertake due diligence on the non-bank entity to protect themselves against the reputation risk to which they are exposed to in such an arrangement.

The instructions/guidelines on KYC/AML/CFT applicable to banks, issued by RBI from time to time, may be adhered to in respect of all cards issued, including co-branded, corporate, and add on credit cards.

Interest Rates and Other Charges

Banks are advised to be guided by the instructions on interest rate on advances issued by RBI and as amended from time to time, while determining the interest rate on credit card dues, the latter being in the nature of non-priority sector personal loans. Banks should also prescribe a ceiling rate of interest, including processing and other charges, in respect of credit cards. In case banks/NBFCs charge interest rates which vary based on the payment/default history of the cardholder, there should be transparency in levying of such differential interest rates. For this purpose, the banks should publicise through their website and other means, the interest rates charged to various categories of customers.

Further, the banks/NBFCs have to adhere to the following guidelines relating to interest rates and other charges on credit cards:

a) Card issuers should ensure that there is no delay in dispatching bills and the customer has sufficient number of days (at least one fortnight) for making payment before the interest starts getting charged. In order to obviate frequent complaints of delayed billing, the credit card issuing bank/NBFC may consider providing bills and statements of accounts online, with suitable security measures. Banks/NBFCs could also consider putting in place a mechanism to ensure that the customer's acknowledgement is obtained for receipt of the monthly statement.

b) Card issuers should quote Annualized Percentage Rates (APR) on card products (separately for retail purchase and for cash advance, if different). The method of calculation of APR should be given with a couple of examples for better comprehension. The APR charged and the annual fee should be shown with equal prominence. The late payment charges, including the method of calculation of such charges and the number of days, should be prominently indicated.

c) Banks/NBFCs should step up their efforts on educating the cardholders of the implications of paying only 'the minimum amount due'. The "Most Important Terms and Conditions" should specifically explain that the 'free credit period' is lost if any balance of the previous month's bill is outstanding.

d) Banks are advised to follow uniform method of determining over-due status for credit card accounts while reporting to credit information companies and for the purpose of levying penal charges viz., late payment charges, etc.,

e) The banks/NBFCs should not levy any charge that was not explicitly indicated to the credit card holder at the time of issue of the card and without getting his/her consent. However, this would not be applicable to charges like service taxes, etc. which may subsequently be levied by the Government or any other statutory authority.

f) The terms and conditions for payment of credit card dues, including the minimum payment due, should be stipulated so as to ensure that there is no negative amortization.

g) There should be transparency (without any hidden charges) in issuing credit cards free of charge during the first year.

Wrongful Billing

The card issuing bank/NBFC should ensure that wrong bills are not raised and issued to customers. In case, a customer protests any bill, the bank/NBFC should provide explanation and, If necessary, documentary evidence may also be provided to the customer within a maximum period of sixty days with a spirit to amicably redress the grievances.

Issue of Unsolicited Cards/Facilities

Unsolicited cards should not be issued. In case, an unsolicited card is issued and activated without the written consent of the recipient and the latter is billed for the same, the card issuing bank shall not only reverse the charges forthwith, but also pay a penalty without demur to the recipient amounting to twice the value of the charges reversed.

In addition, the person in whose name the card is issued can also approach the Banking Ombudsman who would determine the amount of compensation payable by the bank to the recipient of the unsolicited card as per the provisions of the Banking Ombudsman Scheme 2006, *i.e.*, for loss of complainant's time, expenses incurred, harassment and mental anguish suffered by him.

Customer Confidentiality: The card issuing bank/ NBFC should not reveal any information relating to customers obtained at the time of opening the account or issuing the credit card to any other person or organization without obtaining their specific consent, as regards the purpose/s for which the information will be used and the organizations with whom the information will be shared. The application form for credit card must explicitly provide for consent the same.

Reporting to Credit Information Companies (CICs): For providing information relating to credit history/ repayment record of the card holder to a Credit Information Company (that has obtained Certificate of Registration from RBI), the bank/NBFC may explicitly bring to the notice of the customer that such information is being provided in terms of the Credit Information Companies (Regulation) Act, 2005.

Before reporting default status of a credit card holder to a Credit Information Company which has obtained Certificate of Registration from RBI and of which the bank/NBFC is a member, banks/NBFCs should ensure that they adhere to a procedure, duly approved by their Board, including issuing of sufficient notice to such card holder about the intention to report him/ her as defaulter to the Credit Information Company. The procedure should also cover the notice period for such reporting as also the period within which such report will be withdrawn in the event the customer settles his dues after having been reported as defaulter.

Fair practices in Debt Collection: In the matter of recovery of dues, banks should ensure that they, as also their agents, adhere to the extant instructions on Fair Practice Code for lenders (as also BCSBI's Code of Bank's Commitment to Customers (those banks which have subscribed to the BCSBI Code). In case banks have their own code for collection of dues, they should, at the minimum, incorporate all the terms of BCSBI's Code referred above.

Redressal of Grievances: Generally, a time limit of 60 (sixty) days may be given to the customers for referring their complaints/grievances. The card issuing bank/NBFC should constitute Grievance Redressal machinery within the bank/NBFC and give wide publicity about it through electronic and print media. The name and contact number of designated grievance redressal officer of the bank/NBFC should be mentioned on the credit card bills. The designated officer should ensure that genuine grievances of credit card subscribers are redressed promptly without involving delay.

Banks/NBFCs should ensure that their call centre staff is trained adequately to competently handle all customer complaints. Banks/NBFCs should also have a mechanism to escalate automatically unresolved complaints from a call center to higher authorities and the details of such mechanism should be put in public domain through their website.

Internal Control and Monitoring Systems: With a view to ensuring that the quality of customer service is ensured on an on-going basis in banks/NBFCs, the Standing Committee on Customer Service in each bank/ NBFC should review the credit card operations including reports of defaulters to a Credit Information Company which has obtained Certificate of Registration from RBI and of which the bank/NBFC is a member and credit card related complaints on a monthly basis and take measures to improve the services and ensure the orderly growth in the credit card operations.

Fraud Control–Security and Other Measures: Banks/NBFCs should set up internal control systems to combat frauds and actively participate in fraud prevention committees/ task forces which formulate laws to prevent frauds and take proactive fraud control and enforcement measures. With a view to reducing the instances of misuse of lost/stolen cards, it is recommended to banks/ NBFCs that they may consider issuing (i) cards with photographs of the cardholder; (ii) cards with PIN; and (iii) signature laminated cards or any other advanced methods that may evolve from time to time.

Right to Impose Penalty: Reserve Bank of India reserves the right to impose any penalty on a bank/ NBFC under the provisions of the Banking Regulation Act, 1949/the Reserve Bank of India Act, 1934, respectively for violation of any of these guidelines.

HOUSING FINANCE

Introduction: In pursuance of National Housing Policy of Central Government, Reserve Bank of India has been facilitating the flow of credit to housing sector. Since housing has emerged as one of the sectors attracting a large quantum of bank finance, the current focus of RBI's regulation is to ensure orderly growth of housing loan portfolios of banks.

National Housing Policy: As part of the strategy to overcome the colossal housing shortage, the Central Government adopted a comprehensive National Housing Policy which, among other things, envisaged:

i) Development of a viable and accessible institutional system for the provision of housing finance;

ii) Establishing a system where housing boards and development authorities would concentrate on acquisition and development of land and infrastructure; and

iii) Creation of conditions in which access to institutional finance is made easier and affordable for individuals for construction/ buying of houses/flats. This may include outright purchase of houses/flats constructed by or under the aegis of public agencies.

Banks with their vast branch network throughout the length and breadth of the country occupy a very strategic position in the financial system and were required to play an important role in providing credit to the housing sector in consonance with the National Housing Policy.

PRADHAN MANTRI AWAS YOJNA (PMAY)

PMAY is a mission started with an aim 'Housing For All' (HFA) scheme by NDA Government to be achieved by the year 2022, that is when India will be completing its 75 years of Independence. The mission started in 2015 and will be attained in seven years *i.e.*, during 2015–2022.

This Housing for All (HFA) scheme is envisioned by our Honorable Prime Mister Mr. Narendra Modi. "By the time the Nation completes 75 years of its Independence, Pradhan Mantri Awas Yojna will bring a 'Pucca house' for every family in urban cities with water connection, toilet facilities, 24x7 electricity supply and complete access." As addressed by our Prime Minister in the joint session of parliament on 9th June, 2014.

"Housing for all" Mission for Urban area will be implemented during 2015-2022. The Mission will be implemented through four verticals giving options to beneficiaries, ULB and State Governments as under:

I) "In Situ " slum Redevelopment,

II) Affordable housing through credit Linked subsidy,

III) Affordable housing in partnership,

IV) Subsidy for beneficiary–led individual house-construction.

Out of above, affordable Housing through Credit Linked Subsidy will be implemented through Banks/FI, under the mission.

The procedure and practices for Home Loan:

Target Group: Bank can finance home loan to the following;

- All Individuals, Permanent salaried employees, self-employed, professionals, NRIs, An association or group of individuals for meeting their individual needs;
- Proprietorship, HUF on merits, Corporate & Partnership firms for business cum residence provided other requirements of the scheme are fulfilled;
- Indirect housing finance is channelled by way of term loans to housing finance institutions, housing boards, other public housing agencies, etc.,
- Home loan is not available for builders & Real estate for commercial use.

Purpose: Home loan can be financed for the following purposes;

- For purchase of a ready for occupation new house/ flat from any builder/housing board/ Govt. Agency,
- For purchase of an existing house / flat,
- For renovation, addition, extension, alteration, repairs etc.
- Composite loan for purchase of land and construction of house,
- For construction of house on already owned land (land cost treated as margin),
- For repayment of loans from other banks/financial institutions (Takeover of Home loans from other Banks/F.I.s).
- Purchase of house-hold articles for furnishing the new house as a part of housing loan.

Quantum of Loan: The quantum of loan amount is decided by bank based on monthly/annual income of the borrower, Repaying capacity, and cost of the house. CIBIL Score and credit history of borrower to check his past repayment practice is very important now a day.

Age: Banks fix the lower and upper age for availing the loan taking into consideration the remaining period of service for salaried and income earning capacity during the period of loan for others.

Repayment: Repayment will not ordinarily extend beyond a person age of retirement if he is employed or 70 years of age. Banks are offering maximum repayment period for 30 years also subject to age criteria whichever is earlier. As per RBI instruction, Bank will not be levied prepayment charge on home loan on floating interest rate basis w.e.f. 05.06.2012.

Security: Gènerally, the property purchased or constructed out of the bank loan is taken as security by way of mortgage. Sometimes, guarantor is taken for more secure the loan.

LOAN TO VALUE (LTV) RATIO

As a countercyclical measure, the LTV ratios, risk weights and standard asset provisioning rate for individual housing loans sanctioned on or after the date June 7, 2017of this circular shall be as under:

Outstanding loan	*LTV ratio (%)*	*Risk Weight (%)*	*Standard Asset Provision (%)*
Up to ₹ 30 lakh	≤ 80	35	
	> 80 and ≤ 90	50	
Above ₹ 30 lakh and up to ₹ 75 lakh	≤ 80	35	0.25
Above ₹ 75 lakh	≤ 75	50	

PERSONAL LOANS

❍ **Introduction**

Banks are offering loans against personal security without any tangible security. Example: Personal loan to salaried employee, loan to pensioner, loan to professional etc.

❍ **Target Group**

Salaried Employees, Professionals and Self-Employed, Pensioners, Businessmen, High Net worth Individuals, Staff Members etc.

❍ **Purpose**

For meeting personal expenses, purchase of consumer durables, marriage, educational and medical expenses. Sometimes to celebrate family functions and other household expenses.

❍ **Eligible Amount**

The quantum of loan amount is decided by bank based on monthly/annual income of the borrower, repaying capacity and as per their requirement. While arriving the loan amount, the minimum net take home salary/ income is stipulated after proposed EMI.

❍ **Repayment**

Banks allow period of 3 to 5 years for repayment of personal loan. Normally repayment is allowed in EMI.

❍ **Security**

Normally in case of no collateral security, banks demand for guarantee of third person. For pensioners and salaried employee ECS or undertaking, which enable bank to recover the EMI through Employers or salary accounts.

TEST YOURSELF

1. As per RBI guidelines for Credit Card operations, the Credit Card can be issued by:
(a) Banks only
(b) NBFC only
(c) Insurance company
(d) Both banks and NBFC

2. Banks can do so with the approval of their Boards. However, only banks with net worth of ______ and above should undertake credit card business.
(a) ₹ 500 crore (b) ₹ 100 crore
(c) ₹ 200 crore (d) ₹ 500 crore

3. Banks may issue credit cards including other cards such as:
(a) Co-branded credit cards
(b) Add-on credit cards
(c) Corporate credit cards
(d) All of the above

4. Card issuers should ensure that there is no delay in dispatching bills and the customer has sufficient number of days (at least one ______) for making payment before the interest starts getting charged.
(a) week (b) fortnight
(c) month (d) quarter

5. In case, a customer protests any bill, the bank/ NBFC should provide explanation and, if necessary, documentary evidence may also be provided to the customer within a maximum period of ______ with a spirit to amicably redress the grievances.
(a) 30 days (b) 45 days
(c) 60 days (d) 90 days

6. In case, an unsolicited card is issued and activated without the written consent of the recipient and the latter is billed for the same, the card issuing bank shall not only reverse the charges forthwith, but

also pay a penalty without demur to the recipient amounting to ______ the value of the charges reversed.
(a) twice (b) equal
(c) three times (d) four times

7. Which is the correct statements about Issue of unsolicited cards/facilities?
(a) Unsolicited cards should not be issued.
(b) In case, an unsolicited card is issued and activated without the written consent of the recipient and the latter is billed for the same, the card issuing bank shall not only reverse the charges forthwith, but also pay a penalty without demur to the recipient amounting to twice the value of the charges reversed.
(c) The person in whose name the card is issued can also approach the Banking Ombudsman
(d) All of the above

8. With a view to reducing the instances of misuse of lost/stolen cards, it is recommended to banks/ NBFCs that they may consider issuing:
(a) cards with photographs of the cardholder
(b) cards with PIN
(c) signature laminated cards or any other advanced methods that may evolve from time to time.
(d) All of the above

9. PMAY is a mission started with an aim 'Housing For All' (HFA) scheme by NDA Government to be achieved by the year ______.
(a) 2020 (b) 2021
(c) 2022 (d) 2024

10. Pradhan Mantri Awas Yojna will bring a 'Pucca house' for every family in urban cities. Which facilities is not included in house under the scheme?
(a) water connection
(b) kitchen with gas connection
(c) 24 × 7 electricity supply
(d) toilet facilities

11. "Housing for all" Mission for Urban area will be implemented during ______
(a) 2015-2022 (b) 2014-2022
(c) 2015-2023 (d) 2014-2024

12. The Mission will be implemented through four verticals giving options to beneficiaries, ULB and State Governments as under. Which are the correct verticals:
(a) "In Situ" slum Redevelopment.
(b) Affordable housing through credit Linked subsidy.
(c) Affordable housing in partnership.
(d) All of the above

13. Repayment for home loan will not ordinarily extend beyond a person age of retirement if he is employed or ______ of age.
(a) 60 years (b) 65 years
(c) 70 years (d) 75 years

14. Banks are offering maximum repayment period for home loan for ______ also subject to age criteria whichever is earlier.
(a) 30 years (b) 25 years
(c) 20 years (d) 15 years

15. Bank cannot finance home loan to the following;
(a) All Individuals, Permanent salaried employees, self-employed, professionals, NRIs, An association or group of individuals for meeting their individual needs;
(b) Proprietorship, HUF on merits, Corporate
(c) Partnership firms where HUF is a partner
(d) Indirect housing finance is channeled by way of term loans to housing finance institutions, housing boards, other public housing agencies, etc.,

16. Home loan cannot be financed for the following purposes;
(a) For purchase of a ready for occupation new house/flat from any builder
(b) For renovation, addition, extension, alteration, repairs etc.
(c) For purchase of land.
(d) For construction of house on already owned land (land cost treated as margin).

ANSWER

1	2	3	4	5	6	7	8	9	10
(d)	(b)	(d)	(b)	(c)	(a)	(d)	(d)	(c)	(b)
11	**12**	**13**	**14**	**15**	**16**				
(a)	(d)	(c)	(a)	(c)	(c)				

DOCUMENTATION

DOCUMENTATION IN LOAN ACCOUNT

Introduction: It is of utmost importance to obtain appropriate and correctly executed security documents before disbursing an advance to borrowers. In case the borrowers fail to repay, the recovery of Bank's dues, banks will mainly depend upon the enforcement of the security. Banks should, therefore, take necessary care and precaution while obtaining security documents in advance accounts and scrupulously adhere to the instructions/guidelines laid down in this regard. It should be borne in mind that if the Bank is faced with a situation of remedying any defects or irregularities in the security documents at the time of filing a suit, it would be difficult to get the co-operation from the borrowers and guarantors, if any, and the Bank's action against them might be in jeopardy.

DOCUMENT

As per Sec. 3 of Indian Evidence Act 1872, document means any matter expressed or described upon any substance by means of letters, figures or by more than one of these means intended to be used or which may be used for the purpose of recording that matter with an intention of producing the same as evidence.

In common usage Documents are related to written record created for the purpose of evidence while lending the bank funds. Banking relationship is a contract between the Bank & the Customer. Customer should be legally capable of entering into a valid contract.

Need & Importance of Documents: Documents are necessary to be obtained for the following purpose;

- It identifies borrower, guarantor,
- It identifies security, nature of charge
- For creation of Bank's charge on security.
- Written evidence of transaction & hence cannot be disputed by the executant in future.
- It is accepted as an evidence of fact in court of law in any legal proceedings against defaulter. Documentary evidence (Section 64 of the Indian Evidence Act).
- Recording happening of an event/incident.
- Helps Bank to safeguard its interest by incorporating protective clauses as & when felt necessary.
- Under Negotiable Instruments Act 1881, Banker acquires a right to file a money suit based on Demand Promissory Note executed by the borrower.
- Deciding period of limitation.

DIFFERENT TYPES OF DOCUMENTS

Bank obtains different types of documents during opening of accounts and financing an advance to borrower. Documents obtains during an advance can be broadly classified as three types.

1. **Demand Promissory Note (DPN):** DPN is an important loan documents. It is an unconditional promise to repay the loan on demand with agreed rate of interest where no fixed period of time mentioned. Section 4 of the Act defines, "A demand promissory note is an instrument in writing containing an unconditional undertaking, signed by the maker, to pay a certain sum of money to or to the order of a certain person, or to the bearer of the instruments". An instrument to be a promissory note must possess the following elements:

a) It must be a promise to repay a certain sum of money along with agreed rate of interest,
b) It is paid on demand, no time frame for repayment mentioned,
c) Promise to pay must be unconditional,
d) The promise should be to pay in money and money only,
e) It should be signed by the borrower.

2. **Agreements:** It is defined in the Indian Contract Act 1872. Every promise and every set of promises, forming the consideration for each other, is an agreement. An agreement enforceable by law is a contract. All the terms and conditions are mentioned in the agreements. The loan amount, rate of interest, margin, repayment period, moratorium period, details of securities offered are included in the agreement. The agreement attracts a stamp duty as per Indian Stamp Act. During documentation, bankers use different forms of agreements such as term loan agreement, Hypothecation agreement, pledge agreement, guarantee agreement etc.

3. **Forms:** Forms are neither a promise nor an agreement. It is obtained for the purpose of the intention of the borrower. Application for request of a loan by the borrower is also a type of forms. When a loan is granted against the security of a fixed deposit standing in the joint names, one of the depositors gives an authorization to the other to raise a loan on the deposit, such an authorization is taken in a form. If a letter from the borrower authorizing the bank to pay the proceeds by means of drafts, is taken by means of a form. All these forms are used as part of documentation to prove the intention of the borrowers.

STEPS AND PROCESS OF DOCUMENTATION

The following are the precautions, which should be taken care of both by the borrower as well as banker, at the time of preparation, execution and registration of loan documents etc. The systematic process of documentation are as follows;

1) Selection of proper set of Documents and Formats;
2) Stamping;
3) Filling Up;
4) Execution or Signing;
5) Checking & Vetting Recording;
6) Registration;
7) Keeping Documents in Force.

1) **Selection of proper set of documents and formats:** Selection of proper set of documents is important steps of documentation. Selection of full set of documents depending upon the nature of facility, types of security and type of person who will execute the documents. Some documents are common for most of the loans, but some particular documents are relevant for particular credit facility. Documents also depends upon the types of borrowers. Banker needs to be conversant with legal provisions of various Acts. Documents must be in proper format and vetted by the legal department.

2) **Stamping:** The next important steps is stamping of documents. The loan documents should bear proper type of stamps *i.e.*, adhesive, embossed etc. Further value of stamp duty should be adequate, keeping in view the laws of the State in which the documents are executed. The Non-Judicial Stamp papers, if used, should bear the date, prior to its execution and also the date should not be earlier than six months. The text of the agreement may be written on the Stamp papers itself and plain papers (additional sheets) may be used, if required in addition to Stamp papers.

Statutory Requirement: Stamp duty is a form of tax that is levied on documents. Let us understand stamping duty provisions, starting with the Indian Stamp Act 1899. Any instrument which creates, transfers, extends, extinguishes, limits or amends a right or liability is required to be stamped as per the Indian Stamp Act. This extends to the whole of India, except Jammu and Kashmir.

Stamp Duty: Central Government Stamps applicable on the instruments including Demand Promissory Note, Usance Bill of Exchange, Bill of lading, Letter of Credit, Share Transfer Form, Insurance Policy, Money Receipts, the stamp duty will remain the same throughout India.

State Government Stamps applicable on Mortgage, Hypothecation, Guarantee, Pledge, Power of Attorney, Partnership Deed, Agreements etc. Stamp duty in respect of other items (not in union list), the State Government can amend or enact a new Act and prescribe the duty.

Stamping Norms: Section 17 of Indian Stamp Act states that the documents should be stamped before or at the time of execution. Value of stamp will be decided as per the State Act. In the event of doubt, the Collector will decide. All security documents should be properly and adequately stamped before execution. Appropriate stamp refers to using revenue stamps, adhesive stamps or special adhesive stamps or non-judicial stamp paper wherever applicable. Stamp duty is payable on the instrument.

Effect of non-Stamping or under-Stamping: Documents including promissory note, usance bill of exchange and acknowledgement of debt, if unstamped or inadequately stamped, cannot be validated. They will not be admitted in the court of law as evidence. They cannot be validated even after payment of duty. In case of documents like hypothecation agreement, pledge agreement and so on; the difference in stamp duty together with penalty can be paid. However, such payment should be before filing of suit so that it may be admitted as evidence.

Stamp Duty on Documents Executed at Different Place: If documents executed outside India, then after reaching to India again stamping is required within 3 months.

It should be stamped as per state act where it is executed first then to be send to other state, difference to be paid if duty is more in second state. If documents are signed in one state and to be enforced in other state difference to be paid within 3 months of receipt of document.

Cancellation of Stamps: The adhesive stamp which is the revenue stamp on Demand Promissory note and acknowledgement of debt can be cancelled by the executant. This should be done by writing across the stamp so that the stamp cannot be used again.

The special adhesive stamps affixed on top of the hypothecation agreement, pledge, agreement and other bank documents need to be cancelled. The cancellation will be done either by the stamp office or by the Chief Incumbent of the branch or authorised person as per state government notification before or at the time of execution.

Effect of Non-cancellation: Any instrument bearing adhesive stamps that have not been cancelled will be treated as unstamped. Such an instrument will not be admitted in the court of law as evidence.

3) **Filling Up:** The next step of documentation procedure is filling up of the documents before execution. The documents should be filled completely in all respect. No column of the loan documents should be left blank. Date, place, amount, rate of interest, type of facility and security, terms etc. should be filled carefully without any alteration, overwriting and cutting. Entire document should be filled with same ink, in same handwriting by same person. Once the document is executed it becomes a concluded contract and any subsequent filling by bank without the consent of the executant will invalidate it. Place of execution is very important for deciding the jurisdiction of the court. Security documents bearing dates of execution prior to the date affixed by the stamp authority on the special adhesive stamps are invalid.

4) **Execution or Signing:** The next step of documentation procedure is execution or signing of the documents. Person, executing the loan documents must be competent to enter into a contract *i.e.*, he or she should have contractual capacity. Thus, minor, insolvent person, lunatic etc. are not competent persons to execute documents. During the execution of document, it should be ensured that the signature in the documents must tallies with the signature as appearing in the application for the loan and also with the specimen signature available in the deposit account. In case, execution in the representative capacity of sole proprietor or partner or agent or trustee or executor etc, the capacity property should be clearly mentioned. While executing the documents, the borrower must sign in full and in the same flow in which his signatures are available in the bank. The cuttings & over writings must be avoided and if at all, they become unavoidable, they should be authenticated by the borrowers by signing in full. In case the borrowers reside at different places, the loan documents should be got executed through the branches of the bank situated at those stations, after properly verifying the identity of the borrowers. The guarantee form should be executed if so agreed and stipulated as a term of sanction.

Sometimes loan documents are executed by the holder of power of Attorney on behalf of a trading concern, partnership firm, Hindu undivided family (HUF), company, individual etc. In such a case, a notice should be sent to the principal, stating that the attorney has executed the documents on their behalf. A certified copy of Power of Attorney should be kept along with main loan documents. And also, the letter/confirmation received from the principal in this regard, in response to the notice should be preserved.

The borrowers must obtain a copy of the sanction (Sanction letter) and ensure that documents only for those facilities which are sanctioned in their favour are executed.

5) **Checking & Vetting of Documents:** After proper signing or execution of the documents, it should be checked that documents are in proper format, properly filled in all respect and properly executed as per sanction term and conditions. Documents

of the high value of loan amounts should be vetted by the penal advocate. Banks should, scrupulously adhere to the instructions/guidelines laid down in this regard. It should be borne in mind that if the Bank is faced with a situation of remedying any defects or irregularities in the security documents at the time of filing a suit, it would be difficult to get the co-operation from the borrowers and guarantors, if any, and the Bank's action against them might be in jeopardy.

6) **Registration of Loan Documents:** The Registration Act, 1908 was enacted to consolidate the laws relating to the registration of documents. In case of advances of limited companies against his assets, it should be registered to the registrar of companies within 30 days from the date of execution. Similarly, in case of registered mortgage, the mortgage deed is presented for registration within 4 months from date of execution of deed. Equitable mortgage should be registered with CERSAI within 30 days. If these formalities are not done then the bank may have to lose priority over security. The documents may not be admissible as evidence before the competent authority.

7) **Keeping Documents in Force:** After doing all the formalities, the documents should be kept in safe. But, the documents taken by banks for a credit facility do not have perpetual life. The law of limitation as per Limitation Act applied on the documents. For example, the period of limitation for DP Note is three years from date of execution. It means, the bank has to get fresh documents or obtained acknowledgement of debt for extending the period of limitation as per the provision of limitation act. After obtaining of acknowledgement of debt the expiry period of limitation extended for further three years. According to section 3 of Limitation Act, a suit cannot be filed for recovery on the strength of a time barred document.

SECURITISATION

Securitisation means acquisition of financial assets of the NPA account borrower by Securitisation Company. The Securitisation and Reconstruction of Financial Assets and Enforcement of Security Interest Act, 2002 (also known as the SARFAESI Act 2002) is an indian law. The SARFAESI Act 2002 enables the secured creditors (Banks) to enforce security interest for recovery of its dues without intervention of the Court provided that security interest has been properly created in favour of the bank. It allows banks and other financial institution to auction residential or commercial properties to recover loans. Under this act secured creditors (banks or financial institutions) have many right for enforcement of security interest under section 13 of SARFAESI Act, 2002. Under asset securitisation, bank or a financial institution pools and packages individual loans and receivables, creates securities against them, get them rated and sells them to investors in a market. Thus, asset securitisation is nothing but a process of stimulating assets into securities and securities into liquidity on an ongoing basis, increasing thereby turnover of business and profits.

TEST YOURSELF

1. Document is defined in Section 3 of ________.
(a) Indian Contract Act, 1872
(b) Indian Evidence Act 1872
(c) Negotiable Instrument Act, 1881
(d) Transfer of Property Act, 1882

2. As per Indian Evidence Act, document means any matter expressed or described upon any substance by means of letters, figures or by more than one of these means intended to be used or which may be used for the purpose of recording that matter with an intention of producing the same as evidence.
(a) Letters
(b) Figures
(c) More than one of these means intended to be used
(d) All of the above

3. What is the Importance of Documents?
(a) It identifies borrower, guarantor
(b) It identifies security, nature of charge
(c) For creation of Bank's charge on security
(d) All of the above

4. Which is not correct about documents?
(a) It is accepted as an evidence of fact in court of law
(b) Recording happening of an event/incident
(c) Under Negotiable Instruments Act 1881, Banker does not acquires a right to file a money suit based on Demand Promissory Note executed by the borrower
(d) Deciding period of limitation

5. Which is not correct about demand promissory note?
(a) It is paid on demand, no time frame for repayment mentioned
(b) Promise to pay must be conditional,
(c) The promise should be to pay in money and money only
(d) It should be signed by the borrower

6. A demand promissory note is defined in ______ of the NI Act.
(a) Section 4 (b) Section 5
(c) Section 6 (d) Section 7

7. Agreement is defined in the ______.
(a) Indian Contract Act, 1872
(b) Indian Evidence Act 1872
(c) Negotiable Instrument Act, 1881
(d) Transfer of Property Act, 1882

8. All the terms and conditions are mentioned in the ______.
(a) application
(b) forms
(c) agreements
(d) demand promissory note

9. Which is the systematic process of documentation?
(a) Selection of documents, Filling Up, Stamping, Execution or signing, Registration;
(b) Selection of documents, Filling Up, Stamping, Registration, Execution or signing
(c) Selection of documents, Stamping, Filling Up, Execution or signing, Registration;
(d) Selection of documents, Filling Up, Stamping, Checking Execution or signing,

10. Central Government Stamps is not applicable on which of the instruments?
(a) Demand Promissory Note
(b) Usance bill of exchange
(c) Letter of Credit
(d) Guarantee

11. State Government Stamps is not applicable on which of the instruments?
(a) Bill of lading (b) Mortgage
(c) Hypothecation (d) Pledge

12. Value of stamp will be decided as per the State Act. In the event of doubt, the ______ will decide.
(a) Civil court (b) Dy. Collector
(c) Collector (d) Registrar

13. Which types of stamps cannot use by banks?
(a) revenue stamps
(b) postal stamp
(c) special adhesive stamps
(d) non-judicial stamp paper

14. Which is not correct statements about filling up a document?
(a) Filling up of the documents after execution.
(b) The documents should be filled completely in all respect.
(c) Date, place, amount, rate of interest, type of facility and security, terms etc. should be filled carefully without any alteration, overwriting and cutting.
(d) Entire document should be filled with same ink, in same handwriting by same person.

15. Place of execution is very important for deciding the ______.
(a) Address of borrower
(b) Address of the bank
(c) Jurisdiction of the court
(d) Stamps amount

16. Person, executing the loan documents must be ______ *i.e.*, he or she should have contractual capacity.
(a) Borrower
(b) Related to the firm or director of the company
(c) High Net-worth Individual
(d) Competent to enter into a contract

17. Equitable mortgage should be registered with CERSAI within ______.
(a) 30 days (b) 45 days
(c) 60 days (d) 90 days

18. If documents executed outside India, then after reaching to India again stamping is required within ______.
(a) 1 months (b) 3 months
(c) 6 months (d) 12 months

19. It should be stamped as per state act where it is executed first then to be send to other state, difference to be paid if duty is more in second state. If documents are signed in one state and to be enforced in other state difference to be paid within ______ of receipt of document.
(a) 1 months (b) 3 months
(c) 6 months (d) 12 months

20. The borrower if asks for copies of the loan documents:
(a) cannot be given
(b) can be given on demand
(c) It is bank's discretion
(d) Any of the above

ANSWER

1	2	3	4	5	6	7	8	9	10
(b)	(d)	(d)	(c)	(b)	(a)	(a)	(c)	(c)	(d)
11	**12**	**13**	**14**	**15**	**16**	**17**	**18**	**19**	**20**
(a)	(c)	(b)	(a)	(c)	(d)	(a)	(b)	(b)	(b)

DIFFERENT MODES OF CHARGING SECURITIES

CHARGES ON SECURITY

Introduction: For safeguard of their advances, bank accepts different types of securities during the lending and create charge upon them. When land/buildings and fixed assets which is permanently fastened to the earth is offered as a security, it is charged by mortgage in favour of bank. When movable goods are offered as a security, these are charged as pledge or hypothecation. Paper securities are lien or assigned in favour of bank. The law relating to the different types of securities are defined in the concern Acts. Different types of securities, charges and related acts are as under.

Nature of Security	*Types of Security*	*Kind of Charge*	*Defined in Act*	
Immovable Property	Land & Building	Mortgage	Transfer of Property Act (58)	
Actionable Claims (*i.e.* Unsecured Debts)	Book debts, FDR, NSC, Life Policies	Assignment	Transfer of Property Act (130, 135)	
Movable Property/Goods	Plant & Machinery, Stocks, Vehicles etc.	Pledge or hypothecation or lien as agreed between bank and borrower	Lien	Indian Contract Act (170,171)
			Pledge	Indian Contract Act (172)
			Hypothecation	SARFAESI Act 2(n)
Paper Securities	Shares, debentures, mutual fund units, bonds	Lien	Indian Contract Act (170,171)	

MORTGAGE

Definition: Mortgage is defined in Transfer of Property Act 1882 Section 58(a). As per the Act: "A mortgage is the transfer of an interest in specific immoveable property for the purpose of securing the payment of money advanced or to be advanced by way of loan, an existing or future debt, or the performance of an engagement which may give rise to a pecuniary liability".

The transfer or is called a 'mortgagor', the transferee a 'mortgagee'; the principal money and interest of which payment is secured for the time being are called the mortgage-money, and the instrument (if any) by which the transfer is affected is called a 'mortgage-deed'.

Interest in the Property & Possession: The mortgagor only parts with the interest in the property and not the ownership. Mortgage is not merely a contract but it is conveyance of interest in the mortgaged property. As regards the possession, except for usufructuary mortgage, the possession remains with the mortgagor.

Different Types of Mortgage are as under: Types of mortgage defined in Transfer of Property Act 1882 Section 58(b) to 58(g).

1. **Simple Mortgage: Sec. 58 (b) :** Where, without delivering possession of the mortgaged property, the mortgagor binds himself personally to pay the mortgage money, and agrees, expressly or impliedly, that, in the event of his failing to pay according to his contract, the mortgagee shall have a right to cause the mortgaged property to be sold and the proceeds of sale to be applied.
2. **Mortgage by Conditional Sale: Sec. 58 (c) :** In this, the mortgagor ostensibly sells the mortgaged property on conditions that on default of payment of the mortgage money, the sale shall become absolute or on such payment being made, the sale shall become *void* or the buyer shall transfer the property to the seller.
3. **Usufructuray Mortgage: Sec. 58 (d) :** Where the mortgagor delivers possession or of the mortgaged property to the mortgagee, and authorizes him to retain such possession until payment of the mortgage-money, and to receive the rents and profits accruing from the property or any part of such rents and profits and to appropriate the same in lieu of interest, or in payment of the mortgage-money.
4. **English Mortgage. Sec. 58 (e) :** Where the mortgagor binds himself to repay the mortgage-money on a certain date, and transfers the mortgaged property absolutely to the mortgagee, but subject to a proviso that he will re-transfer it to the mortgagor upon payment of the mortgage-money as agree, the transaction is called an English mortgage.
5. **Equitable Mortgage or Mortgage by deposit of title deeds. Sec. 58 (f) :** Where the mortgagor delivers (at notified places) to the mortgagee, the documents of title to immovable property with intention to create a security thereon to secure a loan. The transaction is not to be reduced to writing. In case of non-payment, the mortgagee can sue for sale but he cannot foreclose the mortgaged property. However the Act makes the provisions of this Section applicable only to Bombay, Calcutta, Madras and such other towns as may be notified by the State Governments by notification in the Official Gazette.
6. **Anomalous Mortgage.Sec. 58 (g) :** A mortgage which is not a simple mortgage, a mortgage by conditional sale, an usufructuary mortgage, an English mortgage or a mortgage by deposit of title deeds within the meaning of this section is called an anomalous mortgage.

SUMMARY OF THE DIFFERENT TYPES OF MORTGAGE

Mortgage Type	*Defined in Transfer of Property Act*	*Ownership*	*Personal Liability of Mortgagor*	*Registration with Sub Registrar*	*Mortgage is created by deposit of*
Simple	Section 58(b)	Mortgagor	Yes	Yes	Mortgage Deed
Conditional sale	Section 58(c)	Mortgagor	No	Yes	Mortgage Deed
Usufructuary	Section 58(d)	Mortgagor	No	Yes	Mortgage Deed
English	Section 58(e)	Bank	Yes	Yes	Mortgage Deed
Equitable	Section 58(f)	Mortgagor	Yes	No	Oral Assent

ASSIGNMENT

Assignment is another mode of providing security to the lending banker. Assignment means transfer of a right, property or a debt existing or future. The borrower of the bank may assign any of his right, properties, or debt to the banker to secure a loan. Assignment is also transfer of an actionable claim (such as life insurance policy)), which may be existing or future, as a security for loan. The transferor of such claim is called the 'assignor' and transferee is called the 'assignee'.

Actionable Claim

Actionable claim means a claim to any debt, other than a debt secured by mortgage of immovable property or by hypothecation or pledge of movable property, or to any beneficial interest unmovable property not in the possession, either actual or constructive, of the claimant, which the civil courts recognise as affording grounds for relief, whether such debt or beneficial interest be existent, accruing, conditional or contingent;

PLEDGE

U/s 172 of Indian Contracts Act, pledge is bailment or delivery of goods as security for payment of a debt or performance of a promise. It may be remembered that only goods (movable assets excluding actionable claims (Sec 2(7) of Sales of Goods Act) can be pledged. The bailor in this case is called the "pawnor or pledger". The bailee is called "pawnee or pledgee". Pledge is different from bailment. Bailment is delivery of goods by one person to another for some purpose while the purpose in pledge is performance of a specific promise or security for a debt. The pledgee can sell the goods pledged after giving notice to the pledger while in bailment the goods can be retained or bailer can be sued for charges.

Rights of Pledgee

The pledgee gets the rights of a bailee which include:

a) **Right to Retain:** The pawnee may retain the goods pledged, not only for payment of the debt or the performance of the promise, but for the interests of the debt, and all necessary expenses incurred by him in respect of the possession or for the preservation of the goods pledged. U/s 174, the pawnee shall not (in the absence of a contract to that effect), retain the goods pledged for any debt or promise of other than the debt or promise for which they are pledged.

b) **Right as to Extraordinary Expenses Incurred:** The Pawnee is entitled to receive from the pawnor extraordinary expenses incurred by him for the preservation of the goods pledged.

c) **Right where Pawnor makes Default:** If the pawnor makes default in payment of the debt, or performance, at the stipulated time, the pawnee may bring a suit against the pawnor upon the debt or promise and retain the goods pledged as a collateral security; or he may sell the thing pledged, on giving the pawnor reasonable notice of the sale.

   If the proceeds of such sale are less than the amount due in respect of the debt or promise, the pawnor is still liable to pay the balance. If the proceeds of the sale are greater than the amount so due, the Pawnee shall pay over the surplus to the pawnor.

d) **Defaulting Pawnor Right to Redeem:** If a time is stipulated for the payment of the debt, or performance of the promise, for which the pledged is made, and the pawnor makes default in payment of the debt or performance of the promise at the stipulated time, he may redeem the goods pledged at any subsequent time before the actual sale of them; but he must, on that case, pay, in addition, any expenses which have arisen from his default.

Duties of the Pledgee

Duties of the pledgee are as follows :

a) To return the goods (along with accretion to goods if any) once the money is paid back by the pledger.

b) To take that much care of the goods, which he would have been taking, had the goods belonged to him.

Banker's Right and Other Dues: Bank's right of pledge prevails over any other dues including Govt. dues (Supreme Court State of Bihar vs Bank of Bihar) except workers' wages.

Law of Limitation: The rights of pledgee are not limited by Law of Limitation.

HYPOTHECATION

Hypothecation is defined in Securitisation and Reconstruction of Financial Assets and Enforcement of Security Interest (SARFAESI) Act 2002. As per Sec 2 (n) of SARFAESI Act 2002, 'Hypothecation means a charge in or upon any movable property, existing or future, created by a borrower in favour of a secured creditor without delivery of possession of the movable property to such creditor, as a security for financial assistance and includes floating charge and crystallisation of such charge into fixed charge on movable property',

Hypothecation is an equitable charge, where the borrower is owner and keeps the possession of the security on behalf of the creditor. In hypothecation on the property the ownership as well as possession of the security remains with the borrower. It is applicable on all movable properties like stock, crop, vehicle, machinery, furniture etc.

Hypothecation is Resorted to in the following Cases:

a) When loan is to be raised against work-in-progress, the only way of creating a charge is hypothecation.

b) It is also done in respect of goods which require constant handling in a factory, e.g. rice mills, oil expellers etc.

c) This charge is also convenient, where lending is to be done against goods in a shop or showroom which is required in day to day use.

d) It is easily applicable on vehicle for private or commercial use.

Drawbacks of Hypothecation:

a) The main drawback about this charge is that goods remain in the possession of the borrower and therefore creditor's control over such goods is not practically possible.

b) The borrower may realise and sell the hypothecated stocks and keep only obsolete and slow moving stock.

c) The borrower may hypothecate the same stock for more than on creditor or banker.

d) The realisation of the assets in case of default of payment is a difficult, prolonged and costly affairs.

Precautions to be taken in case of Hypothecation:

a) Banks ensure that firm is not enjoying similar facilities with other banks on the security of same goods.

b) Borrower enjoys facilities from one bank only and an undertaking in writing should be obtained from him.

c) Bank name board should be displayed where the securities are located stating that bank has charge over such goods.

d) Recurring inspection should be conducted by the bank to see that the level of goods being maintained is same as the one declared by the borrower and as per his books.

e) Borrower should submit a stock statement periodically,

f) Such stocks should be insured for fire and other risks.

Possession & Sale

Hypothecation is an equitable charge, where the borrower keeps the possession of the security on behalf of the creditor. If the borrower fails to return the advance against the hypothecation of securities, the bank can take possession of the securities with consent of the borrower and becomes a pledgee. On becoming pledgee, the bank get all the rights of a pledge including right to sell without intervention of the court. Under Securitisation Act, the bank also has got the right to sell the hypothecated securities without intervention of the court, subject to compliance of certain legal formalities.

LIEN

Lien is the right of one person to retain goods and securities in his possession belonging to another until certain legal debts due to the person retaining the goods are satisfied. In other words, it is the right of the creditor to retain the goods and securities in his possession, belonging to a debtor, until the debt due is paid. Lien does not give power of sale but only to retain the property.

- **Particular Lien :** Particular lien is that lien which confers the right to retain that particular commodity in respect of which the particular debt arose.
- **General Lien :** General lien confers a right to retain goods and securities not only in respect of a particular debt incurred in connection with them but in respect of the general balance due by the owner of the goods and securities, to the person in possession of them.
- **Banker's Lien :** As a general rule, the right of lien does not give the person exercising the right, any power or right to sell or dispose of the securities retained. But in case of a bank, it is otherwise. A banker's lien is more than a general lien.

  It is an implied pledge and the banker has a right to sell the property after reasonable notice, provide the property comes into his hands in the ordinary course of his business.
- **Negative Lien :** At the time the advance is made, the banker sometimes asks a borrower to execute a letter declaring that his assets are free from any sort of charge or encumbrance. The borrower also undertakes that the assets stated in the said declaration shall not be encumbered or disposed of without a bank's permission in writing so long as the advance continues. This undertaking is known as a Negative lien.

SET-OFF

Set-off is the right of a debtor to take into account a debt owing to him by a creditor, when claiming a debt due from him to the creditor. In the case of banker, the right of set-off enables him to adjust a debit balance in a customer's account, with any balance outstanding to his credit in the books of the bank. In other words, the banker can adjust his claim from the amount that is payable to the customer.

TEST YOURSELF

1. Mortgage is defined in:
   (a) Section 58 (b) to 58 (g) of Transfer of Property Act 1882
   (b) Section 57 of Transfer of Property Act 1882
   (c) Section 57 of Indian Contract act
   (d) Section 58 of NI act

2. Which of the mortgage is not required to be registered with the registrar of assurance?
   (a) English Mortgage
   (b) Equitable Mortgage
   (c) Simple Mortgage
   (d) Conditional sale

3. In which of the mortgage, mortgagee cannot sale the property but loan can be recovered from income of the property?
   (a) English Mortgage
   (b) Equitable Mortgage
   (c) Simple Mortgage
   (d) Usufructuary Mortgage

4. For creation of equitable mortgage, which is the correct statement?
   (a) An instrument in writing is necessary
   (b) The mortgager will neither sign any documents nor submit any memo in writing at the time of creation of mortgage
   (c) Mortgage will be registered at registrar of assurance
   (d) Mortgage can be created at any place in India

5. Which charge can be created on the book debts by bank?
   (a) Pledge (b) Assignment
   (c) Hypothecation (d) Lien

6. In which of the mortgage, ownership transfers to the mortgagee?
   (a) English Mortgage
   (b) Equitable Mortgage
   (c) Simple Mortgage
   (d) Usufructuary Mortgage

7. In which of the mortgage, mortgagor create the mortgage by oral assent at any notified place in India in favour of the mortgagee?
   (a) English Mortgage
   (b) Equitable Mortgage
   (c) Simple Mortgage
   (d) Usufructuary Mortgage

8. In case of pledge, relationship between banker and customer is:
   (a) Pledger and Pledgee
   (b) Pledgee and Pledger
   (c) Pawnee and Pawnor
   (d) Either 'b' or 'c'

9. Assignment is governed by:
   (a) SARFAESI act
   (b) Transfer of Property Act 1882
   (c) Indian Contract act
   (d) The NI act

10. Charge created on paper securities such as Shares, debenture, bonds and Mutual fund is:
    (a) Hypothecation (b) Assignment
    (c) Lien (d) Pledge

11. After the conversion of hypothecation into pledge, the bank will have the same right as that of:
    (a) Pledgee (b) Pledger
    (c) Hypothecatee (d) Hypothecator

12. At the time the advance is made, the borrower undertakes that the assets stated in the said declaration shall not be encumbered or disposed of without a bank's permission in writing so long as the advance continues. This undertaking is known as a __________.
    (a) Declaration regarding Hypothecation
    (b) Negative lien
    (c) Declaration regarding assignment
    (d) Mortgage

13. __________ is the right of a debtor to take into account a debt owing to him by a creditor, when claiming a debt due from him to the creditor.
    (a) Set-off (b) Lien
    (c) Pledge (d) Assignment

14. __________ is that lien which confers the right to retain that particular commodity in respect of which the particular debt arose.
    (a) Negative lien (b) General lien
    (c) Particular lien (d) Banker's lien

15. A pledgee has further pledged the goods and the original pledger has repaid the loan. What is his right?
    (a) Goods can be received by him subject to charge of the 2nd pledgee
    (b) Goods can be delivered to him even when the 2nd pledgee's loan is outstanding

(c) He is entitle to return the goods
(d) He is not entitle to return the goods

16. In what respect, a charge hypothecation is different from pledge. The goods are:
(a) In possession of bank but ownership with borrower
(b) Both the possession and ownership rest with borrower
(c) There is no difference in regard of possession
(d) None of the above

17. The charge on movable assets to be created is known as:
(a) Set-off (b) Assignment
(c) Mortgage (d) Hypothecation

18. In case of hypothecation, the borrower can:
(a) Take goods out of godown and use them
(b) Keep new goods inside the godown in place of old ones
(c) Sell the goods hypothecated and replenish the stock
(d) All of the above

19. Bank grants a loan against the security of goods relating to a firm, which kind of charge on goods can be created?
(a) Pledge (b) Hypothecation
(c) Assignment (d) Either 'a' or 'b'

20. The person to whom the possession of goods is transferred is called:
(a) Transferee
(b) Bailee
(c) Beneficiary
(d) Bailor

ANSWER

1	2	3	4	5	6	7	8	9	10
(a)	(b)	(d)	(b)	(b)	(a)	(b)	(d)	(b)	(c)
11	**12**	**13**	**14**	**15**	**16**	**17**	**18**	**19**	**20**
(a).	(b)	(a)	(c)	(c)	(b)	(d)	(d)	(d)	(b)

TYPES OF COLLATERALS AND THEIR CHARACTERISTICS

COLLATERAL SECURITIES

Introduction: An advance made by a bank is generally covered by primary or collateral securities. The effectiveness of the security depend on the nature of security. The securities can be classified in two aspects, economic and legal aspect. Economic aspect covers marketability, valuation and other economic factors of the security. The other legal aspect is the validity and enforceability of the security. As per banking terms, the securities can be classified as Primary and Collateral. Primary securities are those assets which are created by bank finance and/or advance is granted against that assets. All assets or security other than the primary security which support and enhance the total value of security is called collateral security. Attributes of good security are as follows:

- **Title of the Security:** The borrower should have a good title to the security.
- **Non Encumbrance:** The security should not have any encumbrance or liability.
- **Marketability:** The security should be easily marketable.
- **Ascertain Ability:** The value of security should be easily ascertainable.
- **Stability of Value:** The security should not be liable to wide price fluctuation.
- **Storability:** Storing of the security should not be difficult.
- **Transferability:** The security should be easily and freely transferable.
- **Durability:** The security should be durable.
- **Transportable:** The security should be easily transportable.

VARIOUS KINDS OF SECURITIES

Bank accepts various kinds of tangible assets as security after creating the charge. Some important types of securities are as under:

1. Land & Building/Real Estate:

It is a common security accepted by bank. During the lending bank mortgaged/creation of charge the landed property in favour of bank. The advantage of these type of securities is that its value generally increases over the time. It is fixed and cannot be shifted to other place. It can be freehold or leasehold property. Valuation of the property is required for accepting as a security in the loan account. The advantages and disadvantages of this form of security cannot be universally applied to all lands and it depends on the nature of the land offered. We shall now discuss both the advantages and disadvantages.

Advantages: The advantage of collateral security of Land & Building are as under:

(i) The advantage that land has over other types of securities is that its value generally increases with time. With every fall in the value of money, the value of land goes up and due to its scant availability in developing areas its value is bound to increase.

(ii) It cannot be shifted, a fact which sometimes is also a disadvantage.

(iii) The securitisation of the mortgaged property can be done without court intervention under SARFAESI Act 2002.

Disadvantages: The disadvantage of collateral security of Land & Building are as under;

(i) Valuation is at Times Difficult: The value of a building depends on several factors such as location, size of property, amenities, etc., this makes the valuation very difficult. Buildings and the materials used in the buildings are not alike. In fact, buildings must be valued on a conservative basis because of limited market in the event of sale.

(ii) Ascertaining the Title of the Owner: The banker cannot obtain a proper title unless the borrower himself has title to the property to be mortgaged. In India, the laws of succession particularly those relating to Hindus and Muslims being very complicated, it is difficult to ascertain whether a person has a perfect title to the property or not. Title verification, must also be done to know whether the property was encumbered. Bank's advocate has to be done by verifying record with the Registrar's office, which involves expense and time. In the case of agricultural land, with the introduction of land ceiling legislation, legislation protecting the tenants' rights, absence of up-to-date and proper land records, it has become less valuable as a security.

(iii) Difficult to Realize the Security: Land is not easily and quickly realizable, due to the lack of ready market. It may take months to sell and sometimes if the market is not favourable, it may fetch a lower price than what was anticipated. After the SARFAESI Act 2002, now the bank can securitise the mortgaged property without intervention of court.

(iv) Creating a Charge is Costly: The security can be charged either by way of legal mortgage or by way of an equitable mortgage. An equitable mortgage may be created by a simple deposit of title deeds with or without a memorandum. Since the remedies under a legal mortgage are better than those under an equitable mortgage. However, completing a legal mortgage involves expenses including stamp duty and lot of formalities.

Precautions to be taken by the Banker: Before immovable property is accepted as security, banker should take the following precautions.

(i) Borrower's Title: The banker should get a penal advocate report to verify the title to the property and the right of the borrower to mortgage. Advocate has to certify that the person in whose property stands has a good, valid, subsisting and marketable title over the over the property, that the property is free from all encumbrances and is not subject to any litigation or attachment from any court or statutory authorities.

(ii) Enquiry Regarding Prior Charges: The borrower should produce a certificate from the Registrar's office listing the charges over the property over a period of time (generally 30 years) that the property is free from encumbrances. This is commonly understood as non-encumbrance certificate. If any prior charges exist the banker's right will be subject tosuch prior charges.

(iii) Freehold or Leasehold: A freeholder is the absolute owner of his land and is able to deal with it as he likes. A leasehold property is one, which is taken on lease for a period and a leaseholder derives a legal status for a term of years from the freeholder and is free to deal with the land when acting within the terms of the lease and within the law during that period. When the lease expires, the land reverts to the freeholder. In the case of leasehold property, the unexpired period of the lease is an important consideration. The longer the unexpired period of the lease, greater is the value of the security. The bank should also ensure that there are no onerous covenants such as the necessity of taking the freeholder's consent before mortgaging the property. The banker should also obtain the last ground receipt to ensure that the lease is active.

(iv) Valuation of the Property: Valuation of the property is necessary to consider as collateral security. Valuation should be done by bank approved valuers who would be engineers or architects. Valuation report must be comprehensive, realistic and on the basis of the following points.

a) The location and site of property
b) Area of the land and building
c) The nature and cost of construction
d) Age of the building, Present status and future life
e) Tax and other obligations

(v) **Documentations:** The mortgage deed must be drafted carefully considering all the legal stipulations. It should be witnessed by at least two persons. In case of simple mortgage it attracts ad-valorem stamp duty.

(vi) **Verification of Tax Receipts:** The banker should request the borrower to produce latest tax receipts since any arrears of tax constitute a preferential charge on property.

(vii) **Insurance of the Property:** To avoid loss of security by fire, natural calamities, it is prudent that in the case of buildings the banker insist on the insurance of the property for its full value at the borrower's expense.

2. Goods/Stocks

The banker gets a tangible form of security, which in case of default by the borrower, can be realised by sale of pledged goods. Banker acquires a good title to the goods when dealing with customers of repute and standing. Banker should take care while accepting the goods as a security because certain goods are liable to perish or deteriorate in quality over a period of time, thus resulting in reduction of the value of the security. Advance against goods may be extended by way of goods as pledge or hypothecation. Advance are given based on the stocks and their value declared in monthly stock statement. Stock statement must be verified by factory or godown inspection.

Merits of this Security: Merits of this collateral security are as under;

(i) Goods have a ready market and as such can be easily sold unlike other kinds of security.

(ii) Valuation of the goods can be easily done.

(iii) The banker gets a tangible form of security compared to unsecured advances, which in case of default by the borrower, can be realized by sale of pledged goods.

(iv) Barring a few states where the stamp duty is heavy, creating a charge on the security is less costly and involves minimum formalities.

Demerits of this Security: Demerits of this collateral security are as under;

(i) Certain goods are liable to perish or deteriorate in quality over a period, thus resulting in reduction of the value of the banker's security.

(ii) The value of the security in certain cases more particularly electronic consumer goods are subject to wide fluctuations. Therefore, the valuation of such goods is difficult.

(iii) In some cases, the banker may find it difficult to store the goods.

(iv) Transporting the goods from the borrower's premises to the banker's premises and thereafter to the market in case of sale is a considerably costly and time-consuming affair.

(v) If the goods are warehoused, the warehouse keeper enjoys a lien over the goods for any unpaid charges. The banker therefore, has to ensure periodically that all charges are duly paid.

Precautions to be taken while goods are considered as collateral security:

(i) Advances against goods should be restricted to genuine traders and not to speculators.

(ii) Loans must be given for short periods, since the quality and thereby the value of the security is likely to diminish.

(iii) The banker must have a working knowledge and gather information of the several types of goods regarding their character, price movements, storage value, etc.

(iv) The banker should confirm the state of goods.

(v) The goods should be insured against loss by theft or fire.

(vi) The banker should verify and confirm the title of the borrower to the goods by inspecting the invoices or cash memos.

(vii) The banker as a Pawnee is liable, if reasonable care is not taken of the goods pledged. He should therefore, take proper care for their storage and take reasonable steps to protect them from damage and pilferage.

(viii) The price of the goods must be accurately ascertained.

(ix) Necessary margin must be taken by the banker to protect him against fluctuations in the price of goods.

(x) The banker must obtain absolute or constructive possession of the goods.

(xi) In the case of hypothecated goods, the bank should obtain from the borrower a written undertaking that the goods are not charged to any bank or creditor and will not be so charged if the borrower is indebted to the bank. The banker should obtain at regular periods certificates regarding the quantity and valuation of the goods, which should be physically verified by the banker.

Inspection of Stocks: Inspection of the stock must be done regularly. Verification of hypothecated/pledged stock is required at regular interval or monthly basis. In case goods are stored in bags, the inspecting official of the bank should count the number of bags and if necessary a few of the bags selected at random may be ordered to be opened to ensure that the goods stated to have been stored are actually held in bags.

Valuation: Normally, valuation of the stock is done on the basis of cost price or market price whichever is less.

Margin: Maintaining an adequate margin on the stock as stipulated in the sanction. Drawing power is calculated after deducting the margin to be maintained.

3. Documents of Title to Goods

As per the Section 2(4) of the Sale of Goods Act, 1930, a document of title to goods is 'a document used in the ordinary course of business as a proof of possession or control of goods authorizing or purporting to authorize either, by endorsement or delivery, the possessor of the documents, to transfer or receive the goods thereby represented.'

Thus, the essential requisites of a document of title to goods are:

(i) The mere possession of the documents creates a right either by virtue of law or trade usage, to possess the goods represented by the documents.

(ii) Goods represented by the documents can be transferred by endorsement and/or delivery of the documents.

(iii) The transferee of the documents can take delivery of the goods in his own right.

(iv) Although they appear to be negotiable instruments, documents of title to goods are not negotiable instruments. The title of bona fide transferee for value can be affected by defects in the title of transferor. They may be called quasi-negotiable instruments.

Examples of documents of title to goods are bills of lading, dock warrant, warehouse-keeper's certificate, railway receipts, delivery orders, etc. Documents of title to goods must be distinguished from other documents like the warehouse-keeper's non-transferable receipts, which are mere acknowledgement of the goods.

Merits of this Security

(i) By mere pledge of the instruments the goods are pledged and serve as a good security.

(ii) The person in possession of the document can transfer the goods by endorsement and/or delivery. The transferee thereafter is entitled to take delivery of the goods in his own right.

(iii) The documents are easily transferable, and the formalities involved are less compared to mortgage or assignment.

Demerits of this Security

(i) **Possibility for Fraud and Dishonesty:** Since the bill of lading or a railway receipt or a warehouse-keeper's certificate does not certify or guarantee the correctness of the contents of the bags or packages, the banker will have no remedy against the carrier or warehouse-keeper, if they turn out to be containing worthless goods.

(ii) **Forged and Altered Documents:** The documents might be forged ones, or even if genuine, the quantity may be altered.

(iii) **Not Negotiable Documents:** The document being "Not Negotiable", the transferee of such documents will not get a better title than that of the transferor. Therefore, if the person who pledged the documents has a defective title, the banker will not acquire a better title.

(iv) **Unpaid Vendor's Right of Stoppage in Transit:** Under the Sale of Goods Act, 1930, an unpaid vendor has the 'right of stoppage in transit' and he is entitled to direct the carrier that the goods need not be delivered, if not already done. If this right is exercised by the unpaid vendor, the banker cannot obtain the goods and his security is of no value.

Precautions to be taken by the Banker

(i) The documents must be examined thoroughly to ensure that they are genuine and of recent origin. In the case of bills of lading, they are prepared generally in triplicate and as such all the copies must be obtained by the banker. Otherwise, the carrier is released from his obligation by delivering the goods on the presentation of any one copy containing ostensibly regular endorsements.

(ii) The banker should ensure that the documents do not contain any onerous clauses or prejudicial remarks about the condition of goods received.

(iii) Banker should ensure that the goods are adequately covered by insurance for full value against risks of theft, fire, damage in transit, etc., and in the case of goods shipped by sea, all the marine risks should be covered.

(iv) Banker should ensure to get consignee copy and banks name being entered as consignee, so that endorsement/transfer of title is specific.

Trust Receipt: Whenever the bank releases documents of title to goods to the borrower without payment being made, then a 'Letter of Trust' should be taken. So also in the case of goods hypothecated to the bank. The reasons are as follows:

(i) The borrower on sale of the goods has to hold proceeds in trust for the banker.

(ii) The goods taken under such trust receipts or the sale proceeds thereof, are not available to the official receiver in case the borrower becomes insolvent.

A Trust Letter incorporates the following Clauses:

(i) Borrower's recognition, of bank's rights in the goods as security and in case of sale, the proceeds, thereof.

(ii) Borrowers, undertaking to hold the goods or sale proceeds thereof, in trust for the banker.

(iii) Borrower's undertaking, to ensure proper storage and insurance, at his cost.

(iv) Borrower's undertaking to direct the buyer to pay the monies directly to the banker, if so required by the banker.

(v) Borrower's undertaking to return unsold goods on banker's request or dispose of the same as directed by the banker.

4. Life Insurance Policy

A life insurance policy is generally taken for both financial security and saving purpose. The assignment of the policy in favour of the banker requires very few formalities and the banker obtains a perfect title. The policy is tangible security and in the custody of the bank. The security can be realised immediately on the borrower's default of payment by surrendering the policy to the insurance company. In the event of the borrower's death, the debt is easily liquidated from the proceeds of the policy.

Advantages

(i) Life insurance business being highly regulated and permitted only to companies having sound financial health, the banker need not doubt the realisation of the policies, which will be done without any difficulty, if the policy and the claim are in order.

(ii) The assignment of the policy in favour of the banker requires very little formalities and the banker obtains a perfect title.

(iii) The longer the period for which the policy has been in force, the greater the surrender value. It is also useful as an additional security because, in the event of the borrower's death, the debt is easily liquidated from the proceeds of the policy.

(iv) The security can be realized immediately on the borrower's default of payment by surrendering the policy to the insurance company.

(v) The policy is a tangible security and is in the custody of the bank. The banker only has to ensure that regular payment of premiums is made.

Disadvantages

(i) If the premium is not paid regularly, the policy lapses and reviving the policy is complicated.

(ii) Insurance contracts being contracts of utmost good faith, any mis-representation or non-disclosure of any particulars by the assured would make the policy void and enable the insurer to avoid the contract.

(iii) The person (proposer) who has obtained the policy must have an insurable interest in the life of the assured or the contract is void.

(iv) The policy may contain special clauses, which may restrict the liability of the insurer.

(v) When the banker accepts a policy coming under Married Women Property Act he must ensure that all the parties sign in the bank's form of assignment.

(vi) There is facility to obtain the duplicate policy if the original is lost. This can be misused by persons by obtaining duplicate policies. Banker should therefore, verify that no duplicate policy has been issued and there are no encumbrances on the policy.

Precautions to be taken by the Banker

(i) The policy must be assigned in favour of the bank and should be sent directly to the insurance company for registration and ensured that only authorized office of Insurance Company has noted assignment.

(ii) The bank should see that the age of the assured is admitted.

(iii) The banker should ensure the regular payment of premium.

5. Book Debts

Borrowers can take advance by assigning book debt in favour of the bank. The assignment must be in writing and signed by the transferor or his duly authorised agent. The assignment may be absolute or by way of charge. As an actionable claim include future debt, there can be a valid assignment of future debt as well. The value of security depends on the solvency of the debtor and his right of set off, if any. The banker must enquire into both aspects.

Legal Implication of Assignment

(i) The assignee can sue in his/their own name and can give a valid discharge

(ii) The debtor can exercise any right of set off against the assignee, which but for such transfer, he could have exercised against assignor

(iii) As an actionable claim includes future debts, there can be a valid assignment of future debts as well.

Precautions to be taken by the Banker

(i) The value of the security depends on the solvency of the debtor and his right of set off, if any. The banker must enquire into both aspects.

(ii) The instrument of assignment must be in writing and duly signed in the presence of the banker, signed by the assignor or his duly authorized agent

(iii) The banker must serve notices of assignment on debtors, who must be asked to acknowledge its receipt and confirm:

a) The amount of the debt

b) His right of set off, if any, and

c) Whether he has received notice of prior assignments, if any

(iv) An undertaking from the borrower should be taken that the amount of debts collected directly if any by him will be passed on to the banker, towards the loan account and operations in account be controlled to ensure this compliance

(v) Where the book debts are as assigned by a joint stock company, the charge must be registered with the Registrar of Joint Stock Companies.

6. Share/Debenture

Banks normally accepted only quoted shares as security. Value of the security can be ascertain easily and creating of charge on share is less expensive. In case of debenture, a charge is created on the assets of the company issuing such debenture in favour of a trustee who is responsible to take care of the interest of individual investors.

Advantages: The advantage of collateral security of Share are as under;

(i) Value of the security can be ascertained without any difficulty.

(ii) In normal times, stocks and shares enjoy stability of value and are not subject to wide fluctuations.

(iii) Stocks and shares require very little formalities, for taking them as security.

(iv) It is easier compared to real estate to ascertain the title, more so with the advent of depositories.

(v) Creating a charge of this is less expensive than real estate.

(vi) They yield income by way of dividends, which can be appropriated towards the loan account.

(vii) Being a tangible form of securities they are more reliable.

(viii) The release of such securities involves very little expense and formality.

Disadvantages: The disadvantage of collateral security of Share are as under;

(i) Being easy to realize, they are fraud prone and as such they must be properly secured.

(ii) In the case of partly paid shares, the following demerits are there:

(a) The banker may have to pay the calls.

(b) Partly paid shares are subject to violent price fluctuations.

(c) They are not easily realizable because of the restricted market for such shares.

Precautions while taking Stocks and Shares as Security: Banker must take the following precautions while advancing against stocks and shares. In the case of partly paid shares;

(i) The banker should never register them in his name.

(ii) He must ensure that pending calls are paid.

(iii) Sufficient margin should be taken to avoid any future loss or change in the value of the security.

(iv) The banker should verify share certificate and ensure that the calls, are paid properly and entered in the space provided for the same.

Other Precautions

(i) Update the list of shares which the particular bank is willing to lend against on a regular basis.

(ii) Updating the amount that can be lent against a particular share which is called the card limit at regular intervals.

(iii) Yearly review of the portfolio or more frequent review depending upon the volatility in the capital market.

7. Term Deposit Receipt

TDR is most common security accepted by a bank. This security is certainly most valuable, as the money represented by the receipt is already with the bank. It is easy know the present value and liquidation of a TDR. The banker normally grant the advance only to the person in whose name the money is deposited. Banker should not advance against fixed deposit receipt of other bank. If deposit is in the joint names the request for the loan must come from all of them.

When the deposit receipt is taken as security, the banker should ensure that all the depositors duly discharge it on the back of the instrument. In addition of this, the banker should obtain letter of appropriation which authorises the banker to appropriate the amount of the deposit on maturity or earlier towards the loan amount. Bank has to lien the TDR before disbursement of loan.

Precautions to be taken by the Banker

(i) The banker should grant the advance only to the person in whose name the money is deposited. Banker should not advance against fixed deposit receipts of other banks.

(ii) If, the deposit is in joint names the request for loan must come from all of them.

(iii) After granting the advance, the banker must note his lien in the fixed deposit register to avoid payment by mistake and the lien, must also be noted on the receipt itself.

(iv) Advance should preferably not be made against fixed deposit receipt in the name of a minor, unless a declaration is taken from guardian, that loan will be utilized for benefit of the minor.

(v) Sometimes, a person may approach for advances by offering the fixed deposit receipts held by third parties as security. In such a case, the fixed deposit receipt must be duly discharged, by the third party, *i.e.*, FD holder and he should declare in writing the bank's right to hold the deposit receipt as security, and also to adjust the deposit amount towards the loan account on maturity or on default in repayment of instalment if any.

8. Supply Bills

Supply bills arise in relation to transaction with the Government and public sector undertaking. A party might have taken a contract for execution, and he is entitled to progressive payment based on work done, for which he has to submit bills in accordance with the term and condition of the contract. Similarly, parties who have accepted tenders for supply of goods over a period are entitled to payment on the supply of goods, for which they submit bills in accordance with the term of the contract. These bills are known as supply bills. Advance against supply bills should be made only to borrowers who have sufficient experience in Government business and Government regulations. The banker should obtain a power of attorney from the supplier authorising him to receive the money. The same should be registered with appropriate Government department.

Risks Involved in Advancing Against Supply Bills

(i) Although the advance is self-liquidating in nature, in certain cases it can take quite some time before the advance is realized because of administrative and other Governmental procedures.

(ii) It is virtually a clean advance and the bank may not realize the full amount, because of the possibility of counter claim or the right of set off by the Government, as the charge is only by way of assignment.

(iii) Sometimes, the Government may not pass the bills for full payment because of the unsatisfactory quality of goods or defective work done by the contractor or delays in the completion of work.

Precautions to be taken by the Banker

(i) Advances against supply bills should be made only to borrowers who have sufficient experience in Government business and Government regulations.

(ii) The contract between the supplier and the Government department should be scrutinized by the banker, to know the volume of transaction, period of supply, rates agreed upon and various other terms and conditions. The Government will not pass the bills unless there is faithful adherence to the terms and conditions by the supplier.

(iii) The banker should obtain a power of attorney from the supplier authorizing him to receive the money. The same should be registered with the appropriate Government department.

(iv) The banker should obtain the inspection note or the engineer's certificates along with the bills. There should be no adverse remarks in the inspection report regarding the quality and quantity of goods supplied.

(v) Banker must reserve the right of demanding the repayment of advance, if the bills remain unpaid for a specified period. The banker, in other words, treats the bills as only items for collection and the advances are recovered.

9. Gold Ornaments

Banks give loan against gold ornaments for agriculture as well as non-agriculture purpose. Bank pledge the gold and allow loan or overdraft against the security of gold ornaments. Now a days, Bank also accept Gold bond as a security.

10. Paper Security

Bank accept various types of deposit receipt such as NSC, KVP, UTI Bond etc as a security and financed against them. Bank must create charge on such paper during the financing.

TEST YOURSELF

1. Which of the following is a characteristic of good security?
   (a) Marketability (b) Storability
   (c) Transferability (d) All of the above
2. Which of the following security is not a self-liquidating security?
   (a) Bank's TDR (b) LIC policy
   (c) Land & Building (d) NSC
3. The nature of charge created while granting advance against security of goods is:
   (a) Hypothecation (b) Pledge
   (c) Lien (d) Both 'a' & 'b'
4. Hypothecation is defined in:
   (a) Transfer of property act
   (b) SARFAESI act
   (c) Indian contract act
   (d) It is not defined in any act
5. Charge creation on LIC policy is:
   (a) Assignment (b) Pledge
   (c) Lien (d) Hypothecation
6. Which is not a character of a good security?
   (a) The security should have encumbrance or liability.
   (b) The security should be easily marketable.
   (c) The value of security should be easily ascertainable.
   (d) The security should not be liable to wide price fluctuation.
7. Which is an attributes of a good security?
   (a) The security should be easily and freely transferable.
   (b) The security should be durable.
   (c) The security should be easily transportable.
   (d) All of the above
8. Which of the following value of LIC policy is taken while taking as a security?
   (a) Maturity value (b) Face value
   (c) Surrender value (d) Insured value
9. Advance against shares can be made if shares are:
   (a) In physical form (b) Party paid shares
   (c) Fully paid shares (d) All of the above
10. ________ arises in relation to transaction of sales of goods, with government and public sector undertaking.
   (a) Supply bills (b) Accommodation bills
   (c) Trust receipt (d) Inspection notes
11. Dock warrants, bills of lading, Warehouse receipt are the example of:
   (a) Documents are title to negotiable instrument
   (b) Documents are title to goods
   (c) Documents are title to immovable property
   (d) Documents are title to movable property
12. Charge creation on Land & building and Plant & Machinery permanent fasten to earth is:
   (a) Assignment (b) Pledge
   (c) Mortgage (d) Hypothecation
13. Which of the following is preferable security from liquidity point of view?
   (a) Immovable property (b) Debenture
   (c) Quoted equity shares (d) Stocks
14. The bank is considered to be Pawnee in case of which of the following securities?
   (a) Stocks of goods (b) Shares
   (c) Immovable property (d) Debenture
15. On which of the following security, the charge hypothecation, pledge or lien can be created?
   (a) Stocks of goods (b) Book debts
   (c) Immovable property (d) Bank's TDR
16. Bank accept which types of deposit receipt as a security and financed against them?
   (a) NSC (b) KVP
   (c) UTI Bond (d) All of the above

ANSWER

1	2	3	4	5	6	7	8	9	10
(d)	(c)	(d)	(b)	(a)	(a)	(d)	(c)	(c)	(a)
11	**12**	**13**	**14**	**15**	**16**				
(b)	(c)	(c)	(a)	(a)	(d)				

NON-PERFORMING ASSETS

PRUDENTIAL NORMS

Introduction: In line with the international practices and as per the recommendations made by the Committee on the Financial System (Chairman Shri M. Narasimham), the Reserve Bank of India has introduced, in a phased manner, prudential norms for income recognition, asset classification and provisioning for the advances portfolio of the banks so as to move towards greater consistency and transparency in the published accounts.

The policy of income recognition should be objective and based on record of recovery rather than on any subjective considerations. Likewise, the classification of assets of banks has to be done on the basis of objective criteria which would ensure a uniform and consistent application of the norms. Also, the provisioning should be made on the basis of the classification of assets based on the period for which the asset has remained non-performing and the availability of security and the realisable value thereof.

Banks are urged to ensure that while granting loans and advances, realistic repayment schedules may be fixed on the basis of cash flows with borrowers. This would go a long way to facilitate prompt repayment by the borrowers and thus improve the record of recovery in advances.

NON-PERFORMING ASSETS

An asset, including a leased asset, becomes non-performing when it ceases to generate income for the bank. A non-performing asset (NPA) is a loan or an advance where;

1. **Loan Account:** For loan account, if the Interest and/or instalment of principal remain 'overdue' for a period of more than 90 days.

   Overdue Status: Any amount due to the bank under any credit facility is 'overdue' if it is not paid on the due date fixed by the bank.

2. **Cash Credit or Overdraft Account :** The account remains 'out of order' for a period of more than 90 days.

   Out of Order Status: Either the outstanding balance remains continuously in excess of the sanctioned limit/drawing power or there are no credits continuously for 90 days as on the date of Balance Sheet or credits are not enough to cover the interest debited during the same period.

3. The Limit is not reviewed within 180 days from the due date of renewal.
4. Where stock statement has not been received for 90 days or more in case of Cash Credit Accounts.
5. **Bills:** The bill remains overdue for a period of more than 90 days from due date of payment.
6. **For Direct Agricultural Loans:** For short duration crops the Interest or instalment remaining overdue for 2 crops seasons & for long duration crop the Interest or instalment remaining overdue for 1 crop season.
7. The credit facilities backed by the Guarantee of Central Govt. though overdue, may be treated as NPA only when the Govt. repudiates its guarantee when revoked.
8. The credit facilities backed by the Guarantee of State Govt. become NPA normally.
9. In the case of bank finance given for industrial projects, housing loan or for agricultural

plantations etc. where moratorium is available for payment of interest, payment of interest becomes 'due' only after the moratorium or gestation period is over.

Advances under Consortium Arrangements: Asset classification of accounts under consortium should be based on the record of recovery of the individual member banks and other aspects having a bearing on the recoverability of the advances.

Classification of the Loan against Term Deposits, NSCs, KVPs/IVPs, etc.: Advances against term deposits, NSCs eligible for surrender, IVPs, KVPs and life policies need not be treated as NPAs, provided adequate margin is available in the accounts. Advances against gold ornaments, government securities and all other securities are not covered by this exemption.

Classification will be done Borrower-wise & not Facility-wise: When only one facility to a borrower/one investment in any of the securities issued by the borrower becomes a problem credit/investment and not others. Therefore, all the facilities granted by a bank to a borrower and investment in all the securities issued by the borrower will have to be treated as NPA and not the particular facility/investment or part thereof which has become irregular.

In case of loans to PACS/FSS Classification will be done Facility-wise: In respect of advances granted by banks to PACS/ FSS under the on-lending system, only that particular credit facility granted to PACS/ FSS which is in default will be classified as NPA and not all the credit facilities sanctioned to a PACS/ FSS.

Reversal of Income: If any advance, including bills purchased and discounted, becomes NPA, the entire interest accrued and credited to income account in the past periods, should be reversed if the same is not realised. This will apply to Government Guaranteed advances also. In respect of NPAs, fees, commission and similar income that have accrued should cease to accrue in the current period and should be reversed with respect to past periods, if uncollected.

Leased Assets: The finance charge component of finance income [as defined in 'AS 19 Leases' issued by the Council of the Institute of Chartered Accountants of India (ICAI)] on the leased asset which has accrued and was credited to income account before the asset became non performing, and remaining Unrealised, should be reversed or provided for in the current accounting period.

Appropriation of Recovery in NPAs: Interest realised on NPAs may be taken to income account provided the credits in the accounts towards interest are not out of fresh/ additional credit facilities sanctioned to the borrower concerned.

In the absence of a clear agreement between the bank and the borrower for the purpose of appropriation of recoveries in NPAs (*i.e.* towards principal or interest due), banks should adopt an accounting principle and exercise the right of appropriation of recoveries in a uniform and consistent manner.

Interest Application: On an account turning NPA, banks should reverse the interest already charged and not collected by debiting Profit and Loss account, and stop further application of interest. However, banks may continue to record such accrued interest in a Memorandum account in their books. For the purpose of computing Gross Advances, interest recorded in the Memorandum account should not be taken into account.

COMPUTATION OF NPA LEVELS

Banks are advised to compute their Gross Advances, Net Advances, Gross NPAs and Net NPAs, as per the format in Annex-1.

1. Gross Advances = Standard Asset Plus Gross NPA
2. Gross NPAs as a percentage of Gross Advances = Gross NPA/Gross Advances
3. Net Advances = Gross Advances – Deductions
4. Deductions
   a) Provisions held in the case of NPA Accounts
   b) DICGC / ECGC claims received and held pending adjustment
   c) Part payment received and kept in Suspense Account or any other similar account
   d) Balance in Sundries Account (Interest Capitalization – Restructured Accounts),
   e) Floating Provisions
   f) Provisions in lieu of diminution in the fair value of restructured accounts classified as NPAs
   g) Provisions in lieu of diminution in the fair value of restructured accounts classified as standard assets
5. Net NPAs = Gross NPAs minus Deductions (listed above)
6. Net NPAs as percentage of Net Advances = Net NPAs/ Net Advances (in %)

Upgradation of Loan Accounts Classified as NPAs: If arrears of interest and principal are paid by the borrower in the case of loan accounts classified as NPAs, the account should no longer be treated as non-performing and may be classified as 'standard' accounts.

Early Recognition of Stress: Before a loan account turns into a NPA, banks are required to identify incipient stress in the account by creating three sub-categories under the Special Mention Account (SMA) category as given in the table below:

SMA Sub-categories	*Basis for classification*
SMA-0	Principal or interest payment not overdue for more than 30 days but account showing signs of incipient stress.
SMA-1	Principal or interest payment overdue between 31-60 days.
SMA-2	Principal or interest payment overdue between 61-90 days.

ASSET CLASSIFICATION

Banks are required to classify non-performing assets further into the following three categories based on the period for which the asset has remained non-performing and the realisability of the dues:

i) Substandard Assets

ii) Doubtful Assets

iii) Loss Assets

Sub-Standard Assets : Account which has remained in NPA category for a period of not more than 12 months. As to realisability these accounts show credit weakness and there is distinct possibility that the Bank will sustain some loss if the deficiencies are not corrected.

Doubtful Assets : Account which remained in NPA category for more than 12 months. A loan classified as Doubtful has all the weaknesses inherent to Sub-Standard assets with added characteristic that the full recovery of the advance is highly improbable due to erosion of security value or fraud or such other reasons.

Loss Assets : Account where Loss has been identified by the bank or Internal Auditors or External Auditors or by RBI Inspector but the amount has not been written off. It is an asset which is considered uncollectible although there may be some salvage or recovery value.

Accounts where there is Erosion in the Value of Security/Frauds Committed by Borrowers: In respect of accounts where there are potential threats for recovery on account of erosion in the value of security or non-availability of security and existence of other factors such as frauds committed by borrowers it will not be prudent that such accounts should go through various stages of asset classification. In cases of such serious credit impairment the asset should be straight away classified as doubtful or loss asset as appropriate:

i) Erosion in the value of security can be reckoned as significant when the realisable value of the security is less than 50 per cent of the value assessed by the bank or accepted by RBI at the time of last inspection, as the case may be. Such NPAs may be straightaway classified under doubtful category and provisioning should be made as applicable to doubtful assets.

ii) If the realisable value of the security, as assessed by the bank/ approved valuers/ RBI is less than 10 per cent of the outstanding in the borrowal accounts, the existence of security should be ignored and the asset should be straightaway classified as loss asset. It may be either written off or fully provided for by the bank.

DETERMINATION OF ASSET CLASSIFICATION AND HEALTH CODE

To Determine the correct Asset Classification of an NPA borrower two aspects are Important:

1. "NPA Since" Date and,
2. "Value of Security"

Note: When RVS (Both Primary & Collateral) falls below 10% of the O/S balance the account, the account is straightway classified as **'LOSS'** and when RVS is above 10% but less than 50% of the O/S balance, it is straightway classified as **'DOUBTFUL'**.

1. RVS: Value of Security (Realisable Value of Security) for the purpose of reckoning NPA is the sum total of the amounts of security available in each accounts of the borrower:

1. Value of Principal (Primary) Security,
2. Value of Security, other than Primary Security,
3. Value of Credit/Cash Margin,
4. Value of Guarantee (only of the Nature of Guarantee Cover obtaining in the account *i.e.*, (ECGC), (DICGC) (CGFMU) and (CGTMSE).

NET OUTSTANDING (NOS) = Total Outstanding less amount of Unrealised Interest (URI).

Determination of Asset Classification and Assets Code from Standard to NPA as under;

1. Where NPA since date is up to 12 months from the Current Date:

(a) Asset Code will be determined as 21 Sub-Standard (Secured), except for as at 'b' below.

(b) Asset Code will be determined as 22 Sub-Standard (Unsecured), if the unsecured portion/ RVS as stipulated & ascertained is not more than10% abinitio (star clean Personal loan, clean OD etc.).

(c) Asset Code will be determined as 31 Doubtful, if erosion of RVS is more than 50% of the value accepted in the last inspection.

(d) Asset Code will be determined as 40 Loss, if erosion of RVS is more than 90% of the value accepted in the last inspection.

2. Where NPA since date is more than 12 months and up to 24 months from the current date:

(a) Asset code will be determined as 31 Doubtful if the RVS is not less than 10% of the NOS.

(b) Asset code will be determined as 40 Loss, if the RVS is less than 10% of the NOS.

3. Where NPA since date is more than 24 months and up to 48 months from the current date:

(a) Asset code will be determined as 32 Doubtful, if the RVS is not less than 10% of the NOS.

(b) Asset code will be determined as 40 Loss, if the RVS is less than 10% of the NOS.

4. Where NPA since date is more than 48 months from the current date:

(a) Asset code will be determined as 33 Doubtful.

(b) Asset code will be determined as 40 Loss, if the RVS is less than 10% of the NOS.

CATEGORIES, CODE AND PERIODS OF NPA ASSETS

Category	*Assets Code*	*Period in category*
Sub-Standard (Secured)	21	Up to 1 year from NPA date
Sub-Standard (Unsecured)	22	Up to 1 year from NPA date
Doubtful I (D1)	31	Above 1 year to 2 years from NPA date
Doubtful II (D2)	32	Above 2 years to 4 years from NPA date
Doubtful III (D3)	33	More than 4 years from NPA date
Loss	40	No time limit

PROVISIONING NORMS

The primary responsibility for making adequate provisions for any diminution in the value of loan assets, investment or other assets is that of the bank managements and the statutory auditors.

Loss assets: Loss assets should be written off. If loss assets are permitted to remain in the books for any reason, 100 per cent of the outstanding should be provided for.

Doubtful assets: Provision for doubtful assets should be done as under;

(i) 100 per cent of the extent to which the advance is not covered by the realisable value of the security to which the bank has a valid recourse and the realisable value is estimated on a realistic basis.

(ii) In regard to the secured portion, provision may be made on the following basis, at the rates ranging from 25 per cent to 100 per cent of the secured portion depending upon the period for which the asset has remained doubtful.

Sub-standard assets: Provision for Substandard assets should be done as under;

i) A general provision of 15 per cent on total outstanding should be made without making any allowance for ECGC guarantee cover and securities available.

ii) The 'unsecured exposures' which are identified as 'substandard' would attract additional provision of 10 per cent, *i.e.*, a total of 25 per cent on the outstanding balance.

iii) However, in view of certain safeguards such as escrow accounts available in respect of infrastructure lending, infrastructure loan accounts which are classified as sub-standard will attract a provisioning of 20 per cent instead of the aforesaid prescription of 25 per cent.

Standard Assets: Provision on Standard Assets is done as under;

(i) The provisioning requirements for all types of standard assets stands as below. Banks should make general provision for standard assets at the following rates for the funded outstanding on global loan portfolio basis:

a) Direct advances to agricultural and Small and Micro Enterprises (SMEs) sectors at 0.25 per cent;

b) Advances to Commercial Real Estate (CRE) Sector at 1.00 per cent;

c) Advances to Commercial Real Estate – Residential Housing Sector (CRE - RH) at 0.75 per cent;

d) Housing loans extended at teaser rates and restructured advances as per latest norms;

e) All other loans and advances not included in (a), (b) and (c) above at 0.40 per cent.

(ii) The provisions on standard assets should not be reckoned for arriving at net NPAs.

(iii) The provisions towards Standard Assets need not be netted from gross advances but shown separately as 'Contingent Provisions against Standard Assets' under 'Other Liabilities and Provisions Others' in Schedule 5 of the balance sheet.

Advances covered by ECGC guarantee: In the case of advances classified as doubtful and guaranteed by ECGC, provision should be made only for the balance in excess of the amount guaranteed by the Corporation.

Advance covered by guarantees of Credit Guarantee Fund Trust for Micro and Small Enterprises (CGTMSE) or Credit Risk Guarantee Fund Trust for Low Income Housing (CRGFTLIH): In case the advance covered by CGTMSE or CRGFTLIH guarantee becomes non-performing, no provision need be made towards the guaranteed portion.

SUMMARY OF PROVISION IN NPA ACCOUNTS

Asset Code	*NPA Category*	*Provision Amount (RBI Guideline)*
21	Sub-Standard (Secured)	15% of Net Outstanding
22	Sub-Standard (Unsecured)	25% of Net Outstanding
	Unsecured Exposures in respect of Infrastructure loan accounts where certain safeguards such as Escrow accounts are available	20% of Net Outstanding
31	Doubtful I (Fully secured by RVS)	25% of Net Outstanding
31	Doubtful I (Partly secured by RVS)	25% of RVS plus 100% of the unsecured Portion (NOS less RVS)
32	Doubtful II (Fully secured by RVS)	40% of net Outstanding
32	Doubtful II (Partly secured by RVS)	40% of RVS plus 100% of the Unsecured Portion (NOS less RVS)
33	Doubtful III	100% of net Outstanding
40	**Loss**	**100% of net Outstanding**

TEST YOURSELF

1. A loan accounts becomes NPA, if the Interest and/or instalment of principal remain __________ for a period of more than 90 days.
(a) due (b) overdue
(c) out of order (d) not deducted

2. Which is not a correct statements? A loan accounts becomes NPA, if:
(a) The Limit is not reviewed within 90 days from the due date of renewal.
(b) Where stock statement has not been received for 90 days or more in case of Cash Credit Accounts.
(c) The bill remains overdue for a period of more than 90 days from due date of payment.
(d) The credit facilities backed by the Guarantee of Central Govt. though overdue, may be treated as NPA only when the Govt. repudiates its guarantee when revoked.

3. A direct agriculture account becomes NPA if:
(a) For short duration crops the Interest or instalment remaining overdue for 2 crops seasons
(b) For long duration crop the Interest or instalment remaining overdue for 1 crop season.
(c) The Limit is not reviewed within 180 days from the due date of renewal.
(d) All of the above

4. Which loan account becomes NPA as per IRAC norms?
(a) Advances against term deposits
(b) Loan against NSCs, IVPs, KVPs
(c) Advances against life policies
(d) Advances against gold ornaments,

5. Which is not the correct statements as per IRAC norms?
(a) Classification of NPA will be done facility-wise & not borrower-wise.

(b) The credit facilities backed by the Guarantee of Central Govt. though overdue, may be treated as NPA only when the Govt. repudiates its guarantee when revoked.

(c) The credit facilities backed by the Guarantee of State Govt. become NPA normally.

(d) In case of loans to PACS/FSS classification will be done facility-wise.

6. On an account turning NPA, banks should:

(a) Reverse the interest already charged and not collected by debiting P & L account

(b) Stop further application of interest.

(c) Provision is required in the account

(d) All of the above

7. Which is not the correct classification of live NPA assets by banks:

(a) Substandard Assets (b) Write-off Assets

(c) Doubtful Assets (d) Loss Assets

8. As per RBI, SMA-2 accounts are those accounts, where Principal or interest payment overdue between ________ days.

(a) 1-30 (b) 31-60

(c) 61-90 (d) 91-120

9. Sub-Standard Assets are those account which has remained in NPA category for a period of not more than ________.

(a) 6 months (b) 12 months

(c) 24 months (d) 30 months

10. Which is not the assets code of doubtful assets?

(a) 31 (b) 32

(c) 33 (d) 40

11. If a standard asset slipped to NPA, Asset Code will be determined as _____ Sub-Standard (Unsecured, if the unsecured portion/RVS as stipulated & ascertained is not more than 10% abinitio:

(a) 12 (b) 21

(c) 22 (d) 40

12. If a standard asset slipped to NPA, Asset Code of secured loan will be determined as _______, if erosion of RVS is more than 50% of the value accepted in the last inspection.

(a) 21 Sub-Standard (b) 31 Doubtful

(c) 32 Doubtful (d) 40 Loss

13. If a standard asset slipped to NPA, Asset Code of secured loan will be determined as _______, if erosion of RVS is more than 90% of the value accepted in the last inspection.

(a) 21 Sub-Standard (b) 31 Doubtful

(c) 32 Doubtful (d) 40 Loss

14. NPA account is remain in Assets Code Doubtful II (D2) From ________ from NPA date.

(a) 2 years to 4 years (b) 2 years to 3 years

(c) 2 years to 5 years (d) 3 years to 4 years

15. Which is defined by Narsimham Committee on Financial Sector Reforms (1991) under Prudential Accounting Norms?

(a) Income Recognition (b) Asset Classification

(c) Provisioning Norms (d) All of the above

16. As per RBI guideline, provision for Sub-Standard (Unsecured) is:

(a) 20% of Net Outstanding

(b) 25% of Net Outstanding

(c) 25% of Secured assets

(d) 40% of Secured assets

17. As per RBI guideline, provision for Assets Code Doubtful III (D3) is:

(a) 40% of Net Outstanding

(b) 25% of Net Outstanding

(c) 100% of Net Outstanding

(d) 40% of Secured assets

18. If an NPA accounts Net Outstanding is ₹ 12 lakh and RVS is ₹ 8 lakh categorized as Assets Code Doubtful II (D2), the provision amount will be:

(a) ₹ 4.80 lakh (b) ₹ 7.20 lakh

(c) ₹ 9.60 lakh (d) ₹ 3.20 lakh

19. If an NPA accounts Net Outstanding is ₹ 10 lakh and RVS is ₹ 7 lakh categorized as Assets Code 21 Sub- Standard (Secured), the provision amount will be:

(a) ₹ 1.50 lakh (b) ₹ 2.50 lakh

(c) ₹ 4.05 lakh (d) ₹ 3.20 lakh

20. The provisioning requirements for all types of standard assets. Provision for direct advances to agricultural and Small and Micro Enterprises (SMEs) sectors at:

(a) 0.10 per cent (b) 0.25 per cent

(c) 0.40 per cent (d) 1.00 per cent

ANSWER

1	2	3	4	5	6	7	8	9	10
(b)	(a)	(d)	(d)	(a)	(d)	(b)	(c)	(b)	(d)
11	**12**	**13**	**14**	**15**	**16**	**17**	**18**	**19**	**20**
(c)	(b)	(d)	(a)	(d)	(c)	(c)	(b)	(a)	(b)

FINANCIAL INCLUSION & FINANCIAL LITERACY

FINANCIAL INCLUSION

Introduction: Providing universal access to banking services and improving the forms of credit delivery, especially for the weaker sections of the population, form the basis of the Reserve Bank's financial inclusion agenda. With a view to achieving sustainable and scalable financial inclusion, multiple strategies are being used such as appropriate relaxations in guidelines, provision of new products and other supporting measures.

Financial Inclusion: Policy Approach and Interventions: RBI First Bi-monthly Monetary Policy Statement, 2014-15 announced on April 1, 2014 which stated that 'On financial inclusion, the fourth pillar, the recommendations of the Mor Committee on accelerating the flow of credit to those at the bottom of the pyramid and enlargement of catchment area of the Business Correspondents (BCs), including through possible inclusion of new entities as BCs, are under examination. To overcome the challenge of cash management of BCs which is impeding the scaling up of the BC model, the Reserve Bank will collate best practices and issue a fresh set of guidelines to commercial banks'.

The Reserve Bank has since the last decade made the following policy interventions in the area of financial inclusion.

Providing Banking Services in Villages with Population more than 2,000: In order to provide door step banking facilities in all the unbanked villages in the country, a phase wise approach has been adopted. During Phase-I (2010-13), all unbanked villages with population more than 2,000 were identified and allotted to various banks (public sector banks, private sector banks and regional rural banks) through State Level Bankers' Committees (SLBCs) for coverage through various modes – Branch or BC or other modes such as ATMs, mobile vans, etc.

Opening Banking Outlets in Unbanked Villages with Population less than 2,000: After the completion of the first phase of the roadmap, the second phase (2013-16) to provide banking services in unbanked villages with populations less than 2000 was rolled out. About 4,90,298 unbanked villages with population less than 2000 have been identified and allotted to various banks (public sector banks, private sector banks and regional rural banks) through SLBCs across the country for coverage in a time bound manner. As on June 30, 2016, as reported by SLBCs, 4,52,151 villages have been provided banking services; 14,976 through branches, 4,16,636 through BCs and 20,539 by other modes viz. ATMs, mobile vans, etc. thereby achieving 92.2% of the target.

Roadmap for Opening Brick and Mortar Branches in Villages with Population more than 5,000 without a Bank Branch of a Scheduled Commercial Bank: For increasing banking penetration and financial inclusion, brick and mortar branches are an integral component and hence it has been decided to focus on villages with population above 5000 without a bank branch of a scheduled commercial bank. Therefore, SLBC Convener Banks have been advised to identify villages with population above 5000 without a bank branch of a scheduled commercial bank in their State. As reported by SLBCs, 6,593 villages were identified and allotted among SCBs (including RRBs) for opening branches. The opening of brick and motar branches under this Roadmap is to be completed by March 2017.

Financial Inclusion Plans: All domestic Scheduled Commercial Banks (SCBs) – both in the public sector and private sector – were advised to draw up board-approved Financial Inclusion Plans (FIPs) as an integral part of their business strategy based on their competitive advantage. FIPs are submitted to the Reserve Bank and are implemented over blocks of three years. These plans broadly include self-set targets with respect to: opening rural brick and mortar branches; Business Correspondents (BCs) employed; coverage of unbanked villages through branches/ BCs/ other modes, opening of Basic Savings bank deposit accounts (BSBDAs) including through BC-ICT; issuance of Kisan Credit Cards (KCC) and General Credit Cards (GCC) and other specific products aimed at the financially excluded segments.

Relaxed Know Your Customer (KYC) Requirements: Recognising that the KYC requirements and related documentation may potentially become a hindrance in encouraging sections of the population in opening bank accounts, KYC for opening bank accounts was simplified to the extent possible. Consequently, small accounts could be opened with self-certification in the presence of bank officials. Further, Aadhaar, the unique identification number allotted by the Unique Identification Authority of India (UIDAI), Government of India was allowed to be used as one of the eligible documents for meeting KYC requirement for opening a bank account.

Committee on medium-term Path on Financial Inclusion: The Committee on Medium-term Path on Financial Inclusion (CMPFI) constituted by Reserve Bank of India submitted its report in December 2015. Among the various recommendations made by the committee, some of the important ones that have been implemented include:

- Framework on BC Registry and BC Certification issued to Indian Banks' Association (IBA).
- Introduction of a Movable Asset Registry.
- Universal crop insurance and satellite imagery for crop mapping and damage assessment as a part of the Pradhan Mantri Fasal Bima Yojana (PMFBY).
- Registration of mobile numbers through ATMs connected with NFS.
- Celebration of financial literacy week at regional offices.

Some of the recommendations that are under implementation include introduction of a system of professional credit intermediaries/advisors for MSMEs, a survey for assessing the level of financial literacy and inclusion across the country, a pilot project for installing kiosks (30 interactive and 70 non-interactive) at 100 locations to encourage self-learning by people newly inducted into the financial system, impact assessment of the financial literacy camps and preparing a curriculum for training programmes for lead literacy officers by the College of Agricultural Banking (CAB), Pune.

Streamlining the Flow of Credit to Micro and Small Enterprises: In order to provide timely financial support to Micro and Small Enterprises (MSEs) facing financial difficulties during their life cycles, banks were advised in August 2015 to review their existing lending policies to the MSE sector.

Allowing Business Correspondents (BCs) Banking: The Reserve Bank permitted banks to utilise the services of intermediaries in providing banking services through the use of business facilitators and Business Correspondents (BCs). The BC model allows banks to do 'cash in-cash out' transactions at a location much closer to the rural population, thus addressing the problems of last mile reach.

The banks may formulate a policy for engaging Business Correspondents (BCs) with the approval of their Board of Directors. Due diligence may be carried out on the individuals/entities to be engaged as BCs prior to their engagement. The due diligence exercise may, inter alia, cover aspects such as;

a) Reputation/market standing,
b) Financial soundness,
c) Management and corporate governance,
d) Cash handling ability and
e) Ability to implement technology solutions in rendering financial services.

Eligible Individuals/Entities: The banks may engage the following individuals/entities as BC.

a) Individuals like retired bank employees, retired teachers, retired government employees and ex-servicemen, individual owners of kirana / medical /Fair Price shops, individual Public Call Office (PCO) operators, agents of Small Savings schemes of Government of India/Insurance Companies, individuals who own Petrol Pumps, authorized functionaries of well-run Self Help Groups (SHGs) which are linked to banks, any other individual including those operating Common Service Centres (CSCs);
b) NGOs/ MFIs set up under Societies/Trust Acts and Section 25 Companies ;
c) Cooperative Societies registered under Mutually Aided Cooperative Societies Acts/Cooperative Societies Acts of States/Multi State Cooperative Societies Act;
d) Post Offices; and

e) Companies registered under the Indian Companies Act, 1956 with large and widespread retail outlets, excluding Non-Banking Financial Companies (NBFCs).

BUSINESS CORRESPONDENTS (BC) MODEL

While a BC can be a BC for more than one bank, at the point of customer interface, a retail outlet or a sub-agent of a BC shall represent and provide banking services of only one bank. The terms and conditions governing the contract between the bank and the BC should be carefully defined in written agreements and subjected to a thorough legal vetting. While drawing up agreements, banks should strictly adhere to instructions contained in the guidelines on managing risks and code of conduct in outsourcing of financial services by banks, issued by Reserve Bank of India on November 3, 2006. The banks will be fully responsible for the actions of the BCs and their retail outlets / sub agents.

Scope of Activities: The scope of activities may include :

(i) Identification of borrowers;

(ii) Collection and preliminary processing of loan applications including verification of primary information/data;

(iii) Creating awareness about savings and other products and education and advice on managing money and debt counselling;

(iv) Processing and submission of applications to banks;

(v) Promoting, nurturing and monitoring of Self Help Groups/ Joint Liability Groups/Credit Groups/ others;

(vi) Post-sanction monitoring;

(vii) Follow-up for recovery,

(viii) Disbursal of small value credit,

(ix) Recovery of principal/collection of interest

(x) Collection of small value deposits

(xi) Sale of micro insurance/mutual fund products/ pension products/other third party products and

(xii) Receipt and delivery of small value remittances/ other payment instruments.

The activities to be undertaken by the BCs would be within the normal course of the bank's banking business, but conducted through the BCs at places other than the bank premises/ATMs.

FINANCIAL LITERACY INITIATIVES

In India, financial literacy has been regarded as a process that provides demand side support for financial inclusion. To assess the extant level of financial literacy and inclusion, a pan-India survey is being conducted by the Reserve Bank. Target-specific content for five target groups viz. farmers, small entrepreneurs, self-help groups (SHGs), school students and senior citizens is also being designed for tailored financial literacy programmes conducted by Financial Literacy Centres (FLCs). A pilot project for setting up 100 Centres for Financial Literacy (CFL) at the block level to scale up the existing FLC infrastructure has been initiated.

Functioning of Financial Literacy Centres (FLCs): Guidelines for banks' financial literacy centres and the operational guidelines for conducting camps by FLCs and rural bank branches were revised in January 2016. Banks have been advised to put in place board approved policies for stronger FLC architecture in terms of providing basic infrastructure to FLCs as well as appointing FLC counsellors. As on March 2016, 1,384 FLCs were operational.

Pilot project on setting up Centres for Financial Literacy (CFLs): Given the challenges of skewed distribution of existing FLCs in a few states, limited outreach and to have an exclusive focus on financial literacy at the ground level, the Reserve Bank is encouraging banks to set up CFLs at the block level on a pilot basis in a few states. The key elements of this block level CFL project are:

a) Area based approach (block)

b) Schedule of camps

c) Skilled workforce

d) Partnerships with NGOs

e) Use of technology

f) Common name and logo 'Moneywise Centre for Financial Literacy'

The pilot project to set up 100 CFLs across 10 states with support from the Financial Inclusion Fund has been initiated. Possibilities of partnerships with eligible NGOs/institutions are being explored to bring in innovative and more efficient approaches/ methods for conducting financial literacy activities.

Technical Group on Financial Inclusion and Financial Literacy: A Technical Group on Financial Inclusion and Financial Literacy of the FSDC sub-committee was set up to co-ordinate the efforts on financial inclusion and literacy at the policy level. The group is chaired by the Deputy Governor, Reserve Bank of India and has representatives from all regulators and the Finance Ministry. A National Centre for Financial Education (NCFE), comprising representatives from all financial sector regulators has been set up to implement the National Strategy on Financial Education (NSFE).

NCFE's main role is to create material on financial education and conducting financial education campaigns across the country.

Some of the initiatives undertaken under the aegis of the Technical Group are:

Kiosk Project: About 100 kiosks (30 interactive kiosks and 70 non-interactive LFDs) are being set up in five states on a pilot basis in public places like banks, post offices, collector's offices and primary health centres to promote financial awareness. The kiosks will display messages in different languages controlled from a central location.

Financial Education in School Curriculum: In collaboration with CBSE, NCFE has prepared financial education workbooks for classes VI to X; these are in the process of getting CBSE's final approval. Meanwhile, NCFE and the Reserve Bank are pursuing with state education boards for the adoption of the financial education workbooks in the school curriculum in their jurisdictions by appropriately integrating them with different subjects. Four state governments viz. Goa, Meghalaya, Jammu and Kashmir and Mizoram have agreed in principle to include financial education topics in state board school curricula. Talks with other state governments are at different stages.

Improving Financial Literacy Levels: Going forward, Reserve Bank envisages further steps for improving the financial literacy levels which include, among others, designing and implementing capacity building programmes for FLC counsellors and bank branch heads in rural areas and conducting surveys for obtaining insights on financial knowledge, attitudes and behaviour of the people.

USE OF MOBILE IN FINANCIAL INCLUSION DRIVE

India has followed bank-led model to achieve financial inclusion (FI) and made steady gains. However, given the enormous population and the demographic and geographical diversity of the country, there is still substantial ground to be covered. A synergetic approach is the need of the hour with banks leveraging the high mobile density in the country to offer basic banking services on the one hand and both banks and non-banks offering mobile-based prepaid instrument (PPI)/e-money products for easy accessibility on the other. In addition, a simple mobile banking registration process and the use of application-based mobiles as a Point of sale (PoS) are potent instruments for achieving the goal of financial inclusion. The Committee is of the view that the desirable level of financial inclusion would be difficult to achieve without a combination of the sustained efforts of conventional banking as well as mobile-based products and services offered by both banks and authorised non-bank entities.

The higher the share of cash, the larger the national cost and, hence, the payments policy should facilitate the transition towards a less-cash society: An important component of the payment segment has traditionally been cash, which entails significant costs in terms of production, distribution and other logistics that are not apparent to the final consumer and, therefore, not factored in while choosing this alternative over others since the cost is borne by the intermediaries. With the Digital India initiative aspiring to provide free wi-fi across India over the next few years, mobile money/e-money will have the advantage of lowering transactions costs while offering convenience of access and thereby enhancing financial inclusion. Thus, in the near future, mobile money has the potential to offer a low-cost alternative to cash.

In order to achieve financial inclusion, the unbanked should be covered by any channel that provides financial service of which payment and remittance is a critical component. A simple process of mobile banking registration is required to facilitate customer adoption. Since a huge segment of the population has been added to the formal banking system under the PMJDY, banks can provide them with ease of banking by introducing mobile banking applications that are non-smart phone-based for simple financial transactions.

Government-to-Person (G2P) Payments: In a number of countries, governments have sought to increase the use of electronic means for payments and to promote greater financial inclusion. While the two agendas have by no means converged, in practice they have often been translated into a single objective of increasing the proportion of recipients of government social cash transfers who receive payment directly into their bank accounts. This direct government cash transfer into bank accounts serves two benefits. Electronic payments are likely to reduce the cost of payment for government and make delivery more targeted and convenient for recipients compared to the prevalent cash-based schemes, which require recipients to be in a particular place at a particular time to receive payment.

Meaningful Financial inclusion is not Feasible without Social Cash Transfer: Given the low level of personal disposable income, the Committee is of the view that meaningful financial inclusion will be elusive without social cash transfers from the Government-to-Person (G2P). Substantial infrastructure has already been put in place by the opening of accounts and biometric identity creation through Aadhaar. The Committee believes that this approach is consistent with the government's vision. This would entail increasing the digitization of government payments and the consolidation of various benefits, which could put significant disposable income in the hands of the marginalized sections of society at regular intervals.

RURAL SELF EMPLOYMENT TRAINING INSTITUTES (RSETI)

RSETIs are managed by Banks with active co-operation from the Government of India and State Government. Dedicated institutions designed as to ensure necessary skill training and skill up gradation of the rural BPL youth to mitigate the unemployment problem. These are promoted and managed by banks with active cooperation from state governments. One RSETI is established in every district in the country. Concerned bank is the lead bank in the district takes responsibility for creating and managing it. Government of India will provide one time grant assistance, upto a maximum of ₹ 1 crore for meeting the expenditure on construction of building and other infrastructure. After successful completion of the training, they will be provided with credit linkage assistance by the banks to start their own entrepreneurial ventures.

The Objective of RSETIs are:

(i) Rural BPL youth to be identified and turned for self-employment;

(ii) The training offered to the demand driven;

(iii) Area in which training to be provided to the trainee to be decided after assessment the candidate's aptitude;

(iv) Hand holding support to be provided for assured credit linkage with bank;

(v) Escort services to be provided for at least for two years soon to ensure sustainability of Micro Enterprise Trainees;

(vi) The trainees to be provided intensive short-term residential self-employment training programmes with free food and accommodation.

Infrastructure: The common minimum infrastructure of each RSETI will be 2-3 classrooms with toilet facilities (separate for women and physically challenged friendly). Two workshops, two dormitories with bath facilities. Adequate physical infrastructure for training, admini-stration, hostel, staff quarters etc.

Programme Structure & Contents: Each RSETI should offer 30 to 40 skill development programmes in a financial year in various avenues. The programmes are of short duration ranging from 1 to 6 weeks and could fall into the categories listed below:

- **Agricultural Programmes :** Agriculture and allied activities like dairy, poultry, apiculture, horticulture, sericulture, mushroom cultivation, floriculture, fisheries, etc
- **Product Programme :** Dress designing for men and women, Rexene articles, incense sticks manufacturing, football making, bag, bakery products, leaf cup making, recycled paper manufacturing, etc.
- **Process Programmes :** Two-wheeler repairs, radio/TV repairs, motor rewinding, electrical transformer repairs, irrigation pump-set repairs, tractor and power tiller repairs, cell phone repairs, beautician course, photography and videography, screen printing, domestic electrical appliances repair, computer hardware and DTP.
- **General Programmes :** Skill development for women.
- **Other Programmes :** Related to other sectors like leather, construction, hospitality and any other sector depending on local requirements.

Training programmes will be decided by the institute based on the local resource situation and potential demand for the products/services. A uniform standardized curriculum would be developed and circulated among the institutes. There shall be two sets of training curriculums in all the RSETIs:

a) Basic orientation programme courses for SGSY SHGs.

b) Skill development programmes for micro enterprise and wage employment/placement.

Soft skill training shall be an integral part in all the training programmes.

Selection of Trainees & Batch Size: At least 70% of the trainees should be from the rural BPL category certified by the DRDA. Proper weightage, as per SGSY guidelines will be given to SC/STs, minorities, physically challenged and women. An ideal size of a batch should be 25-30 candidates. Shramadan/Yoga, presentation of MILLY would become a common input in training module.

Recognition of RSETI Trainees: Certificates issued by an RSETI will be recognised by all banks for purposes of extending credit to the trainees. It means that RSETI trained rural youths will be free to access any scheduled bank for loan/credit.

Credit Linkage: Credit needs of trainees will be appraised by RSETIs and the sense will be conveyed to the bank branches. The trainees could avail bank loans under SGSY or any other government sponsored programmes.

TEST YOURSELF

1. What is Financial Inclusion Plans (FIPs) for bank?
(a) Coverage of unbanked villages through branches/ BCs/other modes,
(b) Opening of Basic Savings bank deposit accounts (BSBDAs)
(c) Issuance of Kisan Credit Cards (KCC) and General Credit Cards (GCC)
(d) All of the above

2. The services which will not offer under Financial Inclusion Plans?
(a) Deposit account
(b) Small Agriculture loan accounts
(c) Vehicle Loan
(d) Remittances services

3. The Reserve Bank permitted banks to utilise the services of intermediaries in providing banking services through the use of:
(a) Business facilitators
(b) Business Correspondents (BCs)
(c) Both business facilitators and Business Correspondents (BCs)
(d) None of the above

4. The Committee on Medium-term Path on Financial Inclusion (CMPFI) constituted by Reserve Bank of India submitted its report in ________.
(a) December 2013 (b) September 2014
(c) December 2015 (d) September 2016

5. Various recommendations made by the committee on Medium-term Path on Financial Inclusion (CMPFI) are:
(a) Introduction of a Movable Asset Registry
(b) Registration of mobile numbers through ATMs connected with NFS.
(c) Celebration of financial literacy week at regional offices.
(d) All of the above

6. After the completion of the first phase of the roadmap, the second phase (2013-16) to provide banking services in unbanked villages with populations less than ________ was rolled out.
(a) 2000 (b) 3000
(c) 5000 (d) 10000

7. SLBC Convener Banks have been advised to identify villages with population above 5000 without a bank branch of a scheduled commercial bank in their State. As reported by SLBCs, 6,593 villages were identified and allotted among SCBs (including RRBs) for opening branches. The opening of brick and motar branches under this Roadmap is to be completed by ________.
(a) December 2014 (b) March 2017
(c) December 2015 (d) September 2016

8. Due diligence may be carried out on the individuals/ entities to be engaged as BCs prior to their engagement. The due diligence exercise may, inter alia, cover aspects such as:
(a) Reputation/market standing
(b) Financial soundness,
(c) Cash handling ability
(d) All of the above

9. The banks may not engage the following individuals/ entities as BC.
(a) NGOs/ MFIs set up under Societies/ Trust Acts
(b) Post Offices
(c) Small banks
(d) Companies registered under the Indian Companies Act, 1956 with large and widespread retail outlets, excluding Non-Banking Financial Companies (NBFCs).

10. The scope of activities of BCs may not include:
(a) Identification of borrowers
(b) Post-sanction monitoring;
(c) Follow-up for recovery
(d) None of these

11. The key elements of financial literacy of this block level CFL project are:
(a) Schedule of camps (b) Skilled workforce
(c) Use of technology (d) All of the above

12. Government of India will provide one-time grant assistance, up to a maximum of ________ for meeting the expenditure on construction of building and other infrastructure.
(a) ₹ 1 crore (b) ₹ 2 crores
(c) ₹ 3 crores (d) ₹ 5 crores

ANSWER

1	2	3	4	5	6	7	8	9	10	11	12
(d)	(c)	(c)	(c)	(d)	(a)	(b)	(d)	(c)	(d)	(d)	(a)

MODULE–C
BANKING TECHNOLOGY

ESSENTIALS OF BANK COMPUTERIZATION

INTRODUCTION

Renovation in Indian banks is taking place from all aspects and is being refined as time proceeds and the products of the banking industry are enthusiastically modifying the face of banking. As the Indian banking and financial systems develop and get integrated with the international similar markets, the computerisation and networking has become inevitable. The banks in India are gearing up to adopt IT-based systems on the lines of what has been done by the banks in other parts of the world.

HISTORY OF BANK COMPUTERIZATION

The Reserve Bank of India had appointed a committee on computerisation under the Chairmanship of Dr. C Rangarajan, the then Governor, RBI, in 1983 to look into the modalities of drawing up phased plan of computerisation for the banking industry covering the period 1985 to 1989. The Committee submitted its report in 1984, recommended introduction of computerisation at branch and controlling offices of banks. The RBI in 1988 constituted the Second Rangarajan Committee to draw up a porspective plan for computerisation in banks and to suggest modalities for implementing on-line computerisation, especially at branch-level, to indicate application-areas like funds transfer, electronic mail, BANK NET, SWIFT, ATMs etc.

The Committee submitted its report in 1989, and recommended that the thrust of bank-computerisation for the next five years should be to computerise around 2000 to 2500 large branches located at high activity centres, computerisation of RO/ZO/HO (Regional Office/Zonal Office/Head Office), use of BANK NET for several intra-bank and inter-bank applications like funds transfer, 'Single Window Concept', ATMs at strategic locations such as airports/railway-stations etc. on shared basis by banks.

The computerisation settlement of October 1993 was signed between the IBA and bank employees' unions to reduce the resistance from labor-unions for computerisation as suggested by the Rangarajan Committee viz to computerise 2500 to 3000 branches in urban and metropolitan centres. The settlement also provided scope for 'Single Window Concept' at branches, networking within and among branches, terminals at customers locations, enquiry terminals for valued customers, ATMs bank-wise and on pool basis, note-counting and signature verification equipment and use of latest communication facilities available under BANK NET/RBI NET, I-NET, SWIFT etc.

The RBI had appointed a Committee (in 1994) on Technology Issues related to payment systems, under the Chairmanship of W S Saraf, the then ED, RBI. The objective of the committee was to suggest ways and means to improve payment systems with the help of technology. The Committee had suggested far reaching changos relating to payment systems, cheque clearing, securities settlement, technology and training in technology for the banking industry. It had also recommended that the use of electronic communications network-based reporting of currency chest transactions. To examine various issues pertaining to technology upgradation in the banking and financial sector, and to suggest steps for a time-bound implementation of schedule of the Narasimham Committee's recommendations, the RBI had setup a Committee in the Department of IT under the chairmanship of Dr. A Vasudevan (ED, RBI).

One of the terms of reference (which was related to computer-security and audit) was, to suggest necessary security systems and standards for various network-based banking applications. The committee submitted its report in July 1999, and re-emphasised the recommendations made by earlier committees. Some of the important recommendations related to computer-security and computer-audit are:

- There should be an appropriate institutional arrangement for key-management and authentication, by way of a certification agency.
- Banks should adopt widely used standard of cryptography procedures to prevent data-tamper during transmission. These standards would require to be periodically reviewed.
- Each bank needs to devise a manual on computer-audit and develop appropriate methodologies/systems for conducting computer-audit.
- All new applications should be subject to pre-installation and post-installation audit in addition to periodical audits.
- The capabilities of the CPPD/IT department for selection of applications for out sourcing, choice of vendors, negotiation, managing the contract and post-installation of the software managing future computer-based solutions etc., have to be reviewed on an ongoing basis or at least once in three years.

The total number of branches of Indian public-sector banks identified for full branch computerisation up to March 2000 is around 7827. However, by March 1999, the number of fully computerised branches was increased to the level of 4620. Banks are also concentrating on interconnecting branches with one another using Leased-lines or VSATs (Very Small Aperture Terminals), which give banks control over their operations from a central place. The foreign banks operating in India, Urban Co-operative banks, newly established private banks and other private sector banks have also undertaken computerisation and networking of their branches.

The administrative offices of banks viz. Head/Zonal/Regional offices are doing a lot of data processing work to help the concerned authorities to analyse the available information, to monitor business activities and to make decisions. In India, computers are being used for selective activities in administrative offices of banks viz. Processing of statutory returns under RBI Act, monthly/quarterly performance reports from branches, credit information, statistical returns, interbank transactions, personnel inventory, provident fund accounting, profit & loss accounts, cash and investment management, stationery stock accounting, and branch house-keeping. Most bank shave operationalised software packages for these purposes.

Need for Computerisation

The four major objectives of computerisation in banking are to improve:

(a) Customer service;
(b) Housekeeping;
(c) Decision-making;
(d) Productivity and profitability.

Back Office Application: The first step of RBI towards bank computerisation, was implementation of the Back-office application in the banking sector. The Back-office application uses computers only for data entry operations and a few calculative operations. It also stores customer's data and uses dos base Fox Pro to calculate interest and develop the pay roll system to calculate the employees' salary. This application was not beneficial to the banks customers because it was not providing them any kind of service. Due to this system the working. hours of bank employees were increased due to daily data entry of all/few manual transactions. It is also observed that in this system daily/weekly/monthly back up was required. In case of failure in backup files, management may not get proper information at a given point of time. Overall observation is that, the back-office application was not that beneficial to bank employees as well as bank customers.

Total Branch Automation: Another step taken by RBI was Total Branch Automation in which the bank should have TBA s/w being used in branches that are covering 80% of the total business of a bank. These branches should have a single customer ID concept using which all the accounts of the customer can be retrieved. The bank should start collecting the customer-related information for customer information system. Also training the employees in the areas of customer relationship, marketing at the customer touch points should be started. In case of TBA bank can also provide ATM facility, but that ATM facility is restricted to that branch only which provide ATM centers. Because in TBA data centre is not established so customer's data is available only at particular branch. So customer can withdraw their cash only at particular branch's ATM centre in which the customer has his/her account. Due to this restriction although the ATM facility is available customer cannot take the advantage of anywhere banking. In TBA each branch needs to take the back up of their data and send the same data backup copy in the form of soft copy on CD or pen drive or by using any storage device to the head office of the bank. Now a days many cooperative banks are still working on total branch automation system. It indicates that TBA is more convenient method of bank transaction as compare to back office application.

Stand-alone Computer System: The stand-alone computer system is used by only one person at a time. Stand-alone systems are best suited for the decision-making process, which involves processing and analysis of data. Today's stand-alone systems are also capable of handling multimedia, high-quality graphics, fax messages, etc.

Multi-User Systems: The multi-user systems are computers on which several people can work at the same time. Mini computers, Main Frame Computers, Micro-computers and the more powerful Super Computers all fall under this category.

Multi-user Computer Networking: In such some system computers are based on the centralised processing concept. All information is kept and processed at the main central machines and various terminals are attached to the main computer. The main computer can store a huge amount of information and possesses high-processing speeds enabling a large number of users to be connected to the main central computer. Each user has his/her own terminal. Most of the banking systems are developed using the centralized computing concept.

The advantages of using a centralised data processing system:

(a) Availability of corporate level information at one location is possible;

(b) Cost of acquiring hardware, software and other infrastructure is more profitable than acquiring the same for individual departments;

(c) Due to the high volume of data processing the computing resources can be fully utilized;

(d) Technical manpower can also be efficiently managed at a central level;

(e) Costly resources like leased telephone lines, satellite links, etc., can be shared among the various departments Branch-level Computerisation.

Computerisation at the branch level can be used to:

(a) Provide better and speedy customer service;

(b) Improve house keeping services;

(c) Analyse the branch-level data for decision making;

(d) Generation of various reports.

Computerisation at Regional/Circle/Zonal Office: RO/ZO acts in between branches and the head office. The most common tasks performed by the regional office/zonal office are:

(a) Branch profile;

(b) Inter-branch reconciliation;

(c) Credit monitoring;

(d) Personnel data management, etc.

Computerisation at Head Office Level: The head office of a bank is responsible for bank level planning, and control functions, policy decisions. The head office activities are divided into different functional areas like:

(a) Operations;

(b) Planning;

(c) Personnel;

(d) International business;

(e) Services, etc.

The computerisation at various functional areas may include application areas:

(a) Personnel management and administrative support;

(b) Funds management;

(c) Investment portfolio management;

(d) Branch profiles;

(e) Credit information system, etc.

LOCAL AREA NETWORK (LAN)

The computer network that links computers and peripherals within a localised area say, within a building is known as LAN. Generally, LAN will not extend beyond 150 metres. However, it can be up to a maximum spread of 1 km and the number of devices supported may also vary from 2 to as many as 1000.

In LANs, each independent system is known as a node and when such nodes are interconnected, it is known as a LAN. Usually, there will be one central node (Server) providing and controlling all the services of the network. The client nodes route their requests to the server and obtain the necessary services.

TOPOLOGY (LAYOUT)

The way in which the devices are interconnected is known as topology:

Bus Topology: All devices on the network are connected to a single continuous cable. Transmission from any station travels the length of the bus in both directions and is received by all other stations. The main advantage of bus topology is that it is quite easy to set up. Further, if one station on the LAN fails, it will not affect the rest of the network Data transmission is possible in one direction only. The breakdown of any one station on the ring can disable the entire LAN.

Star Topology: In a star topology, the central node is often the master. Each of the other nodes is joined to the master by separate links. It cannot handle large traffic as every transaction has to pass through the central node. However, if one node fails, it will not affect the network.

Ring Topology: In a ring topology, the devices are connected in a closed loop and information is passed from one node to the other in series. Data transmission is possible in one direction only. As the packet circulates the destination recognise its address and copies the packet contents onto it. The breakdown of any one section on the ring can disable the entire LAN.

Tree Topology: Tree topology resembles like a tree in the real world. This topology has a root node, intermediate nodes and leave nodes. Root node is a head node of this structure. The leaves nodes are the last nodes and do not have any child nodes. This structure is constructed in a hierarchical form and any node can have any number of child nodes.

Protocols

The protocols are the rules for communication between similar modules of processes, usually in different nodes. Protocols define message formats and the rules for message exchange. It controls priority and sequence of transmission, errors in transmission, and the process of beginning and concluding conversion. The network protocols depend on the adapters. Some of the commonly used types of adapters are Ethernet and Token-Ring. A multiplexer is used to receive signals from several communication lines and pass on to one communication line and vice versa.

Network Operating System

The function of the networking software is to set up some computers as hosts, or servers, and some computers as clients to those hosts. The servers manage the printer sharing, file sharing and communications link sharing to their clients.

The advantages of using LANs in banks are that:

(a) The expensive resources such as computer hardware and software can be shared by several users. This brings down the overall cost of computerisation.

(b) The information stored on the host computer is available to all users of the system. Therefore, there is no necessity of duplication of databases.

(c) Since all the terminals are intelligent terminals, the processing load is shared between the various machines and there is no overloading on any single machine.

There are also a few shortcomings of a LAN, such as:

(a) Complicated software has to be installed for data management.

(b) Security risks are higher, since each user access the host computer independently.

(c) Maintenance cost of such a system is high, since it has to be done frequently.

WIDE AREA NETWORK (WAN)

Wide Area Networks (WAN) are defined as a large-scale computer network spread over a span of sizeable geographic area, normally utilising the telecommunication network. In the banking sector, the WANs are generally used to interconnect branches with the regional offices, and regional/zonal offices to head office, etc.

UNINTERRUPTED POWER SYSTEM (UPS)

Uninterrupted power system provides clean and reliable AC power to the computer systems protecting them from power blackouts, brownouts, swells, sags, surges, and interface. In case of a power failure, the UPS attached with the file server automatically takes over the power supply to the file server or to the main computer to eliminate the chance of data loss.

CORE BANKING SOLUTION

After the turn of consolidated databases (Back office Application) and networks (Total Branch Automation) the next term is core banking applications. Core banking applications (CBS) in Banks provide the complete front-end and back-end automation of banks. These applications also help the banks to achieve centralised processing of each and every service of the customer. "Core banking applications provide anywhere, anytime 24 by 7 non-stop services, which is not possible with traditional localized branch automation systems. These applications also provide automation across multiple delivery channels.

Core banking is a newly developed concept adopted by banks. Core banking is a centralised system that provides accounting, customer information management and transaction processing functions. It provides a central operational database to bank's assets and liabilities, a transaction processing engine and a system for the financial management of the bank. In core banking, a branch will become a service outlet like an ATM booth. Thus, the importance of physical branches will be reduced. In case of core banking, customer can operate their account from various locations like-customer can open an account at one location and can deposit a cheque, check bank balance, withdraw cash, get demand draft, get account statement, transfer funds, other transactions from various different locations of different cities. Implementation of core banking in banking sector allows inter connectivity of branches with the centralised data centre. Core banking is just one part of a fairly complex architecture of today's banking which takes care of the essential banking activities. The major Banks in India, both in the private and public sectors are moving towards core banking solutions.

Basically, core banking means performing accounting transactions like depositing, withdrawals, availing loan, repayment of bills, statement of account etc. through the multiple delivery channels like ATMs, Internet banking, and new branches. For the last couple of years the focus is on Core banking. With the implementation of core banking systems across banks, the usage level of IT for customer management has increased. The Core banking system has enabled banks to launch & targeting new products and services at specific customer segment, after understanding their banking and investment requirements. Core banking therefore all about knows the customer's needs. It is providing them with the right products at the right time, through the right channels, 24 hours a day, 7 days a week.

A super breed of core banking systems has emerged, which offer functionality in addition to core banking. These systems, called universal banking systems, can accommodate combinations of banking services such as retail, wholesale, private banking and securities trading. An advantage of using a universal system is that the data can be transferred easily between the different modules, so a bank can identify customer trends or selling opportunities. For example, if a customer has high levels of cash balances and also performs securities trading then there may be a sales opportunity for private banking services. A disadvantage is that it is unlikely that a single vendor is able to offer modules that are 'best of breed' in each function. The alternative approach is to use a core banking system and supplement its functionality by using 'best of breed' packages for the specific functionality needed such as foreign exchange trading or portfolio management etc. The following modules are offered by the Core Banking Solutions (CBS):

Customer Information Files Management: This module provides centralised access to all customer-related information. This transaction allows the bank to change the information fields without modifying the underlying software.

Deposit Management: This transactional module offers automated, real-time posting and highly efficient deposit processing for all the balance-based liability products. It also provides back up support for opening, settling, and closing card and check account contracts.

Loan Management: Loan management is an automated process for many lending products like secured and unsecured loans. It helps the bank in creating a flexible/tailor made product portfolio and stream lining the processes according to the customer's need.

Security Management: This facility helps banks to manage the following products and security processes like:

- ❍ Security agreements such as real estate liens, registered liens, pledges, assignments, and guarantees;
- ❍ Security amounts;
- ❍ Encumbrances by the banking institution or a third party;
- ❍ Declaration of purpose (specific or global);
- ❍ Relationships between assets, transactions, and security agreements–including guarantee pools;
- ❍ Assignment and deletion of guarantee;
- ❍ Relevant calculations–including security cover, security distribution, loan-to value ratios, free security and security shortfalls.

Reserve for Bad Debts: This module supports risk monitoring, provisioning, and realization of bad-debt charges.

Limit Management: This module indicates the liability limits and actual liability levels of business units and partners. Limit management checks the transactions against liability limits assigned to the borrowers.

Financial Accounting: The Financial Accounting function supports the general ledger transactions and finance management transactions at all the organizational levels, thus improving the management control and reporting.

Complementary Third-party Products: Complementary third-party products are also available to help the bank by managing the teller machines and payments.

Business Components

a) To have retail customer banking modules;

b) Deposits, loans, bills, remittances, locker, clearing, etc.;

c) Trade finance/forex modules;

d) Government business modules;

e) To have corporate finance and service branch modules;

f) To have enhanced MIS modules;

g) To have modules for business intelligence;

h) To integrate with the existing ATMs, tele-banking, debit card, kiosks and other delivery Channels;

i) To have any branch banking, Internet banking and call centre;

j) To interface with existing corporate systems like treasury, IBR, centralised accounting system, HRMS, ALM, credit appraisal and management, credit monitoring and NPA management, etc.

k) To interface with systems like NDS, SFMS, RTGS, CFMS, etc.

Benefits

a) Enables the establishment of a reliable centralised data repository for the bank;

b) Facilitates data warehousing and data mining technologies for business intelligence;

c) Easy implementation of integrated customer centric services like online ATMs, tele-banking, internet banking, any branch banking, kiosk banking, cash management services, etc.;

d) Enables centralised management information, decision support and executive information systems;

e) Efficient and effective MIS, ALM, risk management, etc., using the central data pool;
f) Enables centralised management and control with centralised data;
g) Standardization of the branch automation software using a single version. Quick adoption of software changes as changes are done only at the central site;
h) Facilitates business process re-engineering (BPR) to streamline the existing processes;
i) Relieves branches of jobs like data backup, MIS generation, etc.;
j) Requires infrastructure at the central location, backup location and at branches;
k) Servers are not mandatory at branch locations;
l) Attracts higher investment in the beginning;
m) Cost of implementation for further branches and delivery channels relatively cheaper;
n) Core infrastructure can be used for future expansions; No extra cost for implementation of SFMS, RTGS, CFMS, etc.

TEST YOURSELF

1. The Reserve Bank of India had appointed a committee on computerisation under the Chairmanship of Dr. C Rangarajan, the then Governor, RBI, in ______ to look into the modalities of drawing up phased plan of computerisation for the banking industry covering the period 1985 to 1989.
(a) 1981 (b) 1982
(c) 1983 (d) 1984

2. What is the meaning of VSAT?
(a) Very Small Aperture Terminals
(b) Very Sensitive Aperture Terminals
(c) Various Small Adjustable Terminals
(d) Various Satellite Aperture Terminals

3. The major objectives of computerisation in banking are to improve:
(a) Customer service
(b) Housekeeping
(c) Productivity and profitability
(d) All of the above

4. The multi-user systems are computers on which ______ can work at the same time.
(a) Single person (b) Two persons
(c) Several people (d) None fo the above

5. Key board of the computer is known as:
(a) Hardware (b) Software
(c) Shareware (d) Digital ware

6. Computerisation at the branch level can be used to:
(a) Provide better and speedy customer service
(b) Generation of various reports.
(c) Analyze the branch-level data for decision making
(d) All of the above

7. RO/ZO acts in between branches and the head office. The most common tasks not performed by the regional office/zonal office are:
(a) Branch profile
(b) Inter-bank reconciliation
(c) Credit monitoring
(d) Personnel data management

8. The head office of a bank is responsible for bank level planning, and control functions, policy decisions. The head office activities are divided into different functional areas like:
(a) Operations (b) Planning
(c) Customer dealing (d) Personnel

9. The computer network that links computers and peripherals within a localised area say, within a building is known as ______.
(a) LAN (b) WAN
(c) MAN (d) TAN

10. In a ______ topology, the central node is often the master. Each of the other nodes is joined to the master by separate links.
(a) Bus (b) Star
(c) Tree (d) Ring

11. Core banking applications provide anywhere, anytime ______ non-stop services, which is not possible with traditional localized branch automation systems.
(a) 12 by 7 (b) 24 by 6
(c) 24 by 7 (d) 12 by 6

12. What is the meaning of UPS?
(a) Uniform Power System
(b) Unchanged Power System
(c) Uninterrupted Pressure System
(d) Uninterrupted Power System

ANSWER

1	2	3	4	5	6	7	8	9	10	11	12
(c)	(a)	(d)	(d)	(a)	(d)	(b)	(c)	(a)	(b)	(c)	(d)

PAYMENT SYSTEMS AND ELECTRONIC BANKING

PAYMENT SYSTEMS

The Digital India programme is a flagship programme of the Government of India with a vision to transform India into a digitally empowered society and knowledge economy. "Faceless, Paperless, Cashless" is one of professed role of Digital India. In a transformative attempt to weed out black money and corruption from public life, the Government of India has constituted a Committee of Officers to enable 100 per cent conversion of Government–Citizen Transactions to the digital platform.

In India, the payment and settlement systems are regulated by the Payment and Settlement Systems Act, 2007 (PSS Act) which was legislated in December 2007. The PSS Act as well as the Payment and Settlement System Regulations, 2008 framed there under came into effect from August 12, 2008.

The Reserve Bank has taken many initiatives towards introducing and upgrading safe and efficient modes of payment systems in the country to meet the requirements of the public at large. The dominant features of large geographic spread of the country and the vast network of branches of the Indian banking system require the logistics of collection and delivery of paper instruments. These aspects of the banking structure in the country have always been kept in mind while developing the payment systems.

ELECTRONIC PAYMENTS SYSTEMS

The initiatives taken by RBI in the mid-eighties and early-nineties focused on technology-based solutions for the improvement of the payment and settlement system infrastructure, coupled with the introduction of new payment products by taking advantage of the technological advancements in banks. The continued increase in the volume of cheques added pressure on the existing set-up, thus necessitating a cost-effective alternative system.

Automated Teller Machine (ATM)

Automated Teller Machine is a computerized machine that provides the customers of banks the facility of accessing their account for dispensing cash and to carry out other financial & non-financial transactions without the need to actually visit their bank branch.

White Label ATMs (WLAs)

ATMs set up, owned and operated by non-banks are called White Label ATMs. Non-bank ATM operators are authorized under Payment & Settlement Systems Act, 2007 by the Reserve Bank of India.

Difference between ATM and WLA (White Label ATM):

(i) In White Label ATM scenario, logo displayed on ATM machine and in ATM premises pertain to WLA Operator instead of a bank. However, for a customer, using WLA is just like using the ATM of other bank (bank other than card issuing bank).

(ii) Acceptance of cash deposits at the WLAs is not permitted at present.

The rationale of allowing non-bank entities for setting up of WLAs: The rationale of allowing non-bank entity to set up White Label ATMs has been to increase the geographical spread of ATM for increased/ enhanced customer service.

Convenience of ATMs/WLAs to the Customers: ATMs are the integral part of the bank customer in modern digital era. Following convenience of ATMs are available by the banks to their Customers:

(a) 24 × 7 access availability;

(b) Less time for transactions (less queue);

(c) Privacy in transactions;

(d) Any branch/anywhere banking enabled;

(e) Acceptability of card across multiple bank ATMs, even foreign tourists can access

(f) Maestro/VISA / ATMs.

Convenience of ATMs to the Bank: Following convenience of ATMs are available for bank in the age of CBS.

(a) Cost of setting up ATMs is lower than setting up a branch;

(b) Migration of the routine transactions to the ATMs frees the bank staff for more productive work;

(c) ATMs serve as the crucial touch point for cross-selling of the bank's products;

(d) Enables the bank to display products on the screen and serves as a media for publicity for the bank;

(e) Less hassle in handling cash.

The following components of the ATM provide the Customer Interface:

(a) Video Display Monitor;

(b) Keyboard/Keypad;

(c) Touch Screen;

(d) Slots.

Slots: There are slots in the ATM for various purposes as detailed below:

(a) Card Reader;

(b) Cash Dispenser;

(c) Envelope Dispenser;

(d) Deposit Slot.

Services/Facilities available at ATMs/WLAs: In addition to cash dispensing, ATMs/WLAs may offer many other services/facilities to bank customers. Some of these services include:

(a) Account Information;

(b) Cash Deposit (Acceptance of deposits are not permitted at WLAs);

(c) Regular Bills Payment (not permitted at WLAs);

(d) Purchase of Re-load Vouchers for Mobiles (not permitted at WLAs);

(e) Mini/Short Statement;

(f) PIN change;

(g) Request for Cheque Book.

How can one transact at an ATM/WLA?

For transacting at an ATM/WLA, the customer inserts / swipes his/her Card in the ATM/WLA and enters his/her Personal Identification Number (PIN). Usually the transactions are menu driven for facilitating easy operation. The cards issued by banks in India may be used at any bank / white label ATM in the country.

Customers Entitled to Any Free Transactions at ATMs

With effect from November 01, 2014, a bank must offer to its savings bank account holders a minimum number of free transactions at ATMs as under:

I. **Transactions at a Bank's own ATMs at any location:** Banks must offer their savings bank account holders a minimum of five free transactions (including both financial and non-financial) in a month, irrespective of the location of ATMs.

II. **Transactions at any other Banks' ATMs at Metro locations:** In case of ATMs located in six metro locations, viz. Mumbai, New Delhi, Chennai, Kolkata, Bengaluru and Hyderabad, banks must offer their savings bank account holders a minimum of three free transactions (including both financial and non-financial transactions) in a month.

III. **Transactions at any other Banks' ATMs at Non-Metro locations:** At other locations, banks must offer the savings bank account holders a minimum of five free transactions (including both financial and non-financial transactions) in a month at other bank ATMs.

RBI has mandated only the minimum number of free transactions at ATMs. Banks may offer more number of transactions free of cost to their customers.

The above does not apply to Basic Savings Bank Deposit Accounts (BSBDA) as withdrawals from BSBDA are subject to the conditions associated with such accounts.

What should be done if Card is lost/stolen?

The customer should contact the card issuing bank immediately on noticing the loss/theft of the card and should request the bank to block the card. Banks are required to display the name and the contact numbers of concerned officers/toll free numbers /help desk numbers in the ATM premises. Similarly, in WLAs, contact number of officials/toll free numbers/ helpline numbers are also displayed for lodging any complaint regarding failed/disputed transactions.

What steps should a customer take in case of failed ATM transaction at other bank/white label ATMs, when his / her account is debited?

The customer should lodge a complaint with the card issuing bank at the earliest. This process is applicable even if the transaction was carried out at another bank's/non-bank's ATM. In case of WLAs, the contact number/toll free numbers are also available for lodging complaints regarding failed transactions at their ATMs.

Compensation for delays beyond 7 working days

Effective from July 1, 2011, banks have to pay compensation of ₹ 100/- per day for delays in re-crediting the amount beyond 7 working days from the date of receipt of complaint for failed ATM transactions. The compensation has to be credited to the account of the customer without any claim being made by the customer. If the complaint is not lodged within 30 days of transaction, the customer is not entitled for any compensation for delay in resolving his / her complaint. The customer can take recourse to the Banking Ombudsman, if the grievance is not redressed by his/ her card issuing bank.

Grievance Redressal Mechanism available to users of WLAs in case of failed/disputed WLA transactions

The Grievance Redressal Mechanism available to users of WLA is same as that available to users of banks' ATMs for failed/disputed transactions. While the primary responsibility to redress grievances of customers relating to failed transactions at such WLAs will vest with the card issuing bank, the sponsor bank will provide necessary support in this regard, ensuring that White Label ATM Operator (WLAO) makes available relevant records and information to the Issuing bank.

What should be done to the ATM card when the card is expired or the account is closed?

Customer should destroy the card upon card expiry or closure of account, cut it into four pieces through the magnetic strip/chip before disposing it off.

Customers should observe following Do's and Don'ts to keep their transaction safe and secure at ATM/WLA:

- Customer should conduct any ATM/WLA transaction in complete privacy;
- Only one card holder should enter and access ATM/WLA kiosk at a time;
- He/she should never lend his/her card to anyone;
- Do not write PIN on the card;
- Never share PIN with anyone or seek help from anybody by handing over the card and revealing the PIN;
- Never let anyone see the PIN while it is being entered at the ATM;
- Never use a PIN that could be easily guessed. e.g. his/her birthday, birthday of spouse or telephone number;
- Never leave card in the ATM/WLA;
- Register mobile number with the card issuing bank for getting alerts for ATM /WLA transactions. Any unauthorized card transaction in the account, if observed, should be immediately reported to the card issuing bank;
- Beware of any extra devices attached to the ATMs/WLAs. These may be put to capture customer's data fraudulently. If any such device is found, inform the security guard / bank/ white label ATM entity maintaining it immediately;
- Keep an eye on suspicious movements of people around ATMs/WLAs. Customer should beware of strangers trying to engaging him/her in conversation or offering assistance / help in operating the ATM;
- Remember that bank officials will never ask for card details or PIN over telephone / email. So, do not respond to any vishing / phishing mails from people indicating that they represent your bank.

HWAK (The Intelligent Auto-teller and Netware Management System)

Intelligent auto-teller systems are a special breed of auto-teller machines capable of thinking for themselves, that means they are fast, impose less demands on your banking systems and serve the customers more like a personal banker than less sophisticated auto teller systems. HWAK provides unsurpassed service even without benefit of a reliable communication network.

NATIONAL PAYMENTS CORPORATION OF INDIA (NPCI)

National Payments Corporation of India (NPCI), an umbrella organisation for operating retail payments and settlement systems in India, is an initiative of Reserve Bank of India (RBI) and Indian Banks' Association (IBA) under the provisions of the Payment and Settlement Systems Act, 2007, for creating a robust Payment & Settlement Infrastructure in India.

Considering the utility nature of the objects of NPCI, it has been incorporated as a "Not for Profit" Company under the provisions of Section 25 of Companies Act 1956 (now Section 8 of Companies Act 2013), with an intention to provide infrastructure to the entire Banking system in India for physical as well as electronic payment and settlement systems. The Company is focused on bringing innovations in the retail payment systems through the use of technology for achieving greater efficiency in operations and widening the reach of payment systems.

The ten core promoter banks are State Bank of India, Punjab National Bank, Canara Bank, Bank of Baroda, Union Bank of India, Bank of India, ICICI Bank, HDFC Bank, Citibank N. A. and HSBC. In 2016 the share holding was broad-based to 56 member banks to include more banks representing all sectors.

NPCI, during its journey in the last seven years, has made a significant impact on the retail payment systems in the country. Dedicated to the nation by our former President, Shri Pranab Mukherjee, endorsed by the Hon'ble Prime Minister, Shri Narendra Modi and later made the card of choice for the ambitious Pradhan Mantri Jan Dhan Yojana, RuPay is now a known name. With Immediate Payment Service (IMPS), India has become the leading country in the world in real time payments in retail sector. Needless to mention, National Financial Switch (NFS) and Cheque Truncation System (CTS) continues to be the flagship products of NPCI. Unified Payments Interface (UPI) has been termed as the revolutionary product in payment system and Bharat Bill Payment System (BBPS) has also been launched in pilot mode. The other products include RuPay Credit Card, National Common Mobility Card (NCMC) and National Electronic Toll Collection (NETC). With these products the aim is to transform India into a 'less-cash' society by touching every Indian with one or other payment services. With each passing year we are moving towards our vision to be the best payments network globally.

RUPAY

The Indian market offers huge potential for cards penetration despite the challenges. RuPay Cards will address the needs of Indian consumers, merchants and banks. The benefits of RuPay debit card are the flexibility of the product platform, high levels of acceptance and the strength of the RuPay brand-all of which will contribute to an increased product experience.

Lower Cost and Affordability: Since the transaction processing will happen domestically, it would lead to lower cost of clearing and settlement for each transaction. This will make the transaction cost affordable and will drive usage of cards in the industry.

Customized Product Offering: RuPay, being a domestic scheme is committed towards development of customized product and service offerings for Indian consumers.

Protection of Information related to Indian Consumers: Transaction and customer data related to RuPay card transactions will reside in India.

Provide Electronic product options to Untapped/ Unexplored Consumer Segment: There are under-penetrated/untapped consumers segments in rural areas that do not have access to banking and financial services. Right pricing of RuPay products would make the RuPay cards more economically feasible for banks to offer to their customers. In addition, relevant product variants would ensure that banks can target the hitherto untapped consumer segments.

Inter-Operability between Payment Channels and Products: RuPay card is uniquely positioned to offer complete inter-operability between various payments channels and products. NPCI currently offers varied solutions across platforms including ATMs, mobile technology, cheques etc and is extremely well placed in nurturing RuPay cards across these platforms.

PERSONAL IDENTIFICATION NUMBER (PIN)

A personal identification number (PIN) is a numeric or alpha-numeric password or code used in the process of authenticating or identifying a user to a system and system to a user. PIN is commonly used in mobile phones where after three tries of entering the pin code the user is asked to inter the Personal unblocking code.

The personal identification number has been the key to flourishing the exchange of private data between different data-processing centers in computer networks for financial institutions, governments, and enterprises. PINs may be used to authenticate banking systems with card holders, governments with citizens, enterprises with employees, and computers with users, among other uses.

In common usage, PINs are used in ATM or POS transactions, secure access control (e.g. computer access, smart phone access, door access, car access), internet transactions, or to log into a restricted website.

ELECTROMAGNETIC CARDS

A magnetic stripe card is a type of card capable of storing data by modifying the magnetism of tiny iron-based magnetic particles on a band of magnetic material on the card. The magnetic stripe, sometimes called swipe card or magnetic stripe, is read by swiping past a magnetic reading head. Magnetic stripe cards are commonly used in credit cards, identity cards, and transportation tickets. They may also contain an RFID tag, a transponder device and/or a microchip mostly used for business premises access control or electronic payment.

- **Credit Card:** It allows the card holder to pay for goods and services based on the holder's promise to pay for them. The issuer of the card creates a revolving account and grants a line of credit to the card holder, from which the user can borrow money for payment to a merchant or as a cash advance. The size of most credit cards is 3 3D 8 × 2 1D 8 in (85.60 × 53.98 mm). It allows the consumers a continuing balance of debt, subject to interest being charged.
- **Charge Card:** Transactions are accumulated over a period of time, generally a month and the total amount charged, *i.e.*, debited to the account. The credit card holder is given about 25 to 50 days' time to credit his account in case there are insufficient funds in his account at the time of debit. Since the transactions are accumulated, it is only charged, *i.e.*, not debited to the account immediately, such cards are called charge cards.
- **Debit Card:** A debit card (also known as a bank card or check card) is a plastic payment card that provides the card holder electronic access to their bank account(s). Payments using a debit card are immediately transferred from the card holder's designated bank account.
- **Electronic Purse:** Type of smart card which, with an embedded microchip, provides multiple options, such as debit card or credit card type payments.
- **Smart Card:** A smart card is a payment card embedded with a computer chip, essentially functioning like a mini-computer on a card. The memory and the computing power of the chip on the card could transform payments in many ways. The chip, a true technological break-through, holds at least 80 times more data than the magnetic stripe on existing credit cards.

ELECTRONIC BANKING

Unlike the magnetic stripe, the chip can process data as well as store it, and because each program on the chip runs on independent software, several different programs can operate on the same card at the same time.

- **An added Bonus:** The smart card is a more secure method of payment that protects the card holder's account information from fraudulent use.
- **Electronic Cheque:** The smart card can be used during electronic fund transfer at the point-of-sales (EFTPOS). At a retailer's checkout, the card is placed in the reader, where it automatically goes through authentication sequences.
- **Electronic Cash:** Funds can be loaded into a card for use as cash. This electronic cash can then be used for making purchases.
- **Electronic Token:** The principle here is that a prepaid area is set aside to store electronic units of time or electronic tickets, etc., for a specific service or item. Magnetic strip cards are often used with public telephones, parking meters and vending machines.

Anytime Banking: ATMs have eliminated the time limitations of customer service, and offer a host of banking services, including deposits, withdrawals, requisitions, instructions and transfers. HSBC Ltd., for instance, has taken the concept of remote banking further by providing a service called Hexagon, which allows the customer to access his accounts from a PC that is installed at his office or at his home–that is desktop banking–for the customer.

Anywhere Banking: With the introduction of ATMs and tele-banking, financial details can be accessed from remote locations and basic transactions can be effected even outside the bank.

Corporate Banking: At present, by utilising remote banking facility, corporate customers will be able to get the following services:

(a) Getting their current balance or getting their statement of accounts for any pre-defined;

(b) Period;

(c) Ordering cheque books;

(d) Ordering intra-bank and inter-bank fund transfers;

(e) Instructing stop payments of cheques;

(f) International remittances;

(g) Opening letter of credits.

CHEQUE TRUNCATION SYSTEM

Truncation is the process of stopping the flow of the physical cheque issued by a drawer at some point by the presenting bank en-route to the paying bank branch. In its place an electronic image of the cheque is transmitted to the paying branch through the clearing house, along with relevant information like data on the MICR band, date of presentation, presenting bank, etc. Cheque truncation thus obviates the need to move the physical instruments across bank branches, other than in exceptional circumstances for clearing purposes. This effectively eliminates the associated cost of movement of the physical cheques, reduces the time required for their collection and brings elegance to the entire activity of cheque processing.

Cheque Truncation in India: Cheque Truncation speeds up the process of collection of cheques resulting in better service to customers, reduces the scope of loss of instruments in transit, lowers the cost of collection of cheques, and removes reconciliation-related and logistics-related problems, thus benefitting the system as a whole.

With the other major products being offered in the form of RTGS and NEFT, the Reserve Bank has created the capability to enable inter-bank and customer payments online and in near-real time. However, cheques continue to be the prominent mode of payments in the country. Reserve Bank of India has therefore decided to focus on improving the efficiency of the cheque clearing cycle. Offering Cheque Truncation System (CTS) is a step in this direction.

In addition to operational efficiency, CTS offers several benefits to banks and customers, including human resource rationalization, cost effectiveness, business process re-engineering, better service, adoption of latest technology, etc. CTS, thus, has emerged as an important efficiency enhancement initiative undertaken by Reserve Bank in the Payments Systems arena.

Status of CTS implementation in the country: CTS has been implemented in New Delhi, Chennai and Mumbai with effect from February 1, 2008, September 24, 2011 and April 27, 2013 respectively. After migration of the entire cheque volume from MICR system to CTS, the traditional MICR-based cheque processing has been discontinued across the country.

Benefits of CTS to Customers of Banks: The benefits are many. With the introduction of imaging and truncation, the physical movement of instruments is stopped. The electronic movement of images can facilitate reduction in the clearing cycles as well. Moreover, there is no fear of loss of instruments in transit. Further, limitations of the existing clearing system in terms of geography or jurisdiction can be removed, thus enabling consolidation and integration of multiple clearing locations managed by different banks with varying service levels into a nation-wide standard clearing system with uniform processes and practices.

Under grid-based Cheque Truncation System clearing, all cheques drawn on bank branches falling within in the grid jurisdiction are treated and cleared as local cheques. No outstation cheque collection charges/Speed Clearing charges to be levied if the collecting bank and the paying bank are located within the jurisdiction of the same CTS grid even though they are located in different cities.

CTS also benefits issuers of cheques. The Corporates if needed can be provided with images of cheques by their bankers for internal requirements, if any.

CTS thus brings elegance to the entire activity of cheque processing and clearing. The benefits from CTS could be summarized as follows :

- Shorter clearing cycle;
- Superior verification and reconciliation process;
- No geographical restrictions as to jurisdiction;
- Operational efficiency for banks and customers alike;
- Reduction in operational risk and risks associated with paper clearing;
- No collection charges for collection of cheque drawn on a bank located within the grid.

CURRENCY-COUNTING MACHINE

A currency-counting machine is a machine that counts money—either stacks of bank notes or loose collections of coins. Counters may be purely mechanical or use electronic components. The machines typically provide a total count of all money, or count off specific batch sizes for wrapping and storage.

Currency counters are commonly used in vending machines to determine what amount of money has been deposited by customers.

In some modern automated teller machines, currency counters allow for cash deposits without envelopes, since they can identify which bills have been inserted instead of just how many. The user is given the chance to review the automatic counter's idea of the quantity and kinds of the inserted bank notes before the deposit is complete.

MICROFICHE

Microfiche is a thin photographic film, usually four by five inches, which is capable of storing information in miniaturized form. This technique is used in preserving fragile materials such as archival documents, journals, books, newspapers and magazines, as well as a method of saving space in libraries and other archives.

Microfiche is easy to use and does not require specialized knowledge or software to use it. The documents are photographed and stored in the small space of the microfiche card. The images are too small to be read by the naked eye. In order to read the information on the microfiche, a special device is used to greatly magnify the contents. Like microfilm, microfiche is available as positive and negative images, although negative images are more common.

There are many advantages when microfiche is used, like easy storage. Many documents can be stored in a small space, as a single sheet can store numerous images. It also provides an easy and convenient way to access grouped documents. Updating is also easy, as a new sheet can be added to the file at any point of time, and this helps in keeping the documents organized. This is one of the biggest reasons for using it for archiving photos, newspapers, journals and other documents. Microfiche is a flat film sheet and does not require the spinning of film onto reels, as in case of microfilm. Microfiche also takes less space and has fewer storage requirements compared to microfilm.

One of the major disadvantages of using microfiche is the portability factor. It requires special devices for reading and duplicating the cards, and the special equipment is expensive. Microfiche is also more expensive than microfilm to produce.

TEST YOURSELF

1. The PSS Act as well as the Payment and Settlement System Regulations, 2008 framed there under came into effect from August 12, ________.

(a) 2007 (b) 2008
(c) 2009 (d) 2010

2. What is the meaning of ATM?

(a) Automatic Teller Machine
(b) Automated Transfer Machine
(c) Automatic Talking Machine
(d) Automated Teller Machine

3. ATMs set up, owned and operated by non-banks are called ________.

(a) White Label ATMs
(b) Black Label ATMs
(c) Off-site ATM
(d) On-site ATM

4. ATMs are the integral part of the bank customer in modern digital era. Which of the following convenience of ATMs are not available by the banks to their Customers:

(a) 24 x 6 access availability
(b) Less time for transactions
(c) Privacy in transactions
(d) Any branch/anywhere banking enabled

5. The following components of the ATM does not provide the customer interface:

(a) Video Display Monitor
(b) Keyboard/Keypad;
(c) Touch Screen
(d) Mouse

6. There are slots in the ATM for various purposes. Which is not available?

(a) Card Reader
(b) Cash Dispenser
(c) Coin Dispenser
(d) Deposit Slot

7. Which is correct about PIN of ATM?

(a) It is four-digit alfa-numerical code
(b) It is five-digit numerical code
(c) Bank requests to customer to change the pin on first use
(d) PIN can't changed

8. What steps should a customer take in case of failed ATM transaction at other bank/white label ATMs, when his/her account is debited? The customer should lodge a complaint with the card ________ at the earliest.

(a) Issuing bank
(b) Paying bank
(c) Master/Visa card
(d) NPCI

9. Effective from July 1, 2011, banks have to pay compensation of ₹ 100/- per day for delays in re-crediting the amount beyond ________ days from the date of receipt of complaint for failed ATM transactions.

(a) 5 (b) 7
(c) 5 working (d) 7 working

10. National Payments Corporation of India (NPCI), an umbrella organisation for operating retail payments

and settlement systems in India, is an initiative of Reserve Bank of India (RBI) and ______ under the provisions of the Payment and Settlement Systems Act, 2007.
(a) Govt. of India
(b) Indian Banks' Association (IBA)
(c) IIBF
(d) NABARD

11. Considering the utility nature of the objects of NPCI, it has been incorporated as a "Not for Profit" ______.
(a) Company (b) Trust
(c) Society (d) Firm

12. The benefits of RuPay debit card are the flexibility of the product platform, high levels of acceptance. Find the benefits of RuPay:
(a) Lower cost and affordability
(b) Customized product offering
(c) Protection of information related to Indian consumers
(d) All of the above

13. Which is not used as a magnetic stripe card?
(a) Credit Card
(b) Charge Card
(c) Electronic Purse
(d) All of the above

14. The principle here is that a prepaid area is set aside to store electronic units of time or electronic tickets, etc., for a specific service or item is called:
(a) Electronic Cheque
(b) Electronic Cash
(c) Electronic Token
(d) Electronic Card

15. At present, by utilising remote banking facility, corporate customers will be able to get which of the following services:
(a) Getting their current balance or statement of accounts
(b) Opening letter of credits
(c) Ordering intra-bank and inter-bank fund transfers
(d) All of the above

16. Which are the benefits from CTS (Cheque Truncation Systems)?
(a) Shorter clearing cycle
(b) Superior verification and reconciliation process
(c) No geographical restrictions
(d) All of the above

ANSWER

1	2	3	4	5	6	7	8	9	10
(b)	(d)	(a)	(a)	(d)	(c)	(c)	(a)	(d)	(b)
11	**12**	**13**	**14**	**15**	**16**				
(a)	(d)	(d)	(c)	(d)	(d)				

DATA COMMUNICATION NETWORK AND EFT SYSTEMS

INTRODUCTION

Data communication through the telephone network can reach at any point in the world. The volume of overseas fax transmission is increasing constantly, and computer network that link thousands of business, government and universities are universal. Transmission over such distance are not generally accomplished with a direct wire digital link, but rather with digitally modulated analog carrier signals. This technique makes it possible to use existing analog telephone voice channels for digital data.

DATA COMMUNICATION

Data communications are the exchange of data between two devices via some form of transmission medium such as a wire cable. For data communications to occur, the communicating devices must be part of a communication system made up of a combination of hardware (physical equipment) and software (programs). The effectiveness of a data communications system depends on four fundamental characteristics: delivery, accuracy, time lines, and jitter.

1. **Delivery:** The system must deliver data to the correct destination. Data must be received by the intended device or user and only by that device or user.
2. **Accuracy:** The system must deliver the data accurately. Data that have been altered in transmission and left uncorrected are unusable.
3. **Timeliness:** The system must deliver data in a timely manner. Data delivered late are useless. In the case of video and audio, timely delivery means delivering data as they are produced, in the same order that they are produced, and without significant delay. This kind of delivery is called real-time transmission.
4. **Jitter:** Jitter refers to the variation in the packet arrival time. It is the uneven delay in the delivery of audio or video packets.

Components

A data communications system has five components.

1. **Message:** The message is the information (data) to be communicated. Popular forms of information include text, numbers, pictures, audio, and video.
2. **Sender**: The sender is the device that sends the data message. It can be a computer, workstation, telephone handset, video camera, and so on.
3. **Receiver:** The receiver is the device that receives the message. It can be a computer, workstation, telephone handset, television, and so on.
4. **Transmission Medium:** The transmission medium is the physical path by which a message travels from sender to receiver. Some examples of transmission media include twisted-pair wire, coaxial cable, fiber-optic cable, and radio waves.
5. **Protocol:** A protocol is a set of rules that govern data communications. It represents an agreement between the communicating devices.

Data Transmission Modes

Data transmission occurs in one of three modes. Communication between two devices can be simplex, half-duplex, or full-duplex.

1. **Simplex:** In simplex mode, the communication is unidirectional, as on a one-way street. Only one of the two devices on a link can transmit; the other can only receive. Keyboards and traditional monitors are examples of simplex devices. The keyboard can only introduce input; the monitor can only accept output. The simplex mode can use the entire capacity of the channel to send data in one direction.
2. **Half-Duplex:** In half-duplex mode, each station can both transmit and receive, but not at the same time. When one device is sending, the other can only receive, and vice versa. In a half-duplex transmission, the entire capacity of a channel is taken over by whichever of the two devices is transmitting at the time. Walkie-talkies and CB (citizens band) radios are both half-duplex systems. The half-duplex mode is used in cases where there is no need for communication in both directions at the same time; the entire capacity of the channel can be utilized for each direction.
3. **Full-Duplex:** In full-duplex both stations can transmit and receive simultaneously. The full-duplex mode is like a two-way street with traffic flowing in both directions at the same time. In full-duplex mode, signals going in one direction share the capacity of the link: with signals going in the other direction. One common example of full-duplex communication is the telephone network. When two people are communicating by a telephone line, both can talk and listen at the same time. The full-duplex mode is used when communication in both directions is required all the time. The capacity of the channel, however, must be divided between the two directions.

Communication Media

Communication media are the physical channels through which information is transmitted between computers in a network. Media may be classified as bounded (*i.e.*, wires, cables and optical fibres) or unbounded (*i.e.*, ether or airwaves) through which radio, Transmitted data can move along simplex, half-duplex or full-duplex lines depending on the needs and protocols involved.

1. **Bound Media:** Twisted-pair of wires are inexpensive media used in voice grade telephone lines. They are used for low speed transmission of signals of the order of 1200 bps. Coaxial cables can be used for high-speed data transmission over distance of several kms. Coaxial cables have wide bandwidth of the order of 400 MHz. They may be used in LAN at transmission rates of about 1 Mega bps. Fibre Optics cables are glass fibres that provide high quality transmission of signals at very high speeds of nearly 1000 Megabits per second (Mbps) for distances up to 25 miles.
2. **Unbound Media:** Radio wave in the very high frequency band (VHF) at about 300 MHz is used for communication between computers in inaccessible locations or for short-range communications. Micro-waves are used for wide bandwidth line-of-sight communication. Rates of transmission up to 20 Giga bps is possible with this media. Communication satellite acts as microwave relay station is the sky. Transponders on the satellite are used to receive, amplify and retransmit signals sent from an earth station. The main advantage of satellite is its wide coverage of a large area and thus it may be used from inaccessible location. A transponder has a very large capacity and can handle about 400 channels, each channel having 64 kbps speed.

Communication Components

Followings are the Communication Components:

1. **Modems:** A MODEM is a Modulation Demodulation device that converts the discrete stream of digital "on-off" electric pulses used by computers into the analog wave patterns used for transmission of the human voice. Demodulator (recovers) the digital data from the transmitted signal. A special type of MODEM called an acoustic coupler is often used in libraries and information units with portable machines, but internal and external direct-connect MODEMs are generally used at permanent stations.
2. **Multiplexers:** A multiplexer is a device used for transmission of several messages over a single channel using predetermined frequencies within the full bandwidth. The multiplexer operates on the principle that individual channel may require only a small account of actual transmission time; thus, the multiplexer acts almost as a time-share computer allocating use of the single communication lines on a priority basis. A multiplexer is capable of accepting as many as 45 separate channels for transmitting data on a single communication line.

3. **Concentrators (Data Switch):** A concentrator is a switch that allocates a particular input to a particular output. While a multi-plexer combines the inputs on a high-speed line; the concentrator allocates a particular input to the line for the duration of its information transfer. The allocation of the output line to a specific input depends on when the request is made, the speed of the input line, and the class or importance of the request.

4. **Front-end Processors:** Front-end processors are installed to handle communication related functions for a mainframe computer so that the later can be fully used for processing applications, be it an inquiry to a database, a printing job or updating a master file, etc... The aim of the front-end processor is to provide an inter-face between the mainframe computer and the network so that the data is passed to and from the mainframe efficiently. The front-end processor is responsible for supervision of the input/output controllers or channels attached to the network, for providing buffering and partial processing of in-coming and outgoing data, for the assembling and dissembling of messages and for error handling.

DATA COMMUNICATION NETWORKS IN INDIA

The progress in networking in India has been rather slow due to the poor extension of telecommunication networks and overwhelming use of resources and expertise that are available. However, the scene is changing fast. The Department of Telecommunication is setting up a Public Data Network (PDN) and has plans to expand and revamp the existing telephone system. The potential of data networks in India has already been recognized, and few networks have already come into operation.

Networks that are already in operation or in various stages of development may be classified into the following two categories depending upon their scope and objectives:

1. **National Informatics Centre Network (NICNET):** The satellite based National Informatics Network (NICNET) was set upto provide informatics services to the Central and State Government Departments and its organisations. The NICNET provides computing and two-way data communication infrastructure to aid planning and monitoring of schemes and decision-making activities in the Government.

   The NICNET has expanded as a dedicated network having more than 500 nodes geographically distributed over the country, to address the rapidly growing awareness to computerization in different sectors of the Government. Each district information centre consolidates information for monitoring the socio-economic development of the district. Each district is connected to its State's information centre for flow of information from district level to State level. The State centre in turn sends processed information to the regional and the national centres and is also connected to other States. Hence, any user connected to a remote or master earth station can link to any other remote micro earth station. The national centre at the New Delhi is repository of all information systems and conducts research and development of relevant software and hardware tools.

2. **INDONET:** The INDONET data network was engineered by CMC Limited for the computer user community in India. It is an integrated information management and distributed data processing facility. The INDONET aims to provide facility for distributed data processing on all India basis to large organizations in the network using the CMC computers for their data processing operations. It also plans for provision of data comm-unications between its users in their respective locations in the network, even if the users are not accessing CMC's nodal computers. Distributed databases in various subjects and access to specialized applications software locally, or in remote locations obviate the need for duplication of software and hardware facilities at each location. The INDONET nodes at Bangalore, Mumbai, Delhi, Hyderabad and Pune are connected to the GPSS of the Videsh Sanchar Nigam Limited, thereby facilitating entry to Public Data Networks of other countries.

   In phase I, an experimental INDONET Pilot Satellite Network (IPSN) incorporating all the features of the proposed INDONET was worked out. IPSN connects nodes in Mumbai, Kolkata, Chennai, Delhi, Hyderabad, Bangalore, Vishakhapatnam, Ahmedabad and Pune with IBM 436 computers and MUXs/cluster controllers. The network uses IBM's Computers and Systems Network Architecture and 4800 bps leased lines, 9600 bps packet radio links for intra-city connection.

   In the second phase, the INDONET would operate as a Star Network with control point in Delhi using root top 3-m earth stations and packet switching. Beside SNA, it will also support X. 25 protocols satellite and radio communication the INDONET is expected to cover 35 major cities of India. The CMC Ltd. is closely involved with NISSAT activities in library networking programmes in Kolkata and Delhi.

3. **VIKRAM:** Vikram is the packet switched public data network under development by the Department of Telecommunications. This network will initially have 8 switching nodes in Delhi, Mumbai, Kolkata, Chennai, Bangalore, Hyderabad, Ahmedabad and Pune and 12 remote access nodes with its network management centre located at Delhi. It will support packet switching interface to CCITTs X.25, X.28, X.29 and X.75 recommendations.

4. **BANKNET:** The Bank recognised the pressing need to harness information technology for intra-bank and inter-bank communications in the 1980s and set up BANKNET. The design and implementation of BANKNET was entrusted to M/s. CMC.

   Commissioned in 1991, BANKNET is a packet switched X.25 based network with nodes at Mumbai, Delhi, Chennai and Kolkata, and a switching centre at Nagpur with a mesh topology. In addition, Bangalore and Hyderabad are connected to Chennai through remote PADs. IBM 4381 mainframes at the 4 NCCs, connected to nodal Packet Switch Exchanges (PSEs) through Front-End processors using NCP/NPSI (Network Control Program/Network Packet Switching Interface), provide messaging facility. BANKNET uses a store-and-collect transmission logic, provided by the Message Transfer Utility(MTU), in the systems.

5. **RBI Net:** RBI Net, a communication software, developed in 'C' and available for both DOS and UNIX machines, allows free format messaging and file transfer on the existing BANK NET infrastructure with the help of UNIX servers installed at the 4 NCCs. Each RBI Net user interacts with the local UNIX server through PADs connected to the X.25 switch. The UNIX servers in turn communicate with each other using TCP/IP over the X.25 protocol. The software allows free format messaging without any restrictions on the length of the message, enables file transfer of both ASCII-text and Binary (spread sheets, data bases, programs etc.) files, facilitates dial-up access, and has security features such as end-to-end encryption, audit trail, etc.

   RBI Net is also being used by several Departments of the Bank for various applications such as:

   (i) Transmission of Sec 42(2) of the RBI Act, 1934, data by commercial banks to Regional offices of Department of Banking Operations and Development (DBOD) and furnishing of consolidated data by the Regional offices of DBOD to Central DBOD;

   (ii) Press Relations Division daily news summary of important financial matters;

   (iii) Department of Economic Analysis and Policy Macro Economic Indicators on a weekly basis.

EMERGING TRENDS IN COMMUNICATION NETWORKS FOR BANKING

The Reserve Bank has been taking a number of initiatives for upgradation of technology and bringing the masses under the banking system. Towards this, banks are being encouraged to computerize their operation and connect the branch under the core banking solution so that the branch can provide efficient services by participation in all India funds transfer network like RTGS/NEFT/ECS, etc. But the rural branches have remained largely outside core banking due to connectivity problem. The problem is more for the bank branches in the North Eastern Region.

The Reserve Bank, while playing its developmental role is considering a proposal to provide incentive to banks to provide network connectivity to their existing branches in the under banked districts. There is also a proposal to incentives the banks to open new branches at these locations and bring them under core banking solution right from the beginning.

Satellite Connectivity

As opposed to terrestrial link, satellite connectivity involves use of transponder space on the satellite and communication equipment called Very Small Aperture Terminal (VSAT) at the place being connected for data communication. VSAT is particularly useful in the regions where leased line connectivity cannot be established like hilly areas, ocean, and desert. VSAT technologies ensure link security and reliability. The benefits of VSAT are:

a) Faster relocation;
b) Quick establishment of new sites;
c) Rapid installation of equipment at the customer's premise with limited infrastructure;
d) Reduced Network implementation time;
e) Availability (99.9%) is far better than the availability of ground networks - reliability of data network;

f) Lowest TCO over terrestrial for multistage applications;

g) Highest uptime;

h) Security-VSAT networks are very secure and the ideal option for confidential, business sensitive data transfer;

i) Bandwidth on demand—the bandwidth channels can be regulated Independence from earth networks and infrastructure; and

j) Reduced operational cost.

Some of the important aspects on which the terms of reference of the Committee mainly concentrated on relate to issues such as network architecture and application architecture, for the Indian Financial Network (INFINET). The Committee therefore held detailed deliberations on the strategies to be followed on the following issues:

a) The components of the financial system backbone and the need for integration of INFINET and terrestrial links keeping in view the future traffic needs, backup and disaster management system.

b) The type of applications to be given priority for implementation on the backbone being provided by the Institute for Development and Research in Banking Technology (IDRBT) set up by the Reserve Bank of India.

c) The technology plan for the financial sector.

d) Optimal utilisation of network resources.

INFINET-Network component

In order to upgrade the country's payment and settlement systems, the Reserve Bank of India took the initiative of providing a communication backbone in the form of a satellite network based on VSAT technology to the Banking and Financial Sector and entrusted the work to IDRBT. As the bandwidth at present on INFINET is limited, it may have to be optimally used. This would need allocation of bandwidth to various users and appropriate configuration of ports for dealing with different types of applications viz., burst, transaction oriented, streams by employing appropriate Access Mechanism.

Three access modes viz., the aloha mode, the transaction reservation mode and the stream mode, would be in place in the VSAT based INFINET.

Financial Network Architecture

A Financial Network in the form of a reliable communication backbone facilitates running different applications/services, which eventually result in:

a) Banking and Financial services independent of their location;

b) Extended banking business reach and hours as well as increased business volume and better fund utilisation, thereby facilitating reduced operational cost;

c) Increased security;

d) Reduction/elimination of payment risks;

e) Efficient Housekeeping;

f) Improvement in decision making process;

g) Innovative customer-oriented delivery mechanisms.

The primary objective of INFINET for the banking and financial sector is to enhance efficiency and productivity on the one hand and provide state-of-the-art customer services through innovative delivery channels such as Internet banking, home banking etc., on the other.

Both the inter-bank and intra-bank applications that will use the INFINET are still in the development stage. As time progresses, both the RBI and participating banks would go for bandwidth hungry applications. The total bandwidth available currently will be shared by all the participating banks. Apart from the State Bank of India (SBI), and public-sector banks, other banks, financial institutions, non-banking finance companies, Primary/Satellite dealers in Government Securities which need to communicate with the RBI are also keen to have connectivity to INFINET. The participating banks would in course of time connect their regional/controlling offices with currency chest branches and branches with other commercially critical activities.

Integration of VSAT and Terrestrial Network

While the INFINET should ideally be a blend of different types of media with seamless integration so that the backbone is transparent to the users of the network, the existing rules of the regulatory Authority permit intra-city link to VSATs only through leased lines. Public Switched Telephone Network (PSTN) dial-up link with intra-city and inter-city links to VSATs are not allowed. However, a bank's existing network can be linked to the Hub site through leased lines. The current restrictions result in a major bottleneck in providing cost effective connectivity to the users. This matter has to be vigorously pursued with the regulatory Authority, by the Reserve Bank of India and Indian Banks Association, and the constraints removed. The need for Integrated Subscribers Digital Network (ISDN) connection to VSAT—both inter and intra-city—should also be pursued with the regulatory Authority.

ELECTRONIC FUNDS TRANSFER (EFT) SYSTEM

The system was started in 1996 between Mumbai and Chennai to facilitate transferring of funds between these two cities, across branches and banks. Although the system is inter-bank in orientation, intra-bank transfer would also be possible. In this system, banks can accept request from their customers irrespective of whether the beneficiary happens to be an account holder or another bank. Customers of around 2500 branches of nationalised banks are getting benefited. This scheme works on the principle of Next Day Availability of Funds. The beneficiary gets funds on the next day. Transaction has to be up to ₹ 5,00,000. Those banks which are not computerised can also be linked with the scheme with the help of their service branches. RBI NET is being used for transmitting EFT-messages. RBI acts as a service-provider as well as regulator.

SOCIETY FOR WORLDWIDE INTER-BANK FINANCIAL TELECOMMUNICATION (SWIFT)

India was the 74th country to join the Society for Worldwide Inter-bank Financial Telecommunication (SWIFT) network on December 2, 1991. The initial membership of Banks in India was 34. Using advanced data-processing and telecommunications technology, the SWIFT system is based on the following features:

a) it is available worldwide, 24 hours a day, 7 days a week;
b) standard message formats for transactions enable members to avoid language and interpretation problems and permit the automated handling of messages;
c) delivery of a message is very 'swift';
d) ensures a high level of security while transmitting all messages;
e) assumes financial liability for the accuracy, completeness and timely delivery of all validated messages.

Each country has a SWIFT gateway called the SWIFT Access Point (SAP) to which the individual users' terminals are connected. The users are connected to the SAP through leased lines with PSTN as backup. The SAPs are connected to the Regional Processors, which in turn are connected on-line to mother operating centres in the USA and Netherlands from where the messages are distributed to the ultimate destination address indicated in each message.

SWIFT has 9 types of Standard Message Categories. Each broad Message category has various message types for specific uses. A majority of the forex related messages are sent to correspondent banks abroad through SWIFT.

AUTOMATED CLEARING HOUSE (ACH)

An automated clearing house (ACH) is an electronic funds-transfer system run by the National Automated Clearing House Association (NACHA). This payment system deals with payroll, direct deposit, tax refunds, consumer bills, tax payments and many more payment services.

The use of the ACH network to facilitate electronic transfers of money has increased the efficiency and timeliness of government and business transactions.

1. **Clearing House Inter-Bank Payments System (CHIPS)**: The Clearing House Inter-bank Payments System (CHIPS) is the primary clearing house in the U.S. for large banking transactions. As of 2015, CHIPS settles over 250,000 of trades per day, valued in excess of $1.5 trillion in both domestic and cross-border transactions. CHIPS and the Fedwire funds service used by the Federal Reserve Bank combine to constitute the primary network in the U.S. for both domestic and foreign large transactions denominated in U.S. dollars.
2. **Clearing House Automated Payments System (CHAPS):** Clearing House Automated Payments System (CHAPS) is a British company that facilitates the trading of European currency. CHAPS provide same-day fund transfers for the sterling and the euro. CHAPS transfers are used when money needs to be moved from one account to another. CHAPS transfers are fairly costly, with an average fee of 30 pounds per transfer. CHAPS eliminate float time that occurs with check writing and prohibits the sender from rescinding the payment.
3. **Clearing House Automated Transfer System (CHATS):** The Clearing House Automated Transfer System, or CHATS, is a Real Time Gross Settlement (RTGS) system for the transfer of funds in Hong Kong. It is operated by Hong Kong Inter-bank Clearing Limited, a private company jointly owned by the Hong Kong Monetary Authority (HKMA) and the Hong Kong Association of Banks. Transactions in four currency denominations may be settled using CHATS: Hong Kong dollar, renminbi, euro, and US dollar.

ELECTRONIC CLEARANCE SYSTEM (ECS)

ECS is an electronic mode of payment/receipt for transactions that are repetitive and periodic in nature.

ECS is used by institutions for making bulk payment of amounts towards distribution of dividend, interest, salary, pension, etc., or for bulk collection of amounts towards telephone / electricity / water dues, cess / tax collections, loan instalment repayments, periodic investments in mutual funds, insurance premium etc. Essentially, ECS facilitates bulk transfer of monies from one bank account to many bank accounts or vice versa. Electronic clearance system is again categorized into two categories like ECS (credit) and ECS (Debit).

ECS (Credit): ECS (credit) is a new method of payment introduced by Reserve Bank of India which provides customers an option to collect their monthly/ quarterly/half yearly/yearly interest/dividend/ salary / pension directly through their bank accounts. The customer's bank account would be credited through the new payment mechanism, on the due date. In this system payment instruction would be issued by the bank electronically through the banker to the Clearing Authority and the Clearing Authority would supply credit reports to the bank with which customer maintains the specified account. The branch will credit the customer's account and indicate the credit entry as 'ECS' in his passbook/ statement of account. Individual transactions without any monetary ceiling would be covered under the Scheme. If customers maintain more than one bank account, payment can be received at any of these accounts. The customer need not open any new bank account for the same. This would only be an additional mode of payment and would be optional. The customer can have the right to withdraw from this mode of payment by giving an advance notice of 6 weeks.

ECS (Debit): In this scenario, the Reserve Bank of India has implemented an off-line electronic funds transfer system allowing paperless direct debit and credit transactions by banks, viz. Electronic Clearing Service. After successful implementation of ECS-Credit scheme, Reserve Bank of India initiated the ECS-Debit, a facility of payment of pre-authorised debits through ECS. ECS Debit Clearing Scheme approved by Committee on Technology Issues in Banking Industry (Payment System and Cheque Clearance System) under the chairmanship of Shri W.S. Saraf, the then Executive Director, Reserve Bank of India, was introduced. This ECS allows customer to pay their monthly/quarterly/half yearly/yearly utility bills like telephone, electricity, loan installments, insurance premium etc directly through their bank accounts. The customer's bank account would be debited through the new payment mechanism right on the due date. The customer would be advised in the usual manner to pay the bill. The payment instruction would be issued by us electronically through our banker to the Clearing Authority and the Clearing Authority would supply debit reports to the bank with which customer maintain the specified account. The branch will debit the customer's account and indicate the debit entry as 'ECS' in customer's passbook/statement of account. If the customer maintains more than one bank account, payment can be received from any of these accounts. The customer need not open any new bank account for this purpose. This would only be an additional mode of payment and would be optional. The customer would have the right to withdraw from this mode of payment by giving an advance notice of 2 weeks. The customer's complaint, if any, (the scope of which is very limited) would be immediately dealt with and in that situation the bank assures the customer to give a reply within 15 days.

NATIONAL ELECTRONIC FUNDS TRANSFER (NEFT) SYSTEM

Introduction: National Electronic Funds Transfer (NEFT) is a nation-wide payment system facilitating one-to-one funds transfer. Under this Scheme, individuals, firms and corporates can electronically transfer funds from any bank branch to any individual, firm or corporate having an account with any other bank branch in the country participating in the Scheme.

Reserve Bank of India has introduced an electronic funds transfer system called "National Electronic Funds Transfer" System (hereinafter referred to as "NEFT System" or "NEFT" or "System", as appropriate). A set of procedures to be followed by various stakeholders to the system are detailed in this document.

Objective: The objective of the NEFT System is to establish an electronic funds transfer system to facilitate an efficient, secure, economical, reliable and expeditious system of funds transfer and clearing in the banking sector throughout India, and to relieve the stress on the existing paper-based funds transfer and clearing system.

Coverage: These procedural guidelines shall apply to all NEFT-enabled participating banks/and branches in the system as notified by Reserve Bank of India from time to time on its official website.

Limit on the amount that could be transferred using NEFT: There is no limit either minimum or maximum on the amount of funds that could be transferred using NEFT. However, maximum amount per transaction is limited to ₹ 50,000/- for cash-based remittances within India and also for remittances to Nepal under the Indo-Nepal Remittance Facility Scheme.

Operating hours of NEFT: From July 10, 2017 settlements of fund transfer requests in NEFT system is done on half-hourly basis. There are twenty-three half-hourly settlement batches run from 8 am to 7 pm on all working days of week (Except 2nd and 4th Saturday of the month).

NEFT System Operation

NEFT system is operating in following steps:

Step-1: An individual / firm / corporate intending to originate transfer of funds through NEFT has to fill an application form providing details of the beneficiary (like name of the beneficiary, name of the bank branch where the beneficiary has an account, IFSC of the beneficiary bank branch, account type and account number) and the amount to be remitted. The application form will be available at NEFT enabled originating bank branch. The remitter authorizes his/her bank branch to debit his account and remit the specified amount to the beneficiary. Customers enjoying net banking facility offered by their bankers can also initiate the funds transfer request online. Some banks offer the NEFT facility even through the ATMs. Walk-in customers will, however, have to give their contact details (complete address and telephone number, etc.) to the branch. This will help the branch to refund the money to the customer in case credit could not be afforded to the beneficiary's bank account or the transaction is rejected/returned for any reason.

Step-2: The originating bank branch prepares a message and sends the message to its pooling centre (also called the NEFT Service Centre).

Step-3: The pooling centre forwards the message to the NEFT Clearing Centre (operated by National Clearing Cell, Reserve Bank of India, Mumbai) to be included for the next available batch.

Step-4: The Clearing Centre sorts the funds transfer transactions destination bank-wise and prepares accounting entries to receive funds from the originating banks (debit) and give the funds to the destination banks (credit). Thereafter, bank-wise remittance messages are forwarded to the destination banks through their pooling centre (NEFT Service Centre).

Step-5: The destination banks receive the inward remittance messages from the Clearing Centre and pass on the credit to the beneficiary customers' accounts.

INDIAN FINANCIAL SYSTEM CODE (IFSC)

IFSC or Indian Financial System Code is an alpha-numeric code that uniquely identifies a bank-branch participating in the NEFT system. This is an 11-digit code with the first 4 alpha characters representing the bank, and the last 6 characters representing the branch. The 5th character is 0 (zero). IFSC is used by the NEFT system to identify the originating / destination banks / branches and also to route the messages appropriately to the concerned banks / branches.

REAL TIME GROSS SETTLEMENT (RTGS)

The acronym 'RTGS' stands for Real Time Gross Settlement, which can be defined as the continuous (real-time) settlement of funds transfers individually on an order by order basis (without netting). 'Real Time' means the processing of instructions at the time they are received rather than at some later time; 'Gross Settlement' means the settlement of funds transfer instructions occurs individually (on an instruction by instruction basis). Considering that the funds settlement takes place in the books of the Reserve Bank of India, the payments are final and irrevocable.

RTGS is different from National Electronics Funds Transfer System (NEFT): NEFT is an electronic fund transfer system that operates on a Deferred Net Settlement (DNS) basis which settles transactions in batches. In DNS, the settlement takes place with all transactions received till the particular cut-off time. These transactions are netted (payable and receivables) in NEFT whereas in RTGS the transactions are settled individually. For example, currently, NEFT operates in hourly batches. [There are twelve settlements from 8 am to 7 pm on week days and six settlements from 8 am to 1 pm on Saturdays.] Any transaction initiated after a designated settlement time would have to wait till the next designated settlement time Contrary to this, in the RTGS transactions are processed continuously throughout the RTGS business hours.

Minimum and Maximum Amount Stipulation for RTGS Transactions: The RTGS system is primarily meant for large value transactions. The minimum amount to be remitted through RTGS is ₹ 2 lakhs. There is no upper ceiling for RTGS transactions.

Time taken for Effecting funds transfer from one account to another under RTGS: Under normal circumstances the beneficiary branches are expected to receive the funds in real time as soon as funds are transferred by the remitting bank. The beneficiary bank has to credit the beneficiary's account within 30 minutes of receiving the funds transfer message.

IMMEDIATE PAYMENT SERVICE (IMPS)

Immediate Payment Service (IMPS) is an instant inter-bank electronic fund transfer service through mobile phones. It is also being extended through other channels such as ATM, Internet Banking, etc. The facility is available to all registered users of SBI Anywhere Personal having transaction rights on one or more accounts.

MMID: Mobile Money Identification Number (MMID) is a seven-digit number of which the first four digits are the unique identification number of the bank offering IMPS.

Beneficiary details the customer requires to effect an IMPS remittance from Person to Person: Following beneficiary details are required:

(a) MMID of the beneficiary,

(b) Mobile number of the beneficiary

(c) Name of the beneficiary

Beneficiary details the customer requires to effect an IMPS remittance from Person to Account: The beneficiary details required are:

(a) Name of the beneficiary

(b) Account Number of the beneficiary

(c) IFS Code of the beneficiary bank

Restrictions for activation of a Beneficiary added by a user

A customer can add and approve only one beneficiary in a calendar day, which will be activated by the internet banking system within 4 hours, if approved by you using OTP during the period from 6.00 AM to 8.00 PM (IST). Beneficiary approved after 8.00 PM will be activated on the next day after 8.00 AM (IST). You can commence funds transfer to the new beneficiary only after its activation. During the first 4 days after activation, you can transfer a total sum of ₹ 1,00,000/- to a new beneficiary if activated by the system.

DIGITAL SIGNATURE

A digital signature (not to be confused with a digital certificate) is a mathematical technique used to validate the authenticity and integrity of a message, software or digital document. The digital equivalent of a handwritten signature or stamped seal, but offering far more inherent security, a digital signature is intended to solve the problem of tampering and impersonation in digital communications. Digital signatures can provide the added assurances of evidence to origin, identity and status of an electronic document, transaction or message, as well as acknowledging informed consent by the signer. In many countries, including the United States, digital signatures have the same legal significance as the more traditional forms of signed documents. The United States Government Printing Office publishes electronic versions of the budget, public and private laws, and congressional bills with digital signatures.

How Digital Signatures Work? Digital signatures are based on public key cryptography, also known as asymmetric cryptography. Using a public key algorithm such as RSA, one can generate two keys that are mathematically linked: one private and one public. To create a digital signature, signing software (such as an email program) creates a one-way hash of the electronic data to be signed. The private key is then used to encrypt the hash. The encrypted hash along with other information, such as the hashing algorithm is the digital signature. The reason for encrypting the hash instead of the entire message or document is that a hash function can convert an arbitrary input into a fixed length value, which is usually much shorter. This saves time since hashing is much faster than signing.

TEST YOURSELF

1. The effectiveness of a data communications system depends on four fundamental characteristics. Which are not the fundamental characteristics:

(a) Delivery (b) Accuracy
(c) Protocol (d) Jitter

2. A data communications system has five components. These are:

(a) Message
(b) Transmission medium
(c) Protocol
(d) All of the above

3. A ____________ is a set of rules that govern data communications. It represents an agreement between the communicating devices.

(a) Protocol (b) Delivery
(c) Message (d) Jitter

4. Which is not the Data transmission modes?

(a) Simplex (b) Half-duplex
(c) Full-duplex (d) Triplex

5. In ______ mode, the communication is unidirectional, as on a one-way street. Only one of the two devices on a link can transmit; the other can only receive.

(a) Simplex (b) Half-duplex
(c) Full-duplex (d) Triplex

6. A _________ is a device used for transmission of several messages over a single channel using predetermined frequencies within the full bandwidth.

(a) MODEM
(b) Multiplexer
(c) Concentrator
(d) Front-end processors

7. The satellite based ________ was set upto provide informatics services to the Central and State Government Departments and its organisations.
(a) INDONET (b) VIKRAM
(c) NICNET (d) BANKNET

8. The Bank recognised the pressing need to harness information technology for intra-bank and inter-bank communications in the 1980s and set up BANKNET.
(a) INDONET (b) RBINET
(c) NICNET (d) BANKNET

9. Electronic Funds Transfer (EFT) System was started in ________ between Mumbai and Chennai to facilitate transferring of funds between these two cities, across branches and banks.
(a) 1996 (b) 1997
(c) 2007 (d) 2008

10. India was the 74th country to join the Society for Worldwide Inter-bank Financial Telecommunication (SWIFT) network on December 2, ________.
(a) 1990 (b) 1991
(c) 1992 (d) 1993

11. The Clearing House Inter-bank Payments System (CHIPS) is the primary clearing house in ________ for large banking transactions.
(a) Britain (b) India
(c) U.S. (d) Hong Kong

12. From July 10, 2017 settlements of fund transfer requests in NEFT system is done on ________ basis.
(a) Half-hourly (b) Hourly
(c) Two-hourly (d) Three-hourly

ANSWER

1	2	3	4	5	6	7	8	9	10	11	12
(c)	(d)	(a)	(d)	(a)	(b)	(c)	(d)	(a)	(b)	(c)	(a)

ROLE OF TECHNOLOGY UPGRADATION AND ITS IMPACT ON BANKS

INTRODUCTION

Today Indian Banking Sector is a flourishing industry. It is mainly focused on new banking technological innovations. Banks created to use technology to provide effective quality and services to the customer and get high speed. Today all the banks started with the different channels, like ATM, Credit Cards, Debit Cards, Mobile Banking, Internet Banking, etc. But Net Banking made it an easy way for customers to do their banking transaction from various places.

Technology and banking are inseparable now in India. The transformation from brick and mortar banking to technology driven banks has been fairly rapid during the last two decades. Economic liberalization and the integration with international best practices in banking and finance gave the much-needed push to a largely stagnating computerization program. It was also understood that if banking was to become efficient and penetrative the aid of technology was crucial. Challenges of diverse nature were faced to achieve the current status though it can safely be said that much is still to be done. Banking in India had fairly laid-back approach prior to the emergence of the reform period during the mid 1990s.

Objectives of Technology Development in Banks

The main objectives of the technology development in banks are:

1. To promote industrial growth;
2. To develop backward areas;
3. To create more employment opportunities;
4. To generate more exports and encourage import substitution;
5. To encourage modernization and improvement in technology;
6. To promote more self-employment projects;
7. To revive sick units;
8. To improve the management of large industries by providing training;
9. To remove regional disparities or regional imbalance;
10. To promote science and technology in new areas by providing risk capital;
11. To improve capital market in the country.

INNOVATION IN INDIAN BANKING

Nowadays the Indian banking sector has seen number changes. Most of the Banks began to take an innovative challenge towards banking with the objectives, to create more customers, and consequently to the banks. The government result of regulations, tax policies, globalization, liberalization, privatization to raise risk in the monetary market. The financial innovation in development and design the implementation of innovative financial process. In the recent years, innovative banking sector are using Internet Banking, Mobile Banking, Debit Card, Credit Card, Automatic teller machine, Fund Transfer, RTGS, NEFT, EFT, ECS, Advisory Services, Payment Utility bills, fund Transfer, Insurance Schemes, Cheque

Books, Travel Cheques and value-added services. Today's digital age and hyper-connected environment requires banks to reimagine their business continuously, and Indian banks are leading the pack when it comes to transforming from digital to truly digital. The year 2017 will be no different for the Indian banking sector. There are growth fuelled by innovative initiatives such as Unified Payments Interface (UPI) and technology. Our top picks for major technology trends that will reshape Indian banking are as follows:

1. **Open Banking:** A connected ecosystem for financial and non-financial services with multiple under lying service providers is the future of banking.
2. **Banking Strategy:** Banks are already making gaits in cloud adoption. Technologies are changing the face of business. Big Data, block chain, artificial intelligence (AI), will be leveraged using cloud computing. Business models for merging banks will also be largely driven by the strategy.
3. **Block Chain:** The banks try to meet the increasing demands of customers; block chain will be one of the enablers for reimagining processes. The current year 2018 will increasingly move some project, product and leverage block chain to automate inter-organizational processes. The new Emirates NBD and ICICI Bank Partnership to launch a block chain pilot network for international remittances and trade finance is advancing in this technology.
4. **Artificial Intelligence**: It has the potential to transform both front office and back office operations with its self-improving programs at ICICI Bank. The banks will explore the concepts to integrate the conversational interface into their Omni Channel Strategy.
5. **More things to Bank:** The year 2016 was the year of mobile-first strategy. Indian banks leveraged the increasing adoption of mobile to provide customized offerings on their apps.
6. **Banking Architecture Simplification:** The new technology is the bedrock of banking architectural simplification. The new year will see banks move to componentization instead of the traditional monolithic architecture. In other words, complex architecture will be broken up into smaller bite sized pieces for ease of deployment and upgrade for specific functionalities. The Indian government has made it clear that India will be yanked away from a cash-based economy. GST rollout will give further impetus to the Indian economy.

In 2018, banks will not only have to keep up with the growing expectations of a billion connected customers, but they'll also have to make sure that they are leagues ahead of the emerging competition.

DATA WAREHOUSING AND DATA MINING

In computing, an enterprise data warehouse (EDW), it is a method used for reporting and data analysis. Integrating data from one or more distinct sources creates a central repository of data, a data warehouse (DW). Data warehouses store current and historical data and which are used for creating reports for senior management individuals such as yearly and quarterly evaluations. DM an interdisciplinary sub-field of computer science (CS), is the computational procedure of discovering models in large data sets (DSs) involving techniques at the junction of artificial intelligence (AI), machine learning (ML) and database systems (DBs). The overall goal of the data mining process is to extract information from a data set and transform it into an understandable structure for further use. Aside from the rare analysis step, it involves database and data management characteristics, data pre-processing, model and inference considerations, complexity considerations, post-processing of discovered structures, and visualization.

Data Warehouse Architecture: Banks need a diversity of solutions ranging from a fully integrated global data warehouse (DW), to not integrated data marts (DMs) for the rising needs of the divisions. Both of these extreme solutions have important disadvantages along with their advantages, so it is worth considering the indirect alternative presented here based on Operational Data Store (ODS), a global DW and DMs.

Architecture of Data Mining: DM is described as a process of discover or extracting interesting knowledge from large amounts of data stored in multiple data sources such as file systems, databases, data ware-houses etc. This knowledge contributes a lot of benefits to business strategies, scientific, medical research, governments and individual. The steps involved in architecture are:

a) Client gives the data;
b) Data assembling is done;
c) Data verification;
d) Task assignment by team leader to employees;
e) Finally data is dispatched.

RECENT TRENDS IN BANKING

The Indian banking business has changed dramatically over the past 25 years, due in large part to technological change. The various factors of innovations in banking and financial market are ECS, RTGS, NEFT, ATM, and Retail Banking. Etc., and including more product and services.

1. **ATM:** The automated teller machine or ATM, is an important tools for banking services. Automatic Teller Machine enables the customers to withdraw their money 24 hours a day, 7 day a week. ATMs can be used for cash withdrawal, payment of utility bills, funds transfer between accounts, deposit of cheques and cash into accounts, balance enquiry etc.
2. **Electronic Payment Services:** It is mainly based on the e-governance, e-mail, e-commerce, e-tail etc. EPS Being developed in US for introduction of e-cheque Negotiable Instruments Act.
3. **Real Time Gross Settlement (RTGS) and NEFT:** Introduced in India Since March 2004. It is Nationwide Payment System for fund transfer. It is operated by RBI for transfer funds from one account to the account of another bank.
4. **Electronic Funds Transfer (EFT):** EFT is a system whereby anyone who wants to make payment to another person/company etc. Details required in EFT are receiver's name, bank account number, account type (savings or current account), bank name, city, branch name etc. RBI is the service provider of EFT.
5. **Point of Sale Terminal:** It is linked online to the computerized customer information files in a bank. Plastic transaction cards are used for payment, where customer's account is debited and the retailer's account is credited.
6. **Tele Banking:** It is entire non-cash related banking on telephone. Automatic Voice Recorder, manned phone terminals are used in it.
7. **Electronic Data Interchange (EDI):** The electronic exchange of business documents like purchase order, invoices, shipping notices, receiving advices etc. in a standard, computer processed, universally accepted format between trading partners.
8. **Customer Management:** Banks need to clearly articulate and measure the expected benefits from the winning strategies which would be dependent on the value various initiatives provide customers. These include: Customer segmentation, Co-creation, CRM to customer experience, use of alternative channels, and effective cross and upsell the third party products.
9. **Risk Management and Information Security:** Risk management methods include; MIS, Credit systems, ALM, Enterprise Risk Management Systems, Liquidity risk systems etc.
10. **Technology in Training and e-Learning:** Increase in investment on training and development by banks in India. Banks are adopting new technology—e-learning for knowledge updating among staff members.

IMPACT OF TECHNOLOGY IN BANKING SECTOR

Technology has revolutionized every aspect of human activity. One of these is the introduction of information technology in the capital market. The Internet is changing banking, the banking sector and a major impact on the banking relationship. Web is important for financial services to retail customers as well as many other industries.

- **Retail Loan Development:** Retail Banking in India is the individual maturation over time, more products could be next. Technology upgradation in banks launches various new retail loan products in banking sector. The housing sector's busiest, witnesses of ruinous competition. The home loans are popular because they allow you to achieve your most cherished dreams. Interest rates in market has dropped and I saw some innovative products as well. Other retail banking products, personal loans, mortgages and vehicle loans education.
- **Plastic Money:** Plastic money is a delightful gift for the Indian market. Giving relief from carrying too much cash. Now some new features added to the plastic money to make it more attractive. Formula works on buy now pay later. There are several facts of synonyms plastic credit card, money for everyone.
- **Credit Card:** Credit is a financial instrument that can more than once used to lend money or buy products and services on credit. Banks, retailers and other rule in this matter. On the basis of their credit limit, are of different species, such as Classic, Gold or Silver.
- **Charge Card:** They have almost the same properties as credit cards. The fundamental difference is, you cannot move payments from general higher credit limit, or sometimes without credit limits. Like Debit Card this card can be used as a mobile ATM. Account holder will be called, for this you need a bank account with a credit card.

Over the years, the banking sector in India has seen many changes. Most banks have started to themselves innovative approach for banks with the goal of creating more value for customers and then the banks. Some of the most important changes in the banking sector are discussed below.

Mobile Banking: Among the benefits of the booming market for mobile phones and mobile services, banks have more mobile phones introduced. Mobile Banking allows customers to perform banking transactions. For example, the HDFC SMS services introduced. Mobile banking operation is especially focused on people who travel frequently and deal with their banks.

Agriculture and Land Development Banking: One of the innovative system of rural banks was called into life by the Kisan Credit Card (KCC) SCHEME began in 1994-1995 fiscal year from NABARD. Revised KCC is implemented with effect from May 12, 2012. KCC-mode makes it easier for authors to gain more agricultural inputs. In addition to normal agricultural loans, banks offer a variety of other Products targeted to the needs of the rural population. In the recent changes ATM must be issued to all KCC account holder. KCC can be disbursed through both ATM, POS and internet Kiosks in rural areas. Private banks also saw the potential of rural market.

NRI Services: With a significant number of Indians who have relatives abroad have begun to banks, services, expatriate Indians to send money to relatives India can offer cost-effective to transfer one of the most important improvements of the report.

E-Banking: E-banking is becoming increasingly popular among retail banking customers. E-banking helps to reduce costs by providing cheaper and faster way to deliver products to customers. It also helps the customer to the place, time and method that will use the services and gives power, the provision of services by multi-channel banking. This e-banking is "driven by two engines" of the client-bank-pull and push.

Technology is one of the most important factors for the development of mankind. Information technology and communication is the biggest volumes in the field of technology, the phone is for the processing, storage and dissemination of information by electronic means. Banking is growing rapidly with the use of technology in the ATM, bank, online banking, mobile banking, etc. Plastic card is a banking product provided for the needs of the retail segment has seen its numbers grow in geometric progression in recent years. This growth has been strongly influenced by developments in technology, without which this would have been possible, of course it will change our way of life in the coming years.

The Indian banking sector has improved the terms and new Technology. The innovative banking technology changing reforms have changed the face of Indian banking and financial sector. The banking system has improved the manifolds in terms of product and services, technology, banking system, trading facility etc. It is the evident that the banking system has grown in India to compare with other country. Future, the banks compare hands their customer and bank will be meeting their requirements. Indian Banking Sector provide better services with other developed banks.

TEST YOURSELF

1. The main objectives of the technology development in banks are:
(a) To promote industrial growth
(b) To develop backward areas
(c) To create more employment opportunities
(d) All of the above

2. A connected ecosystem for financial and non-financial services with multiple underlying service providers is the future of banking is called:
(a) Open banking
(b) Block chain
(c) Artificial Intelligence
(d) Banking architecture simplification

3. __________ has the potential to transform both front office and back office operations with itsself-improving programs at ICICI Bank. The banks will explore the concepts to integrate the conversational interface into their Omni Channel Strategy.
(a) Open banking
(b) Block chain
(c) Artificial Intelligence
(d) Banking architecture simplification

4. __________ store current and historical data and which are used for creating reports for senior management individuals such as yearly and quarterly evaluations.
(a) Computer science
(b) Data warehouses
(c) Data Mining
(d) File systems

5. Tele-Banking is entire ______ related banking on telephone. Automatic Voice Recorder, manned phone terminals are used in it.
(a) Non-cash
(b) Cash
(c) Both cash & non-cash
(d) Account inquiry

6. ______ is mainly based on the e-governance, e-mail, e-commerce, e-tail etc. EPS Being developed in US for introduction of e-cheque Negotiable Instruments Act.
(a) Electronic Funds Transfer
(b) Electronic Payment Services
(c) Tele Banking
(d) Electronic Data Interchange

7. ______ is linked online to the computerized customer information files in a bank. Plastic transaction cards are used for payment, where customer's account is debited and the retailer's account is credited.
(a) Electronic Funds Transfer
(b) Electronic Payment Services
(c) Point of Sale Terminal
(d) Electronic Data Interchange

8. ______ is a financial instrument that can more than once used to lend money or buy products and services on credit. Banks, retailers and other rule in this matter.
(a) Debit Card (b) Credit Card
(c) Chard Card (d) Prepaid Card

9. Which is correct statements about E-banking?
(a) E-banking is becoming increasingly popular among retail banking customers.
(b) E-banking helps to reduce costs by providing cheaper and faster way to deliver products to customers.
(c) It also helps the customer to the place, time and method that will use the services and gives power, the provision of services by multi-channel banking.
(d) All of the above

ANSWER

1	2	3	4	5	6	7	8	9
(d)	(a)	(c)	(b)	(a)	(b)	(c)	(b)	(d)

SECURITY CONSIDERATIONS

INTRODUCTION

Information security issue is the most important one in using Internet and it becomes more crucial while implementing the Internet in banking sectors. This research revealed a lot of risks and threats to the security of online banking information which are increasing day by day. The demand for high security in banking & financial services creates both challenges and new business opportunities. Information security is the process by which an organization protects and secures its systems, media, and facilities that process and maintain information vital to its operations. Financial institutions and banks protect their information by instituting a security process that identifies risks, forms a strategy to manage the risks, implements the strategy, tests the implementation, and monitors the environment to control the risks.

RISK CONCERN AREAS

Information security in finance and banking can be increased by striving certain objectives like availability, integrity, confidentiality, accountability and assurance. Security objectives can be achieved by Information Security Risk Assessment, Strategy, Controls Implementation, Monitoring & Process Monitoring and Updating. Monitoring and updating makes the process continuous instead of a one-time event. Security risk variables include threats, vulnerabilities, attack techniques, financial institution operations and technology, and the financial institution's defensive posture. These standards provide systematic management approach to adopt the best practice controls, quantify the level of acceptable risk and implement the appropriate measures which protect the confidentiality, integrity and availability (CIA) of information. Technical control improves security by Identity Authentication Management, Access Control Technology, Firewall Technology & Encryption technology (key technology). Internal control reduces the harm caused by internal personnel morals risk, the system resources risk and the computer virus.

CONTROLS MECHANISM IN IT ENVIRONMENT

Every bank and FI should identify the events and circumstances whose occurrence could result in a loss to that organisation. These are called exposures. Controls are those acts which the organisation should implement to minimize the exposures. In addition to knowing the cause(s) of exposure that a particular control is intended to act upon, it is also useful to know the type of role the control is intended to perform. There are basically four categories of control:

Deterrent: These controls are designed to deter people (internal as well as external to the organisation) from undesirable behaviour. For example, written policies to deter people from doing undesired activities.

Preventive: These controls prevent the cause of exposure from occurring, or at least minimize the possibility. For example, security-controls at various levels like hardware, system software, application software, database, network etc.

Detective: When a cause of exposure has occurred, detective controls report its existence in an effort to minimize the extent of the damage. Certain fire precautions (such as heat detectors, smoke detectors etc.) fall into this category. Even auditing function can many times be also treated as a detective control.

Corrective: These controls are necessary to recover from a loss situation. For example, without corrective controls in place (in the form of Disaster Recovery Management System), the bank has risk of loss of business and other losses (which could even result in bank going out of business) due to its inability to recover essential IT-based services, information and other resources, after the disaster strikes.

COMPUTER AUDIT

Management should use the audit function as an independent arbiter to measure compliance with policies, standards, and guidelines as well as to assess the adequacy of information security. Management must concern itself with safe guarding the information resources under its jurisdiction.

Computer Audit (sometimes it is also called as Electronic Data Processing Audit *i.e.*, EDP Audit or Information Technology Audit *i.e.*, IT-Audit or Information-Systems Audit *i.e.*, IS Audit), assumes greater importance in the context of accelerated pace of computerisation taking place in Indian banking sector. Even though computerisation leads to improvement in customer service, housekeeping, productivity and profitability, it need not be construed as apanacea for all the problems being faced by the banking industry, or its implementation is not going to be without attendant problems or areas of concern. Uncontrolled use of computer can cause loss of important data. Inaccurate or untimely data can lead to incorrect decision making. Computer abuses/frauds caused by outsiders or employees can land the bank in serious trouble and in the absence of any vigilant machinery, detection of computer frauds/abuses can be left to chance. Protecting the IT related assets viz. hardware, software and data is of vital importance. Computer error can prove to be costly in the long run and loss of confidential data can attract claims for compensation. Hence, there was urgent need felt for banks to have IT systems with proper audit/control over such systems. Computer Audit could be defined as a process of collecting and evaluatlng evidence to:

1) Determine whether a computer system could safeguard assets through adoption of adequate security and control measures,
2) Maintain data integrity, achieve the goals of the organisation effectively, and
3) Result in efficient use of resources available. Data integrity implies that data having certain attributes like completeness, accuracy, time-liness, effectiveness and reliability are con-sistently maintained during input, processing, storage, retrieval and communications.

INFORMATION SECURITY POLICIES

Information Security Policies are the corner stone of information security effectiveness. The Security Policy is intended to define what is expected from an organization with ,respect to security of Information Systems. The overall objective is to control or guide human behaviour to reduce the risk to information assets by accidental or deliberate actions. Information security policies underpin the security and well being of information resources. They are the foundation, the bottom line, of information security within an organization.

We all practice elements of data security. At home, for example, we make sure that deeds and insurance documents are kept safely so that they are available when we need them. All office information deserves to be treated in the same way. In an office, having the right information at the right time can make the difference between success and failure. Data Security will help the user to control and secure information from inadvertent or malicious changes and deletions or unauthorized disclosure. There are three aspects of data security:

Confidentiality: Protecting information from unauthorized disclosure like to the press, or through improper disposal techniques, or those who are not entitled to have the same.

Integrity: Protecting information from unauthorized modification, and ensuring that information, such as a beneficiary list, can be relied upon and is accurate and complete.

Availability: Ensuring information is available when it is required. Data can be held in many different areas, some of these are:

- Network Servers;
- Personal Computers and Workstations;
- Laptop and Hand held PCs;
- Removable Storage Media (Floppy Disks, CD-ROMS, Zip Disks, Flash Drive etc.);
- Data Backup Media (Tapes and Optical Disks).

Data Loss Prevention: Leading causes of Data Loss:

- Natural Disasters
- Viruses
- Human Errors
- Software Malfunction
- Hardware & System Malfunction

Computers are more relied upon now than ever, or more to the point the data that is contained on them. In nearly every instant the system itself can be easily repaired or replaced, but the data once lost may not be retraceable. That's why of regular system backups and the implementation of some preventative measures are always stressed upon.

Natural Disasters

While the least probable cause of data loss, a natural disaster can have a devastating effect on the physical drive. In instances of severe housing damage, such as scored platters from fire, water emulsion due to flood, or broken or crushed platters, the drive may become unrecoverable. The best way to prevent data loss from a natural disaster is an off-site back up. Since it is nearly impossible to predict the arrival of such an event, there should be more than one copy of the system back up kept, one onsite and one off. The type of media back up will depend on system, software, and the required frequency needed to back up. Also be sure to check backups to be certain that they have properly backed up.

Viruses

Viral infection increases at rate of nearly 200-300 new Trojans, exploits and viruses every month. With those numbers growing every day, systems are at an ever-increasing risk to become infected with a virus.

There are several ways to protect against a viral threat:

- Install a Firewall on system to prevent hacker's access to user's data.
- Install an anti-virus program on the system and use it regularly for scanning and remove the virus if the system has been infected. Many viruses will lie dormant or perform many minor alterations that can cumulatively disrupt system works. Be sure to check for updates for anti-virus program on a regular basis.
- Back up and be sure to test backups from infection as well. There is no use to restore virus infected back up.
- Beware of any email containing an attachment. If it comes from anonymous sender or don't know from where it has come or what it is, then don't open it, just delete it & block the sender for future mail.

Human Errors

Even in today's era of highly trained, certified, and computer literate staffing there is always room for the timelessness of accidents. There are few things that might be followed:

- Be aware. It sounds simple enough to say, but not so easy to perform. When transferring data, be sure it is going to the destination. If asked "*Would you like to replace the existing file*" make sure, before clicking "yes".
- In case of uncertainty about a task, make sure there is a copy of the data to restore from.
- Take extra care when using any software that may manipulate drives data storage, such as: partition mergers, format changes, or even disk checkers.
- Before upgrading to a new Operating System, take back up of most important files or directories in case there is a problem during the installation. Keep in mind slaved data drive can also be formatted as well.
- Never shut the system down while programs are running. The open files will, more likely, become truncated and non-functional.

Software Malfunction

Software malfunction is a necessary evil when using a computer. Even the world's top programs cannot anticipate every error that may occur on any given program. There are still few things that can lessen the risks:

- Be sure the software used will meant ONLY for its intended purpose. Misusing a program may cause it to malfunction.
- Using pirated copies of a program may cause the software to malfunction, resulting in a corruption of data files.
- Be sure that the proper amount of memory installed while running multiple programs simultaneously. If a program shuts down or hangs up, data might be lost or corrupt.
- Back up is a tedious task, but it is very useful if the software gets corrupted.

Hardware Malfunction

The most common cause of data loss, hardware malfunction or hard drive failure, is another necessary evil inherent to computing. There is usually no warning that hard drive will fail, but some steps can be taken to minimize the need for data recovery from a hard drive failure:

- Do not stack drives on top of each other—leave space for ventilation. An overheated drive is likely to fail. Be sure to keep the computer away from heat sources and make sure it is well ventilated.
- Use an UPS (Uninterruptible Power Supply) to lessen malfunction caused by power surges.
- NEVER open the casing on a hard drive. Even the smallest grain of dust settling on the platters in the interior of the drive can cause it to fail.
- If system runs the scan disk on every reboot, it shows that system is carrying high risk for future data loss. Back it up while it is still running.

- If system makes any irregular noises such as clicking or ticking coming from the drive. Shut the system down and call Hardware Engineer for more information.

ABOUT VIRUSES

A virus is a form of malicious code and, as such it is potentially disruptive. It may also be transferred unknowingly from one computer to another. The term Virus includes all sorts of variations on a theme, including the nastier variants of macro-viruses, Trojans, and Worms, but, for convenience, all such programs are classed simply as virus.

Viruses tend to fall into 3 groups :

Dangerous: Such as 'Resume' and 'Love letter' which do real, sometimes irrevocable, damage to a computer system files, and the programs and data held on the computer's storage media, as well as attempting to steal and transmit user ID and password information.

Childish: Such as 'Yeke', 'Hitchcock', 'Flip', and Diamond, which do not, generally, corrupt or destroy data, programs, or boot records, but restrict themselves to irritating activities such as displaying childish messages, playing sounds, flipping the screenup side down, or displaying animated graphics.

Ineffective: Those, such as 'Bleah', which appear to do nothing at all except reproduce themselves, or attach themselves to files in the system, thereby cloggingup the storage media with unnecessary clutter. Some of these viruses are ineffective because of badly written code, - they should do something, but the virus writer did not get it quite right.

Within all types there are some which operate on the basis of a 'triggered event' usually a date such as April 1st, or October 31st, or a time such 15 : 10 each day when the 'Tea Time' virus activates.

Protection of computer from virus infection :

- Make regular backups of important data.
- Install antivirus software on computer and use it daily.
- Update the antivirus software with the latest signature files on weekly/fortnightly basis. Antivirus software does no good unless it is frequently updated to protect against the most recent viruses.
- Upgrade the antivirus software when new releases are provided.

Never open or execute a file or e-mail attachment from an unidentified source. If user is unsure of the source, delete it. Recent viruses have been written so that they come from friends and colleagues. Be cautious with attachments even from trusted sources. If it was sent knowingly, an attachment could still contain a virus. Saving it as a file and running the virus scan software will catch any virus that it has been set up to find, therefore will catch most of them.

INFORMATION SYSTEMS AUDIT (IS AUDIT)

'The Working Group on Information Systems Security for the Banking and Financial Sector' constituted by Reserve Bank of India enumerated that each Bank in the country should conduct 'Information Systems Audit Policy' of the Bank. Accordingly Information Systems Audit and Security cell prepare Information Systems Audit Policy. The fundamental principle is that risk and controls are continuously evaluated by the owners, where necessary, with the assistant of IS Audit function.

The business operations in the Banking and Financial sector have been increasingly dependent on the computerized information systems over the years. It has now become impossible to separate Information Technology from the business of the banks. There is a need for focused attention of the issues of the corporate governance of the information systems in computerized environment and the security controls to safeguard information and information systems. The developments in Information Technology have a tremendous impact on auditing. Well-planned and structured audit is essential for risk management and monitoring and control Information systems in any organization.

IS Audit Objectives: Auditing is a systematic and independent examination of information systems environment to ascertain whether the objectives, set out to be achieved, have been metor not. Auditing is also described as a continuous search for compliance. The objective of the IS audit are to identify risks that an organization is exposed to in the computerized environment. IS audit evaluates the adequacy of the security controls and informs the management with suitable conclusions and recommendations. IS audit is an indopondont subset of the normal audit exercise. Information systems audit is an ongoing process of evaluating controls; suggest security measures for the purpose of safeguarding assets/resources, maintaining data integrity, improve system effectiveness and system efficiency for the purpose of attaining organization goals. Well-planned and structured audit is essential for risk management and monitoring and control of information systems in any organization.

Safeguarding IS Assets: The Information systems assets of the organization must be protected by a system of internal controls. It includes protection of hardware, software, facilities, people, data, technology, system documentation and supplies. This is because hardware can be damaged maliciously, software and data files may be stolen, deleted or altered and supplies of negotiable forms can be used for unauthorized purposes. The IS auditor will be require to review the physical security over the facilities, the security over the systems software and the adequacy of the internal controls. The IT facilities must be protected against all hazards. The hazards can be accidental hazards or intentional hazards.

Maintenance of Data Integrity

Data integrity includes the safeguarding of the information against unauthorized addition, deletion, modification or alteration. The desired features of the data are described hereunder:

a) **Accuracy:** Data should be accurate. Inaccurate data may lead to wrong decisions and thereby hindering the business development process.

b) **Confidentiality:** Information should not lose its confidentiality. It should be protected from being read or copied by anyone who is not authorized to do so.

c) **Completeness:** Data should be complete.

d) **Reliability:** Data should be reliable because all business decision are taken on the basis of the current database.

e) **Efficiency:** The ratio of the output to the input is known as efficiency. If output is more with the same or less actual input, system efficiency is achieved, or else system is inefficient. If computerization results in the degradation of efficiency, the effort for making the process automated stands defeated. IS auditors are responsible to examine how efficient the application in relation to the users and workload.

It summarizes the influence elements introducing the concept of information technologies in financial and banking industries and analyze the relationship of information technology risk factors. It explores why information security should be a priority for businesses and deals with how a security expert can model potential losses for their organization. It also provides guidelines for professionals to make well informed decisions.

TEST YOURSELF

1. Every bank and FI should identify the events and circumstances whose occurrence could result in a loss to that organisation. These are called exposures. ________ are those acts which the organisation should implement to minimize the exposures.
(a) Audit (b) Controls
(c) Confidentiality (d) Completeness

2. There are basically four categories of control. These are:
(a) Deterrent (b) Preventive
(c) Detective (d) All of the above

3. ________ controls are designed to deter people (internal as well as external to the organisation) from undesirable behaviour.
(a) Deterrent (b) Preventive
(c) Detective (d) All of the above

4. Ensuring information is available when it is required. Data can be held in many different areas, some of these are:
(a) Network Servers
(b) Personal Computers and Workstations
(c) Laptop and Hand held PCs
(d) All of the above

5. Which are the leading Causes of Data Loss:
(a) Natural Disasters (b) Human Errors
(c) Software Malfunction (d) All of the above

6. 'Resume' and 'Love letter' are which type of Virus?
(a) Dangerous (b) Childish
(c) Ineffective (d) Effective

7. ________ is a systematic and independent examination of information systems environment to ascertain whether the objectives, set out to be achieved, have been met or not.
(a) Controlling (b) Auditing
(c) Protecting (d) Checking

8. ________ includes the safeguarding of the information against unauthorized addition, deletion, modification or alteration.
(a) Data integrity (b) Confidentiality
(c) Auditing (d) Checking

9. The desired features of the data are:
(a) Accuracy (b) Confidentiality
(c) Reliability (d) All of the above

ANSWER

1	2	3	4	5	6	7	8	9
(b)	(d)	(a)	(d)	(d)	(a)	(b)	(a)	(d)

OVERVIEW OF IT ACT

RBI GUIDELINE ON IT ACT FOR BANKING

The RBI guideline is useful for all banks and financial institutions incorporating IT operations and support to meet their business objectives. The guidelines are important to be complied and followed sincerely to maintain the trust level of the customer by assuring the security of their information residing with these financial institutions. The guidelines can also be used by advisory & auditing firms for consulting and audit purpose.

In today's Indian scenario, banking sectors are rapidly utilizing IT services for their operations. Automation of various processes no doubt has given lots of advantages to these banking and financial institutions but has given rise to many risks as well.

Technology risks not only have a direct impact on a bank as operational risks but can also exacerbate other risks like credit risks and market risks. Given the increasing reliance of customers on electronic delivery channels to conduct transactions, any security related issues have the potential to undermine public confidence in the use of e-banking channels and lead to reputation risks to the banks. Inadequate technology implementation can also induce strategic risk in terms of strategic decision making based on inaccurate data/information. Compliance risk is also an outcome in the event of non-adherence to any regulatory or legal requirements arising out of the use of IT. These issues ultimately have the potential to impact the safety and soundness of a bank and in extreme cases may lead to systemic crisis.

Keeping in view the changing threat milieu and the latest international standards, it was felt that there was a need to enhance RBI guidelines relating to the governance of IT, information security measures to tackle cyber fraud apart from enhancing independent assurance about the effectiveness of IT controls. To consider these and related issues, RBI announced the creation of a Working Group on Information Security, Electronic Banking, Technology Risk Management and Tackling Cyber Fraud in April, 2010. The Group was set up under the Chairmanship of the Executive Director Shri. G. Gopalakrishna.

GOPALAKRISHNA COMMITTEE RECOMMENDATIONS

Looking at the IT challenges and information security concerns today, RBI introduced guidelines to enhance the governance of IT and institute robust information security measures in the Indian banking sector. Following were the major reasons for introducing the guidelines for the bank:

a) Information technology (IT) risk assessment and management was required to be made a part of the risk management framework of a bank.

b) Internal audits/information system audits needed to independently provide assurance that IT-related processes and controls were working as intended.

c) Given the instances of cyber fraud in banks recently, it was necessary to improve controls and examine the need for pro-active fraud risk assessments and management processes in commercial banks.

d) With the increase in transactions in electronic mode, it was also critical to examine the legal implications for banks arising out of cyber laws and steps that were required to be taken to suitably mitigate the legal risks.

e) Considering the above mentioned issues, creation of a Working Group on Information Security, Electronic Banking, Technology Risk Management and Tackling Cyber Fraud took place.

This working group was formed with the following vision to:

a) Undertake a comprehensive assessment of extant IT and e-banking related guidelines vis-à-vis international guidelines/best practices and suggest suitable recommendations.
b) Suggest recommendations with respect to information security to comprehensively provide for a broad framework to mitigate present internal and external threats to banks.
c) Provide recommendations for effective and comprehensive Information Systems Audit related processes to provide assurance on the level of IT risks in banks.
d) Suggest scope for enhancement of measures against cyber fraud through preventive and detective mechanisms as part of the fraud risk management framework in banks.
e) Identify measures to improve business continuity and disaster recovery related processes in banks.
f) Assess the impact of legal risks arising out of cyber laws, the need for any specific legislation relating to data protection and privacy and whether there is an Indian equivalent of the Electronic Fund Transfer Act in the US.
g) Consider scope to enhance customer education measures relating to cyber fraud.

The working group decided to address IT issues across multiple dimensions arising out of the use of IT and provide recommendations in these areas. These dimensions and provided recommendations were elaborated in the following 9 chapters of the guideline :

Chapter 1 : Information Technology Governance
Chapter 2 : Information Security
Chapter 3 : IT operations
Chapter 4 : IT services outsourcing
Chapter 5 : IS Audit
Chapter 6 : Cyber frauds
Chapter 7 : Business Continuity Planning
Chapter 8 : Customer education
Chapter 9 : Legal issues

The report further is divided into different chapters and each chapter contains introduction, associated roles and responsibilities and the desired control recommendations from the RBI for banks to implement mandatorily. The recommendations are not "one-size fits-all" and the implementation of these recommendations need to be based on the nature and scope of activities engaged by banks and the technology environment prevalent in the bank and the support rendered by technology to the business processes.

The key recommendations of the Report include and pertain to:

- Approach to capacity building in banks and non-banks;
- Enhancing Human Resources Management practices;
- Creation of position of Chief Learning Officer in banks and concept of return on learning;
- Strategies for addressing issues of replacement or replenishment of talent in banks;
- Process and steps for skill development;
- Training strategy and need for expert trainers to help build capacities;
- Coaching and mentoring including mentoring programme for Top Management of banks;
- Entry point qualifications at recruitment stage, development of competency standards and certification or accreditation in various areas of training;
- Conducting a common Banking Aptitude Test (BAT) at entry levels;
- Qualifications for generalists and specialists;
- E-learning as an important constituent for building capacity and imparting training;
- Training and learning Infrastructure oriented to banking;
- Proposal for setting up a Centre of Excellence for Leadership Development in banking sector;
- Fostering research on skill development in banking sector and evolving a monitoring frame-work for capacity development in banking sector;
- Creation of skills registry for the banking sector.

The committee was constituted with an objective to implement non-legislative recommendations of the Financial Sector Legislative Reforms Commission (FSLRC) relating to capacity building in banks and non-banks, streamlining training intervention and suggesting changes thereto in view of ever increasing challenges in banking and non-banking sectors.

The objectives also included evolving an appropriate certification mechanism in the realm of training, where feasible, examining possible incentives for undertaking such certification and covering all stages of hierarchy-from the lowest rung to the Board level executives.

TEST YOURSELF

1. RBI announced the creation of a Working Group on Information Security in April, _______ under the Chairmanship of the Shri G. Gopalakrishna.
   (a) 2008 (b) 2010
   (c) 2012 (d) 2014
2. Shri G. Gopalakrishna is a former _______ of RBI.
   (a) Executive Director (b) Dy. Governor
   (c) Governor (d) Regional Director
3. Which were not the major reasons for introducing the IT guidelines for the bank:
   (a) Information technology (IT) risk assessment and management was required to be made a part of the risk management framework of a bank.
   (b) Internal audits/information system audits need not to independently provide assurance that IT-related processes and controls were not working as intended.
   (c) Given the instances of cyber fraud in banks recently, it was necessary to improve controls and examine the need for pro-active fraud risk assessments and management processes in commercial banks.
   (d) With the increase in transactions in electronic mode, it was also critical to examine the legal implications for banks arising out of cyber laws and steps that were required to be taken to suitably mitigate the legal risks.
4. This working group was formed with the following vision to:
   (a) undertake a comprehensive assessment of extant IT and e-banking related guidelines vis-à-vis international guidelines/best practices and suggest suitable recommendations
   (b) Provide recommendations for effective and comprehensive Information Systems Audit related processes to provide assurance on the level of IT risks in banks
   (c) Identify measures to improve business continuity and disaster recovery related processes in banks
   (d) All of the above
5. The working group dimensions and provided recommendations were elaborated in the following _______ of the guideline.
   (a) 7 chapters (b) 8 chapters
   (c) 9 chapters (d) 10 chapters
6. Third Chapters of the recommendation deals with:
   (a) Information Technology Governance
   (b) IT operations
   (c) IS Audit
   (d) Cyber frauds
7. To consider these and related issues, RBI announced the creation of a Working Group on Information Security, _______ in April, 2010.
   (a) Electronic Banking
   (b) Technology Risk Management
   (c) Tackling Cyber Fraud
   (d) All of the above
8. The key recommendations of the Report include and pertain to:
   (a) Enhancing Human Resources Management practices
   (b) Creation of position of Chief Learning Officer in banks and concept of return on learning
   (c) Process and steps for skill development
   (d) All of the above

ANSWER

1	2	3	4	5	6	7	8
(b)	(a)	(b)	(d)	(c)	(b)	(d)	(d)

PREVENTIVE VIGILANCE IN ELECTRONIC BANKING

INTRODUCTION

The dictionary defines Vigilance as being watchful and cautious to detect danger; being ever awake and alert. While being vigilant is important in all walks of life, the observance of vigilance becomes more critical in the financial sector and particularly for institutions like banks, which deal with public money.

Banks, which act as an intermediary between depositors and lenders, are duty bound to observe the highest standards of safeguards to ensure that money accepted from depositors are not mis-utilized and are put to gainful use or are available with them to be paid on demand. To ensure this, banks are not only required to do due diligence on the borrowers but are also expected to put in place appropriate safeguards to ensure that the transactions being undertaken by the staff are as per laid down guidelines. The watchfulness enforced by the vigilance function is required to ensure that public money, which banks hold in fiduciary capacity is not allowed to be misused by the delinquent elements in any manner.

VIGILANCE FUNCTION IN BANKS

The need to have a dedicated body to investigate vigilance and anti-corruption issues in public sector undertakings was felt way back in the early 1960s when Government of India set up the Committee on Prevention of Corruption [popularly known as Santhanam Committee] on whose recommendation the Central Vigilance Commission (CVC) was set up in February 1964 as an Apex Body with its vigilance units headed by Chief Vigilance Officers. The Commission was since accorded statutory status on August 25, 1998 through the Central Vigilance Commission Ordinance, 1998 which was substituted by Central Vigilance Commission Act, 2003.

Public Sector banks fall under the jurisdiction of Central Vigilance Commission because of their incorporation and operation as public-sector entities. Further, RBI also issued guidelines in May 2011 advising all the private sector banks to evolve suitable structure within their organization which would scrutinize all cases where any foul play is suspected from vigilance angle. This mechanism is intended to ensure that reckless decisions resulting in loss of money and reputation to the bank are identified and suitable action is initiated against the delinquent employees promptly and effectively. The existence of a credible and responsive vigilance system acts as an effective deterrent to disorderly conduct.

The guidelines on vigilance administration are issued by the Central Vigilance Commission. The Chief Vigilance Officers in the respective organisations have been authorised to decide upon the existence of a vigilance angle in individual cases, at the time of registration of the complaint. Once a complaint has been registered as a vigilance case, it will have to be treated as such till its closure, irrespective of the outcome of the investigation. Although formulation of a precise definition is almost impossible, generally a vigilance angle could be perceptible in cases characterized by:

- Commission of criminal offences like demand and acceptance of illegal gratification, possession of disproportionate assets, forgery, cheating, abuse of official position with a view to obtaining pecuniary benefits advantage for self or for any other person;
- Irregularities reflecting adversely on the integrity of the public servant;
- Lapses involving gross or willful negligence, recklessness, failure to report to competent authorities, exercise of discretion without or in excess of powers/jurisdiction, cause of undue loss or a concomitant gain to an individual or a set of individuals/a party or parties and flagrant violation of systems and procedures.

PHISHING ATTACK

Phishing is a type of social engineering attack often used to steal user data, including login credentials and credit card numbers. It occurs when an attacker, masquerading as a trusted entity, dupes a victim into opening an email, instant message, or text message. The recipient is then tricked into clicking a malicious link, which can lead to the installation of malware, the freezing of the system as part of a ransomware attack or the revealing of sensitive information.

An attack can have devastating results. For individuals, this includes unauthorized purchases, the stealing of funds, or identify theft.

Moreover, phishing is often used to gain a foothold in corporate or governmental networks as a part of a larger attack, such as an advanced persistent threat (APT) event. In this latter scenario, employees are compromised to bypass security perimeters, distri-bute malware inside a closed environment, or gain privileged access to secured data.

An organization succumbing to such an attack typically sustains severe financial losses in addition to declining market share, reputation, and consumer trust. Depending on scope, a phishing attempt might escalate into a security incident from which a business will have a difficult time recovering.

Phishing Attack Examples: The following illustrates a common phishing scam attempt:

1) A spoofed email ostensibly from my university.edu is mass-distributed to as many faculty members as possible.
2) The email claims that the user's password is about to expire. Instructions are given to go to myuniversity.edu/renewal to renew their password within 24 hours.

Several things can occur by clicking the link. For example:

a) The user is redirected to myuniversity.edurenewal.com, a bogus page appearing exactly like the real renewal page, where both new and existing passwords are requested. The attacker, monitoring the page, hijacks the original password to gain access to secured areas on the university network.

b) The user is sent to the actual password renewal page. However, while being redirected, a malicious script activates in the background to hijack the user's session cookie. This results in a reflected XSS attack, giving the perpetrator privileged access to the university network.

Phishing Techniques: Email phishing is a numbers game. An attacker sending out thousands of fraudulent messages can net significant information and sums of money, even if only a small percentage of recipients fall for the scam. As seen above, there are some techniques attackers use to increase their success rates.

For one, they will go to great lengths in designing phishing messages to mimic actual emails from a spoofed organization. Using the same phrasing, typefaces, logos, and signatures makes the messages appear legitimate.

In addition, attackers will usually try to push users into action by creating a sense of urgency. For example, as previously shown, an email could threaten account expiration and place the recipient on a timer. Applying such pressure causes the user to be less diligent and more prone to error.

Lastly, links inside messages resemble their legitimate counter parts, but typically have a misspelled domain name or extra subdomains. In the above example, the myuniversity.edu/renewal URL was changed to myuniversity.cduronowal.com. Similarities between the two addresses offer the impression of a secure link, making the recipient less aware that an attack is taking place.

Spear Phishing: Spear phishing targets a specific person or enterprise, as opposed to random application users. It's a more in depth version of phishing that requires special knowledge about an organization, including its power structure.

An attack might play out as follows:

1. A perpetrator researches names of employees within an organization's marketing department and gains access to the latest project invoices.

2. Posing as the marketing director, the attacker emails a departmental project manager (PM) using a subject line that reads, Updated invoice for Q3 campaigns. The text, style, and included logo duplicate the organization's standard email template.
3. A link in the email redirects to a password-protected internal document, which is in actuality a spoofed version of a stolen invoice.
4. The PM is requested to log in to view the document. The attacker steals his credentials, gaining full access to sensitive areas within the organization's network.

By providing an attacker with valid login credentials, spear phishing is an effective method for executing the first stage of an APT.

Phishing Protection

Phishing attack protection requires steps be taken by both users and enterprises. For users, vigilance is key. A spoofed message often contains subtle mistakes that expose its true identity. These can include spelling mistakes or changes to domain names, as seen in the earlier URL example. Users should also stop and think about why they're even receiving such an email.

For enterprises, a number of steps can be taken to mitigate both phishing and spear phishing attacks:

- Two-factor authentication (2FA) is the most effective method for countering phishing attacks, as it adds an extra verification layer when logging in to sensitive applications. 2FA relies on users having two things: something they know, such as a password and user name, and something they have, such as their smartphones. Even when employees are compromised, 2FA prevents the use of their compromised credentials, since these alone are insufficient to gain entry.
- In addition to using 2FA, organizations should enforce strict password management policies. For example, employees should be required to frequently change their passwords and to not be allowed to reuse password for multiple applications.

Educational campaigns can also help diminish the threat of phishing attacks by enforcing secure practices, such as not clicking on external email links.

TEST YOURSELF

1. The dictionary defines __________ as being watchful and cautious to detect danger; being ever awake and alert.

(a) Vigilance (b) Alertness
(c) Attentiveness (d) Awareness

2. The Central Vigilance Commission (CVC) was set up on recommendation of which committee?

(a) Narsimhan (b) R V Gupta
(c) Santhanam (d) Murty

3. Government of India set up the Committee on Prevention of Corruption on whose recommendation the Central Vigilance Commission (CVC) was set up in __________ as an Apex Body with its vigilance units headed by Chief Vigilance Officers.

(a) 1962 (b) 1964
(c) 1970 (d) 1978

4. The Commission was since accorded statutory status on August 25, 1998 through the Central Vigilance Commission Ordinance, 1998 which was substituted by Central Vigilance Commission Act, __________.

(a) 2003 (b) 2004
(c) 2005 (d) 2006

5. Phishing is a type of social engineering attack often used to steal __________, including login credentials and credit card numbers.

(a) User details
(b) User data
(c) User money
(d) User account

6. Spear phishing targets a __________ person or enterprise, as opposed to random application users.

(a) Common (b) General
(c) Specific (d) Group

ANSWER

1	2	3	4	5	6
(a)	(c)	(b)	(a)	(b)	(c)

MODULE–D

SUPPORT SERVICES—MARKETING OF BANKING SERVICES/PRODUCTS

MARKETING – AN INTRODUCTION

INTRODUCTION

India has a diversified financial sector undergoing rapid expansion, both in terms of strong growth of existing financial services firms and new entities entering the market. The sector comprises commercial banks, insurance companies, non-banking financial companies, co-operatives, pension funds, mutual funds and other smaller financial entities. The banking regulator has allowed new entities such as payments banks to be created recently thereby adding to the types of entities operating in the sector. However, the financial sector in India is predominantly a banking sector with commercial banks accounting for more than 64 per cent of the total assets held by the financial system.

The banking services sector has undergone significant changes in the last years. These changes are due not only to large bank mergers and strategic alliances between banking groups, but also to the increasing legislative deregulation of the banking market and the decreasing the state intervention in banking affairs; the above have led to the creation of a new market which is characterized by a slight increase in primary demands and less legislative restrictions. The preservation and mainly the increase of market shares constitute the primary objective of all banking institutions and many strategies have been implemented in order to maintain their clients. In this effort, bank managers have been creating new products and services. Yet as such innovations involve significant expenses and banking costs, it has been supported that a better approach would be to focus on client trust, by offering better quality of services and aiming at satisfying clients to the maximum extent.

MARKETING

Marketing is the process by which companies create customer interest in products or services. It generates the strategy that underlies sales techniques, business communication, and business development. It is an integrated process through which companies build strong customer relationships and create value for their customers and for themselves.

Whilst the American Marketing Association states: *'Marketing is the activity, set of institutions, and processes for creating, communicating, delivering, and exchanging offerings that have value for customers, clients, partners, and society at large'.*

Marketing author and academic Philip Kotler defines marketing as: '*Satisfying needs and wants through an exchange process*'. The management process through which goods and services move from concept to the customer. It includes the coordination of four elements called the 4 P's of marketing :

(1) Identification, selection and development of a **product**,

(2) Determination of its **price**,

(3) Selection of a distribution channel to reach the customer's **place**, and

(4) Development and implementation of a **promotional** strategy.

For example, new Apple products are developed to include improved applications and systems, are set at different prices depending on how much capability the customer desires, and are sold in places where other Apple products are sold.

In order to promote the device, the company featured its debut at tech events and is highly advertised on the web and on television. Marketing is based on thinking about the business in terms of customer needs and their satisfaction. Marketing differs from selling because (in the words of Harvard Business School's retired professor of marketing Theodore C. Levitt) "Selling concerns itself with the tricks and techniques of getting people to exchange their cash for your product. It is not concerned with the values that the exchange is all about. And it does not, as marketing invariable does, view the entire business process as consisting of a tightly integrated effort to discover, create, arouse and satisfy customer needs." In other words, marketing has less to do with getting customers to pay for your product as it does developing a demand for that product and fulfilling the customer's needs.

MARKETING MANAGEMENT

Market: Market is a place where buyers and sellers meets and goods and services sales and buys producers.

Marketing: It is a total system of business activities design to plan promote and distribute want satisfying goods and services to target market.

Marketing Management: It can be define as an art and science of choosing target volume and getting keeping and growing customer to creating delivering and communicating superior customer value.

Marketing Process: Marketing is a process that marketing managers execute. In a number of instances, a marketing manager does not manage people, but manages the marketing process. A product manager is an example of such a marketing manager; he manages the marketing process for a product within a larger marketing organization. We, as consumers, see the results of that processing the form of products, stores, shopping malls, advertisements, sales pitches, promotions, prices, etc. This process usually involves four phases.

a) **Analysis:** Markets must be understood, and this understanding flows from analysis. Marketing managers spend weeks analyzing their markets before they undertake the development of marketing plans for influencing those markets.

b) **Planning:** Once a market is understood, marketing programs and events must be designed for influencing the market's customers and consumers, and even the firm's competitors.

c) **Execution:** The marketing events are executed in the markets: advertisements are run, prices are set, sales calls are made, etc.

d) **Monitoring:** Markets are not static entities and thus must be monitored at all times. After events execute, they need to be evaluated. The planning assumptions upon which the upcoming events are based must be continually tested; they are no longer true then the events may need modification.

SERVICES MARKETING

The world economy nowadays is increasingly characterized as a service economy. This is primarily due to the increasing importance and share of the service sector in the economies of most developed and developing countries. In fact, the growth of the service sector has long been considered as indicative of a country's economic progress.

Economic history tells us that all developing nations have invariably experienced a shift from agriculture to industry and then to the service sector as the main stay of the economy. This shift has also brought about a change in the definition of goods and services themselves. No longer are goods considered separate from services. Rather, services now increasingly represent an integral part of the product and this inter connectedness of goods and services is represented on a goods-services continuum.

Definition and Characteristics of Services: The American Marketing Association defines services as - "Activities, benefits and satisfactions which are offered for sale or are provided in connection with the sale of goods." The defining characteristics of a service are:

Intangibility: Services are intangible and do not have a physical existence. Hence services cannot be touched, held, tasted or smelt. This is most defining feature of a service and that which primarily differentiates it from a product. Also, it poses a unique challenge to those engaged in marketing a service as they need to attach tangible attributes to an otherwise intangible offering.

1. **Heterogeneity/Variability:** Given the very nature of services, each service offering is unique and cannot be exactly repeated even by the same service provider. While products can be mass produced and be homogenous the same is not true of services. e.g.: All burgers of a particular flavor at McDonalds are almost identical. However, the same is not true of the service rendered by the same counter staff consecutively to two customers.

2. **Perishability:** Services cannot be stored, saved, returned or resold once they have been used. Once rendered to a customer the service is completely consumed and cannot be delivered

to another customer. e.g.: A customer dissatisfied with the services of a barber cannot return the service of the haircut that was rendered to him. At the most he may decide not to visit that particular barber in the future.

3. **Inseparability/Simultaneity of Production and Consumption:** This refers to the fact that services are generated and consumed within the same time frame. E.g.: a haircut is delivered to and consumed by a customer simultaneously unlike, say, a take away burger which the customer may consume even after a few hours of purchase. Moreover, it is very difficult to separate a service from the service provider. E.g.: the barber is necessarily a part of the service of a haircut that he is delivering to his customer.

Difference between Goods and Services

Goods	*Services*
A physical commodity	A process or activity
Tangible	Intangible
Homogenous	Heterogeneous
Production and distribution are separation from their consumption	Production, distribution and consumption are simultaneous processes
Can be stored	Cannot be stored
Transfer of ownership is possible	Transfer of ownership is not possible

MARKETING IN BANKING SERVICES

In case of the banking industry, customer retention plays the critical role in customer service. Customer retention is potentially an effective tool that banks can use to gain a strategic advantage and survive in today' sever-increasing banking competitive environment. The key factors influencing customers' satisfaction and ensuring customer retention of a bank include the range of services, rates, fees and prices charged. It is apparent that superior service alone is not sufficient to satisfy customers. Prices are essential, if not more important than service and relationship quality.

There are compelling arguments for bank management to carefully consider the factors that might increase customer retention rates in India. Unless a bank can extend its product quality beyond the core service with additional and potential service features and value, it is unlikely to gain a sustainable competitive advantage. Thus, the most likely way to both retain customers and improve profitability is by adding value via a strategy of differentiation while increasing margins through higher prices. Today's customers do not just buy core quality products or services; they also buy a variety of added value or benefits. This forces the service providers such as banks to adopt a market-orientation approach that identifies consumer needs, and designs new products and redesigns current ones.

Quality of Personnel: In businesses where the underlying products have become commodity-like, quality of service depends heavily on the quality of their personnel. This is well documented in a study by Leeds, who documented that approximately 40 per cent of customers switched banks because of what they considered to be poor service. Indeed, customer satisfaction has for many years been perceived as a key to determine why customers leave or stay with an organisation. Organisations, especially banks, need to know how to keep their customers, even if they appear to be satisfied.

Services Under One Roof: Innovation and renovation are the keys to success in service marketing including banks. The provision of all the financial services under one roof is the concept of modern banking. The banks are now not just the clearing houses, but are the best marketable places too. Foreign banks have realised this fact long ago and they have been providing the best services as per the requirement of their customers. The competitive scenario has made banks to provide customized products and services. Customers have many options today.

In today's banking, the role of information desk has become very important. Customers may require some assistance in various transactions, in which the help desk should be able to provide services promptly with dignity and honour.

TEST YOURSELF

1. Marketing is the process by which companies create customer _____ in products or services.
   (a) Involvement (b) Activity
   (c) Interest (d) Image

2. Marketing generates the strategy that underlies _____.
   (a) Sales techniques
   (b) Business communication
   (c) Business development
   (d) All of the above

3. The management process through which goods and services move from concept to the customer. It

includes the coordination of four elements called the 4 P's of marketing. Which is not the part of 4 P's?

(a) Product (b) Planning
(c) Price (d) Promotional strategy

4. Markets must be understood, and this understanding flows from ________.

(a) Analysis (b) Planning
(c) Price (d) Promotional strategy

5. ________ is a place where buyers and sellers meets and goods and services sales and buys producers.

(a) Marketing
(b) Marketing management
(c) Analysis
(d) Market

6. ________ can be define as an art and science of choosing target volume and getting keeping and growing customer to creating delivering and communicating superior customer value.

(a) Marketing
(b) Marketing management
(c) Analysis
(d) Market

7. Markets are not static entities and thus must be ________ at all times. After events execute, they need to be evaluated.

(a) Monitored (b) Planning
(c) Analyzed (d) Involvement

8. Which is not a part of Marketing Process?

(a) Analysis (b) Planning
(c) Inquiry (d) Monitoring

9. Which is not the features of Goods?

(a) Tangible
(b) Homogenous
(c) Cannot be stored
(d) Transfer of ownership is possible

10. Which is the features of Services?

(a) Tangible
(b) Homogenous
(c) A process or activity
(d) Can be stored

11. Which is not the features of Services?

(a) Transfer of ownership is not possible
(b) Heterogeneous
(c) A process or activity
(d) Can be stored

12. This forces the service providers such as banks to adopt a ________ that identifies consumer needs, and designs new products and redesigns current ones.

(a) market-orientation approach
(b) market-segmentation approach
(c) market-satisfaction approach
(d) market-interest approach

ANSWER

1	2	3	4	5	6	7	8	9	10	11	12
(c)	(d)	(b)	(a)	(d)	(b)	(a)	(c)	(c)	(c)	(d)	(a)

SOCIAL MARKETING/NETWORKING

INTRODUCTION

The base for any media to succeed is to make conversation impactful. Social Media Marketing (SMM) is the new method of marketing, which is based on the common principle of Word of Mouth (WOM). SMM is the latest innovation in the marketing world. Social media is defined as "a group of Internets based on the ideological and technological foundations and allow the creation and exchange of user generated content." Social media are a means for consumers to share text, images, audio, and video information with each other and with companies and vice versa. Social media allow marketers to establish a public voice and presence on the web and reinforce other communication activities.

Because of their day-to-day immediacy, they can also encourage companies to stay innovative and relevant. Therefore, business must learn how to use social media in a way that is consistent with their business plan. This is especially true for companies striving to gain a competitive advantage. The popularity of social media for marketing purposes can be attributed to several advantages associated with social media when compared to traditional marketing channels.

SCOPE OF SOCIAL MEDIA MARKETING (SMM)

Since opening up for everyone to sign up on September 26, 2006, Facebook just crossed 2 billion monthly active users as of quarter two of 2017. Even though the world population has grown to over 7.5 billion, by now, one out of every four humans on this planet has a facebook account. Facebook, quite literally, is beginning to take over the world. 62% of people in North America use the platform, and the percentages for similar countries are equally staggering.

92% of marketers declared that social media marketing plays a vital role for their business. 97% of marketers are showing interest by participating social media. 62% of the marketers said Social media played dynamic role in marketing past 6 months. As per the statistics an average of 42 minutes were spent by users on Facebook daily. The above statistics exhibits a vast prospective of social media marketing to surge sales.

According to the recent studies, companies recognized the importance and role of social media marketing and planned to increase social media budgets for next 5 years. It is a best medium to convey our information easily and effectively online. From last 7 or 8 years we have seen a sudden increase and progression on Social Media sites. Presently the most diversified Social Media Networks are Facebook, Twitter, Google+ and Linkedin etc.

India is World's 7th largest in Internet Market; there are 21 million people in India who are estimated to visit social media sites regularly which is 60.3% of the total active Indian Internet audience. More than 90% of Indian online users belong to 18-45 age group which has high purchase power and high disposable income. The social media websites in India are growing by almost 100% year after year.

Methodology: The paper is conceptual in nature. Data collection was achieved by online websites and the data is filtered to improve the quality of paper. The interpretations are made by the authors with the help of guide.

Few Popular Social Media Networks are:

- **Facebook**: Marketing campaigns on Facebook can make your social presence more visible and vivacious. FB marketing solutions consists of integrated Facebook advertising campaign, Facebook application development, page design, paid advertising, viral marketing and a lot more.
- **Twitter:** Twitter provides innovative marketing services which can help to increase your followers and make your products and services more visible in several social media platforms. It provides your business to engage your product or service with millions of users at a time.
- **Linkedin:** Linkedin promotes services helps you link with your targeted audience. The innovative strategies and ideas can play an active role in enhancing your social presence and make it better than your opponent.
- **Google+ and You Tube Marketing:** Google+ and You Tube offers an exciting opportunity by which any organization can competently promote their business. By using these networking platforms, we promote the services and products of our clients and improve their visibility and brand equity online.

OPPORTUNITIES BY SOCIAL MEDIA MARKETING

- **Blogger/Copywriter:** The post and articles you read on the internet were written by people. Working as a blogger or online writer means managing a varied workload and keeping track of plenty of deadlines, but it's hard to argue with the convenience of working from your home computer.
- **App Developer:** App development is typically a humble field but offers a significant potential for success. A great idea, if given enough effort and exposure, can grow a tiny start-up into a wildly popular social media giant. At the very least, though, developers can be satisfied knowing that their work is making the Internet a better, more diverse place.
- **Web Designer:** A great idea for the Next Big Thing in social media may be technically sounds, but it won't do much good unless it's presented in an accessible, user - friendly package. This is where the web designer comes in. Designers create the layout and aesthetic of a site, essentially building a bridge between the codes that makes the site work and ordinary users.
- **Hacker/Security Specialist:** It's generally more about stealing and destroying top-secret files, extorting money from large corporations and government institutions, and often, flying through wire-frame environments. The reality is a lot less fantastic, but real-world hacking is invaluable to today's social media and is an honest, paying job, to boot.
- **Digital Marketer:** Digital marketers focus on the critical task of studying internet trends and using them to cleverly draw traffic to a site. As social media's influence on society has grown, more and more businesses have recognized the importance of building their web presence, so opportunities for digital marketers are more widespread than ever.

Issues of Social Media Marketing:

- Choosing appropriate Brand Ambassador for the organization;
- In social media it involves high budget to promote product effectively;
- Ignorance of advertisements from customers in social media to save time;
- Faceless relationships with customers;
- Fake news and false promises in social media leads to decrease in reputation of organization.

SOCIAL MEDIA MARKETING PROSPECTS IN INDIA

Social Media Marketing is possible when there is an active participation among the people in general. It is very much important to have interested consumers for active conversation. This population can be referred to as "Active Internet Users". According to the research data released by Global Web India in March 2014, India is the country which comes 3rd when it comes to social networking and photo sharing. While United States and China are the biggest market, the next level of growth is expected out of India. As the country is poised for a 4G launch and with 500+ mobile phone penetration across the billion plus people populated country, it's only a matter of time that the adoption of internet and social media comes via mobile and other devices as well.

SMM SERVICES

Social Media Marketing Services are the services which helps the organization in enhancing the usability of the company's website using integration with social tools and application; improve site likability; allow easy sharing of site content on popular social sites; increase visibility on custom and niche search engines (Technorati etc.);

easy tracking of updates on your website; encouraging discussions on the site and a whole lot more. SMM Services helps positioning one's business on social networks to improve online brand visibility, brand protection / reputation management, leads and /or sales generation and increase quality inbound links. Some of the major SMM Services are:

- Social media audit;
- Social media optimization;
- Optimized blog development, design, maintenance and promotion;
- Brand management using social media monitoring;
- Social media profile creation and management (Twitter, Facebook, You Tube, etc.);
- Community building and monitoring;
- Linkedin Direct Ads;
- Facebook Advertisement;
- Social bookmarking;
- Social media distribution: leveraging social channels besides the regular channels to promote press releases and newsworthy content.

Everybody is a winner in the Social Media Space, no doubt about it. But one thing that is to be remembered by the Brand Managers that average consumer is far more vocal today. He does not need a Letter to the Editor to voice his opinion. His voice is far stronger than what it is today. All he needs to do is sneeze which will create a viral effect. One blog on any platform can make or mar your image. So just don't sit there and bombard him with marketing initiatives. Listen to him and talk to him. That's how he likes it.

Conclusion: Social media marketing is emerging rapidly to promote the products and services in online through various social networks like LinkedIn, Facebook, twitter, Instagram etc. Major benefit of social media marketing, which results in increasing profit of your company, is improving sales, regardless if you own an online shop or you want to encourage people to visit your business a specific location. So basically, the organizations must adopt social media strategies to sustain in the market. A job in social media is likely to be fast-paced and challenging, but it can be quite rewarding, monetarily and otherwise. If you know what kind of position to look for, social media could just be the source of your dream career.

TEST YOURSELF

1. Social media is defined as "a group of ________ on the ideological and technological foundations and allow the creation and exchange of user generated content."
(a) Mobile based
(b) Internets based
(c) Computer based
(d) Relation based

2. Since opening up for everyone to sign up on September 26, ______, Facebook just crossed 2 billion monthly active users as of quarter two of 2017.
(a) 2002 (b) 2004
(c) 2006 (d) 2008

3. The social media websites in India are growing by almost ________ year after year.
(a) 100% (b) 150%
(c) 200% (d) 300%

4. Which is not the Popular Social Media Networks?
(a) Facebook (b) Xender
(c) Linkedin (d) Twitter

5. Which are the opportunities by social media marketing?
(a) Blogger/Copywriter (b) App Developer
(c) Web Designer (d) All the above

6. Which are the scope of Social Media Marketing Services?
(a) Social media audit
(b) Social media optimization
(c) Community building and monitoring
(d) All the above

ANSWER

1	2	3	4	5	6
(b)	(c)	(a)	(b)	(d)	(d)

CONSUMER BEHAVIOUR AND PRODUCT

INTRODUCTION

Satisfying needs and wants of consumers whether tangible or intangible products/ services, is the major concern of all marketing firms. In other words, consumer's satisfaction is the essence of every service provider. Product forms the focal point of an organization's effort in satisfying its customers' needs. Satisfaction refers to the outcome of efforts put in by the banks and other service delivery concerns to deliver goods and services satisfactorily.

India has one of the largest saving rates to GDP. But still Indians prefer safety and liquidity over returns. They would still prefer to invest in so called safe investment products like bank deposits, post-office schemes, gold and land. Only a little of total investments gets into equity markets. That's why it is said that Indians are wise savers but poor investors. This paper explores the relationship between the various financial products and the underlying consumer behaviour for choosing the particular investment product. It first describes the various investment products available to the Indian consumers and then plots these products in Consumer Behavior Matrix developed by Antony Beckett. On the basis of the Consumer Behaviour matrix, it tries to conclude why customers are averse for making investments into equity markets and still prefer safe investment options.

CONSUMER BEHAVIOUR

If we define consumer behaviour as activities realized in the process of selecting, purchasing and using products and services, then the role of the bank image in relation to consumer behaviour is relatively complicated. From the point of view of consumers' behaviour research, the image may be viewed either as an independent variable, *i.e.*, the customers' behaviour determinant (the bank image influences decisions of customers), as a dependent variable (it is a result of the customer's experience with the bank and a reflection of the degree of their satisfaction or dissatisfaction) and of course also as an intervening variable (it works as a filter which influences the perception of the bank and judging of the information concerning the bank). The image thus may be studied in many contexts.

While at the initial stages of research into corporate image attention was mainly paid to its influence over consumer decisions and to image creation through marketing communication, later the attention of many authors writing about the services sector shifted to the relationship between corporate image and customer loyalty. Understanding the image as the impression created at a particular time at a particular level of abstraction, it appears to be necessary to better understand the character of customers' relationship to banks and the consequences of this relationship for consumer behaviour. With respect to the fact that "corporate image is formed in a consumer's mind through a procedure whereby information is processed and organized into meaning on the basis of stored categories."

MASLOW'S HIERARCHY OF NEEDS THEORY

Abraham Maslow is well renowned for proposing the Hierarchy of Needs Theory in 1943. This theory is a classical depiction of human motivation. This theory is based on the assumption that there is a hierarchy of five needs within each individual. The urgency of these needs varies. These five needs are as follows :

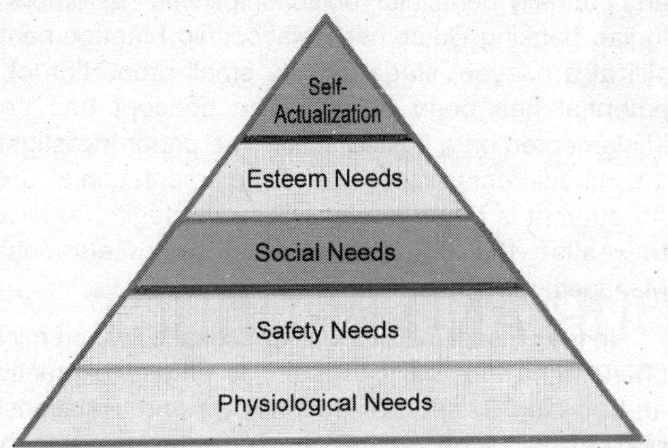

1. **Physiological Needs:** These are the basic needs of air, water, food, clothing and shelter. In other words, physiological needs are the needs for basic amenities of life.
2. **Safety Needs:** Safety needs include physical, environmental and emotional safety and protection. For instance-Job security, financial security, protection from animals, family security, health security, etc.
3. **Social Needs:** Social needs include the need for love, affection, care, belongingness, and friendship.
4. **Esteem Needs:** Esteem needs are of two types: internal esteem needs (self-respect, confidence, competence, achievement and freedom) and external esteem needs (recognition, power, status, attention and admiration).
5. **Self-actualization Need:** This include the urge to become what you are capable of becoming/ what you have the potential to become. It includes the need for growth and self-contentment. It also includes desire for gaining more knowledge, social-service, creativity and being aesthetic. The self-actualization needs are never fully satiable. As an individual grows psychologically, opportunities keep cropping up to continue growing.

According to Maslow, individuals are motivated by unsatisfied needs. As each of these needs is significantly satisfied, it drives and forces the next need to emerge. Maslow grouped the five needs into two categories—Higher-order needs and Lower-order needs. The physiological and the safety needs constituted the lower-order needs. These lower-order needs are mainly satisfied externally. The social, esteem, and self-actualization needs constituted the higher-order needs. These higher-order needs are generally satisfied internally, *i.e.*, within an individual. Thus, we can conclude that during boom period, the employees lower-order needs are significantly met.

PRODUCT

Definition: A product is the item offered for sale. A product can be a service or an item. It can be physical or in virtual or cyber form. Every product is made at a cost and each is sold at a price. The price that can be charged depends on the market, the quality, the marketing and the segment that is targeted. Each product has a useful life after which it needs replacement, and a life cycle after which it has to be re-invented. In FMCG parlance, a brand can be revamped, re-launched or extended to make it more relevant to the segment and times, often keeping the product almost the same.

Products in Bank: The concept of product packages is by considering customers' behaviour. Generally, a customer comes to the bank simply for a product but basically for solving the problems and to satisfy the needs. Customer needs are varied, complex and multi dimensional needs. A bank should offer multi-dimensional product otherwise called product package. In the place of offering one or two or a large number of products to the customers, it is by understanding all bank related needs of a customer and then evolve a comprehensive product package which can take care of his entire spectrum of needs. Hence once the bank gives a tailor-made product it will definitely cultivate a psychological ownership on the customer's mind. Another aspect required in a product policy is local touch that is, by considering local peculiarities, product must be local-oriented.

Marketing concept asserts to identify consumers' needs before the product is produced so that the product developed can meet the needs. It can be said that the consumer is the pivot around which the whole marketing system revolves. Modern marketing therefore begins with an understanding of consumer needs. The real problem is to learn what consumer needs. The real problem is to learn what a consumer takes into consideration when he chooses a particular brand. All the behaviour of human beings during the purchase may be turned as buyer's behaviour.

Factors influencing the consumer behaviour are internal like needs, motives, perceptions and attitudes as well as external. The major external factors are family social group, culture economics, business influence etc. To be more specific the peripheral services need frequent innovations, since this would be helpful in excelling competition. The product portfolio designing is found significant to maintain the commercial viability of the public sector banks. The banks professionals need to assign due weightage to their physical properties. They are supposed to look smart active and attractive.

Price: Price is a critical and important factor of bank marketing mix due numerous players in the industry. Most consumers will only be prepared to invest their money in search of extraordinary or higher returns. They are ready to pay additional value if there is a perception of extra product value. This value may be improved performance, function, services, reliability, and promptness for problem solving and of course, higher rate of return.

Promotion: Bank Marketing is actually is the marketing of reliability and faith of the people. It is the responsibility of the banking industry to take people in favour through Word of mouth publicity, reliability showing through long years of establishment and other services.

Place: The choice of where and when to make a product available will have significant impact on the customers. Customers often need to avail banking services fast for this they require the bank branches near to their official area or the place of easy access.

Bank Marketing Strategies: The marketing research considered being a systematic gathering, recording and analysis of data makes ways for making and innovation the marketing decisions. The information collected from the external sources by conducting surveys helps bank professional in different wants.

In the bank services, the formulation of overall marketing strategies is considered significant with the view point of tapping the potentials, expanding the business and increasing the marketing share. The increasing domination and gaining popularity banks, the popularity banks, the profitable schemes of the non-banking organization mounting craze among the customers for private banks have made the task of influencing the impulse of customers a bit difficult.

The marketing research simplifies the task of studying the magnitude of competition by opinion surveys and the feedback customers, the multi dimensional changes in the services mix can be made productive if it is based on marketing research.

CUSTOMER RELATIONSHIP MANAGEMENT (CRM)

Introduction: Customer Relationship Management has become inevitable for growth and profitability of Banks in present scenario marked by rising competition, technological advancement and empowered customers. The CRM practices are adopted to generate better understanding of the customer for product development, segmentation, appropriate targeting, campaign management and maintenance of long term profitable and mutually beneficial relationships with customers. In Indian banking Customer Relationship Management is still at a nascent stage. A very small proportion of its potential has been utilized. The concept has been implemented on a limited scale. The paper investigates the impediments to successful implementation of CRM. An attempt is made to chart out a strategic framework to realise the benefits of Customer Relationship Management.

In the present Indian Banking Scenario, two prominent phenomena are the focal point to emerging practices and policies. These are 'Technology' and 'Relationship Marketing'. The power of technology that has revolutionized banking services and practices. 'Relationship Marketing' is seen as the only differentiating factor given the almost commoditization of banking services. On observation of the recent restructuring, rebranding and re-engineering efforts of many banks, we find that the key motive towards these is to utilize customer centricity as a strategy. Further, catalyzing the importance of Technology and Relationship marketing is the Core Banking Solution (CBS). All the banks have overcome the teething troubles of CBS and it has become the axis of banks' growth and performance. Going further, most of the Banks have invested in technology enabled Customer Relationship Management Software to utilize CBS generated customer information for enhancing business opportunities, access to customers and support. Thus, CRM is a logical progression of CBS for Indian banks. Although, at a nascent stage it is developing swiftly.

Customer Relationship Management is the integration of these two cornerstones of Indian banking viz. technology and relationship marketing. It has a potential to bring about dynamic changes in marketing practices of banks in near future, with the objective of business growth through managing customers as assets, Systematically collecting, analyzing and disseminating customer information and use of this customer information for acquiring, retaining and better servicing customers. An understanding of the current status of the CRM initiative in majority of banks suggests that only a minuscule of the potential of CRM has been realised. The key impediment is the lack of understanding and acceptance of CRM as an organisation wide strategy and need for reorientation of organisation structure to adopt this. The paper attempts to investigate these issues and suggests a framework for reaping the benefits of this investment in CRM by various banks.

Definitions of Customer Relationship Management (CRM): CRM is the strategy for building, managing and strengthening loyal and long-lasting customer relationships. CRM is a customer centric approach based on customer insight. Its ultimate objective is toward 'Personalized' handling of customers as distinct entities through the identification and understanding of their differentiated needs, preferences and behaviour. A few more definitions which clarify CRM concept are :

According to Philip Kotler, CRM is the process of carefully managing detailed information about individual customers and all customer 'touch points' to maximize customer loyalty.

It can also be described as a business strategy comprised of process, organizational and technical change to better manage business around customer behaviour.

Types of CRM

Broadly, three types of CRM are adopted by banks:

1. **Operation CRM :** In this, CRM software packages are used to track and efficiently organise inbound and outbound interactions with customers including the management of marketing campaigns and call centres. Operational CRM supports frontline processes in sales, marketing and customer service, automating communications and interactions with the customers. They record contact history and store valuable customer information to ensure a consistent picture of customer's relationship with the bank that can be retrieved by staff as per requirement. The major benefits of operational CRM to banks are:
   (a) Sales Force Automation;
   (b) Customer Service and Support;
   (c) Enterprise Marketing Automation.

2. **Analytical CRM :** It is about analysing customer information to better address marketing and customer service objectives and deliver the right message to the right customer at the right time through the right channel. It involves the use of data analysis to extract knowledge for optimising customer relationships.

   The major benefits of Analytical CRM to banks are:
   (a) Customer Retention;
   (b) Fraud Detection;
   (c) Optimising marketing efforts as per customer life time value;
   (d) Credit Risk Analysis;
   (e) Segmentation and targeting;
   (f) Development of customised new products matching the specific preferences and priorities of customers.

3. **Collaborative CRM :** These involve systems facilitating customers to perform services on their own through a variety of communication and interactive channels. It brings people process and data together and enables channeling of data and information appropriately to bank staff for proactive decision making and enhanced informed customer service and support activities. It provides a means of information sharing to all concerned in timely manner and includes customer as a creator of service. The major benefits of collaborative CRM to banks are:
   (a) Providing efficient customer communication across a variety of channels
   (b) Online services to reduce customer service costs
   (c) Providing access to customer data while interacting with customers.

Thus, CRM can be understood as a catalyst enabling transformation of Banking from traditional 'Transactional banking' to 'Relationship Banking' by use of technology.

CRM in Banking for Indian Scenario

Although significance of Relationship Marketing practices and optimising and maintaining customer relationships across diverse customer segments has been realised and practiced by all banks in India, the technology enabled CRM is still at a developing stage. Different Banks are at different levels of CRM adoption and implementation and majority of them can be considered to be at preliminary stages. Operational CRM is the most wide spread, but collaborative CRM is most evident in internet banking, mobile banking, ATM functions, POS devices and initiatives like availability of pass book printing machines to enable customers to update their passbooks themselves. Also SMS alerts at various significant customer service events are proliferating. Analytical CRM is being utilised but not by all banks. Here also a few illustrations of Indian banks using CRM will define a clearer picture of CRM in Indian banking.

Issues and Challenges of CRM in Banking

CRM is a strategic initiative which has organisation wide implication. Many banks are still struggling to make proper use of this very useful mechanism. However, the adoption and utilisation is dependent on a number of factors and impediments. Broadly the issues are pertaining to: People, Processes, Data and Technology. Also a major draw back is the general perception of CRM being a Technology imperative. There is a great need to understand that technology is only the enabler to CRM. In the real sense it is an organisation wide strategy. The success of this depends on a careful integration of Organisation's goals, structure, systems, processes and resources.

TEST YOURSELF

1. Abraham Maslow theory is a classical depiction of human motivation. This theory is based on the assumption that there is a hierarchy of ______ needs within each individual.
   (a) three (b) four
   (c) five (d) six
2. What is the least pressing in Maslow's Hierarchy of Needs?
   (a) self-actualization (b) safety needs
   (c) physiological needs (d) social needs
3. Consumer purchases are influenced strongly by cultural, social, personal, and:
   (a) psychographic characteristics
   (b) psychological characteristics
   (c) psychometric characteristics
   (d) supply and demand characteristics
4. Product involvement refers to ______ or personal relevance of an item.
   (a) A consumer's perception of the importance
   (b) The need of the product
   (c) The price the product
   (d) The amount of people who bought the product
5. If the purchase is for a high-involvement product, consumers are likely to develop a high degree of ______ so that they can be confident that the item they purchase is just right for them.
   (a) Brand loyalty (b) Society
   (c) Product knowledge (d) References
6. Bank's products marketing influences which of the following factors?
   (a) Price (b) Promotion
   (c) Place (d) All of the above
7. Which types of CRM are adopted by banks in India?
   (a) Operation CRM (b) Analytical CRM
   (c) Collaborative CRM (d) All of the above
8. The major benefits of operational CRM to banks are except:
   (a) Sales Force Automation
   (b) Credit Risk Analysis
   (c) Customer Service and Support
   (d) Enterprise Marketing Automation
9. The major benefits of Analytical CRM to banks are:
   (a) Customer Retention
   (b) Segmentation and targeting
   (c) Fraud Detection
   (d) All of the above
10. Different products remain in existence for a different limitation period is called:
    (a) Product life cycle
    (b) Product life
    (c) Product maturity
    (d) Product decline

ANSWER

1	2	3	4	5	6	7	8	9	10
(c)	(a)	(b)	(a)	(c)	(d)	(d)	(b)	(d)	(a)

PRICING

PRICING IMPORTANCE

One of the elementary considerations any business startup has to attend to immediately after it has been established is what price it will charge for its principal product, as this is the primary means to cover raw material or other input costs, generate revenues, cover expenses, attract consumers, pay employees etc. in brief, to become a sustainable and profitable enterprise. Even though it is a fundamental decision, few choices a company will ever make are so essential in determining the bottom line it will report, the number of consumers it will have, and the ultimate performance it records and mistakes or errors here could have potential disastrous ramifications all across the board.

Pricing strategy refers to method companies use to price their products or services. Almost all companies, large or small, base the price of their products and services on production, labor and advertising expenses and then add on a certain percentage so they can make a profit. There are several different pricing strategies, such as penetration pricing, price skimming, discount pricing, product life cycle pricing and even competitive pricing.

A small company that uses penetration pricing typically sets a low price for its product or service in hopes of building market share, which is the percentage of sales a company has in the market versus total sales. The primary objective of penetration pricing is to garner lots of customers with low prices and then use various marketing strategies to retain them. For example, a small Internet software distributor may set a low price for its products and subsequently email customers with additional software product offers every month. A small company will work hard to serve these customers to build brand loyalty among them.

Pricing Definition: Price is the value that is put to a product or service and is the result of a complex set of calculations, research and understanding and risk taking ability. A pricing strategy takes into account segments, ability to pay, market conditions, competitor actions, trade margins and input costs, amongst others. It is targeted at the defined customers and against competitors.

PRICING OBJECTIVES

Setting prices for your products or services doesn't simply come down to a simple calculation. Prices can be practical tools for making ends meet or they can be marketing tactics for communicating something about the quality of your offerings. To figure out the best way to set prices, it's worthwhile to take a step back and examine your pricing objectives to develop a clear idea of what you want your pricing strategy to achieve. Four types of pricing objectives are as follows:

1. **Profit-Oriented Pricing:** In a sense, all pricing is profit-oriented because, even if you set prices with other objectives in mind, you still need to earn a profit to stay in business. However, profit-oriented pricing makes profit the top priority when figuring out the ideal price to set. A profit-oriented pricing strategy looks for the sweet spot that allows you to charge as much as possible for your offerings without charging so much that you alienate potential customers and lose money through missed sales. This type of pricing objective can either aim to maximize profit per

unit relative to cost of goods sold and other operating costs, or it can aim to maximize overall profit by setting a price that is competitive enough to increase the overall number of units you sell.

2. **Competitor-Based Pricing:** Competitor-based pricing uses the price you set to appeal to customers and define your niche relative to your competitors. It doesn't necessarily rely on setting a lower price than other available options, although this strategy will certainly make your products appeal to customers who shop on the basis of price alone. You can also use competitor-based pricing effectively by setting a price that's in the same ball park as other products in the same niche, or by choosing a higher price to send the message that your product is superior and worth the extra money.

3. **Market Penetration:** A market penetration pricing strategy is geared towards getting a foothold in a competitive market, usually by offering a low initial price. If you start out by attracting customers on the basis of price, you can get more people to try your products, and then start building a reputation and clientele that will allow you to eventually charge more. A market penetration strategy can be risky because customers don't like growing accustomed to a low price and then being asked to pay more. However, this approach can be successful if your products really do have qualities other than price that will make customers want to buy them, such as unique features or unusually high quality.

4. **Skimming:** A skimming pricing strategy uses the opposite logic from one based on market penetration. Although market penetration uses low prices to attract attention, skimming uses a reputation that has already been built to charge high prices from early adopters. If customers are passionate about your products and willing to pay extra to be the first to have them, you can charge initial high prices when you first introduce a new innovation or a new line, and then lower the prices once you've already attracted the people who are willing to pay more.

PRICING METHODS

The term pricing method in the context of compiling price indices would probably be regarded by most price statisticians as a common concept. The different pricing methods are discussed below :

1. Cost-Based Pricing

Cost-Based Pricing refers to a pricing method in which some percentage of desired profit margins is added to the cost of the product to obtain the final price. In other words, cost-based pricing can be defined as a pricing method in which a certain percentage of the total cost of production is added to the cost of the product to determine its selling price. Cost-based pricing can be of two types, namely, cost-plus pricing and markup pricing.

These two types of cost-based pricing are as follows:

(i) **Cost-plus Pricing:** Refers to the simplest method of determining the price of a product. In cost-plus pricing method, a fixed percentage, also called mark-up percentage, of the total cost (as a profit) is added to the total cost to set the price. For example, XYZ organization bears the total cost of ₹ 100 per unit for producing a product. It adds ₹ 50 per unit to the price of product as profit. In such a case, the final price of a product of the organization would be ₹ 150.

Cost-plus pricing is also known as average cost pricing. This is the most commonly used method in manufacturing organizations.

In economics, the general formula given for setting price in case of cost-plus pricing is as follows:

P = AVC + AVC (M)

AVC = Average Variable Cost

M = Mark-up percentage

AVC (m) = Gross profit margin

Mark-up percentage (M) is fixed in which AFC and net profit margin (NPM) are covered.

AVC (m) = AFC+ NPM

For determining average variable cost, the first step is to fix prices. This is done by estimating the volume of the output for a given period of time. The planned output or normal level of production is taken into account to estimate the output.

The second step is to calculate Total Variable Cost (TVC) of the output. TVC includes direct costs, such as cost incurred in labor, electricity, and transportation. Once TVC is calculated, AVC is obtained by dividing TVC by output, Q. [AVC = TVC/Q]. The price is then fixed by adding the mark-up of some percentage of AVC to the profit [P = AVC + AVC (m)].

The advantages of cost-plus pricing method are as follows:

a) Requires minimum information
b) Involves simplicity of calculation
c) Insures sellers against the unexpected changes in costs

The disadvantages of cost-plus pricing method are as follows:

a) Ignores price strategies of competitors

b) Ignores the role of customers

(ii) Markup Pricing: Refers to a pricing method in which the fixed amount or the percentage of cost of the product is added to product's price to get the selling price of the product. Markup pricing is more common in retailing in which a retailer sells the product to earn profit. For example, if a retailer has taken a product from the wholesaler for ₹ 100, then he/she might add up a markup of ₹ 20 to gain profit.

It is mostly expressed by the following formulae:

a. Markup as the percentage of cost = (Markup/ Cost) × 100

b. Markup as the percentage of selling price = (Markup/Selling Price) × 100

c. For example, the product is sold for ₹ 500 whose cost was ₹ 400. The mark up as a percentage to cost is equal to (100/400) × 100 = 25. The mark up as a percentage of the selling price equals (100/500) × 100 = 20.

2. Demand-Based Pricing

Demand-based pricing refers to a pricing method in which the price of a product is finalized according to its demand. If the demand of a product is more, an organization prefers to set high prices for products to gain profit; whereas, if the demand of a product is less, the low prices are charged to attract the customers.

The success of demand-based pricing depends on the ability of marketers to analyze the demand. This type of pricing can be seen in the hospitality and travel industries. For instance, airlines during the period of low demand charge less rates as compared to the period of high demand. Demand-based pricing helps the organization to earn more profit if the customers accept the product at the price more than its cost.

3. Competition-Based Pricing

Competition-based pricing refers to a method in which an organization considers the prices of competitors' products to set the prices of its own products. The organization may charge higher, lower, or equal prices as compared to the prices of its competitors.

The aviation industry is the best example of competition-based pricing where airlines charge the same or fewer prices for same routes as charged by their competitors. In addition, the introductory prices charged by publishing organizations for textbooks are determined according to the competitors' prices.

4. Other Pricing Methods

In addition to the pricing methods, there are other methods that are discussed as follows:

i) **Value Pricing:** Implies a method in which an organization tries to win loyal customers by charging low prices for their high-quality products. The organization aims to become a low-cost producer without sacrificing the quality. It can deliver high-quality products at low prices by improving its research and development process. Value pricing is also called value-optimized pricing.

ii) **Target Return Pricing:** Helps in achieving the required rate of return on investment done for a product. In other words, the price of a product is fixed on the basis of expected profit.

iii) **Going Rate Pricing:** Implies a method in which an organization sets the price of a product according to the prevailing price trends in the market. Thus, the pricing strategy adopted by the organization can be same or similar to other organizations. However, in this type of pricing, the prices set by the market leaders are followed by all the organizations in the industry.

iv) **Transfer Pricing:** Involves selling of goods and services within the departments of the organization. It is done to manage the profit and loss ratios of different departments within the organization. One department of an organization can sell its products to other departments at low prices. Sometimes, transfer pricing is used to show higher profits in the organization by showing fake sales of products within departments.

PRICING STRATEGIES

There are several pricing strategies. These are the four basic strategies, variations of which are used in the industry.

1. ***Premium pricing:*** High price is used as a defining criterion. Such pricing strategies work in segments and industries where a strong competitive advantage exists for the company. Example: Porsche in cars and Gillette in blades.

2. ***Penetration pricing:*** Price is set artificially low to gain market share quickly. This is done when a new product is being launched. It is understood

that prices will be raised once the promotion period is over and market share objectives are achieved. Example: Mobile phone rates in India; housing loans etc.

3. ***Economy pricing:*** No-frills price. Margins are wafer thin; overheads like marketing and advertising costs are very low. Targets the mass market and high market share. Example: Friendly wash detergents; Nirma; local tea producers.
4. ***Skimming strategy:*** High price is charged for a product till such time as competitors allow after which prices can be dropped. The idea is to recover maximum money before the product or segment attracts more competitors who will lower profits for all concerned. Example: the earliest prices for mobile phones, VCRs and other electronic items where a few players ruled attracted lower cost Asian players.

Costing and Pricing in Indian Banks

Over the years, the relationship between costs and benefits offered by the banks in India has been very hazy. Banks have been known for cost consideration. Costing had not made its appearance in the Indian banks till very recently. The study group had made its appearance in the Indian banks. The study Group on banking costs, set up by the banking commission, the PEP committee on banking and several other studies provide a useful insight into the costing and pricing aspects of services in banks in India.

TEST YOURSELF

1. _____ is the value that is put to a product or service and is the result of a complex set of calculations, research and understanding and risk-taking ability.
   (a) Selling (b) Price
   (c) Marketing (d) Promotion
2. Which are not the types of pricing objectives?
   (a) Profit-Oriented Pricing
   (b) Competitor-Based Pricing
   (c) Demand based Pricing
   (d) Market Penetration
3. Which is not the advantages of cost-plus pricing method?
   (a) Requires minimum information
   (b) Ignores the role of customers
   (c) Involves simplicity of calculation
   (d) Insures sellers against the unexpected changes in costs
4. When single price is charged for all consumers without any discrimination is known as:
   (a) Fixed price (b) Single price
   (c) Price strategy (d) Dynamic price
5. Which of the following is affected by the pricing, in case of a business concern?
   (a) Growth (b) Profit
   (c) Sustainability (d) All of the above
6. __________ refers to a pricing method in which the price of a product is finalized according to its demand.
   (a) Cost-plus pricing method
   (b) Demand-based pricing
   (c) Competition-based pricing
   (d) Value-based pricing
7. The pricing which helps in achieving the required rate of return on investment done for a product is called:
   (a) Target Return Pricing
   (b) Value Pricing
   (c) Going Rate Pricing
   (d) Transfer Pricing
8. Price is set artificially low to gain market share quickly. This is done when a new product is being launched is called:
   (a) Premium pricing (b) Penetration pricing
   (c) Economy pricing (d) Skimming strategy
9. Which of the following is not an external factor in pricing by a firm?
   (a) Buyer's behaviour (b) Competitor's policy
   (c) Social consideration (d) None of the above
10. Which of the following objective is generally not served by the pricing, in a business organization?
    (a) Profit (b) Survival
    (c) Market Share (d) None of the above

ANSWER

1	2	3	4	5	6	7	8	9	10
(b)	(c)	(b)	(a)	(d)	(b)	(a)	(b)	(d)	(d)

DISTRIBUTION

INTRODUCTION

The Information Technology hurricane which has impacted banking globally has also impacted the Indian banking sector and has made this colossus to wake up and embrace the new gift of the millennium for bringing in operational convenience of banking to the door step of the customer. Technological innovation not only enable a broader reach for consumer banking and financial services in Indian banking sector, but also enhances its capacity for continued and inclusive growth. E-developments in the arena of ATMs, Debit Cards, Credit Cards, Internet Banking and Mobile Banking are changing the way businesses work. While customers get the convenience of 24 × 7 banking, the bank saves in heavy real estate and manpower costs when compared to establishing a branch. The results are indicative of technology invasion in banks as is obvious from increasing number of ATMs, debit and credit cards.

DISTRIBUTION

In marketing, distribution is the process of moving a product from its manufacturing source to its customers. Four important Ps of marketing are Product, Promotion, Price and Place or Distribution. In the economic terms, any product, being capable of giving customer satisfaction needs to have 'place' and 'time' utility. This is provided by the 'Distribution' function of marketing mix.

Distribution Channels

A distribution channel is a chain of businesses or intermediaries through which a good or service passes until it reaches the end consumer. The path through which goods and services travel from the vendor to the consumer or payments for those products travel from the consumer to the vendor. A distribution channel can be as short as a direct transaction from the vendor to the consumer, or may include several interconnected intermediaries along the way such as wholesalers, distributors, agents and retailers. Each intermediary receives the item at one pricing point and moves it to the next higher pricing point until it reaches the final buyer.

Distribution Channels for Banking Services

Distribution channels are various technology based means through which the customers can transact their business with the Bank at their convenience anywhere and at any time of the day or night. Thus, customers have the choice of transacting business through ATM, Internet Banking, Telebanking, Mobile banking or through plastic cards such as Credit Card, Debit Card Smart Card etc.

In tune with various needs of the customers, different channels for delivery of service have evolved. Choice of delivery channels depends on several factors such as:

- Convenient time as ATMs, Telebanking, Internet Banking and Mobile Banking are available round the clock. ATMs must be accessible 24 × 7. Likewise Internet Banking and Mobile Banking must be accessible 24 × 7.
- Delivery channels should be easily accessible to customers. For eg., The ATM location must be spread across the area of operation for easy accessibility. These channels can be accessed

at multiple locations, including overseas locations.

- Delivery channel technology should be user-friendly. Customer should feel comfortable with the technology. The technology should have simple process for authentication and verification. Channels could have instructions in regional language, use biometrics, special facilities for the physically handicapped etc.
- All efforts must be made to ensure that service levels are met at all times to build customer confidence over a period of time. For eg., Managing cash replenishment to ensure ready availability of cash at all times is of utmost importance in ATM management. Cash management is essential when there are continuous bank holidays. Where the difference between peak and lean periods can widely vary. Care must be taken to ensure that customer should not have conflicting experiences across various channels.
- Bank should provide integrated platform that can accept information from various other platforms used by various product groups of the bank. For eg., The balance in the account should be correctly displayed when requested through any delivery channel.
- Channels must continuously offer to customers increased services, for eg., Mobile top-ups, purchase of railway tickets, investment in mutual funds, payment of bills through ATMs etc.
- Customer education on delivery channels is necessary. Customers need to be educated on topics like channel potential, channel usage through and-holding at least for the initial period. This improves confidence of the customer and induces them to use the channel.
- Continuous improvement to remove customer inconvenience by following simple "don't do's" need to be followed by banks. For eg., Avoiding calls at odd hours, avoiding mobile alerts at odd hours, process and systems improvements for reducing prolonged wait times at Phone Banking.
- Seamless service integration between the front-line (branches/phone banking) and back-office (operations units) is essential. Integration with back-end to deliver a one-bank experience to the customer across various channels, across various product lines is required. For managers to function in an informed environment there is need to create a single view of the customer across channels. This will enable the manager to act in a more proactive manner.

Reasons for Various Delivery Channels in Bank: Bank management is keen on implementation of delivery channels for various reasons such as:

- Bank can deliver the services simpler;
- Bank can deliver the services faster;
- Bank can acquire new customers;
- Bank can retain existing customers;
- Bank can keep customers highly satisfied on the services provided;
- Bank can lower operational costs and transaction processing costs;
- Bank can have a wider customer base regardless of geographies;
- Bank can improve profitability.

TYPES OF DISTRIBUTION CHANNELS FOR BANKING SERVICES

A distribution channel is a route to the market for a supplier. In the case of a bank, the distribution channel is the way the banking product or service takes from the bank to the customer. Most banks have multiple channels to serve their customers. Today, they can choose between branches, contact centers, ATMs and online channels, portals and web banks.

Types of Distribution Channels: Different types of distribution channels are as under:

1. **Branches:** These are the face of the bank and the place where the client meets the bank. The distribution is made by the traditional counter. Human beings. Without us none of these products and services would exist at all. The dialogue banking concept is built on the basis that, for the foreseeable future at least, people prefer to interact with other humans. Live dialogue builds assurance and trust, and answers to what customers feel are important questions can be obtained much more rapidly. Staffing models are evolving in response to the migration to new distribution channels, and it is the universal banker or relationship banker (also called a "universal agent or relationship agent") model that is shaping up to be the dominant type for branch staff going forward. Relationship bankers are expected to have a different skill-set to the traditional tellers, with versatility, a personable/sales-orientation, and confidence in educating customers how to use modern banking technology a must. Universal bankers working in dialogue towers with cash recyclers constitutes an Assisted Full-Service option. In this respect, the branch is a distribution channel where the human factor plays a dominant role.

2. **Specialized Branches:** These branches have been created as an alternative for the classic branches. These specialized branches are focused on a certain type of activity such as: operations for individuals, for small business or for corporate clients. Banks have opened such branches in super markets or malls. The main reason for establishing such branches was to have a close relationship with these corporate customers and to provide services of interests for their clients. Their primary activities are the consumer loans and basic operations for individuals (payments, foreign exchanges etc.).

3. **Micro Branches:** The micro branch has earned its own right to be considered a distribution channel, because a full-size branch wouldn't fit into the market places where micro branches really make a difference. In addition to their versatility, micro branches give a guaranteed return on investment. Micro branches are smaller, more cost-effective versions of their "small branch" counterparts. They can be fully-automated via advanced terminals, with a single relationship agent available to sell products and services. Micro branches can be strategically placed in targeted market places inside larger stores, malls, or even hotels. When properly designed with compelling retail communications and brand merchandising, a micro branch can stand out in a crowd and exudes convenience.

4. **Business Correspondents / Business Facilitators (BCBF) Model:** Financial Inclusion Programme was launched by Government of India as more than 40% of the country's population did not have any access to Banking services. With the objective of ensuring greater financial inclusion and increasing the outreach of the banking sector, in Jan. 2006 based on the recommendations of Khan Commission, the Reserve Bank of India issued a new set of guidelines allowing banks to employ two categories of intermediaries—Business Correspondents (BCs) and Business Facilitators (BFs)—to expand their business. According to the guidelines scheduled commercial banks including Regional Rural Banks (RRBs) and Local Area Banks (LABs) have been permitted to use the services of intermediaries in providing financial and banking services throughout the country and even in remote areas.

   In this model BCs are permitted to carry out transactions on behalf of the bank as agents, the BFs can refer clients, pursue the clients' proposal and facilitate the bank to carry out its transactions, but cannot transact on behalf of the bank. Recently Reserve Bank of India (RBI) has permitted all Business Correspondents (BCs) working for one particular bank; perform business for other banks too.

   As reported by the banks under their financial inclusion plans nearly 2,48,000 BC agents had been deployed by banks as on March 31, 2014 which are providing services through more than 3,33,000 BC outlets. Nearly 117 million basic saving bank deposit accounts (BSBDAs) opened through BCs remained outstanding as on March 31, 2014.

5. **Video/Call Centers:** Call centers are one of the most preferred support channels, probably because making a telephone call is very quick and convenient. As video ITM's and Assisted Self-Service (advanced) terminals become more common, financial institutions can potentially convert service and support calls into sales. This means the universal banker model for branch staffing can also be applied in call centers. With improvements in quality of support, a target per cent rate of support-to-sales-conversions can be established, and call centers will become a significant distribution channel. One drawback is that the option of telephone support is usually only offered to premium account holders, but as conversion targets are met it's expected that a larger segment of customers will be able to receive phone support. Expanding this option to the entire customer base may be instrumental in growing the call center as a major sales channel, with specially trained staff and full video capability. Even without quality improvements, the call center is a legitimate distribution channel, serving both advice and sales, with emphasis on customer service.

6. **Advanced Terminal and ATM Kiosks:** According to the IBM Institute for Business Value, 65% of all banking customers regularly use ATM's. This is significant, and it indicates that the ATM will be relevant as a stand alone distribution channel for years to come. The latest technology (the advanced terminal) can perform a wide range of banking tasks and envelope-free deposits. Advance Studies on Financial Services have stated that advanced terminals offer banks the opportunity to generate additional revenue streams by using "self-service terminals to sell products such as mobile recharge, transit tickets, theater tickets, and prepaid cards". ATM's are slowly evolving towards a scenario where

the ATM would be either an advanced multifunction ATM, or else would function as a cash safe controlled by a tablet (or even a smartphone) used by a customer. This is true ATM-mobile integration and is viewed by industry commentators as an inevitable aspect of the banking omnichannel.

7. **EFTPOS (Electronic Funds Transfer at Point of Sale):** It is a payment method that can be described as a distribution channel. EFTPOS is a system by which the clients pay the services they acquired just by using a bank card. This system is very used when shopping, travelling, buying tickets. In a society where time is money, there has been a huge request from the customers for more accessible distribution channels. The computers and the mobile phones were the best choice. As a result the banks have made considerable investments in the development of services that are not based in the branch and which are accessible through the Internet or mobiles phones. The client has the possibility of choosing from a large variety of channels: phone, ATM, POS, Internet. As a result, a new form of banking has appeared.

8. **Digital and Mobile:** Mobile and online transactions are merging with those performed on an ATM. Banking website The Financial Brand reported in April, 2015 that 39% of adults say they use their smartphone for mobile banking, but it is speculated that smartphone usage for online banking may plateau as smartphones have saturated the market. Nevertheless, customers will continue to engage in online banking of various types, including tablet, laptop and desktop banking, regardless of stagnating growth in smartphone sales. Digital banking is a huge part of the omnichannel, with modern financial institutions' websites, banking apps, social media accounts, SMS notifications, chat support and more presenting a unified voice and appearance to consumers. With detachable tablets like the Surface Pro predicted to grow by 75% in 2016, digital banking is set to keep growing, and demand for a seamless, parallel, device-switchable banking experience will grow with it.

9. **BHIM (Bharat Interface for Money):** BHIM is a mobile app developed by NPCI, based on the Unified Payment Interface (UPI) and was launched on 30 December 2016. It is intended to facilitate e-payments directly through banks and as part of the drive towards cashless transactions. BHIM allow users to send or receive money to other UPI payment addresses or scanning QR code or account number with IFSC code or MMID (Mobile Money Identifier) Code to users who do not have a UPI-based bank account. BHIM allows users to check current balance in their bank accounts and to choose which bank account to use for conducting transactions, although only one can be active at any time. Users can create their own QR code for a fixed amount of money, which is helpful in merchant transactions.

10. **Innovations in Branch Banking through Intelligent Robotic Assistant:** As per latest RBI reports, AI (Artificial Intelligence) and robotics have the potential to transform data analytics and customer experience in banking. Until recently, application of robotics was unheard of in banking and was considered for application primarily in the manufacturing & medical sectors. With use of Intelligent Robotic Assistant (IRA), robotics are being brought into the main stream of customer service and support. IRA is designed to assist branch staff in large branches, which have high footfalls, by guiding customers to carry out their banking transactions. AI is becoming an integral part of the banking system, functions, processes and customer interactions. Both Robotics and AI will help banks manage both internal and external customers much more effectively and help reduce operational costs exponentially in the future. The potential of AI and Robotics based solutions is enormous and will revolutionize the way people do banking.

11. **Plastic Cards:** Credit Cards and Debit Cards facilitate the banking transactions of a certain nature, to be done outside the banking premises and at the time suitable to the customer. These serve as a means for credit services becoming available at the merchant establishments located away from the branches.

As we could see, most banks operate through various distribution channels. The expectation was that customers would eventually conduct most of their business online or by phone. However, current studies suggest that customers still prefer the branches. Over the last decade, banks have made considerable investments in the development of services that are not based in the branch. Multichannel banking is, therefore, more relevant than ever. Multichannel banking is more than just offering multiple channels, but offering integrated channels, with the optimal balance of services, prices and offer across channels. Banks should have the ability to deliver the right service at the right time in the right channel.

MOBILE BANKING

Mobile banking is a service provided by a bank or other financial institution that allows its customers to conduct financial transactions remotely using a mobile device such as a smartphone or tablet. Unlike the related internet banking it uses software, usually called an app, provided by the financial institution for the purpose. Mobile banking is usually available on a 24-hour basis. Some financial institutions have restrictions on which accounts may be accessed through mobile banking, as well as a limit on the amount that can be transacted.

Mobile phones, as a medium for extending banking services, have attained greater significance because of their ubiquitous nature. The rapid growth of mobile users in India, through wider coverage of mobile phone networks, have made this medium an important platform for extending banking services to every segment of banking clientele in general and the unbanked segment in particular.

In order to ensure a level playing field, Reserve Bank brought out a set of operating guidelines for adoption by banks. For the purpose of the instructions contained in this Master Circular, 'Mobile Banking transaction' means undertaking banking transactions using mobile phones by bank customers that involve accessing / credit / debit to their accounts. Banks are permitted to offer mobile banking services (through SMS, USSD or mobile banking application) after obtaining necessary permission from the Department of Payment & Settlement Systems, Reserve Bank of India. Mobile Banking services are to be made available to bank customers irrespective of the mobile network.

Regulatory & Supervisory Issues: Banks which are licensed, supervised and having physical presence in India, are permitted to offer mobile banking services. Only banks who have implemented core banking solutions are permitted to provide mobile banking services. The services shall be restricted only to customers of banks and/or holders of debit/credit cards issued as per the extant Reserve Bank of India guidelines. Only Indian Rupee based domestic services shall be provided. Use of mobile banking services for cross border inward and outward transfers is strictly prohibited.

Banks may also use the services of Business Correspondent appointed in compliance with RBI guidelines, for extending this facility to their customers. The guidelines issued by the Reserve Bank on 'Risks and Controls in Computers and Telecommunications' will apply *mutatis mutandis* to Mobile Banking. The guidelines issued by Reserve Bank on "Know Your Customer (KYC)", "Anti Money Laundering (AML)" and "Combating the Financing of Terrorism (CFT)" from time to time would be applicable to mobile based banking services also.

Registration of Customers for Mobile Service: Banks shall put in place a system of registration of customers for mobile banking. Banks should strive to provide options for easy registration for mobile banking services to their customers, through multiple channels, thus minimizing the need for the customer to visit the branch for such services. The time taken between registration of customers for mobile banking services and activation of the service should also be minimal.

MPIN Generation: In order to address the challenges in extending the facility of MPIN generation to the customers registered for mobile banking, banks have to explore various options. In order to quicken the process of MPIN generation and also widen the accessibility to their mobile banking registered customers, banks can consider adopting various channels/ methods such as:

a) Through the ATM channels (similar to option available for change of PIN on their own ATMs as well as in inter-operable ATM networks);
b) Through an option provided in the USSD menu for mobile banking (both their own USSD platform, if any, as well as under the inter-operable USSD Platform for mobile banking);
c) Banks' own internet banking website, with necessary safeguards;
d) Use of MPIN mailers (like PIN mailers for cards);
e) Common website can also be designed as an industry initiative.

Banks may also undertake customer education and awareness programme in multiple languages through different channels of communication to popularise their process of mobile banking registration/activation and its usage etc.

Information Security is most critical to the business of mobile banking services and its underlying operations. Therefore, technology used for mobile banking must be secure and should ensure confidentiality, integrity, authenticity and non-reputability.

Inter-Operability: Banks offering mobile banking service must ensure that customers having mobile phones of any network operator is in a position to avail of the service, *i.e.*, should be network independent. Restriction, if any, for the customers of particular mobile operator(s) are permissible only during the initial stages of offering the service, up to a maximum period of six months subject to review.

The long-term goal of mobile banking framework in India would be to enable funds transfer from account in one bank to any other account in the same or any other bank on a real time basis irrespective of the mobile network a customer has subscribed to. This would require interoperability between mobile banking service providers and banks and development of a host of message formats. To ensure interoperability between banks, and between their mobile banking service providers, banks shall adopt the message formats like ISO 8583, with suitable modification to address specific needs.

INTERNET BANKING

Internet banking (e-banking) facilitates customers to avail various small and large value banking products and services through electronic channels. Internet banking comprises banking activities or services which can be availed by the customers at any point of time and from any places with their convenience, it is also called PC banking, online banking, cyber banking, virtual banking, etc. Internet banking delivers banking services through the open access computer network *i.e.*, Internet, directly to customers' home that can be used with different electronic devices such as personal computer, mobile phone with a browser or desktop software, digital television. So, we can say that Internet banking is about using banking facilities via the internet with the help various electronic devices.

Benefits of using Internet Banking

Using Internet banking is beneficial for both *i.e.*, Customers as well as banks. The benefits of adopting internet banking are mentioned below:

(A) Benefits for Costumers : The customer has following benefits with Internet Banking.

- **Less Waiting Time:** It offers less waiting time and more convenience as compared to the traditional banking system and significantly lowers the cost structure than traditional delivery channels. It also reduces the time and place limitation and it provides various benefits to consumers so that they feel convenient while doing banking activities.
- **Ease and Convenience:** Internet banking is considered as more efficient in term of ease of use and access. It allows the consumers to make transactions on internet provide them comfort of home or office without going outside. It also enables consumers to keep an eye on their transactions or account activities from their home, office or else where so they can feel satisfied and convenient. Even non-transactional facilities like ordering check. books online, updating accounts, inquiring about interest rates of various financial products etc. have become much simpler on the internet.
- **24 × 7 Availability:** With the help of internet banking, costumer can access their banking facilities and services all around the clock *i.e.*, 24 hours and 365 days from any where any time. They don't need to wait for timing of bank branches.
- **Self-Service Channel:** Internet banking provides their customer a self-service channel for various banking services they have not to depend on the bank's staff and other depending process to avail their services. Internet banking is one of the most popular self-service banking technologies. Continued use of self-service technology is positively affected by buyers' perceived usefulness.
- **Save Time and Money:** Now customers don't have to go to branch to avail banking services it consists various advantages such as: it will save time, save fuel, do away from traffic, save the environment in term of reducing the use of motor vehicles and reduce waiting time.

(B) Benefits for Banks: The banks are benefits with internet banking services.

- **Increased Profitability:** Adoption of internet helps the banks to increase their profitability. Banks with Internet banking have better operating efficiency ratios and profitability as compared to banks, which are not using internet facilities. The banks can provide banking services to the consumers using internet banking at a far lower cost as compared to the traditional banking.
- **Cost Effective Mechanism:** The internet banking provides an opportunity of self-service channel to the consumers. This help the banks to cut their work force up to a particular extent that results in reducing the administrative costs bear by the banks. Compared to traditional banking system, internet banking is cost-effective as it reduces the administrative costs and paperwork needed for the bank transactions. Many studies show that electronic banking has successfully reduced operating and administrative cost and fees.
- **Reach where there is no branch:** Internet banking has expanded their geographical reach and may increase customer base through deploying electronic delivery channels at lower cost. Actually, some banks are doing in that way, they are providing banking services

exclusively via the Internet in some areas because they do not have bank branches in these areas. Whereas many financial institutions are using the Internet banking as a branchless banking to satisfy their existing customers and attract new customers in the perspective of convenience and cost effectiveness.

- **Improve Customer Relationship:** Maintaining the relationship with consumers has become a strategic priority for most of the banks. Using the internet banking technology and facilities can provide a means for banks to develop and maintain a good relationship with their customers by offering easy access to a wide range of products and services. Managing a good relationship with the customers may help to make customer loyalty, customer retention and improve cross-selling. Internet banking facilities have become a useful tool for improving customer satisfaction and increasing cross-selling opportunities.
- **Eco-friendly Image:** Another important benefit of internet banking is that it is eco-friendly in nature. Internet banking cuts down the paper usage and reduces pollution as people do not have to travel physically and also does not add carbon emissions. Implementing the e-banking facilities in the banks show the concern of the bank to wards the environment, which further, will help the banks to create an eco-friendly image.

CURRENT SCENARIO OF INTERNET BANKING / E-BANKING IN INDIA

Internet Banking has become an integral part of banking system in India. The concept of e-banking is of fairly recent origin in India. Till the early 90's traditional model of banking *i.e.*, branch based banking was prevalent, but after that non-branch banking services were started. The Indian government enacted the IT Act, 2000, with effect from the 17th October, 2000. Most of the banks have already implemented the e-banking facilities, as these facilities are beneficial to both *i.e.*, banks as well as consumers. But the adoption of e-banking by the consumers is still at the early stage due to various challenges. The challenges such as security risk, privacy risk, trust factor and less awareness among consumers about e-banking are acting as hurdle in the adoption of e-banking facilities. Considering the challenges and risk related to e-banking, the Government of India along with various government agencies is making an effort to make e-banking more safe, secure and reliable.

TEST YOURSELF

1. In marketing, _________ is the process of moving a product from its manufacturing source to its customers.

(a) promotion (b) distribution
(c) marketing (d) selling

2. Bank management is keen on implementation of delivery channels for various reasons such as:

(a) Bank can deliver the services faster
(b) Bank can acquire new customers
(c) Bank can retain existing customers
(d) All of the above

3. Most banks have multiple channels to serve their customers. Which is not the distribution channel of banking services for customer?

(a) Branches
(b) Specialized branches
(c) Micro Branches
(d) Head office

4. Bank facilitate payment services available at merchant establishments through which of the following?

(a) ATM (b) Branches
(c) Debit cards (d) All of the above

5. Bank make credit services available at merchant establishments through which of the following?

(a) Branches (b) Credit Card
(c) Debit Cards (d) All of the above

6. In a credit card or debit card, where the cash is actually used is called:

(a) Point of sale (b) ATM
(c) Point of distribution (d) All of the above

7. __________ is a mobile app developed by NPCI, based on the Unified Payment Interface (UPI) and was launched on 30 December, 2016.

(a) Bharat Code (b) BHIM
(c) PAYTM (d) PAYPAL

8. As per latest RBI reports, __________ have the potential to transform data analytics and customer experience in banking.

(a) AI (Artificial Intelligence) and robotics
(b) Mobile and online transactions
(c) Bharat Code
(d) EFTPOS (Electronic Funds Transfer at Point of Sale)

9. In order to quicken the process of MPIN generation to their mobile banking registered customers, banks can consider adopting various channels/methods such as:
(a) Through the ATM channels
(b) Banks' own internet banking website, with necessary safeguards
(c) Use of MPIN mailers (like PIN mailers for cards)
(d) All of the above

10. Using Internet banking is beneficial for both *i.e.*, Costumers as well as banks. The benefits for customers of adopting internet banking are mentioned below:
(a) 24x7 Availability
(b) Increased Profitability
(c) Cost effective mechanism
(d) All of the above

ANSWER

1	2	3	4	5	6	7	8	9	10
(b)	(d)	(d)	(c)	(c)	(a)	(b)	(a)	(d)	(a)

CHANNEL MANAGEMENT

CHANNEL MANAGEMENT

Definition: The term Channel Management is widely used in sales marketing parlance. It is defined as a process where the company develops various marketing techniques as well as sales strategies to reach the widest possible customer base. The channels are nothing but ways or outlets to market and sell products. The ultimate aim of any organization is to develop a better relationship between the customer and the product.

Goal of Channel Management

Channel management helps in developing a program for selling and servicing customers within a specific channel. The aim is to streamline communication between a business and the customer. To do this, you need to segment your channels according to the characteristics of your customers: their needs, buying patterns, success factors, etc. and then customize a program that includes goals, policies, products, sales, and marketing program.

The goal of channel management is to establish direct communication with customers in each channel. If the company is able to effectively achieve this goal, the management will have a better idea which marketing channel best suits that particular customer base. The techniques used in each channel could be different, but the overall strategy must always brand the business consistently throughout the communication.

A business must determine what it wants out of each channel and also clearly define the framework for each of those channels to produce desired results. Identifying the segment of the population linked to each channel also helps to determine the best products to pitch to those channels.

Distribution Channel Management in Bank

In order to sustain profitability, financial institutions and, in particular, retail and wholesale banks need to offer a unique value proposition and provide exceptional customer experience across all distribution channels. Retaining and winning new clients is not only a matter of tailoring new financial products and services to client's needs, but also ensuring that the services provided are aligned across all distribution channels, providing positive and personalized customer interaction regardless of how the customer contact is made (branch, call center, online banking, mobile banking and business partners). This is the biggest challenge in a modernized, omni-channel architecture.

CHANNEL LEVELS

Channel level refers to the intermediary in marketing distribution channel between the producer/manufacturer and the end consumer. Every channel level plays a role in making the good available to the end consumer. The number of channel levels between the producer and consumer could be 0, 1, 2, 3 or more.

A zero-level channel is a direct marketing channel where there is no intermediary and the producer sell directly to the consumer. For example – direct mails, telemarketing etc. A one level channel has one intermediary, typically a retailer between a manufacturer and consumer. Similarly, a 2-level channel and a 3-level channel have 2 and 3 intermediaries respectively.

The different levels of the basic distribution channels can be given as below:

Zero Channel	*One Level*	*Two Level*	*Three Level*
No Intermediary	One Intermediary	Two Intermediaries	Three Intermediaries
Sell directly to the consumer	Seller → Retailer → Customer	Seller → Wholesaler → Retailer → Customer	Seller → Wholesaler → Agent → Retailer → Customer

CHANNEL DYNAMICS

Distribution channels do not stand still. New wholesaling and retailing institutions emerge, new channels systems evolve. Channels can be vertically, horizontally and through multi-channels. In the recent days, banks are using the hybrid channels. They use all the channel alternatives for marketing their services.

a) **Vertical Marketing Systems (VMS):** Vertical marketing systems is a kind of cooperation that exists between the distribution channels that are available in various levels with different members working together for promoting the efficiency and also the scale of economies in way that the products can be promoted towards customers, products get inspected, credit can be provided to the customers and also can be delivered to the customers.

b) **Horizontal Marketing Systems:** A horizontal marketing system is a distribution channel arrangement whereby two or more organizations at the same level join together for marketing purposes to capitalize on a new opportunity. For example: a bank and a supermarket agree to have the bank's ATMs located at the supermarket's locations; two manufacturers combining to achieve economies of scale otherwise not possible with each acting alone to meet the needs and demands of a very large retailer; or two wholesalers joining together to serve a particular region at a certain time of year.

c) **Multi-Channel Marketing Systems:** When distributing a product, each "channel" is an additional avenue to reach customers. Thus, multi-channel distribution management is a strategy to provide customers with multiple ways to purchase the same product. A multi-channel distribution management system is the set of business processes that enable profitable, sustainable development of multiple distribution channels. Many multi-channel distribution systems benefit from the support of technology. However, the "system" includes more than just software that supports the execution of a multi-channel strategy. It also includes strategic business planning to help shape the creation and improvement of that execution.

ADVANTAGES OF CHANNEL MANAGEMENT

When a customer is considering buying a product he tries to access its value by looking at various factors which surround it. Factors like its delivery, availability etc which are directly influenced by channel members. Similarly, a marketer too while choosing his distribution members must access what value is this member adding to the product. He must compare the benefits received to the amount paid for using the services of this intermediary. These benefits can be the following:

a) **Cost Saving:** The members of distribution channel are specialized in what they do and perform at much lower costs than companies trying to run the entire distribution channel all by itself.

b) **Time Saving:** Along with costs, time of delivery is also reduced due to efficiency and experience of the channel members. For example, if a grocery store were to receive direct delivery of goods from every manufacturer the result would have been a chaos. Everyday hundreds of trucks would line up outside the store to deliver products. The store may not have enough space for storing all their products and this would add to the chaos. If a grocery wholesaler is included in the distribution chain then the problem is almost solved. This wholesaler will have a warehouse where he can store bulk shipments. The grocery store now receives deliveries from the wholesaler in amounts required and at a suitable time and often in a single truck. In this way cost as well as time is saved.

c) **Customer Convenience:** Including members in the distribution chain provides customer with a lot of convenience in their shopping. If every manufacturer owned its own grocery store then customers would have to visit multiple grocery stores to complete their shopping list. This would be extremely time-consuming as well as taxing for the customer. Thus, channel distribution provides accumulating and assorting services, which means they purchase from many suppliers the various goods that a customer may demand. Secondly, channel distribution is time saving as the customers can find all that they need in one retail store and the retailer.

d) **Customers can buy in Small Quantities:** Retailers buy in bulk quantities from the manufacturer or wholesaler. This is more cost effective than buying in small quantities. However, they resell in smaller quantities to their customers. This phenomenon of breaking bulk quantities and selling them in smaller quantities is known as bulk breaking. The customers therefore have the benefit of buying in smaller quantities and they also get a share of the profit the retailer makes when he buys in bulk from the supplier.

Customers Receive Financial Support

Resellers offer financial programs to their customers which makes payment easier for the customer. Customers can buy on credit, buy using a payment plan etc.

TEST YOURSELF

1. ________ is defined as a process where the company develops various marketing techniques as well as sales strategies to reach the widest possible customer base.
(a) Distribution (b) Channel Management
(c) Sale Promotion (d) None of these

2. Find the incorrect statements about Channel management:
(a) Channel management helps in developing a program for selling and servicing customers within a various channel.
(b) The aim is to streamline communication between a business and the customer.
(c) To do this, you need to segment your channels according to the characteristics of your customers: their needs, buying patterns, success factors, etc.
(d) After segmentation, customize a program that includes goals, policies, products, sales, and marketing program.

3. A ________ channel is a direct marketing channel where there is no intermediary and the producer sell directly to the consumer.
(a) zero-level (b) one-level
(c) two-level (d) three-level

4. The type of distribution channel Seller ⇨ Retailer ⇨ Customer is called:
(a) zero-level (b) one-level
(c) two-level (d) three-level

5. New wholesaling and retailing institutions emerge, new channels systems evolve. In the recent days, banks are using the hybrid channels. These channels are:
(a) Vertical marketing systems
(b) Horizontally marketing systems
(c) Multi-channels marketing systems
(d) All of the above

6. A ________ is a distribution channel arrangement whereby two or more organizations at the same level join together for marketing purposes to capitalize on a new opportunity.
(a) Vertical marketing systems
(b) Horizontally marketing systems
(c) Multi-channels marketing systems
(d) Wider marketing systems

7. When distributing a product, each "channel" is an additional avenue to reach customers. Thus, ________ is a strategy to provide customers with multiple ways to purchase the same product.
(a) Vertical distribution management
(b) Horizontally distribution management
(c) Multi-channels distribution management
(d) Wider distribution management

8. Advantages of Channel Management are:
(a) Cost Saving
(b) Time Saving
(c) Customer Convenience
(d) All of the above

ANSWER

1	2	3	4	5	6	7	8
(b)	(a)	(a)	(b)	(d)	(b)	(c)	(d)

PROMOTION

INTRODUCTION

In marketing, promotion refers to any type of marketing communication used to inform or persuade target audiences of the relative merits of a product, service, brand or issue. The aim of promotion is to increase awareness, create interest, generate sales or create brand loyalty. It is one of the basic elements of the market mix, which includes the four P's: price, product, promotion, and place. Promotion is also one of the elements in the promotional mix or promotional plan. These are personal selling, advertising, sales promotion, direct marketing publicity and may also include event marketing, exhibitions and trade shows. A promotional plan specifies how much attention to pay to each of the elements in the promotional mix, and what proportion of the budget should be allocated to each element.

Role of Promotion in Marketing in Banking Services

In the formulation of marketing mix the bank professionals are also supposed to blend the promotion mix in which different components of promotion such as advertising, publicity, sales promotion, word-of-mouth promotion, personal selling and tele-marketing are given due weightage. The different components of promotion help bank professionals in promotion the banking business.

Banks have a unique challenge when it comes to marketing because they do not offer tangible products for consumers. Promoting a bank requires convincing consumers to trust a bank with their money and make customers feel like they are getting the most value for their money. Once customers invest with a bank, the bank must work to keep customers and get them to buy-in to additional products.

KINDS OF PROMOTION

The promotion efforts aim to encourage the customer to move through various stages of the decision-making process towards buying the offering made by the bank. The companies having different objectives choose different kinds of promotion. These are:

(a) **Informative Promotion:** The primary objective of every promotional activity is to disseminate information about the product, product line, brand, and the company. The marketers adopt this promotion strategy to convince customers to try a product at least once. It is based on the notion that the customer will purchase the product only if he has the adequate information about it.

(b) **Persuasive Promotion:** The persuasive promotion is prevalent at the growth stage of a product where the primary objective of the management is to persuade people to buy. The basic purpose of this promotion strategy is to stimulate purchase and create a positive image of the product in the minds of customers in order to influence their long-term behaviours.

(c) **Reminder Promotion:** The reminder promotion is often adopted at the stage when a product reaches its maturity. The purpose of such promotion is to keep the product alive in the minds of the customers. Here, the firm emphasizes on the product's utility, features, brand names with the intent to make customers remind the product.

d) **Buyer behaviour Modifications:** The effect of promotional strategies could be accessed through the modifications in the consumer behaviour. The constant personal selling and repeated advertisements could be used to measure the effectiveness of such promotional schemes.

Thus, the companies can choose any of the promotions depending on the nature of the product and the pursued objectives.

COMPONENTS OF PROMOTION MIX

One of the most important element of marketing mix of services is promotion which is consist of personal selling, advertising, public relations, and selling promotional tools.

a) **Personal Selling:** Due to the characteristics of banking services, personal selling is the way that most banks prefer in expanding selling and use of them. The personal selling is found instrumental in promoting the banking business. It is just a process of communication in which an individual exercise his/her personal potentials, tact, skill and ability to influence the impulse buying of the customers. Since we get in immediate feedback, the personal selling activities energies the process of communication very effectively.

The personal selling in an art of persuasion. It is a highly distinctive form of promoting sale. In personal selling, we find inter-personal or two-way communication that makes the ways for a feedback. There is no doubt in it that the goods or services are found half sold when the outstanding properties are well told. This art of telling and selling is known as personal selling in which an individual based on his/her expertise attempts to transform the prospects into customers.

b) **Advertising:** Like other organizations, the banking organizations also use this component of the promotion mix with the motto of informing, sensing and persuading the customers. While advertising, it is essential that we know about the key decision-making areas so that its instrumentality helps bank organization both at micro and macro levels.

Banks have too many goals which they want to achieve. Those goals are for accomplishing the objectives as follows in a way that banks develop advertising campaigns and use media.

1. Conceive customers to examine all kinds of services that banks offer;
2. Increase use of services;
3. Create well fit image about banks and services;
4. Change customers' attitudes;
5. Introduce services of banks;
6. Support personal selling;
7. Emphasize well service.

Advertising media and channels that banks prefer are newspaper, magazine, radio, direct posting and outdoor ads, TV commercials and Social media. In the selection of media, target market should be determined and the media that reach this target easily and cheaply must be preferred.

c) **Selling of Promotional Tools:** Another element of the promotion mixes of banks is improvement of selling. Mostly used selling improvement tools are layout at selling point, rewarding personnel, seminaries, special gifts, premiums, contests.

d) **Direct Marketing:** Direct marketing represents one of the most productive ways of market communication of the bank with actual and potential customers for a product from the bank selection offer. It is based upon the client precise target segments. Thereby, the key mechanism is the database on clients (actual and potential ones). Database marketing includes the names, addresses, telephone numbers, faxes and e-mails of individual and potential customers, with the aim of market communication as well as results in sales and profit.

e) **Public Relations:** Almost all the organization need to develop and strengthen the public relations activities to promote their business. We find this component of the promotion mix effective even in the banking organizations. We can't deny that in the banking services, the effectiveness of public relations is found of high magnitude. It is in this context that we find a bit difference in the designing of the mix of promoting the banking services. Of course, in the consumer goods manufacturing industries, we find advertisements occupying a place of outstanding significance but when we talk about the service generating organizations in general and the banking organizations in particular, we find public relations and personal selling bearing high degree of importance. It is not meant that the banking organizations are not required to advertise but it is meant that the bank executives unlike the executives of other consumer goods manufacturing organizations focus on public relations and personal.

f) **Sales Promotion:** The term "promotion" is usually an expression used internally by the marketing company, but not normally to the public or the market-phrases like "special offer" are more common. Promotion is one of the market mix elements, and a term used frequently in marketing. It is the specification of five promotional mix or promotional plan. These elements are personal selling, advertising, sales promotion, direct mail marketing, and publicity. A promotional mix specifies how much attention to pay to each of the five categories, and how much money to budget for each.

FACTORS INFLUENCING THE PROMOTION MIX

The Promotion Mix is the blend of several promotional activities (Advertising, personal selling, sales promotion, public relations, direct marketing) used by business to create, maintain and increase the demand for a product. Main factors influencing promotion mix has been briefly discussed as under:

1. **Types of Product:** The different type of product requires different promotional tools. Such as, for the industrial products viz. Machinery, equipment or land personal selling is more appropriate as a great deal of pre-sale and after-sale services is required to sell and install such products. On the other hand, advertising and publicity are more suitable for the consumer goods, especially the convenience goods.
2. **Nature of Market:** The number and location of customers greatly influence the promotion mix. In case the group of potential customers is small and are concentrated in a particular locality, then personal selling is more likely to be effective. Whereas, if the customer base is large and widespread, then the blend of advertising, personal selling, and the sales promotion is required to sell the product.
3. **Stage of Product's Life:** The promotion mix changes as the product moves along its life cycle. During the introduction stage, the principal objective of the promotion is to create the primary demand by emphasizing the product's features, utility, etc. therefore, the blend of advertising and publicity is required. As the product reaches its maturity stage the advertising and personal selling is required to maintain the demand of the customers.
4. **Availability of Funds:** The marketing budget also decides the promotion mix. If the funds available for the promotion are large, then the blend of promotional tools can be used, whereas in the case the funds are limited then the management must choose the promotional tool wisely.
5. **Nature of Technique:** Each element of the promotional mix has unique features that significantly influences the purpose of promotion. Such as, the advertising is an impersonal mode of communication that reaches a large group of customers. Its expression can be amplified with the use of colours and sound that helps in developing the long-lasting brand image in the minds of the customer.
6. **Promotional Strategy:** The promotion mix largely depends on the company's promotional strategy, *i.e.*, whether it accepts the Push Strategy or a Pull Strategy.

   Push Strategy: In a Push strategy, the manufacturer forces the dealers to carry the product and promote it to the customer, *i.e.*, convince the potential buyers to buy it. Here, personal selling and trade promotion are likely to be more effective.

   Pull Strategy: In the case of a Pull Strategy, the consumers ask the dealers to carry the product, *i.e.*, customers themselves purchase the product. Here, advertising and consumer promotion are more appropriate.
7. **Readiness of Buyer:** Different promotional tools are required at different stages of buyer readiness. Such as, at the comprehension stage, the blend of advertising and personal selling plays a vital role. Whereas at the conviction stage, personal selling is more effective. At the time of sales closure, the blend of sales promotion and personal selling is likely to be more effective.

Hence, the advertising and publicity are more effective at the early stages of buying decision process while the sales promotion and personal selling are more effective during the later stages.

TEST YOURSELF

1. In marketing, __________ refers to any type of marketing communication used to inform or persuade target audiences of the relative merits of a product, service, brand or issue.
   (a) promotion (b) promotion mix
   (c) distribution (d) advertisement
2. The aim of promotion is to increase awareness, create interest, generate sales or create brand loyalty. It is one of the basic elements of the market mix, which includes promotion, and others such as:
   (a) price (b) product
   (c) place (d) All of the above
3. Banks have a unique challenge when it comes to marketing because they do not offer __________ products for consumers.
   (a) hypothetical (b) tangible
   (c) intangible (d) physical
4. Which of the following is not a part of the promotion process in marketing?
   (a) reminding (b) information
   (c) reinforcing (d) None of these
5. A bank offers discount coupons to the customers availing consumer loan from the bank. This kind of marketing mix is called:
   (a) personal selling (b) advertising
   (c) sales promotion (d) direct marketing
6. A promotion strategy which is directed to the final customer to induce them to purchase the product is called:
   (a) push strategy (b) pull strategy
   (c) selling strategy (d) marketing strategy
7. A promotion strategy which is directed at channel members to induce them to purchase the product and sell them to the final consumer is called:
   (a) push strategy (b) pull strategy
   (c) selling strategy (d) marketing strategy
8. If a bank offers its customers discounted rate of interest for their home loan, this kind of marketing mix is called:
   (a) personal selling (b) advertising
   (c) sales promotion (d) direct marketing
9. __________ represents one of the most productive ways of market communication of the bank with actual and potential customers for a product from the bank selection offer. It is based upon the client precise target segments.
   (a) personal selling
   (b) advertising
   (c) sales promotion
   (d) direct marketing
10. Another element of the promotion mixes of banks is improvement of selling. Mostly used selling improvement tools are layout at selling point, rewarding personnel, seminaries, special gifts, premiums, contests. It is called:
    (a) Direct Marketing
    (b) Selling of Promotional tools
    (c) Public Relations
    (d) Personal Selling

ANSWER

1	2	3	4	5	6	7	8	9	10
(a)	(d)	(b)	(d)	(c)	(b)	(a)	(c)	(d)	(b)

ROLE OF DIRECT SELLING AGENT/ DIRECT MARKETING AGENT IN A BANK

DIRECT SELLING AGENT

Direct Selling Agent (DSA) are persons or body corporate engaged by financial institutions or a business to act as sales agents on its behalf. A Direct Selling Agent is different from an in-house sales persons in that the DSA would not be on the rolls of the company, would have a fixed period of contract and would have a performance based compensation. On the other hand, a sales person would be employed by the business, have a fixed monthly pay and can be terminated only as per the terms of employment and labour laws in India.

Definition of Direct Selling

Direct selling is characterized by a consultant or representative that utilizes their personal connections to sell a product or service directly to consumers and is compensated for the sales they make. Direct selling is based on making and keeping personal relationships with the people you sell to, encouraging repeat business from customers. The one-on-one communication with your customers makes selling a product that much easier since you can pull from personal experience to give examples of ways to use the product and share your impressive results.

Definition of Direct Marketing

Direct marketing is focused on advertising a product with the hopes that the advertisement will encourage a consumer to purchase a certain product or service. What makes this type of marketing direct is the audience that it targets—with direct marketing, a company does not intend their marketing material to spread worldwide, but rather throughout a certain region, or specifically to a certain type of person. Direct marketing is not necessarily meant to sell a product immediately, but rather set a consumer up to purchase the product in the future.

Benefits of Direct Marketing

Some of the strengths of direct marketing include:

a) **Targeting:** You can send specific messages to particular groups of customers and potential customers based on demographics and buying behaviour. The more targeted your campaigns, the more successful they are likely to be.

b) **Personalisation:** Reach your audience with a personal touch. Direct mail or email can be addressed to a specific person, and even include details like past orders. A phone call can engage a customer in conversation to start building a relationship with your business.

c) **Affordable:** Tactics like email marketing or leaf letting can be very cost effective. Most direct marketing will be more cost effective for SMEs than mass media advertising campaigns.

d) **Measurable:** If your marketing messages ask the recipient to take a particular action or use a specific voucher code, you can easily track the success of campaigns. This can help you plan future campaigns.

e) **Informative:** You can deliver detailed information on your products, services and prices unlike other forms of advertising.

ROLES OF DIRECT SELLING AGENT REPRESENTATIVE IN BANKS

In the primary responsibility of the Banking Direct Selling Agent/Representative is branch management and in-branch services, teller and platform services, financial product sales, customer services, and management of lending risk to retail customer base. He builds a client base for banking direct sales through prospecting, networking, and referrals.

A typical job description for the Banking Direct Selling Agent Representative role may include:

1. Develops new business prospects in specific geographic areas through cold calls.
2. Interacts with existing customers to increase sales of the bank's products and services.
3. Requires a high school diploma or equivalent and 2-4 years of experience in the field or in a related area.
4. Familiar with standard concepts, practices, and procedures within a particular field.

IBA MODEL CODE OF CONDUCT FOR DIRECT SELLING AGENTS

Code of Conduct for Direct Selling Agents (DSAs) lays down a clear and transparent policy stating the model code of conduct for DSAs while operating as agents of the Bank. This code will be applicable to all persons who are involved in marketing and distribution of any loan or other financial product of the Bank. DSA and its Tele-Marketing Executives (TMEs) and field sales personnel, known as Business Development Executives (BDEs) will have to agree to abide by this Policy before they undertake any direct marketing operations on behalf of the Bank.

In case of violation of any clause given in this Policy by any TME/BDE, the concerned person may be blacklisted from participating in any marketing operation undertaken by the Bank. Failure to comply with the requirements may result in permanent termination of business between the Bank and the concerned DSA. It may also attract permanent blacklisting by the industry.

1. Tele-calling a Prospect (a Prospective Customer): A prospect is to be contacted for sourcing a bank product or bank related product only under the following circumstances:

a) When prospect has expressed a desire to acquire a product through the bank's internet site/call centre/Branch or through the Relationship Manager at the bank or has been referred to by another prospect/customer or is an existing customer of the bank who has given consent for accepting calls on other products of the bank.

b) When the prospect's name/telephone no./address is available & has been taken from one of the lists/directories/databases approved by the DSA Manager/Team leader, after taking his/her consent.

c) The Tele-Marketing Executives (TMEs) should not call a person whose name/number is flagged in any "do not disturb" list made available to him/her.

2. When you may contact a Prospect on Telephone: Telephonic contact must normally be limited between 09:30 Hrs and 19:00 Hrs. However, it may be ensured that a prospect is contacted only when the call is not expected to inconvenience him/her. The DSA shall ensure that calls outside of prescribed hours are placed only when the Prospect has explicitly authorized the TME/BDE for the same either in writing or orally.

3. Privacy of Prospective Customers: DSA should respect a prospect's privacy. The prospect's interest may normally be discussed only with the prospect and any other individual/family member such as prospect's accountant/secretary /spouse, authorized by the prospect.

4. Leaving Messages and Contacting Persons other than the Prospect: Calls must first be placed to the prospect. In the event the prospect is not available, a message may be left for him/her. The aim of the message should be to get the prospect to return the call or to check for a convenient time to call again. Ordinarily, such messages may be restricted to:

Please leave a message that __________ (Name of officer) representing __________ Bank called and requested to call back at __________ (phone number)".

As a general rule, the message must indicate, that the purpose of the call is regarding selling or distributing a bank product of __________ Bank.

5. No Misleading Statements/Misrepresentations Permitted: TMEs and BDEs shall not use misleading statements or use any misrepresentations while dealing with the Prospect. The TME/BDE shall not:

- Mislead the Prospect on any service/product offered;
- Mislead the Prospect about the nature of business or the organization's name;
- Misrepresent or inadequately represent themselves;
- Mislead the Prospect by making a false or unauthorized commitment on behalf of the Bank regarding any products or services.

6. Telemarketing Etiquettes: TMEs shall ensure that any communication with the Prospect follows proper etiquettes and meet all the provisions as given in this Policy document. The model behaviour that the TMEs needs to follow are given as follows:

Pre Call:

- No calls prior to 0930 Hrs or post 1900 Hrs unless specifically requested;
- No serial dialing;
- No calling on lists unless list is cleared by team leader.

During Call:

- Identify yourself, your company and your principal;
- Request permission to proceed;
- If denied permission, apologize and politely disconnect;
- State reason for your call;
- Always offer to call back on landline, if call is made to a cell number;
- Never interrupt or argue;
- To the extent possible, talk in the language which is most comfortable to the prospect;
- Keep the conversation limited to business matters;
- Check for understanding of "Most Important Terms and Conditions" by the customer if he plans to buy the product;
- Reconfirm next call or next visit details;
- Provide your telephone no, your supervisor's name or your bank officer contact details if asked for by the customer;
- Thank the customer for his/her time.

Post Call:

- Customers who have expressed their lack of interest for the offering should not be called for the next 3 months with the same offer;
- Provide feedback to the bank on customers who have expressed their desire to be flagged "Do Not Disturb";
- Never call or entertain calls from customers regarding products already sold. Advise them to contact the Customer Service Staff of the bank.

7. Gifts or Bribes: TME/BDE's must not accept gifts from prospects or bribes of any kind. Any TME/ BDE offered a bribe or payment of any kind by a customer must report the offer to his/her management.

8. Precautions to be Taken on Visits/Contacts: The BDE shall take the following precautions while dealing with a Prospect:

- Respect personal space 1– maintain adequate distance from the prospect;
- Not to enter the prospect's residence/office against his/her wishes;
- Not visit in large numbers – *i.e.*, not more than one BDE and one supervisor, if required;
- Respect the prospect's privacy;
- If the prospect is not present and only family members/office persons are present at the time of the visit, he/she should end the visit with a request for the prospect to call back;
- Provide his/her telephone number, supervisor's name or the concerned bank officer's contact details, if asked for by the customer;
- Limit discussions with the prospect to the business – Maintain a professional distance.

9. Other Important aspects such as Appearance & Dress Code: BDE's must be appropriately dressed :

For men this means:

- Well ironed trousers;
- Well ironed shirt, shirt sleeves preferably buttoned down.

For women this means:

- Well ironed formal attire (Saree, Suit etc.);
- Well-groomed appearance.

Jeans and/or T Shirt, open sandals are not considered appropriate.

10. Handling of Letters & Other Communication: Any communication sent to the prospect should be only in the mode and format approved by the Bank.

DELIVERY CHANNELS IN A BANK

Bank customer can access his account through the various channels and operates his accounts. Customer can give an instruction to the bank for issue of cheque book, transfer fund to another account through various delivery channels. Banks offer the following delivery channel for its services:

a) Net Banking;

b) Mobile Banking;

c) ATM Counters;

d) E-gallery and Kiosk;

e) POS Machine;

f) Cash Management Service;

g) Call centres;
h) RTGS/NEFT/SWIFT;
i) Single Window Systems;
j) Online Trading Accounts etc.

Activities that should not be Out Sourced

Banks which choose to outsource financial services should however not outsource core management functions including Internal Audit, Compliance function and decision-making functions like determining compliance with KYC norms for opening deposit accounts, according sanction for loans (including retail loans) and management of investment portfolio.

Evaluating the Capability of the Service Provider

In considering or renewing an outsourcing arrangement, appropriate due diligence should be performed to assess the capability of the service provider to comply with obligations in the outsourcing agreement. Due diligence should take into consideration qualitative and quantitative, financial, operational and reputational factors. Banks should consider whether the service providers' systems are compatible with their own and also whether their standards of performance including in the area of customer service are acceptable to it. Banks should also consider, while evaluating the capability of the service provider, issues relating to undue concentration of outsourcing arrangements with a single service provider. Where possible, the bank should obtain independent reviews and market feedback on the service provider to supplement its own findings.

Due diligence should involve an evaluation of all available information about the service provider, including but not limited to :

- Past experience and competence to implement and support the proposed activity over the contracted period;
- Financial soundness and ability to service commitments even under adverse conditions;
- Business reputation and culture, compliance, complaints and outstanding or potential litigation;
- Security and internal control, audit coverage, reporting and monitoring environment, Business continuity management;
- External factors like political, economic, social and legal environment of the jurisdiction in which the service provider operates and other events that may impact service performance;
- Ensuring due diligence by service provider of its employees.

Responsibilities of DSA/ DMA/ Recovery Agents

Code of conduct for Direct Sales Agents formulated by the Indian Banks' Association (IBA) could be used in formulating their own codes for Direct Sales Agents / Direct Marketing Agents/ Recovery Agents. Banks should ensure that the Direct Sales Agents / Direct Marketing Agents/ Recovery Agents are properly trained to handle with care and sensitivity, their responsibilities particularly aspects like soliciting customers, hours of calling, privacy of customer information and conveying the correct terms and conditions of the products on offer etc.

TEST YOURSELF

1. Who can become a Direct Selling Agent (DSA) engaged by financial institutions or a business to act as sales agents on its behalf.
(a) an individual
(b) a group of persons
(c) body corporate
(d) Any of the above

2. ____________ is characterized by a consultant or representative that utilizes their personal connections to sell a product or service directly to consumers and is compensated for the sales they make.
(a) Direct selling (b) Direct selling agent
(c) Direct marketing (d) Distribution

3. _________ is focused on advertising a product with the hopes that the advertisement will encourage a consumer to purchase a certain product or service.
(a) Direct selling (b) Direct selling agent
(c) Direct marketing (d) Distribution

4. Benefits of direct marketing are:
(a) Personalization (b) Affordable
(c) Measurable (d) All of the above

5. In case of ________ of direct marketing, you can send specific messages to particular groups of customers and potential customers based on demographics and buying behaviour.
(a) Personalization (b) Affordable
(c) Targeting (d) Measurable

6. A typical job description for the Banking Direct Selling Agent Representative role may not include:
(a) Develops new business prospects in specific geographic areas through cold calls.

(b) Interacts with existing customers to increase sales of the bank's products and services.

(c) Requires a Post Graduate Degree or equivalent and 2-4 years of experience in the field or in a related area.

(d) Familiar with standard concepts, practices, and procedures within a particular field.

7. As per IBA model code of conduct for DSA, Telephonic contact must normally be limited between

(a) 09:00 Hrs and 20:00 Hrs
(b) 09:30 Hrs and 19:00 Hrs
(c) 09:00 Hrs and 1900 Hrs
(d) 10:30 Hrs and 19:30 Hrs

8. TMEs and BDEs shall not use misleading statements or use any misrepresentation while dealing with the Prospect. Find the wrong statements:

(a) The TME/BDEshall not mislead the Prospect on any service/product offered;

(b) The TME/BDEshall not mislead the Prospect about the nature of business or the organization's name;

(c) The TME/BDEshall misrepresent or inadequately represent themselves;

(d) The TME/BDEshall not mislead the Prospect by making a false or unauthorized commitment on behalf of the Bank regarding any products or services.

9. The model behaviour that the TMEs needs to follow during call are given as follows:

(a) Identify yourself, your company and your principal
(b) Request permission to proceed, if denied permission, apologize and politely disconnect
(c) State reason for your call
(d) All of the above

10. Customer can give an instruction to the bank for issue of cheque book, transfer fund to another account through various delivery channels. Banks offer the which of the following delivery channel for its services:

(a) Net Banking
(b) ATM Counters
(c) Call centres
(d) All of the above

ANSWER

1	2	3	4	5	6	7	8	9	10
(d)	(a)	(c)	(d)	(c)	(c)	(b)	(c)	(d)	(d)

MARKETING INFORMATION SYSTEMS— A LONGITUDINAL ANALYSIS

INTRODUCTION

A marketing information system (MKIS) is a management information system (MIS) designed to support marketing decision making. The online business dictionary defines that Marketing Information System (MKIS) is a system that analyzes and assesses marketing information, gathered continuously from sources inside and outside an organization or a store.

All businesses are operating under conditions of risk and uncertainty. The success or failure of any firm or company depends on many factors like economic situation, the changing tastes of customers, the extent and nature of competition and competitive activities and more. Business decisions and especially marketing decisions, are actually the decisions about the future of a company. The management of successful companies always focuses on each of the aspects of their business in order to make achievable decision. Marketing is usually that area of a company which requires lots of attention. Company sales depend on marketing so company must use adequate solutions for the more effective promotion of their products. For this purpose companies rely on marketing information system. Marketing information system allows a company to use all relevant information for developing its marketing strategies more effectively.

THE MARKETING INFORMATION SYSTEM PROCESS

Collecting, analyzing, and disseminating marketing information relies on the five steps in the process. These steps are as under:

1. **Determine what metrics to include in your Marketing Information System:** This is a very serious step in creating an effective marketing information system. All data has a cost, both real and opportunity costs, so including the right metrics is critical.

   Measure the wrong things and you'll make bad decisions and waste money. Measure too many metrics and analysis become difficult. Accumulating metrics costs money. Data is only worth its cost when the value it contributes to improved decision-making outweighs the cost of collecting the data and be sure to include the human cost of gathering and analyzing this data to other costs in acquiring the data.

2. **Gather Relevant Data:** Some data comes from internal sources, such as sales records, accounting figures, website analytics, and reports from your sales force. Other data comes from external sources, including competitor results, economic metrics, listening post metrics, and Facebook Insights. Your marketing research data can also form part of your marketing information system, such as recurring surveys of customer satisfaction.

3. **Process The Data:** It's very difficult to make decisions based on raw data because the data contains invisible patterns that might otherwise indicate appropriate actions. For instance, it's hard to see a downward trend in customer

satisfaction without graphing the data until the decline is substantial and by then it might be too late to reverse the trend. Processing data allows managers to quickly detect changes in critical metrics over time. Sure, you can use the graphing function of Excel or other data program, but newer data visualization software makes the job even easier. Some even create dashboards to bring all your marketing metrics to one place, making decision-making even easier.

4. **Communicate Results:** The more people who have the information from your marketing information system, the better. But, not everyone is going to understand tables of raw data or even visualizations like in the dashboard above. That's because your marketing information system requires interpretation through the lens of marketing knowledge.

5. **Make Marketing Decisions:** The final step in the process is using metrics from your marketing information system to make decisions that optimize your marketing outcomes.

COMPONENTS OF MARKETING INFORMATION SYSTEM

Marketing Information System (MKIS) collects, analyses, and supplies a lot of relevant information to the marketing managers. It is a valuable tool for planning, implementing and controlling the marketing activities. The role of MKIS is to identify (find out) what sort of information is required by the marketing managers. It then collects and analyzes the information. It supplies this information to the marketing manager at the right time. MKIS collects the information through its subsystems. These subsystems are called components. The four main components of Marketing Information System (MKIS) are:

1. **Internal Records System:** The first component of MKIS is 'Internal Record'. Marketing managers get lots of information from the internal-records of the company. These records provide current information about sales, costs, inventories, cash flows and account receivable and payable. Many companies maintain their computerized internal records. Inside records help marketing managers to gain faster access to reliable information.

2. **Marketing Intelligence System:** The second component of MKIS is 'Marketing Intelligence'. It collects information from external sources. It provides information about current marketing-environment and changing conditions in the market. This information can be easily gathered from external sources like; magazines, trade journals, commercial press, so on. This information cannot be collected from the Annual Reports of the Trade Association and Chambers of Commerce, Annual Report of Companies, etc. The salesmen's report also contains information about market trends.

   The information which is collected from the external sources cannot be used directly. It must be first evaluated and arranged in a proper order. It can be then used by the marketing manager for taking decisions and making policies about marketing. So, marketing intelligence is an important component of MKIS.

3. **Marketing Research System:** The third important component of MKIS is 'Marketing Research'. Marketing research is conducted to solve specific marketing problems of the company. It collects data about the problem. This data is tabulated, analyzed and conclusions are drawn. Then the recommendations are given for solving the problem. Marketing research also provides information to the marketing managers. However, this information is specific information. It can be used only for a particular purpose. MKIS and Marketing research are not substitutes of each other. The scope of MKIS is very wide. It includes Marketing Research. However, the scope of Marketing Research is very narrow.

4. **Marketing Decision Support System:** The fourth component of MKIS is 'Marketing Decision Support System'. These are the tools which help the marketing managers to analyze data and to take better marketing decisions. They include hardware, *i.e.*, computer and software programs. Computer helps the marketing manager to analyze the marketing information. It also helps them to take better decisions. In fact, today marketing managers cannot work without computers. There are many software programs, which help the marketing manager to do market segmentation, price fixing, advertising budgets, etc.

THE EFFECT OF MKIS ON SALES PERFORMANCE

Firms that successfully compete in today's ruthless business climate are naturally inclined to focus on customer needs. Because they are customer-focused, successful firms are also inherently more agile than competitors in anticipating and satisfying those needs. Marketing information systems are empowering tools that allow successful firms to drive enhanced sales performance by maintaining customer focus and out maneuvering competitors.

ADVANTAGES OF MARKETING INFORMATION SYSTEMS

With an increasingly competitive and expanding market, the amount of information needed daily by an organization is profound. Thus, they have to establish a Marketing Information system. There are several advantages of Marketing information systems :

1) **Organized Data Collection:** Lots of data can be collected from the market. But the main word here is "Organized". Organizing data is very important else the data is meaningless. Thus, MKIS helps you to organize your database thereby improving productivity.

2) **A Broad Perspective**: With a proper MKIS in place, the complete organization can be tracked which can be used to Analyse independent processes. This helps in establishing a broader perspective which helps us know which steps can be taken to facilitate improvement.

3) **Storage of Important Data:** Several times in pharmaceuticals, when one drug is being produced they may need data of another drug which was produced years back. Similarly, in Media, photographs are stored in archives. This storage of important data plays a crucial role in execution and thus proves again that MKIS is not important only for information but also for execution.

4) **Avoidance of Crisis**: The best way to Analyse a stock (share market) is to see its past performance. Top websites like money control thrive on MKIS. Similarly, MKIS helps you keep tracks of margins and profits. With an amazing information system established, you can know where your organization is moving and probably avert a crisis long before it has taken place. Ignoring hints received from MKIS reports is foolhardy.

5) **Co-ordination**: Consumer durables and FMCG companies have huge number of processes which needs to be coordinated. These companies depend completely on MKIS for the proper running of the organization. There are dedicated people for marketing information systems in such organizations. This is mainly because of the speed required to access information and implement it.

6) **Analysis and Planning**: MKIS is critical for planning. You cannot do planning without information. For planning, the first thing which is needed is the organizations capabilities, then the business environment and finally competitor analysis. In a proper MKIS, all these are present by default and are continuously updated. Thus, MKIS is very important for planning and analysis.

7) **Control**: Just like MKIS can help in a crisis, in normal times it provides control as you have information of the various processes going on and what is happening across the company. Thus, it provides you with a sense of control.

Disadvantages

Maintenance, complexity and setting up a MKIS are one of the major hindrances to Marketing information systems. Furthermore, wrong information being fed in MKIS can become cumbersome and appropriate filters need to be established.

Limitations of MKIS

Kotler and Philip have said that "both primary and secondary researches offer loads of the data and information needed for the marketers, whereas the secondary data sources are relatively superior in quick provision of data at lower cost. Simultaneously, a firm cannot find all the data required by itself, but sometimes can be done with the help of secondary research. However, researchers must assess those data collected from both primary and secondary data sources to enable the accuracy, updates and fairness. Each primary data collection method–observational, survey, and experimental–has its own advantages and disadvantages. Similarly, each of the various research contact methods –mail, telephone, personal interview, and online–also has its own advantages and drawbacks."

TEST YOURSELF

1. A ________ is a management information system (MIS) designed to support marketing decision making. It is the process of providing accurate information to improve marketing planning, execution and control of the business.

(a) marketing system
(b) marketing information system
(c) management system
(d) marketing control system

2. What kind of information is required by a bank under MIS so far as market forces are concerned?

(a) Information about customer
(b) Information about competitors

(c) Information about technology
(d) All of the above

3. The process of MIS are Collecting, analyzing, and disseminating marketing information relies on the five steps in the process. Which is not the process?
(a) Gather relevant data (b) Process the data
(c) Communicate results (d) All of the above

4. The final step in the process is using metrics from your marketing information system to ________ that optimize your marketing outcomes.
(a) Gather relevant data (b) Process the data
(c) Make decisions (d) Communicate results

5. Which are the components of Marketing Information System?
(a) Marketing Intelligence System
(b) Marketing Research System
(c) Marketing Decision Support System
(d) All of the above

6. The third important component of MKIS is ________. It is conducted to solve specific marketing problems of the company. It collects data about the problem.
(a) Marketing Intelligence
(b) Marketing Research
(c) Marketing Decision Support
(d) Internal Records

7. The fourth component of MKIS is ________. These are the tools which help the marketing managers to analyze data and to take better marketing decisions.
(a) Marketing Intelligence System
(b) Marketing Research System
(c) Marketing Decision Support System
(d) Internal Records System

8. Which are several advantages of Marketing information systems?
(a) Organized Data collection
(b) Storage of Important Data
(c) Avoidance of Crisis
(d) All of the above

9. Which are one of the major hindrances to Marketing information systems.
(a) Maintenance
(b) Complexity
(c) Setting up a MKIS
(d) All of the above

10. Just like MKIS can help in a crisis, in normal times it provides ________ as you have information of the various processes going on and what is happening across the company.
(a) control (b) maintenance
(c) planning (d) analysis

ANSWER

1	2	3	4	5	6	7	8	9	10
(b)	(d)	(d)	(c)	(d)	(b)	(c)	(d)	(d)	(a)

MODULE–E
ETHICS IN BANKS AND FINANCIAL INSTITUTIONS

ETHICS, BUSINESS ETHICS & BANKING: AN INTEGRATED PERSPECTIVE

CONCEPT OF ETHICS

Ethics can be defined as a system of criteria and measures examining the values, norms and rules underlying the individual and social relations on such moral grounds as right and wrong or good and bad.

The word ethics is derived from the Greek word 'ethos', which means character. Ethics is a branch of philosophy that is concerned with human character and conduct. It is a discipline dealing with that which is good and bad with moral duty and obligation. Ethics is the embodiment of moral values, which describes, what is right and what is wrong in human behaviour and what ought to be. Thus ethics refers to good character and morality and to generally accept human character and behaviour considered as desirable by contemporary society.

The same action or practice is viewed as ethical or unethical depending upon the school of moral thought to which one subscribes. Further, the perceptions of ethical or unethical change at times because some values are dropped and some values are added over the period. "Ethics is the discipline dealing with what is good and bad and with moral duty and obligation." In this broad sense ethics in business is simply the application of everyday moral or ethical norms to business.

In the era of global competition, ethics in every business is assuming importance. This is because, relationship with suppliers, customers and other stakeholders are shaped by ethical business practices. This builds trust and adds on to image building and long term profitability.

BUSINESS ETHICS

Business ethics is defined as "the process of evaluating decisions, either before or after, with respect to the moral standards of society." Core ethical values include honesty, integrity, fairness, responsible citizenship and accountability. In short, business ethics means "choosing the good over the bad, the right over the wrong, the fair over the unfair, and the truth over the lie".

What is ethical and unethical in general society may not be the same in business. In business operations, ethics is concerned in different environments and with different objectives that are centered on profit and wealth maximization. Business ethics is concerned primarily with the relationship of business goals and techniques to specific human needs. It studies the impact of acts on the good of the individual, the firm, the business community and the society as a whole.

Business ethics studies the special obligations that a man and a citizen accept when he becomes a part of the world of commerce. Business ethics is the study of business situations, activities, and decisions where issues of right and wrong are addressed.

The subject of business ethics is the effect of the social nature of morality, and the feedback effect of business morality on the business environment. Thus, business ethics may be defined as a group of moral actions of an individual, as the element of a collective, that he/she adheres to during all forms of business activities without damaging the business relationships within the business system and the wider environment.

Public attention has lately turned towards debates about business ethics, as the social responsibility of the individual and the collective. The question arises as to whether business has anything to do with the morality of the individual and the collective. Many people deny the connection between ethics and business, believing that the place of morality is within religion, while others perceive the interconnection between morality and religion. Every business activity has certain things in common with morality and moral actions of an individual or groups. Business ethics has two basic dimensions of expression and demonstration:

1. **Collective Ethics:** Collective ethics include the application of ethical principles in the management's decision-making that refers both to external subjects and the environment and the ethical relations within the business system itself.
2. **Individual Ethics**: Individual ethics involve adherence to the norms of customary business morality. If an individual has a deficit of ethical morality it means that they put their interests before the collective and legal norms, and before the norms of customary business morality, which can damage the business climate. Individual ethics is the basic element of group or collective ethics. It is certain that opposed stands regarding the relationship between business and ethics are gaining importance.

The Basic Ethical Principles in Business are:

- **Principle of Mutual Trust:** Principle of mutual trust is of special importance for successful functioning of the business system. Important and valuable deals are very often contracted over the phone, in the absence of witnesses, while the relationship between the participants is dominated by the inviolable principle of mutual trust.
- **Principle of Mutual Benefit and Interest:** It means that none of the partners in a business relationship should feel cheated.
- **Principle of Good Intentions:** It is very important for business ethics and moral behaviour. This principle means that there is no intention to treat the business partner in an immoral way, whether it refers to deception, theft or some other undesirable way of treating a business partner.
- **Principle of Business Compromise and Business Tolerance:** It refers to the harmonization of the conflicting interests of participants in the business process.
- **Principle of Ethical Improvement of Business Behaviour:** It represents the business partner's readiness to accept the mistake that has been made as a result of his own actions. He should admit the mistakes and respond in an appropriate way.
- **Principle of Conflict Between One's Own Interests:** It refers to the inability to relate common to personal interests, with simultaneous adherence to the same ethical values.

Business Ethics in a Global Perspective

ISSUES	EUROPE	UNITED STATES	ASIA
Who is responsible for ethical conduct in business?	Social control by the Collective	The individual	Top management
Who is the key factor in business ethics?	Government, trade unions, corporate associations	The corporation	Government, corporations
What are the key guidelines for ethical behaviour?	Negotiated legal Framework of business	Corporate codes of ethics	Managerial discretion
What are the key issues in business ethics?	Social issues in organizing the framework of business	Misconduct and immorality in single decision situations	Corporate Governance and accountability

Importance of Business Ethics

- With the growing influence and power of business in society, its contribution is also increasing. How, or indeed whether this contribution is made raises significant ethical questions. Business Ethics helps us to find answers to such questions.
- Business Ethics helps us to understand more about the causes and consequences of business malpractices and seeks to address them in a better way.
- Business Ethics can help to improve ethical decision making by providing knowledge and solution to ethical dilemmas faced by business leaders.

- Real life situations have shown that ethical business practices create high returns for the organisation in the long run, by creating trust.
- Business Ethics eventually lead to sustainability.

BANKING ETHICS IN GLOBAL AND INDIAN CONTEXTS

Following the banking law is one of the basic professional requirement for banks. They must also pay close attention to moral concerns in order to make the right ethical decisions on a day-to-day basis. The upholding of an ethical culture in banking is of critical interest to regulators, banks, employees and customers alike. Banking ethics are the moral or ethical principles that certain banks chose to abide by. There is not an ethics ombudsman or a universal code of ethical conduct, but the banks that vaunt their ethical credentials vet the ethical standing of potential investors and partners and also choose the companies that they in turn invest in with their ethical policy in mind.

In this module, I would be discussing the concept of Business Ethics, and its importance in banking. Also the global viewpoint of Business Ethics in different countries. How Business Ethics is viewed in terms of the view point of the employee, customer or management. Also I would be analyzing the importance of Business Ethics on the Banks in general, which includes a specific study of the Business Ethics in the Banks in India.

The financial community has a history of placing moral considerations above legal or opportunistic expedients. But we are often exposed to moral dangers and the dangers of contamination are increasing. Deregulation and the technological revolution are sharpening ethical conflicts. Bankers' role is one of stewardship based on trust. We are trusted by those who ask us to look after their money and we have a duty to lend that money responsibly. Banking is about rewards reflecting real risks and ethical considerations form an important part of our risk-taking activities. The welfare of our borrowing customers, in good times and bad, is of major concern in any business proposition.

We have to let our people know what is expected of them and help them to avoid pressures and temptations. A bank's responsibility extends to Government, customers, shareholders, staff and the community.

Ethical Banking: An ethical bank, also known as a social, alternative, civic, or sustainable bank, is a bank concerned with the social and environmental impacts of its investments and loans. The ethical banking movement includes: ethical investment, impact investment, socially responsible investment, corporate social responsibility, and is also related to such movements as the fair trade movement, ethical consumerism, and social enterprise.

Other areas of ethical consumerism, such as fair trade labelling, have comprehensive codes and regulations which must be adhered to in order to be certified. Ethical banking has not developed to this point; because of this it is difficult to create a concrete definition that distinguishes ethical banks from conventional banks. Ethical banks are regulated by the same authorities as traditional banks and have to abide by the same rules. While there are differences between ethical banks, they do share a desire to uphold principles in the projects they finance, the most frequent including: transparency and social and/or environmental values. Ethical banks sometimes work with narrower profit margins than traditional ones, and therefore they may have few offices and operate mostly by phone, Internet, or mail. Ethical banking is considered one of several forms of alternative banking.

Need of Ethics in Banking: Ontologism based on the concept of good as opposed to evil helps us define the banking business from the point of view of ethics. The idea of awareness or conscience of the need for banking products or services inevitably comes to mind. This simplified parallel leads us to the conclusion that full awareness of and the related ethics about the importance of banking products and services is imminent to all economies, regardless of their economic development.

Importance of Business Ethics in Banking: The main aspects that signifies the importance of Business Ethics in Banking are as under:

- To define acceptable behaviour;
- To promote high standards of practice;
- To provide a benchmark for self-evaluation;
- To establish a framework for professional behaviour and responsibilities;
- As a vehicle of occupational identity;
- Ethics corresponds to basic human needs;
- Law cannot protect society, ethics can;
- It creates credibility with the public;
- It gives management credibility with employees;
- It helps in better decision-making.

Conclusion: Finally to conclude, we can say that business ethics in banking is viewed differently by different types of people. If "Loyalty to your organisation" is business ethics for the management, then for employees its "faith in their profession" and for employees it's "Justice to those with whom you deal". We can also say that integrity, humane values and honesty are the major qualities that people associate with a manager who is ethical in his approach or dealings. We have also seen the need or importance of business ethics in banking. The most important aspect of the study is that people feel that profit maximisation and business ethics can go together without any hindrances.

TEST YOURSELF

1. Which one of these is not a basic ethical principle in business?
   (a) Principle of good intentions.
   (b) Principle of business intolerance.
   (c) Principle of mutual trust.
   (d) Principle of conflict between one's own interests.
2. Entity responsible for ethical conduct in business in Asia is ______.
   (a) Top Management.
   (b) Social Control by collective.
   (c) Government Decisions.
   (d) Individual.
3. What is business ethics?
   (a) The study of business situations, activities, and decisions where issues of right and wrong are addressed.
   (b) Defined as decisions organisations make on issues that could be considered right or wrong.
   (c) Ethics that can be applied to an organization's practices.
   (d) The process of evaluating decisions, either before or after, with respect to the moral standards of society
4. In many cases, rules of business ethics can be determined by ______.
   (a) applicable laws
   (b) company guidelines
   (c) economic requirements
   (d) rules of conduct that apply in everyday life
5. The economic character of business can be seen in its ______.
   (a) trading characteristics
   (b) ethical dimensions
   (c) personal aspects
   (d) legal guidelines
6. Organization in business is characterized mainly by its ______.
   (a) rules (b) hierarchy
   (c) profits (d) products
7. Which are the Basic Ethical Principles in Business?
   (a) Principle of Mutual Trust
   (b) Principle of Mutual Benefit and Interest
   (c) Principle of Good Intentions
   (d) All of the above
8. Which are the Importance of Business Ethics in Banking?
   (a) To promote high standards of practice
   (b) To establish a framework for professional behaviour and responsibilities
   (c) Ethics corresponds to basic human needs
   (d) All of the above
9. The school of thought that says that law and ethics govern two different realms is wrong because ______.
   (a) ethics apply to every field of life
   (b) anything that is legal is also ethical
   (c) anything that is illegal is also unethical
   (d) the law governs every aspect of life
10. It is not ethically sufficient to obey the law because ______.
    (a) the law does not apply to business in general
    (b) ethical constraints sometimes require that the law be ignored
    (c) ethics go beyond what can be legally codified
    (d) the law itself is stricter than ethics

ANSWER

1	2	3	4	5	6	7	8	9	10
(b)	(a)	(d)	(d)	(a)	(b)	(d)	(d)	(a)	(c)

ETHICS AT THE INDIVIDUAL LEVEL

INTRODUCTION

The ethical standards of an organization have a major influence on how it conducts its business. Business ethics are defined by the behavior standards of management and personnel, and the way in which business is carried out at both a strategic and operational level. A positive approach to maintaining ethical standards can lead to competitive market advantage and an enhanced reputation.

ETHICS AT THE INDIVIDUAL LEVEL

An important aspect of organizational strategy and management is empowering a strong sense of ethics at the individual level. Organizations should internally develop a code of conduct and/or ethics statement, provide ethics training, appoint ethics officers, and ensure there is an anonymous way to report ethical problems. Providing intrinsic and extrinsic sources of motivation for individual employees to behave ethically reinforces positive ethical behavior. Hiring and developing employees who have a strong sense of individual professionalism will ensure best practices are achieved from an ethical point of view.

Employees often need to make various moral decisions in the workplace. While many of these workplace decisions have to be made depending on moral obligations, some morally supportable decisions may require courage and need to be performed beyond the generally accepted norms. Understanding the concepts like Value, Norms and Beliefs and their significance for both individuals and business level.

Values: Values are a concept of desirable behaviour or standard or principle by an individual. Values comprise of ideas which are preferred, described in other words, what is good, right, wise or beneficial. Values are generally expressed in terms of 'should'. Values are implanted early in a person's life and once they are fixed, serve as a guide in choosing behaviour and in forming attitudes.

They become part of superego. Values change through day-to-day behaviour, regulated by norms. Values are developed and reinforced and do not develop spontaneously. Values are re-learned, e.g., in group work sessions members re-learn the desirable values. viz., wealth of others should be treated as mud, other's wife should be seen as mother, and the like. Social work has its own values which are embedded in democratic values.

Norms: Norms mean any rule or standard that defines appropriate and acceptable behaviour, what people should or should not do, think or feel in any given situation. Norms seen as expression of values are standards of behaviour shared by a larger segment of society. Norms are formally expressed through law.

The social or subjective norm thus captures the perception of what important others expect the individual to do. Norms can be studied by observing the behaviour of a certain group of individuals in a society and knowing how others respond to that behaviour. A person who violates norms beyond a certain limit is labelled as 'abnormal'.

Beliefs: Beliefs are ideas about the nature of social world, supernatural reality, a person or an object which one believes to be true and acts accordingly. Beliefs may be based on facts or may be without factual evidence. According to Ellis (1973), beliefs generate emotions. To cite an example, when Mr. B. abuses Mr. A, he (Mr. A) gets angry or sad with Mr. B. because he believes that this abuse has lowered his prestige, status, etc.

Sadness/anger is the result of the belief about being abused and not of the event (abusing). Individual beliefs play very important role in the behaviour of a person, therefore, caseworker should try to tackle and manage these beliefs.

Morality: Morality is the human attempt to define what is right and wrong about our actions and thoughts, and what is good and bad about our being who we are.

Morality (from Latin: *moralis, lit*. 'Manner, character, proper behavior') is the differentiation of intentions, decisions and actions between those that are distinguished as proper and those that are improper. Morality can be a body of standards or principles derived from a code of conduct from a particular philosophy, religion or culture, or it can derive from a standard that a person believes should be universal. Morality may also be specifically synonymous with "goodness" or "rightness".

Immorality is the active opposition to morality (i.e. opposition to that which is good or right), while amorality is variously defined as an unawareness of, indifference toward, or disbelief in any particular set of moral standards or principles.

Ethics (also known as moral philosophy) is the branch of philosophy which addresses questions of morality. The word "ethics" is "commonly used interchangeably with 'morality,' and sometimes it is used more narrowly to mean the moral principles of a particular tradition, group, or individual."

Conflict: Conflict is serious disagreement and argument about something important. If two people or groups are in conflict, they have had a serious disagreement or argument and have not yet reached agreement. Conflict is a state of mind in which you find it impossible to make a decision.

A conflict is a clash of interest. The basis of conflict may vary but, it is always a part of society. Basis of conflict may be personal, racial, class, caste, political and international. Conflict in groups often follows a specific course. Routine group interaction is first disrupted by an initial conflict, often caused by differences of opinion, disagreements between members, or scarcity of resources. At this point, the group is no longer united, and may split into coalitions. This period of conflict escalation in some cases gives way to a conflict resolution stage, after which the group can eventually return to routine group interaction

Integrity: Integrity is the practice of being honest and showing a consistent and uncompromising adherence to strong moral and ethical principles and values. In ethics, integrity is regarded as the honesty and truthfulness or accuracy of one's actions. Integrity can stand in opposition to hypocrisy, in that judging with the standards of integrity involves regarding internal consistency as a virtue, and suggests that parties holding within themselves apparently conflicting values should account for the discrepancy or alter their beliefs. The word integrity evolved from the Latin adjective *integer*, meaning whole or complete. In this context, integrity is the inner sense of "wholeness" deriving from qualities such as honesty and consistency of character. As such, one may judge that others "have integrity" to the extent that they act according to the values, beliefs and principles they claim to hold.

In ethics when discussing behavior and morality, an individual is said to possess the virtue of integrity if the individual's actions are based upon an internally consistent framework of principles. These principles should uniformly adhere to sound logical axioms or postulates. One can describe a person as having ethical integrity to the extent that the individual's actions, beliefs, methods, measures and principles all derive from a single core group of values. An individual must therefore be flexible and willing to adjust these values to maintain consistency when these values are challenged—such as when an expected test result is not congruent with all observed outcomes. Because such flexibility is a form of accountability, it is regarded as a moral responsibility as well as a virtue.

An individual's value system provides a framework within which the individual acts in ways which are consistent and expected. Integrity can be seen as the state or condition of having such a framework, and acting congruently within the given framework.

Dilemma: Dilemma is from a Greek word *di lemma* for "double proposition." It was originally a technical term of logic, but we use it now for any time you have a problem with no satisfactory solution. A dilemma is a problem offering two possibilities, neither of which is unambiguously acceptable or preferable. The possibilities are termed the horns of the dilemma, a clichéd usage, but distinguishing the dilemma from other kinds of predicament as a matter of usage.

It is a forced choice between two (or more) courses of action which are equally disfavored or favored. For example, a choice between debt (which has to be paid back with interest and on schedule, but which generally does not affect owners' control of the business) and equity (which does not have to be paid back but may result in dilution or loss of control to outsiders).

Decision-making: In psychology, decision-making is regarded as the cognitive process resulting in the selection of a belief or a course of action among several alternative possibilities. Every decision-making process produces a final choice, which may or may not prompt action.

Decision-making is the process of identifying and choosing alternatives based on the values, preferences and beliefs of the decision-maker. The thought process of selecting a logical choice from the available options. When trying to make a good decision, a person must weigh the positives and negatives of each option, and consider all the alternatives. For effective decision making, a person must be able to forecast the outcome of each option as well, and based on all these items, determine which option is the best for that particular situation.

Decision-making can be regarded as a problem-solving activity yielding a solution deemed to be optimal, or at least satisfactory. It is therefore a process which can be more or less rational or irrational and can be based on explicit or tacit knowledge and beliefs. Tacit knowledge is often used to fill the gaps in complex decision making processes. Usually both of these types of knowledge, tacit and explicit, are used together in the decision-making process.

THE GOLDEN RULE

The Golden Rule is the principle of treating others as one would wish to be treated. It is a maxim that is found in many religions and cultures.

The oldest golden rule is the Hindu "One should always treat others as they wish to be treated" (Hitopadehsa, from before 2000 BCE) which seems potentially more demanding than the golden rule. Most people would like to be treated better than they expect to be, or are willing to accept.

The Golden Rule can be considered an ethic of reciprocity in some religions, although other religions treat it differently. The maxim may appear as either a positive or negative injunction governing conduct.

Golden Rules of Ethics:

- Everything you want others to do to you, you shall do to others;
- Do not do to others that which you do not wish them to do to you;
- Do not do anything to others that if done to you, would cause harm to you.

Some point out that it cannot be followed literally in all kinds of relationships, such as between employer and employee, parent and child, or teacher and student. Others say that it can be, because it could be interpreted to mean "treat others as you would wish to be treated if you were them, in their social role, relative to you"; i.e. if you are a boss, treat your employees as you would wish to be treated if you were in their position.

Thus, perhaps the Hindu version, "treat others as they wish to be treated" is better worded. But, it doesn't save the day. Some people wish to be treated badly. Others wish to be treated like gods. Few people know what is best for themselves.

TEST YOURSELF

1. __________ are a concept of desirable behaviour or standard or principle by an individual.

(a) Morals (b) Values
(c) Norms (d) Integrity

2. Any rule or standard that defines appropriate and acceptable behaviour, what people should or should not do, think or feel in any given situation is called ______.

(a) Morals (b) Values
(c) Norms (d) Integrity

3. Which is not a correct statement?

(a) Conflict is serious disagreement and argument about something important.
(b) Conflict is a state of mind in which you find it impossible to make a decision.
(c) A conflict is a clash of interest.
(d) The basis of conflict may vary but, it is not always a part of society.

4. Morality may also be specifically synonymous with __________.

(a) Goodness (b) Wrongness
(c) Valueless (d) Moral less

5. ______ is the practice of being honest and showing a consistent and uncompromising adherence to strong moral and ethical principles and values.

(a) Morals (b) Values
(c) Norms (d) Integrity

6. _______ is the human attempt to define what is right and wrong about our actions and thoughts, and what is good and bad about our being who we are.

(a) Morality (b) Values
(c) Norms (d) Integrity

7. A ______ is a problem offering two possibilities, neither of which is unambiguously acceptable or preferable.
   (a) dilemma (b) conflict
   (c) confusion (d) decision-making

8. In psychology, ____________ is regarded as the cognitive process resulting in the selection of a belief or a course of action among several alternative possibilities.
   (a) dilemma (b) conflict
   (c) confusion (d) decision-making

9. Which of these may be a hindrance in reinforcement of positive ethical behavior in an organization?
   (a) Motivational Factors.
   (b) Hiring of Individuals with deep sense of professionalism.
   (c) Development of uniform code of conduct.
   (d) Red-Tapism.

10. Which of these is correct?
   (a) Norms are regulated by norms.
   (b) Values are regulated by norms.
   (c) Both are regulated by each other.
   (d) None of them is regulated by the other.

11. State in which one has to go for either of the two forced choices equally favoured or disfavoured is........
   (a) Conflict. (b) Double Bind.
   (c) Suspicion. (d) Dilemma.

12. Which of these is not a golden rule of Ethics?
   (a) Everything you want others to do to you, you shall do to others.
   (b) Do not do anything to others which if done to you will harm you.
   (c) Always try to do those things which if done to you will displease you.
   (d) Do those things to others which you wish others to do with you.

ANSWER

1	2	3	4	5	6
(b)	(c)	(d)	(a)	(d)	(a)
7	**8**	**9**	**10**	**11**	**12**
(a)	(d)	(b)	(d)	(d)	(c)

ETHICAL DIMENSIONS : EMPLOYEES

INTRODUCTION

The employer-employee relationship should not be looked at simply in economic terms. It is a significant human relationship of mutual dependency that has great impact on the people involved. A person's job, like a person's business, is highly valued possession that affects the lives of the employees and their families. With stakeholders everywhere, the relationship is laden with moral responsibilities. Though the pressures of self-interest are very powerful and compelling, both workers and bosses should guide their choices by basic ethical principles including honesty, frankness, respect and caring.

Customer being the backbone of the banking business, it is essential that both bank and customer understand all ethical dimensions in conducting the banking activities. Customers can be of various types including Individuals, NRIs, HUF, Firms, Companies, and Trust etc. Customers open different types of accounts and conduct their banking activities with the banks.

Ethical dimension refers to the conduct of business in line with the prescribed code of conduct of the respective profession. 'Code of Bank's Commitment to Customers' is prepared by the Banking Codes and Standard Board of India (BCSBI). BCSBI is an independent banking industry watchdog to protect interests of the consumers of banking services in India. Likewise, 'Fair Practices Code for Lenders' is introduced by RBI, the regulator, lays down the process of conducting ethical business while giving loans.

OBLIGATION TO BANK

The relationship between the banker and customer creates some obligations on the part of a bank. The main obligations of the bank towards the customers are as follows:

1. **Obligation to Honour Cheques:** The bank has a statutory obligation to honour the cheques of its customers up to the amount standing to the credit of the customer's account. If a bank wrongfully refuses to honour the cheque of its customer, it shall be liable to compensate the customer. This obligation is subject to some conditions, namely:
   a) There must be sufficient funds of the customer in the hands of the bank.
   b) The funds must be properly applicable for the payment of the customer's cheque.
   c) The cheque must be properly drawn up i.e., it should be complete in all respects.
   d) The cheque must be presented for payment within a reasonable time.
   e) There must be no legal bar preventing the payment of such cheques. If the bank has received any order from a court or any other competent authority prohibiting payment, it is the duty of the bank to obey such orders.
2. **Obligation to Maintain Secrecy:** The relationship between the banker and customer is obligatory. The bank must not disclose to any outsider the details concerning the customer's account; as such disclosures may adversely affect the credit and business of the customer. However, a disclosure can be made under the following two situations:
   a) When the law requires such disclosures to be made, and

b) When the practices amongst the banks permit such disclosure.

3. **Obligation to Follow Customer's Instructions:** The banker is under a legal obligation to follow the instructions of the customer. This is so because there is the contractual relationship between the bank and the customer.

4. **Obligation to Maintain Proper Records:** The banker is under an obligation to maintain accurate record of all the transactions of the customers made with the bank.

5. **Obligation to Give Notice before Closing the Account:** If a bank wishes to close the account of a customer, it must give a reasonable notice to this effect to the customer.

Thus, a bank cannot close the account of a customer on its own, because it may have serious consequences to the customer.

Besides the obligations towards the bank's customers, they also have got the obligation to follow all the laws, guidelines, directives and policies of the regulators.

RIGHT OF THE BANK

For fulfilling the obligations towards the customers, bankers enjoy the following rights:

- **Right of General Lien:** General lien gives the banker the right to retain goods and securities delegated to him in his capacity as a banker, in the absence of a contract contradictory to the right of lien. It extends to all goods/properties placed with him as a banker by his customer which are not particularly identified for another purpose.
- **Right of Set-off:** The banker has the right to set off the accounts of its customer. This enables a debtor (Bank) to set off a debt owed to him by a creditor (customer) before the latter recovers a debt due to him from the debtor. Banks can merge two accounts in the name of the same customer and set off the debit balance in one account with the credit balance in the other. But the funds should belong to the customer.
- **Right of Appropriation:** In the normal course of business, a banker accepts payments from customers. If the customers have more than one account or he/she has taken more than one loan, the customer has the right to direct his banker against which debt the payment should be appropriated/settled. If the customer does not direct the banker and there is more than one debt outstanding in his/her name, the bank can exercise its right of appropriation and apply it in payment of any debt. The banker can apply it against time barred debts also. Once an appropriation has been made it cannot be reversed.
- **Right to Charge Interest:** The banker has an implied right to charge interest on the advances granted to its customer. Bankers generally charge interest monthly, quarterly or half yearly or annually. There may be an agreement between the banker and customer in this case the manner agreed will decide how interest is to be charged.
- **Right to charge Service Charges:** Banks charge customers a particular amount if their balance is below a predetermined amount, for the usage of ATMs and withdrawals.

  Banks are free to charge these but the Reserve Bank of India expects banks to advise their customers of these charges at the time of opening an account and advise them when changes are being made.
- **Right to Close the Account:** If the bank is of the opinion that an account is not being operated properly, it may close the account by sending a written intimation to the customer.

OBLIGATIONS TO THIRD PARTIES

When the bank is outsourcing its banking functions to the third parties, it needs to have clear and transparent contracts with all terms and conditions incorporated in agreement paper. Banks must incorporate especially in service contract that the service level agreement have to be defined minutely and ensure that the third party do not cause an inconvenience to the bank customer.

ABUSE OF OFFICIAL POSITION

Employees are advised to follow code of conduct laid down by the bank. The use of one's official position for personal gain is often an abuse of power. This abuse can exist when a conflict of interest leads to disloyalty. Abuse of official position for personal gains to friends, family members with selfish motive amounts to violation of employee's obligation to the bank. There are some examples of abuse of official position in banks:

- Employee goes for personal travel and claims for official travel;
- False claim beyond fixed perquisites;
- Use of official resources for personal use;
- Accepting bribe in any form either a monetary or another kind of advantage (gifts, training trips,

discounts, etc.) that an official gets for breach of duty.

- Showing discrimination to the customers based on their closeness to the employee;
- Discrimination to the customers for account opening and operations;
- Discrimination in the selection of borrowers during lending.

SEXUAL HARASSMENT

Today's world is accustomed to the term Sexual harassment. Sexual Harassment can be identified as a behavior. It can in general terms be defined as an unwelcome behaviour of sexual nature. Sexual harassment at workplace is a universal problem in the world whether it be a developed nation or a developing nation or an underdeveloped nation, atrocities and cruelties against women is common everywhere. It is a problem giving negative effect on both men and women. It is seen to be happening more with women gender as they are considered to be the most vulnerable section of the society these days.

In simple words, sexual harassment at workplace is an act or a pattern of behaviour that compromises physical, emotional or financial safety and security of a woman worker. Legally speaking, sexual harassment includes such unwelcome sexually determined behaviour as:

(a) Physical contact and advances;

(b) A demand or request for sexual favour;

(c) Sexually coloured remarks;

(d) Showing pornography;

(e) Any other unwelcome physical verbal or non-verbal conduct of sexual nature.

Sexual harassment is also understood to have taken place if a victim has reasonable apprehension of facing humiliation, and health and safety problem at the place of hor work. If the employer or the co-workers by any action or words or gesture create a hostile environment for a woman worker, it amounts to sexual harassment.

The Sexual Harassment of Women at Workplace (Prevention, Prohibition and Redressal) Act, 2013 is a legislative act in India that seeks to protect women from sexual harassment at their place of work.

CONFLICT OF INTEREST

A conflict of interest (COI) is a situation in which a person is involved in multiple interests, financial or otherwise, and serving one interest could involve working against another. Typically, this relates to situations in which the personal interest of an individual might adversely affect a duty owed to make decisions for the benefit of a third party.

It is expected that the top management recognises such conflicts of interest and take some definite pre-emptive measures so that they do not result in inappropriate or adverse consequences on the banks and all stakeholders.

These are some examples for conflict of interest in banks:

- Among employees of a bank or branch;
- Among employees of a branch and administrative offices;
- Employees of a bank and a client;
- Between a given bank and one or more of its clients.

The presence of a conflict of interest is independent of the occurrence of dishonesty. Therefore, a conflict of interest can be discovered and voluntarily defused before any corruption occurs. Many of the above conflicts can be resolved internally by the bank.

FAIR ACCOUNTING PRACTICES

In order to protect bank loan borrowers from unfair lending practices and to hold banks/financial institutions to higher levels of ethical practices, the Reserve Bank of India (RBI) implemented the Fair Practices Code for Lenders in 2003. The guidelines for lending have been finalised and banks/financial institutions have adopted the broad guidelines and framework prescribed in the RBI Fair Practices Code. Banks or Financial Institutions have the freedom of drafting the Fair Practices Code, enhancing the scope of the guidelines, but in no way sacrificing the spirit underlying the following guidelines prescribed by RBI.

All banks and financial institutions must process a loan application based on the following minimum guidelines:

- Banks and financial institutions should provide acknowledgement for receipt of all loan applications.
- Banks and financial institutions should process the loan applications within a reasonable period of time. If additional details or documents are required, they should intimate the borrowers immediately.
- Banks and financial institutions should not discriminate on grounds of sex, caste and religion in the matter of lending. However, this does not preclude lenders from participating in credit-linked schemes framed for weaker sections of the society.

HUMAN RESOURCE MANAGEMENT (HRM) ETHICS

Human Resource Management (HRM) deals with work force management, manpower planning and other employee related activities in an organization. Therefore, we can say that it is a special branch of management where ethics play a crucial role. HRM concerns human issues, especially those related with compensation, development, industrial relations, health and safety issues. However, there are sufficient disagreements in managing HRM issues that stem from various quarters.

HRM Ethics and Market System: Various types of market systems affect business and HR ethics differently and hence, business ethics becomes negotiable. Occupations in which the market conditions do not favour the employees, it becomes necessary to have government and labour union interventions for controlling the possible exploitation of employees.

- Free market systems empower employees and the employers equally. Negotiations are used to create win-win situations for both of these parties. Government or labour union interventions are often harmful in free market systems because they stall the operations and create unnecessary hindrances.
- With the growth of globalization, the concept of globalizing labour has gained importance. Trade unions have ceased to exist and the role of HR as such in issues like employee management, desirable policies and practices has become debatable topics.
- Many people now have the opinion that HR is nothing but a part of the stakeholders, which initiates major strategic and policy decisions to divulge the organization and gear it towards profit making.

There cannot be a single opinion about ethics in HR that is completely convincing. Market is neither an ethical institution nor an unethical one. No policies and procedures can govern and align the markets for human well-being. However, the need of these policies and procedures cannot be denied or ignored because human development is the ultimate aim of all human initiatives.

EMPLOYEES AS ETHICS AMBASSADORS

Encouraging employees to 'do the right thing' and apply their organisation's core values is of utmost importance. How can this be achieved in practice by organisations that employ thousands of employees around the world, who might have to make difficult decisions every day in their job?

Ethics ambassadors are employees selected to assist senior management in promoting and embedding ethics policies, codes of conduct and other related policies. The post of ethics ambassador may be full-time or may be taken on in addition to an employee's day-to-day job. Ethics ambassadors are not part of the ethics function but will normally be positioned throughout the company – across business units, geographical locations and/or the hierarchy of an organisation, and form an informal 'network' of diverse employees with similar responsibilities.

They can provide local knowledge, language and case studies to help make the ethics programme relevant to the needs of the local operating environment. This encourages buy-in from employees and decreases the likelihood of misconceptions which can arise from faulty translations or a clumsy choice of wording. Historical context can be important to the perceived meaning of a word and taking this into consideration is best done by someone familiar with the local culture.

Ethics ambassadors can also act as a local point of contact, so if an employee has a query or an ethical dilemma they can talk to a local person rather than a telephone helpline or a more formal contact within head office. Ambassadors may also deliver training, record and report issues and occasionally help conduct investigations into unethical behaviour. However, as their name suggests, it is as advocates for the ethics programme that ambassadors are most valuable.

MANAGERS AS ETHICAL LEADERS

Leadership is the ability of an individual to influence, motivate, and enable others to contribute towards the effectiveness and success of the organizations of which they are members. A constant change that has become a part of life for many organizations highlights the increasing importance of transformational leadership. Superior performance or performance beyond normal expectations is possible only by transforming followers' values, attitudes' and motives from a lower to a higher plane of arousal and maturity.

The ethical culture from the senior leadership percolates down in the bank. However, the employees do not personally know the senior leaders. They form their opinions based on what they come to know through others or when they listen to the top leaders. Therefore, the senior leadership should convey the importance of ethics in a variety of ways and in such a manner as to reach to every employee in the bank. If senior managers talk about ethics regularly and also walk their talk without exception, they will develop a reputation for their ethical leadership.

TEST YOURSELF

1. ________is an independent banking industry watchdog to protect interests of the consumers of banking services in India.

(a) BCBOB (b) BCBOI
(c) BCCBI (d) BCSBI

2. Which of the following is not an obligation of the bank towards the customers?

(a) Obligation to Follow Customer's Instructions
(b) Obligation to Maintain Proper Records
(c) Obligation not to Maintain Secrecy
(d) Obligation to give Notice before Closing the Account

3. Which of these will not be considered as sexual harassment?

(a) Sexually coloured remarks
(b) Friendliness behaviour
(c) Unwelcome physical verbal or non-verbal conduct of sexual nature
(d) A demand or request for sexual favour

4. Which are the examples for conflict of interest in banks:

(a) Among employees of a bank or branch
(b) Among employees of a branch and administrative offices
(c) Employees of a bank and a client
(d) All of the above

5. In order to protect bank loan borrowers from unfair lending practices and to hold banks/financial institutions to higher levels of ethical practices, the Reserve Bank of India (RBI) implemented the Fair Practices Code for Lenders in______.

(a) 2003 b) 2005
(c) 2007 d) 2009

6. Which is/are the example(s) of abuse of official position in banks:

(a) Employee goes for personal travel and claims for official travel
(b) False claim beyond fixed perquisites
(c) Use of official resources for personal use
(d) All of the above

7. Which is not the main obligation of a bank towards its customers?

(a) Obligation to honour cheques
(b) Right to charge interest
(c) Right to charge service charges
(d) Right to close the account without notice

8. Sexual harassment at workplace is a universal problem in the world whether it be a developed nation or a developing nation or an underdeveloped nation, atrocities and cruelties against women is common everywhere. It is a problem giving negative effect on ________.

(a) Men only
(b) Women only
(c) Both men and women
(d) None

ANSWER

1	2	3	4	5	6	7	8
(d)	(c)	(b)	(d)	(a)	(d)	(d)	(c)

WORK ETHICS AND THE WORKPLACE

INTRODUCTION

Work ethic is a belief that hard work and diligence have a moral benefit and an inherent ability, virtue or value to strengthen character and individual abilities. In its simplest definition, a system of moral principles is called ethics. They affect how people lead their lives, for life is an unbroken stream of decision-making and ethics are concerned with what is the right moral choice, for individuals and for society. This is also known as a moral philosophy.

WORK ETHICS

In a business, an ethical code is a defined set of principles which guide an organization in its activities and decisions and the firm's philosophy may affect its productivity, reputation, and bottom line. Among staff ethical behaviour ensures work is completed with integrity and honesty and staff that are ethical adhere to policies and rules while working to meet the aims of the enterprise.

Traditionally, work ethic has been understood as a value based on hard work and diligence. These values have been challenged and characterized as submissive to social convention and authority, and not meaningful in and of itself, but only if a positive result accrues. An alternative perception suggests that the work ethic is now subverted in a broader, and readily marketed-to society. This perspective has given us the phrase "work smart".

BENEFITS OF ETHICAL BEHAVIOUR

The following are few advantages of ethical behaviour in the workplace:

- **Asset Protection and Assurance:** When the workers possess an ethical working environment and ethical behaviour in the workplace, the company's maintenance cost decreases to a remarkable extend because they are well aware of their duties and responsibilities towards the company. They also realise that they should not do any damage to any of the machines and equipment are given to them as they are quite valuable for the company and doing damage to these things will be a wrong act, so automatically things will be taken care of and everything will work systematically.
- **Productivity will Increase:** When the work staff and the workers value the work given to them and then they will do all the given work in time and achieve their set targets, this will greatly affect the sales and the productivity of the company. Due to this it is assured that you will have a group of people who will sail your business even in the worst of the downfall of the market, and keep the growth of the company and business consistent.
- **Team Work will Develop:** When all the workers do their jobs in a responsible way, then a time comes when they have achieved the target way before the given deadline, then a question arises What Next? So the situation automatically bonds up all the individuals into a team. These individuals now work as a team and work in the benefit of the company for which they will be getting or achieving their incentives. This mutual understanding of the employees is a positive signal that the company will sustain for a very long period in the variable market conditions.

- **Public Image and Brand Value Increases:** Yes if all the members of the company are dedicated to work as well as figure out there values and responsibility towards the environment, then it is for sure that the type of cleanliness and the disposal of the waste product of the company will be unbeatable in the market, hence resulting in attracting a bigger customer base due to the clarity and quality of the services or products. Moreover, increase in the public image and increase in the customer base is directly proportional to an increase in the brand value. In simpler words when you gain popularity amongst your customers you start to develop your company into a brand.
- **Adaptive to Changes:** Workers with professional ethics in the workplace is definitely the master key to the lock of success. The team of understanding, trustworthy, reliable, motivated, concerned and responsible people will definitely adapt themselves into any kind of position and work they are filled with.
- **Decision Making and Implementing is Always Easy:** Whenever there is a need to take a big decision then the best one made is by the advice of the employees of the company, and what will be better than every single employee respecting the decision and supporting the company to go ahead with their decision. This is the power of ethics in the employees who respect the decision of the company and let it go along with the flow. This is very rare in the big companies but where this scene happens; the company turns big brands over the night.
- **Trouble Free Working Environment:** Generally, where everyone is unknown and moreover no one wants to know each other there are higher chances of great trouble and where there is a friendly, respectful and understanding environment between the employees there are fewer chances of troubles from the employee's end.
- **There is No One Left Negative:** When people are detached from one another and someone gets negative regarding the company's work then it has been seen that from that single negative employee many are affected. Thus there is a sudden decline in the working of the employees, but when everything is good to go and everyone is concerned about one another then things become systematic and in case if someone gets negative, the positive and supportive environment works as a boost up for the person and again he/she starts working to their best.
- **Less Legal Issues:** When everything is systematic and functional and in addition your workers are cooperative and understanding then you won't be facing any problems or legal obligations from the employee's end, because all the workers are treated equally and all are well known with their duties which the job requires from them. When everything is managed and systematic then all the paperwork and the legal formalities are the primary things which is considered the most, so there is no question of any legal issues.
- **The company will Touch New level of Success:** When everything is so managed and systematic along with the understanding of the employees because of their strong ethics, the company will surely touch new heights of success and even the growth of your business will be assured.

When your employees become expert in their respective works and respective fields, then their dedication and will to do the work will show true colours and give more fruitful results.

UNETHICAL BEHAVIOUR: CAUSES AND REMEDIES

Unethical behaviour in the workplace doesn't have to be rampant or extravagant to be costly. Corporate scandals that culminate with the arrests of nefarious executives may garner the headlines. But the cumulative damages caused by the seemingly small indiscretions that employees and managers commit every day are just as bad.

- **No Code of Ethics:** Employees are more likely to do wrong if they don't know what's right. Without a code of ethics, they may be unscrupulous. A code of ethics is a proactive approach to addressing unethical behaviour. It establishes an organization's values and sets boundaries for adhering to those values. Everyone is accountable.
- **Fear of Reprisal:** When explaining why they don't report ethical misconduct that they witness, people often say it is because they worry about the ramifications. They don't want to damage their career or incur the wrath of the offender. Or, sometimes, they let the infraction go because they don't know how to report it or they feel that their report may be ignored.
- **Impact of Peer Influence:** If everyone is doing it, it must be right. Or is it? What's to stop someone from padding their expense report when their co-workers do it but don't get caught? Too often people lapse into the bad behaviour of others. People behave unethically because they tend to perceive questionable behaviours exhibited by people who are similar to them like their co-workers to be more acceptable than those

exhibited by people who they perceive as dissimilar, researchers say.

- **Going Down a Slippery Slope:** Misconduct starts small, such as the exaggeration of a mileage report. But the longer it goes unchecked, the worse the offenses become. The little extra money that came from the mileage report may eventually be dwarfed by larger falsified expenses or perhaps even outright embezzlement. People who are faced with growing opportunities to behave unethically are more likely to rationalize their misconduct because unethical behaviour becomes habit.
- **Unrealistic Targets:** As competition keeps intensifying in financial or other sectors, the employees will continue to be pressurized to meet some unrealistic targets. For facing the ire of the reviewing manager during appraisals, some employees find shortcuts by claiming work which was never done or provide some inflated benefits of a financial product or hidden riders and so on. The cause of all these wrong practices in the pressure to achieve some unreasonably high targets on account of growing competition and trying to succeed somehow.
- **Unprincipled Leadership:** Ethical behaviour starts at the top. Employees emulate their leaders, and the most significant factor in ethical leadership is personal character. Corporate leaders who employees view as demonstrating personal character are more likely to be perceived as setting a strong tone, researchers say. If employees see the boss knocking off early every day, they may do likewise.

Ignoring the small stuff will not necessarily lead to the type of scandals that make the news. But ethical misconduct could prove costly if it is not stopped. Identifying these causes of unethical behaviour in the workplace could prevent problems and minimize damages. The following can be tried as some of the remedies to rectify unethical behaviour at workplace.

- Developing ethical behaviour;
- Starting conversation about ethics in the organisation;
- Ideal and cooperative behaviour by the top management;
- Nipping of unethical behaviour in the bud;
- Frequent utilization of the manual;
- Appreciation and rewards for ethical behaviour;
- Care of reputation rather than result.

CODE OF ETHICS MANUAL

A Code of Ethics Manual is a set of rules, which are accepted as guiding principles. A code is adopted by a Corporate, Professional body, and/or a nation. A Company's policy statements define the ethical code. Codes do not produce ethical behavior, unless the ethical practices are understood and practiced in both at individual and corporate levels.

Formal Codes of Ethics: Philosophy of the code envisages and expects:

- Adherence to the highest standards of honest and ethical conduct, including proper and ethical procedures in dealing with actual or apparent conflicts of interest between personal and professional relationships.
- Full, fair, accurate timely and meaningful disclosures in the periodic reports required to be filed by the Bank with government and regulatory agencies.
- Compliance with applicable laws, rules and regulations.
- To address misuse or misapplication of the Bank's assets and resources.
- The highest level of confidentiality and fair dealing within and outside the Bank.

RBI Ethics at Work: The RBI, with the assistance of Professor Dipankar Gupta, who is also a Director on the RBI Central Board, has formulated a Code of Conduct for itself, which we term ethics@work on 10 Jan 2014. You may well ask, why an ethics manual and I quote from the ethics manual.

An Ethics Manual Promotes:

- Solidarity among colleagues;
- Pride and commitment to working for the Organisation;
- Personal Aspirations that are aligned with Organisational goals.

The Ethics Manual is Expected:

- To define and clearly set out what will be deemed to be acceptable behaviour;
- We hope that this will promote and ensure high standards of practice;
- And also establish a benchmark for self-evaluation;
- Lay down the mainframe for professional behaviour and responsibilities;
- Enable a sense of occupational identity Ideals we can clearly ascribe to.

The written code of ethics will be useful for socialization of our new recruits in the organisation, serve as an implement of employee training. Be a benchmark transgression of the same, will invite disciplinary action. It will also help in dispute and conflict management. The moral dilemmas, the approach-approach conflicts will be more easily resolved with reference to the touchstone of the code of ethics. It clarifies the organisation's expectations from the employee and vests on enshrining complete transparency. This is a formal code of business conduct and ethics, to be ascribed to and strictly adhered to by all employees. It is morally incumbent upon them to do so.

Some organisations also have ethics officers but in the ultimate analysis, the foundations of ethical behaviour go well beyond corporate culture and policies. These are rooted in one's moral training, lessons parents and school teachers have taught from early childhood on which affect not just individual behaviour the competitive business environment and indeed society as a whole.

WHISTLE-BLOWING IN BANKS

The Government of India, has authorized the Central Vigilance Commission (CVC), as the Designated Agency to receive written complaints for disclosure on any allegation of corruption for misuse of office and recommend appropriate action. Bank, being a Banking Company established under the Central Act is coming under the jurisdiction of the CVC for the said purpose. In accordance with the aforesaid Resolution of the Government of India, the CVC has formulated norms for acceptance of complaints under the Public Interest Disclosures and Protection of Informer (PIDPI) and keeping the identity of the complainant secret. As a Public Sector Bank coming under the purview of PIDPI, Bank is required to make public to the Employees, Officers and general public the norms thus laid down by the CVC and this Policy is intended to provide for the same.

Policy Statement: All concerned are hereby informed that any complaint which is to be made under PIDPI should comply with the following aspects:

- The complaint should be in a closed/secured envelope.
- The envelope should be addressed to Secretary, Central Vigilance Commission and should be superscribed "Complaint under The Public Interest Disclosure". If the envelope is not superscribed and closed, it will not be possible for the Commission to protect the complainant under the above resolution and the complaint will be dealt with as per the normal complaint policy of the Commission. The complainant should give his/her name and address in the beginning or end of complaint or in an attached letter.
- Commission will not entertain anonymous/pseudonymous complaints.
- The text of the complaint should be carefully drafted so as not to give any details or clue as to his/her identity. However, the details of the complaint should be specific and verifiable.
- In order to protect identify of the person, the Commission will not issue any acknowledgement and the whistle-blowers are advised not to enter into any further correspondence with the Commission in their own interest. The Commission assures that, subject to the facts of the case being verifiable, it will take the necessary action, as provided under the Government of India Resolution mentioned above. If any further clarification is required, the Commission will get in touch with the complainant.

A copy of the public notice issued by the CVC in relation to the above mentioned resolution is available on the website of the http://www.cvc.nic.in. Complaints under the PIDPI Resolution must be sent directly to the CVC, New Delhi, as Bank is not empowered to handle them.

WHISTLE-BLOWING LAWS IN INDIA

Whistle-Blowers Protection Act, 2014 is an act passed in the Parliament of India which provides a mechanism to investigate alleged corruption and misuse of power by public servants and also protect anyone who exposes alleged wrongdoing in government bodies, projects and offices. The wrongdoing might take the form of fraud, corruption or mismanagement. The Act will also ensure punishment for false or frivolous complaints.

The Act was approved by the Cabinet of India as part of a drive to eliminate corruption in the country's bureaucracy and passed by the Lok Sabha on 27 Dec., 2011. The Bill was passed by Rajya Sabha on 21 February 2014 and received the President's assent on 9 May 2014.

An Act to establish a mechanism to receive complaints relating to disclosure on any allegation of corruption or willful misuse of power or willful misuse of discretion against any public servant and to inquire or cause an inquiry into such disclosure and to provide adequate safeguards against victimization of the person making such complaint and for matters connected therewith and incidental thereto.

Salient Features: The Act seeks to protect whistle-blowers, i.e. persons making a public interest disclosure related to an act of corruption, misuse of power, or criminal offense by a public servant.

- Any public servant or any other person including a non-governmental organization may make such a disclosure to the Central or State Vigilance Commission.
- Every complaint has to include the identity of the complainant.
- The Vigilance Commission shall not disclose the identity of the complainant except to the head of the department if he deems it necessary. The Act penalizes any person who has disclosed the identity of the complainant.
- The Act prescribes penalties for knowingly making false complaints.

TEST YOURSELF

1. In a business, an _______ is a defined set of principles which guide an organization in its activities and decisions and the firm's philosophy may affect its productivity, reputation, and bottom line.

(a) Ethical principle
(b) Ethical code
(c) Business code of conduct
(d) Unethical code

2. Which is/are the correct statement(s) regarding complaint which is to be made under PIDPI?

(a) The complaint should be in a closed / secured envelope.
(b) Commission will not entertain anonymous/ pseudonymous complaints.
(c) The text of the complaint should be carefully drafted so as not to give any details or clue as to his/her identity. However, the details of the complaint should be specific and verifiable.
(d) All of the above

3. Which of the following can't be considered as an advantage of ethical behaviour in the workplace?

(a) Increase in productivity.
(b) Adaptive to changes.
(c) Increase in legal issues.
(d) Coductive working environment.

4. Which of the following can't be considered as a reason of unethical behaviour in the workplace?

(a) Weak personal character.
(b) No fear of reprisal.
(c) Realistic targets.
(d) Strong monitoring system in place.

5. One of these is not a remedy to rectify unethical behaviour at workplace.

(a) Care of result rather than reputation.
(b) Appreciation and rewards for ethical behaviour.
(c) Conversation about ethics in the organization.
(d) Punishment for unethical behaviour.

6. Philosophy of the code envisages and expects:

(a) Non-Confidentiality
(b) Improper use and misapplication of organisation's assets.
(c) Non-compliance.
(d) Adherence to set standards and codes.

7. PIDPI stands for.....................:

(a) Public Income Disclosures and Protection of Informer.
(b) Public Information Disclosures and Protection of Income.
(c) Public Interest Disclosures and Protection of Informer.
(d) Public Income Disclosures and Protection of Interest.

8. Whistle-Blowers Protection Act has been drafted and enacted in.........

(a) 2004 (b) 2007
(c) 2014 (d) 2011

ANSWER

1	2	3	4	5	6	7	8
(b)	(d)	(c)	(b)	(a)	(d)	(c)	(c)

BANKING ETHICS: CHANGING DYNAMICS

INTRODUCTION

Ethics in technology is a sub-field of ethics addressing the ethical questions specific to the Technology Age. Technology ethics is the application of ethical thinking to the practical concerns of technology. The reason technology ethics is growing in prominence is that new technologies give us more power to act, which means that we have to make choices we didn't have to make before. While in the past our actions were involuntarily constrained by our weakness, now, with so much technological power, we have to learn how to be voluntarily constrained by our judgment.

ETHICS AND TECHNOLOGY

Technology ethics (tech ethics) is a field of study that seeks to understand and resolve moral issues that surround the development and practical application of mechanical and electronic technology. Tech ethics focuses on subjects such as the relationship between technology and human values and well-being, the condition in which technological advances occur and the social repercussions for technological advancements.

It is often held that technology itself is incapable of possessing moral or ethical qualities, since "technology" is merely tool making. But many now believe that each piece of technology is endowed with and radiating ethical commitments all the time, given to it by those that made it, and those that decided how it must be made and used. Whether merely a lifeless amoral 'tool' or a solidified embodiment of human values "ethics of technology" refers to two basic subdivisions:

- The ethics involved in the development of new technology—whether it is always, never, or contextually right or wrong to invent and implement a technological innovation.
- The ethical questions that are exacerbated by the ways in which technology extends or curtails the power of individuals—how standard ethical questions are changed by the new powers.

In the former case, ethics of such things as computer security and computer viruses asks whether the very act of innovation is an ethically right or wrong act. Similarly, does a scientist have an ethical obligation to produce or fail to produce a nuclear weapon? What are the ethical questions surrounding the production of technologies that waste or conserve energy and resources? What are the ethical questions surrounding the production of new manufacturing processes that might inhibit employment, or might inflict suffering in the third world?

In the latter case, the ethics of technology quickly break down into the ethics of various human endeavours as they are altered by new technologies. For example, bioethics is now largely consumed with questions that have been exacerbated by the new life-preserving technologies, new cloning technologies, and new technologies for implantation. In law, the right of privacy is being continually diminished by the emergence of new forms of surveillance and anonymity. The old ethical questions of privacy and free speech are given new shape and urgency in an Internet age. Such tracing devices as RFID, biometric analysis and identification, genetic screening, all take old ethical questions and amplify their significance. Lastly, we should also remember that ethic's is a very broadly defined term which is incompetent to influence something as fast changing and ever improving field as technology.

DATA SECURITY AND PRIVACY

Banking is one of the most at risk sectors for privacy violations due to the sensitive, and highly personal nature of information that is exchanged, recorded, and retained. Individuals must trust banks with personal identifying information, their financial records, the access information to their accounts, and their credit history. Thus, privacy violations are not taken lightly and heavily impact the individual whose privacy was violated. Ways in which a violation of privacy can take place in the banking sector include: sharing personal information with third parties without consent for marketing purposes, stolen or lost banking number or card, sharing personal information or allowing access to third parties without informed consent, inadequate notification to an individual concerning what will be done with their data, collecting more personal data than is necessary, refusal to provide financial records upon request by client, incorrectly recording personal information, and loss of a client's personal data due to improper security measures.

RBI provided guidelines on Information Security, Electronic Banking, Technology Risk Management and Cyber Frauds to all commercial banks. As part of these guidelines, RBI has advised banks on data security as under:

- Banks need to define and implement procedures to ensure the integrity and consistency of all data stored in electronic form, such as databases, data warehouses and data archives.
- A data security theory seeks to establish uniform risk-based requirements for the protection of data elements. To ensure that the protection is uniform within and outside of the institution, tools such as data classifications and protection profiles can be used.
- Data classification and protection profiles are complex to implement when the network or storage is viewed as a utility. Because of that complexity, some institutions treat all information at that level as if it were of the highest sensitivity and implement encryption as a protective measure. The complexity in implementing data classification in other layers or in other aspects of an institution's operation may result in other risk mitigation procedures being used. Adequacy is a function of the extent of risk mitigation, and not the procedure or tool used to mitigate risk.
- Policies regarding media handling, disposal, and transit should be implemented to enable the use of protection profiles and otherwise mitigate risks to data. If protection profiles are not used, the policies should accomplish the same goal as protection profiles, which is to deliver the same degree of residual risk without regard to whether the information is in transit or storage, who is directly controlling the data, or where the storage may be.
- There should be secure storage of media. Controls could include physical and environmental controls such as fire and flood protection, limiting access by means like physical locks, keypad, passwords, biometrics, etc., labelling, and logged access. Management should establish access controls to limit access to media, while ensuring that all employees have authorization to access the minimum data required to perform their responsibilities. More sensitive information such as system documentation, application source code, and production transaction data should have more extensive controls to guard against alteration (e.g., integrity checkers, cryptographic hashes).
- The storage of data in portable devices, such as laptops and PDAs, poses unique problems. Mitigation of those risks typically involves encryption of sensitive data, host provided access controls, etc.
- Banks need appropriate disposal procedures for both electronic and paper based media. Contracts with third-party disposal firms should address acceptable disposal procedures. For computer media, data frequently remains on media after erasure. Since that data can be recovered, additional disposal techniques should be applied to sensitive data like physical destruction, overwriting data, degaussing etc.
- Banks should maintain the security of media while in transit or when shared with third parties. Policies should include contractual requirements that incorporate necessary risk-based controls, restrictions on the carriers used and procedures to verify the identity of couriers.
- Banks should encrypt customer account and transaction data which is transmitted, transported, delivered or couriered to external parties or other locations, taking into account all intermediate junctures and transit points from source to destination.
- A few other aspects that also needs to be considered include appropriate blocking, filtering and monitoring of electronic mechanisms like e-mail and printing and monitoring for unauthorised software and hardware like password cracking software, key loggers, wireless access points, etc.
- Concerns over the need to better control and protect sensitive information have given rise to a new set of solutions aimed at increasing an enterprise's ability to protect its information assets. These solutions vary in their capabilities and methodologies, but collectively they have been placed in a category known as data leak prevention (DLP). It provides a comprehensive approach covering people, processes, and systems that identify, monitor, and protect data in use (e.g., endpoint actions), data in motion (e.g., network actions), and data at rest (e.g., data storage) through deep content inspection and with a centralized management framework.

Most DLP solutions include a suite of technologies that facilitate three key objectives:

- Locate and catalogue sensitive information stored throughout the enterprise;
- Monitor and control the movement of sensitive information across enterprise networks;
- Monitor and control the movement of sensitive information on end-user systems.

Banks may consider such solutions, if required, after assessing their potential to improve data security.

INTELLECTUAL PROPERTY RIGHTS

Intellectual property rights are the rights given to persons over the creations of their minds. They usually give the creator an exclusive right over the use of his/her creation for a certain period of time.

Intellectual property rights is a right that is had by a person or by a company to have exclusive rights to use its own plans, ideas, or other intangible assets without the worry of competition, at least for a specific period of time. These rights can include copyrights, patents, trademarks, and trade secrets. These rights may be enforced by a court via a lawsuit. The reasoning for intellectual property is to encourage innovation without the fear that a competitor will steal the idea and/or take the credit for it.

PATENTS AND PROPRIETARY RIGHTS

Patent: A Patent is a statutory right for an invention granted for a limited period of time to the patentee by the Government, in exchange of full disclosure of his invention for excluding others, from making, using, selling, importing the patented product or process for producing that product for those purposes without his consent.

The patent system in India is governed by the Patents Act, 1970 (No. 39 of 1970) as amended by the Patents (Amendment) Act, 2005 and the Patents Rules, 2003. The Patent Rules are regularly amended in consonance with the changing environment, most recent being in 2016.

The term of every patent granted is 20 years from the date of filing of application. However, for application filed under national phase under Patent Cooperation Treaty (PCT), the term of patent will be 20 years from the international filing date accorded under PCT..

Proprietary Rights: Proprietary rights, also known as property rights, are the theoretical or legal rights that an entity has to own property, whether tangible or intangible. Property rights are some of the most basic rights in a free society. They give individuals the right to accumulate, own, hold, delegate, rent, or sell their property. Within economics, property rights form the basis for all market exchange, and they don't always refer only to what's lawful. They might also refer to what is ethical or moral.

Property rights of an owner of proprietary information that may be protected under law: In contracting, this term refers to the data belonging to the contractor, and may include financial information, intellectual property (concepts, designs, and techniques), technical documentation, artwork, and the like.

ETHICS OF INFORMATION SECURITY

Information security for banking application of online services is mandatory aspects to protect the information and information system assets of the bank. Protection depends upon the mechanism and aligned tools and technologies with the assets such as networking components and software applications. Online functionalities of banking system is more prone to be attacked due to use of open public network for remote customers and employees to perform the basic functions of banking services.

The major security concerns are confidentiality, integrity, availability, accuracy etc. These security concerns are analyzed with domain of functions and proper and effective mechanisms are devised to mitigate such type of event to happen with assets. Laws and regulation proposed by legislature in this area is also effective to prevent the attackers and hackers to do such violation with the information assets of the bank. The proactive security mechanism is considered as better mechanism to protect the application integrity along with the application. The ethics related with the functional domain of the banking services. The work ethics must be positive with the domain of the role of the system with electronic platform.

CYBER THREATS

A rapid growth has been observed in the adoption of new security measures and transfers to the digital channels by Indian banks after 2010. It has always been a topic of debate that cyber security practices have never been kept in pace with the evolution/adoption of new technologies, because of which quantum of cyber-attacks is increasing every day. The cyber-attacks not only result in the huge financial losses but also erodes the brand value of any organization.

About 70% of India's internet users make an online transaction on these websites. You can't even estimate the number of transactions done per day. These transactions are not online limited to online shopping.

Raise of the bar in cyber threats ultimately made Reserve Bank of India (RBI) realize the need of holistic and integrated approach towards cyber security, resulting in which a circular from RBI inhibiting the guidelines on cyber security came into effect.

RBI Guidelines: Since compliance-centric approach of banks imposing a critical threat to the security. RBI defined proper guidelines on measures of cyber security. The RBI guidelines are followed.

- **Cybersecurity Operations Center (SOC):** RBI understands the need of a secured ecosystem which can ensure proactive Information sharing and a flexible framework. Therefore, RBI guidelines clearly state the need for setting up a cybersecurity operations center. As per guidelines, focus on a secured ecosystem from top management and cyber-aware board is expected.
- **Architect a Strong Governance:** Any implementation to the cybersecurity requires approval/ rejection from board/top level management. Circular clearly defines the necessity of board-level awareness and participation to make them sensitive

about the current state of cybersecurity. It will make cybersecurity as important as investigating in business-enabling technologies.

- **Securing Client Data and Its Usage in Financial Crimes:** RBI has a very clear and strong emphasis on the data security of customers. The banks are required to adopt the highest possible preventive measures to secure customer's data whether it is in motion or freeze state. Guidelines further focus on organizing such programmes where customers can make aware to reduce the incidents of attacks.
- **Proactive Reporting and Collaboration:** RBI have recognized the importance of collaboration between different financial institutions which would help them mutually and make them capable in responding to the attacks proactively and quickly.
- **Infinite Surveillance:** A much important need for continuous surveillance and real-time analysis was required as it helps in taking actions faster when attacked from outside. New guidelines would require banks to implement a 24 × 7 real-time based surveillance. These measures not only reduce the impact of loss but also helps in deciding an effective measure to stop such incidences in the future.
- **Cyber Crisis Management Plan (CCMP):** The RBI circular calls for the establishment of a Cyber Crisis Management Plan to address the full life cycle of detection, response, containment, and recovery.

Successful implementation of guidelines would help banks to protect customer's data, banks would be able to report incidents proactively, and continuous surveillance would arm the existing capabilities of cyber security which would eventually lead to an extended ecosystem.

DIGITAL RIGHTS MANAGEMENT (DRM)

Digital rights management (DRM) is a term which refers to various technologies that are used by software and hardware manufacturers, publishers, copyright holders, and individuals with the intent to control the use of digital content. Digital rights management includes technologies that control the use, modification, and distribution of works, as well as systems within devices that enforce these policies. Copyright holders are allowed to use DRM to safeguard their work being duplicated or utilized by others. However, copyright laws across the world allow fair use of the copyrighted work. Fair use essentially means using the copyrighted work for as part of or for the purposes of a commentary, search engines, criticism, parody, news reporting, research, teaching, library archiving and scholarship etc.

The right to Fair Use has therefore played a very important role. It has helped research, education and general intellectual development. The right to Fair Use now stands threatened. With the emergence of WIPO Internet treaties (World Intellectual Property Organization Copyright Treaty, and World Intellectual Property Organization Performances and Phonograms Treaty), this right to fair use of digital media protected by DRM is penalized by law, irrespective of taking into consideration if it was a fair use or not. DRM is a general term used for a set of technologies, software, and hardware that seek to identify, protect, and manage digital content in terms of access, distribution, consumer usage, and payment. In a very common sense approach, it can be said that Digital Rights Management is the management of rights digitally, i.e. Using the advanced technological measures to manage and control one's rights.

TEST YOURSELF

1. Ways in which violation of privacy can't take place in the banking sector include:
   (a) collecting adequate personal data than is necessary.
   (b) incorrectly recording personal information.
   (c) sharing personal information or allowing access to third parties without informed consent.
   (d) loss of a client's personal data due to improper security measures.
2. Controls for secure storage of data do not include ....
   (a) Behavioural (b) Environmental
   (c) Physical (d) Technical
3. Degaussing is applied for ______
   (a) Application of data (b) Storage of data
   (c) Concealment of data (d) Erasing the data
4. The term of every patent granted is ______ years from date of filing of application:
   (a) 1 (b) 10
   (c) 20 (d) 25
5. The Patent Rules are regularly amended in consonance with the changing environment, most recent being in ______.
   (a) 2010 (b) 2012
   (c) 2014 (d) 2016

ANSWER

1	2	3	4	5
(a)	(a)	(d)	(c)	(d)

Principles & Practices of Banking

Mock Test-1

1. The scheduled banks are those which are included under the ______ Schedule of the Reserve Bank of India Act, 1934.

(a) 2nd (b) 3rd

(c) 4th (d) 5th

2. Primary dealers deal in government securities and deal in ______.

(a) Primary markets

(b) Secondary markets

(c) Both the primary and secondary markets

(d) None

3. The PSS Act, ______ provides for the regulation and supervision of payment systems in India.

(a) 2005 (b) 2007

(c) 2009 (d) 2010

4. The foreign exchange reserve of India are managed by:

(a) Exim Bank (b) RBI

(c) FEDAI (d) SEBI

5. Monetary and credit policy is reviewed by RBI:

(a) On bi-monthly basis

(b) Once in a year

(c) Thrice in a year

(d) Four times in a year

6. The Central Board of RBI comprises, a Governor, ______ Deputy Governors and ______ Directors.

(a) 4, 10 (b) 4, 15

(c) 5, 10 (d) 5, 15

7. Global depository receipts are normally traded on:

(a) US Stock Exchange

(b) European Stock Exchange

(c) Indian Stock Exchange

(d) International Stock Exchange

8. Banking facilities provided to poor and deprived family of the country is called as:

(a) Narrow banking

(b) Financial inclusion

(c) Financial literacy

(d) Universal banking

9. Which of the following can issue participatory notes:

(a) SEBI (b) SGB Holders

(c) FII (d) FDI

10. Commercial Paper can be issued for maturities between a minimum of ______ and a maximum of up to one year from the date of issue.

(a) 7 days (b) 14 days

(c) 30 days (d) 90 days

11. Which is not a correct statement about the Repo and Reverse Repo Market?

(a) Repo (repurchase agreement) was introduced in December 1995.

(b) Repo means selling a security under an agreement to repurchase it at a predetermined date and rate.

(c) Repo transactions are affected between banks and financial institutions and among bank themselves, RBI also undertake Repo.

(d) Reverse Repo means buying a security on a spot basis with a commitment to resell on a forward basis.

12. A Government Security (G-Sec) is a tradeable instrument issued by ______. It acknowledges the Government's debt obligation.

(a) The Central Government only

(b) The State Governments only

(c) The Central Government or the State Governments

(d) None of the above

13. On account of non-delivery of securities by the trading member on the pay-in day, securities are put up for ______ by the exchange.

(a) settlement (b) auction

(c) pay out (d) security

14. SEBI has stipulated the eligibility norms for companies planning an IPO. Which is not a correct statement regarding Entry Norm (Profitability Route)?

(a) Net tangible assets of at least ₹ 5 crore in each of the preceding three full years of which not more than 50% are held in monetary assets.

(b) Minimum of ₹ 15 crore as average pre-tax operating profit in at least three years of the immediately preceding five years.
(c) Net worth of at least ₹ 1 crore in each of the preceding three full years.
(d) The issue size should not exceed 5 times the pre-issue net worth.

15. Headquarters of SEBI is located at ______.
(a) Mumbai (b) New Delhi
(c) Kolkata (d) Ahmedabad

16. The Government's ambitious National Health Protection Scheme (NHPS) to cover 10 crore poor families with ________ health insurance may be lurching for funds as allocations hardly cover the programmes potential expenditure costs.
(a) ₹ 1 lakh (b) ₹ 2 lakh
(c) ₹ 5 lakh (d) ₹ 10 lakh

17. PMJJBY is a lucrative life insurance plan, wherein the insured receives ₹ 2 Lakh cover against an annual premium of ₹ 330 each year. The life risk cover will get terminated after ______.
(a) 50 years (b) 55 years
(c) 58 years (d) 60 years

18. Which is not a part of Factoring service?
(a) Management of receivables
(b) Hands over the entire export bill
(c) Discounting of bills
(d) Collection of bills

19. The letter of credit where packing or anticipatory credit is available against the LC is called ______.
(a) Transferable LC (b) Red clause LC
(c) Back to back LC (d) Revolving LC

20. Which is not a type of liquidity risk?
(a) Funding Liquidity Risk (b) Time risk
(c) Call risk (d) Interest Rate Risk

21. The risks considered for capital requirements under Basel II are ________.
(a) credit risk, market risk, operational risk
(b) transaction risk, credit risk, liquidity risk,
(c) market risk, operational risk, forex risk
(d) liquidity risk, market risk, operational risk

22. At organizational level in each bank, the overall responsibility of risk management is assigned to:
(a) Board of Director
(b) Risk Management Organization
(c) Risk Management Committee
(d) Risk Management Sub-committee of Board of Director

23. CIBIL Trans Union Credit scores range between ______.
(a) 200 and 800 (b) 200 and 900
(c) 300 and 800 (d) 300 and 900

24. Normally our representatives will contact you between ______, unless the special circumstances of your Code of Bank's Commitment to Customers.
(a) 06 am and 07 pm (b) 07 am and 07 pm
(c) 06 am and 08 pm (d) 07 am and 08 pm

25. Equifax is currently headquartered in ______.
(a) Mumbai (b) Delhi
(c) Bangalore (d) Kolkata

26. In general, a CIBIL Trans Union Credit score of ___ or higher is considered good.
(a) 600 (b) 650
(c) 750 (d) 800

27. Which is not a part of demand deposit?
(a) Savings Account (b) Current Account
(c) Recurring Deposit (d) All of the above

28. The transferor of ______ in property, is called a mortgagor and the transferee is called a mortgagee.
(a) ownership
(b) possession
(c) interest
(d) all of the above

29. Term deposits are fixed for a definite term. Minimum period as per RBI is ______. Maximum period as per IBA is ______.
(a) 7 days, 20 years
(b) 14 days, 10 years
(c) 7 days, 10 years
(d) 14 days, No limit prescribed

30. The money laundering cycle can be broken down into three distinct stages; the correct stages of money laundering are the:
(a) Placement; Integration, Layering:
(b) Layering; Placement; Integration:
(c) Placement; Layering; Integration
(d) Integration; Layering; Placement

31. All cash transaction of the value of more than ______ or its equivalent in foreign currency are covered by the act.
(a) 5 lac (b) 10 lac
(c) 20 lac (d) 50 lac

32. The Director of FIU-IND is vested with the power of a ________ under the code of civil procedure.
(a) Civil Court (b) High Court
(c) Supreme Court (d) CBI Court

33. A special power of attorney authorises a person to act in a ______ transaction.
(a) general (b) special
(c) single (d) multiple

34. A mandate in a partnership account can be cancelled by:
(a) All the partners
(b) Any one of the partners
(c) Majority of the partners
(d) Court

35. A comprehensive amendment (The Consumer Protection (Amendment) Act 2002) has been passed on December 17, 2002 implemented effective from March 15, 2003. The day March 15 is celebrated as:
(a) World Consumer Day
(b) World Consumer Rights Day
(c) India Consumer Rights Day
(d) COPRA establishment day

36. Under Consumer Protection Act, the Central Government has established a council known as:
(a) National Commission
(b) State Commission
(c) Central Consumer Protection Council
(d) All of the above

37. The Banking Ombudsman may award compensation not exceeding ________ to the complainant for mental agony and harassment.
(a) ₹ 1 lac (b) ₹ 5 lac
(c) ₹10 lac (d) ₹ 20 lac

38. Customer and bank have to send acceptance of the award within ________ of date of receipt of the award.
(a) 15 days (b) 30 days
(c) 60 days (d) 90 days

39. In India, the Negotiable Instruments Act was passed during 1881 which came into force from ________.
(a) March 01, 1881 (b) March 01, 1882
(c) January 01, 1881 (d) January 01, 1882

40. Bill of exchange is defined under which section of the NI Act?
(a) Section 4 (b) Section 5
(c) Section 6 (d) Section 7

41. Which of the following bills is/are allowed grace period under section 22 of NI Act?
(a) Usance bill (b) Demand bill
(c) Both (d) None of the above

42. As per Indian Companies Act 2013, Maximum number of partners in a firm can be:
(a) 10 (b) 20
(c) 100 (d) 200

43. A company is known as the ________ of another company if it has control over another company.
(a) Holding company (b) Existing company
(c) Other company (d) Foreign company

44. Embodies Company's name, Authorized capital, Objectives of the company, Liability of shareholders are written in:
(a) Certificate of Incorporation
(b) Memorandum of Association
(c) Article of Association
(d) None of the above

45. Demand draft or Pay order of ________ & above in a day should be issued to the debit of an account or cheque and not against cash.
(a) ₹ 10,000 (b) ₹ 20,000
(c) ₹ 50,000 (d) ₹ 100,000

46. Settlement Timings of the NEFT operates in ________ batches.
(a) half hourly (b) hourly
(c) two hourly (d) three hourly

47. The RTGS system is primarily meant for large value transactions. The minimum amount to be remitted through RTGS is ________.
(a) ₹ 50000 (b) ₹ 1 lakh
(c) ₹ 2 lakh (d) ₹ 5 lakhs

48. The relationship between bank and customer in case of Safe Deposit Vault is:
(a) Principal and Agent (b) Lessor and Lessee
(c) Bailee and Bailor (d) Debtor and Creditor

49. The designer of Indian Rupee Sign is:
(a) Hitendra Swami
(b) Udaya Kumar Dharmalingam
(c) Panduranga Kumarlingam
(d) None of the above

50. Where the RBI has no branch the bank which can act as its agent is?
(a) Any commercial bank
(b) Any nationalised bank
(c) SBI
(d) Indian bank

51. Which is the correct statement about 'Public Company'?
(a) Its share is listed in stock exchange
(b) Minimum seven members, no limit of maximum number
(c) Minimum three directors, maximum no limit
(d) All of the above

52. As per Indian Contract Act 1872, who is not competent to contract?
(a) Minor (b) Insolvent
(c) Insane (d) All of the above

53. ________ is the rate banks receive for depositing funds with the Central Bank:
(a) Reverse repo rate (b) Repo rate
(c) Interest rate (d) All of these

54. Whose signature appears on Indian ₹ 100 note?
(a) Finance Minister (b) RBI Governor
(c) Finance Secretary (d) None of the above

55. Indian banks are offering cash management services like;
(a) Electronic funds transfer services
(b) Provision of cash related MIS reports
(c) Cash pooling services
(d) All of the above

56. Vetting of the document is being carried out by:
(a) A senior officer
(b) Empaneled Lawyer
(c) Any Lawyer
(d) Chartered Accountant

57. Bank Guarantee is not written in Balance Sheet as:
(a) It is a contingent liability
(b) It is not a liability
(c) It is an asset
(d) It is backed by security

58. Within the 18% target of agriculture, target of 8% is prescribed for Small & Marginal Farmer, to be achieved ________ by March 2017.
(a) 7% (b) 8%
(c) 10% (d) 12%

59. Scheduled Commercial Banks having any shortfall in lending to priority sector shall be allocated amounts for contribution to the ________.
(a) RIDF (b) SEDF
(c) SIDBI (d) NHB

60. In November 1974, the banks were advised to raise the share of priority sectors in their aggregate advances to the level of ________ by March 1979.
(a) 30 per cent (b) 33.3 per cent
(c) 40 per cent (d) 50 per cent

61. Banks may consider sanctioning KCC loans on hypothecation of crops up to card limit of ________ without insisting on collateral security in case of tie-up advances.
(a) ₹ 1.00 lakhs (b) ₹ 2.00 lakhs
(c) ₹ 3.00 lakhs (d) ₹ 5.00 lakhs

62. Which of the following stages of the crop and risks leading to crop loss are not covered under the PMFBY scheme?
(a) Prevented Sowing/ Planting Risk
(b) Malicious Damage
(c) Post-Harvest Losses
(d) Localized Calamities

63. Pradhan Mantri Fasal Bima Yojana (PMFBY), to be implemented from ______.
(a) 1st Jan. 2016 (b) 1st April 2016
(c) 1st Jan. 2017 (d) 1st April' 2017

64. Investment in plant & machinery more than ₹ 5 crores but not to exceed ₹10 crore is classified as:
(a) Manufacturing Micro Enterprise
(b) Services Small Enterprise
(c) Manufacturing Small Enterprise
(d) Manufacturing Medium Enterprise

65. Functions of Reserve Bank are:
(a) Bankers bank
(b) Banker to Government
(c) Lender of the last resort
(d) All the above

66. The following is a mechanism for injecting liquidity by RBI to the financial system:
(a) Reverse Repo
(b) Hike in CRR
(c) Hike in interest rate
(d) Repo

67. Under Minor Irrigation schemes, Loan cannot be financed for the purpose of
(a) Power threshers
(b) Construction of pump house
(c) Electric motor & pump set
(d) Lift irrigation

68. Credit rationing is a ______ method of credit control.
(a) quantitative credit control
(b) qualitative credit control
(c) direct credit control
(d) continuous credit control

69. The GOI and SIDBI as settlors of the Trust have committed a corpus of ₹ 2,500 crore in the ratio of to the CGTMSE.
(a) 4:1 (b) 1:4
(c) 1:2 (d) 2:1

70. MSMED Act, 2006 was notified in India on________.
(a) April 1, 2006 (b) October 2, 2006
(c) April 1, 2007 (d) October 2, 2007

71. DAY-NRLM would provide Revolving Fund (RF) support to SHGs in existence for a minimum period of ________ and follow the norms of good SHGs.
(a) 1 to 2 months (b) 1 to 3 months
(c) 3 to 6 months (d) 6 to 9 months

72. The primary function of Central Bank is to ______ of the country.
(a) control the system
(b) resulate the monetary system
(c) plan the monetary system
(d) None of these

73. Rural area, PMEGP Scheme to be implemented by:
(a) KVIC (b) KVIB
(c) DIC (d) All of the above

74. In case of special SHGs i.e., groups in the difficult areas, groups with disabled persons, and groups formed in remote tribal areas, this number may be a minimum of ______.
(a) 4 persons (b) 5 persons
(c) 6 persons (d) 7 persons

75. All loan to SHG is categorised as ______.
(a) Agriculture loan (b) MSME loan
(c) Weaker sections loan (d) KCC loan

76. Banks may issue credit cards including other cards such as:
(a) Co-branded credit cards
(b) Add-on credit cards
(c) Corporate credit cards
(d) All of the above

77. PMAY is a mission started with an aim 'Housing For All' (HFA) scheme by NDA Government to be achieved by the year ______.
(a) 2020 (b) 2021
(c) 2022 (d) 2024

78. As per RBI guidelines for Credit Card operations, the Credit Card can be issued by:
(a) Banks only
(b) NBFC only
(c) Insurance company
(d) Both Banks and NBFC

79. Agreement is defined in the ______.
(a) Indian Contract Act, 1872
(b) Indian Evidence Act 1872
(c) Negotiable Instrument Act, 1881
(d) Transfer of Property Act, 1882

80. Equitable mortgage should be registered with CERSAI within ______.
(a) 30 days (b) 45 days
(c) 60 days (d) 90 days

81. State Government Stamps is not applicable on which of the instruments?
(a) Bill of lading (b) Mortgage
(c) Hypothecation (d) Pledge

82. Which of the following is preferable security from liquidity point of view?
(a) Immovable property (b) Debenture
(c) Quoted equity shares (d) Stocks

83. A direct agriculture account becomes NPA if:
(a) For short duration crops the Interest or instalment remaining overdue for 2 crops seasons
(b) For long duration crop the Interest or instalment remaining overdue for 1 crop season.
(c) The Limit is not reviewed within 180 days from the due date of renewal.
(d) All of the above

84. Which is not the correct classification of live NPA assets by banks:
(a) Substandard Assets (b) Write-off Assets
(c) Doubtful Assets (d) Loss Assets

85. The services which will not offer under Financial Inclusion Plans?
(a) Deposit account
(b) Small Agriculture loan accounts
(c) Vehicle Loan
(d) Remittances services

86. What is the meaning of VSAT?
(a) Very Small Aperture Terminals
(b) Very Sensitive Aperture Terminals
(c) Various Small Adjustable Terminals
(d) Various Satellite Aperture Terminals

87. ATMs set up, owned and operated by non-banks are called ______.
(a) White Label ATMs (b) Black Label ATMs
(c) Off-site ATM (d) On-site ATM

88. In ______ mode, the communication is unidirectional, as on a one-way street. Only one of the two devices on a link can transmit; the other can only receive.
(a) Simplex (b) Half-duplex
(c) Full-duplex (d) Triplex

89. ______ has the potential to transform both front office and back office operations with its self-improving programs at ICICI Bank. The banks will explore the concepts to integrate the conversational interface into their Omni Channel Strategy.
(a) Open banking
(b) Block chain
(c) Artificial Intelligence
(d) Banking architecture simplification

90. ______ is a systematic and Independent examination of information systems environment to ascertain whether the objectives, set out to be achieved, have been met or not.
(a) Controlling (b) Auditing
(c) Protecting (d) Checking

91. Spear phishing targets a ______ person or enterprise, as opposed to random application users.
(a) Common (b) General
(c) specific (d) Group

92. The management process through which goods and services move from concept to the customer. It

includes the coordination of four elements called the 4 P's of marketing. Which is not the part of 4P's?
(a) Product (b) Planning
(c) Price (d) Promotional strategy

93. Which is not the Popular Social Media Networks?
(a) Facebook (b) Xender
(c) LinkedIn (d) Twitter

94. What is the least pressing in Maslow's Hierarchy of Needs?
(a) Self-actualization (b) Safety needs
(c) Physiological needs (d) Social needs

95. Which are not the types of pricing objectives?
(a) Profit-Oriented Pricing
(b) Competitor-Based Pricing
(c) Demand Based Pricing
(d) Market Penetration

96. In a credit card or debit card, where the cash is actually used is called:
(a) Point of sale (b) ATM
(c) Point of distribution (d) All of the above

97. A ________ channel is a direct marketing channel where there is no intermediary and the producer sell directly to the consumer.
(a) zero-level (b) one-level
(c) two-level (d) three-level

98. A promotion strategy which is directed to the final customer to induce them to purchase the product is called:
(a) push strategy (b) pull strategy
(c) selling strategy (d) marketing strategy

99. As per IBA model code of conduct for DSA, Telephonic contact must normally be limited between ________
(a) 09:00 Hrs and 20:00 Hrs
(b) 09:30 Hrs and 19:00 Hrs
(c) 09:00 Hrs and 1900 Hrs
(d) 10:30 Hrs and 19:30 Hrs

100. The third important component of MKIS is ________. It is conducted to solve specific marketing problems of the company. It collects data about the problem.
(a) Marketing Intelligence
(b) Marketing Research
(c) Marketing Decision Support
(d) Internal Records

ANSWER

1	2	3	4	5	6	7	8	9	10
(a)	(c)	(b)	(b)	(a)	(d)	(b)	(b)	(c)	(a)
11	**12**	**13**	**14**	**15**	**16**	**17**	**18**	**19**	**20**
(a)	(c)	(b)	(a)	(a)	(c)	(b)	(b)	(b)	(d)
21	**22**	**23**	**24**	**25**	**26**	**27**	**28**	**29**	**30**
(c)	(c)	(d)	(b)	(a)	(c)	(c)	(c)	(c)	(c)
31	**32**	**33**	**34**	**35**	**36**	**37**	**38**	**39**	**40**
(b)	(a)	(c)	(b)	(b)	(c)	(a)	(b)	(b)	(b)
41	**42**	**43**	**44**	**45**	**46**	**47**	**48**	**49**	**50**
(a)	(c)	(a)	(b)	(c)	(a)	(c)	(b)	(b)	(c)
51	**52**	**53**	**54**	**55**	**56**	**57**	**58**	**59**	**60**
(d)	(d)	(a)	(b)	(d)	(b)	(a)	(c)	(a)	(b)
61	**62**	**63**	**64**	**65**	**66**	**67**	**68**	**69**	**70**
(c)	(b)	(b)	(c)	(d)	(d)	(a)	(b)	(a)	(b)
71	**72**	**73**	**74**	**75**	**76**	**77**	**78**	**79**	**80**
(c)	(b)	(d)	(b)	(c)	(d)	(c)	(d)	(a)	(a)
81	**82**	**83**	**84**	**85**	**86**	**87**	**88**	**89**	**90**
(a)	(c)	(d)	(b)	(c)	(a)	(a)	(a)	(c)	(b)
91	**92**	**93**	**94**	**95**	**96**	**97**	**98**	**99**	**100**
(c)	(b)	(b)	(a)	(c)	(a)	(a)	(b)	(b)	(b)

Mock Test-2

1. The minimum total capital under Basel III is ___ % of total risk weighted assets.
(a) 7% (b) 8%
(c) 9% (d) 10%

2. Basel is a city found in Basel-City, ______.
(a) Brazil (b) Switzerland
(c) France (d) USA

3. Which of the elements of Tier 2 capital other than undisclosed reserves?
(a) Revaluation Reserves
(b) Hybrid Debt Capital Instruments
(c) Subordinated Debt
(d) All of the above

4. Banking Codes and Standards Board of India (BCSBI) is registered as ______.
(a) Firm (b) Company
(c) Govt. Undertaking (d) Society

5. RBI, in its Monetary Policy Statement in April ____ announced setting up of the Banking Codes and Standards Board of India (BCSBI).
(a) 2005 (b) 2006
(c) 2007 (d) 2008

6. How many Credit Information Companies work in India?
(a) 2 (b) 3
(c) 4 (d) 5

7. While taking physical possession of securities the bank becomes _____ and the customer _____.
(a) bailee, bailor
(b) bailor, bailee
(c) trustee, beneficiary
(d) beneficiary, trustee

8. A NRE account can be opened by ________.
(a) Foreign national only
(b) Foreign Institutional investors only
(c) NRI and Foreign national
(d) NRI and PIO

9. Which is a type of term deposit?
(a) Monthly Interest Deposit
(b) Short-Term Deposits
(c) Flexi Recurring Deposit
(d) All of the above

10. As per PMLA Act 2002, preserving records for ____ from the date of each transaction between bank & clients or for 5 years after business relationship ended.
(a) 3 years (b) 5 years
(c) 8 years (d) 10 years

11. At the ________ stage, the money re-enters the mainstream economy in legitimate-looking form. It appears to come from a legal transaction.
(a) Placement (b) Integration
(c) Layering (d) Smurfing

12. Which types of risk is not involved with money laundering?
(a) Reputational Risk (b) Compliance Risk
(c) Credit Risk (d) Operational Risk

13. Which is categorised as Low Risk Customer?
(a) Statutory Bodies (b) Trust
(c) Charities (d) Non resident customer

14. Particular lien gives the creditor right to retain ____ increase the expenses incurred is not valid.
(a) All goods (b) Specific goods
(c) Some goods (d) Ordered goods

15. A Garnishee Order is an order issued by ________.
(a) Police officer (b) Court
(c) Revenue officer (d) CBI

16. If a customer maintains more than one account with a bank and he deposits some amount then he has the first right to indicate to which account the amount should be credited. This right is called:
(a) Power of Attorney (b) Right of Set-off
(c) Lien (d) Right of Appropriation

17. Lien is the ________ of one person to retain goods and securities in his possession belonging to another until certain legal debts due to the person retaining the goods are satisfied.
(a) right (b) interest
(c) obligation (d) instrument

18. A power of attorney may be ________.
(a) Specific (b) General
(c) Both (d) None

19. For filling a complaint under COPRA, Limitation period is _____from the date of cause of action *i.e.* purchase of goods/hiring of services.
(a) 2 years (b) 1 year
(c) 6 months (d) No time limitation

20. All costs of the Banking Ombudsman office are borne by________.
(a) State Bank of India
(b) All Commercial Banks of the area
(c) RBI
(d) All Commercial Banks & RRB of the area

21. Appeal against the order of banking ombudsman may be filed by a bank only with the prior sanction of the ______ or any other officer of equal rank.
(a) Chairman (b) MD or CEO
(c) ED (d) Any of the above

22. According to Section 13 (a) of the Act, Negotiable Instruments means:
(a) Promissory Note (PN),
(b) Bill of Exchange (BOE)
(c) Cheque
(d) All of the above

23. Number of parties in a bill of exchange is ______.
(a) 2 (b) 3
(c) 4 (d) None

24. Present validity period of cheque, as per RBI and w.e.f. 01.04.2012 is _____.
(a) 2 months (b) 3 months
(c) 4 months (d) 6 months

25. In a Government company, number of shares held by the Government at least:
(a) 50% (b) 51%
(c) 75% (d) 100%

26. While giving a loan to a club or society or school the bank should study:
(a) Bye-laws (b) Copy of resolution
(c) Rules & Regulation (d) All of the above

27. A company which is established before the Company Act 1956 is called ________.
(a) Holding Company
(b) Subsidiary Company
(c) Existing Company
(d) Foreign Company

28. Which is not a statutory company in India?
(a) Reserve Bank of India
(b) Tata Iron & Steel Company
(c) The Life Insurance Corporation of India
(d) The Food Corporation of India

29. Which is not necessary for financing a Private Company?
(a) Memorandum of Association
(b) Article of Association
(c) Certificate of commencement of business
(d) Board resolution

30. For opening of bank account, registration of a partnership firm is:
(a) Optional
(b) Compulsory
(c) Not required
(d) As per partnership deed

31. The relationship between bank and customer in case of Safe Deposit Vault is:
(a) Principal and Agent (b) Lessor and Lessee
(c) Bailee and Bailor (d) Debtor and Creditor

32. Period of Credit in case of NEFT, the beneficiary should get credit within ________ from the time of completion of batch *i.e.* on B+2 basis on the same day.
(a) 1 hour (b) 2 hours
(c) 4 hours (d) 6 hours

33. Safe Deposit Vault is governed by provisions of ________.
(a) Transfer of Property Act
(b) Indian Contract Act
(c) NI Act
(d) Banking Regulation Act

34. In a Government company, number of shares held by the Government at least:
(a) 50% (b) 51%
(c) 75% (d) 100%

35. Which is not a statutory company in India?
(a) Reserve Bank of India
(b) Tata Iron & Steel Company
(c) The Life Insurance Corporation of India
(d) The Food Corporation of India

36. For opening of bank account, registration of a partnership firm is:
(a) Optional
(b) Compulsory
(c) Not required
(d) As per partnership deed

37. While giving a loan to a club or society or school the bank should study:
(a) Bye-laws (b) Copy of Resolution
(c) Rules & Regulation (d) All of the above

38. The originating member should release the payment message from their system to the RTGS central system within _____ of debiting a customer's account.
(a) 30 minutes (b) 60 minutes
(c) 120 minutes (d) 180 minutes

39. Duplicate DD have to be issued to the purchaser within _______ of the request subject to completion of formalities.
(a) 14 days (b) 21 days
(c) 30 days (d) 45 days

40. Indian banks are not offering which type of cash management services?
(a) Cash collection services
(b) Guaranteed credit arrangements
(c) Tax payment services
(d) None of the above

41. Credit Monitoring starts from the moment:
(a) The loan sanctioned
(b) The account converts as SMA 1.
(c) The loan disbursed
(d) The possibility of a new advance is visualized.

42. When more than one banks are allowing credit facilities to one party in coordination with each other under a formal arrangement, this type of finance is called:
(a) Consortium (b) Multiple
(c) Syndication (d) Participation

43. Within the MSME target, Micro Enterprises will be ____ of ANBC or Off- Balance Sheet exposure, whichever is higher to be achieved.
(a) 7% (b) 7.5%
(c) 8% (d) 10%

44. Foreign banks with less than 20 branches have to achieve the total Priority Sector Target 40 percent of ANBC to be achieved in a phased manner by _____.
(a) 2018 (b) 2019
(c) 2020 (d) 2021

45. Housing Loan for Repairs for priority sector, loans for repairs to damaged dwelling units up to ____ in metropolitan centres and up to ___ in other centres.
(a) ₹ 4 lakh, ₹ 2 lakh
(b) ₹ 5 lakh, ₹ 2 lakh
(c) ₹ 5 lakh, ₹ 3 lakh
(d) ₹ 10 lakh, ₹ 5 lakh

46. Agri-clinics provide support in which of the following areas?
(a) Soil health (b) Cropping practices
(c) Plant protection (d) All of the above

47. Premium Rates under the PMFBY scheme for Kharif Season are ____ of SI or Actuarial rate, whichever is less.
(a) 1.5% (b) 2.0%
(c) 2.5% (d) 5%

48. Under Dairy Development Scheme, the loan cannot financed to:
(a) Agriculture labourers (b) Co-operative Society
(c) Limited Company (d) Charitable Trust

49. Which is not excluded schemes under CGTMSE?
(a) Consortium Finance
(b) SRTO
(c) Educational Institutions
(d) Self Help Group

50. Subsidy available under PMEGP scheme for General Category in Rural area is___ Project Cost.
(a) 15% (b) 25%
(c) 30% (d) 35%

51. Which one of the banker's bank?
(a) RBI (b) Federal Bank
(c) Union Bank (d) Bank of India

52. Which one is the custodian of foriegn balances of country?
(a) RBI (b) Fedral Bank
(c) Union Bank (d) Bank of India

53. The revised KCC Scheme is effective from _____.
(a) 12 May 2012 (b) 12 May 2013
(c) 12 May 2014 (d) 12 May 2015

54. CGTMSE is applicable to those loan account if:
(a) No primary Security obtained
(b) No third party guarantee taken
(c) Sanctioned Limit up to 200 lac
(d) Any credit facility having ROI more than 14%

55. Credit Guarantee Fund Trust for Micro & Small Enterprises (CGTMSE) for MSE loans iş affected from which date?
(a) 2nd July 2006 (b) 2nd July 2007
(c) 2nd July 2008 (d) 2nd July 2010

56. Which one is the controller of credit?
(a) RBI (b) Federal Bank
(c) Union Bank (d) Bank of India

57. Under DAY-NRLM scheme 2nd dose of CIF will be __________ of existing corpus and proposed saving during the next 12 months or ₹ 1 lakh, whichever is higher.
(a) 2-3 times (b) 4-8 times
(c) 5-10 times (d) 8-12 times

58. Which is the part of 'Panchasutra' for SHG?
(a) Regular meetings
(b) Regular savings
(c) Regular internal lending
(d) All of the above

59. Definition of Family is applicable for PMEGP Scheme is:
(a) Beneficiary & spouse
(b) Beneficiary, spouse & children
(c) Beneficiary, spouse & parents
(d) Beneficiary, spouse dependent children

60. As per operational guidelines of NABARD, SHGs may be sanctioned savings linked loans by banks varying from a saving to loan ratio of 1:1 to____.
(a) 1:2 (b) 1:3
(c) 1:4 (d) 1:5

61. A self-help group (SHG) is a village-based financial intermediary usually composed of ______ local women.
(a) 5–10 (b) 5–20
(c) 10–20 (d) 10–15

62. Banks are offering maximum repayment period for home loan for ____also subject to age criteria whichever is earlier.
(a) 30 years (b) 25 years
(c) 20 years (d) 15 years

63. Card issuers should ensure that there is no delay in dispatching bills and the customer has sufficient number of days (at least one______) for making payment before the interest starts getting charged.
(a) week (b) fortnight
(c) month (d) quarter

64. Pradhan Mantri AwasYojna will bring a 'Pucca house' for every family in urban cities. Which facilities is not included in house under the scheme?
(a) water connection
(b) kitchen with gas connection
(c) 24x7 electricity supply
(d) toilet facilities

65. The borrower if asks for copies of the loan documents:
(a) cannot be given
(b) can be given on demand
(c) It is bank's discretion
(d) any of the above

66. Person, executing the loan documents must be _____ *i.e.*, he or she should have contractual capacity.
(a) Borrower
(b) Related to the firm or director of the company
(c) High Net-worth Individual
(d) Competent to enter into a contract

67. Value of stamp will be decided as per the State Act. In the event of doubt, the ______will decide.
(a) Civil court (b) Dy. Collector
(c) Collector (d) Registrar

68. Hypothecation is defined in:
(a) Transfer of property act
(b) SARFAESI act
(c) Indian contract act
(d) It is not defined in any act

69. Charge creation on LIC policy is:
(a) Assignment (b) Pledge
(c) Lien (d) Hypothecation

70. ______ arises in relation to transaction of sales of goods, with government and public sector undertaking.
(a) Supply bills (b) Accommodation bills
(c) Trust receipt (d) Inspection notes

71. On an account turning NPA, banks should:
(a) Reverse the interest already charged and not collected by debiting P&L account
(b) Stop further application of interest
(c) Provision is required in the account
(d) All of the above

72. Which is not the assets code of doubtful assets?
(a) 31 (b) 32
(c) 33 (d) 40

73. If an NPA accounts Net Outstanding ₹ 12 lakh and RVS is ₹ 8 lakh categorized as Assets Code Doubtful II (D2), the provision amount will be:
(a) ₹ 4.80 lakh (b) ₹ 7.20 lakh
(c) ₹ 9.60 lakh (d) ₹ 3.20 lakh

74. The Committee on Medium-term Path on Financial Inclusion (CMPFI) constituted by Reserve Bank of India submitted its report in________.
(a) December, 2013 (b) September, 2014
(c) December, 2015 (d) September, 2016

75. The key elements of financial literacy of this block level CFL project are:
(a) Schedule of camps
(b) Skilled workforce
(c) Use of technology
(d) All of the above

76. The computer network that links computers and peripherals within a localised area say, within a building is known as _______.
(a) LAN (b) WAN
(c) MAN (d) TAN

77. In a ______ topology, the central node is often the master. Each of the other nodes is joined to the master by separate links.
(a) Bus (b) Star
(c) Tree (d) Ring

78. Considering the utility nature of the objects of NPCI, it has been incorporated as a "Not for Profit" __________.
(a) Company (b) Trust
(c) Society (d) Firm

79. Which is not used as a magnetic stripe card?
(a) Credit Card (b) Charge Card
(c) Electronic Purse (d) All of the above

80. The Bank recognised the pressing need to harness information technology for intra-bank and inter-bank communications in the 1980s and set up BANKNET.
(a) INDONET (b) RBINET
(c) NICNET (d) BANKNET

81. A connected ecosystem for financial and non-financial services with multiple underlying service providers is the future of banking is called:
(a) Open banking
(b) Block chain
(c) Artificial Intelligence
(d) Banking architecture simplification

82. ______ includes the safeguarding of the information against unauthorized addition, deletion, modification or alteration.
(a) Data integrity (b) Confidentiality
(c) Auditing (d) Checking

83. RBI announced the creation of a Working Group on Information Security in April, ______ under the Chairmanship of the Shri G. Gopalakrishna.
(a) 2008 (b) 2010
(c) 2012 (d) 2014

84. Phishing is a type of social engineering attack often used to steal ______, including login credentials and credit card numbers.
(a) User details (b) User data
(c) User money (d) User account

85. Which is the features of Services?
(a) Tangible
(b) Homogenous
(c) A process or activity
(d) Can be stored

86. If the purchase is for a high-involvement product, consumers are likely to develop a high degree of __________ so that they can be confident that the item they purchase is just right for them.
(a) Brand loyalty (b) Society
(c) Product knowledge (d) References

87. The major benefits of operational CRM to banks are except:
(a) Sales Force Automation
(b) Credit Risk Analysis
(c) Customer Service and Support
(d) Enterprise Marketing Automation

88. The pricing which helps in achieving the required rate of return on investment done for a product is called:
(a) Target Return Pricing
(b) Value Pricing
(c) Going Rate Pricing
(d) Transfer Pricing

89. _________ is a mobile app developed by NPCI, based on the Unified Payment Interface (UPI) and was launched on 30 December 2016.
(a) Bharat Code (b) BHIM
(c) PAYTM (d) PAYPAL

90. A ______ is a distribution channel arrangement whereby two or more organizations at the same level join together for marketing purposes to capitalize on a new opportunity.
(a) Vertical marketing systems
(b) Horizontally marketing systems
(c) Multi-channels marketing systems
(d) Wider marketing systems

91. A promotion strategy which is directed at channel members to induce them to purchase the product and sell them to the final consumer is called:
(a) Push strategy (b) Pull strategy
(c) Selling strategy (d) Marketing strategy

92. Customer can give an instruction to the bank for issue of cheque book, transfer fund to another account through various delivery channels. Banks offer the which of the following delivery channel for its services:
(a) Net Banking (b) ATM Counters
(c) Call Centres (d) All of the above

93. The process of MIS are collecting, analyzing, and disseminating marketing information relies on the five steps in the process. Which is not the process?
(a) Gather relevant data
(b) Process the data
(c) Communicate results
(d) All of the above

94. When goods or machinery are purchased by customer on long term credit and payment is to be made in instalments which type of guarantee is to be issued by the bank?
(a) Financial guarantee
(b) Performance guarantee
(c) Deferred Payment guarantee
(d) None of the above

95. PMJJBY is a lucrative life insurance plan, wherein the insured receives ₹ 2 Lakh cover against an annual premium of ₹ 330 each year. The life risk cover will get terminated after _____.
(a) 50 years (b) 55 years
(c) 58 years (d) 60 years

96. The issue of new securities to existing shareholder at a ratio to those already held is known as _____.
(a) Bonus issue (b) Right issue
(c) Preference issue (d) None

97. A foreign exchange transaction other than by which there may be a change in asset or liabilities outside India of a person resident in India as per FEMA 1999, is called:
(a) Capital account transaction
(b) Foreign direct investment
(c) Foreign currency transaction
(d) Current account transaction

98. Global depository receipts are normally traded on:
(a) US Stock Exchange
(b) European Stock Exchange
(c) Indian Stock Exchange
(d) International Stock Exchange

99. All SCBs are required to submit to Reserve Bank a provisional Return of CRR in Form 'A' within _____ from the expiry of the relevant fortnight.
(a) 5 days (b) 7 days
(c) 10 days (d) 14 days

100. Monetary control is exercised by RBI in India through:
(a) Payment system
(b) Issue of currency
(c) Cash reserves and liquid reserve ratios
(d) Repo rate and reverse repo rate

ANSWER

1	2	3	4	5	6	7	8	9	10
(c)	(b)	(d)	(d)	(a)	(c)	(a)	(d)	(d)	(10)
11	**12**	**13**	**14**	**15**	**16**	**17**	**18**	**19**	**20**
(b)	(c)	(a)	(b)	(b)	(d)	(a)	(c)	(a)	(c)
21	**22**	**23**	**24**	**25**	**26**	**27**	**28**	**29**	**30**
(d)	(d)	(b)	(b)	(b)	(d)	(c)	(b)	(c)	(b)
31	**32**	**33**	**34**	**35**	**36**	**37**	**38**	**39**	**40**
(b)	(b)	(a)	(b)	(b)	(b)	(d)	(a)	(a)	(d)
41	**42**	**43**	**44**	**45**	**46**	**47**	**48**	**49**	**50**
(d)	(a)	(b)	(c)	(b)	(d)	(b)	(d)	(b)	(b)
51	**52**	**53**	**54**	**55**	**56**	**57**	**58**	**59**	**60**
(a)	(a)	(a)	(a)	(b)	(a)	(c)	(d)	(a)	(c)
61	**62**	**63**	**64**	**65**	**66**	**67**	**68**	**69**	**70**
(c)	(a)	(b)	(b)	(b)	(d)	(c)	(b)	(a)	(a)
71	**72**	**73**	**74**	**75**	**76**	**77**	**78**	**79**	**80**
(d)	(d)	(b)	(c)	(d)	(a)	(b)	(d)	(d)	(d)
81	**82**	**83**	**84**	**85**	**86**	**87**	**88**	**89**	**90**
(a)	(a)	(b)	(b)	(c)	(c)	(b)	(a)	(b)	(b)
91	**92**	**93**	**94**	**95**	**96**	**97**	**98**	**99**	**100**
(a)	(d)	(d)	(c)	(b)	(b)	(d)	(b)	(b)	(c)